Technical Fouls

Interventions:
Theory and Contemporary Politics
Stephen Eric Bronner, Series Editor

Technical Fouls:
Democratic Dilemmas and Technological Change,
John Kurt Jacobsen

Freedomways Reader:
Prophets in Their Own Country,
edited by Esther Cooper Jackson and Constance Pohl

Notes from the Minefield,
Irene Gendzier

Business and the State in International Relations,
edited by Ronald W. Cox

Television and the Crisis of Democracy,
Douglas Kellner

Technical Fouls

Democratic Dilemmas and Technological Change

JOHN KURT JACOBSEN

University of Chicago

Westview Press

A Member of the Perseus Books Group

Interventions: Theory and Contemporary Politics

Published in 2000 in the United States of America by Westview Press, 5500 Central Avenue, Boulder, Colorado 80301–2877, and in the United Kingdom by Westview Press, 12 Hid's Copse Road, Cumnor Hill, Oxford OX2 9JJ

Find us on the World Wide Web at www.westviewpress.com

Library of Congress Cataloging-in-Publication Data
Jakobsen, John Kurt, 1949–
    Technical fouls : democratic dilemmas and technological change / John Kurt Jacobsen.
        p.   cm. — (Interventions: theory and contemporary politics)
    Includes bibliographical references and index.
    ISBN 0-8133-1999-4
    1. Technology and state.   2. Technology—Social aspects.   3. Democracy.   I. Title.
II. Series.

T49.5. J33 2000
303.48'3—dc21   00-029619

10   9   8   7   6   5   4   3   2   1

Contents

Acknowledgments

I would like to thank Charles Lipson and Duncan Snidal of the University of Chicago's Program on International Politics, Economics, and Security (PIPES), from whose core concerns this project seemingly departs, but not really all that much. The analytical scope of the topics treated at PIPES is, fortunately for me, quite breathtaking. Through graduate school Lloyd Rudolph humored, guided, and grounded my interest in technological change. For useful comments on all or parts of the manuscript I am indebted to series editor Stephen Bronner, David Edgerton, and three anonymous referees. The London School of Economics made its fine facilities available to me over several summers while I was there as an academic visitor. Chapter 2 is an updated and revised version of an article that first appeared in the *British Journal of Political Science*. A small portion of Chapter 4 appeared in *The Guardian*. An abridged version of Chapter 5 appeared in the British journal *Imprints*.

I also am grateful for various reasons to Alba Alexander, Helmuth Berking, Glenn Fong, John Freeman, Roger Gilman, Ira Katznelson, Joel Krieger, Bill Leahy, Desmond and Skylla MacNamara, Robert Melville, Carine Minne, Brendan O'Leary, Kenneth Prewitt, Adam Przeworski, Susanne Rudolph, Philippe Schmitter, Sabine Schweinitz, Brian Trench, Daniel Verdier, Michael Wallerstein, and Jack and Nell Wendler. I particularly thank Leo Wiegman of Westview Press for his display of sublime patience, and I thank David McBride for his exacting role. Many authors whom I haven't met but who have influenced me over the years are amply cited herein. The usual disclaimer applies.

Although I introduce original material, this work is intended foremost to be a critical synthesis of an important field of scholarship. Readers are encouraged to follow the relevant footnotes as they burrow their way further into the nooks and crannies of these extremely tricky debates.

John Kurt Jacobsen

Introduction

"There is no economic system," scientist J. D. Bernal tartly observed, "which is willing to pay scientists just to amuse themselves." By the start of the twentieth century the huge sums required to conduct cutting-edge scientific work exceeded the means of the wealthiest individuals while the high risks made all but a few of the most powerful corporations shy away.[1] The state everywhere had to step in with public monies and other aids to spur research, and so the question of the "social function" of science became a legitimate topic for political debate.[2] What social needs and values should science serve, and in what priority? *Technical Fouls* investigates how modern democratic states govern the development of science and technology and examines especially the dilemmas—"choices or situations involving choices between equally unsatisfactory alternatives"—that daunt citizens and policymakers regarding four vital and frequently interrelated issues: automation, military procurement, genetic engineering, and ecological backlash.[3]

The notion that science should have a social function of any kind deviates from contemporary celebrations of the perfect wisdom of "market forces" and instead ushers us into a rich historical realm to track down the determinants of decisions about the *choice* of technologies—choices that always affect the distribution of power and wealth in societies. Contrary to what John Kenneth Galbraith nicely terms the "convenient wisdom," choices cannot be based on the perfectly neutral criterion of pure efficiency because there rarely is one best way to perform any given task.[4]

This volume will therefore challenge portrayals of scientific activity as nothing but a dispassionate quest for knowledge of, and control over, nature. That is not to deny that scientists are ever dispassionate and cannot pass lie detector tests to that effect, but in major research projects far more is at stake than many of them are ready, willing, or able to perceive. Intentions alone tell us very little in the absence of knowledge of the circumstances in which research is conducted. "A thing," as John Ruskin shrewdly observed, "may be judged according to the conditions under which it was built."[5] A society ruled by profit-seeking will apply this priority to all its products, and it is "only natural" that managers will embrace

1

technologies that embody their own agenda of controlling the workforce and beguiling consumers. Scientists and, increasingly, physicians are *employees* who rarely control the conditions under which they work, let alone the purposes to which their research eventually will be put. A project that is savored as "technically sweet" (as Robert Oppenheimer said of the atomic bomb project) always contains other crucial dimensions that analysts outside the lab must assess, such as whether it is economically profitable, militarily applicable, socially feasible, or—perish the thought— morally responsible.

My central argument is that technologies, and the criteria by which we evaluate them, are politically shaped in subtle but decisive ways. This is not to say that technological systems can be molded and reshaped as easily as if they were an electronic form of Silly Putty®. Technological policy decisions, whether taken in government halls or corporate boardrooms, often result in unplanned and contradictory impacts in work places, laboratories, societies, and international relations.[6] When a decision is made, and a physical apparatus is in place, a technological system begins to act according to its own (albeit human-installed) logic and thereby discourages, and even forecloses, other options. Although technology emphatically is a "creature of our Art and craft," it also can generate effects that are no part of any conceivable human intention.[7] Science and technology, like their human practitioners, are both good and evil, depending on circumstance, aim, and context. How could it be otherwise?

Machines are, in social-science jargon, path-dependent creatures that run remorselessly along the grooves initially set for them. Nonetheless, a disappointing or disastrous performance can force their minders to circle back so as to reconsider abandoned or ignored alternatives. The objective here is not to bewail or decry technological change in itself (which would be foolish) but rather to expose the manufacture of self-serving *images* of technology, their causes and consequences, and to venture beyond the narrow ambit of conventional wisdom, which ensnares us in *false* dilemmas, and draw attention to new options and expand access to decisionmaking.

A volume of this modest size cannot treat every imaginable aspect of science and technology. So why choose to scour automation, military weaponry, genetic engineering, and ecology? These topics encompass the key concerns that recur in every debate about science policy, including the question whether nonspecialists can participate meaningfully in deciding how to resolve often arcane disputes. All four topics promise to be pertinent ones well into the new century. The automation chapter examines the basis for fears of technologically caused unemployment. Military procurement raises the issue of trade-offs of domestic prosperity for defense of external frontiers in a post–cold war era. Genetic engineering, in contrast, penetrates our most intimate internal frontiers; how societies are to guide this extraordinary new power to manipulate the codes of life is a pressing question. Ecology brings into sharper focus the delicate web of feedback loops between the manmade world and our "natural" environment, which, as the quotation marks suggest, is a highly porous boundary. In each policy area we will explore differences in the relations of markets, expertise, and democracy. What is the proper balance among these influences? Is such a balance possible or desirable?

Explanatory Approaches

For the sake of brevity a wide variety of theories of technological change can be condensed into three basic explanatory approaches.[8] The most common approach insists that any technology, no matter how immense or complex, is an instrument to be used for good or ill according to the designs of those who apply it. The deceptively simple and appealing idea here is that a personal computer or interballistic missile—and the technical and social systems in which they are embedded—is merely a tool, rather like a hammer or a skilsaw, only a tad more sophisticated and expensive. (The cautionary tale of the sorcerer's apprentice ought to spring to mind.) Technology is believed to be malleable and easily controlled. So goes this attractive but incomplete story.

A second and no less familiar approach, associated in the scholarly literature with philosopher Jacques Ellul, asserts that untamed technology already has evolved into an autonomous process that develops deliriously in accordance with its own inner laws, to which dependent societies—elites and masses alike—must adjust. Management, labor, and politicians capitulate to the logic of their own demonic machinery. This melodramatic B movie vision (viz. Fritz Lang's cinematic classic *Metropolis*) exemplifies what Marx called the "fetishism of commodities," whereby people attribute autonomy to things they have created in an alienating way that makes these very people proportionately powerless.[9] Technology becomes a debilitating process that shrinks the range of human choice by determining the values ("instrumental rationality," quantitative criteria, and the idolatry of reductionist methods) by which we appraise the world and our own activities in it.[10] The ultimate power of technical metaphors is expressed in self-rationalization, that is, the insidious process of "seeing oneself more and more as a computer."[11] If people are persuaded that they are nothing but a bundle of programs or a vehicle for selfish genes, they then become easier prey for highly pedigreed bullies and charlatans aiming to "reprogram" them to serve their purposes.[12] Oddly enough, unprofitable technologies never seem to dominate anything or anyone, a fact that should alert us that the social context is extremely relevant in any analysis of the sources and the consequences of technical change.[13] So we have ample reason to be skeptical toward the scenario of technology running amok.

The third explanatory approach asserts that technologies arrive with a "social history" and an interest-laden agenda already inscribed within them; that is, they comply with the values of elites who have set their acceptable operating limits. This critical perspective, I argue, comes closest to the actual state of affairs regarding technological change, although allowances also must be made for the role of accidents, unforeseen events, and popular resistance. As memorably expressed in *The Wizard of Oz,* amidst all the bellowing smoke and blazing fireworks there is usually someone—a tangible and identifiable interest—at the control panel concealed behind a curtain, and they don't always know exactly what they are doing. On this point such acute but contentious analysts of technology and society as Max Weber, Lewis Mumford, and Herbert Marcuse are very much in accord.

At the core of every policy debate are tacit theoretical conceptions about how a society ought to array its technical capabilities to achieve its objectives. Authorities assure us that their supreme goal regarding weapons acquisition is "security" for the public good, and corporate CEOs plead that, although they admittedly do seek profits, this concern is wholly in tune with greater prosperity for everyone. These bright and glittery claims need to be scrutinized, and in order to detect self-interested motives we require critical paradigms by which to appraise their decisions.

Technological decisions are the product of a blend of material interests and ideologies of those potent actors who strive to strike a balance between technical requirements for effective performance and for their own need to retain or augment their power. By power I refer not only to formal political offices but to private economic and organizational resources devoted to influencing public policy agendas and outcomes.[14] The machine is a social product, and experts are far more often "on tap" than on top. "The mode of production," as Marx noted, determines "the general character of all else"; an "imperative" in technology is a reflection of the imperatives of economic influence, although even the best-laid plans, as Robert Burns put it, often go astray.

Technologies emerge within an intricate web of cultural constructs that they in turn affect, so that they are both agents and products of cultural change. Any technology is shaped by a surrounding social system in which certain demands—and, as feminists point out, a certain gender—have been privileged over others.[15] Contrary to mere economic logic, numerous examples exist of deliberate trade-offs of efficiency for the sake of power. Bernal cited cheap miner's lamps that raised the rates both of worker accidents and of company profits; certain kinds of machine tools are favored that have maximized managerial control at the cost of productivity; hybrid corn was devised so as to render farmers dependent on a few seed suppliers; mass production ("Fordism") was not the only or the most efficient production arrangement available; the life of fluorescent light tubes was shortened from 10,000 to 1,000 hours at the same cost to stir sales.[16] In the late 1990s the Monsanto Corporation developed a so-called Terminator gene yielding sterile seeds, which would force farmers, whatever their income, to return to the company for constant replenishment—and the agribusiness giant backed off only under the fiercest public opposition and boycotts.[17] The American health system arguably is the most scandalous example of a swap of efficiency and equity for the many for the sake of profits for a few.

Chapter Contents

The opening chapter examines competing critiques of technical change. All models do have their blind spots. My argument is that neo-Marxist analyses provide the most interesting critical accounts but need to be supplemented by other perspectives in order to come to grips with the dialectical dimension of technologies that, once in place, tend to take on a dynamic of their own. A technology is usually selected because it suits both the criteria of technical viability and the power designs of influential groups. This is as true for bureaucratic socialist systems as for democratic capitalist societies. Any adequate theory of the social control of technology must deal with the vexing phenomenon of "reverse adaptation" of human purposes to those permitted by the structure of the technological system (and, behind that, its sponsors).[18] The recent Y2K uproar, stemming from the original programmers' need in the 1960s to conserve limited computer memory, demonstrates that these kinds of adaptations are inadvertent at least as often as they are willed.[19]

Throughout history there have been genuine alternatives—in the sense of technical, not political, feasibility—to those promoted by powerful hierarchical organizations. These choices were backed by groups whose clout within political institutions or in the design process made the outcomes seem, in retrospect, "inevitable."[20] But this depiction is distinct from one that asserts these results were the optimal and/or necessary outcomes. As manufacturing in the "post-Fordist era" became more flexible—in that a single set of equipment makes many products for multiple purposes—there also are potential options serving different social priorities for different—or a wider inclusion of—groups. It is important in democracies for elites to resort to ideologically resonant arguments to persuade other citizens that there is an irresistible sense of "fate" in the triumph of specific direction or pattern of technological change. This book offers a theoretical synthesis of critiques of technology and a theory of how ideas are employed by groups in order to enhance their own power. By no means would I claim, however, that ideas alone dictate decisions.

Chapter 2 investigates the specter of "automation"—a scare word with a good deal of substance. Capitalism, according to a controversial school of thought, generates "long waves" of economic change based on "bunchings" of technical innovations that propel expansionary upswings and prosperity. What is even more controversial is whether these upturns occur naturally or else require state intervention. Conflicts over technological choice consist of competing groups trying to control debates and to impose their own revitalizing project. The pursuit of productivity is spurred by competition with industrial states and with relatively low-cost Third World producers. An abiding concern during downturns is whether the United States is seen to suffer primarily from "unfair competition" or whether it must rearrange internal economic relationships (between government, industry, union, universities, and communities) in order to spur beneficial technological change.

Each historical long wave is associated with a social structure of control, so that what is at stake is who gains the power to shape the next stage.[21] The microchip revolution today is the celebrated "carrier" of such an upswing. Chapter 2, however, challenges the routine policy response of subsidizing this or that project, building this or that science park or business center, and which industry to favor with tax breaks. The analysis extends from shopfloor struggles to industry policy debates to international bargaining. The key dilemma is the "automate or die" imperative. Yet it is not the microchip but the social context into which it is introduced that determines where benefits and costs are conferred.

Chapter 3 examines innovation in military technology. Historians, who agree about little else, concur that technical progress was sparked through warfare and the perpetual pursuit of preparedness. War, not a cyclical upturn, pulled the West out of deep economic depression in the 1930s. Science was mobilized for national services in World War I, yielding poison gas, radar, airplanes, submarines, and organizational ties between government and corporations. Generations of Americans grew up with the strong implicit belief that, within the current system, prosperity for the average family requires high military expenditure and all the risks that it entails. The dilemma is obvious. Dare one oppose military spending if it comes at the cost of one's job? Yet today the stimulus of "preparedness" no longer seems persuasive and may be viewed more as a retardant on economic progress.

Chapter 3 zeroes in on President Ronald Reagan's Star Wars scheme and cites relevant historical episodes to illustrate the role of military procurement in selecting those technologies most amenable to hierarchical control. I also address the "Calley syndrome," wherein complex chains of command result in a confusion—and, therefore, absolution—of responsibility of all actors for misdeeds. This is Hannah Arendt's aptly labeled "rule by nobody."[22] Even among the most unworldly scientists toiling away in the remotest recesses of laboratories, responsibility must be designated so that any remedial measures can more readily be assured to be the right ones. The chapter also investigates the fleeting (and now fled) opportunity in the post–cold war era to channel a chunk of defense funds to other public uses.

Chapter 4 reviews the extraordinarily sordid story of the pseudoscience of eugenics and its links via strong cultural beliefs and professional predilections to genetic engineering. The uncritical celebration today of genetic determinism, researchers find, "is part of the wider medicalization of people's behavior which is a feature of the late twentieth century."[23] Eugenics proved to be nothing more than class prejudice and group vanity masquerading as science, yet first-rate scientists and physicians heartily endorsed this racial reductionist creed in the belief that they were pursuing the unsullied truth.[24] Curiosity—normally a praiseworthy trait—pursued odious lines of research. Nazi scientists were most avid to learn at what altitudes or temperatures men would die, although some fussy souls wondered whether Jews and Gypsies, who were favorite specimens, ought to be used inasmuch as "their different racial make-up could produce results which are not absolutely applicable to all men."[25] The mantra that one should behave dispassionately helped to coax functionaries to overcome any remaining scruples and participate in "special actions" in the name of higher scientific principles.[26] In fact, the United States, not Germany, originated the eugenics movement and a mindset that recurs worrisomely within modern genetics. The dilemma posed for democratic decisionmakers today is that close monitoring of eugenical tendencies may obstruct the technical progress on which prosperity (however unevenly distributed) depends, while unchecked experimentation may corrode civil liberties and concepts of human identity and responsibility.

Chapter 5 scrutinizes ecological mishaps. Oil spills, Bhopal, Chernobyl, hazardous waste dumps, and the greenhouse effect are the offspring of specific philosophical and political patterns of technological application. At the philosophical root of ecology is the critique of anthropocentrism (and what to substitute for this myopic belief that nature exists solely for our use). At the political core of every ecological problem is the issue of internalizing formerly excluded costs of production, technically termed "externalities." While agreeing on trivialities such as placing paper and bottles in separate containers, lead-free gasoline, or resisting toxic dumps in their "backyards," the variegated members of environmental movements are rarely alert to the class or international issues involved in the politics of regulation.[27] The chapter thus considers the differences among eco-anarchists, liberal critics, neo-Marxists, and conservatives who trust that the market will sort it all out. The question arises of what is an adequate definition of efficiency. Are we undergoing what German sociologist Ulrich Beck calls "reflexive modernization," whereby citizens are compelled by circumstance to be more enlightenedly self-aware of their interdependence with each other and with the natural world?

Finally, in regard to alternatives, a key source I draw upon is Andre Gorz on the strategic pursuit of "non-reform reforms." Public acquiescence to elite designs usually stems from a fatalism that no realizable alternative exists. Yet there always are forces at work that open up possibilities. Trade unions in several European countries have brought the design stage of technology into the bargaining agenda—even if in fits and starts. Grassroots community organizations form to compel ameliorative changes in their neighborhoods.[28] The issue of energy alternatives to nuclear power is back on the agenda. The "Sussex School" urges implementing a Keynesian approach, focusing on changes in organizational processes, and urges a democratic monitoring and input into policy decisions. We need to sharpen our ability to detect the influences at work and their rhetorical strategies for promoting interest-laden technological options. Norbert Wiener's words of warning still ring true,

> whether we entrust our decisions to machines of metal or machines of flesh and blood which are bureaus and vast laboratories and armies. We shall never receive the right answers to our questions unless we ask the right questions. . . . For the man who is not aware of this, to throw his responsibility on the machine, whether it can learn or not, is to cast his responsibility to the winds, and to find it coming back on the whirlwind.[29]

Notes

1. And it remains true that "business simply will not fund long-term high-risk basic research," according to James Senenbrunner, Republican chairman of the House Committee on Science. *Issues in Science and Technology* 13, 4 (Summer 1997): 7.

2. J. D. Bernal, *The Social Function of Science* (London: Macmillan, 1939), p. 1.

3. *Webster's Third New International Dictionary* (New York: G & C Merriam Co., 1961), p. 633.

4. See John Kenneth Galbraith, *Economics and the Public Purpose* (Boston: Houghton-Mifflin, 1973), and *The Culture of Contentment* (Boston: Houghton Mifflin, 1992).

5. Cited in Tracy Kidder, *The Soul of a New Machine* (New York: Random House, 1985), p. 272.

6. See Edward Tenner, *Why Things Bite Back: Technology and the Revenge of Unintended Consequences* (New York: Knopf, 1996). The insight is usually attributed to sociologist Max Weber.

7. Harry Collins and Trevor Pinch, *The Golem: What You Should Know About Science* (Cambridge: Cambridge University Press, 1993), p. 1. On this basis I disagree with their characterization of science (or technology) as a "lumbering fool which knows neither his own strength nor the extent of his clumsiness and ignorance" and therefore is not independently subject to blame.

8. All condensations of material, alas, come at a sacrifice in content. For a survey of the literature that emphasizes the distinction between innovation and technique-in-use see David Edgerton, "From Innovation to Use: Ten Eclectic Theses on the Historiography of Technique," *Annales—Histoire, Sciences Sociales* 4, 5 (July–October 1998): 1–24.

9. "There is a physical relation betwen physical things but it is different with commodities. The commodity form . . . is simply a definite social relation between men that assumes, in their eyes, the fantastic form of a relation between things"; Tom Bottomore and Maximilien Rubel, eds., *Karl Marx: Selected Writings on Sociology and Social Philosophy* (London: Penguin, 1961), p. 183.

10. There seems no better term than idolatry for the overvaluation of reductionism. Critical works written long ago about this tendency and its social consequences are as applicable as ever. See Abraham Maslow, *The Psychology of Science: A Reconnaissance* (New York: Harper & Row, 1966), and David Bakan, *On Method: Toward a Reconstruction of Psychological Investigation* (New York: Jossey-Bass, 1974).

11. Theodore Roszak, *The Cult of Information: The Folklore of Computers and the True Art of Thinking* (London: Lutterworth, 1986), pp. 18, 40.

12. Theodor Adorno, *Minima Moralia: Reflections from Damaged Life* (London: Verso, 1974), p. 40.

13. See chapter 3 in my *Dead Reckonings: Ideas, Interests and Politics in the "Information Age"* (Atlantic Highlands, N.J.: Humanities Press, 1997).

14. On the relation of American political influence to corporate funding see Thomas Ferguson, *Golden Rule: The Investment Theory of Democracy* (Chicago: University of Chicago Press, 1995).

15. See Urs E. Gattiker, ed., *Women and Technology* (New York: de Gruyter, 1994); Cheris Kramarae, *Technology and Women's Voices* (London: Routledge & Kegan Paul, 1988); and Joan Rothschild, ed., *Machina Ex Dea: Feminist Perspectives on Technology* (New York: Pergamon Press, 1983). Anyone underestimating women's contributions would do well to peruse Autumn Stanley, *Mothers and Daughters of Invention: Notes for a Revised History of Technology* (London: Scarecrow Press, 1993), and Anne L. MacDonald, *Feminine Ingenuity: Women and Invention in America* (New York: Ballantine, 1993).

16. On machine tools see David F. Noble, *Forces of Production: A Social History of Automation* (New York: Oxford University Press, 1985), pp. 269–318; on hybrid corn see Richard Lewontin, *The Doctrine of DNA: Biology as Ideology* (London: Penguin, 1993), pp. 54–56; on mass production assembly see Charles Sabel and John Zeitlin, "Historical Alternatives to Mass Production: Politics, Markets and Technology," *Past & Present* 108 (1985): 133–176; on medicine see Robert Sherrill, "Medicine and the Madness of the Market," *Nation*, 9–16 January 1995; Mark Clark, "Suppressing Innovation: Bell Laboratories and Magnetic Recording," *Technology and Culture* 34 (1993): 516–538; and on fluorescent lights see Vance

Packard, *The Waste Makers* (New York: David McKay Co., 1960). For an overview see George Balassa, *The Evolution of Technology* (Cambridge: Cambridge University Press, 1988).

17. John Vidal, "How Monsanto's Mind Was Changed," *Observer*, 9 October 1999, p. 15.

18. Langdon Winner, *Autonomous Technology: Technics-Out-of-Control as a Theme in Political Thought* (Cambridge, Mass.: MIT Press, 1977), p. 229.

19. James Fallows, "Hurry Up Please It's Time," *New York Review of Books*, 23 September 1999, p. 29.

20. See Noble, *Forces of Production*, and his *America by Design: Science, Technology and the Rise of Corporate Capitalism* (New York: Oxford University Press, 1977).

21. David Gordon, Michael Edwards, and Michael Reich, *Segmented Work, Divided Work* (Cambridge: Cambridge University Press, 1982). The same may be said of the stakes of global wars. The winner "is able to establish an all-pervasive framework of the postwar political and economic order"; Karen A. Rasler and William Thompson, *War and State Making: The Shaping of the Global Powers* (Boston: Unwin Hyman, 1989), p. 4.

22. Hannah Arendt, *On Violence* (New York: Harcourt, Brace & World, 1969), p. 26.

23. Anne Kerr, Sarah Cunningham-Burley, and Amanda Amos, "Eugenics and the New Eugenics in Britain: Contemporary Professionals' Accounts," *Social Studies of Science* 23, 2 (Spring 1998): 193.

24. See Gunnar Broberg and Nils Roll-Hansen, *Eugenics and the Welfare State: Sterilization Policy in Denmark, Sweden, Norway and Finland* (East Lansing: Michigan State Press, 1996).

25. Bapbaz Distel and Ruth Jakusch, eds., *Concentration Camp Dachau, 1933–1945* (Brussels: Comite International de Dachau, 1974), p. 146.

26. These casually racist models, Sander Gilman observes, "are found not only in crackpot pamphlet literature of the time; they are present in virtually all discussions of pathology from 1880 to 1930"; Gilman, *Freud, Race and Gender* (Princeton: Princeton University Press, 1993), p. 5.

27. See Andrew Ross, *Strange Weather: Culture, Society and Technology in the Age of Limits* (London: Verso, 1991).

28. See Michael H. Schuman, *Going Local: Creating Self-Reliant Communities in a Global Age* (New York: Free Press, 1998).

29. Norbert Wiener, *The Human Use of Human Beings* (Boston: Houghton Mifflin, 1950), p. 254.

1

Technology as a Cultural System

We're not sure who discovered water but we're pretty sure it wasn't a fish.

—Marshall McLuhan

The primary problem in the "social control of the sciences," Nigel Calder observed, is reconciling "specialist expertise and long-range planning with the generalism of democracy in a way where ordinary citizens' wishes are heeded and experts neither bow nor dictate to administrative authority."[1] Technology conjures double-edged visions: prosperity and pollution, medical elixirs and chemical poisons, cheap plentiful energy and hair-triggered nuclear obliteration. Until the rise of conservative political regimes in Britain and the United States near the start of the 1980s social analysts assumed as a matter of course that national planning was necessary so that their societies could cope competently with imminent waves of technological and economic change.

Planning in modern societies is unavoidable. Corporations never have been particularly hostile to planning—only to *public* planning that might form a democratic counterweight to unhampered pursuit of profit.[2] This pursuit duly is portrayed by corporate public relations wizards as compelled both by market competition and technological "imperatives."[3] Yet technological transformations always occur according to values that will favor some actors over others. Neutral words like "pragmatic" and "efficient" are really value-laden ones that tend to cater to social groups according to the slot they occupy in the distribution of power and wealth. So the key questions motivating any serious inquiry into technical change are: Who controls what and whom else, on what grounds, and for what ends?

11

What range of "inputs" is deemed relevant for decisionmaking? What constitutes adequate feedback? Finally, how inclusive must planning procedures be in an age when omissions can jar the seamless web as brutally as do clumsy interventions?

I begin this chapter with an instructive glance back at social forecasting several decades ago to ferret out the perennial problems daunting our best guesswork about the shape of things to come. These prophets predictably were blinkered less by their vantage point in time than by the organizational interests they served and the ideas they accordingly promoted. I then tap more fully into historical accounts to appraise the major scenarios for future governance that these forecasters beheld: autonomous technology, technocracy, class domination, or a more participatory democracy. "More of the same" is yet another option.

Science today is widely regarded as the sole rational means for acquiring knowledge, and many enthusiasts have deduced from this powerful status the political lesson that there is likewise a single best way to organize society to promote material progress. However, I will draw upon the work of historians and philosophers of science who demonstrate that the natural world always has been filtered, simplified, and interpreted for human purposes and therefore "that different ways of representing nature are always possible"—and with different accompanying agendas for social control or democratic empowerment.[4] Finally, I probe the perils of "technological fixes" and underline how difficult the intrinsic problems are that technological change poses for even the most competent and sensitive specialists.

Futurism Isn't What It Used to Be

Since the 1960s social forecasting forays have formed a thriving quasi-academic industry and a favorite media pastime.[5] Scholars and pundits scurried to invent catchy names for a nonetheless nebulous future.[6] A few optimists even foretold that new technologies would nourish the "greening" of unblossomed democratic ideals.[7] The advent of a leisure society, they imagined, would enable the unparalleled enrichment of cultural life through devices rather more meaningful than a multiplication of television channels.[8] But the tension between technological change and democratic control was depicted more often by these academic sages as a struggle between an irresistible force and an acquiescent object. The outlook for democracy was very dim if by that term one meant meaningful participation by nonelites in decisionmaking. Forecasters favored Joseph Schumpeter's definition of "formal democracy," which denoted a polity run by competing elites who work out among themselves the policies to be imposed on the citizenry.[9]

Most forecasters saw future forms of rule as an extension of prevailing arrangements, only slightly modified according to the forecaster's political taste, methodological bias, or sources of income. Hannah Arendt, though, cautioned readers that such predictions are always projections, that is, "occurrences that are likely to come to pass if men do not act and if nothing unexpected happens; every action, for better or worse, and every accident necessarily destroys the whole pattern in whose frame the prediction moves and where it finds its evidence [and so the] danger is that these theories are not only plausible because they take their evidence from actual discernible present trends but that, because of their inner consistency, they have a hypnotic effect; they put to sleep our common sense."[10]

Ivy League experts advised that the future ought to be guided by, well, Ivy League experts, which is not so surprising because experts tend to define tasks in terms of their specific skills, values, and professional interests.[11] Citizens must acknowledge the sheer reasonableness of their right to rule, prudently retreating into a private world of hedonistic mass consumption. Events, however, worked out differently over ensuing decades. Since the late 1960s Americans with average incomes, instead of basking in plenty and leisure (except in the involuntary form of unemployment), suffered declines in real wages and job security.[12] (This widening gap in income and wealth was blamed on a mysterious process called "globalization" that, by chance, increasingly enables huge banks and firms to escape all public forms of control.)[13] A horde of prophets rushed forward, but surpassing them all in terms of public notice were Daniel Bell, author of *The Coming of Post-Industrial Society,* and Zbigniew Brzezinski, author of *Between Two Ages* and later President Jimmy Carter's National Security Adviser.[14] What they scribbled—sometimes rashly, sometimes shrewdly—deserves a close look for having set the scholarly agenda for the rest of the century.

Bell stated that the technologically driven transition from a manufacturing-based society to a service-based one signified a profound change in citizens' relations to leaders, each other, and their productive base. He asserted that "centrality of theoretical knowledge is the axis around which new technology, economic growth, and stratification of society is organized."[15] Skills, not property ownership, would be the decisive criterion for acquiring power, or so he strongly implied. Bell was alert to social tensions attending change, such as friction between the professional class and the rest of the populace because demands for rights were bound to multiply among minority groups—correctly anticipating the advent of "identity politics."[16] Despite the necessity of specialized knowledge, he thought that it would remain "the politician, not technocrats, who ultimately hold power." Bell (who qualifies his statements so well that he is maddeningly difficult to pin down) appeared to believe that a new intelligentsia would be incapable of indulging in ideological fancies or excesses. Nor would they always heed their paymasters, about whom Bell had little to say except to dismiss them as obsolete holdovers of the past.

Brzezinski, reflecting his foreign policy bent, charted a future when major states maneuvered gingerly between the poles of political fragmentation and the temptations of hypercontrol. He heralded what he called a "technetronic era" when technology and electronics become the principal determinants of social change. One had to wonder when reading Brzezinski whether his rules of scientific etiquette forbade not only looking backward but glancing from side to side too. Brzezinski's technetronic society, like Bell's, boasted the "end of ideology," which rather than diminish the importance of ideas and ideals, ushered in an age in which abstract issues about the meaning of personal and social life become intensely important.

Bell perceptively argued that planning would generate political strife because the act of planning in itself sharpens available choices without providing consensual standards by which to make them. This emergent society would exhibit "contradictory impulses toward equality and rationality."[17] Unlike critics who thought that these factors will reintroduce ideology to the political fray, Brzezinski assumed that citizens would seek security the moment that they came face-to-face with intimidating complexities.[18] This would mean that fewer citizens will pester or challenge the experts, and that, in his view, was a commendable state of affairs.[19] The system was self-correcting so long as the unlettered rabble did not meddle very much with it.

Technetronic society requires a "mobilization of the ablest" who adhere to the Faustian mandate to orchestrate greater and greater control over nature.[20] Society should be a meritocracy, doubtless comprised of the genetically elect (a notion explored in Chapter 4). Education will be application oriented. Those intellectuals who shun the reprehensible role of social critic will enlist instead as well-rewarded "house ideologues" contriving clever rationales for the mysterious activities of the meritocracy. Brzezinski observed that traditionally the dispersal of authority courted problems of poor coordination, but, just in case any unauthorized personnel imagine they'll get away with anything, he stipulated that "techniques of coordination make possible both increased authority at the lower levels and almost instantaneous national coordination."[21]

Citizens who prize incremental change must bow to the wisdom "of this progressive symbiosis of the institutions of society and government." The United States will emerge from an age of transition as the global disseminator of the technetronic revolution whose essence "derives from the unprecedented scientific power over both man's environment and man himself." There being but one sensible future, what choice does one have but to rejoice in it? This high mandarin attitude, mixing an elitist arrogance with a complacent faith in technology, permeates several of the four competing scenarios of technological politics that we next review.

Autonomous Technology

The most melodramatic scenario—redolent of science-fiction tales from Karl Capek's *RUR* to Aldous Huxley's *Brave New World*—is society succumbing to a technological juggernaut. This is the dismal fate forecast by Jacques Ellul, who defines technology as "the totality of methods rationally arrived at and having absolute efficiency at any given stage of human development." Once in motion, technologies embark on a relentless search for the "one best way" to attain designated goals: Construct a car, kill germs, or concoct and peddle an antidepressant. Ellul apotheosizes the deadening form of rationality that Max Weber a century earlier feared would bring about a world ruled by "specialists without spirit, sensualists without heart."[22] These harrowingly narrow beings were the callous culmination of a long process of rationalization, and for Auschwitz survivor Primo Levi they represented the "century's most dangerous type"—for "without the Hoeses, the Eichmanns, the Kesselrings, without thousands of other faithful and blind executors of orders, the great savage beasts, Hitler, Himmler, and Goebbels" would have been badly hampered in carrying out the streamlined slaughter of the Nazi death camps.[23]

Modernization, however, was traditionally equated with human maturation and seemed just as inevitable. The "icy waters of egotistical calculation," as Karl Marx and Friedrich Engels phrased it, invade puerile primitive cultures to transform them, however painfully, into mature emancipated societies.[24] Modernization was marked by the functional differentiation of primary group structures into a new social structure capable of peacefully institutionalizing technical change. It spurs (1) the division of labor, (2) the differentiation of associations and interests, (3) bureaucratization, (4) centralized government, and (5) a dramatic change in social values, including a shift from the importance of ascriptive ties to achievement-based status.

Modern society was beheld as a delicate bundling of mutual interdependencies in which all the members perform integrated tasks serving the needs of the complex whole. Affective (emotional) ties are reformulated and gratified through new social organizations. Sociologist Emile Durkheim essentially measured modernization according to a society's capacity to master, or shelter itself from, nature.[25] Hence, modern society was seen in a benevolent light as man's progressive liberation from environmental and tribal tyrannies. Durkheim foresaw a harmonizing of individual needs with social demands through a happily benign process whereby each person enjoyed liberty within their own "bubble" inside the larger society. But a long shadow fell between this pleasant scenario and a more rambunctious reality. Whether technological civilization today exemplifies signs of maturity or protracted adolescence is, or ought to be, a pertinent question.

German sociologist Max Weber described history as a narrative of the progressive imposition of a legal-rational modern state upon society. Rational organizations—driven by warfare—leveled ascriptive roles, culminated in the advent of capitalism, and surged toward an all-embracing and all-smothering bureaucracy. Rationalization, as he grimly saw it, was a potent propelling force that was bereft of brakes. He foresaw the bureaucratic usurpation of all significant political activity in a centralizing state and, on reflection, found it "horrible to think that the world could one day be filled with nothing but those little cogs, little men clinging to little jobs and striving towards bigger ones. [The] passion for bureaucracy . . . is enough to drive one to despair."[26]

Bureaucratic centralization, in Weber's reckoning, annihilates organizational alternatives. Relationships are reduced to the administration of things and/or persons who are treated as things. The state, according to this glum account, bulldozes any barrier impeding control in order to direct its institutional energies to tax collection and the waging of expansionist wars. Weber characterized the full-fledged modern state as one that exhibited a precise legal order, an administrative apparatus that conducted business according to legislative rules, a compulsory jurisdiction over a territory, and the monopolization of the legitimate use of violence. In order to achieve this dominant status the state had to dissolve all feudal obstructions to the growth of commerce and of its own power.

If new capitalist entrepreneurs were dependent upon the ruler to provide a secure environment for abundant business opportunities, the ruler was almost equally dependent upon the support of these economic interests. These groups demanded a clear legal system that would be free of both administrative arbitrariness and aristocratic interference, that would offer guarantees of the legally binding character of contracts, and that, in consequence of these factors, would function in a calculable way.[27] But one should not forget that this love for law ends where disadvantages begin. Today the process of economic globalization relies "overwhelmingly on ad hoc, discretionary, closed and non-transparent legal forms fundamentally inconsistent with a minimally defensible conception of the rule of law."[28] This occurs because a porous and open-ended legal system provides economic giants with a considerable leeway of action against weaker actors and agencies.

Rationalization also marked the transition from agricultural societies to mercantile and, eventually, industrial societies. Industrialization forced people from farms into factories and into a new network of relationships on the job and in the community that were to be based on the strictest utilitarian calculation. Superstition, small-group tyranny, and other medieval bedevilments dissolved slowly—and with a good deal of resistance—into a money-based economy. Rights of citizenship and the provision of public services soon arose to cushion the collision between the individual and this gradual "disenchantment" of the world, a remorseless process whose economic dimension Marxists would call commodification.[29]

Rationalization acquired an appealing aura of worldly salvation as its enthusiasts dreamed of constructing a cornucopic and, often more important, orderly future. But rationalization, and the technologist's tools, also could become animated by seemingly alien purposes to threaten to erase any trace of human control, creativity, or conscience. In the "worst case" scenario of rationalization, science itself is reduced to the subservient status of a cold-blooded instrument of technology, rather than serving human or humane purposes. In Jacques Ellul's glum view, even a technocratic state would be seen as an optimistic outcome if this scenario entailed the rash belief that such a polity could be governed by human beings at odds in the minutest fashion with the implacable imperatives of technique, which he characterized as autonomous, monistic, self-augmenting, universal, and irreversible.[30] Technique, as Ellul beheld it, evolves "in a purely causal way," he wrote. "The combination of preceding elements furnishes the new technical elements. There is no purpose or plan that is progressively being realized. To pose arbitrarily some goal is to divest technique of its character and its strengths."

The political realm evaporates like misty morning dew. Ellul was unable to imagine any realistic political challenge to the omnivorous imperium of technique, which reduces everything to a dimension amenable to the application of available methods. Choice is an illusion: Rulers, no less than the *hoi polloi*, fall under a spell that promises untold power but really shrinks human horizons to fit the boundaries that technique already has drawn. The classical analogy is the bed of Procrustes, where hapless guests had their limbs agonizingly stretched or lopped to fit the size of the recliner. Langdon Winner nicely labels this inverted relation between technologies and human purposes as "reverse adaptation" (although reverse adaptation usually suits powerful groups).[31]

Technique compels states, whatever their original composition and constitution, to deform themselves into pale totalitarian entities. In the supreme interest of coordinating the entire ensemble of techniques, the state must intrude into every crevice of everyday life so as to prevent disruption. This formidable form of organization is a relentless process assigning appropriate tasks to specialized individuals so as to attain, in an efficient and economic way, and by coordination and combination of all activities, the objectives agreed upon. But agreed by whom? This standardization of all economic and administrative life, as Antoine Mas perceptively noted, "means resolving *in advance* all the problems that might possibly impede the functioning of an organization. It is not a matter of leaving to inspiration, ingenuity, nor even intelligence to find a solution."[32]

Technology triumphs utterly when human beings replicate the standards of technique within their own consciousness—when they internalize the machine.[33] German sociologist Karl Mannheim long ago spotted the crucial implication that "functional rationalization of objective activities ultimately leads to self-rationalization [and that] the more industrialized a society is and the more advanced its division of labour and organization, the greater will be the number of spheres of human activity which will be functionally rational and hence also calculable in advance."[34] He lamented the suffocating impact that *functional* rationality ("blind subordination of all means to a single goal") exerted upon *substantive* rationality ("intelligent insight into the interrelations of events in a given situation") and that impeded assessment of the true rationality and desirability of chosen goals.

Technique is the purest distillate of Weberian rationalization and is toxic to any cultural system that deviates from the naive notion that "the one way of gaining access to reality is by cleansing ourselves of all subjective distortion."[35] For technology constitutes not just a physical apparatus but a cultural system; that is, a delimited way of experiencing, seeing, and thinking about the world. Scientific technique succeeded in divorcing the quantitative aspect of things from their surrounding qualitative sphere and found favor with authorities who enforced this distinction to the point of forcing other realms into virtual eclipse.[36] Where men do not surrender to scientific doctrines of the day, they are, as Brzezinski scornfully indicated, nothing more than obstinate scribblers of graffiti on the sparkling vehicle of human progress. In this instance, at least, Ellul's harsh portrait of "a civilization committed to the quest for continually improved means to carelessly examined ends" seems well justified.[37]

This is where the rub lies in portrayals of technology as autonomous, and depictions of technocrats as pursuers of truth. Technologies (and their designers) are embedded in social systems and are inflected by the distribution of power within them. (This does not imply that technology is the product solely of the tastes and demands of a ruling class or, moreover, a class untroubled by internal conflicts.) Contemporary alternatives should extend beyond facing a repugnantly rational destiny with the passive fortitude of Max Weber or, like Ellul, piously witnessing oneself being devoured by a profoundly stunted form of rationality.

Yet technology does impose its values—values conducive to its own expansion—so that a correspondence develops between technology and patterns of social organization. Technology, as I will describe in the next two chapters, requires anticipatory changes in organization in order to work optimally, or at all.[38] Yet the historical paths of technological change—which often could have turned out otherwise—are invoked as if inevitable. One can imagine distressed analysts who gritted their teeth in Weberian anguish rather than appear to be hostile toward an unconditionally valid definition of scientific and technological progress. Yet science and technology are not the same thing. Ellul (like the Frankfurt scholars discussed below) noted that technology actually degrades science. Until recently, to dare to question the direction of technological growth was to invite scorn similar to that heaped upon those who in the past violated religious laws.

Technology filled the lofty role formerly held by heralds of human emancipation. A materialistic "emancipation"—via consumer goods and work-control techniques—displaced humanistic visions and took on the mantle of a mechanized world spirit moving toward a mystic culmination in divine gadgetry. "Myths about the future are, after all, in large part a secularization of religious expectations of an afterlife—the bringing of eschatology down to earth—have essentially the same effect as supernaturalism."[39] Ellul's weak plea for human intervention may demand too much from awesome systems that promise to alleviate all the material causes of human misery. One easily can concede with Frankfurt School scholar Herbert Marcuse that the sacrifice paid off handsomely at least in economically advanced areas: "The conquest of nature is practically complete, and more needs of a greater number of people are fulfilled than ever before. Neither the mechanization and standardization of life, nor the mental impoverishment, nor the growing destructiveness of present-day progress provides sufficient ground for questioning the 'principle' which has governed Western Civilization."[40]

If technological systems can perform this wonderful feat, the impulse is to let them proceed and to fret about side effects later. However, a healthy and vibrant political system *must* scrutinize means and ends. In complex technological societies the nagging question of the competence of the citizenry always arises. Even if an absolutely superb educational system should dispense skilled citizens capable of untangling all kinds of Gordian knots, there will remain numerous decisions that teasingly or tormentingly remain outside the immediate scope of public understanding. In these cases, the public must rely on, and weigh, the testimony of competing scientists and specialists who are made democratically accountable.

"I do not see any way for the average citizen to judge the substantive issues relevant to judge the vast sums for research and development, medicine, space exploration and technical training," social critic Paul Goodman admitted, "but it would be helpful if he understood the interests and politics involved."[41] With regard to one area of science, however, it is essential that citizens do learn to judge the substantive issues; this is human ecology, combining physical science, physical and mental hygiene, sociology, and political economy to analyze problems of urbanism, transportation, pollution, degenerative disease, mental disease, pesticides, indiscriminate use of antibiotics and other powerful drugs, and so forth. These matters are too important to be delegated to experts.

But have citizens been thoroughly intimidated or gulled by the blandishments of "scientism"? This important term refers to applications of scientific methods beyond their proper domain as well as to any perversion of scientific activity. Scientism consists of "(1) the assumption that the mathematical science of natural phenomena is a model to which all other sciences ought to conform, (2) that all realms of being are accessible to the methods of the science of phenomena [and] (3) that all reality which is not accessible to the science of phenomena is either irrelevant or, in the most radical form of the dogma, illusionary."[42] The fusion of scientistism with technology has been a key rhetorical ingredient in the antidemocratic thrust of political debate. To paraphrase the military strategist Carl von Clausewitz: "Science is not merely a scientific activity, but also a political instrument, a continuation of political relationships, a carrying out of the same by other means." If scientism and technology combine to displace politics as the orderer of priorities, societies will be in grave danger of losing touch with reality and embarking on dangerous paths.[43] Scientism animates technocratic ambitions.

The Phantom of Technocracy

Another vision of the political future, exemplified by Brzezinski, is that by default as much as by merit a "knowledge elite" is destined to govern us. Whether experts merely polish liquid crystal displays on control panels or actually do put their hand on the steering column is an intriguing question. Complexity and information overload supposedly deny citizens any significant role in policy decisions except perhaps to answer the questionable queries of pollsters. Society is entrusted to "the best and the brightest" (a term that acquired a bitter taint in reference to the Kennedy-Johnson advisers who misguided the Vietnam War).[44] The "brightest" were experts who were deemed to be immune to corruption and all the wicked temptations of daily politicking.[45] If knowledge, and not property or might, is the new source of power, then those who sported the credentials of knowledge must move from being "on tap" to "on top." The hitch is that there is very little evidence for this claim. Jean Meynaud in a classic study admitted the "impossibility of totally mechanizing decisions" but nonetheless noted that the "risk—the only one, in fact—is that man will become a slave of those who feed these machines with information and make use of the results."[46] There is a useful distinction to be made between technical experts who "feed the machine" and administrative experts who "make use of the results." The relationship between these elites is not always clear and requires investigation from case to case.[47] Still, the boss usually wins.

During the Vietnam War, President Lyndon Johnson's aversion to bad news was so well known that underlings apparently generated distorted and, eventually, disastrous underestimates of enemy strength.[48] Nor is a technocratic scenario borne out by decisionmaking patterns since the development of the atomic bomb. The lure of the "technically sweet" in the Manhattan Project was far too tempting for scientists, engineers, and technicians to resist.[49] Scientists who after the defeat of German fascism fretted about the possibly gratuitous use of nuclear weapons, went unheeded. Although there is scant reason to believe that the spirit of conformity is much less prevalent among technical experts than other occupations, the need to meet purely professional standards can indeed clash with the need to accede to the will of the state or of the entrepreneur. This point should not be exaggerated; accommodations do get worked out over time among the state, industries, and the professions. In his study of seventeenth-century science, Robert Merton emphasized the stimulative role played by a rising merchant class who valued science and technologies as handy devices by which to augment their wealth.[50] But scientists cautiously trod the path of least resistance:

> Under the conditions of ideological impasse that were reached in England in 1640 scientists found themselves in a situation in which it was increasingly useful to adopt Baconianism as a strategy of survival . . . natural science served as a symbol of a neutral meeting ground. Official support of science in France and elsewhere on the continent derived from absolutist conservative rulers. The insistence on the strict neutrality of science and the specificity which made it accessible only to experts was, therefore, a condition for the freedom of scientific inquiry.[51]

One rueful legacy is that it "discouraged the scientist from critically examining his own metaphysical assumptions [and] even fomented the delusion that he had none."[52] Epitomized in Lord Kelvin's exhortation, scientists instead strived to advance knowledge "one more decimal place." They substituted an evolutionary optimism for an analysis of the relationship of their work to particular social contexts. A utopian impulse was absorbed into positivistic science and expressed through its parched terminology.[53]

Indeed Thomas Hobbes in sixteenth-century England had envisioned a Leviathan uniting society so that the "war of all against all" became a tidier "war of one against all." Hobbes foresaw the political utility of a controlled public vocabulary—a premonition of "image management" and spin doctoring.[54] Jean-Jacques Rousseau later sought to destroy the fetters of group life by isolating men in separate pores of the body politic, thereby melding libertarian and authoritarian principles in a "general will." This ambition to control everything reflected the preoccupations of people whose "passion for geometrical symmetry, inherited from Cartesian philosophy, drove them beyond a reform of the currency system, beyond standardization of weights and measures, to a rational standardization of the very units of men's social and political lives."[55]

History came to be read in the United States in a more hopeful light as a process leading toward universal equality. In the early nineteenth century, Alexis de Tocqueville even mused that the major threat to liberty was tyranny of the majority.[56] But elites believed that the truly grave dangers lay elsewhere. By the late 1870s, Indians, immigrants, and freed blacks "asserted in their different ways the desire to control the conditions and terms of their labor—as opposed to requirements of the new industrial system as defined by its managers and owners."[57] Frontiers closed, and sporadic class struggles erupted. Elites wanted immigrants to be loyal without "demanding an undivided social acceptance into Anglo-American society [and] without his demanding a greater return for his labor and a fairer allocation of the system's material wealth."[58] The Indian wars shifted "the grounds of controversy from the ideological frame in which progress and right order are presumed to emerge from the widest possible diffusion of property and political power to one in which progress depends on the exclusion/extermination of a congenitally regressive type of humanity and an aggrandizement of a privileged race or group."[59]

Science would act, it was hoped, as the absorber and adjudicator of conflicts between proletariat and capitalists.[60] The Progressive movement hailed science as the moral link that would ensure stability on managerial terms. Its leaders were commercial men who thought of their work as an evangelical extension of business practices to government.[61] Even Thorstein Veblen, who elucidated many foibles of his age, was not immune. He reached vitriolic heights in attacking manipulative "captains of finance" for generating waste at the expense of the general welfare, but his proposed remedy was an angelic host of engineers.[62] Although engineers might retain a bit of latitude within business organizations, they typically reflect their employers' values, and it would be astonishing if it were otherwise. It was never necessary for specialists to "distort (scientific) truth in their particular area of concern," David Rappaport writes. "To serve the interests of power, they need only neglect the truth or values outside their areas of concern."[63] Soviet communism likewise eagerly adopted Frederick Winslow Taylor's obsessive time and motion techniques—note Lenin's naive formula: "Soviets plus electrification equal communism"—to prod workers to maximum productive expenditure of energies. The USSR's politburo thwarted the threat of an antiparty technocracy through the deliberate creation of a hardy, loyal, and prudently unimaginative corps of "red experts."[64]

The latest rendition of this stubborn technocratic faith are "epistemic communities"—defined as networks of knowledge-based experts sharing normative and principled beliefs, causal notions, notions of validating truth, and a common enterprise motivated "presumably out of the conviction that human welfare will be enhanced as a consequence."[65] Proponents of this approach are pleased to behold evident increases in scientific staffing of government and an "increasing deference" paid to technical experts and scientists. Public attitudes toward experts, however, are quite ambivalent, which is wise because the historical record on such experts does not compare very well to less credentialed citizens with regard to moral courage, foresight, or any other civic virtue.[66] In any case, research data are usually ambiguous, and scientists are frequently divided concerning environmental, energy, and other issues.

The epistemic approach is the latest manifestation of a model of elites designed by elites and for elites. This approach is driven by a misplaced faith in the critical inclinations of like-minded experts. Evidence instead suggests that experts who are closest professionally to controversial issues tend to be less critical than warranted. More physicists than biologists consider recombinant DNA research risky, and more physicists than biomedical scientists consider nuclear plants safe; a researcher ascribes these tendencies "to the influence of social networks within disciplines rather than to expertise" itself.[67] The implication is that communities of any kind—the mafia, the bridge club, or American Medical Association—are unlikely to encourage dissent within their ranks. Lay citizens ought to ponder the lesson that it is not an epistemic community *per se* but rather the clashes among "communities" from different disciplines of science and (as Jurgen Habermas urges) conducted in the public sphere that produce the most valuable and democratically useful input into policy decisions.[68] Nonetheless, a yearning for a trustworthy expert or band of experts—from Plato's philosopher-kings to Thorstein Veblen's "Soviet of engineers"—seems a persistent feature of modern life.[69]

Mumford's Megamachine

Lewis Mumford's *The Myth of the Machine* is a guardedly optimistic version of Weberian rationalization. The pyramid age of Egypt is pictured as the apex of a process whereby a rigidly centralized organization consisting of coerced human parts comprised the first "megamachine."[70] The army became the model upon which society was to be arranged. Bureaucracies sprang from the need to delegate royal powers to officials who administered resource-gathering in a growing empire. Religion, which in primitive societies at times acted as a restraining power to tyranny over people and the environment, was recruited into the pharaohs' service. "Commitment to the power complex and relentless pursuit of pecuniary gains, in both direct and indirect forms, define the power system and prescribe its only acceptable goal," Mumford writes. "That goal, fitly enough, belongs to the same memorable series of alliterations—progress. In terms of the power system, progress means simply more power, more profit, more productivity, more paper property, more publicity—all convertible into quantifiable units."[71]

Mumford defined man as far more than a toolmaker. Primitive people, according to Mumford's psychoanalytically informed view, channeled their excess of libidinal energy into constructive pursuits by developing the extraordinary harness of language. Repetitive activities create a ritually enriched order in what otherwise is a moral and cultural void. Language became the central expression of our mental activity, contained and shaped imagination, and preserved the memory of collective experience. Tools became benign regulators of our relationship with the universe, and thus men and women fashioned inchoate impulses into a coherent human identity. But the megamachine would slip out of all these harnesses.

The problem was the advent of a "mechanical worldview" that wrenched quantitative reality out of its surrounding sphere of collective cultural development. Feminist scholars note that Mumford offers a "more holistic view" than many male colleagues because he emphasized the vital role that gender and "softer" (less rational) values played—even when consciously suppressed—in modifying the course of technological development.[72] Men constructed a singular form of scientific reality without acknowledging any debt to their subjective consciousness (dreams, wishes, impulses, religious motives) for employing "objective" devices. Mumford welcomed the discipline of technics in overcoming certain kinds of cultural biases and opening the visible world to systematic observation. But science pulverized a partial representation of a finite world and presented it as the only legitimate account of reality, thus submerging more nurturing, integrative, and realistic views of our relation with the universe.

The blinding renunciation of qualitative dimensions of life was arguably a precondition for the triumph of capitalism. Organized political power, backed by coercion—which is the preserve of private property—served to expand markets through which the leaders accumulate profits. Money by nature is a limitless aim that ruptures the feedback systems that a society requires to maintain self-correcting solvency. Warfare "corrects" imbalances whenever overproductivity threatens the internal gyroscope of the megamachine. Now men would choreograph reality from a majestically detached perch. At these heights, Hannah Arendt warned, all "activities, watched from a sufficiently removed vantage point in the universe, would appear not as activities of any kind but as processes [so that] the action of scientists, since it acts into nature from the standpoint of the universe, and not into the web of human relationship, lacks the revelatory character of action as well as the ability to produce stories and become historical, which together form the very source from which meaningfulness springs into and illuminates human existence."[73]

A pluralist paradigm reigned in the 1950s and 1960s, when Mumford and Arendt scribbled their key critiques, as social scientists celebrated group politics.[74] Any social phenomena not bound up in dominant institutions tended to be labeled as irrational or Red-inspired. Peaceful mediation among interest groups became imbued with the power to divine the needs of society, and the evident sag in class conflict signaled "the exhaustion of political ideas in the 1950s."[75] The bad old versions of capitalism bit the dust, and the new welfare states smoothed economic fluctuations, encouraged innovation, and protected the vulnerable.[76] Loose ends would be tucked in. Big science, large organizations, and blind faith in progress underpinned this complacent vision.

Impartial science is one thing; callous detachment is quite another. According to Mumford, the human roots of this technological drive for power are familiar ones: anxiety and insecurity. Individuals beset by these ancient harpies are unlikely to acknowledge Weber's recognition that order is brought to chaos in relation to the observer's cultural values. In a scientific age these values are as invisibly pervasive as the air one is able to breathe. So is it possible or necessary, as Mumford urged, to balance demands for democratic participation against likewise legitimate demands for free inquiry?

Interrogating Science

In Thomas Kuhn's classic work, a "normal science," for which a paradigm is a necessary condition, is an enforced orthodoxy, a directive for, and a constraint on research—the boundary maker of the conceptual boxes into which paradigm workers dutifully attempt to force reality.[77] To be ordained a paradigm, which is "universally recognized achievements that for a time provides model problems and solutions to a community of scientists," a candidate must be unprecedented, open-ended and have an explanatory capacity superior to competitors although it need not and never does explain all the facts with which it is confronted.[78] "A paradigm governs, in the first instance, not a subject matter but rather a group of practitioners," Kuhn argues.[79]

So "precision" is simply a demand made within a particular context at a given time and in response to a definite question or problem. And that presupposes an ontology, a view of reality, of the nature of the target phenomenon in it, and a view of how it is to be described. Euban perceived that Kuhn's analysis suggests that the "behavioralism is a paradigm, which like all paradigms is simultaneously prescriptive and descriptive, normative and empirical, a partially (in two senses) articulated framework for analysis, as to mutually-reinforcing images of man and politics. . . . Realism becomes an implicit and unargued conservativism, the best and perhaps only kind."[80]

Paul Feyerabend goes Kuhn one better in arguing that significant research always violates rules.[81] Feyerabend relies on historical studies to demonstrate how standard methods were suspended by successful scientists. Galileo's heliocentrism, Newton's gravitational theory, and Bohr's atomic model fail to satisfy positivism's criteria for scientific conduct. In Galileo's case the reigning Ptolemaic theory not only displayed superior empirical content but the only visible means of support of his hypothesis, the telescope, was so primitive that it could not provide trustworthy evidence.[82] (The church, to put it perversely, had a point.) Indeed, E. A. Burtt reckoned that "empiricists, had they lived at the time, would have been the first to scoff out of court the new philosophy of science."[83]

Bruno Latour likewise stresses that scientists' stories about research are retrospective recreations and idealizations of the processes by which they actually operate: "[S]cientific reality is a pocket of order, created out of disorder by seizing on signals which fit what has already been disclosed and by enclosing it, albeit at a cost."[84] In a study of a laboratory in the 1970s Latour and a coauthor were moved to ask ironically what was *not* social about science when the word social "refers equally to a pen's inscription on graph paper, to the construction of a text and to the gradual elaboration of an amino-acid chain?"[85] None of these activities existed in a research zone devoid of social influence and import. Scientists, when all is researched and recorded, are employees too.[86]

Galileo's triumph is attributed to cunning rhetorical skills by which he attracted support from a rising commercial class, eluded challenges to his law of circular inertia, and thereby promoted a view that at the time absurdly claimed that the earth rotates on its axis. Stealth, guile, and cunning may be indispensable if a new or revitalized theory is to insinuate itself into the prevailing framework, at least until that framework is displaced by a cumulative process of subversion.[87] Even if the challenge fails, the contest would improve the older theory by subjecting it to rigorous critique. There is a deeply dialectical core to Feyerabend's argument; a liberatory motive explicitly guides his analysis. His project aims at restoring historical tension to the concept of reason; this objective is identical with that of critical theorist Herbert Marcuse:

When the historical content enters into the dialectical concept . . . ontological tension between essence and appearance, between "is" and "ought," becomes historical tension, and the "inner negativity" of the object world becomes understood as the work of the historical subject—man in his struggle with nature and society. Reason becomes historical reason. It contradicts the established order of men and things on behalf of existing societal forces that reveal the irrational character of the order—*for "rational" is a mode of thought and action which is geared to reduce ignorance, destruction, brutality and oppression.*[88]

Feyerabend argues that only the proliferation of methods will encourage and fortify the protective institutions of a dynamic democracy. David Bloor similarly promotes what he calls a "strong programme" of inquiry whereby "rational and irrational ideas, insofar as collectively held, should be equally the object of sociological curiosity, and should be explained by reference to the same kind of causes."[89]

Feyerabend also displays an affinity with the "social construction of science" position, as recently marked out by Trevor Pinch, emphasizing the "interpretative flexibility" of artifacts, which means that a given technology can be "subject to radically different meanings co-extensive with social groups."[90] The desirability of a device will be experienced differently from the standpoint of various groups, professions, and classes (which sounds remarkably Marxist, though social constructionists may deny any link).

In prescribing highly unorthodox means to reach emancipatory ends, Feyerabend intended to make science so conscious of the ways in which knowledge is constructed and employed within systems of domination that the spread of this consciousness will nourish a wider democratic struggle. The Frankfurt School scholars endorsed this goal.

Critical Theory and Technological Society

The critical theorists of the Frankfurt School attacked ahistorical images of scientific enterprise and exposed how asymmetrical power relationships (within scientific community and encompassing them) are disguised. Max Horkheimer and Theodor Adorno asserted that if the "truth" of scientific knowledge must be tested by its consequences, it ultimately is evaluated in a circular fashion by the technology it produces—and thus science dwindles into "instrumental" reason. But what counts as "instrumental," as useful, is always tied to human interests. If economic and political institutions are controlled by a rigged game of class interests, then scientific knowledge unconsciously, but all the more powerfully, will promote the interests of those who dominate the "exchange process."[91]

Horkheimer and Adorno argue that the Enlightenment view of reason was at first a liberating belief that, eventually, became a stumbling block. Marcuse condemned Auguste Comte's *Cour de philosophie positive*, which heralded science as "the only positive knowledge of reality," for viewing men and institutions as "neutral objects" governed by "natural necessity."[92] This implies that the status quo is always rational—a verdict that critical theorists regard as plainly preposterous. The primacy of "utility" is built into the concept of instrumental reason: People are valuable if they are useful (to whom?); they are useful only if predictable (to whose benefit?); and knowledge is useful only if its applications make people useful, that is, makes them predictable means to ends determined by someone else.[93] We are no longer dealing with citizens but with scientific specimens and economic units. Ends that serve nonutilitarian values are ignored.[94] The utility of activity becomes more important than its social purposes.

The critical theorists repudiated this positivist view as both deeply flawed and morally repugnant. The world of objects exists, but it always is a world of human interpretations too. The "given" is mediated by a consciousness full of needs—full of human interests, and conflicts among them—a consciousness that has a specific history, which is the product of an entire social practice, which includes noninstrumental values. The knowledge process cannot be severed from the historical struggle of humans with nature or with one another—at least not without distortion. *What is suppressed in positivism is the potentiality of things.* Instrumental reason ignores the alternative meanings that subjects can give to their actions; it ignores the alternative ways of organizing social life, including the organization of science. It denies that the act of evaluating is also an intimate part of describing and explaining.

Science becomes ideology ("scientism") when it masks contradictions that work to the advantage of dominant groups and/or when it arbitrarily cuts off inquiry, as reductionist-oriented positivists are so wont to do (as we shall see). Claiming to represent a "common interest" in knowledge-seeking or to deal only in "hard facts" or to say that reality is basically harmonious and "natural" are ploys that conceal inequalities and contradictions. Any form of knowledge, including the very language we use, exists in part as a product of some politically and historically bounded method. Indeed, as the "linguistic turn" put it, citizens should become conscious of how power and authority are secured in the language "through which individuals speak and are spoken."[95] Horkheimer concludes that only a full-fledged classless society can guarantee the existence of a democratically invigorating variety of these practices. Science is valuable, but it is only one among many "traditions" informing and shaping humanity, neither good nor bad as such.

A Participatory Democracy?

Of what does a participatory democratic politics consist? True politics requires tensions and diversity and is characterized by anomalies to which scientism is utterly inhospitable. Politics, Bernard Crick writes, "can be simply defined as the activity by which differing interests within a given unit of rule are conciliated by giving them a share in proportions to their importance to the welfare and the survival of the whole community . . . a political system is that type of government where politics proves successful in insuring reasonable stability and order."[96]

Democracy implies that all those affected by a decision must have a voice in that decision so that power is legitimated and the decisionmakers are held publicly accountable.[97] A mature democracy is inhabited by what C. Wright Mills calls "genuine publics": self-cognizant, rationally insightful, self-cultivating men and women who could maintain their "given unit of rule" against the atomization of mass society and the blandishments of power.[98] "The objective of political democracy becomes that of making harmonious and effective the various group allegiances which exist in society, not sterilizing them in the interest of an artificial political community."[99]

Arendt, with her peculiar mix of romanticism and critical acumen, commended the evanescent Greek polis as the ideal standard by which to assess all other political forms. The polis is humankind's elegant answer to infinity. Finite men are motivated to unite in a framework within which to fashion enduring monuments; only those men who strived for immortal fame were thought fully "human." The polis freed (some) men from nature's necessities—the sphere of sheer toil—that prevented them from engaging in genuine action. Necessity was the enemy of all that is human.[100] The private household therefore was the antonym of the active public life.

The polis enabled an equality among peers, whereas the household, writes Arendt, "resembles nothing so much as the equality of household members before the despotic power of the household head." Politics was the exclusive sphere of freedom. All other activities were the prepolitical foundation upon which the liberated terrain of the political rested. Men then strove through unique deeds and creations to distinguish themselves from all others and to prove themselves the best of all. The public realm was the only place where men could demonstrate unequivocally who they really were. "It was for the sake of the chance," Arendt continues, "and out of love for a body politic that made it possible for them all, that each was more or less willing to share in the burden of jurisdiction, defense, and the administration of public affairs."[101]

Property provided a private place of one's own and enabled men (not slaves or women) to participate in public life. Arendt is easy to criticize for downplaying this point. But a polis that at the time was built upon slavery could now be founded on the free time allowed by machinery and automation. (Feminist scholars, though, raise the question whether labor-saving machinery really has made the modern household any easier to run.[102]) If the property-owner chose instead of using it to lead a public life, "it was as though he willingly sacrificed his freedom and became voluntarily what the slave was against his own will, a servant of necessity."[103] Arendt therefore called the modern state "a nation-wide administration of house-keeping" in which "action" is ground down into "behavior, where man by virtue of swelling numbers in modern societies became statistics and where the distinction of public and private realms is blurred together into a centralized states." As Ellul argued, the "necessary" and the ephemeral have invaded and negate the political realm. The choice of efficiency, for example, is no choice at all. "If politics is defined as the art of the possible, nowadays it is the technician whom determines with growing authority what is possible," he writes.[104]

Technique steamrolls toward a myopic absolute, and technocracy seeks to spread a spurious "precision." Politics generates, maintains, and conciliates diversified institutions and groups. Politics, as well as guarding privacy from unwarranted public action, provides for effective public action. Victor Ferkiss presciently warned that the danger is that "instead of a dominant total government riding roughshod over an inert society, public purposes will be lost sight of in the feudalistic struggle of competing interests."[105] Theodore Lowi inveighed against a "market" system of politics that stultifies rational policy planning by encouraging upper-tier compromise and informal bargaining, frequently at the cost of public welfare and the loss of the public's trust.[106]

Less government does not automatically result in more popular power and participation. Corporate interests fill any power vacuums and decide "when industries will eliminate labor and what human functions will be replaced by the computer," Ferkiss observes. Today, even more so than twenty-five years ago, there "simply is no basic acceptance of the legitimacy of such decisions being made by the conscious action of the whole community rather than by incremental decisions of individual and there is no institutional mechanism for eliciting, weighing and implementing popular decisions on such matters."[107]

Neither epistemic communities nor freshly minted systems of technocratic domination will win over politically alienated citizens. A technological society releases itself from popular sovereignty through the guise of rationalization: increasing the autonomy of decisionmakers in the state and private sector. In both private and public sectors "New Mandarins" cherish a top-down orientation and define the problems they confront by the techniques they have mastered. They typically answer adversity by administering a larger or more streamlined dose of the same medicine to the apparent malady. Yet citizens cannot pledge allegiance to coteries of private interests or anonymous administrators engaged in the irresponsible pursuit of technetronic age plunder. John Schaar poses the diagnosis:

> Intricate division of labor reduces common experience, producing both pluralistic ignorance and fragmentation of the work process . . . the relativization,

materialization, and secularization of values makes it impossible for men to relate to one another on the basis of shared commitments to transcendent and demanding purposes and values. . . . Authorities cannot pretend to speak for the public and objective goods, but must accept the popular equation of private desire with public right. . . . Hence the basic features and tendencies of modernity have produced a situation in which the established processes and formal structure of control are at war with the conditions necessary for authority. In this battle, legitimacy is destroyed.[108]

The notion of a genuinely democratic participative structure slowly fades. Even if "pop sociological" schemes to computerize decisionmaking personal computer link-ups in every home were actually enacted, this measure may only be negated by an in-built "one-dimensional" blanket that smothers dissent and imagination. A divided society only drives affluent citizens further into a refuge of privatized and hedonistic isolation—instead of Kafka' s Castle we get, at best, Kafka's playground. The steering column is relegated to private corporations, or a mix of the state functionaries and private economic interests.

Yet there is no disembodied "principle" dictating development. The goals and ideologies of men guide technological progress, not mechanistic marionette strings. Men make history, as Marx observed, but not according to conditions of their choosing. C. Wright Mills added that men are free to make history but that obviously some are freer than others.[109] "Technics and civilization as a whole are a result of human choices and attitudes and striving." Mumford writes: "deliberate as well as unconscious, often irrational when they appear most objective and scientific, but even when they are uncontrollable they are not external. . . . No matter how completely technics relies upon the objective procedures of the sciences, it does not form an independent system, like the universe; it exists as an element in human culture."[110]

Freedom requires access to the means of decisionmaking and the power by which decisions are implemented. "We must not think of the problem in terms of a choice between being determined and being free," Ellul writes. "We must look at it dialectically and say that man is indeed determined, but that it is open to him to overcome necessity, and that act is freedom. Freedom is not static, but dynamic, not a vested interest but a prize continually to be won."[111]

The Paradox of Technological "Fixes"

Technology does not operate in the perfectly friction-free environment that alone would enable Ellul's dire vision to come to pass. From the 1970s onwards it became apparent that the megamachine was teetering on the edge of a panoply of poorly understood limits. Unrestrained progress inflicted shocking setbacks with names like Vietnam, Bhopal, and Three Mile Island. The social feedback mechanisms required for prudent regulation obviously were impaired. Contradictions proliferated in the forms of human protest and environmental degradation. In the 1960s French sociologist Michel Crozier identified a fundamental tension afflicting all elitist grand schemes: "[P]eople have power over other people insofar as the latter's behavior is narrowly limited whereas their own is not [but as] long as some uncertainty remains in carrying out a task, the most menial subordinate retains some slight discretion, and in a way as long as the human being is preferred over the automatic machine there will be some uncertainty"— and noted that unheeded subordinates always will fight to retain and expand their degree of discretion.[112] This simple but lucid insight underlines the ineradicability of uncertainty and bargaining in human affairs, even in the most sophisticated organizations. Indeed, in any skewed social structure "increased rationality" for one group (such as managers) can mean increased insecurity for another group (line workers) whose resistance consequently produces "irrational" outcomes.[113]

Daniel Bell noted that planning "demands explicit recognition of value commitments and value priorities and often brings into the open value conflicts that remain hidden in the more impersonal and less conscious workings of the market system."[114] (This partly accounts for the rhetorical corporate enthusiasm for "restoring" a free market so as to conceal business-oriented agendas.) But the premier anomaly gestates within technology itself. Technology works in a finite system and, with its shiboleth of efficiency, jeopardizes human survival because nature through countless millennia of evolution simply has never been efficient. Survival has been achieved through maintenance of reserves, exploration of many potentials, proliferation of the species, and unpredictable divergences and mutations, both biological and social.[115]

Each solution to a technosocial problem proves to be only a quasisolution that triggers a host of residue problems. Technologists who view each problem as an isolated thing in an open system are in serious error. When parameters are expanded "to include the myriad of relationships with other processes and materials within a closed system, as is required for a realistic approach to the technological process, the solution is no longer complete."[116] Solutions are incomplete inasmuch as improvements are always possible and usually necessary. The augmentation of the original problem arises "when a higher-order problem is engendered by the completion of a solution" at which time the general problem demands a different type of solution. Another source of residue problems are the consequences when in solving an original problem, a number of secondary effects occur—some foreseen, others unexpected, some recognized, some not.[117]

Each successive set of new residue problems is more difficult to handle than the predecessors because of the dynamics of technology, increased complexity, increased cost, decreased resources, growth and expansion, requirements for greater control, and inertia of social institutions. Eugene Schwartz noted that when nature's cycles are broken or disturbed, authorities assume that only an application of more man-imposed order can prevent the breakdown of life-sustenance which these cycles serve. Yet imposed order overwhelms and undermines it with resulting threat of chaos. As each new successive technosocial solution requires controls, the institutions of control interfere with new solutions because of prior "commitments" and time lag. So the prudent course is not always, as technocratically minded elites believe, to refine the instruments at hand so as to do things somehow better but rather to do things differently or, in some cases, not at all.

Conclusion

Who or what rules? Sovereignty is diffused among a multitude of decision-making centers. Each group harbors interests that are not always congruent with other components, so friction is visible. But, as Ferkiss notes, these competing interests may be ultimately reconcilable. The groups composing the institutional order need not be monolithic—as in an Oliver Stone movie—yet still can exercise effective power over the way we live and, no less important, the way we think about the way we live. The governing of America and other advanced industrial societies is best characterized by a rise and fall of temporarily irresponsible groups, irresponsible because "many activities in their scope are essentially unaccountable in the democratic process, in a system of minimal accountability and minimum consent."[118]

So what John Kenneth Galbraith terms the technostructure—a "bureaucratic symbiosis" of private firms and public agencies—serves the interests (which it also works to shape) of "significant publics." The poor, the unskilled, the marginal, and the displaced workers are deemed insignificant, and the somewhat luckier "average citizen" is thought to be ignorant or easily swayed. Those who enjoy closest access to decisionmaking usually have the least reason to challenge or change the standards or procedures by which decisions are made. Thus a kind of triangular domination arises of technological imperatives, political "technocrats," and private economic interests.

Notes

1. Nigel Calder, *Technopolis* (New York: Simon & Schuster, 1969), p. 271.
2. John Kenneth Galbraith, *The Galbraith Reader* (London: Andre Deutsch, 1977).
3. The political effect of this special form of rationality is "to remove the total social framework of interests from view." Jurgen Habermas, "Science and Technology as Ideology," in *Toward a Rational Society* (Boston: Beacon Press, 1974), p. 82.

4. David Bloor, "Anti-Latour," *Studies in History and Philosophy of Science* 30, 1 (March 1999): 90.

5. See Hamish McCrae, *The World in 2020* (London: HarperCollins, 1994). Note the steady stream of publications by Alvin and Heidi Toffler, John Naisbitt, and other pop prognosticaters.

6. In addition to his own neologism Daniel Bell lists posteconomic, postcapitalist, postmodern, postbourgeois, postcollective, and posttraditional. See Daniel Bell, *The Coming of Post-Industrial Society* (London: Penguin, 1973), p. 52.

7. See Ronald Inglehart, *Culture Shift in Advanced Industrial Society* (Princeton: Princeton University, 1992).

8. On the misestimation of leisure in a postindustrial society see Juliet Schor, *The Overworked American: The Unexpected Decline of Leisure* (New York: Basic Books, 1994).

9. This definition is found in Joseph Schumpeter, *Capitalism, Socialism and Democracy* (New York: Harper, 1942). There is plenty of tacit support in the upper reaches of society for the sentiment frankly expressed by the first chief justice of the Supreme Court that "the people who own the country ought to govern it." Quoted in Noam Chomsky, *Necessary Illusions: Thought Control in Democratic Societies* (London: Pluto Press, 1989), p. 36.

10. Hannah Arendt, *On Violence* (New York: Harcourt, Brace & World, 1969), pp. 7–8.

11. On the scholarly need to pay attention to the beliefs, norms, and self-images of technical elites in order to explain national and sectoral variations in policy outcomes see J. Nicholas Ziegler, *Governing Ideas: Strategies for Innovation in Germany and France* (Ithaca: Cornell University Press, 1997), p. 16.

12. While the average manufacturing wage fell slightly over 1981–1990 (and Americans in poverty increased a quarter) the after-tax income of the upper 20 percent rose from $73,000 to $91,000. John Kenneth Galbraith, *The Culture of Contentment* (Boston: Houghton Mifflin, 1992), p. 105. See also William Julius Wilson, *When Work Disappears* (New York: Alfred Knopf, 1996).

13. On the United States see Edward N. Wolff, *Top Heavy* (New York: Twentieth Century Fund, 1995). On Britain see Will Hutton, *The State We're In* (London: Vintage, 1995). Regarding financial sector schemes to "move effective decision-making entirely out of the political arena and into the hands of technicians and market 'players,'" see Louis W. Pauly, *Who Elected the Bankers?* (Ithaca: Cornell University Press, 1997).

14. See Zbigniew Brzezinski, *Between Two Ages: America's Role in the Technetronic Arena* (New York: Viking Press, 1970); and Daniel Bell, *The Coming of Post-Industrial Society* and his *The Cultural Contradictions of Capitalism* (London: Penguin, 1976).

15. Bell, *Coming of Post-Industrial Society*, p. 112.

16. *Ibid.*, p. 123.

17. *Ibid.*, pp. 8, 256.

18. *Ibid.*, p. 128; and Victor Ferkiss, *Technological Man: The Myth and the Reality* (New York: Mentor Books, 1968).

19. Today as in the 1960s "the vast majority of experts" in science, medicine, and technology "have a stake in their own authority going unchallenged." See John Abraham and Julie Shepherd, "Democracy, Technocracy and the Secret State of

Medicine: Expert and Non-expert Perspectives," *Science, Technology and Human Values* 22, 2 (Spring 1997): 147.

20. Brzezinski, *Between Two Ages,* p. 264. Bell more cagily anticipated a shift from property and/or political criteria to knowledge as "the basis of *new* power"; see Bell, *Coming of Post-Industrial Society,* p. 343. What happens to possessors of the "old" power?

21. Brzezinski, *Between Two Ages,* p. 259.

22. Jacques Ellul, *The Technological Society* (New York: Knopf, 1964), pp. 17–18. On Weber's morose life see Arthur Mitzman, *The Iron Cage* (New York: Grosset & Dunlap, 1971). For a work that surpasses Ellul's pessimism, see Friedrich Georg Juenger, *The Failure of Technology* (Chicago: Henry Regnery Press, 1956).

23. Primo Levi, *The Mirror Makers* (New York: Schocken Books, 1989), p. 86.

24. Karl Marx and Frederick Engels, *The Communist Manifesto* (London: Verso, 1998), p. 37.

25. Emile Durkheim, *The Division of Labor in Society* (New York: Free Press, 1957).

26. Cited in Reinhard Bendix, *Max Weber: An Intellectual Portrait* (New York: Doubleday, 1962), p. 464.

27. *Ibid.,* p. 406.

28. William Scheurman, "Economic Globalization and the Rule of Law," *Constellations* 6, 1 (March 1999): 3.

29. On commodification and "decommodification" see Sam Bowles and Herb Gintis, "The Crisis of Liberal Democratic Capitalism," *Politics and Society* 11, 2 (1982).

30. Jacques Ellul, *The Technological Society* (New York: Knopf, 1964), p. 135.

31. Winner defines reverse adaptation as "the adjustment of human ends to match available means." Langdon Winner, *Autonomous Technology: Technology-Out-Of-Control as a Theme in Political Thought* (Cambridge, Mass.: MIT Press, 1977), p. 229.

32. Ellul, *The Technological Society,* p. 11.

33. Other notable works include Joseph Weizenbaum, *Computer Power and Human Reason* (New York: Freeman, 1975), and Theodore Roszak, *The Cult of Information* (London: Butterworth Press, 1986). Also see Bruno Bettelheim's case study "Joey the Mechanical Boy," in *The Empty Fortress* (New York: Free Press, 1967), pp. 233–342.

34. Karl Mannheim, *Man and Society in an Age of Reconstruction* (New York: Harcourt, Brace & World, 1951), p. 55.

35. See Theodore Roszak, *The Making of a Counter-Culture: Reflections on the Technocratic Society and Its Youthful Opposition* (New York: Anchor Books, 1969); and Clifford Geertz, "Ideology as a Cultural System," in *The Interpretation of Cultures* (New York: Basic Books, 1973).

36. See Floyd W. Matson, *The Broken Image: Man, Science and Society* (New York: Doubleday, 1964).

37. Robert K. Merton cited in Ellul, *The Technological Society,* p. 6.

38. This is a theme in Giovanni Dosi, Christopher Freeman, Richard Nelson, Gerald Silverberg, and Luc Soete, eds.,*Technical Innovation and Economic Change* (London: Frances Pinter, 1991).

39. Ferkiss, *Technological Man,* p. 26.

40. Herbert Marcuse, *Eros and Civilization* (New York: Random House, 1955), p. 3.

41. Paul Goodman, *People or Personnel and Like a Conquered Province* (New York: Random House, 1968), p. 315.

42. The definition is supplied by Ernst Voegelin. Cited in William H. Whyte, *The Organization Man* (New York: Simon and Schuster, 1956), p. 23.

43. For the most extreme example of this combination in action see Jeffrey Herf, *Reactionary Modernism* (Cambridge: Cambridge University Press, 1984).

44. See David Halberstam, *The Best and The Brightest* (New York: Vintage, 1975). Also James William Gibson, *The Perfect War* (New York: Atlantic Monthly Press, 1986), pp. 64, 332; and Neil Sheehan, *The Pentagon Papers* (New York: Bantam Books, 1971), p. 241.

45. For a discussion of technocracy in terms of political theory see chapter 4 in Winner, *Autonomous Technology*.

46. Jean Meynaud, *Technocracy* (London: Faber & Faber, 1968), pp. 293, 294. On Soviet ambivalence regarding technocracy see Kendall Bailes, *Technology and Society Under Lenin and Stalin* (Princeton: Princeton University Press, 1978), pp. 1–25, 106.

47. Ziegler, *Governing Ideas*, pp. 17–39.

48. Sam Adams, *War of Numbers: An Intelligence Memoir* (South Royalton, VT.: Steelforth Press, 1994).

49. See Robert Jungk, *Brighter Than a Thousand Suns* (London: Penguin, 1982).

50. Robert Merton, *Science, Technology and Society in the Seventeenth Century* (New York: Howard Fertig, 1938); and James R. Jacob, "The Political Economy of Science in Seventeenth Century England," in Margaret C. Jacob, ed. *The Politics of Western Science, 1640–1990* (Atlantic Highlands, N.J.: Humanities Press, 1994).

51. Joseph Ben-David, *The Scientist's Role in Society* (New York: Prentice-Hall, 1972), pp. 74, 86.

52. Lewis Mumford, *The Myth of the Machine: The Pentagon of Power* (New York: Harcourt Brace, 1970), p. 115.

53. For more nuanced discussions of utopias and technology see Harold P. Segal, *Technological Utopianism in American Thought* (Chicago: University of Chicago, 1985); and Patrocinio Schweckart, "What If . . . Science and Technology in Feminist Utopias" in Joan Rothschild, ed., *Machina Ex Dea: Feminist Perspectives on Technology* (New York: Pergamon, 1983), pp. 198–212.

54. Euban, "Political Science and Political Silence," in Phillip Green and Sanford Levinson, eds., *Power and Community: Dissenting Essays in Political Science* (New York: Random House, 1968), p. 67.

55. *Ibid.*, p. 159.

56. Alexis de Tocqueville, *Democracy in America* (New York: Doubleday, 1969), pp. 56–57, 246–261.

57. Richard Slotkin, *Gunfighter Nation: The Myth of the Frontier in America* (New York: Atheneum, 1992), p. 20.

58. Michael Parenti, "Assimilation and Counter-Assimilation," in Green and Levinson, *Power and Community*, p. 192.

59. Slotkin, *Gunfighter Nation*, p. 21.

60. Reinhard Bendix, *Work and Authority: Ideologies of Management in Industrialization* (New York: Harper, 1963).

61. Dwight Waldo, *The Administrative State* (New York: Ronald Press, 1948), p. 70.

62. Thorstein Veblen, *The Engineers and the Price System* (New York: Viking, 1940).

63. David Rappaport, "Have Intellectuals a Class Interest?" in Hans Peter Dreitzel, *Recent Sociology #1* (London: Macmillan, 1969), p. 229.

64. The Soviet Union in the Stalinist 1930s experienced its own conflict between the reductionist-minded "mechanists" and the opposing "Deborinites." See Bailes, *Society and Technology Under Lenin and Stalin*, p. 43. The result was "conciliarism," which amounted to truth by committee vote. Lenin, however, believed that "natural scientists spontaneously practiced dialectical materialism" and saw no need to interfere in research so long as they did not interfere with the party.

65. Peter Hass and Emmanuel Adler, eds., special issue on epistemic communities, *International Organization* 43, 2 (Autumn 1991): 11.

66. Regarding Harris polls indicating a steep decline in public esteem for practitioners of science and medicine, see Sheila Jasonoff, "The Dilemma of Environmental Democracy," *Issues in Science and Technology* (Fall 1996): 64. Also see Leonard A. Cole, *Politics and the Restraint of Science* (Totowa, N.J.: Rowman & Allanheld, 1983).

67. Allan Mazur, *The Dynamics of Technical Controversy* (Washington, D.C.: Communications Press, 1981), pp. 81–82.

68. This accords with Geertz's comment that "competing ideologies are at least as important a check on ideological claims" as is scientific analysis. Quoted in Clifford Geertz, "Ideology as a Cultural System," in *The Interpretation of Cultures* (New York: Basic Books, 1973), p. 230.

69. See Thorstein Veblen, *The Engineers and the Price System* (New York: Viking Press, 1940). On the attraction of German engineers to Nazi ideology, see Herf, *Reactionary Modernism*, pp. 152–188.

70. See Lewis Mumford, *The Myth of the Machine: Technics and Human Development* (New York: Harcourt, Brace & World, 1967), pp. 193–222.

71. Mumford, *The Pentagon of Power*, p. 165. For a similar but feminist critique of the triumph of this tradition, see Carolyn Merchant, *The Death of Nature: Women, Ecology and the Scientific Revolution* (New York: Harper & Row, 1980).

72. Joan Rothschild, "Introduction," in Rothschild, *Machina Ex Dea*, p. xxii.

73. Hannah Arendt, *The Human Condition* (Chicago: University of Chicago Press, 1958), pp. 242–243.

74. For a cogent critique, see Michael Paul Rogin, *The Intellectuals and McCarthy* (Cambridge, Mass.: MIT Press, 1967), especially chapter 9.

75. This is the subtitle of Daniel Bell's *The End of Ideology* (Glencoe: Free Press, 1956). In this vein, see Rolf Dahrendorf, *Class and Class Conflict in Industrial Society* (Stanford: Stanford University Press, 1959). For a critique, see Anthony Giddens, *Class Structure in Advanced Industrial Societies* (London: Hutchinson, 1973).

76. See Anthony Shonfield, *Modern Capitalism: The Changing Balance of Public and Private Power* (New York: Oxford University Press, 1965).

77. Thomas S. Kuhn, *The Structure of Scientific Revolutions* (Chicago: University of Chicago, 1962), p. 5. Also see Imre Lakatos and Alan Musgrave, eds., *Criticism and the Growth of Knowledge* (Cambridge: Cambridge University Press, 1969).

78. Kuhn, *The Structure of Scientific Revolutions*, pp. 10–11.

79. *Ibid.*, p. 180.

80. Euban, "Political Science and Political Silence," in Green and Levinson, *Power and Community*, pp. 19, 21–22.

81. Paul Feyerabend, *Against Method* (London: New Left Books, 1975), pp. 41, 47, 204.

82. *Ibid.*, p. 117.

83. E. A. Burtt, *The Metaphysical Foundations of Modern Science* (Garden City, N.Y.: Doubleday Books, 1954), p. 38.

84. See Bruno Latour and Stephen Woolgar, *Laboratory Life: The Construction of Scientific Fact*, 2d ed (Princeton: Princeton University Press, 1986), p. 246. Also see Latour, *Science in Action* (Milton Keynes: Open University Press, 1987).

85. Latour and Woolgar, *Laboratory Life*, p. 281.

86. *Ibid.*, p. 229.

87. See Feyerabend, *Against Method,* chapters 1, 3, 4, 6, 8–11, and 13. Also see Feyerabend, *Science in a Free Society* (London: Verso, 1978), Part 1, chapters 5 and 6, and Part 2, chapters 6 and 9.

88. Herbert Marcuse, *Eros and Civilization* (New York: Vintage, 1956), p. 112.

89. Bloor, "Anti-Latour," p. 90.

90. Trevor Pinch, "The Social Construction of Technology: A Review," in Robert Fox, ed., *Technological Change: Methods and Theory in the History of Technology* (Amsterdam: Harwood Academic Publishers, 1996), p. 26.

91. The enlightenment view is of "a science that is universal" because it is produced by structures of the mind common to us all. The knowledge produced when particulars are dominated by the abstract is a means-to-ends (instrumental) form of reason. Its purpose is control of one's passions and will, and of the physical and social worlds. This form of reason inevitably produces a technology of control as the manifestation of its adequacy, or "reasonableness."

92. Herbert Marcuse, *Reason and Revolution* (Boston: Beacon Press, 1960), p. 343.

93. See Michel Crozier, *The Bureaucratic Phenomenon* (Chicago: University of Chicago Press, 1967).

94. Horkheimer, *Critical Theory: Selected Essays* (New York: Herder and Herder, 1972), p. x. Leszek Kolakowski, *Positive Philosophy* (New York: Penguin, 1972), offers an account of versions of positivist tradition from which reductionism stems.

95. Henry A. Giroux, *Disturbing Pleasures: Learning Popular Culture* (London: Routledge, 1994), p. 113.

96. Bernard Crick, *In Defence of Politics* (London: Penguin, 1962), p. 21.

97. See C. Wright Mills, *The Sociological Imagination* (New York: Oxford University Press, 1959), chapter 10.

98. See Richard Flacks, "On Participatory Democracy," *Dissent* (November–December 1966); and Paul Jacobs and Saul Landau, *The New Radicals* (New York: Random House, 1966), pp. 154–157.

99. Flacks, "On Participatory Democracy," p. 70.

100. Arendt, *The Human Condition* , p. 35.

101. *Ibid.*, p. 38.

102. Ruth Schwartz Cowan, *More Work for Mother: The World of Household Technology from the Open Hearth to the Microwave* (New York: Basic Books, 1983), p. 9.

103. Arendt, *The Human Condition*, p. 59.

104. Jacques Ellul, *The Political Illusion* (New York: Knopf, 1968).

105. Ferkiss, *Technological Man*, p. 131.

106. Theodore Lowi, *The End of Liberalism* (New York: Norton, 1969).

107. Ferkiss, *Technological Man*, p. 151.

108. John H. Schaar, "Legitimacy in the Modern State," in Green and Levinson, *Power and Community*, pp. 297, 311.

109. Mills, *The Sociological Imagination*, p. 181.

110. Lewis Mumford, *Technics and Civilization* (New York: Harcourt, Brace & World, 1934), p. 6.

111. Ellul, *The Technological Society*, p. xxxiii.

112. Crozier, *The Bureaucratic Phenomenon*, pp. 158, 162. "A human being," Crozier says, "does not only have a hand and a heart. He also has a head, which means that he is free to decide to play his own game. This is what almost all proponents of human relations theories, as well as their early rationalist opponents, tend to forget."

113. Yehonda Shenhau, "Manufacturing Uncertainty and Uncertainty in Manufacturing: Managerial Discourse and the Rhetoric of Organizational Ideology," *Science in Context* 7, 2 (Summer 1994): 290.

114. Daniel Bell, *Coming of Post-Industrial Society;* and Emmanual Mesthene, *Technological Change: Its Impact on Man and Society* (Cambridge, Mass.: Harvard University Press, 1970), p. 45.

115. Eugene S. Schwartz, *Overskill: The Decline of Technology in Civilization* (Chicago: Quadrangle Books, 1971).

116. *Ibid.*, p. 59.

117. *Ibid.*, p. 61.

118. Tom Hayden and Marc Pilisuc, "Is There a Military-Industrial Complex Which Prevents Peace?: Consensus and Countervailing Power in Pluralistic Systems," in Robert Perucci and Marc Pilisuc, *The Triple Revolution* (Boston: Little, Borwn, 1968), p. 90.

2

The Specter of Automation

Never have so many been so completely at the mercy of so few.
—Aldous Huxley

In early nineteenth-century England desperate workers deliberately damaged the new power looms and threshers that were displacing them. These Luddites, named after mythical rebel Ned Ludd, became identified in history with futile resistance to technological progress. At the time, however, Great Britain was ruled by landowners and industrialists who crafted the laws exclusively to suit their (sometimes conflicting) interests. A new ideology of laissez-faire blessed this world where the powerful aided each other and the weak were forced to fend for themselves. Bringing labor-saving machinery into such a deeply skewed social milieu could not help but spread misery and stir resistance. Yet the sufferers were angry not so much at things (machines) as at what spokesman William Cobbet called "the Thing, the whole conspiracy of the rich against the poor."[1] Living and working conditions would improve as a result of a long bouts of violent protest, political agitation, and legislative reforms. Machinery alone was never the villain, but new technology afterward retained an underlying sense of menace, especially in hard times.

During the Great Depression of the 1930s and in the economically erratic 1950s, controversies erupted again about the nature of the impact of technology on ordinary people's livelihoods. The threatening image of technology as a "job killer" ebbed away in the 1960s when jobs abounded, living standards shot up, and what some critics called the military-industrial complex grew unchecked (particularly during the Vietnam War).[2] Analysts hailed the new talent of modern capitalist states to smooth economic fluctuations through the clever use of Keynesian interventionist techniques.

The "violence of the marketplace"—economic fluctuations, sudden firings, wage cuts, work speed-ups, employer tyranny—promised to be nothing more than museum exhibits in those prudent polities that regulated macro-economic policy, installed welfare systems, and coordinated the activities of public authorities with private firms in order to minimize market uncertainties, resource misallocation and, especially, unemployment.[3] Everyone would make a good living under fair conditions in a humane system, or so it happily appeared.

The linchpin of the "social democratic compromise" (that is, the peaceful institutionalization of class conflict in collective bargaining in the workplace and party competition in the political realm) was the post–World War II commitment by industrial states to sustain full employment through the bad patches that any dynamic economy undergoes. Many European societies recognized that the benefits of growth did not automatically extend to all, or even a majority, of citizens, so that state mechanisms must be in place to ensure spreading of new wealth in ways that serve the public good. In a giddy climate of constant economic growth it would not seem far-fetched to foresee an "end of ideology" or, even later, an "end of history" culminating in liberal market-oriented democracies.[4] So technical change, which since the awesome onset of the industrial revolution sparked justifiable fears among vulnerable workers, came to be viewed more or less as benign. But, reflecting on the 1950s automation debate, which may well have been more premature than preposterous, anthropologist Jules Henry provocatively observed

We misuse automation, for instead of using the increased productivity resulting from it to lower prices, and expand consumption, and hence production and employment, it is being employed to displace workers, while much of the savings made possible by the new techniques are distributed to profits. This has always been the case when new technology has been invented. And it always takes a century and terrifying depression to alter the situation. . . . We must not be bamboozled by the 'spectre of automation,' for it becomes manageable when viewed against the background of all economic possibilities, including the gigantic powers of government.[5]

In the aftermath of the OPEC oil crises in the 1970s, and particularly the epidemic of corporate "downsizing" from the 1980s onward, the latent fear of technological unemployment revived. A widely hailed "information revolution" ignited a fresh round in the automation debate in which optimists (who always seem to occupy secure posts) acclaimed microelectronics as the "carrier" of a new "long wave" of prosperity while a pessimist camp foresaw steady erosion in the number and quality of decently paid jobs. Modern states, the latter said, face a "microchip dilemma" that stipulates

that in a competitive global economy, slow adoption by firms of new productive technologies would cause more job losses than its rapid adoption.[6]
The excruciating choice posed for citizens is to embrace new technology
now and lose some jobs or else fail to adopt it with necessary haste and so
lose many more jobs in the long run. In an unbridled era of Schumpeterian
"creative destruction," industries must, as the dire slogan warns, "automate or evaporate."[7]

Still, one must always be wary of extrapolations from present trends and
attentive to the *contingent* character of technical change (that is, the degree
to which outcomes depend upon a host of contributing causes that themselves are changeable). A European government report, for example, detected in the microelectronics revolution "a contradiction between employment and foreign trade" (because the policy measures needed to improve
competitiveness eliminate jobs), but it also took pains to identify the *social*
determinants that combined to create this plight.[8] That study—the Nora
Report—will serve as a useful foil against which to assess various ap-
praisals in the automation debate.[9] In this chapter I also incorporate examples from case studies of the United States, Britain, France, and Japan, because a broad canvas enables us to trace the impact of policy decisions
down to the workplace level, and back again, and to tease out the effects of
the same technical changes in different settings.

Technology policy debates usually focus on the most suitable policy mix
by which to stimulate the expansion and diffusion of cutting-edge microelectronics firms and products in order to hone a national competitive advantage. This narrow and conventional emphasis brushes aside vital social
questions as to the nature of the impact of technology on broader objectives
of national welfare. Quite a few studies have tried to correct (in some cases,
over-correct) this presumably pragmatic trend by emphasizing, among other
things, that the effective use of new productive technology requires a multitude of preceding changes in managerial habits, organizational structures,
and workplace practices. One doesn't drop a machine into a functioning
work environment and expect it to operate without a hitch. What is called
"architectural innovation" also is needed to properly shift the relationship
among separate manufacturing elements into a coherent process.[10] This
theme also is a staple one in studies of military innovations and their integration within battlefield units and headquarters strategy.

This chapter pays particular attention to members of what I dub the
"Sussex School," who operate at or congregate around critical themes developed primarily at the Science Policy Unit of the University of Sussex.
They, of course, are not alone in arguing that policy analysis must pay
acute attention to the "societal context: including economic, but also social
and ethical factors which will set the conditions within which technological
change will be adapted, even selected."[11] As an American scholar likewise

found in Japan, "politics shaped the context of the rights and roles to which people resort in deciding how the economy should be organized; [machine tool industry workers] came to interpret industrial options and producers to adopt strategies to promote economic recovery in ways ultimately rooted in ideologies and power struggles affecting industrial choices."[12]

The Sussex School and like-minded critics demonstrate that contrary to conventional wisdom, "efficiency" actually increases when public policy emphasizes "equity enhancing" economic measures. Market forces, though undeniably important, cannot suffice to improve competitiveness while maintaining social stability too. Bear in mind that job loss is not necessarily a symptom of grave problems. A dynamic economy can shed as many as one in every ten jobs each year; the displaced workers should soon be absorbed elsewhere in more productive and profitable activities. But this placid scenario assumes that workers' skills are transferable, that adequate provisions for retraining assure a redistribution of labor to needed posts, and that the added wealth is spread among all income groups. Another strained assumption is that labor is mobile or else that the productive machinery is—but not too much so (i.e., going offshore). Unemployment only becomes a policy problem when (1) the rate of displacement outruns the pace of job creation over a protracted period, and (2) when pressure is brought to bear on policymakers who are institutionally capable of responding with ameliorative measures.

Beneath the more visible causes of economic turbulence there is a second "great transformation" (the first being the industrial revolution) under way in which, as Karl Polanyi noted, a "double movement" occurs: (1) a relentless reassertion of the market as the supreme organizing principle (extremely so in what formerly were the Soviet Union and the Eastern bloc nations), and (2) a resurgence of countermovements organized on the basis of the principle of social protection, that is, aiming to reform their social systems to operate, as E. F. Schumacher once put it, "as if people mattered."[13] In this chapter I contend that the microchip dilemma can be tamed under conditions that I identify, particularly changes in institutional structures and in the ideas that guide industrial policies and practices.[14]

High Tech: Military Origins, Commercial Imperatives

The glamorous label of "high technology" is applied to those industries in which "product development involves large development costs, long lead times, and considerable technological uncertainty" and that rely on "knowledge that is close to the frontiers of present-day scientific research."[15] These industries include computers, robotics, fiber optics, genetic engineering, aerospace, artificial intelligence, and telecommunications. Head-spinningly rapid in pace of development and amazingly wide in scope of applications, microelectronics is deemed to be by far the most vital element because it undergirds, pervades, and enhances other technologies and promises to revitalize such classic "low-tech" industries as steel, automobiles, and garments.

Yet private enterprise did not originate it. The U.S. government—primarily the Department of Defense—played the crucial role nurturing this risky and expensive industry through grants and procurement policies so that microelectronics soon became "the most outstanding success story in terms of government policy to stimulate technical progressiveness, growth and employment in the postwar period."[16] Savvy analysts answer with "a fairly clear 'no'" the question whether private interests could develop the computer industry even remotely at the pace of this generously state-aided program.[17] Military Keynesianism, which is explored in depth in the next chapter, is a camouflaged form of state aid for private industries. During the height of the cold war any spending proposal linked to the sanctifying cause of national security won not only the approval of conservative legislators but also the consent of liberals who feared being labeled "soft" on defense.

After the abrupt collapse of the Soviet Union in 1991 defense programs instead were "sold to Congress as a response to industry's eroding technological leadership."[18] Since one barely can imagine a high-tech product devoid of defense applications, this tactic remains a very attractive rationale by which free-market devotees especially in the United States and Britain can keep their fiscal principles at bay while dispensing lavish funds to favored firms (which enjoyed paying a steadily declining share of total tax during the cold war years). By 1997 defense research and development (R&D) was 16 percent less than in 1992 while total federal spending for R&D was down 7 percent.[19] In 1998 the Clinton administration—which boosted annual military research by 2.2 percent—promised to even out a 60–40 split between military and commercial applications of research money. U.S. presidential administrations always have encouraged "dual purpose" programs serving both military and civilian uses.[20]

In the United States, "dual purpose" programs have a long history that includes numerous National Science Foundation projects (which increasingly favor applied research) and the Defense Department's Division of Applied Research and Advanced Projects (DARPA), which, in turn, bankrolled the Very High Scale Integrated Circuits (VHSIC) project, the 1980s Strategic Computing Initiative, and a share in the public-private Semtech corporation. The state dispensed valuable favors in other ways, too. Antitrust regulations were relaxed to facilitate mergers in general and the formation in particular of an industrial consortium, the Microelectronics and Computer Technology Corporation. At that time these measures were motivated as much by economic competition with Japan, which was viewed as an almost supernaturally strong economy, as by fear of likely military rivals. Even for staunchly conservative European governments Japan's announcement in the 1980s of its ambitious "fifth generation" project "made it respectable to use public funds on a large scale" in such projects as France's *Plan Filiere Electronique* and Britain's Alvey scheme, which both just happened to have a significant defense component.[21] President Ronald Reagan's Strategic Defense Initiative (SDI) in 1983 dangled before potential participants the seductive prospect of reaping subsidized technical advantages. An elementary question posed by those few who were not queuing up for lucrative defense contracts was whether this money would be well-spent relative to alternative uses.

Economic historian Nathan Rosenberg, among many others, found that Reagan's audacious "Star Wars" Initiative only reinforced "the impression that the military and civilian sectors confront increasingly divergent needs" because today's "unique military requirements are of little use or relevance to manufacturers of civilian products."[22] If this is so, the urgent task instead is to align new investments with an invigorating "long wave" of commercial technical advances. According to this innovation-based theory of economic growth, microelectronics and computers are the successors to the "basic innovations" (steam and power looms, coal and transport, steel and autos, oil and consumer durables) propelling previous waves of technical change and economic growth.[23] Microelectronics advances have pushed continuously decreased production costs (though costs of chip-making equipment and laboratories soared), greater packing density per chip, price falls, and improvements in reliability, custom capability, and power consumption.

A virtual consensus on policy reforms quickly emerged among elites across the advanced industrial states. An eminent European observer advised Americans to shift resources from "sheltered" industries—which make complex custom-made products for a few sophisticated customers—to "exposed" commercial enterprises that compete in world markets. These two kinds of firms work in arenas characterized by different logics of competition; their products and processes do not cross the boundary easily. Since the mid-1960s analysts had spotted a trend toward declining commercial payoffs from defense research. Indeed, after deducting defense funds from total R&D over the period 1961–1985 it turns out that U.S. research spending had been surpassed by France, Japan, and West Germany.[24] By 1990 U.S. nondefense R&D comprised 2 percent of gross national product (GNP) versus Japan's 2.9 percent and Germany's 2.6 percent.

The traditional direction of spin-offs between military and civilian applications had reversed. So the Defense Department funded the VHSIC research program and the Strategic Computing Initiative in hope of capturing vital know-how from commercial enterprises. In turn these firms would use the research results to develop marketable products—a process that so far has proved unsatisfactory.[25] Among the remedies urged are more grants, more tax breaks (especially for R&D), and creation of a special government department to improve the commercial technology base. In the aftermath of the cold war the problems of adjusting professional and organizational cultures from military to civil purposes loom dauntingly large. "There's a big difference in these kinds of thinking," said a senior research fellow at Hoover Institute. "The military is high-tech, almost regardless of cost. But in any commercial calculation, cost is always primary. These guys don't have the right mindset."[26]

Before Japan's financial calamities in the 1990s, European analysts had urged Americans to collaborate with European partners in order to fend off the rising sun—which U.S. firms instead were embracing in a multitude of joint ventures (very nearly including the purchase of a White House–approved stake in a manufacturer of nuclear weapons components).[27] But joint ventures alone allow proficient foreign firms to acquire physical and intellectual capital from weaker partners while maintaining control of their local strategies. This hardly aids the home front. So, according to critics, there seems to be no substitute for an activist state policy.

The need for state aid is such that even in pre-Blairite Britain a doctrinaire laissez-faire government grudgingly became a "coordinater and catalyst," appointed a minister for information technology, and launched a five-year project, called Alvey, to stimulate the indigenous computer industry. More catalyzing then coordinating took place. Alvey's director noted how "ironic" it was that the university cutbacks imposed by Tories cut down the engineering and computer personnel that the state, through other policies, aimed to expand.[28] After the Alvey project elapsed, British policies remained rigorously uncoordinated even if they did improve on an earlier attitude, recalled by a Department of Industry official.[29]

> In 1979 Keith Joseph asked me and my division to produce a report on information technology. . . . We put the report together which, infelicitously, we headed "A Strategy for information technology." I remember Lord Trenchard, the industry minister, responding: "Atkinson, what is this bloody nonsense? We don't have strategies in this government."

Alvey intended to foster a "collaborative culture" of academics and industrialists. The supreme task was to divine "how to organize Britain's effort to the best advantage of industry." What happened? Academic institutions forked out more money than anticipated in yet another subsidy to industries. A study found that academics performed their part creditably whereas huge firms like GEC, Plessey, and British Telecom came and went as they pleased.[30] The Alvey case typified a pervasive line of thought that supposed that when competitiveness goals are met, everything else magically will sort itself out. What became clear was that anointing business people, even from the august Business Roundtable or the Confederation of Business Industries, to carry out public policy was not a very reliable way to tackle the problems of accommodating new technology.

Riding the Fifth Wave: Radical Critiques

A dominant theme in contemporary research on innovation is that socio-organizational changes (institutional, managerial, legal, and educational) are essential if technical innovations are to flourish in socially beneficial ways. So spurring progress is not merely a matter of finding the right promotional schemes. This alternative view is most cogently stated by the Sussex School critics. Christopher Freeman and associates have focused squarely on the job-generating aspect of long waves and offered what they call "radical Keynesian prescriptions" to cope with a volatile environment in which technical change is eroding the empirical basis for neoclassical economics.[31] The Sussex critics add technical change to the customary list of impediments to steady (equilibrium) growth: time lags, undetermined expectations, limited factor substitution, and wage and price inelasticities due to oligopolistic practices. They unabashedly raise the heretical "possibility of technological unemployment which results from technical change but is dependent on institutional constraints to adaptation."[32]

There are numerous long-wave theories, and all of them are controversial.[33] The version favored by the Sussex researchers posits that during any boom period, industries will exploit the commercial potential of interrelated "technology systems," install new capacity, stimulate capital goods production and secondary investments, and so create lots of jobs. These new and mostly small-to-medium firms are labor intensive (they depend more on workers than machines to increase output) because the technologies still are in a "fluid state" and production has not yet been standardized. But sustained expansion generates labor shortages and inflationary pressures on labor costs, so that profitability

tends to decline and there is increasing induced demand for labour-saving technical innovation throughout the economy. . . . [As] a new industry or technology matures, several factors are interacting to reduce the employment generated per unit of investment. Economies of scale become increasingly important and these work in combination with technical changes and organizational changes associated with increasing standardization. The profits of innovation are diminished both by competition and by pressures on input costs, especially labour costs. A process of concentration tends to occur.[34]

Hard times set in as markets become saturated. Under these straitened circumstances investment will be channeled into productivity-enhancing measures (to obtain the same output from less labor) so that even as investment expands during successive "upswings as a result of Keynesian and other stimuli, it has less effect on employment, unless it is directed to areas of very low capital intensity such as government and administrative services."[35] They supply data attesting that since the 1960s ever higher increments of output, growth, and investment have been required to generate a given level of employment.[36] This troubling trend was apparent in France, West Germany, Italy, and the United Kingdom since the 1970s. The United States created 25 million jobs during the period 1975–1985 but at a high cost in productivity—and the quality of these jobs, and of those created under the recent Clinton boom, is a source of great controversy.[37] Jobs are nothing to cheer about if you need two or three of them to pay your bills. Even Japan, with its highly touted lifetime employment schemes (which applied to a fraction of firms and were never guaranteed), came under sway of this corrosive trend by the late 1970s.

But the fundamental problem for researchers as well as policymakers is an ongoing shift in the "techno-economic paradigm," which the Sussex critics define as the "cluster of interrelated technical, managerial and organizational innovations, whose advantages are to be found not only in a new range of products and systems, but most of all in the dynamics of the relative cost structure of all possible inputs to production." This paradigm shift is ushering societies from reliance on technologies based on cheap energy to those "predominantly based on cheap inputs of information derived from advances in microelectronics."[38] Ignoring the profound nature of this change leads to foolish policy choices. How is this so?

The Sussex authors argue that President Jimmy Carter's 1977–1978 "reflation in one country" strategy (a Keynesian injection of state spending)—which was repeated with the same unhappy inflationary result in France in 1981–1983—exemplified the futility of interventionist measures that are insensitive to the uneven distribution and the differential impact of technical change across sectors with varying capital, marketing, and research resources.[39] But a return to mythical good old days of free markets was even less advisable. Monetarist policies were deemed even more pernicious because, apart from their human toll, they protract periods of low demand and, accordingly, depress business expectations. Nothing—not taxes, wage levels, or regulative activity—is more important to investors than demand expectations, because the prospect of sustained demand augers high sales and profits. In slack periods, firms often carry out an excessive scrapping of unused assets, a rational short-term act that only will impede the next economic upturn because of a consequent shortage of productive potential to meet demand. Inflationary pressure increases and so will the temptation to inflict severe austerity policies—and the vicious cycle continues.

Prime minister Margaret Thatcher's Britain was the premier laboratory for free-market nostrums well into the 1990s. The uninspiring result was that the manufacturing share of GNP dropped from 29.5 percent in 1978 to 21.9 percent by 1987; the celebrated "leaner, fitter" survivors exhibited a condition "more like emaciation."[40] All firms obviously are not the same, and it does no good for governments to treat them as if they were. The different capacities of firms to absorb innovations meant that (1) those powerful firms with high expansive potential could exploit opportunities, (2) industries with low expansive potential resorted instead to labor-saving forms of equipment and organization, and (3) small firms, which were unable or unwilling to install new equipment, intensified their work processes. None of these routes is calculated to generate many jobs (and instead in the 1990s a mania for "downsizing" pervaded industry). Hence, the Sussex critics urge that governments devise and adopt sectorally sensitive sets of technology policies.

In Britain over the past quarter-century, workplace rationalization was more important than technical change as a cause of job loss.[41] What is crucial to recognize is that this was by no means a straightforward response to market forces but was as much a result of a Tory government strategy to change the balance of power between labor and management in the latter's favor, and thereby alter the calculations that managers would make about the merits of different types of investment.[42] The upshot is that if a government, in order to instill "discipline," curbs the bargaining power of labor both through legislation favoring management and by deflationary policies that encourage unemployment (which reduces workers' value) it also diminishes the incentives for industrialists to invest in new technologies.[43] Unless global demand for local products suddenly counteracts the loss in domestic purchasing power, companies cut back production or gear existing technologies so as to produce the same amount with less labor and, at the next upturn, resort to hiring cheaper labor rather than try to improve their technological base. The legacy is that well into a new Labour government's term British workers endure the longest work week in the European Union and under conditions of high insecurity and unenviable wages. The number of people working two jobs in order to survive doubled between 1984 to 1999.[44] (Beholding this, some observers suggest there may well be a peculiarly punitive, as well as pecuniary, motive driving those groups who confidently peddle these collectively irrational policies.)

So the institutional foundations for low growth were set through deliberate political decisions, not by sheer technological change. Neither standard economic explanations nor an abstract "logic of capitalist development," as some Marxists see it, suffice to explain shifts in forms of productive investment and their adverse employment effects. Public policy, which is the outcome of wider social contests, consciously mediated the internal impact of economic forces all the way down to the shop-floor level. In short, there are distinct *political* causes of "technological unemployment." The Sussex critics also confirm economist Joseph Schumpeter's prediction that the largest firms would "bureaucratize" research to create a "strong feedback loop from successful innovation to increased R&D [leading] to increased market concentration." Small firms always provide key innovations, but the superior capital and marketing power of the behemoths enable them to play the role of "fast imitator" and to buy smaller dynamic firms as "captive suppliers." Again, this is no boon to employment.

Critiques of the Sussex Critics

The Sussex critique itself, of course, can be criticized. Three major objections have been lodged. First, the Sussex critics have committed the "lump of labor" fallacy wherein one ignorantly neglects the price and the productivity elasticities that stand to enlarge demand, output, and job numbers. A National Academy of Sciences study contended, for example, that "reductions in labor requirements per unit of output from new process technologies have been and will continue to be outweighed by the beneficial employment effects of the expansion of total output that generally occurs."[45] Second, analysts should acknowledge that the direction of technical change also can be capital saving. Finally, there is the possibility that growing demand for customized "small batch" goods may undermine corporate concentration and their Fordist organization. This latter term refers to capitalist institutions that have wed mass-production techniques to mass consumption in a sustained growth cycle.[46] (The usual homely example is Henry Ford paying assemblyline workers a relatively high wage, increasing both productivity and the purchasing power of the consumer.)

The Sussex critics respond that what economists call the "price elasticity of output" (demand) and the "productivity elasticity of prices" (the degree to which productivity rises allow prices to fall) are weakened severely by trends toward industrial concentration and oligopolistic practices. So they believe that their case stands. Regarding the second point, capital-saving technologies themselves exert labor-saving effects insofar as they reduce the "depth of production" by eliminating layers of service workers, which indeed is an underlying goal of industries ranging from motor vehicles to banking.[47] (Note that this second objection concedes the implication that technological *design* is a socially determined variable.)

The third objection comes from analysts such as Michael Piore and Charles Sabel, who optimistically foresee that new "flexible specialization" technologies required to meet modern consumer tastes inherently favor small entrepreneurial firms and, consequently, more democratic workplace regimes too.[48] But, as the old song goes, it ain't necessarily so. David Friedman cautiously points out that political struggles throughout society "cumulatively defines the rights that structure an economy toward either mass or flexible specialization."[49]

Flexible specialization is highly touted as the successor to the comparatively rigid Fordist mass production model.[50] Friedman shows that Japanese industrial success was less the product of government savants than of a wide range of commercial contests that were responsible for an expansion of small producers who were able to resort to small-scale general-purpose machinery to build goods more flexibly and thereby enable the state to pursue "an aggressive strategy of constantly differentiating products to break up [and enter] mass markets."[51] There is very little evidence to suggest that the appearance of such flexible producer goods inherently deters industrial concentration or even that they necessarily improve productivity.[52] There are examples supporting the argument that democratized post-Fordist workplaces are superior in productivity to mass production, but that is a very different claim that says nothing about the scale of use and application. Why can't flexible specialization be centralized too?

That these critiques and counterarguments still must be judged as provisional and controversial ones is precisely the Sussex School's point: The direction of technical change is highly dependent upon institutional variables that are politically shaped. In the realm of economic history even three decades is probably too short a span for a complete inventory of costs and benefits, and that is because a host of facilitating changes of social and institutional structures are needed to realize their full potential. In contrast to the literature of the past decade or two, and after a good many trials and errors on the ground, the direction that the debate on high technology has begun to take is not whether to explore but how best to go about accommodating workplace organization to new technology—and, of course, on whose terms and at what cost.

The Ambiguities of Technical Change

The key macro concept deployed by the Sussex critics is "regimes of regulation," which are "the whole set of institutions, private behavior and actual functioning of the various markets channeling the long-term dynamics and determining the cyclical properties of the economy during an historical period for a given society."[53] This term overlaps exactly with what David Gordon, Michael Reich, and Richard Edwards dub the "social structure of accumulation," which refers to the institutional environment within which capital accumulation occurs (including the pattern of state involvement in the economy, the character of class conflict, interindustry relations, and the nature of the money and credit systems).[54] Institutional reconstruction is a rather messy matter of matching organizational structure to new techniques and changed market conditions. This task is inevitably the object of "sharp group conflicts about the distribution of relative costs and benefits," which rival schemes of institutional change will promise.

Each long swing or wave is associated with a distinct social structure of accumulation. Stable growth will resume when the contest over which groups will determine the key features of this new structure, or "regime of regulation," is resolved. Ideological "habits" and traditions also will hamper or bias the search for appropriate institutions and practices. Because there rarely is "one best way" to organize the largest economy or the smallest workplace, economic strategies tend to be varying amalgams of data-based designs and power-retention tactics. Hence there is always a social struggle, however subtle or imbalanced, to control the design of institutions and technologies.[55] When these two aspects of strategy clash, economic logic tends to get short shrift, at least in the short term (witness "Reaganomics").

The Sussex critics point out that in times of uncertainty, technical change increasingly is capital-using so that investment must rise as a fraction of GNP in order to avert a shortage of productive assets while demand must rise as fast or faster than productivity if employment is also to increase. This feat is judged to be beyond the reach of monetarism or standard Keynesianism. Freeman and his colleagues instead argue for a directive mix of macro- and microeconomic intervention, a targeted technology policy via exploratory subsidies (instead of "picking winners"), expanded training programs, diffusion of innovations in the public sector, negotiated "multilateral agreements of prices and incomes on semi-permanent basis," and encouragement of industrial democracy because a broadened responsibility for, and diffusion of the rewards of, technical change can hasten the adoption of "growth-oriented abut anti-inflationary policies."

Reviewing Japan's past successes, Freeman cautions against the knee-jerk adoption of their authoritarian organizational modes, which the business press unabashedly envied. In the corporatistic cases of Scandinavia and Germany (prior to reunification and its burdens), high productivity and skill formation were achieved by strategies that accorded with their domestic institutions and social context, which use institutionalized forums to secure industrial cooperation.[56]

There are two basic ways to go today. German companies meet competition "by concentrating on high quality goods, produced in small batches at high prices" in a flexible specialization style, whereas British firms, because of their low skill levels, were "forced to compete with those in the Third world, producing large quantities cheaply" and at much lower wages.[57]

Critics complain that too many British and American employers individually pursued a low-skill competitive strategy in what collectively amounts to a "race to the bottom." The lesson, however, is that there are alternatives to opting fatalistically for Japan's "militarized approach to social order." Ironically the Fifth Generation project, to get the creative juices flowing, established special work zones in which Japanese researchers could "behave more like relaxed Westerners."[58]

But the search for, and support of, organizational alternatives will be discouraged if citizens (1) are inured to lower expectations, (2) are persuaded that there is, in former British premier Margaret Thatcher's ringing words, "no alternative," or (3) conclude that opposing domestic groups and/or international forces are simply too strong to overcome. If any or all of these judgments occur, the "microchip dilemma" is depoliticized and accepted as defining the situation that citizens face. Still, growing economic adversities could provoke a policy crisis for authorities in charge of reconciling economic activity with political stability. But given the gradual diffusion of technology and, in wealthy countries, the falloff in demographic pressure, this seems a fairly minor threat.

Still, in general popular discourse, the words "progress," "technology," and "market" are saturated with ideologically charged meaning, usually connoting that autonomous forces are at work that compel single optimal responses. The criteria defining what is optimal (for whom and for what purpose) are a crucial concern in the struggle to shape the character of the "social structure of accumulation." Any examination of the assumptions guiding technological design should be inseparable from a scrutiny of the social forces that shaped them. In the political arena, contending groups always strive to portray their own policy preferences as logically irresistible, as practical necessities, and as immaculately attuned to the public interest. A propensity to invoke teleological or deterministic concepts is hardly the unique fault of mechanistic versions of Marxism; it is a common tactic in any policy debate.

Shopfloor workers are no less appreciative than university economists of the potential value and benefits of technological change. It is not technology in itself that is the target of criticism but rather specific societal groups whose interests become embodied at the design stage in proliferating gadgetry. Management tends to be the stronger source of resistance.[59] If anything, workers accede too gracefully to technological "imperatives."[60] Only when technology ceases to be viewed as an autonomous entity can it be seen as the politicized phenomenon it always has been and thus become the legitimate object of struggles at the workplace and national levels to decide its proper purposes. To what extent public debate influences policy outcomes is conditioned by each country's economic institutions, political structures, and economic pressures. Sweden (and, more ambiguously,

Japan) appears at the more dynamic end of the participatory spectrum; the United States, even under Clinton, and the United Kingdom, even under Tony Blair, occupy the other end. France interestingly falls somewhere in the middle.

Shaping Technology: A "Tricky Matter"

The French Nora Report in the early 1980s characterized microtechnology as "practically an alteration of nature" and, on the basis of the evidence it assembled, argued—contrary to textbook economics—that the integration of computers with telecommunications would increase unemployment at the same time that it improved competitive capability. The short-term remedy was to be "a double policy, consolidating hyper-competitive sectors, and generating, through transfers, an increase in amenities and collective consumption [which is, to say the least,] a tricky matter."[61] In light of world market fluctuations and the spread of microtechnologies to the service sector, the authors judged that the chances that market growth could compensate for jobs lost from productivity gains was "hardly plausible." The report routinely acknowledges that adjustment of national structures to international exigencies was imperative, yet it was unusually attentive to problems that new technologies pose for social stability. Successful economic adjustment implies a "massive computerization" that, as the Sussex critics similarly argue, will upset orthodox assumptions about the relation of growth to job creation. Hence a new "model of growth aimed at stimulating new kinds of demand" must be devised.

The Nora model derived from suggestions originally floated within Japan's Ministry of International Trade and Industry (MITI), which went unheeded. The state should aim to establish a "precise mix" between trade-exposed sectors where the premium is on productivity and profit, and trade-sheltered sectors where job creation and perhaps public service has priority. The latter can be expanded to the extent permitted by the level of demand for collective amenities, the import content level, and a social willingness to transfer trading sector surplus to the state for public amenities.[62] This scheme would channel local demand into collective goods projects, which would have the local effect of guarantee outlets for industries treating the home market as a "laboratory" in which to refine products for export. (In effect, this was a strenuously dirigiste version of product cycle theory.)

But this scheme heroically presupposed the achievement of a tight social consensus, a task beyond even (and perhaps especially) the most sophisticated social engineers. Intervention of this kind and at this scale makes the interests driving them more visible, thus mobilizing opposition. Taking the supposedly exemplary Japanese case, Friedman cites a long litany of failures by MITI in the chancy realm of direct investment: "the political strength of the firms involved led to a system in which bureaucrats provided financial incentives while industrialists controlled actual economic activity."[63] Nonetheless this was a form of state-corporate cooperation—even if not quite the form as advertised—and no one denies that such cooperation was crucial to Japanese success.

Regardless who controls whom, states will always intervene. Few industrial democracies can permit external trends to dictate the pace and direction of technical and economic change, or to allocate risks and losses. Even among the ranks of promarket British Tories in the 1990s training became an important concern. Researchers reported huge training gaps between the British and the German (and, less so, with the French and the Dutch) clothing industries, a situation that is "probably typical" of U.K. companies. So the British state squarely confronts a critical "chicken or the egg" question: Do trained workers breed higher profits, or vice versa?[64] Forecasts suggest that the supply of skills does not create their own demand, at least not in a climate of low-demand growth and in the absence of state provisions. British training funds, public and private, were abysmally low.[65] In the long run it may prove to be true that economic competition favors the ubiquitous adoption of a "high-skilled, high-wage" policy in industrial states, but whenever it happens, it will be cold comfort to those who already have lost market shares and jobs.

One policy task is to remedy a perennial collective action problem bedeviling capitalist firms—that is, that the individual units will not supply resources required to promote collective national prosperity if they cannot wholly capture the benefits for themselves. A prudent objective even for a "voluntarist state" is to make compulsory the funding for training that firms are unlikely to provide for themselves. The French have a minimum percentage of company payrolls set aside for upgrading skills. A more activist model was the Swedish Training (Renewal) Fund, enacted in 1985 and financed by a 10-percent levy on company profits.[66] This model stemmed from centralized trade unions in an industrial relations system embedded in an interventionist state, or at least it was one until a carefully concerted offensive by the Swedish employers' association (SAF), whose "resources dwarf that of all the political parties combined," was waged against corporatist compromise and gained the ideological high ground in the early 1990s.[67]

Conquering the "microchip dilemma" demands a keen appreciation of the manner in which policies enacted at state level affect technical choice all the way down to the shop-floor level and upward again. Nothing short of this conceptualization can comprehend the political dynamics of high technology, and as yet no one claims to have hit upon a "completely satisfactory alternative to the dominant theory."[68] The major point, however, is that the dilemma stems neither from pure market forces nor from autonomous technological development. The dilemma is ultimately a political one, and its consequences can be grouped under these four headings: (1) automation, (2) institutional change, (3) ideology, and (4) the international dimension.

Dilemma or Problem?

Automation

The Sussex critics readily concede how difficult it is to distinguish "technological unemployment" from job losses resulting from other causes. They agree that at present macroeconomic causes are more important. One can make a strong case, however, that trade-displaced jobs ultimately are lost because of superior technologies deployed in rival nations.[69] Some early estimates of job loss certainly were overstated, but there is scant reason to believe that future losses automatically will be offset by new jobs of the same or better quality elsewhere.[70] Even a relative optimist finds that "the marginal-employment dividend of new investment in technology is low."[71]

High-tech automation is no panacea for what ails business. The 1950s automation debate was only premature because forecasters did not take into account "long time lags in building up a capital goods supply industry and a components industry on a sufficient scale," misjudged the time needed to train personnel, and erred in estimates of the rate at which the relative costs of labor and capital would begin to favor the latter.[72] The current factors inhibiting investment include high software costs, aversions to invest in rapidly changing technology, reluctance to rely on fragile equipment, skill shortages, and myriad debugging difficulties. As noted above, monetarist policies in the 1980s kicked in to negate the levels of demand, the wage pressures, and the volume of government regulation that motivate firms to replace labor with machinery. On the other hand, the motives to automate include trimming middle management, improving stock quality, economizing on inputs and inventory (including "just-in-time" techniques), increasing safety, and maximizing production flows.[73] But these factors are secondary to, and largely derived from, the scale of available profitable opportunities offered by the national policy environment and by global economic trends.

Marxist critics acerbically argue that a shifting threshold of profitability will keep a scenario of total automation well at bay. Capitalists simply cannot automate to the full degree that the technology allows because if "wage earners push for full employment, production becomes more capital intensive [to avert wage pressure]; if workers push toward liberation of labor power, production becomes more labor intensive [as capitalists strive to avoid transferring "surplus" via the state to "unused labor"].[74] There is a "basic contradiction between the increase in fixed capital and accelerated obsolescence" brought about by continuous innovation and resulting in "valorization" problems, increasing corporate debt, and in a dangerous dependence on state resources.[75] Still, if there is one clear historical tendency in Western capitalism, it is that contradictions usually get counteracted. But this counteracting does not occur naturally and will require many socio-organizational modifications if modern states are to adjust their society's productive structures to new economic patterns in what are politically palatable ways.

Socio-organizational Change

The good news is that the pace of labor displacement is moderated by the foregoing factors; the bad news is that laggard adoption of technology creates cumulative trade difficulties that compel countries to undertake either harsh adjustment schemes or protectionist measures, or a mingling of both. In the absence of policies geared to reconcile social needs with exploitation of technological product "trajectories," the microchip dilemma could take a corrosive hold. Meanwhile, as Pierre Bourdieu notes, "terms like flexibility, globalization, deregulation [succeeded in giving] the appearance of a message of freedom and liberation to a conservative ideology which thinks itself opposed to all ideology."[76] In these circumstances, according to a U.S. congressional study, the effect of the Reagan years was to increase the pay of the top one-fifth of income earners by 11 percent while the bottom one-fifth lost 6 percent. Also during those years, the United States fell from tenth in infant mortality to twenty-second in the world.[77] Poverty shot up so that in the mid-1990s, 21 percent of American children suffered this condition (versus 9.3 percent of Canadians), and 11 percent of elderly Americans were poor (versus 2.2 percent in Canada).[78]

There are some encouraging, if not easily emulated, experiences, particularly in the small European states deploying "domestic compensatory mechanisms" to complement an "aggressive marketing orientation based on specialised export production."[79] Unemployment typically is lowest in nations with extensive welfare states and labor market institutions such as Sweden, Norway, Austria, Finland, and Luxembourg.[80] Industrial policy proponents always have contended that the road to continuous growth is paved with programs that enhance the competitive advantage of skilled labor so as to create a virtuous cycle of following a track of encouraging sophisticated products that in turn demand higher levels of skilled labor.[81]

This is the desired outcome engendered by the "German-Scandinavian model," in which the "rights of employees, enforced by the state, should make it easier for unions in these countries to negotiate changes in the organization of work."[82] Although not wholly immune to rocky times or neoliberal prescriptions, Sweden, Finland, the Netherlands, and France managed to maintain generous social programs while stoking strong economic growth at the close of the twentieth century.[83] Several European Union (EU) members, however, embraced elements of the neoliberal market strategy and despite—or, more likely, *because* of—this tack, unemployment throughout the EU reached 11 percent in 1998. The pay gap between good and bad jobs also has grown in the absence of corrective policies.[84] Marxists, in any case, are highly skeptical as to whether the "high training, high tech" scenario is plausible because it "undermines the entire hierarchical structure of factory and economy, without which the extortion of surplus value from labor is impossible."[85] One need not subscribe to theories of the "iron laws" of capitalism (or generic industrialism) to suspect that management may not welcome the erosion of its authority that an expanded skilled workforce portends.

In her study of service industries Shoshana Zuboff found that "hierarchical power" was the biggest barrier to an unfolding of a democratic division of labor wherein "mental" and "manual" tasks eventually blend. Although some deskilling occurs in the process of automating, these new technologies have the unsettling effect for managers of transferring their functions into a collective knowledge base to which employees must have considerable access if they are to do their jobs well. In short, the workers take on managerial responsibilities—or would if only managers would let them do so.[86] This account accords with David Noble's tale of General Electric's shopfloor war over control of numerically controlled tools, resulting in what appeared to be a conscious tradeoff by management of productivity gains for workplace control. (Other studies indicate situations in which capitalists choose more profits and less efficiency over the reverse distribution as in, for example, the U.S. health care industry.) Noble also contends that technological advance is hindered by an inadequate accounting for socio-organizational influences both at the design stage and at the operational level.[87] How technology is adapted to a given work environment depends on the pattern of authority and the purposes of the most powerful actors.

Piore and Sabel admit that "computers adapt to any environment"—including presumably the authoritarian mass production mode that they so vigorously assert is being superseded by the benign postindustrial force of flexible specialization. In the fullness of time the Fordist mode could be surpassed by firms boasting multiskilled, training-oriented, and participatory work regimes that churn out high productivity and profits. But one cannot sit back and wait for it. Strategies are outlined and concrete examples cited of ways in which unions can take the initiative in putting industrial relations on a footing based on "mutual advantage that capital and labor derive from a productive and efficient enterprise that is grounded in respect for human skill and ingenuity."[88] Among the concrete examples are Australian Telecom, Ericson, German Volkswagen, ESPRIT's project in human-centered CIM systems, and, unfortunately, Swedish Volvo's Uddevala and Kalmar plants, which "despite being quite profitable," were shut down in 1993 and 1994 in order to invest in Asia instead.[89] Like U.S. companies investing in Mexico—where manufacturing wages fell despite increased productivity—Swedish firms avidly were seeking, in Congressman Richard Gephart's words, "21st century technology combined with 19th century working and living conditions."[90] The Swedish Employers Association in 1990 withdrew from corporatist bargaining in the calculated belief that it now had enough muscle in a deregulated environment to disregard labor.[91]

So the catch in the co-operative model is that businesses, once they gain the upper hand in partisan politics, do not always need or want to play along. Among the results is that the Swedish poverty rate doubled to nearly 8 percent from 1987 to 1991 while tax "reforms" (i.e., cuts helping the wealthy) spurred increases in inequality.[92] If an energetically democratic post-Fordist system is to emerge, the rub is that there is probably no substitute for having a labor-controlled party formally in charge of the state—*and* one immune to neoliberal nostrums.

State policy influences the balance of power in workplaces, so it is no surprise that organizational changes—from labor markets to technology agreements—are enacted swiftly in corporatist states with centralized labor organizations and potent labor-oriented parties. In (West) Germany, where labor was incorporated in policy under SPD auspices, the machine tool industry was successfully revitalized and on terms favorable to the use, rather than displacement, of skilled labor.[93] However, in 1985 the European Commission joined with the European Trade Union Confederation to promote a "social dialogue" document on participation in technological decisions. By the 1990s the trade unions simply had ratified the old principle that final decisions on technology belong always to the employer.[94] In the technology agreements forged in Belgium, analysts find that the national agreement had only a "marginal impact" on choices, because the workers "still did not question Management prerogatives" and because technology is "still viewed as an autonomous factor."[95] On the other hand, Europeans, possessing a stronger social democratic tradition, are likelier than Americans to view economic problems in terms of social structures rather than to ascribe them to personal failings.[96] Beliefs matter.

Ideology

The "automate or evaporate" dilemma stems from ideological premises, too. Potent notions can appear to be independent of human agency and capable of constraining human agents. The "free market" is one example; "autonomous technology" is another. When intertwined, these political and cultural categories yield a "Darwinian view of technological development." If existing technologies have ever been

> put to rigorous tests, it has typically been only after the decisions were made to invest social surplus in their development and use, and these decisions were based not only upon mere guesses as to their technical and economic potential but also upon the political interests, enthusiastic expectations, and culturally sanctioned compulsions of those few with the power to make them.[97]

This conception restricts social awareness regarding the inherent variability in technical change, market relations, and especially their interaction, thereby imbuing certain policy preferences with a false sense of fatedness. In short, the microchip dilemma needs to be disentangled from a "damned if you do, damned if you don't" plight and be portrayed more accurately as a *problem* of social power and choice. In, for example, a "right-to-work" system (which employs all comers at a median rather than minimum wage) this requirement would soon find itself reflected (or reacted to) in the future design of productive technologies, workplace organizations, and the structure of decisionmaking from the work site to the state level.[98]

A major benefit of such a demystification would be a reduction in the pressure for protectionism. As the "dislocation costs" of domestic retooling rise, the distribution of costs and the regulation of the pace of adjustment become political issues. Policy debate may then take two not mutually exclusive forms: (1) how to allocate the social surplus generated by new technology to citizens who are "freed" from labor, or (2) how to restore full employment at postwar norms. Whether or not domestic mechanisms can moderate the costs of adjustment, labor unions and labor-oriented parties would be extremely ill-advised to press for anything less than full employment *in advance of socially legitimated arrangements*. No political movement will persuade a majority of the working population in a culture where prestige and status (as well as survival) is so intimately tied to work that it should support "able-bodied" nonworkers. This latter situation is rich fodder for talk show demagoguery.

Full employment—at fewer hours—fortifies efforts not only to arrange introduction of technology on agreeable terms but to share its benefits through public programs in health care, child care, educational upgrading, housing, public works projects, and urban revitalization reaching into inner cities.[99] In France today, for example, the government offers employers relief from national insurance contributions in exchange for shortening the work week and taking on more employees.[100] The upshot is not that societies are "free to choose" productive strategies as they please but rather that the range of choice of one shapes the other and that the range of choices is wider than is usually acknowledged.

International Aspects

Apart from the unlikely advent of a "global Marshall Plan," industrial states will continue to determine, according to their own devices (and social divisions), their competitive strategies in customary ways. The microchip dilemma will be exacerbated by disjointed strategies and the corporate version of globalization. For "obvious reasons business interests do not talk about escaping from the law (it sounds unpatriotic)," as William Grieder notes.[101] "Instead they promote the goal of greater efficiency—a harmonization of national laws that will remove barriers and encourage greater trade." The political thrust is to reduce states' inclinations to protect citizens from the whims of those who wield market power.[102] What is at stake is a "restructuring of the state" either so that it sides preponderantly with unbridled economic elites or it reaches a democratic accommodation meeting the needs of, and spreading the costs among, competing societal groups.

The Sussex School advocates coordinating economic exchange among the Organization for Economic Cooperation and Development (OECD) members and between them and the Third World regarding credit, investment, technology transfer, and trade concessions.[103] One attractive strategy is a Nora Report scenario in which each country permits a moderate expansion of high job-generating domestic sectors along with a brisk free trade in high-tech products, thereby easing the political reaction to declines in unsalvageable industries and creating the effective demand to absorb enhanced production. The collective action problem is that nations will be tempted to free ride and to gain a competitive edge by keeping social spending on the stingy side. It is conceivable, though, that public programs and a robust industrial strategy can yield more competitive benefits than will be reaped by countries taking the "cheap labor" route.

Another joker in the pack is a phenomenon that virtually all these critics cite—that while there is no prospect of a stampede of foreign investors out of Third World locales, new computer integrated systems are enabling First World firms to offset cheap labor advantages abroad.[104] IBM, Motorola, Fairchild, and National Semiconductor are among the firms that returned (or remained rooted) to the United States because of new-found technical capacities to churn out small-batch customized products. "[Computer Integrated Systems] is the key to bringing factories back to the industrialized countries," Jean-Claude Derian jubilantly predicts.[105] This transformation of old industries heralds a progressive shortening of the product cycle, which diminishes the attractiveness of offshore investment and thus possibly adversely affects Third World development overall.[106] Little thought is spared for the implications for the next band of industrializers after the "gang of four" newly industrialized countries (NICs)—South Korea, Taiwan, Hong Kong, and Singapore—and what this might mean for Third World demand, which, after all, is supposed to absorb some of the anticipated increase in First World output. The recent Asian financial meltdown reminds us that their troubles reverberate everywhere.

Conclusion

The microelectronics revolution offers—nay, imposes—opportunities to revitalize the productive bases of modern industrial societies. This chapter stresses that political processes shape the character of technical innovation and also that the "microchip dilemma" is the result of *changeable* patterns of distributions of power and ideas. Macroeconomic policies are not adequate to mediate the powerful social impacts of technical change. Policymakers are urged to test mixes of macro- and microinterventionism if they are to reconcile economic imperatives with social demands in this "information age."

States always shape the impact of external forces upon domestic groups whose political alliances, in turn, determine policy outcomes. The success of a group's project depends upon how preferences match up with the structure of opportunities provided by the global economy, and upon the ability of competing groups to invoke social beliefs to augment the attractiveness of their project to actors whose consent is crucial to the outcome of policy conflicts over technical choices.

If "the search for productivity" is an exogenous factor, dominating the "alternatives of domestic policy" in liberal polities like the United States and United Kingdom, this nonetheless is a condition subject to political change.[107] The post-Fordist scenario envisions an active state, democratic vitality, and competitive industry enhancing one another in a virtuous cycle and is one of several value-laden alternatives, each implying a different distribution of benefits and costs. Japan is something of a cautionary case because there a flexible manufacturing system arose from a confluence of unintended circumstances, of a peculiar balance of domestic forces responding to global exigencies. One result is the flexible team practices that were developed and have been contained (so far) within a hierarchical system.[108] It is hardly what the post-Fordist scholars have in mind, but it is a possible model though hardly one anyone cares to follow these days.

Policy analyses ought to extend beyond who gets this grant or that tax break to illuminate instead the ways in which technical change, market forces, and policy are dynamically linked—tracing the effects from national adjustment actions to strategies in firms to impact the workplace and the

international arena again. This is an ambitious task, but such trail-blazing (with attendant trial and error) is well under way.[109]
Polanyi observed that free trade in the nineteenth century required "an enormous increase in continuous centrally organized and controlled interventionism."[110] As a "protective counter-movement" arises in modern trading states, the existence of "free trade" may well depend on a reliving of this process. Market competitiveness and at least a major (post-Fordist) element in this "counter-movement" are arguably reconcilable. I have argued that in this high-tech era "efficiency" is not opposed to "equity"—and indeed may presuppose improvements in the latter. When several organizational forms are compatible with the same economic goal, politics, not economic logic alone, decides the outcomes. As always, the state will be drawn into contests among social groups to determine this efficiency-equity mix. Certainly, the worst policy is to let "technology" decide.

Notes

1. A. L. Morton, *A People's History of England* (London: Lawrence & Wishart, rev. 1976), p. 370.

2. Among the many books generated during the 1950s and early 1960s debate were Walter Buckingham, *Automation: Its Impact on Business and People* (New York: Mentor, 1965); John Diebold, *Automation* (Princeton: Von Norstrand, 1952); Charles Dechert, *The Social Impact of Cybernetics* (New York: Simon & Schuster, 1965); and Howard R. Bowen and Garth Mangum, eds., *Automation and Economic Progress* (Englewood Cliffs, N.J.: Prentice-Hall, 1966). There was a still earlier edition of the debate during the 1930s depression. On nineteenth-century Luddites, see Brian J. Bailey, *The Luddite Rebellion* (New York: New York University Press, 1998), and Kirkpatrick Sale, *Rebels Against the Future* (Reading, Mass.: Addison-Wesley, 1995).

3. See Andrew Shonfield, *Modern Capitalism* (Oxford: Oxford University Press, 1965); Seymour M. Lipset, *Political Man* (New York: Doubleday, 1960); and Ralf Dahrendorf, *Class and Class Conflict in Industrial Society* (Stanford: Stanford University Press, 1958).

4. See Daniel Bell, *The End of Ideology* (Glencoe, Ill.: Free Press, 1956), and Francis Fukuyama, *The End of History and the Last Man* (New York: Free Press, 1987).

5. Jules Henry, *On Sham, Vulnerability, and Other Forms of Self-Destruction* (New York: Vintage, 1973), p. 145.

6. Richard Cyert and David Mowery, *Technology and Employment: Innovation and Growth in the U.S. Economy* (Washington, D.C.: National Academy Press, 1987), p. 5; see also Stephen S. Cohen and John Zysman, *Manufacturing Matters: The Myth of the Post-Industrial Economy* (New York: Basic Books, 1987), p. 170, and Tom Forester, ed., *The Microelectronics Revolution* (Cambridge, Mass.: MIT Press, 1980), p. 295.

7. On "creative destruction," see Joseph Schumpeter, *Capitalism, Socialism, and Democracy*, 3rd ed. (New York: Harper & Row, 1975).

8. Simon Nora and Alain Minc, *The Computerization of Society* (Cambridge, Mass.: MIT Press, 1980). This originally was a commissioned report to the French president Giscard d'Estaing, composed by two finance inspectors and a team of specialists. It was published in January 1978 and became a best-seller.

9. Giovanni Dosi et al., eds., *Technical Innovation and Economic Change* (London: Frances Pinter, 1988); Christopher Freeman and Luc Soete, *New Explorations in the Economics of Technical Change* (London: Frances Pinter, 1990); Richard Cyert and David Mowery, *Technology and Employment: Innovation and Growth in the U.S. Economy* (Washington, D.C.: National Academy Press, 1987); Jean-Claude Derian, *America's Struggle for Leadership in Technology* (Cambridge, Mass.: MIT Press, 1990); Brian Oakley and Kenneth Owen, *Alvey: Britain's Strategic Computing Initiative* (Cambridge, Mass.: MIT Press, 1989); David Friedman, *Misunderstood Miracle* (Ithaca: Cornell University Press, 1988); Shoshana Zuboff, *In the Age of the Smart Machine* (New York: Basic Books, 1989); and John Matthews, *Tools of Change* (London: Pluto, 1989).

10. J. Nicholas Ziegler, *Governing Ideas: Strategies for Innovation in France and Germany* (Ithaca: Cornell University Press, 1997), p. 160.

11. Richard R. Nelson and Luc Soete, "Policy Conclusions," in Dosi et al., *Technical Innovation and Economic Theory*, p. 633.

12. Friedman, *Misunderstood Miracle*, pp. 17, 161.

13. Karl Polanyi, *The Great Transformation* (Boston: Beacon Press, 1944), pp. 140–141. Also see Martin Bever, ed., *Resistance to New Technology: Nuclear Power, Information Technology, and Biotechnology* (Cambridge: Cambridge University Press, 1995); and Yaron Ezrahi, ed., *Technology, Pessimism and Postmodernism* (Amherst: University of Massachusetts Press, 1995).

14. Even scholars who reject the job "killer" and/or job "de-skiller" arguments foresee persisting mismatches between labor skills and available employment, and they acknowledge many ways in which a haphazard or biased diffusion of new technologies aggravates existing social inequalities. See Harry Braverman's seminal work, *Labor and Monopoly Capital: The Degradation of Work in the Twentieth Century* (New York: Monthly Review Press, 1974).

15. Nathan Rosenberg, *Inside the Black Box: Technology and Economics* (Cambridge, Mass.: MIT Press, 1982), p. xi.

16. *Ibid.*, p. 236; also see Merritt Roe Smith, ed., *Military Enterprise and Industrial Technology* (Cambridge, Mass., MIT Press, 1987), p. 9.

17. Kenneth Flamm, *Targeting the Computer* (Washington, D.C.: Brookings Institution, 1987), p. 18.

18. *Ibid.*, p. 77.

19. Philip Smith and Michael McGerry, "Don't Look Back: Science Funding for the Future," *Issues in Science and Technology* 13, 3 (Spring 1997): 34.

20. James E. Nolan, "Crunch Time for Advanced Arms Experts," *Issues in Science and Technology* 12, 3 (Fall 1996): 24.

21. Oakley and Owen, *Alvey*, pp. 178, 221.

22. Quoted in Derian, *America's Quest for Leadership*, pp. 143–144; also see Richard R. Nelson, "Institutions Supporting Technical Change in the United States," in Dosi et al., *Technical Innovation and Economic Theory*, p. 323.

23. See James R. Kurth, "Product Cycles and Industrial Growth," *International Organization* 33, 1 (Winter 1979): 1–34.

24. Cyert and Mowery, *Technology and Employment*, pp. 37, 38.

25. Derian, *America's Quest*, p. 143; also see David Mowery and Nathan Rosenberg, *Technology and the Pursuit of Growth* (Cambridge: Cambridge University Press, 1989).

26. William J. Broad, "Defense Industry Goes Hustling to Make a Buck Without a Bang," *New York Times*, 8 April 1990.

27. *Ibid.*

28. Oakley and Owen, *Alvey*, p. 60.

29. *Ibid.*, pp. 12–13.

30. *Ibid.*, pp. 186–187.

31. Christopher Freeman, John Clark, and Luc Soete, *Unemployment and Technical Innovation* (London: Frances Pinter, 1982).

32. *Ibid.*, p. 16.

33. Joseph Schumpeter, *Business Cycles: A Theoretical, Historical, and Statistical Analysis of the Capitalist Process* (New York: McGraw-Hill, 1939); Joshua Goldstein, *Long Cycles: Prosperity and War in the Modern Age* (New Haven, Conn.: Yale University Press, 1988); Ernest Mandel, *Late Capitalism* (London: New Left Books, 1975); Gerhard Mensch, *Stalemate in Technology* (Cambridge, Mass.: Ballinger Press, 1979); William R. Thompson, "Long Waves, Technological Innovation, and Relative Decline," *International Organization* 44 (1990): 201–233.

34. Freeman, Clark, and Soete, *Unemployment and Technical Innovation*, pp. 74, 76.

35. *Ibid.*, pp. 79, 97.

36. *Ibid.*, pp. 153–157.

37. See Robert Kuttner, *The End of Laissez-Faire* (New York: Houghton Mifflin, 1990).

38. Christopher Freeman, "Preface To Part II, Evolution, Technology and Institutions: A Wider Framework for Economic Analysis," in Dosi et al., *Technical Change and Economic Theory*, p. 11. The notion of a "techno-economic paradigm" derives from theories of scientific paradigm change.

39. Freeman, Clark, and Soete, *Unemployment and Technical Innovation*, p. 191.

40. *Guardian*, 28 June 1989 and 8 January 1990.

41. Doreen Massey and Richard Meegan, *The Anatomy of Job Loss* (London: Metheun, 1982), p. 225.

42. *Ibid.*, pp. 183–184.

43. See Francis Green, ed., *The Restructuring of the UK Economy* (London: Macmillan, 1989); and Bob Jessop, Kevin Bonner, and Simon Bromley, "Farewell to Thatcherism?" *New Left Review* 179 (1990): 73.

44. Seumus Milne and Larry Elliot, "How Rich and Poor Must Both Pay the Price of a Workplace Revolution," *Guardian* 4 January 1999, p. 7. There are 1.2 million people with two jobs, two-thirds of them women.

45. Cyert and Mowery, *Technology and Employment*, p. 2.

46. Robert Boyer, "Technical Change and the Theory of Regulation," in Dosi et al., *Technical Change and Economic Theory*, p. 73.

47. Giovanni Dosi, "The Nature of The Innovative Process," in Dosi et al., *Technical Change and Economic Theory*, p. 227.

48. Michael Piore and Charles Sabel, *The Second Industrial Divide* (New York: Basic Books, 1987).

49. Friedman, *Misunderstood Miracle*, p. 13.

50. See Michel Aglietta, *A Theory of Capitalist Regulation: The U.S. Experience* (London: Verso, 1979); Alain Liepitz, *Mirages and Miracles: The Crisis of Global Fordism* (London: Verso, 1987); and, a critical appraisal from the left, Robert Bremmer and Mark Glick, "The Regulation Approach: Theory and History," *New Left Review* 188 (1991): 45–120.

51. Friedman, *Misunderstood Miracle*, p. 13.

52. Cyert and Mowery, *Technology and Employment*, p. 29. Scott Lash distinguishes between post-Fordism, which is "a disintegration of Fordist hierarchies into a plethora of smaller firms," and neo-Fordism, which entails only the disaggregation of the functions of the firm, which remain within the physical space of the company, in "Disintegrating Firms," *Socialist Review* 21 (1990): 104. What is at stake is the kind and degree of workplace control. See also Keith Pavitt, "Chips and Trajectories," in Roy McLeod, ed., *Technology and the Human Prospect* (London: Frances Pinter, 1986), pp. 31–54.

53. See Giovanni Dosi and Luis Orenigo, "Coordination and Transformation: An Overview of Structures, Behaviour and Change in Evolutionary Environments," p. 27; Norman Clark and Calestous Juma, "Evolutionary Crises in Economic Thought"; and Christopher Freeman and Carlotta Perez, "Structural Crises of Adjustment: Business Cycles and Investment Behaviour," in Dosi et al., *Technical Change and Economic Theory*.

54. David M. Gordon, Michael Reich, and Richard Edwards, *Segmented Work, Divided Workers: The Historical Transformation of Labor in the United States* (Cambridge: Cambridge University Press, 1982).

55. David Noble, *Forces of Production* (New York: Knopf, 1985); Harley Shaiken, *Work Transformed* (New York: Holt, Rinehart, Winston, 1986); and Friedman, *Misunderstood Miracle*.

56. Freeman, "Japan: A New National System of Innovation," in Dosi et al., *Technical Change and Economic Theory*, p. 344. Also see Ben Dankbaar, "International Competition and National Institutions: The Case of the Automobile Industry," in Freeman and Soete, *New Explorations in the Economics of Technical Change*, p. 170.

57. H. Steedman and K. Wagner in the *Independent*, 2 January 1991.

58. Karel von Wolferen, *The Enigma of Japanese Power* (New York: Knopf, 1989), p. 181.

59. Cyert and Mowery, *Technology and Employment*, p. 133; Forester, *High Tech Society* (Cambridge, Mass.: MIT Press, 1987), p. 217; and Zuboff, *The Age of the Smart Machine*.

60. Heather Rolfe, "In the name of Progress: Skills and Attitudes Toward Technological Change," *New Technology, Work and Employment* 5 (1991): 110–117.

61. Nora and Minc, *The Computerization of Society*, pp. 4–5.

62. *Ibid.*, pp. 42–45.

63. Friedman, *Misunderstood Miracle*, p. 38.

64. *Independent*, 2 January 1991.

65. *Guardian*, 14 February 1990.

66. Matthews, *Tools of Change*, pp. 134–135.

67. Mark Blyth, "The Neoliberal Moment in Sweden: Economic Ideas and the Transformation of the State," paper presented at the Princeton Workshop on Ideas and Politics, May 1998, p. 20. On the success of Swedish adjustments to adversities in the 1970s and 1980s see Barry Bosworth and Alice Rivlin, eds., *The Swedish Economy* (Washington, D.C.: Brookings Institution, 1987).

68. Dosi, "Introduction," in Dosi et al., *Technical Change and Economic Theory*, p. 3.

69. Cyert and Mowery, *Technology and Employment*, p. 62.

70. Forester, *High Tech Society*, pp. 198, 213; see also David Knights and Hugh Wilmott, *New Technology and the Labour Process* (London: Macmillan, 1988), p. 188.

71. Gosta Esping-Andersen, *The Three Worlds of Welfare Capitalism* (Princeton: Princeton University Press, 1990), p. 181.

72. Freeman, Clark, and Soete, *Unemployment and Technical Innovation*, p. 122.

73. See Dosi, "The Nature of the Innovative Process," in Dosi et al., *Technical Change and Economic Theory*, pp. 227–228.

74. Adam Przeworski, "Material Interests, Class Compromise, and the Transition to Socialism," *Politics and Society* 7 (1980): 149.

75. Manuel Castells, *The Economic Crisis and American Society* (Princeton: Princeton University Press, 1980), p. 56.

76. Pierre Bourdieu in *New Left Review* 227 (January-February 1998): 129.

77. Cited in Noam Chomsky, *Deterring Democracy* (New York: Verso, 1992), p. 91.

78. Elaine Bernard, "How Should We Pay?" *Social Policy* 24, 3 (Spring 1994): 24–31.

79. Peter J. Katzenstein, *Small States in the World Economy* (Ithaca: Cornell University Press, 1986).

80. See Esping-Andersen, *The Three Worlds of Welfare Capitalism*; John Freeman, *Democracy and Markets* (Ithaca: Cornell University Press, 1989); and Jan Fagerberg, Adne Cappelen, Lars Mjoset, and Rune Skarstein, "The Decline of Social Democratic State Capitalism in Norway," *New Left Review* 181 (1990): 60–94.

81. Matthews, *Tools of Change*, p. 113.

82. Dankbaar, "International Competition and National Institutions," in Freeman and Soete, *New Explorations*, p. 169.

83. Edmund L. Andrews, "Sweden Bounces Back: Welfare and Entrepreneurship Combine in Powerful Transformation of Economy," *International Herald Tribune*, 9 October 1999, p. 4.

84. James K. Galbraith, "With Economic Inequality for All," *Nation*, 7–14 September 1998.

85. Castells, *The Economic Crisis and American Society*, p. 56.

86. "[These organizations] illustrated the need to defend and reproduce the legitimacy of managerial authority can channel potential innovation toward the conventional emphasis on automation. In this context, managers emphasize machine intelligence and managerial control over the knowledge base at the expense of developing knowledge in the operating workforce. They use the technology as a fail-safe system to increase their sense of certainty and control over both production and organizational functions." Zuboff, *In the Age of the Smart Machine*, p. 390.

87. Noble, *Forces of Production*, p. 65.

88. Matthews, *Tools of Change*, p. 141.

89. Ake Sandberg, "Volvoism at the End of the Road," *Studies in Political Economy* 45 (1994): 1–23.

90. Economic Policy Institute study cited in *Solidarity* (UAW newsletter), April/May 1997: 12.

91. Gregg M. Olsen, "Remodeling Sweden: The Rise and Demise of the Compromise in a Global Economy," *Social Problems* (February 1996): 6.

92. *Ibid.*, p. 7.

93. Ziegler, *Governing Ideas*, pp. 131–132.

94. Dieter Frohlich and Hubert Krieger, "Technological Change and Worker Participation in Europe," *New Technology, Work, and Employment* 5 (1990): 95.

95. Michel Albertijn, Bob Honcke, and Davy Wigaerts, "Technology Agreementsand Industrial Relations in Belgium," *New Technology, Work and Employment* 5 (1990): 6.

96. William Julius Wilson, *When Work Disappears: The World of the New Urban Poor* (New York: Knopf, 1996), p. 160.

97. Noble, *Forces of Production*, p. 164.

98. Esping-Andersen, *The Three Worlds of Welfare Capitalism*, p. 153.

99. Wilson, *When Work Disappears*, p. 205.

100. Victor Keegan, *Guardian*, 19 January 1996.

101. William Grieder, *One World, Ready or Not* (New York: Simon & Schuster, 1997), p. 34.

102. Philip Cerny, "Paradoxes of the Competition State: The Dynamics of Political Globalization," *Government and Opposition* (Spring 1998), pp. 251, 256.

103. Kurt Unger, "Industrial Structure, Technical Change, and Microeconomic Behaviour in LDCs," in Dosi et al., *Technical Change and Economic Theory*, pp. 484–485; Freeman, Clark, and Soete, *Unemployment and Technical Innovation*, pp. 162–182.

104. Jeffery Hendersen, *The Globalization of High Technology* (London: Routledge, 1989), p. 143; Cyert and Mowery, *Technology and Employment*, p. 81; see also Christopher Freeman, "Technical Innovation in the World Chemical Industry and Changes of Techno-Economic Paradigm," in Freeman and Soete, *New Explorations*, pp. 74–92.

105. Derian, *America's Quest*, p. 229.

106. Cyert and Mowery, *Technology and Employment*, pp. 81, 126; and Francois Chenais, "Industrial Structure, Technical Change, and Miocroeconomic Behavior in LDCs," both in Dosi et al., *Technical Change and Economic Theory*, p. 491.

107. Nora and Minc, *The Computerization of Society*, p. 41.

108. A more benign view of Japanese work practices is given in Masahiko Aoki, "A New Paradigm of Work Organizational Coordination," in Stephen Marglin and Juliet Schor, eds., *The Golden Age of Capitalism: Reinterpreting the Postwar Experience* (Oxford: Oxford University Press, 1990), pp. 267–293.

109. Friedman, *Misunderstood Miracle*, p. 13.

110. Polanyi, *The Great Transformation*, p. 140, fn 16.

3

Aimless Accuracy

Technology and the Military

You can ask a computer whether you have the military capacity to accomplish an objective. It will answer whether "yes" or "no." It will never say, "Yes, but it is not a good idea."
—Richard Goodwin, White House
special assistant under Presidents
Kennedy and Johnson

War may not be the mother of invention, but it surely is its most reliable spur. Armed conflict is the crucible of modern states that, in turn, require expensive state-of-the-art arsenals to accomplish their sovereign and, for their citizens, often inscrutable purposes. In the twentieth century, warfare, and perpetual preparations for warfare ("deterrence"), came to be identified not only with destruction, horror, and grief but also with economic vitality, technological progress, and full employment.[1] This paradoxical bundle of beliefs makes the issue of weapons procurement a vexing one indeed.

Nation-states, in an anarchic world filled with untrustworthy rivals, constantly seek a decisive technical edge over both potential adversaries and erstwhile allies.[2] Hence, the means of production are pushed into high gear to devise ample means of destruction through costly basic research that the private sector on its own would shun. The world's militaries since the Second World War thus have employed a quarter to half of all scientists and engineers and have absorbed the bulk of government research funds—a considerable diversion of resources from other useful civil purposes (although it is rash to assume that unneeded defense dollars automatically

would be available for other uses).[3] In the United States today it is clear
even to conservatives that "business simply will not fund long-term high
risk basic research; therefore it is incumbent on the federal government to
step in and fill the void."[4]

War, at least in the short term, mobilizes consent across the social divides
of class, race, and creed in support of new policies ranging from weapons
research to whatever can conceivably be depicted as preparatory steps for
warfare. In this highly militaristic light, education, shelter, and health measures become prized particularly for assuring that sufficient skilled laborers
and military recruits are always available.[5] In wartime Britain, for example,
the desperate fight against foreign fascism became an opportunity for progressive parties to create "a general rise in well-being, happiness and security in human life" by implementing much of the 1942 Beveridge schemes
for universal health care, welfare, and education.[6] Affluent groups, except
in these moments of national peril, rarely succumb to (downward) redis-
tributive social programs without a serious struggle.

Although one controversial social science thesis (and popular cynicism) is
the "diversionary theory of war" whereby rulers preempt domestic dissent
by provoking external conflict, one should not overlook how the wider
populace comes to embrace or acquiesce to hegemonic strategies. That is to
say, the public usually gets however small a payoff too. In the 1930s Nazi
rearmament provided full employment for German citizens who hardly appreciated at the time that in the bargain they or their loved ones later might
suffer misery and death in the smoking ruins of central Europe and the
eastern front.[7] Scientists, patriotic and always eager for funds, displayed remarkably little dismay at the military objectives and policy priorities of
their governments.[8] Science, as Nobel Prize–winning chemist and inventor
of poison gas Fritz Haber bluntly put it, "belongs to humanity in peacetime
and to the Fatherland in war."[9]

In the United States the military-industrial complex arose as a dangerously ambiguous symbol of prosperous times as well as deadly expertise
and unconscionable waste. For it was World War II, not a cyclical upturn,
that ended the protracted agonies of the 1930s depression. Military Keynesianism—accelerated state spending for arms production and its ancillary
activities—afterward became an indispensable device nestled in every
party's policy repertoire. Indeed, in 1940 a sadly bemused John Maynard
Keynes, who had argued for state deficit spending to revive depression-
ridden Western economies, lamented that it seems "politically impossible
for a capitalist economy to organize expenditures at such a scale necessary
to make a grand experiment which would prove my case—except in war
conditions."[10]

Because the "general aspirations and prejudices of particular social
groups are just as important for the history of military technology as are

straightforward problems of technical efficiency," one needs to keep in mind that a sound analysis requires that all groups must be accounted for, despite severe imbalances of power among them.[11] Mobilizing scientific ingenuity for wars produced intimate ties between governments, corporations, and science during unprecedented periods of economic growth.[12] However, a major thematic question, suggested in the preceding chapter, is whether the perpetual stimulus of war-preparedness has become more of a hindrance than a contributor to prosperity, stability, and security.

In a crazily clinical manner of speaking, war can be said to be growth-producing if it draws on underemployed factors (labor, capital, land) of production, stimulates output in industries where economies of scale reduce costs, expands new and ancillary branches of industry, and precipitates financial and organizational development that redistributes income or opportunities to favor innovating enterprises.[13] War becomes a serious retardant on economic growth when extensive physical destruction of the productive base occurs, scarce resources are diverted to unproductive uses, risks and uncertainties increase for enterprises situated beneath bombsights—and, of course, if your side loses.

This highly condensed chapter will leap from the era of chariots and spears to twentieth-century weapons that touchingly often were said to be too hideous for war ever again to be sanely contemplated: artillery, the airplane, poison gas, submarines, and the atomic bomb.[14] We also encounter a scientific mindset of "technification" that is applied with daunting tenacity to the ancient and versatile art of killing. Over the past century, especially, the crucial "difference is the distance" at which weapons kill, which increased steadily so that soldiers barely see their targets except as luminescent blurs on computer screens.[15] Distance makes a crucial difference because a "majority of men in battle would not try to kill the enemy, even to save their own lives or the lives of their friends" even though new technology and training methods enabled the rate of troops pulling the trigger to rise from 15–25 percent in World War II to 55 percent in Korea and more than 90 percent in Vietnam—an "improvement" that residents at, say, My Lai and other villages would not appreciate.[16] Yet even in Vietnam a high firing rate did not necessarily imply that soldiers always were aiming at their human targets.[17]

The flip side of this stubborn reluctance to kill is what I term the "Calley syndrome," whereby the complex chains of command in civilian and military organizations result in a contrived confusion, and absolution, of responsibility by the central authorities for indiscriminate misdeeds.[18] The metaphoric "magic bullet" in medicine is matched by a search for the literal magic bullet or shield. The quest for superior weaponry designed to kill at a sanitary distance probably will remain a vexing one insofar as such research must reckon with civilian critics troubled by the moral and strategic implications. Hence, an airily abstract language obligingly accompanies the deployment of new weapons, providing a "distancing" wall of language that is no less important for combat than the internal intricacy of the devices themselves.[19] Finally in this chapter, I investigate the fleeting opportunity in the early post–cold war era to channel a chunk of defense money to civil purposes.

From Stirrups to Smart Bombs

The story of weaponry is a predictable parade of measures and countermeasures in a long and increasingly lethal succession. The fortunes of empires tended to reflect changes in the military basis of their political power and, of course, in its adroit application.[20] Bronze weapons changed to sturdier iron by 1200 B.C. So simple a device as the stirrup in 600 A.D. enabled horsemen to maneuver and to use lances more effectively, but of course the pike, the long bow, and the crossbow would enable foot soldiers in time to defeat armored cavalry.[21] The Second Lateran Council even banned the crossbow "as too lethal for Christians to use against one another," though one must suspect that the latent threat this weapon posed to class rule had more to do with such ecclesiastical distaste.[22] Commoners wielding longbows had the temerity to cut down the mounted nobility in droves at Crecy in 1346 and again at Agincourt in 1415 and thereby "heralded the downfall of feudalism."[23]

A warrior class historically controlled the bulk of the surplus of production among the peasantry they allegedly protected against other pillagers. Barbara Ehrenreich even suggests that the medieval crusades were probably a deliberate and clever diversion of knightly thuggishness—of warriors as alien to the locals as the most exotic invader—to the promised land, which instead would feel the sublime savagery of chivalric ideals.[24] The seeds of contemporary arms races hark to familiar arrangements between embryonic European states (and city-states) and private manufacturers that extend as far back as the early fourteenth century. Their combined efforts crafted murderous contraptions in such profusion that by the sixteenth century military prowess and personal valor "all but disappeared behind an armour-plated routine."[25] Gunpowder-based artillery in the late fifteenth century readily made a sieve of formerly impregnable castle walls and also endowed European armies with the capacity to defeat the nomadic mounted invaders galloping in from Eastern empires:

Besides the destructive power of artillery, there was also its capacity for concentrating wealth in a few major kingdoms, and thus of influencing social conditions by centralizing power. It was, in fact, the combination of the new breed of 'chemical propulsion engines' in conjunction with the economic machinery of early capitalism that defeated the nomads because only a State apparatus could afford the economic investment to avail of them.[26]

Military elites pay close attention to new gimmicks (particularly when opponents employ them effectively), but the best tactics for employing them to full advantage are not always very obvious.[27] Long before the advent of mass production, military elites faced perplexing choices between standing pat or adopting innovative weapons with all the attendant tasks of learning fresh, unproven, and often unwelcome ways of conducting warfare.[28] Killing at ever-increasing distances also eroded the warrior's cherished code of honor, however fictitious or selective it actually was in practice.

War stimulated industrialization. The American system of manufactures stemmed from the Civil War, creating the mass assembly of small arms and artillery as well as numerous significant improvements in firing and loading mechanisms.[29] The American Civil War was a technological war in which the infantry rifle, for example, evolved from an erratic, cumbersome weapon to a lighter, sleeker one capable of a 60-percent hit rate at 75 yards so that, blended with more accurate artillery fire, 30–40 percent of combatants became casualties. Eric Hobsbawm summarizes:

> The wars of the 1860s already employed the railroad to good effect for mobilisation and transport, had the telegraph available for rapid communications, developed the armoured warship and its pendant, heavy armour-piercing artillery, could use mass-produced firearms, including the Gatling machine gun (1861) and modern explosives—dynamite was invented in 1866—with significant consequences for the development of industrial economies.[30]

By the 1890s smokeless powder and quick-firing artillery came along. But not every newfangled device would be welcomed by stodgier peacetime armies. The U.S. Ordnance Department rejected the Lewis, Maxim, and Browning machine guns and remained stoutly skeptical about the weapon's utility until reports arrived of the battle of Omdurman in Sudan, wherein six British Maxims mowed down 11,000 Dervish warriors in minutes, with the loss of only a few dozen Tommies.[31] Yet it was not until the First World War slaughters on the Somme, Ypres, Verdun, and Paeschendele that it became obvious that the machine gun was a superb scythe that could butcher European boys just as quickly and easily as it did swarthy tribesmen. The commanders, despite certain exceptions such as British field marshal Horatio Kitchener, could hardly help in their distant dugouts but to suffer delusions as to the exorbitant toll that modern mechanized warfare actually exacted in blood, treasure, and legitimacy.[32]

Weapons research and development, above all, required a strong industrial structure and a large tax base. In the run-up to the First World War, marked by a dreadnought-building race between Britain and Germany, the British arms industry benefited from the much wider tax base instituted by Lloyd George's 1909 budget both to fund armaments *and* new social provisions, the first modern instance of providing (and linking) guns and butter. The arms and shipbuilding industries, which were heavily labor intensive, consequently were viewed as the heralds of prosperity. By 1913 the jobs of one in every six British industrial workers depended on naval contracts, and rises in military spending spread beneficial "multiplier effects" throughout economies (even though these effects were not fully understood in this pre-Keynesian era).[33]

In 1914 the typical aristocratic officer corps of Europe were "neither professional nor technical, if by that one means deference to the weight of objective technological, professional, and modernizing criteria that compels revision in traditional concepts and modes of conduct." This was grotesquely proven in the killing fields of France, where Allied troops clambered "over the top" to stride straight into machine-gun massacres, inflicting 8,246 British casualties in a single day in September 1915 versus nary a single German scratched.[34] Military leaders firmly believed when the First World War began that the "determination to take heavy casualties would result in victory."[35] Several nations instead suffered losses of legitimacy and increasing disorder during these protracted slaughters. In spring 1917 mutinies on the western front spread especially among the French while the outright revolt of Russian troops on the eastern front sparked the Bolshevik Revolution.

Mechanized warfare cranked into gear in 1918 and is credited—along with American entry—with breaking the stalemate.[36] Chemical warfare showed mixed results: It inflicted more than half a million (mostly temporary) enemy casualties, but uncontrollable mustard and phosgene gas clouds also could float backward so that 2,500 British soldiers managed to gas themselves in one such errant incident.[37] Zeppelin raids in 1915 were to be the first manifestations of popular science-fiction visions of awesome air power. German Zeppelins and Gotha bombers, however, dropped barely 74 tons of bombs on Britain throughout the First World War, which barely amounted to a single raid's work early in the Second World War.[38]

In 1909 a British army analyst, trying his hand at forecasting, opened up perhaps the most muddled theme of modern weaponry when he argued that new airships, which he thought likely to make war more terrible, also might mercifully make warfare "more localised in its destruction (that is to say, more humane) more decisive and more rapid. By skillfully directing artillery fire, by more accurate location of enemy's position, and by discharge of aerial projectiles, the destruction will be more closely restricted to combatants, and there will be far less of the cruel slaughter of non-combatants and useless destruction of property."[39] (Artillery, not the machine gun, was the main killer in the First World War.) According to his peculiarly cheery forecast, the very terror of aerial warfare will serve to provide a pause for sober thought, which might help countries to avert plunging into unnecessary hostilities. Yet, as one senses the author suspects, this vaunted accuracy also makes the incentive to go to war even more attractive.

Before and immediately after the First World War a scenario of a perfectly impenetrable defense vied against a rival vision of aerial armadas of bombers that "always get through" to pulverize enemies. Colonel Billy Mitchell became the legendary American proponent of the Italian general Douhet's audacious doctrine that bombers would wield "an offensive force so great that it defies imagination."[40] At Washington hearings in 1925 Mitchell insisted that air battles will be "so decisive [that] the nation losing there will be willing to capitulate without resorting to any further contact on land or water on account of the degree of destruction which would be sustained if the country is subjected to unrestrained air attack."[41]

An army general quaintly but no doubt earnestly protested that the United States wouldn't "bomb cities because the world will not stand for that sort of thing," and an admiral plaintively asked if Americans "are to become the 'baby killers' and the 'boches' of the future?"[42] Both officers indignantly stated that the "theory of ruthlessness" underlying air warfare was a repugnant one, as if that ended the matter. Indeed it did so far as an independent air force was concerned, but at a rather less apocalyptic level, Mitchell's aerial vision did concentrate many more orthodox military minds on the prospect of very cheaply creating through combined air and naval power a strong protective zone around the United States and its sea lanes.

Three key lessons were evident to those willing to see them. First, the British found, contrary to dire expectations, that bombing raids strengthened civilian determination to resist. Second, analysts took note of the carnage that a tactical blend of aircraft working with ground forces could wreak, including a Royal Air Force (RAF) attack on Turkish troops in September 1918 that "degenerated into a slaughter which made many pilots sick who took part," testimony echoed by Desert Storm pilots about strafing Iraqi troops in retreat on the road to Basra.[43] Third, the bombings in Abyssinia, China, and Spain in the 1930s ought to have dispelled lingering illusions about delicately sparing population centers. Indeed, Douhet offered a perfectly democratic rationale for killing civilians: It was, after all, the "sovereign people who waged war," wasn't it? So weapons became ever more accurate, longer-ranged, and consequently more abstract for those well outside the line of fire. Even if not, anything was thought better than the relentless hell of trench warfare.

The Second World War

In the late 1930s the U.S. Navy allegedly rejected an applicant for a chemist's post because the department already had one. This story is, if not apocryphal, exaggerated. The United States in 1916, let alone 1938, spent a sixth of the national budget on the navy to police and protect its borders.[44] The United States had only the world's eighteenth-largest army, but this is because this force was more than adequate to keep the likes of Canada and Mexico at bay and to police new possessions in the Pacific and the Caribbean. Like Britain, America's power was premised on a formidable navy and, increasingly, the airplane. Technology invisibly exceeded the boundaries of strategy, as in the case of the B–17 bomber, which was explicitly designated, if not designed, for "coastal defense" of a resolutely neutral United States but also had the capacity for long-range missions (e.g., from British airfields to Berlin).

For all the myths of abject unpreparedness, President Franklin D. Roosevelt in March 1933 already had ordained naval rearmament an integral part of public works, since 85 percent of shipbuilding costs went to labor and every state benefited.[45] By November 1938 Roosevelt set a goal of 10,000 military planes annually as a cheap deterrent that in conjunction with a naval blockade on axis powers, matched the British strategy.[46] From then on there was public support for ample air force expenditures, though far less for an army expansion. Between 1937 and 1940 the chief executive authorized 17 new battleships and, after the fall of France, 10 new aircraft carriers. This financial maneuver secured the bonus for FDR at this time of strong isolationist attitudes (a selective isolationism applying only to Europe, not the Pacific) of evading congressional authority concerning naval and aircraft construction.[47]

Memories of the vile horrors of trench warfare affected all former combatants although in markedly different ways. One reaction was the profoundest reluctance to venture into a ghastly replay of barbed wire horizons where metallic shards minced whole battalions in minutes flat. *Kriegpsychose* in Germany induced Adolf Hitler to adopt a "half-hearted centralization" in order to keep consumer goods flowing as well as winning his favor for mobile blitzkrieg tactics.[48] Britain, unlike Germany, mobilized totally for a long war designed to drain German resources, and it soon managed to out-produce Germany in most weapons categories, including, despite blitz-era myths, aircraft.[49]

Hitler's robust arms buildup was a militaristic Keynesian solution to German economic woes, if an autarkic, imperialist, and incomplete one. Hermann Goering, asked by Allied interrogators what key factors won the war, allegedly replied "Detroit," indicating that the productive capacity of the United States supplied the decisive edge.[50] Scientists served their countries with admirable ingenuity. Radar, proximity fuses, jet aircraft, rockets (the V–1 and V–2), code-breaking computers, and the atomic bomb resulted. Technology alone, of course, did not destroy the Axis; this task also required motivated forces, vast amounts of especially Soviet blood (over 20 million dead), adequate strategy, and a good deal of luck.

Strategic air power was grasped at as the perfect way to dissolve future trench stalemates. Yet in May 1940—contrary to propaganda films celebrating pinpoint accuracy—a British bomber became so hopelessly lost that it bombed an RAF airfield in the belief that it was German. A July 1941 bombing survey found that only 1 in 5 aircraft claiming to have hit their target actually came within 5 miles of the bullseye—and only 1 in 15 on moonless nights.[51] It worked, or malfunctioned, both ways: A radar-equipped German bomber crew blithely landed in Suffolk under the assumption that they were in Holland, which was a nice intelligence boon to RAF Bomber Command.[52]

Nonetheless, Bomber Command lost nearly as many airmen (47,268 in combat and 8,040 more in "non-operational" flights) as Britain did from combined German air and rocket strikes (about 60,000). American air services lost 52,173 men (of a total of 291,557 battle deaths) and 35,946 more in accidents. Only a quarter of all British and American bomber crews completed their tours intact, which makes Yossarian's plight in the novel *Catch-22* a vivid one indeed.[53] The doctrine of U.S. daylight precision bombing operated against 1930s data that tactical support for troops was the best use. Contrary to the fondest prewar hopes for air power, in World War I the percentage of civilian casualties was 15 percent; in World War II, it ballooned to 65 percent (and has since leveled out at a steep 90 percent).[54]

The RAF, forced by heavy losses into a night bombing regimen, dubbed their highly imprecise mayhem as "dehousing the enemy"—a task comprising half their hazardous missions.[55] Radio navigational aids and a ground-scanning radar in 1942 failed to improve accuracy, so Bomber Command continued to resort to littering cities with incendiaries and high explosives.[56] The allied bombing campaign against Germany alone eventually killed 900,000 noncombatants and left 25 million homeless.[57]

It was neither the volume, accuracy, or attrition of the bombing campaign that decisively aided the allied war effort but rather the diversion of enemy resources. Eighty percent of the German air force, which rapidly was shot out of the air once fighter escorts with drop tanks accompanied bombers, was assigned to bomber defense; anti-aircraft crews drained manpower badly needed elsewhere. Air raids resulted in 70,000 recorded deaths in Hamburg, 80,000 at Dresden, and 225,000 in two raids on Tokyo.[58] Racism against Japanese, which was returned in kind, doubtless eased the task of razing 63 cities and the killing of nearly a million civilians.[59]

The Nazis' avid pursuit of miracle weapons proceeded with a "bewildering variety of as many as 425 different aircraft models that were very difficult to mass produce. German production remained inflexible, unrationalized and excessively bureaucratic."[60] By 1944, 42 aircraft types were reduced to five, and a dozen antitank guns reduced to one, as the minister for armament and war production, Albert Speer, pushed forward mass production runs.[61] The superb ME–262 fighter jet, which appeared too late to affect the result, required complete engine overhauls after only 10 to 24 hours of real flight time. An obsession to pursue "excellence for its own sake" was, under the circumstances, a fatal German flaw. Richard Overy contends that the "allies stuck with the weapons of the late 1930s and pushed them to their limits, in most cases matching the performance of Germany's most sophisticated weaponry."[62] Still, the teasing promise of "war-winning" miracle weapons worked to sustain German morale until the crushing final Soviet assault on Berlin in April 1945.

By 1944 the United States was producing 60 percent of the allies' munitions and 40 percent of the world's arms.[63] Through the war's end the nation churned out "some 5600 merchant ships, 80,000 landing craft, 100,000 tanks and armored cars, 300,000 airplanes, 370,000 artillery weapons, 2.4 million trucks, 2.6 million machine guns, 20 million small arms, 434 million tons of steels, 41 billion rounds of ammunition and 6 million tons of bombs."[64] Wartime technology and fabrication laid the sturdy foundations for postwar growth in aerospace, electronics, plastics, chemicals, communications, and nuclear industries.

So-called "dollar a year" businessmen (who retained company pay) reaped for their companies a bonanza of war contracts, subsidized facilities, and a lasting institutional influence inside the deepest recesses of government. The top 100 American firms accounted for 70 percent of defense contracts by 1943, thereby increasing concentration of their economic power.[65] About two-thirds of new manufacturing plants built in the war were sold at cut-rate bargains.[66] "The War had to be won. Dr. New Deal— with all of FDR's talk of economic royalists—goodbye. Dr. Win The War, hello," said the head of FDR's Civilian Requirements Division. "The government gives in. The military, of course, is much more sympathetic to business. They're the same kind of boys."[67] John Kenneth Galbraith recalls,

> We have a public picture of the businessman as a dynamic figure, always ready for action. [In actuality in war he] was somebody who could never bring himself to action as the situation required. He would come to the conference and say, "Let us wait awhile. I think this is something we can accomplish in a voluntary basis. I'm sure business will see its responsibility for radical action." We really had to fight them all the way.[68]

The postwar business campaign dimmed public memory about business culpability for the agonies of the Great Depression and identified prosperity with confident capitalism.[69] Yet in 1942 the proportion of war spending grew from 15 percent to 33 percent, and the next year "federal spending for goods and services exceeded the total product of the economy in 1933."[70] The federal government provided two-thirds of all industrial financing during the 1940–1943 expansion.[71] The synthetic rubber industry, like shipbuilding, aircraft, and other war-related industries, depended heavily on government assistance. Federal expenditures soared elevenfold, from $9 billion to $98 billion, and formed one-half of the GNP, with executive-branch power expanding accordingly.[72]

This remarkable feat of amnesia about the state's role was more difficult to accomplish in conquered fascist or fascist-occupied countries where major industrialists had worked closely with tyrants and profited immensely from slave labor. In postwar Europe the Allies and the USSR both scrambled to milk dry the considerable scientific resources of the former Nazi apparatus.[73] Cold-war exigencies lifted pressure on West Germany to denazify. In 1948 a German court acquitted I. G. Farbin's director on the excuse that he did not know the exact purposes for which Zyklon B was used—though 70 percent of this poisonous agent was shipped to Auschwitz. (At least a quarter of a million Germans were involved directly in war crimes, but only about 36,000—5,200 in West Germany—were convicted.[74]) As for the lengthy list of Japanese war crimes, there is evidence that in exchange for its data, the United States offered legal immunity to a notorious Japanese bacteriological warfare unit, whose members were the "best and the brightest" of their authoritarian culture, that had operated freely in China throughout the war.[75]

Conservatives managed to avert the fair taxation of profits to fund the war, seeking to rely instead on loans to be paid back primarily by average wage-earners.[76] Nonetheless, the wartime boom had exerted a "modest leveling effect on incomes."[77] Conservatives also succeeded in thwarting the growth of a full-scale welfare state by containing social policy demands in the GI Bill of Rights (which some legislators fretted would improve the lot of "uppity" blacks). Still, the overarching domestic policy goal was to prevent a widely feared postwar economic downturn. "The American soldier is depression-conscious," *Fortune* reported in 1943, "and worried sick about postwar joblessness."[78] Roosevelt's "fireside chat" in July 1943 laid plans "for the return to civilian life of our gallant men and women of the armed services. They must not be demobilized into an environment of inflation and unemployment." The GI Bill signed on June 22, 1944, became a homegrown substitute for the Beveridge Act in England, providing loans and educational benefits for the 25 percent of Americans who were veterans.[79] From 1947 to 1950 GI Bill funds at $7 billion a year were half as large as the defense budget, providing a vital cushion of demand for the sudden spending dropoff, too.

As we saw in the previous chapter, it is not technological change alone but commercial patterns and decisions to stoke demand that matter most in creating prosperity. New products do not automatically provide the means to purchase themselves. The cornerstone of security became military Keynesianism. Michael Sherry observes that "well into the 20th century military expenditures in production took 0.4 to 0.9% of GNP although it did comprise 20 to 25% of federal spending from the 1880s to the 1920s—but only 3% of GNP before the 1920s compared to 10% in the post-world war II era."[80] (Compare this to a sixth of 1 percent of R&D spent on the much-denigrated poverty programs in the 1960s, and less than 1 percent overall.[81])

The Marshall Plan was another foresightful response to fear of recession, providing dollars and goods to restore European economic and political stability—and therefore stoke demand for American products—although President Harry Truman in 1946 had to "scare the hell out of the American people" to enact it.[82] As the defense budget dwindled from $80 billion to $11.7 billion in the first three postwar years, war scares were trumpeted in 1946 and 1948, and finally in 1950 a "police action" got underway in Korea.[83] The institutional culture of secrecy enabled the Pentagon to generate its own threats to justify desired arms acquisitions ever afterward. The public, and particularly the labor unions, equated prosperity with a steady flow of military production.[84] U.S. legislators found that they had to camouflage public purposes in the language of military defense: Measures to improve public health, education, or services only got by a phalanx of vigilant conservatives in Congress when presented as building bulwarks against the Red menace abroad or next door.

The Manhattan Project, which secretly constructed the atomic bomb at Los Alamos, New Mexico, embodied the alienated and compartmentalized character of weapons production. The momentum of this massive $2 billion expenditure itself made nuclear weapons use extremely likely—regardless of the intimidating effect it might also exert upon the Soviet Union.[85] At one precarious point scientists Robert Oppenheimer and Edward Teller fretted that a nuclear explosion might result in igniting the entire atmosphere, which they calculated at a three-in-a-million chance—a risk deemed worth taking.[86] In this daring light it becomes possible to suggest that when Oppenheimer at the Alamogordo test in July 1945 uttered the words "I am become death, destroyer of worlds," he was thinking not about the bomb itself but in career terms. The next ground-level witnesses were the incinerated citizens of Hiroshima; a few years later those detonations became a sight-seeing event.[87] In a calculatedly paranoid and persecutory McCarthyist climate, possession of the bomb may only have deterred the United States from reaching a rational accommodation with the Soviets, thus spurring avoidable destruction in a host of proxy wars.[88]

On the domestic front key science policy adviser Vannevar Bush vied with progressive New Dealers regarding postwar public institutional arrangements for determining the uses of scientific and technological resources. Contrary to Bush, who wanted science policy completely insulated from popular control, the New Dealers envisioned the National Science

Foundation (NSF) as a nonmilitary and democratized alternative agency to organize basic research to meet basic social needs, with social science included in the mix to study the policy consequences.[89] In 1950 the NSF was established, but with a relatively meager budget of $15 million (a third the proposed amount) as compared, say, to the $85 million appropriated for the Office of Naval Research alone.[90]

Even so, the NSF remained the only public institutional restraint on the military domination of science as "the proliferation of knowledge of the natural and social worlds coincided with an extension of the hierarchical control over its production and distribution."[91] The United States so thoroughly outmatched the war-ravaged Soviets that opportunistic politicians zestily resorted to domestic persecutory activities—McCarthyism—to prevent Russia from ever "catching up" via espionage, real or imaginary. One result is that "today's soft money researchers," who are dependent on government funding and carefully monitored in their role as an elite reserve labor force, "provide an authoritative voice on scientific ideas, ratifying the advice given to politicians on all technical matters."[92] Here then is Brzezinski's imposing vision of the technetronic elite come to pass.

Lessons of Military Keynesianism

The outbreak of the Korean War in June 1950 cemented the new military-industrial complex by enabling the implementation of the hawkish manifesto, National Security Council document 68, which had been prepared months earlier.[93] This founding document of the cold war aimed to institutionalize an arms buildup—projected to exceed the whole of the federal budget for 1950—to oppose a devastated Soviet Union, to which it insistently attributed the most predatory designs.[94] A military buildup ensued that surpassed the needs of the so-called police action in Korea and which only "grudgingly" provided funds for Korea inasmuch as the real target remained the Soviets in Europe. The United States, which spent 4.8 percent of the GNP on defense in 1950, *added* 9 percent of the GNP by the end of the Korean War, a hike from $13.7 billion to $52.8 billion.[95] Only about a tenth of the new money was channeled to soldiers fighting in Korea.

> Instead the defense establishment spent mightily on weapons such as the B–47, the first nuclear bomber (useless in Korea where fighter planes were needed), and on vast quantities of tanks which, like the B–47, were sent off to the quiet European front. Half of all Korean casualties were created by frostbite because they hadn't decent boots nor did they have a decent anti-tank weapon.[96]

In Korea the air force, which got the largest share of new funds, bombed without restriction but failed to play the decisive strategic—as opposed to tactical ground support—role it assiduously claimed for itself.[97] "We burned down just about every city in North and South Korea both," said Air Force General Curtis LeMay. "We killed over a million civilian Koreans and drove several million more from their homes."[98] But the population did not capitulate under severe bombing that ranged from napalming cities to destroying power stations to busting huge irrigation dams. The war ended in a draw, leaving Korea in utter ruin and suffering losses proportionally higher than the Soviet Union suffered under the Nazi invasion. The alleged threat of use of nuclear weapons played little or no role in the eventual armistice.[99] President Dwight Eisenhower, a fiscal conservative and savvy military man, adopted a cheap deterrent doctrine of "massive retaliation," in which reliance on nuclear weapons was preferred to a much more expensive conventional arms buildup.[100]

The Sputnik satellite launch in October 1957 aroused acute public anxieties about Soviet military domination of space and so generated, among many other things, a quadrupling of academic research funding and the nominally nonmilitary but glamorous NASA space program, which by 1961 would absorb $20 billion.[101] By then the U.S. nuclear arsenal contained the equivalent of 10,000 times the destructive power expended in World War II. Eisenhower in his farewell speech that year memorably warned that "the military establishment, not productive itself, necessarily must feed on the energy, productivity and brainpower of our country, and if it takes too much, our total strength declines." Ike, former supreme commander of Allied Forces in Europe, soberly cited the trade-offs of schools, houses, and other foregone civil needs for each and every gleaming new bomber, but his speech went unheeded in a relatively prosperous nation in which dissenting views had been rigorously suppressed in the name of anticommunism.

By 1968 the 100 largest defense contractors garnered two-thirds of all defense dollars; 40 percent was scooped up by the top ten. Ninety percent of procurement contracts were awarded to firms without competitive bidding. Lubricating this interlocking administrative machinery were more than 2,000 retired military officers at or above the ranks of colonel or Navy captain who were employed by the top 100 defense contractors. One hundred and thirty-nine members of Congress in the early 1960s also held reserve military commissions, including several generals.

A muck-raking biography of John F. Kennedy charges that corporate blackmail of the randy president secured a crucial company contract for a new fighter-bomber.[102] If true, the firm hardly needed to resort to such crude measures. "The evidence is persuasive that the Secretary of Defense awarded the TFX plane contract to General Dynamics, against the unanimous recommendation of the Joint Chiefs of staff that it be given to Boeing," Richard Barnet writes, "in order to rescue a ranking contractor from probable collapse (which had lost 400 million earlier on Convair)."[103] Secrecy also enabled the Pentagon to feed whatever information it pleased to Congress and the public, conjuring imaginary "bomber gaps" and "missile gaps" (not to mention the "mineshaft gap" of *Dr. Strangelove* lore).[104]

Bruce Franklin attests that as a Strategic Air Command (SAC) officer in 1957–1958 his main task was "helping to conceal from the American people, particularly our own SAC crews, the almost certain knowledge that the Soviets still had neither operational intercontinental bombers nor missiles."[105] In 1961 a satellite revealed that the USSR had a far skimpier arsenal than was advertised: 44 intercontinental ballistic missiles (ICBMs) and 155 heavy bombers versus America's 156 ICBMs, 144 submarine-born Polaris missiles, and 1,300 bombers. U.S. officials told the Soviets—though not the American public—that they knew very well that the gap was lopsided in America's favor. Soviet prime minister Nikita Khruschev responded by dispatching nuclear missiles to Cuba in 1961 to offset an intolerable advantage, which brought the world within a whisker of all-out nuclear war.[106] Unknown to Kennedy and his often bellicose advisers, the Soviets in Cuba already possessed megaton-level nuclear devices for at least 20 missiles that could strike as far north as Washington, D.C., plus nuclear artillery and short-range rockets that the local units were authorized to use as they saw fit against a U.S. invasion force.[107]

The reigning logic of "erring on the safe side" to counter weapons that the foe *might* build was profitable for defense firms, expensive for the country, and hazardous for the planet. A Treasury Department secretary acknowledged this reality when he rejected the 1957 Gaither Report (which briefly intrigued Kennedy) recommendation of a $22 billion fallout shelter program inasmuch as the Soviets, or what we imagine about them, will "make us spend ourselves into bankruptcy." Egged on by think-tank gurus such as Herman Kahn to "think about the unthinkable" conduct of a purportedly rational nuclear exchange in step-by-step progress up an escalatory ladder to "war-gasm," the Kennedy administration entertained the illusion that a "counter-force strategy" (targeting silos and military sites, rather than "counter-value" cities) really might work.[108]

Among the snags is that nuclear weapons weren't sanitarily precise; the foe need not courteously respond in kind; and, in the absence of massive retaliatory capacity, it induced preemptive attack to protect one's own deterrent. Given a rapid Soviet catch-up program after the Cuban fiasco, the major nuclear powers settled into the nervous stability of the doctrine of mutually assured destruction (MAD), whereby every adversary knows with certainty that an attack invites unacceptable losses from the foe's surviving "second strike" weapons. What the MAD doctrine failed to deter was an unrelenting arms race and cumulative (and provocative) improvements in missile technology.

Enabling Vietnam:
Technology, Arrogance, and Attrition

The cold-war confrontation instead moved superpowers toward a discreet series of proxy conflicts conducted in the Third World. "Bluntly put," Devereaux argues, "the Vietnam War initially appeared to be a vital component of a plan to immediately stimulate high growth in the economy without resorting to tax cuts, as such."[109] The trouble, as a business executive reminded President Johnson, is that arms spending "is more selective and less diffuse than tax cuts"—and encouraged foolish global policing schemes. In Third World anticolonial conflicts, technology could be said to have played, in pop psychological jargon, the role of "enabler" for arrogant, ignorant, unrealistic, and, in terms of international law, criminal policies.

At a press conference in May 1962 Defense Secretary Robert McNamara boasted that he was confident of victory in Vietnam because every "quantitative measurement we have shows that we're winning this war."[110] Machines, and machinelike thinking, were formed within the restricted range of purposes and values tolerated by powerful authorities. Mathematical data become a deceptive substitute for rare ground-level knowledge. High officials "playing it safe" within their own institutions plunged countless other actors into harm's way amid the recalcitrant or tampered data of the Southeast Asian conflict.[111] These latter-day Lord Kelvins often knew little of local conditions other than what was "countable," such that the Viet Cong were destroyed three times over according to certain "reliable" estimates.[112] On wargaming exercises Colonel Harry G. Summers tells a possibly apocryphal but highly instructive story:

> When the Nixon administration took over in 1969 all the data on North Vietnam was fed into a Pentagon computer—population, GNP, manufacturing capacity, number of tanks, ships, and aircraft, size of the armed forces and the like. The computer was asked: "When will we win?" It took only a moment to give the answer: "You won in 1964."[113]

The motivating assumption—once the notion of deploying special forces alone proved futile—was that sheer technological superiority in the form of massive aerial bombing such as Operation Rolling Thunder (an extension of attacks going on since 1961) plus new airmobile tactics would shatter the enemy's will to resist, rather than strengthen it (as was the case in every other war).[114] Given such a mindset, a considerable degree of racism, and enormous technological power, there was little chance of overturning erroneous assumptions about the nature of the conflict, the enemy, and the enormously counterproductive American war effort itself.[115] A *mechanistic fallacy*, Robert Lifton observes, "pervaded much of American thinking about Vietnam" so that indignant media references to "lack of leadership" to explain the misadventure were as if one

> were discussing a massive machine in which a few gears (leaders) were missing, with the implication that if WE (Americans) "instill leadership" in THEM (Vietnamese), they would then fight and all would be well. The fallacy is a means of dismissing the more fundamental human dimensions of the problem. . . . Americans are reluctant to look beyond the immediate "operation" into the chasm, preferring to reinforce at every point the circle of deception.[116]

Carpet bombing a rural economy did not produce the desired results. "It cost the U.S. 9.6 dollars to inflict $1 of damage on North Vietnam in 1966 as compared with $6.6 in 1965," McNamara reckoned.[117] There was no halting the few tons of arms needed daily to carry on. The kill ratio on the Ho Chi Minh "trail"—an improvised and farflung network of crisscrossing paths—was 1 infiltrater per 300 bombs, at a cost of $140,000 each—making it seem a wiser, saner, and cheaper proposition to have posted officials at "reverse toll booths" along the trail to bribe the enemy to go away.[118] From 1965 to 1969 the United States dropped 6.5 times the bomb tonnage on the vast free fire zone that was Vietnam as it had in Korea.[119]

The Tet offensive in January 1968 profoundly shocked Americans and turned a majority against the intervention; only a month earlier a Harris poll found that 40 percent had opposed even peaceful and legal antiwar demonstrations.[120] President Richard Nixon in 1969 started the gradual withdrawal of American ground troops ("Vietnamization") but also expanding the bombing, a move that went largely unchallenged because the high-technology air war "was not very tangible to the average American."[121] In Indochina, encompassing both Vietnams, Laos, and Cambodia and which is roughly the size of Texas, the United States dropped 8 million tons of bombs—four times the amount dropped in all of World War II—at a loss of 3,720 aircraft and some 5,000 helicopters. Chemical defoliants poisoned millions of acres of rich farmland as well as dense jungle. Nixon always bragged that his 1972 Christmas bombings of North Vietnam forced the final peace settlement, although there was virtually no change from the terms offered not just three months but three years earlier.[122] The bombing, which cosmetically tried to make a failed venture seem a success, was conducted to appease a rancorous right wing at home and a resistant South Vietnamese leadership abroad as much as it was to pummel the North Vietnamese.[123]

In a wildly indiscriminate war of "pacification," where body counts were the macabre measure of success, the numerical costs were the lives of more than 58,000 Americans, 250,000 ARVN troops, 4,400 South Koreans, 1,000 Australians and New Zealanders, and, at minimum, 1.5 million

Vietnamese civilians (and three times as many wounded). In South Vietnam 40 percent of the populace became hapless refugees. By 1969 American defense reached 9.5 percent of the GNP, with 37 percent accounted for by Vietnam. The total monetary cost was approximately $150 billion in military spending (and perhaps four times that figure when adding in indirect costs), a newly ignited inflation, a 2-percent drop in the average wage earner's standard of living, the incalculable price of foregone investment sorely needed elsewhere, and a deeply divided home front.[124] Here was an unnecessary war that, as Martin Luther King Jr. sadly pointed out, featured the "cruel irony of watching Negro and white boys on TV screens as they kill and die together for a nation that had been unable to seat them together in the same schools."[125]

In Vietnam only 22 percent of American soldiers were line combat troops, compared to 36 percent in World War II, which attested to the more than proportional substitute of firepower for manpower.[126] Still, the gruesome necessity of enduring 60 days or more of continuous combat became common only in the industrialized twentieth century.[127] Some 850,000 veterans reported suffering posttraumatic stress disorder syndrome—about 30 percent of all veterans—which matches the numbers serving in or dangerously near combat zones.[128] Technology could not always provide an adequate disguise for their grim business. "I felt the worst thing that happened to me there was what could happen to any soldier in Vietnam," remarked one veteran. "I learned to see the Vietnamese as people."[129] Few soldiers, understandably worried about survival from one minute to the next, could do likewise.

U.S. military expenditure as a percentage of GNP reached 9.3 percent in 1968 and, with the end of the war, slid to 4.9 percent by 1980, President Jimmy Carter's last year in office. (The anticipated "peace dividend" never materialized.) That same year Carter, beset by the second Arab oil embargo, a hostage crisis in Iran, and Soviet military intervention in Afghanistan, pledged to spend more defense dollars than his opponent Ronald Reagan actually would: 4.5-percent annual increases for five years; the deployment of new MX, Cruise, and Trident missiles; and a new Rapid Deployment Force organized to "get it right" this time in Third World interventions.

The oft-lamented decline in defense spending after Vietnam is highly exaggerated. According to the Office of Management and Budget, average expenditure from 1962 to 1982 was $78.95 billion in constant (1976) dollars. In the peak year of the Vietnam buildup (1969), the figure hit $107.7 billion. In the next six years the annual average was $70 billion. Considering that expenditures were $77.2 billion in 1962 and $76.6 billion in 1981, the annual rates were consistent.[130] Still, in Reagan's first term, spending shot from $199 billion to $264 billion, or from 5.2 percent to 6.6 percent of

GNP.[131] His pugnacious administration, refashioning Vietnam into a "noble cause," went on the prowl for intervention targets in Central America only to find itself thwarted by a rock-solid majority opposition in the early 1980s.

Creeping Toward Star Wars

In the late 1930s, B-movie actor Ronald Reagan starred in *Murder in the Air,* where he heroically picked off circling enemy aircraft with a super weapon described as "an inertial projector whose rays were to make America invincible in war."[132] Almost half a century after, in March 1983, President Reagan made his startling "Star Wars" proposal, officially dubbed the Strategic Defense Initiative (SDI), to create an impenetrable antimissile shield composed of similar science-fiction devices. Apart from several speculative conversations between Reagan and Edward Teller, the Star Wars proposal was rooted in the Starbird Memorandum of the 1960s, which had been crafted to sell Congress an expensive Sentinel antiballistic missile (ABM) system (defense secretary Robert McNamara decided the contraption was unfeasible, technically and economically). The 1972 ABM Treaty—permitting each side a single ABM site—put the "perfect shield" notion to rest for a decade.

No magic interception devices existed. The price tag of a trillion dollars for this B-movie vision was equivalent to eight Manhattan Projects: Vast sums must be raised in order to build a shield of interlocking lasers, satellites, and super-speed projectiles with nuclear-powered beams. The rub was that "a perfect astrodome defense is not a realistic thing," as even the head of the SDI program admitted a year later.[133] The initiative really aimed at assuring the survival of missile silos and command posts, not the citizenry. The SDI initiative, by definition, broke with MAD doctrine and therefore upset the stable balance of threat between the nuclear superpowers. A reporter discovered a decade afterward that the Pentagon in 1984 had planted a remote-control explosive device aboard a target missile to rig a "successful" Star Wars test. The administration officials retorted that "it was more important for the Soviets to believe that we could intercept their missiles in flight than it was for the US to actually have the capability to do so."[134]

The installation of SDI, workable or not, frightened the Soviets. Unlike the American "triad" system of spreading nukes among land-, air-, and sea-based launchers, the Soviet system kept the vast majority of its devices in silos. Whereas a first strike might leave 300 missiles—an ample deterrent—an ABM system working at 90-percent effectiveness would reduce this to 30. The Soviets grew edgy because there are aggressive elements in every polity willing to take daft chances. The intoxicating idea of a space shield only encouraged trigger-happy mentalities. Hence, technical innovation (indeed, the *prospect* of technical innovation) combined with a zealous government to bring about a more dangerous strategic situation.

Cumulative increases in accuracy eroded the ABM limitation of the SALT I treaty because submarine-based weapons (formerly thought of as second-strike "city-busters") could become first-strike "silo-busters." The Reagan administration favored nuclear use theory (NUTS), based on beliefs in selective targeting, a spiffy ABM system, a need for nuclear superiority, distrust of arms control—and the stockpiling of morphine and opium for survivors. Reagan officials actually predicted that it would take two to four years to recover from an all-out nuclear war. The Congressional Office of Technology Assessment, however, estimated that in the first thirty days of a nuclear exchange, some 70 to 160 million Americans would perish.

Reagan touted SDI as a jobs and renovation program for smokestack industries as well. Boeing, which received $100 million for Star Wars laser work and a five-year, $300 million extension, played along. A company ad burbled: "If a laser can destroy a missile half a world away, imagine what it could do to a cancer cell as small as a few centimeters." The ad suggested that a Boeing-type laser would "treat disease, and also in surgical and diagnostic procedures," although a spokesmen soon hedged this by saying the "company was not actually pursuing them at the moment."[135]

The Pentagon hailed spin-offs such as "the development of autos, food preservation, oil wells, heart defibrillators, leg braces, blood purifiers, kidney-stone breakers and even instruments that can track killer bees" (presumably the sort that its surveillance equipment mistakes for incoming Soviet missiles).[136] Mishaps have ranged from nuclear submarine collisions to identifying geese as Soviet ICBMs to losing nuclear bombs at sea. Analysts uncovered "numerous instances of safety violations, unanticipated operational problems, bizarre and dangerous interactions, and unordered risk-taking by both junior and senior commanders."[137] The navy report on the Iraqi exocet attack on USS *Stark* in 1987 admitted that "glitches in the ship's radars and electronics may have contributed to the disaster" and that "the launching of the two exocets was undetected although the Iraqi Mirage was."[138] The Aegis radar system in 1988 shot down an Iranian Airbus that was mistaken for an F–14 a third its size and pictured as descending to attack instead of climbing; the smart Maverick missile once locked onto a campfire where soldiers were cooking beans.[139] The Soviet record is, if anything, far worse.

The first ABM proposal was designed to meet a nonexistent Soviet threat at a chastening time when economic pressures made U.S. elites aware that they should curb ambitions. The MAD "doctrine" was a sober recognition of grim realities resulting from a global stand-off by two superpowers possessing overwhelming offensive capabilities. The United States in the 1980s wielded an overkill capacity 46 times the mega-tonnage needed to destroy the Soviet Union—and a third was "survivable" after a successful Soviet strike. The evolution of nuclear destructiveness is such that the Defense Department in the 1960s thought 100 missiles would destroy 59 percent of Soviet industrial capacity and that 300 hits would demolish 77 percent. But by the 1980s three Minutemen II missiles and seven Poseidon missiles with multiple warheads would destroy 73 percent of such capacity.

The Poseidon carries 6 to 14 warheads, and the Trident I carries 8 warheads with a greater range and double the yield. The Trident II is a "hard-target kill capacity" with 480-foot circular error probability (CEP); the MX was more accurate but less potent. Some 40–50 percent of nuclear subs were "on station at any one time and able to deliver some 2,500 warheads."[140] The bomber force acquired "stand-off" cruise missiles as the Reagan buildup rapidly created smaller weapons, greater accuracy, and higher yield-to-weight ratios.

The phenomenon of "technological creep" came into play. The CEP of missiles shrank to pickle-barrel proportions. Devices boasted an imputed accuracy of 100 yards for "clean, surgical weapons." (The CEP refers to a statistical situation of *half* the missiles falling in the designated area with the advertised accuracy, but only if nothing so much as a snowflake brushes against them.[141]) The pursuit of increased accuracy for Trident II, MX, and Minutemen III made these weapons appear to be silo-busters and neutralizers of a Soviet counterstrike. The defense stirred the dangerous illusion that flawless interception of missiles was possible.

Military dollars also were an inadvisable way of creating jobs. The military created 48,000 jobs per billion dollars spent. The same billion generates 76,000 jobs in sewer construction, 76,000 in public housing, 100,000 jobs for teachers, 77,000 jobs for specialized nurses, or 151,000 places in the Job Corps.[142] Reagan spent 75 percent more on aircraft to get 9 percent more planes.[143] Numerous studies found these military products far too specialized to spin off in civilian markets.

Despite a General Accounting Office report decrying "massive overclassification" of documents, Reagan also reclassified hordes of them.[144] In 1987 the National Academy of Sciences said that government secrecy cost the economy dearly because restricted items were gotten elsewhere and it impeded dissemination of knowledge. By 1988 the undeclared "black budget" of the Pentagon grew eightfold to $36 billion—more than the military budget of any nation but the USSR, which was a tax of $150 on every American, with no right to know how their money was being spent.[145] By 1985 over 7,000 concerned American scientists pledged to refuse to work on SDI. In 1982 Gallup polls showed that a majority of business executives welcomed detente as an opportunity to cut excessive defense spending.[146] A 1982 nuclear freeze referendum passed in eight of the nine states in which it was considered. Mass demonstrations took place in many major cities. The Reagan buildup stirred a nuclear freeze movement in the United States and Western Europe, with 60 percent or more of the citizenries favoring it, which coaxed reluctant U.S. authorities to carry the START talks, begun in 1982, into a phase of earnest negotiations.[147]

Does Technology Prevent Peace Dividends?

"When it comes to conversion," Barnet wrote in the early 1970s, "most Americans are Marxists. They do not believe that the present levels of prosperity or employment can be maintained except by a war economy."[148] One in five jobs depended on the Department of Defense; 3.4 million served in the armed forces, and 1.3 million civilian defense workers plus 3.8 million more were in defense-related industries—and many more were involved in indirect ways. At the height of the Vietnam war, Barnet estimated that

> 70 cents of every tax dollar [is being spent] on present, past and future wars. The American people are devoting more resources to the war machine than is spent by all federal, state, and local governments on health, and hospitals, education, old-age and retirement benefits, public assistance and relief, unemployment and social security, housing and community development, and the support of agriculture. If one wonders why inner city ghettoes, farm bankruptcy, and educational cuts must occur, it lies here.[149]

The government and the defense sector have strived to convey the impression that there has been a 40-percent cut in the military budget since 1987, the peak year of the bloated Reagan buildup. In fact, cuts have only returned the Pentagon budget to the pre-Reagan cold war norm.[150] The United States spends seven to eight times more on the military than do Russia, France, Japan, Germany, and Britain combined. After the Soviet collapse in 1991 the United States still accounted for 40 percent of world military spending, justified by an ambitious two-regional-war strategy of preparedness.

The 1991 Gulf War constituted a sensational global advertisement for the performance of U.S. weapons systems—and a partially misleading one. The Patriot antimissile systems adulated by a meticulously censored media turned out not to have scored a single confirmed SCUD kill.[151] The army, "alerted by Patriot missile manufacturer Raytheon, even attempted to gag the MIT professor who released the discouraging news."[152] Furthermore, British destroyers "picked up Stealth planes from 40 miles away. U.S. radar identified Stealth crafts from five times that distance."[153] The aerial hunt for the Iraqi SCUD missiles was far less successful than claimed. But the ground assault certainly owed much of its stunning success to round-the-clock air strikes that inspired mass desertions of Iraqi conscripts long before the Allied armored columns cranked into deadly gear. From 125,000 to 175,000 Iraqis fled their desert posts and left 25,000 comrades to face 400,000 well-trained and well-equipped professional Allied troops. The hapless Iraqi forces suffered at least 100,000 killed and perhaps another 300,000 wounded, according to Defense Department intelligence estimates.[154] The American public was treated to a six-week television commercial for military expenditures—(partly offset by Allies' contributions) in order to restore an authoritarian monarchy to its "rightful" throne. And it now appears that the depleted uranium rounds that devastated Iraqi armor may be a contributor to the notorious "Gulf war syndrome" inflicting postwar casualties on Allied soldiers.[155]

Under President Clinton the defense budget did shrink relative to the peaks of the 1980s but, on returning to late-1970s levels, were projected to rise again. The pattern of post–cold war cuts has been personnel first, weapons systems last. U.S. troops in Europe fell from 304,000 in 1990 to 133,700 by 1994—and fell overall to 1.4 million. The defense budget remains unchallenged at a hefty level of half of discretionary federal spending, with $377 billion allocated for past expenses (veterans' benefits plus debt interest, which is 80 percent military) and $286 billion in 1996 for the Defense Department, not to speak of ponying up for the Central Intelligence Agency (CIA), Department of Energy, and less explicit channels for arms-related expenditures.[156] Senator Charles Grassley declared that the Pentagon, with $33 billion in "problem disbursements," was virtually unauditable; Franklin Spinney, a Defense Department analyst, decried a "time bomb being fueled by the Pentagon's corrupt budget numbers."[157] Arms manufacturers riposted by playing the job loss card inasmuch as "both Congress and the White House increasingly view defense as a federal jobs program" for high-tech employees, and so the B–2 bomber, Seawolf submarine, C–17 transport, F–22 fighter, V–22 Osprey, Milstar satellite, E–8A reconnaissance plane, and Trident II missile flourish despite the Soviet collapse.[158]

The mechanisms of influence are familiar ones. Defense-sponsored political action committees (PACs) gave Congress $7.5 million over 1993–1994, with one-third targeting 42 members of the House National Security Committee; between 1989 and 1994 each Senate Armed Services Committee member reaped $108,000 from these generous PACs.[159] U.S. military procurement dropped 50 percent between 1987 and 1995 (from $104 billion to $47 billion), but arms exports held steady at $10 billion a year as the U.S. share of world military exports rose to three-fifths from one-quarter only ten years earlier via aggressive marketing schemes.[160] In 1995 Clinton approved a government-backed $125 billion loan-guarantee fund and a $200-million-a-year tax break for foreign arms purchases even though arms exports accounted for just 300,000 jobs as compared to the 1.8 million jobs lost through military downsizing.

Randall Forsberg, urging a 40-percent budget cut, points out the "vicious circle to keep arms industries open" through "promoting national exports that are bound to be matched by others that will create the very military threats whose potential future existence is suppose to justify arms industries."[161] Defense-stimulated employment fell from 7 million in 1987 to 4.8 million (and another million indirectly) versus 128 million other workers—a 20 to 1 ratio of those who gain versus those who lose. Robert McNamara and William J. Kauffman at the Brookings Institute argue that the budget could safely be sliced in half—a 5-percent cut per year (adjusted for inflation) would free $100 billion for tax cuts, social spending, or deficit cutting. More than 60 percent of Americans want to fight "drugs and homelessness, 21 percent to reduce the deficit, and 10 percent to cut taxes." In a focus group poll in November 1994 most people favored cuts in military spending but feared the potential loss of jobs in the absence of a solid conversion plan.

There is no convincing evidence that exports are needed to lower procurement costs, and job losses mount as mergers proceed merrily on, notably Lockheed and Martin Marietta in 1995. By then, the United States held 64 percent of the world arms market (versus 46.5 percent U.K., 20.8 percent Russia, 8.3 percent China, and 5.6 percent France). In a standard deal with Turkey for F–16s the asking price was $4.3 billion, of which 75 percent was provided by U.S. loans and grants.[162] Saudi Arabia typically does not deal without enjoying a minimum 25-percent offset, and some offsets amount to 100 percent. Yet these indulgent arms deals amount to only 1.5 percent of merchandise exports.[163] These exports entail hiving off American jobs. Prior to 1991 the United States had shipped $1.5 billion in licensed arms to Iraq, which also captured more sophisticated weaponry in Kuwait. There simply is no technical fix for national security.

Conclusion: Smart Weapons, Dumb Choices?

"The industrialization of war," William McNeill observes, "scarcely more than a century old, has erased the old realities of soldiering without altering concurrent, inherited psychic aptitudes for the collective exercise of force. This constitutes a dangerous instability."[164] The modern military goal is to remove the soldier from the line of fire, the better to improve the rate of slaughter as well as to deflect any misgivings that citizens may have about the often puzzling purposes served by the deployment of their tax dollars, sons, and, increasingly, daughters.[165]

The Berlin Wall fell in 1989, the USSR dissolved in December 1991, and the cold war ended, luckily, with a whimper. There was no victory parade to "help free us of the illusion that a large military force is still needed" and that it was high time to attend to all the opportunities foregone in the cold war, such as "schools that were never built, the gaps in the welfare safety net that were not filled, [and] the parks that were not tended."[166] National Science Foundation director Neal F. Lane points out that domestic discretionary spending (parks, prisons, highways, food safety, etc.) fell from a quarter of the budget thirty years ago to just one-sixth today and is slated to be cut to one-seventh in what appears to be "a high risk experiment to see if our nation can scale back its investment in critical areas such as research and education and still remain a world leader."[167] So a Stealth bomber that "fails crucial tests and can't tell a mountain from a rainstorm but is funded at $2.2 billion per plane," slouches ahead, regardless of costs.[168] As a constituent aptly, if crudely, told the secretary of labor, Robert Reich, in the early 1990s: "Shit, man. Jus' make one less of those big bombers and you got work for every poor kid in America."[169]

Notes

1. "It is not facetious to say that if the United States has a full employment policy, it is war." David Cameron in Thomas Ferguson and Joel Rogers, eds., *The Political Economy: Readings in the Politics and Economics of American Public Policy* (Arrack, N.J.: M. E. Sharpe, 1984). Also see Seymour Melman, *The Permanent War Economy* (New York: Touchstone, 1974), pp. 1–25. For broad histories see Karen A. Rasler and William Thompson, *War and State Making: The Shaping of the Global Powers* (Boston: Unwin Hyman, 1989); John Nef, *War and Human Progress* (Cambridge, Mass.: Harvard University Press, 1950); and J. M. Winter, *War and Economic Development* (Cambridge, Mass.: Cambridge University Press, 1995).

2. This is a standard characterization in "realist" models of international relations. For critiques see Justin Rosenberg, *The Empire of Civil Society* (London: Verso, 1994), and J. K. Jacobsen, *Dead Reckonings* (Atlantic Highlands, N.J.: Humanities Press, 1997), pp. 188–212.

3. Brian Martin, "Science, Technology and Nonviolent Action: The Case for a Utopian Dimension in the Social History of Science and Technology," *Social Studies of Science* 27, 2 (June 1997): 440.

4. Congressman F. James Sennenbrunner (R-Wis.), letter to the editor, *Issues in Science and Technology* 13, 3 (Spring 1997): 7.

5. Charles Tilly observes that war-making also led, however inadvertently, to "a civilization of government and domestic politics" because of concessions that rulers made to civilians in order to extract resources. Charles Tilly, *Coercion, Capital and European States, A.D. 990–1990* (London: Basil Blackwell, 1990), p. 206.

6. *Persuading the Public* (London: HMSO, 1995), p. 11. On Beveridge see Peter Calvocoressi, Guy Wint, and John Pritchard, *Total War: The Causes and Consequences of the Second World War* (London: Viking, 1989, 2d ed), pp. 451–455.

7. Mary Fulbrook, *The Fontana History of Germany: The Divided Nation, 1918–1990* (London: Fontana, 1991), pp. 82–83. On the "rattenkrieg" and extinction of a Nazi Army, see Antony Bevor, *Stalingrad* (London: Viking, 1998), esp. pp. 145–165.

8. In a critical survey of Britain that is applicable elsewhere, David Edgerton judges "the pronouncements of scientific intellectuals on the relations of science and war display a combination of arrogance and ignorance which is as difficult to credit as it is to understand." See his "British Scientific Intellectuals and the Relations of Science, Technology and War," in Paul Forman and Jose M. Sanchez-Ron, eds., *National Military Establishments and the Advancement of Science and Technology: Studies in 20th-Century Science* (Dordrecht: Kluwer Academic Publishers, 1996), p. 26.

9. See Fritz Stern's essay "Fritz Haber: The Scientist in Power and Exile," in his *Dreams and Delusions* (London: Weidenfeld & Nicolson, 1988), p. 63.

10. Quoted in Robert W. DeGrasse, *Military Expansion, Economic Decline: The Impact of U.S. Military Spending on U.S. Economic Performance* (New York: M. E. Sharpe, 1983), p. 2.

11. John Ellis, *The Social History of the Machine Gun* (New York: Pantheon, 1976), p. 9.

12. See David Dickstein and David Noble, *The New Politics of Science* (New York: Pantheon, 1984).

13. Rasler and Thompson, *War and State Making*, p. 156.

14. This view persists among designers of nuclear weapons. See Jo Ann Schroyer, *Secret Mesa: Inside Los Alamos National Laboratories* (New York: John Wiley & Sons, 1998), p. 15; and Hugh Gusterson, *Nuclear Rites: A Weapons Laboratory at the End of the Cold War* (Berkeley: University of California, 1996), p. 220. The inventor of the neutron bomb, however, candidly observed, "On a surface level I've rationalized my fascination with nuclear weapons by saying it's important for the security of my country and so there are no qualms to be had. If I went down another level in my psyche, I wouldn't know what to say—I've done it because I wanted to." Robert Del Tridici, *At Work in the Fields of the Bomb* (New York: Harper & Row, 1987), p. 47.

15. Lt. Col. Dave Grossman, *On Killing: The Psychological Cost of Learning to Kill in War and Society* (New York: Little, Brown, 1995), p. 106.

16. *Ibid.*, pp. 4, 160. One notices, from the standpoint of the U.S. military, that the outcomes did not improve accordingly.

17. A 9th Infantry Division veteran who served in the Mekong Delta recounted to me a story of a lone Vietnamese—presumed a "Viet Cong" in this free fire zone—running hundreds of yards through volleys from his squad. "We must have fired two thousand rounds, and when we finally hit him and found the body there was a single bullet hole in it." His point was there were plenty of excellent marksmen, including himself, who could have shot the man with the first round or two. Since no squad members were in danger, everyone slacked off, hoping someone else would kill him. For testimony as to the inherent misconduct of the war, see Richard Stacewicz, *Winter Soldiers: An Oral History of the Vietnam Veterans Against the War* (New York: Twayne Publishers, 1996).

18. Lieutenant William Calley commanded the American troops who massacred approximately 500 unarmed Vietnamese villagers in My Lai on 16 March 1968. The public believed that Calley, while guilty enough, was made the scapegoat for higher authorities. Opinion polls indicated that only 15 percent favored prosecution of Calley. See Richard A. Falk, Gabriel Kolko, and Robert Jay Lifton, eds., *Crimes*

of War (New York: Vintage, 1971), pp. 6, 24. Also see Seymour Hersh, *My Lai 4: A Report on the Massacre and Its Aftermath* (New York: Random House, 1970); and Herbert Marcuse, "Reflections on Calley," in George Katsiaficas, ed., *Vietnam Documents: American and Vietnamese Views of the War* (London: M. E. Sharpe, 1992), pp. 138–139.

19. Michael S. Sherry, *The Rise of American Air Power: The Creation of Armageddon* (New Haven: Yale University Press, 1987), p. 226.

20. See the references above to McNeill, Mumford, and Nef.

21. See Lynn T. White, *Medieval Technology and Social Change* (Oxford: Clarendon Press, 1962).

22. William H. McNeill, *The Pursuit of Power: Technology, Armed Forces and Society Since A.D. 1000* (Chicago: University of Chicago Press, 1982), p. 68.

23. J.C.F. Fuller, *Armaments and History* (New York: Da Capo Press, 1945), p. 76.

24. Barbara Ehrenreich, *Blood Rites: Origins and History of the Passions of War* (New York: Henry Holt, 1997), p. 169.

25. McNeill, *The Pursuit of Power*, p. 130. Also see Martin Van Crevald, *Technology and War* (New York: Free Press, 1991).

26. Manuel De Landa, *War in the Age of Intelligent Machines* (New York: Zone Books, 1991), pp. 12–13.

27. See the mitigating case made for the military viewpoint in Stephen Peter Rosen, *Winning the Next War: Innovation and the Modern Military* (Ithaca: Cornell University Press, 1991), pp. 180–181. His explanation as to why drop tanks for fighter escorts were not used sooner in the Second World War is persuasive, but other examples of evident obtuseness, such as denial of parachutes to allied airmen in the First World War, are harder to justify on rational grounds.

28. McNeill, *The Pursuit of Power*, p. 141.

29. *Ibid.*, p. 232. Also see Merritt Roe Smith, "Army Ordnance and the 'American System' of Manufacturing, 1815–1861," in Smith, ed., *Military Enterprise and Technological Change: Perspectives on the American Experience* (Cambridge, Mass.: MIT Press, 1985).

30. Eric J. Hobsbawm, *The Age of Capital, 1848–1877* (London: Weidenfeld and Nicolson, 1975), p. 99.

31. Ellis, *The Social History of the Machine Gun*, pp. 79, 87.

32. Observing the African carnage caused by artillery and machine guns in 1898, Kitchener was duly apprehensive of what would happen when British soldiers "had to undertake the offensive under similar conditions." Rosen, *Winning the Next War*, p. 113.

33. McNeill, *The Pursuit of Power*, p. 285.

34. Gabriel Kolko, *Century of War: Politics, Conflicts and Society Since 1914* (New York: New Press, 1994), p. 20; Alan Clarke, *The Donkeys* (London, Pimlico, 1990), p. 173.

35. John Keegan, *The First World War* (London: Hutchinson, 1998), p. 194. On the French mutinies in spring 1917 see pp. 346–360.

36. Fuller, *Armaments and History*, pp. 140–142. "The technology [of the tank] was not resisted by military commanders," Stephen Rosen argues. "The problem was not in deciding to produce limited numbers but in learning how to evaluate the weapon's strategic merit relative to competing modes of warfare" Rosen, *Winning the Next War*, pp. 109–129. This begs the question regarding a military mindset

that took so long—over 40 months—to effectively integrate the new mechanized weapon within a new "combined army doctrine."

37. Edward Speirs, *Chemical Warfare* (London: Macmillan, 1986), p. 15. These chemicals hurt the home front too. In British mustard gas factories "90% of the workforce were voiceless and about 50% coughed constantly. Conjunctivitis was almost universal, and most workers suffered from red, peeling skin which was itching and made sleep 'almost impossible'" (p. 27). L. F. Haber, son of the famous German chemist Fritz Haber, whose attitude to war was "jingoistic," estimated that between 500,000 and 800,000 soldiers suffered from gas attacks, although the vast majority recovered quickly. Still, at least 26,000 died on the western front alone. L. F. Haber, *The Poisonous Cloud: Chemical Warfare in the First World War* (Oxford: Clarendon Press, 1986), p. 243.

38. J. M. Spraight, *Air Power in the Next War* (London: Geoffrey Blos, 1938), p. 75.

39. R. P. Hearne, *Aerial Warfare* (London: John Lane Cooper Publishers, 1909), pp. xxix, 130.

40. Giulio Douhet, *The Command of the Air* (London: Faber and Faber, 1943; first published 1921), p. 24.

41. Cited in J. M. Spraight, *Air Power and the Cities* (London: Longman, Green & Co, 1930),p. 7.

42. *Ibid.*, pp. 8–9.

43. Spraight, *Air Power in the Next War*, p. 34.

44. William McBride, "The Unstable Dynamics of a Strategic Technology: Disarmament, Unemployment and the Interwar Battleship," *Technology and Culture* 38, 2 (April 1997): 386, 389. "With regard to the Navy Roosevelt was like a small boy given the run of the candy store" (p. 401).

45. *Ibid.*, p. 405.

46. Sherry, *The Rise of American Air Power*, p. 77.

47. On selective isolationism see Franz Schurmann, *The Logic of World Power: An Inquiry into the Origins, Currents and Contradictions of World Power* (New York: Pantheon, 1974).

48. Calvocoressi, Wint, and Pritchard, *Total War*, p. 234. On the Nazis' concern about "war psychosis" in the 1930s see William Sheridan Allen, "The Collapse of Nationalism in Nazi Germany," in John Breuilly, ed., *The State in Germany* (London: Longman, 1992), pp. 147–149. Also see Kolko, *Century of War*, pp. 75, 184. On other factors involved in blitzkrieg warfare see John Mearsheimer, *Conventional Deterrence* (Ithaca: Cornell University Press, 1986).

49. See David Edgerton, *England and the Aeroplane: An Essay on a Militant and Technological Nation* (London: Macmillan, 1991); and Clive Ponting, *1940: Myth and Reality* (London: Hamish Hamilton, 1990), pp. 120–137.

50. See Ellis, *Brute Force*; Richard Overy, *Why the Allies Won* (New York: Norton, 1995); and Sherry, *The Rise of American Air Power*.

51. S. P. MacKenzie, "On Target: The Air Ministry, RAF Bomber Command and Feature Film Propaganda" 1940–42 *War and Society* 15, 2 (October 1997), pp. 48, 52. The films are: *Target for Tonight, One of Our Aircraft is Missing, The Big Blockade*.

52. Geoffry Reagan, *The Guinness Book of Air Force Blunders* (London: Guinness Publishers, 1997), p. 74.

53. Sherry, *The Rise of American Air Power*, p. 198; Charles Messinger, *Bomber Harris and The Strategic Bombing Offensive 1939–45* (London: Arms and Armoury Press, 1984), p. 190

54. Ehrenreich, *Blood Rites*, pp. 206, 227.

55. Messinger, *Bomber Harris and The Strategic Bombing Offensive*, p. 213. Thus, necessity became a virtue and virtue became a habit. By late 1944, as bombing accuracy allegedly improved, the RAF persisted in striking cities rather than oil refineries and other bottleneck industries. See Rosen, *Winning The Next War*, pp. 26–27.

56. John Ellis, *Brute Force: Allied Strategy and Tactics in the Second World War* (London: Andre Deutsch, 1990), p. 172.

57. Sherry, *The Rise of American Air Power*, p. 154.

58. Grossman, *On Killing*, p. 97.

59. Sherry, *The Rise of American Air Power*, p. 115. Also see John Dower, *War Without Mercy: Race and War in the Pacific* (New York: Pantheon, 1986); and William Manchester's Pacific warfare memoir *Goodbye Darkness* (Boston: Little, Brown, 1980).

60. Overy, *Why the Allies Won*, p. 210.

61. See Albert Speer's memoir *Inside the Third Reich* (New York: Avon, 1970). Also see Gita Sereny, *Albert Speer: His Battle with Truth* (New York: Knopf, 1995).

62. Overy, *Why the Allies Won*, p. 243.

63. Richard J. Barnet, *Economy of Death* (New York: Atheneum, 1969), pp. 21, 26.

64. Overy, *Why the Allies Won*, p. 45.

65. Barnet, *Economy of Death*, p. 51.

66. Kolko, *Century of War*, p. 80.

67. Joe Marcus, in Studs Terkel, *The 'Good War': An Oral History of World War Two* (New York: Pantheon, 1984), p. 328.

68. Terkel, *The 'Good War,'* p. 325.

69. Bradley F. Smith, *The War's Long Shadow: The Second World War and Its Consequences* (New York: Touchstone, 1986), p. 145.

70. John Morton Blum, *V Was for Victory: Politics and American Culture During World War II* (New York: Harcourt, Brace, Jovanovich, 1976), p. 91.

71. John W Jeffries, *Wartime America: The World War II Home Front* (Chicago: Ivan R Dee, 1997), p. 55.

72. *Ibid.*, p. 16.

73. Between 1945 and 1955 more than 700 German scientists, engineers, and technicians—many of them former Nazis—were brought to the United States under government auspices. See Christopher Simpson, *Blowback: America's Recruitment of Nazis and Its Effect on the Cold War* (London: Weidenfeld & Nicolson, 1988), p. 38.

74. Clive Ponting, *Armageddon: The Second World War* (London: Sinclair-Stevenson, 1995), pp. 337, 341.

75. Peter Williams and David Wallace, *Unit 751: The Japanese Army's Secret of Secrets* (London: Hodder & Stoughton, 1989), pp. xv, 36, 286. The victims of Unit 751 were termed "maruta" (blocks of wood).

76. See Alba Alexander, "Playing Fair: American Taxation and Social Citizenship" (Ph.D. dissertation, University of Chicago, 1994).

77. Richard Polenberg, *War and Society: The United States 1941–45* (New York: J. B. Lippincott, 1972), p. 86; on the social impact of the war see pp. 131–156.

78. Blum, *V Was for Victory*, p. 89. Only 29 percent of returning soldiers expected prosperity to continue. Richard Severo and Lewis Milford, *Wages of War* (New York: Simon & Schuster, 1989), pp. 283, 284.

79. Smith, *The War's Long Shadow*, p. 141. Theda Skocpol nonetheless is correct that these measures did not place the United States on anything like an equal footing with the emergent welfare states of Europe. See her *Protecting Soldiers and Mothers* (Cambridge: Belknap Press of Harvard University Press, 1992), p. 7.

80. Sherry, *In the Shadow of War*, pp. 5–6.

81. Mary Ames, *Outcome Uncertain: Science and the Political Process* (Washington, D.C.: Communications Press, 1977), p. 22.

82. Stephen E. Ambrose, *Rise to Globalism: American Foreign Policy, 1938–1980* (New York: Penguin, 1981), p. 132.

83. Barnet, *Economy Of Death*, p. 71.

84. DeGrasse, *Military Expansion, Economic Decline*, p. 2.

85. On the Manhattan Project see Richard Rhodes, *The Making of the Atomic Bomb* (New York: Touchstone, 1986); Robert Jungk, *Brighter Than a Thousand Suns* (New York: Penguin, 1982, rev. ed.); and John Newhouse, *War and Peace in the Nuclear Age* (New York: Knopf, 1989). On Soviet nuclear weapons development see David Hollway, *Stalin and the Bomb: The Soviet Union and Atomic Energy, 1939–1956* (New Haven: Yale University Press, 1994).

86. Sherry, *Rise of American Air Power*, p. 202.

87. David E. Nye, *American Technological Sublime* (Cambridge, Mass.: MIT Press, 1994), p. 233.

88. Gar Alperowitz and Kai Bird, "The Centrality of the Bomb," *Foreign Policy* 94 (Spring 1994): 4.

89. See Vannevar Bush, *Science: The Endless Frontier* (Washington, D.C.: National Science Foundation, 1960, first published 1945). Also see his *Modern Arms and Free Man* (Cambridge, Mass.: MIT Press, 1968, first published 1949).

90. Jessica Wang, "Liberals, the Progressive Left, and the Political Economy of Postwar American Science: The NSF Debate Revisited," *Historical Studies in Physical and Biological Sciences* 26, 1 (1995): 142, 144.

91. Herbert N. Foerstel, *Secret Science: Federal Control of American Science and Technology* (Westport, Conn.: Praeger, 1997), p. 2.

92. *Ibid.*, p. 7.

93. On NSC–68 see Callum MacDonald, *Korea: The War Before Vietnam* (New York: Free Press, 1986), pp. 22–39; and Bruce Cumings, *The Origins of the Korean War: The Roaring of the Cataract* (Princeton: Princeton University Press, 1990, vol. 2).

94. On exaggerations by Western intelligence agencies of Soviet strength see, for example, Matthew Evangelista, "Stalin's Postwar Army: A Reappraisal," *International Security* 15, 7 (Winter 1982–1983): 110–138; and John J. Mearsheimer, "Why the Soviets Cannot Win Quickly in Central Europe," *International Security* 7, 1 (Summer 1982): 3–39.

95. Fred Block, "Economic Instability and Military Strategy: The Paradox of the 1950 Rearmament Decision," *Politics and Society* 10 (1980): 35–80; and DeGrasse, *Military Expansion, Economic Decline*, p. 111.

96. Alexander Cockburn and Ken Silverstein, *Washington Babylon* (New York: Verso, 1996), p. 157.

97. David M. Hart, *Science, Technology and Economic Policy in the United States, 1921–53* (Princeton: Princeton University Press, 1998), p. 195.

98. Quoted in MacDonald, *Korea*, p. 235.

99. "Nothing on the diplomatic front or the battlefield, where the Chinese continued to launch attacks and counterattacks up to the signing of the armistice in July 1953, indicated that they were intimidated by the threat of nuclear weapons or by the US Air Force's massive conventional bombing of the North Korean dam-irrigation system in May. To the contrary, they were determined to avoid even the appearance of having caved in and were therefore committed to resist nuclear blackmail. The armistice agreement itself, which as a compromise, indicated that both sides had acknowledged the military stalemate." Jeffrey Kimball, *Nixon's Vietnam War* (Lawrence: University of Kansas Press, 1998), p. 84.

100. Talbot, *Master of the Game*, pp. 70–73.

101. Roger L. Geyer, "What Happened After Sputnik?: Shaping University Research in the United States," *Minerva* 35, 4 (Winter 1997): 365.

102. Seymour Hersh, *The Dark Side of Camelot* (New York: Little, Brown, 1998), pp. 318–322.

103. Barnet, *Economy of Death*, pp. 120–121.

104. On the "missile gap" see Fred Kaplan, *Wizards of Armageddon* (New York: Simon & Schuster, 1983), pp. 156–161.

105. Bruce Franklin, *War Stars: The Superweapon and the American Imagination* (Oxford: Oxford University Press, 1988), p. 181.

106. Richard Rhodes, "The General and World War II," *New Yorker,* August 1995.

107. *Ibid.* On the missile crisis see Graham Allison, *Essence of Decision: Explaining the Cuban Missile Crisis* (Boston: Little, Brown, 1971) and the recently released Kennedy tapes.

108. See Herman Kahn, *Thinking About the Unthinkable* (New York: Horizon, 1962), and his *On Escalation: Metaphors and Scenarios* (New York: Praeger, 1965). On Kahn's background, see Kaplan, *Wizards of Armageddon*, pp. 220–231. On the faultiness of his logic see Philip Green, *Deadly Logic: The Theory of Nuclear Deterrence* (New York: Schocken Books, 1968).

109. Eric Devereaux, "Industrial Structure, Intermediation, and the Collapse of the Cold War Consensus: Business, Media and Vietnam," in Ronald Cox, ed., *Business and the State in International Relations* (Boulder: Westview Press, 1996), pp. 16, 21.

110. Neil Sheehan, *A Bright Shining Lie* (New York: Random House, 1988), p. 290. On his "disenchantment" by autumn 1966, when he privately called for a "coalition government in Saigon that includes elements of the Viet Cong," see Neil Sheehan, *Pentagon Papers* (New York: Bantam Books, 1971), pp. 510–511, 514.

111. Kolko, *Century of War*, pp. 15, 20, 417.

112. Richard Barnet, *Roots of War* (New York: Atheneum Press, 1972), p. 128.

113. Quoted in Thomas B. Allen, *War Games* (New York: McGraw-Hill, 1987), p. 166. The point is that "models do not increase our knowledge of the real world we live in. Human beings gain knowledge by experience and their own sense" (p. 192).

114. James Clay Thompson, *Rolling Thunder: Understanding Policy and Program Failures* (Chapel Hill: University of North Carolina Press, 1980), p. 19.

115. On these rueful themes see Noam Chomsky, *American Power and the New Mandarins* (New York: Vintage, 1969); Frances Fitzgerald, *Fire in the Lake* (Boston: Little, Brown, 1972); Jonathan Schell, *The Military Half* (New York: Knopf, 1968); James William Gibson, *The Perfect War: The War We Couldn't Lose and How We Did* (New York: Atlantic Monthly Press, 1986); Gabriel Kolko, *Anatomy of a War: Vietnam, the United States and the Modern Historical Experience* (New York: Pantheon, 1985); and Falk, Kolko, and Lifton, *Crimes of War.*

116. Robert J. Lifton, *History and Human Survival* (New York: Random House, 1970), p. 216.

117. Paul Joseph, *Cracks in the Empire*, (Boston: South End Press, 1981), p. 125.

118. Michael MacLear, *The Ten Thousand Day War* (New York: St. Martin's Press, 1981), p. 183.

119. Falk, Kolko, and Lifton, *Crimes of War*, p. 412. "Stated another way, in 1968 and 1969 the US used about 7,700 to 7,800 tons of ground and air ordnance during an average day. At the time of the 1968 Tet Offensive the Pentagon estimated that the NLF forces were consuming 27 tons of ammunition a day, and half that amount during an average day in April 1969. Roughly, this is a ratio of 250 to 500 to one" (p. 413).

120. Tom Wells, *The War Within: America's Battle over Vietnam* (Berkeley: University of California Press, 1974), p. 253. By April 1971 a majority polled felt the war was "morally wrong" (p. 491).

121. Raphael Littauer and Norman Uphoff, eds., *The Air War in Indochina* (Boston: Beacon Press, 1971), p. v.

122. Kimball, *Nixon's Vietnam War*, pp. 364–365. A rarely mentioned aspect of the Christmas bombings were the heavy losses: 15 B–52s and 26 American aircraft overall in eleven days.

123. Thompson, *Rolling Thunder*, p. 156.

124. Melman, *The Permanent War Economy*, pp. 66–67.

125. Martin Luther King, "A Time to Break Silence," in Reese Williams, ed., *Unwinding the Vietnam War* (Seattle: Real Comet Press, 1987), p. 429.

126. Kolko, *Century of War*, p. 61; Richard Holmes, *Firing Line* (London: Jonathan Cape, 1985), p. 76.

127. Grossman, *On Killing*, p. 50.

128. J. T. Hansen, A. Susan Owen, and Michael Patrick Madden, *Parallels: The Soldier's Knowledge and the Oral History of Contemporary Warfare* (Hawthorne, N.Y.: Aldine De Gruyter, 1992), p. 28.

129. Grossman, *On Killing*, p. 123.

130. *New York Times*, 24 October 1982, p. 18.

131. David N. Gibbs, "The Military-Industrial Complex: Sectoral Conflict and the Study of U.S. Foreign Policy," in Cox, *Business and the State in International Relations*, p. 51.

132. Sherry, *In the Shadow of War*, p. 406.

133. Matthew Rothschild and Keenen Pick, "Star Wars: The Final Solution," *Progressive*, July 1985, p. 22.

134. William Hartnung, "Reagan Redux: The Enduring Star Wars Myth," *World Policy Journal* 15, 3 (Fall 1998): 19. The reporter was Tim Weiner of the *New York Times*.

135. William J. Broad, "Defense Industry Goes Hustling to Make a Buck Without a Bang," *New York Times*, 8 April 1990, p. 1.

136. *Ibid.*

137. Scott D. Sagan, *The Limits of Safety: Organizations, Accidents, and Nuclear Weapons Prevention* (Princeton: Princeton University Press, 1993), p. 115; and Louis Rene Beres, *Apocalypse* (Chicago: University of Chicago, 1980).

138. John A. Adams, "New Radar Systems Peer Farther, Hide Their Signatures," *International Herald Tribune*, 15 December 1987, p. 3.

139. On the Aegis system see Chris Hables Gray, *Postmodern War: The New Politics of Conflict* (London: Guilford Press, 1997), pp. 64–69; Cockburn and Silverstein, *Washington Babylon*, p. 176.

140. *Bulletin of Atomic Scientists*, August/September 1984: 10.

141. See James Fallows, *National Defense* (New York: Random House, 1981), pp. 148–152.

142. Leonard Silk, "Cost-Effective Job Creation," *New York Times*, 18 September 1983, p. 30. Estimates by then-Representative Les Aspin.

143. Sherry, *The Rise of American Air Power*, p. 402.

144. Foerstel, *Secret Science*, p. 21.

145. Tim Weiner, *Blank Check: The Pentagon's Black Budget* (New York: Warner Books, 1990), p. 6.

146. Noam Chomsky, *Deterring Democracy* (New York: Verso, 1992), p. 93.

147. U.S. policymakers, always ahead of a "reactive" Soviet Union, displayed little interest in enacting genuine measures to reduce or control arms until Gorbachev surprised them by agreeing to deeply asymmetrical cuts in Soviet forces. Matthew Evangelista, *Innovation and the Arms Race* (Ithaca: Cornell University Press, 1988), p. 263. For an argument that the Reagan buildup did not "spend the Soviets into collapse," see Robert G. Herman, "Identity, Norms and Security: The Soviet Foreign Policy Revolution and the End of the Cold War," in Peter Katzenstein, ed., *The Culture of National Security* (New York: Columbia University Press, 1996).

148. Barnet, *Economy of Death*, p. 150.

149. *Ibid.*

150. Randall Forsberg, "Force Without Reason," *Boston Review* 20, 3 (Summer 1995): 3. Also see Randall Forsberg, ed., *The Arms Production Dilemma: Contraction and Restraint in the World Combat Aircraft Industry* (Cambridge, Mass.: MIT Press, 1994).

151. Peter Beaumont, "Gulf of Despair," *Observer*, 14 January 1996. At the time Israeli authorities reported 44 percent accuracy destroying, not just intercepting, SCUDs. The army and manufacturer Raytheon claimed an 80 percent-plus "kill" rate. See Gray, *Postmodern War*, p. 40. Also see Trevor Pinch and Harry Collins, "A Clean Kill?: The Role of the Patriot in the Gulf War," in *The Golem at Large: What You Should Know About Technology* (Cambridge: Cambridge University Press, 1998), pp. 7–29; and Theodore Postol, "Lessons of the Gulf War Patriot Experience," *International Security* 16, 3 (Winter 1991/2): 119–171.

152. Tim Weiner, "Army Cracks Down on Patriot's Critic," *Chicago Tribune*, 20 March 1992, p. 16.

153. Cockburn and Silverstein, *Washington Babylon*, p. 170.

154. Sherry, *In the Shadow of War*, p. 474.

155. Bill Mesler, "Pentagon Poison: The Great Radioactive Ammo Cover-Up," *Nation*, 26 May 1997; and "The Gulf War's New Casualties," *Nation*, 14 July 1997.

156. *Nation*, 26 April 1996.

157. Column by Anthony Lewis, *Guardian*, 23 January 1996, p. 17.

158. *Ibid.*

159. Cockburn and Silverstein, *Washington Babylon*, p. 164. The Department of Defense is paying for industrial restructuring costs by buying up excess capacity but, according to undersecretary of defense Paul Kaminsky, "is not directing the restructuring of the defense industry. Our role has been to provide industry with honest and detailed information about the size of the market so industry can plan intelligently. Dod permits contractors to include restructuring costs in contracts where it can be shown that savings generated over 5 years exceed the costs." Letter to the editor, *Issues in Science and Technology* 13, 3 (Spring 1997): 6.

160. Jayne E. Nolan, "Crunch Time for Control of Advanced Arms Exports," *Issues in Science and Technology* 12 (Fall 1996): 24.

161. Forsberg, "Force Without Reason," p. 4.

162. *Boston Sunday Globe*, 11 February 1996, p. 1.

163. David E. Rosenbaum, "Peace Dividend: A Dream for Every Dollar," *New York Times*, 18 February 1990, p. 10.

164. McNeill, *The Pursuit of Power*, p. viii.

165. See Gray, *Postmodern War*, pp. 43, 175, 241.

166. Henry M. Sapolsky, Mike Trahan, Eugene Gholz, and David T. Burbach, "Let's Have a Parade," *Breakthroughs* 6, 1 (Spring 1997): 3.

167. James F. Neal, NSF director in letter to editor, *Issues in Science and Technology* 13, 3 (Spring 1997): 7.

168. Lewis, *Guardian*, 23 January 1996.

169. Robert Reich, *Locked in the Cabinet* (New York: Knopf, 1997), p. 108.

4

Weeding Them Out

The Curious Case of Eugenics
and Genetic Engineering

Was this possible or that possible? You cannot imagine what this means to an investigator, what an intellectual passion grows upon him. You cannot imagine the strange colourless delight of these intellectual desires. The thing before you is no longer an animal, a fellow-creature, but a problem.
—H. G. Wells, *The Island of Dr. Moreau*

The Victorians took a hearty pride in looking hard facts in their hairy faces, which especially to these nineteenth-century British observers tended to look rather Irish.[1] It was not entirely clear to white Anglo-Saxon Protestant scientists whether Greeks, Italians, or Jews were full-fledged members of the white race either.[2] Even British South Africans during the Boer War (1899–1902) suspected that rebellious Dutch Afrikaaners were not quite "white" enough.[3] The facts that investigators found usually reaffirmed the disdain they already harbored for subordinate classes, races, and women.[4] The underlying thematic thrust of research was that any group situated low on the social scale was to be designated as a biological problem foremost and only then—to the extent it posed a threat or nuisance to respectable folk—as a social problem.

The rigor of research too often reflected the depth of the pockets of the specimens under study: The poorer the subjects, the more slipshod the work about them. Biological value coincided neatly with class or racial "worth," and this concordance produced a particularly tenacious legacy of explanatory determinism, which has resurged in the past two decades.[5]

This biological form of determinist thought can be defined as a spurious "attempt at a total system of explanation" and as a severely reductionist view "in which the arrows of causality run from genes to humans and from humans to humanity."[6] That is to say, everything that we do is rooted in and controlled by our genetic structure so that nothing intervening between that structure and our actions makes any significant difference.

What appealed to so many highly cultivated minds of the time, reared in restricted social worlds of comfort, was the flattering scientific self-image that they gazed unflinchingly at raw truths—painful truths, although painful mostly for "lesser breeds." Though humanity, after Charles Darwin's work on natural selection was popularized, had to digest (despite biblical fundamentalists) the unsavory news of its direct descent from apes, some human groups were deemed less descended than others. An anti-enlightenment notion of "nature red in tooth and claw" became quite an attractive rule for elites to read into human conduct, for it absolved elites for all action or inactions in a harsh new world in which industrial capitalism erased older social ties and obligations and replaced them with impersonal market relations and a law of contracts based on the legal fiction of equality among all parties.

A new batch of "rational" managerial ideologies enabled many employers to repudiate all social responsibilities (except philanthropy, which entails no obligations), treat labor as nothing but an expendable factor of production, and ride roughshod over the unmoneyed populace in good conscience, knowing that this was nature's way.[7] Subordinate groups were viewed as what economists term "externalities," which may be defined as anything or anyone that one can afford to ignore in calculating one's own interest when choosing a course of action. An "externality" isn't so much a technical concept as a social one whose boundaries reflect the state of the play of power in a society.

Nature answers our questions in relation to the values by which we have learned—consciously or unconsciously—to understand those answers. "Just as it was natural for medieval thinkers to view nature as subservient to men's knowledge, purpose and destiny," historian E. A. Burtt observed, "so now it has become natural to view her as existing and operating in her self-centred independence [and] to consider his knowledge and purpose somehow provoked by her, and his destiny wholly dependent on her."[8] This modern concept of nature was no more "the whole story," of course, than the one it succeeded. Indeed, the questions that researchers ask of nature reflect their social backgrounds as well as professional training, and it is only with a great deal of self-scrutiny and humility that some come to understand how their own inbred attitudes and tacit beliefs affect their work.[9] That scientists excel in studying the natural world is no guarantee that they understand their own nature, let alone those of other people, or the intricate interaction of their specialized subject matter with the social environment.

Scientists as a group (exceptions always exist) usually accede to the reigning beliefs about race, gender, class, and creed in the particular milieus in which they grow up, even to the point of acquiring Nazi armbands, Klan robes, or party membership cards.[10] In short, like the vast majority of citizens—though often having more to lose in status and resources—they tend to conform to whatever standards are deemed to be socially approved and professionally advantageous. Nuclear physicists or molecular biologists are just as inclined to confuse their own self-interest or petty prejudices with the general welfare of the community as are television evangelists or used-car salesmen.

But scientists, technicians, and physicians, unlike most other citizens, have the additional barrier of formidable credentials deterring them from prudent acknowledgment of their own fallibility and foibles. Hence, in the history of science we sometimes encounter pure conceit posing as principle. In any field the members of a scientific community, who view themselves as the epitome of objectivity, certainly scrutinize each other's work very carefully. But what happens when such a community preponderantly favors a seriously flawed assumption, finding, or model? It's all too easy for technically astute personnel to mistake their own sincerity for clear-sighted objectivity. An unacknowledged danger of distortion lurks inside the ingenuous notion of the objective observer, as when Hannah Arendt warned against imagining oneself perched on Olympian heights from which to observe the distant whirling earth, a lofty stance that sorely tempts the observer to think of human beings as insignificant creatures—all but for those doing the observing and interpreting.[11] Hence, one frequently finds scientists—caught up in a romance with their own fascinating specialty—handing down perfectly assured verdicts that humanity is nothing but a bundle of genes or nerve twitches or chemicals or conditioned responses or some other factor that they happen to study. This temptation is hard to resist.

No historical episode embodied this temptation so luridly as eugenics, which was a social engineer's dream of refining other human beings to a state of perfection resembling nothing so much as these well-meaning engineers themselves (or, rather, how they would like to see themselves). These Industrial Age inquirers, who generally knew precious little of their own inner motives and desires (especially before Freud and his followers pried open the unruly unconscious), sought to divine the universe's secrets but too often only as they were already inclined to find them.[12]

The drives for fame, fortune, and approval of colleagues also play strong roles in a scientific enterprise whose methods alone cannot provide a foolproof framework for deciding which goals are worth pursuing.[13] In this instance Jacques Ellul is terribly apt when he describes technological processes as increasingly refined means to achieve carelessly examined ends.[14] The application of scientific energy to a subject carries with it a powerful presumption that whatever it does is unquestionably worth doing.[15] In any case, the specific topics that scientists study are usually suggested by problems afflicting their society, problems which depend for their resolution on available resources and ideologies, as Marx remarked in a rather broader context.

A scientific theory, and the popular discourse arising around it, is always liable to be linked in tendentious ways to prevailing political agendas. This linking takes place in two fashions: (1) as research reports reach the public through the media they inadvertently—sometimes deliberately—take on a different character or stronger claim than scientists support, or else (2) when organizations pounce on congenial research findings and diffuse them into the public realm with a self-interested twist.[16] In the 1920s Burtt noted that "the precise notions and assumptions of modern scientific thinking itself have not as yet become the object of really disinterested, critical thought."[17] The advent of sociology of science, critical theory, and cultural studies have improved matters a good deal. Cultural studies, rather than refute laws of gravity or portray them as a figment of imagination, draw attention to the variability of the conduct of scientific investigations in relation to personal and institutional constraints.[18] Sources of distortion are legion. Scientists can operate with the most scrupulous care inside the lab only to see their results misshapen by a media keen for headlines about "revolutionary" breakthroughs and to reinforce popular misconceptions about science. There is no more widespread misconception—albeit one stoked by a faction in the scientific community—than the reductionist dogma that smallest possible units of biological activity totally control human behavior. Scientific findings—or the way they are reported—color political judgment and shape public policy. The greatest care must be taken in wielding tentative findings, and one is well advised to err on the side of generosity when it comes to delivering verdicts with regard to human development, because these verdicts are self-fulfilling in their consequences.

In this chapter I examine the rise, fall, and resurgence of the project of biological "improvement"—a quest stretching back to the speculations of Socrates and Plato. Science alone cannot tell us whether we should clone living creatures, decide the social destinies of our children on the basis of IQ tests, or fix insurance premiums to gene testing results. But there are potent organizations who want the citizenry to believe that science provides absolutely trustworthy answers to controversial social questions. The chapter reviews the extraordinarily sordid history of "racial hygiene" and socially driven mischaracterizations of mental abilities.

Eugenics displays signs of a comeback in a suitably subtle form and under nicer names. Scientists have proclaimed the discoveries of "definite" genetic causes for phenomena as intricate and disparate as homosexuality, shyness, homelessness, schizophrenia, manic-depression, and autism and perhaps even for the arrogance to advance such extravagant claims. Not long ago and with no less reliable evidence scientists confidently announced single gene explanations for the social scourges of thalassophilia ("urge for sea-faring"), drapetomania ("irrational urge by slaves to run off"), Jewish facial expressions, "shiftlessness," and chicken stealing.[19] It pays to be wary of anyone who defines problems exclusively in terms of the techniques he or she has mastered.

The identification of hereditary diseases is a task that poses thorny moral and legal issues, especially about privacy. Behold the prospect of "designer children" in whose pursuit fashion models allegedly have peddled their eggs on the Internet to all comers. The same ambition that spurred the eugenics movement motivates the Human Genome Project to obtain control of the architecture of life; it seems as if life were regarded as a technical puzzle that when solved would yield no more problems. The historical link between eugenics and modern genetic engineering is much stronger than contemporary scientists care to acknowledge, but a "cultural amnesia" about eugenics is cultivated with ease in a commercial culture that prizes short-term thinking and even briefer memories.[20]

Why are certain groups so tempted to assume humanity is "hard-wired" for every possible trait? The answer lies in the far from solely biological predisposition of elites to accumulate power in the natural and the social worlds and, perhaps no less important, also in a common human desire, which owes more to sheer moral laziness than to a "selfish gene," to shirk responsibility for one's own actions and for the welfare of others.[21] It also may be a good deal easier and more financially rewarding for scientists to study genes alone than it is to study their interaction within and among organisms in a variety of complex environments.

The Advent of Eugenics

Throughout the nineteenth century industrialization, urbanization, and state expansion proceeded hand in hand. By the 1870s a growing middle class in Western Europe and America had begun (through personal practices that often entailed deep frustration) to limit their families, unlike the unbridled "lower orders" who seemed to breed madly. As diets improved, public hygiene measures were enacted, and medical care became more widely available, infant mortality fell and more children of the "masses" survived to adulthood. In the United States a declining middle-class birth rate was coinciding with a northward migration of recently freed blacks.

A massive migration of Eastern and Southern Europeans to the United States also got underway from the 1880s onward.[22] These alien influxes, as they always do, annoyed and worried the locals. Commentators at the time remarked on the "deep cultural pessimism" pervading the apprehensive middle classes, which stemmed from their feeling of being under siege by teeming *untermenschen* camped at the edges of their genteel communities. In 1913, for example, Henry Goddard, author of a renowned eugenics text, solemnly advised American authorities that of the immigrants pouring through Ellis Island, at least 83 percent of the Jews, 80 percent of the Hungarians, 79 percent of the Italians (especially Southern Italians), and 87 percent of the Russians were without doubt feebleminded.[23]

Socialist, labor, and suffragette movements erupted during this turbulent time and were met with harsh repressive measures, particularly in the United States. This knee-jerk inhospitality became a well-rehearsed phenomenon by the late 1870s, when, as Richard Slotkin summarizes,

Indians (versus Custer), ethnic immigrants (via strikes) and Blacks (in the collapse of Reconstruction, unfortunately) all asserted in their different ways the desire to control the condition of terms of their labor as opposed to the requirement of the new industrial order as defined by its owners and managers. . . .

The substitution of the symbolism of "savage war" for that of class war shifts the grounds of controversy from the ideological frame of the democratic tradition to that of race war, from a frame in which progress and right order are presumed to emerge from the widest possible diffusion of property and political power to one in which progress depends on the exclusion/extermination of a congenitally regressive type of humanity and aggrandizement of a privileged race or group. [24]

Eugenics bestowed the warm blessings of science on the self-aggrandizing designs of privileged groups. President Theodore Roosevelt was always as strenuous a eugenicist as he was a sportsman. In *The Winning of the West* Roosevelt surmised regarding the extermination of Native Americans that "if we fail to act as the 'superior people' then . . . barbaric acts and savagery and squalid obstruction will prevail over most of the globe."[25] He also feared that "inferior segments" of the white population would swamp this newly cleansed country. President Grover Cleveland shared Roosevelt's exciting vision. In 1912 Woodrow Wilson in his inaugural presidential speech proclaimed that "the whole nation has awakened to and recognized the extraordinary importance of the science of heredity, as well its application to the ennoblement of the human family."[26] (The Ku Klux Klan, which underwent a revival, held "better babies" contests that same year.) Presidents Warren Harding and Calvin Coolidge approvingly invoked such rabid eugenics tracts as Madison Grant's *The Passing of the Great Race*.[27]

Eugenics appealed to dominant social groups because, apart from flattering them, it promised to transfer conflicts stemming from clashing material and cultural interests to a serene biological realm where impartial "science" supposedly would hold sway. Decisions would be based on the unassailable truth. This rather disingenuous trend formed part of a larger Progressive movement in American politics aiming to design an "administrative state" whose exponents hoped that their own awesome expertise would displace the crude and messy war of interests.[28]

In Britain at this heady time Francis Galton, cousin of Darwin and heir to a manufacturing and banking fortune, was sorely distressed by a declining birth rate among what he deemed to be the "best families." The rate commenced a long slow fall from 34 per 1,000 in the 1870s to 15 per 1,000 by the economically stricken 1930s, or from six children per family to slightly more than two.[29] In 1869 Galton published *Hereditary Genius*, "the first work to treat the subject in a statistical manner," which stated with enviable lack of doubt that genius was a wholly inherited phenomenon and that elites were elected by nature, not circumstances or luck.[30] Galton wanted genetically correct people to take charge of society, a stance that fell well short of a revolutionary one since he believed they already possessed all political and economic power. Nonetheless, even biologically blessed elites could not afford to be even momentarily complacent.

The term eugenics, meaning "well-born" or "noble in heredity," was coined by Galton to "signify social uses to which the science of heredity could be put."[31] The supreme objective of eugenics was to improve the racial "stock" through a finely calibrated blend of negative measures (to discourage the "unfit" from reproducing) and positive ones (to encourage those ordained "fit" to breed). People were pretty much like poultry or fruit flies except that some imperfect specimens, unfortunately, could vote.

The eugenics movement was founded on the deceptively commonsensical doctrine that mental characteristics (intelligence, diligence, sobriety, etc.) pass from one generation to another as reliably as physical ones, such as blue eyes or brown hair. Nature trumped nurture; environment counted for nothing. An allied assumption was that races—such that they exist outside their social construction as such—were arrayed in a natural hierarchy, extending from the ever-ascendant European whites on downward.[32] Galton knew with perfect assurance that black servants in U.S. households tended to be half-witted because every book that he had ever read that took any notice of them had described them as such; obversely, for Galton "a high reputation is a pretty accurate test of high ability."[33] Eugenicists cooperate "with the workings of nature by seeing that humanity is represented by the fittest races," Galton declared. "What nature does blindly, slowly, ruthlessly, man may do premeditatedly, quickly and kindly."[34] The goal was to tame life through gaining control of the biological composition, and thus the behavior, of humanity.

Galton had trained in mathematics and medicine—fields unfriendly to "soft" humanist approaches—and latched onto the kindred philosophy of Herbert Spencer, who in Malthusian fashion preached the hard doctrine of the survival of the fittest (although eugenics and social Darwinism would not fit together as easily as one might, at first glance, think).[35] Galton, like Spencer, denounced such palliatives as private philanthropy and the public health movement as unconscionable wastes of good money. Eugenicists patiently explained that they were observing the highest dictates of science when they opposed old age pensions, free public schooling, the minimum wage, and even the prohibition of alcohol, inasmuch as it slows the plunge of lower breeds to their genetically designated doom.[36]

The average citizen, as Galton sized him or her up, was "too base for the everyday work of modern civilization and should maintain celibacy" because the irresponsible procreation of children "inferior in moral, intellectual, and physical qualities" renders their feckless parents fit "to be considered enemies of the states, and to have forfeited all claims to kindness."[37] Galton, in effect, toiled to legitimize a "natural" world where predators determined the exact conditions under which their prey existed. Yet at another, and highly contradictory, level he promoted conditions for reproduction that logically led to a world consisting of nothing but predators, of nothing but wolves: an unsustainable world. But logic had little hold over the evangelical eugenicists.

Galton was never more revealingly naive than when interpreting photos of Jewish immigrant children: "I felt, rightly or wrongly, that every one of them was coolly appraising me at market value, without the slightest interest of any other kind." (Might that match, one wonders, the cold-bloodedness characterizing the average band of bankers, country club board, or fraternity/sorority rush committee?) Galton echoed his social class's favorite self-absolving creed when he attributed blame for all the drawbacks of commercialized life to highly vulnerable Jews.[38] Indeed, eugenicists solemnly identified Jewish "inbreeding" as a prime cause weakening the "stock."[39] In nineteenth-century medicine, in fact, "Jewish disease" was a legitimate category: "For fin de siecle medical science Jewish racial differences was statistically measurable," Gilman writes, "Jewish pathologies were statistically evident."[40] A personal concern may have intruded in Galton's proudly objective analysis. He embraced the view that infertility was an inherited characteristic afflicting mostly women, which consolingly must have meant that his childless marriage wasn't really his "fault."[41]

Galton believed that each mental and physical characteristic a child inherited—and absolutely everything was inherited—was a blend of traits of the parents and of their ancestors. The problem for eugenics is that this implied a regression to the mean, which ominously augured a loss of prized characteristics over generations. Not only did the "finest" people need to be browbeaten to breed prolifically (within marriage) but they had to con-

trive to maintain "desirable" traits too. A tall order. The way out of this co-
nundrum was to incorporate the Lamarckian notion of inheritance of acquired characteristics, which Galton thought required no more than three
generations to fasten firmly in any fit organism.[42] Thus, one theoretically
could arrange social patterns of reproduction in such a way as to stir elites
to breed like bunnies and yet strengthen the traits that eugenicists valued,
or rather those traits they claimed that nature valued. Still, even on its own
dubious terms this would be a tricky maneuver.

To this grand end Galton generously founded and funded an institute to
study characteristics and locate the exact mechanisms of their transmission.
He willed his fortune to finance the London Eugenics Laboratories, where
statistician Karl Pearson carried on his crusade. (Statisticians flocked to eugenics, which a number of "giants" such as Yerkes, Terman, Thorndike,
and Gini wholeheartedly endorsed.) Galton also bankrolled *The Eugenics
Review* and the Eugenics Education Society. This latter and unabashedly
snobbish organization nevertheless could count on attracting many grassroots plebs seeking a scientific basis for their own cracker-barrel bigotry.
The first International Congress of Eugenics in London in 1912, however,
was presided over by the lordly Leonard Darwin, son of Charles. Winston
Churchill, Alexander Graham Bell, and the presidents of Harvard and Stanford Universities helped to legitimate the executive council.

Tainted Breeds, Tainted Deeds

Darwinian thought appealed to all sides of the political spectrum. For capitalists a theory of evolution propelled by natural selection spelled out the
necessity of the free market, and for mechanistic Marxists this theory
hailed the inevitability of progressive social change. History was on your
side, whichever one you were on. Here was an enormously enticing vision,
grounded in impeccable statistical studies, for improving the breeding
stock, if not always the lot, of mankind.

The suffragettes employed eugenics theories as persuasive rhetorical elements in their brave campaigns for birth control and, by extension, population control. (It is often rash to assume an oppressed group is sensitive to
different forms of subjection applied to others.) Eugenics, viewed as preventive medicine, seemed completely compatible with the fight not only for
women's rights but for socialist goals. Supporters of eugenics included such
icons of sexual liberation and equality as Havelock Ellis, Margaret Sanger,
Maria Stopes, and Ellen Key. One cannot ignore otherwise progressive literary figures such as George Bernard Shaw and H. G. Wells (recall the mor-
locks and eloi in *The Time Machine*) as well as the Fabian socialists with
whom they consorted. Neither a high IQ nor the best intentions guarantee
that any person can achieve a capacity to reflect critically on his or her own

social conditioning or cherished beliefs. "If the rich were infertile because they were rich," reasoned the British scientist J.B.S. Haldane, "they might become less so if they were made less rich" and the taxed funds poured into a free and universal school system in which people from every social class were encouraged to flourish and thereby show that genetically they were the right stuff. But few eugenists rushed to take up this logical if waggish suggestion.[43]

Public interest in eugenics ignited in Britain during the Boer War when dismayed military recruiters found that of "every nine men examined, four were quite unfit, three being described as physical wrecks and one as a physical invalid."[44] This alarming rejection rate signaled to some experts that a degeneration of the British "race" was well under way. This diagnosis meant that uppercrust reformers could call for drastic preventive measures to stem the biological tide rather than take a painful look—in terms of the costs to themselves of instituting reforms—at the lack of decent working conditions, nutrition, and housing for classes suffering from a maldistribution of wealth and political power. Eventually, the 1904 Interdepartmental Committee on Physical Deterioration brought into the open many of the real problems of living conditions responsible for the ill-health of working-class Britons. Though the committee could not formally endorse the pessimistic degenerationist view, its members subscribed to much of the eugenical creed.[45]

In the United States a sudden flood of biased and wildly colorful studies stoked a morbid sense of impending biological apocalypse. From the titillating family sagas of the crazy "Jukes" (1877) through the feebleminded and promiscuous "Kallikaks" (1912), purse-lipped WASP investigators imbued what they viewed as innately sociopathic hillbillies with every imaginable vice.[46] The Jukes family was accused of costing taxpayers $1.3 million for the care or incarceration of all its depraved generations. Author William Dugdale actually believed that environment counted a great deal for the hill folk's insalubrious ways, but a second edition in 1915 conjured 2,000 more fertile family members, half of whom were designated feebleminded.[47] On meeting a poor Kallikak boy dressed in rags, a field investigator decided that "a glance was sufficient to establish his mentality, which was low," and she foresaw that he "would produce many feeble-minded children with which to clog the wheels of progress."[48] These sensational studies consisted of far more fabrication than fact, with the result that country bumpkins, like Eastern European immigrants or black migrants, were beheld as being indelibly subhuman. (The film *Deliverance* traded on this slack-jawed image for its dramatic kick.) Many kindred studies were conducted, supported by the Rockefellers, the Harrimans, the Carnegie Institute, and other plutocrats who were deeply interested in learning how to bring the disorderly lower classes to heel. Harriman money also funded the Eugenics Records

Office started in 1910 in Cold Harbor Springs on Long Island, directed by Charles Davenport.

A severe puritanical mindset pervaded the cultural politics informing these alarmist diagnoses so that, as exemplified by the Kallikak field investigation earlier, any immoral acts, imputed or otherwise, committed by social inferiors were viewed as damning evidence of mental defect, not as consequences of living conditions (or short-sighted diagnostic procedures).[49] Delinquent behavior became rooted in the highly seductive theory of defective "germplasm" (a term preceding and roughly approximating the gene), which posited that feebleminded folk inherently were criminals and therefore that social policy must establish institutions to segregate and hold them.[50]

There were two major strains of eugenics ideology: (1) a fatalistic social Darwinist version, and (2) an improvement-oriented version; both strains won staunch supporters, for different reasons, across the political spectrum. In day-to-day practice, eugenicists quite evidently were less concerned with survival of the fittest than with the survival of whomever they deemed fit.[51] Leonard Darwin admitted that in eugenics doctrine the "fittest" designates whomever *ought* to survive in the evolutionary sense. "Natural selection seems to take no thought as to what is 'good' whilst in eugenic problems the moral qualities of men should be the primary consideration," he remonstrated, "to make a man a noble being."[52] In other (and deeply contradictory) words, nature the supreme arbiter needs a helping hand.

Apart from the Holocaust, never did so eminent a group of authorities assemble to think so cretinously about attaining so dubious an objective. (Marxist historian Joseph Needham impishly challenged the natural "fitness" of rich shareholders in companies that inflict unemployment, low wages, and poor safety conditions upon fellow citizens.[53]) The goal of "racial betterment" boosted the growth of a new professional middle class by providing it with an administrative role in utilizing biological deviants as raw material to fill asylums and prisons. The image of the "unrestrained fertility of those of tainted stock" breeding licentiously at taxpayers' expense was calculated to rouse public ire and attention. The rise of the centralized state stimulated the rapid spread of asylums for the feebleminded although it exerted a considerable and unwelcome strain on local coffers too.[54] Nonetheless, here was scapegoating rigorously refined and sanctified by science.

The "degenerationist" dogma assumed that mental qualities were rooted in the physical structure of the brain and "placed considerable weight on physical stigmata, partial sight, deafness, dyslexia and left handedness" as signs of disease.[55] The objective was to persuade the citizenry that a child "is defective not because the parent is alcoholic [which, heretically, implies environmental effects] but because it is the product like the parent of a defective germ plasm" [which is satisfyingly irremediable] even though it would "be difficult," as researchers honestly admitted, "to differentiate any hereditary influence, cross, toxic, and environmental influence on the basis of the present material."[56] The poor, according to this uncharitable doctrine, were not "demoralized because of living conditions, they were degenerate."[57] For enthusiasts of genetic determinism it did not matter that "all the facts" were not in at that time any more than it does today.

What is clear is that neither direct experience nor scientific theorizing assured that a judicious view would be taken of the complex mysteries of causation. In Britain a Royal Commission on Care and Control of the Feeble Minded in 1904 backed the hypothesis of hereditary causes because a majority of witnesses had "attached supreme importance to heredity as a factor in causation [although] their views were based largely on the theories which they held."[58] Eugenicists, who initially welcomed the advent of Mendelian genetics at the start of the twentieth century, needed to believe that neuropathic (i.e., undesirable) characteristics were transmitted in a relatively straightforward way.

Franz Kallman drove these tentative findings to their logical conclusion when he called for the sterilization of "all relatives of schizophrenics who by virtue of their known genetic constitution are certain of carrying a latent factor for the disease."[59] Wasn't it self-evident that a better body carried a purer spirit or superior soul? This socially dangerous assumption was consistent with the medical model—a purely biological view of life that presupposes, among other things, an exact correspondence between brain cells and thoughts. This radical physicalistic approach

> viewed the mind simply as a product of the brain, much as bile is a product of the liver. . . . By the close of the 19th century, European physicians were convinced that most mental illnesses were of organic origin and that racial (as well as familial) degeneracy played a major role in predisposing any individual to risk. . . . Even in those cases where no clear somatic illness could be shown, where only a functional deficit was known, one assumed some underlying organic lesion.[60]

Likewise, the field of psychiatry confidently attributed every mental disorder to hereditary degenerative tendencies, and the only question was whether it was individual, familial, or racial in origin. So, on the basis of partial and disputable evidence, public policies were recommended that, if and when enacted, promised to inflict irreversible damage on targeted populations. Harry Laughlin, Davenport's successor as head of the Eugenics Record Office, took a graduated approach, demanding the sterilization of the "lowest" 10 percent of the population because low status—as demonstrated by relative lack of wealth, which is easy for statisticians to mea-sure—proved that they were unfit to reproduce. Once this task was accom-plished by whatever means necessary, he then would have culled the next lowest 10 percent.[61] It was not clear where this progressive decimation was supposed to end.

Degeneration and Its Discontents

Eugenicists toiled to clinch their case by meticulously linking mental and physical maladies in a vast outpouring of daunting quantitative studies. Every eugenical text was crammed with statistical charts and bar graphs calculated to convey the impression of solid and unassailable research. Re-searchers would prove to their own satisfaction the existence of a "close correspondence" between inheritance of insanity and that of pulmonary tu-berculosis or that "25 to 40% of the offspring of insane people are them-selves insane."[62]

Obviously, the fact that "mentally defective offspring occur in families in which neuroses, alcoholism, or insanity are more frequent [leads to the con-clusion that there is] an inherited tendency to general degeneracy."[63] Statisti-cian Karl Pearson, who ecumenically was as anti-Irish ("stolid oxen") as he was anti-Semitic ("a parasitic race"), lobbied the British Parliament to de-vote money to controlling parentage because this tack would eliminate the TB scourge more quickly than would establishing a sanitarium in every township.[64] He was proven dead wrong, but it is difficult to convey today just how much shame, fear, and loathing were attached to those who con-tracted the disease and how much needless pain was inflicted on tuberculosis sufferers by ideologues in white lab coats who sported such attitudes.[65]

It is important to note that the eugenical doctrine by no means went un-contested even in its heyday. But researchers who detected no evidence of hereditary degeneration found that their results received precious little pub-licity. Geneticists, who by 1915 had begun to unlock the actual complexi-ties of heredity, were slowly turning away, but the "general public was not made aware of the declining scientific status of eugenics."[66] Kuhl, however, reports that in the 1920s even biologists and geneticists "who distanced themselves from the organized movement still tended to express eugenical ideas."[67] Until the outbreak of the Second World War "leading biologists generally agreed with, or at least did not publicly oppose [eugenicist formu-lations,] and this attitude was shared by many prominent American psychologists and sociologists."[68]

In 1880 German biologist August Weismann demonstrated the continu-ity of traits in the "germ plasm" and that for a given trait, the traits of either parent could dominate without blending, which only made "negative eugenics" more attractive because it decisively undermined the Lamarckian theory of acquired characteristics.[69] Austrian botanist Gregor Mendel's pea hybridization experiments were rediscovered in 1900 and provided the basis for modern genetics.[70] Mendelism at first was interpreted so as to confirm hereditary patterns exactly as prominent eugenicists conceived them. Charles Davenport, first head of the Cold Harbor eugenics research center, seized on Mendel to claim that even one really bad gene—because it would not blend—could ruin an entire stock.[71] But modern Mendelian research soon produced the key notion of discontinuities and mutations, rendered by geneticist Hugo De Vries (a protégé of British Mendelian William Bateson, who coined the term "genetics.")[72]

Scientists found that a stable genotype can correspond to continuous variations in phenotype and that "many symptoms regarded as pathological might only arise from interaction of genotype with surrounding conditions."[73] That a "genotype cannot always be derived from phenotype" was an earth-shaking finding that should have demolished the entire theoretical basis for eugenics. Wilhelm Johennsen, a leading Danish geneticist, derived the lesson that "the complexity of society made it impossible that one single human type should be the best. We need all different types of humanity." [74] One hardly could draw a more democratic conclusion—or one more studiously ignored by eugenicists. Prior to the discovery of chromosomes, those seeking to trace hereditary influences relied heavily on mere appearance—a handy line of thought inasmuch as any aspiring Nazi could wield a pair of calipers.

Refutations mounted, but almost invisibly. In 1930 a British study reported that mental defects occurred proportionately across social classes in population, not mostly among the poor; three years later the British Medical Association formally rejected the notion of the inheritance of feeblemindedness. In 1935 the American Neurological Association too rejected eugenics as a scientifically untenable creed.[75] None of these repudiations made much impact in public or professional attitudes.

Eugenics, to be sure, was beset by internal conflicts. The movement drew much of its popular support from a morally conservative base that opposed birth control, which led to internal contradictions and conflicts.[76] Hence, the Catholic Church—which wasn't keen even on the rhythm method of birth control—strongly opposed some of the edicts of eugenics. Taxpayers were eager to stanch the rising costs of institutional care. In the southern United States, where the existence of extended families placed less pressure on institutions, eugenics did not meet the acclaim one might expect (perhaps because the races already were separated by ferocious Jim Crow laws). Enthusiasm ebbed somewhat in the 1920s, but partly because so many eugenic propositions were taken for granted.

Sterile Environments

Historians mention a dramatic change in public attitudes toward eugenics from one of cautious support in 1929 to ardent approval by 1935, a change related to the onset of desperately hard times and a hardening attitude toward the poor.[77] Up to that point the trouble, as one eugenicist lamented, was that the principles of the science of breeding were "reserved for and restricted to domesticated animals and birds."[78] Birth-control propaganda was aimed at the lower classes but, as an author daintily advised, "it is pleasanter to avoid references to social stratification, a subject which always creates much intellectual heat and smoke."

Eugenics reformers sought to "improve the very nature of man of the future, without reference to nurture," but why cease questioning at this point? If whatever nature does is right, why does nature require a helping hand? One unusually candid eugenics exponent even admits with an almost audible harrumph that "the demand for ability does not in any way equal supply" in our world and that "the notion that children follow their parents into professions from doctor, lawyer, actor, or burglar is genetic is pure poppycock. What matters is influence, luck, and ability in that order."[79] Nothing much has changed in this respect, according to recent research.[80]

What would an ideal eugenical society look like, anyway? A "sagacious government" would consult medical opinion as to how hereditary factors determine "health, longevity, stature, good eyesight and hearing, and resistance to disease generally."[81] Happily unaware that scientific opinion was divided about eugenics, a British psychologist opined that the decline of civilizations ultimately derive from "aberrations on the distribution in mental capacity" and that all "breakdowns" in civilization result from a most unfortunate multiplication within them of slavering "submen." Yet mighty Rome, which he admired, fell to these "submen" who included the Germanic "races" that later put into macabre practice the remedies that he preached. So then, are German-Slavic tribes meant to be perpetually inferior, or are they improvable? Contradictions pile up.

Eugenicists were dismissive of poverty, overcrowding, and dietary deprivations except as natural aids in culling the flock. In the evacuations of children during the Blitz from cities to rural areas, many middle-class families were startled on viewing the dreadful poverty so many working-class children also had escaped.[82] Many middle-class Americans likewise recall their profound shock at meeting so many malnourished and ill-educated young men in recruiting offices and draft boards—and who were assigned disproportionately to infantry combat units.[83] Otherwise, however, those ensconced in "good stock" families accepted eugenical beliefs because, for example, "if the right children were in secondary schools there would be no need to increase the accommodation." This spares the affluent the cost of supporting public schools; the quantity of talent is fixed, and that is all there is to it. Here was a reckless rationality remorselessly at work; to oppose or quibble with eugenic truths was merely a sad display of "emotional resistance to the truth that heredity limits our endowment."[84]

In 1937 British eugenicist R. B. Cattell reiterated Galton's implacable lament that "300 years from now half the population will be mentally defective."[85] His befuddled futurism typified a strong strain of public opinion at the brink of the Second World War. That same year a *Fortune* survey reported that 66 percent favored sterilization for mental defects, and 63 percent sterilizing criminals; only 15 percent opposed sterilization, period.[86] "If we really want to build an A1 nation," urged Cattell, "we must take this matter to its logical conclusion and employ the whole machinery of our medical services, not merely for 'preventative medicine' in the narrow sense, not even for ante-natal hygiene but for large-scale efforts along eugenic lines—and just such an epic effort was going into action in Germany," was it not?[87]

With Liberty, or Sterilization, for All

Eugenicists everywhere expressed undisguised admiration for "oligarchic Germany where the community boldly acts upon the wisdom of the biologist and the medical men and where eugenics laws are instantly put into operation."[88] Germany had the honor to be "first to adapt sterilisation with a positive emphasis on racial improvement," although the "Scandinavian countries, Holland, and Switzerland are equally advanced in the practice of sterilisation." Come to think of it, Cattell noted, the "USA seems to have been the first country in which sterilization has been legalized."[89]

In the 1890s American penal and mental institutions began castrating inmates to suppress their sexual appetites. The search for a less repulsive procedure culminated in the first vasectomy, performed at Indiana State Reformatory. Vasectomies facilitated sterilization because they did not conjure the same ugly imagery among the public as did castration. Indiana legalized compulsory sterilization in 1907; it was followed in 1909 by California and Connecticut; in 1911 by Nevada, Iowa, and New Jersey; in 1912 by New York; and in 1913 by Kansas, Michigan, North Dakota, and Oregon. After 1918 another fifteen states joined the biological mission to preserve "home europaeus." Far from an ignorant lynch mob in maniacal motion, here was a form of mob rule enacted by an impeccably professional community. *Scientific American* advocated compulsory sterilization in five editorials between 1911 and 1914.[90]

All did not always go smoothly for these earnest biological improvers. "Between 1913 and 1918 court challenges were brought for violating equal protection, due process and cruel and unusual punishment resulted in repeal of such laws" so that by the 1920s just ten states still had the law.[91] In 1927, however, the U.S. Supreme Court in *Buck v. Bell* approved involuntary sterilization for prisoners. The eugenical momentum resumed on the pretext of preventing the rampant scourge of feeblemindedness. The definition of feeblemindedness in Louisiana was "an inborn defect so pronounced that he is incapable of managing himself or his affairs, or being taught to do so, and requiring supervision control and care for his own welfare, or the welfare of others, or of the welfare of the community."[92] Laws were draconian. In Connecticut in 1890 a pauper—automatically defined as congenitally feebleminded—who inveigled sexual relations with a woman under the age of 45 was liable to three years' imprisonment.[93]

Medical technology produced an imposing arsenal of drastic answers for badly posed questions. In Switzerland's Burgholzl Hospital, August Forel castrated violent patients; in the 1890s in Freiberg, Germany, professor of obstetrics Alfred Hagar performed ovariectomies, or female castration, to "cure" hysteria. (Freud's Dora was luckier than she, or Freud's legion of critics, appreciated.) Craniectomies quickly became a fad for curing retardation despite its deplorable 15–25 percent death rate.[94] In this same decade the clitoris of a seven-year-old 'masturbater' would be removed as a preventive measure by the chief consulting surgeon of a hospital in Ohio.[95] The physician who later invented Kellogg's corn flakes—as a happily bland alternative to spicier and, he presumed, sexually stimulative foods—performed this surgery too. In an era justly described as one of outright "medical terrorism," numerous medical texts, authored by the most distinguished scientists and physicians, solemnly related masturbation and nocturnal emissions to the onset of insanity.[96]

Medical progress marched unflinchingly on. In 1889 a Kansas state hospital castrated 44 boys and mutilated 14 girls before word got out and a public outcry put a stop to it.[97] Institutes for the mentally retarded in Pennsylvania and Arkansas sterilized 58 boys with what they proudly claimed was "in almost every case, marked improvement both mental and physical." The medical purpose had been "masturbation prevention," so a problem was solved, as a historian points out, that was created and ensured by the very nature of the institution itself.[98] But this realization was well beyond the wit, the training, and the financial interests of most surgeons.

The California State Board of Charities and Corrections in 1906 said "most physicians agree that feeble-mindedness is generally inherited, and that a feeble-minded mother especially will have feeble-minded offspring."[99] Sterilizers invariably report that after snippings, the patients were happier, healthier, and more grateful than words could express. California by 1927 was sterilizing 5,000 patients a year—more than the rest of the world combined.[100] The medical profession faced a classic conflict between the patients' best interests and the good of the community, but it dealt with it in strictly utilitarian terms. Physicians seemed singularly untroubled about the choices. Further, patients in this eugenical milieu were treated as if they suffered infectious diseases, which made the physician's choice more obvious.

Eugenical hard-liner Harry Laughlin, Davenport's successor at the eugenics center in Cold Harbor, contributed to passage of the highly restrictive 1924 U.S. Immigration Act by testifying that the foreign-born and poor people inevitably and disproportionately occupied prisons—though one Midwestern senator drolly pointed out to Southern colleagues that Danes, Norwegians, Dutch, and Germans were far more literate than the average southerner. In fact the U.S. Army suppressed an impolitic report in the 1920s that Southern blacks scored higher in intelligence tests than did Southern whites.[101]

The cry to defend the purity of Nordic blood resonated in Scandinavia too. In 1929 Denmark became the first European country to approve sterilization on the basis of the assumption that paupers, prostitutes, and feeble-minded inherited their "defects." The Danes urged sterilization for schizophrenics, certain cases of epilepsy, Huntington's chorea, psychopaths, alcoholics, and habitual criminals of normal intelligence. In 1927 the Swedish Social Democrat party even petitioned the government to study American eugenics and advocated sterilization as a way of conserving public resources for health care.[102] Norway passed a sterilization act in 1934, and there was no perceptible resistance by Norwegians to a 1941 Nazi sterilization law during the occupation.[103] After Hitler's seizure of power, Harry Laughlin, who received an honorary doctorate from Heidelberg, staunchly opposed "exceptional admission for Jews who are refugees from persecution."[104] It was not only German Nazis who applauded the 1924 U.S. Immigration Act for "preserving Nordic blood."

How did American democracy fare in the course of this pseudobiological warfare? "Instead of protecting the rights of minorities," Ellen Brantlinger notes, the government "acted to protect dominant groups from them."[105] Half the states approved involuntary sterilization "not only of MR [mentally retarded] people but of criminals, epileptics, and promiscuous people as well—and involuntary sterilizations occurred at the same rate in states with no legislation."[106] Yet most mentally retarded children are born to normal parents, and most mentally retarded parents have normal children. Indeed, mental retardation "is not necessarily a 'disease' but partly a social construct that evolved to deal with differences in intellectual competence."[107] The incidence of mental retardation had not grown over time. The American Neurological Association showed as early as 1937 that these people lived much shorter lives, and with low marriage and fertility rates. The panic was based on a manufactured myth.

The promise of preventing feeblemindedness was ill-founded and known to be so even at the time. "Unfortunately more people probably read a bigoted judge's blathering in one week than real genetics textbooks in an entire year," Philip Reilly writes.[108] The movement grew out of the callous class-bound values and was exacerbated by ignorance and fear. Sterilization actually cannot prevent the reappearance of a trait in the next generation. As Herbert J. Muller, a socialist who flirted a while with eugenics, explained:

> If we assume 200,000 people in the US owe their condition to some regressive gene Z, eight generations of feeblemindedness are required to cut numbers by half—and 20 generations overall to cut them by half again (75,000), and subsequent diminution slows and slows—because the genes are carried in ten million in latent state. After a thousand years of sterilizing of only the outright feeble-minded there would still be about 4 million apparently carrying the gene for feeblemindedness. . . .
>
> As soon as we undertook the ratings of different traits, according to their relative merits or demerits, we are brought face to face with the fact that which characteristic shall be considered defective and which normal, and which superior, depends upon one's point of view. . . . Great differences in intelligence may exist but they are not stratified into different social classes as some geneticists fondly imagine.[109]

Muller concluded that eugenics lends a "false appearance of a scientific basis to advocate of race and class prejudice. . . . Even the least unreasonable of the professional supporters of modern eugenics have taken no clear stand against the atrocities recently proposed and carried out in its name."[110]

The Third Reich and "Life Unworthy of Life"

The Eugenics Society applauded Nazi programs up to the outbreak of war. "Many far-sighted men and women in both America and England," wrote an enthusiast, "have long been working toward something very like what Hitler has now made compulsory."[111] The sterilization discussion prior to the Nazi Law on Preventing Hereditarily Ill Progeny was strongly influenced by American models, especially those in California.[112] German medical students—not unlike those in most Western professions—were notoriously anti-Semitic, and since the turn of the century "the superiority of German racial stock was a textbook cliché."[113]

The key German eugenics text of the era was Erwin Bauer, Eugen Fischer, and Fritz Lenz's *Human Heredity and Racial Hygiene*. Hitler had read Fischer's *The Principles of Human Heredity and Race* in prison. Fisher directed the Berlin Institute of Anthropology, Human Heredity and Eugenics, where in 1942 his successor hired Josef Mengele as an assistant. Lenz, professor of racial hygiene in Munich, fretted that Americans were far too fixed on whites, versus Nordics, who were indeed superior to other whites. As for Jews, well, they "cannot transform themselves into Germans by writing books on Goethe."[114]

After the First World War the Rockefeller Foundation "saved genetic research in Germany" and elsewhere in Europe, including the Galton Laboratory, Penrose's Institute at Colchester, and the Institute of Human Genetics in Copenhagen.[115] In the 1920s the foundation established the Kaiser Wilhelm Institute for Psychiatry and the Kaiser Wilhelm Institute for Anthropology, Eugenics and Human Heredity and provided a major donation for a building for an Institute for Psychiatry in Munich devoted to research on neurologic traits for criminality, which then was supported by a Jewish philanthropist until 1940![116] (A Jewish scientist was expelled from the Kaiser Institute for Anthropology but, good scientist that he was, could not bring himself to reject eugenics in principle.) The overarching purpose of the foundation's funding, according to director Warren Weaver in 1934, was the "rationalization of social control" through understanding and gaining control of the mechanisms of heredity.[117]

The 1933 German law required sterilization for the retarded, schizophrenics, manic-depressives, epileptics, the deaf, alcoholics, and assorted other "defectives." From 1934 to mid-1937 over 200,000 people were sterilized in Germany (compare this to Denmark, where 1,380 were sterilized during 1935–1939).[118] From 1933 to 1945, over 3.5 million forced sterilizations were done in Germany.[119] The Third Reich inaugurated its campaign to purify the Aryan race by murdering 75,000 German patients; in August 1941, protests brought it to a halt—though it secretly resumed. (In France in 1935, Nobel Prize–winner Alexis Carrel published a modest book calling for the "ideal solution" of "little economic gas chambers" for "all those with bad genes."[120])

Nonetheless, 70,000 to 100,000 "defective" Germans were killed prior to 1945, and a quarter of a million were killed in Europe overall. Euthanasia and eugenics snuffed what Nazi arbiters termed "life unworthy of life." On the "positive" side they conducted the *lebensborn* ("fount of life") programs to breed unblemished Aryan children, which included kidnapped foreigners who fit their rigorous racial criteria.[121] The German state also provided families with "positive" incentives in the form of loans, child support for third and fourth children, and tax breaks.

Racism permeated people in lab coats who by their own self-understanding were carrying out legitimate and dispassionate research. These cool, calm, and collected researchers went so far as to attempt to detect homosexual and Gypsy blood so that the carriers could be traced and rubbed out.[122] The German Medical Association even promised Nazi leaders that they could eventually detect disguised Jews via blood tests.[123] These vile exercises demonstrate that one cannot always separate science as an investigative activity from science as an institutional network steeped in particular contexts. No professional group was more supportive of the unfolding Nazi blueprint than was the medical establishment.[124] The lure was the promise of a definitive biological answer as to how, not whether, humans were to be bred and utilized. The ultimate irony is that the vast bulk of the German Army—which was actively complicit in the "final solution"—was crushed in the titanic bloodbath on the eastern front by the "subhuman Slavic races" they had set out to enslave.[125]

Science, in the reductive way in which it was exclusively understood, made murder easier to perform. "Is it difficult to understand how scientists, physicians, and health care workers could destroy human life in the name of racial purity," a historian asks. His answer is that "they were normal human beings but part of a scientific ethos which over decades has sanctioned violence in the name of racial purity." Lest we be misled by the recent resurgence of national guilt arguments we would do well to recall that a majority (62 percent) of Germans opposed the Nazis until they seized power in 1933.[126] The desk murderers *(schreibtischaten)*, like Himmler and Eichmann, emerged in droning droves to direct those who herded the inmates, pulled the triggers, and sprinkled Zyklon B crystals into gas chambers. Millions died and many more suffered horribly. The rest of the hideous story should need no recounting here.

After the Holocaust

German physicians and scientists were hardly exceptional. In America the eugenics activists included "biologists, geneticists, psychiatrists, zoologists and physicians. Five presidents of the American Association for the Advancement of Science served on the advisory board the Eugenics society."[127] Many professionals shied away from eugenics because of its totalitarian taint but endorsed eugenical policies that were shorn of obvious racial biases.

Physicians on trial at Nuremberg for ghastly camp experiments embarrassingly cited American examples to prove that the ambition of eliminating "inferior elements" was not unique to Germany. Nuremberg prosecutors, many of whom themselves were under sway of eugenicist notions, did not prosecute the Nazi doctors for the sterilizations, only for outright killings.[128] As elsewhere in Germany, as the cold war revved up, many of these Nazi physicians returned to prominent posts. Reilly notes that "international science critics failed to question the aim of race improvement in principle."[129] After World War II, renowned scientist Julian Huxley, brother of Aldous, insisted that eugenics "had not been proved wrong, it had merely been wrongly applied."[130] The reductionist thrust to genetics research continued, and reductionism remained as liable as ever to be taken as the *only* legitimate view of science.

Revulsion at Nazi racial policies did not really curb American steriliza-tion; rather, the cause was a wartime shortage of physicians.[131] (From 1907 to 1927 a total of 8,500 patients were sterilized in the United States, rising in the 1930s to about 2,500 a year and 4,000 at its peak, after which there was a tapering off to 1,500 annually in the 1950s.) The postwar baby boom ended all the fuss about depopulation. Totalitarianism, not eugenics in it-self, put the latter in disrepute. Still, the flagship journal *Eugenics* discreetly retitled itself as the *Journal of Social Biology*.

By the end of World War II new research findings demonstrated that many mental disorders originated as much or more from material depriva-tion or other environmental sources as from inherited characteristics.[132] Scientists became more aware of race as a constructed category rather than a biological essence—and especially so in medicine, where the latter view had led to abuses such as the notorious Tuskegee experiment.[133] There the United States Public Health Service had enrolled some 400 black men with syphilis to treat them for "bad blood."[134] The service deliberately denied proper treatment in a deceitful experiment hatched to watch how syphilis ran its course and that lasted from 1932 to 1972. (The Danes already had run similar experiments, so this cruel study was also redundant.) In 1997 President Clinton issued an apology for a government study that was "so clearly racist" and had the long-term repercussion of creating "suspicion in the black community of Federal intent in other medical problems such as AIDS/HIV."[135]

A "new" round of genetic determinist exploits has been accompanied by very little skepticism. Once again the media revel in reporting that in the nature versus nurture controversy "a wealth of new research has tipped the scale overwhelmingly toward nature"—although a careful reading always reveals an Olympic degree of back-pedaling on what is thought, let alone proven, to be heritable.[136] The Human Genome Project has received $3 bil-lion in funding with the goal of providing a complete map of the nucleotide system for all the genes in our bodies—the better to improve them, they say.[137] (A gene is a long sequence of elements called nucleotides, of which there are only four kinds, identified by letters A, T, C, and G. Each se-quence specifies what the constitution of our body will be.) Genome project proponents primly oppose any government control, which then places re-search and its "payoffs" in scientists' and private corporate hands, such as they are distinguishable. And every molecular geneticist promises that available genetic techniques *will* be used.[138]

Will corporations thereby gain control of the human gene pool? What becomes of the individual's right to privacy? (One corporation at the time of writing was setting up a centralized database for the entire gene pool of Iceland.)[139] Will the products of genetic technologies be made available only to the rich? The present holds out "an industrial conception of living matter which subordinates it to the commodity form."[140] In 1991 the National Institute of Health announced a program of patent applications on human gene fragments—or "express tag sequences"—on 2,375 fragments, representing about 5 percent of all human genes. Control of these fragments would block any use of the corresponding full gene, even if the identity of these genes was unknown. Should these genes be owned by those possessing the technology to manipulate them? All these questions ultimately hinge on cultural understandings and misunderstandings of science—including a subtle yet quite zealous religious dimension that investigators have brought to light.[141]

Law professor Lori Andrews, who ultimately resigned in protest, recounts her unsettling experience as chair of the Human Genome Project's work group on ethical, legal, and social implications, which was consistently underfunded and undermined by project directors.[142] Her successor, Troy Duster, a University of California sociologist, found it difficult to reconcile dishing out "$8 million to this lab and $12 million to that lab" while pinching pennies ($25 thousand) when it came to the working group, which hardly bespoke an intent that it be anything more than an in-house device for deflecting public criticism.[143] The project directors reportedly got in a tizzy because the work group planned an anthology critically evaluating Charles Murray and Richard Herrnstein's The Bell Curve—evidently fearing that casting any doubt even on this screed might diminish support for public funds to do whatever they pleased.

The popularized view that humans are only fleshy vehicles for genes is credible only if one succumbs to an artificial atomistic view of the world.[144] The trouble with it is that "the properties of the parts cannot be understood except in their context in the whole because the environment of the organism is constantly being remade by the life of the organism," Richard Lewontin notes.[145] So there simply is no "general genetic superiority—different environments bring out different degrees of superiority."

Disease supplies the perfect moral justification to resume a purportedly kinder, gentler eugenics creed.[146] What else is control of reproduction for except improvement of "the" race? Does a fetus with an unsound genotype have the right to be born? Cystic fibrosis, Duchesne disease, muscular dystrophy, myotonic dystrophy, Huntington's disease, Tay-Sachs disease, and Down's syndrome are single-gene disorders, but most disorders are hugely complex and are not related in an invariant way to genes.[147] People all carry predispositions for specific diseases that may never appear, or only appear in conjunction with specific environmental stimuli. One must still ask, are all diseases transmitted genetically, or are many of them acquired behaviors based on the familial and social milieu of the individual? Then there is the virtually incalculable problem of sussing out how these physiological dispositions blend with environmental cues to cause a given disease.

In this wider framing, genetic determinism is exposed as an appealing illusion and appalling ideology. Today, as a century ago, the "medical model of deviance provides even the most cynical state apparatus with a legitimate tool to control the behaviour of individuals."[148]

Sensationalized reports of genetic causation routinely occur when research hits the media, partly because proponents sincerely subscribe to this impoverished view of humankind. The nineteenth-century practitioners were true believers too.[149] It is front-page news when a genetic cause is lodged, and page-10 news when retracted, as the Breggins observe about the still-elusive gene for alcoholism.[150] Claims for a manic-depressive gene have been retracted, and a gene for depression detected in Amish families turned out to have occurred within a single extended family, which of course reintroduces socialization as a culprit.[151] The gene, if any, for schizophrenia is as elusive as ever.[152] The "gay" gene has never been corroborated.[153] Nor has a gene for autism been found.[154] But ask someone either on the street or in the corridors of power, and they will likely say that scientists have found exact genetic causes for all these maladies. The publicized suspicion that an extra male Y chromosome caused aggression in "XYY syndrome" people also came to an ignominious dead end.

Genetic intervention poses thornier problems than the media usually convey. The gene for sickle cell anemia in blacks actually extends to all the peoples who inhabited malaria-ridden regions in Africa and the Middle East and serves a protective function against malaria. Curing sickle cell, if possible, raises the problem of pleiotropy, where "negative" genes have positive effects that also will be lost.[155] But the majority of diseases with a genetic component are polygenic disorders and are extremely likely to involve some significant degree of interaction with the environment. This fact, when acknowledged, raises the question of which end—environmental or molecular—one should start at to analyze or alleviate a medical problem. Genetics studies alone are not enough. From Cyril Burt's controversial data to the present day, the tendentious misuse of "twins studies," so as to prove predesignated conclusions on genetic causation, is one of the most disputatious arenas in the history of science.[156]

The future holds out the spectacle not of coercion but of a "eugenics of the free market."[157] Parents dearly want normal children, but what is normal is determined by the values of the social circle, not by a gene map. Under Nazi eugenics we supposedly would get SS officers; under modern genetics we would get *Beverly Hills 90120* clones—a world populated by soap opera stars with ethics, sensitivity, and compassion to match. For all the eugenicist—and middle-class parental—fuss, a high IQ has never been the supreme quality for worldly success; rather, a passable intelligence will do nicely if born into an affluent family and/or wed to a cunning conformity to reigning dogmas.[158] Innovation in most fields is prized insofar as it does not threaten gatekeepers and therefore one's own career. Are there genes for conformity or cunning or bigotry or integrity? To ask the question about such complex human qualities is to answer it.

Genetic engineering, as conveyed in popular media, is an embodiment of a constricted methodology of reductionism, which is extremely useful and indeed indispensable as a research tool but dangerously naive when mistaken as the entirety of the scientific apparatus and applied to the complexity of the social world. Genetics *as a discipline* jettisons man as end in himself, rendering him a means to an end. Genetics misapplied *as a total philosophy* does likewise. The essential problem is not biology per se but the mindset of manipulators who have melded a reductionist method to a singularly resilient "mechanistic model."

In the 1960s Arthur Koestler offhandedly asserted that man suffers from a "form of paranoia" built into the wiring of the brain. A critic astutely replied that his view was only the latest in a long line of resurrections of "nineteenth century-style, organic-instinctual theories of violence."[159] Koestler and (former Nazi) Konrad Lorenz wanted to discard history and espouse the "mechanistic fallacy," which is "denial of man's fundamental need to render into viable psychic form (that is, recreate and symbolize) all that he experiences." Lifton explains,

> One must then consider the symbols and forms man requires in order to make sense of his world and act upon it—and the way in which these combine elements of emotion ("faith") and reason ("logic"). As Susanne Langer has emphasized, man's lifelong mental task is one of continuous "transformation" of the "data" reaching him from within and without.[160]

Denial of this symbolic realm is the essence of genetic determinist creeds, which are themselves a particular symbolization of nature posing as the whole truth. In the 1930s psychiatry encouraged the application of violent somatic treatments such as electric shock and insulin shock based on the familiar assumption that mental disorders stemmed primarily from traceable organic defects.[161] In the 1990s "psychiatric geneticists began to propose genetic anticipation, the tendency of some illness-causing genes to expand in size when passed from generation to generation, as the mechanism behind the increasing severity of schizophrenia or manic-depressive illness as handed down by a family tree. This was the exact equivalent," historian Edward Shorter writes, "of 'degeneration' in the first biological psychiatry. The schizophrenogenic mother was truly dead!"[162] It's perfectly fine, then, to revive a dubious diagnostic tendency in order to exculpate parents from in anyway adversely affecting their children. Perhaps this owes something to the fact that parents form lobbying organizations and kids do not?

The American Psychiatric Association (APA) sought and received drug company support to prove "psychological suffering is a biologically based medical problem"; in 1991 and 1992 the pharmaceutical behemoth Upjohn alone contributed $1.5 million to the grateful APA.[163] Thus, the fundamental problem cannot be defined as family conflicts or lousy schools (rooted in bad social conditions); the child instead is blamed—with the very best of professional intentions—as carrier of a disease or a misshapen gene, which supports the venerable biopsychiatric inclination to "reduce human conduct and social conflict to grossly sluggish neurotransmitters in a particular type of nerve cell."[164] It's not begging the question, it's genetic.

In the 1960s psychologist Arthur Jensen opined that blacks congenitally were less intelligent than whites, that intelligence was 80 percent heritable, and that "compensatory education has been proved to be false," all of which are unproven or false statements.[165] William Shockley, cowinner of a Nobel Prize for physics, stepped well outside his field in 1965 to quote the Kallikak study as if it were pristine social research and to lament, like Galton at the turn of the century or Cattell prior to World War II, that the quality of the human race is in precipitous decline. Hans Eysenck in London and Richard Lynn in Belfast doggedly argue that "whites and Asians are generally more intelligent and family-oriented than blacks and that a higher black crime rate is related to lower intelligence."[166] In the 1990s archconservatives Charles Murray and Richard Herrnstein published *The Bell Curve*, which was exasperatingly and disturbingly greeted in the mass media as though it were an unprecedented work.[167]

Conclusion

Eugenics was and is propelled by a profoundly antidemocratic worldview. It is not possible to accept the crude propositions deriving from a reductionist mode of modern genetics and not be drawn into this political stance. The highest likelihood of irreversible harm is in store for those who are successfully targeted by genetic edicts. Scientists, in this respect, are just another interest group; fortunately, they are divided over the conduct, interpretation, and ethics of their research. Science obviously should be a voice—indeed a medley of voices—but should never be taken as the last word in determining policy. Recall that it was the "careful argument of experts" that helped to free reluctant Nazis of any lingering revulsion for the eugenics program.[168]

One likewise should beware of scientists pleading, like the inventor of the cloning process that yielded Dolly the sheep, that ethical and social implications are irrelevant on the grounds that one is "only a scientist." What this maneuver represents is the development of an artificial construct—a social construct—which supports the reductionist notion that we can segregate all of our human activities, including science, from a social context and that science does not have social responsibilities . . . in the case of genetic engineering, we are also talking about a science which has been initiated and funded by government tax money.[169]

Many geneticists endorsed muted forms of eugenics long after World War II. In 1970, 67 percent of American physicians agreed that "forcible sterilization of criminally insane, retarded and feeble-minded was a desirable social policy."[170] The *Boston Globe* in 1982 found that half of those surveyed favored sterilizing the feebleminded and criminals.[171] Involuntary sterilizations continued in the United States into the 1960s, in Canadian provinces until 1978, and in Sweden until 1975. Today one "hears no hatred in the eugenical voice, just pragmatic selection," Professor Hilary Rose observes. "The difference is that today there is a huge resistance."[172]

The eugenics episode, at the cost of so many lives, may act as a powerful cautionary reminder that averts greater crimes in the future because it shows how fallible scientists can be. One can always ferret out a correlation between proteins that can be associated with particular symptoms—as well as between a genotype and a specific threat—and this correlation will more likely than not be a social construct.[173] The eugenics story needs to be told so that the community weighs *all* the risks in this high-stakes issue and brings to bear the necessary degree of skepticism to claims stemming from a scientistic, not a truly scientific, attitude.

Middlebrow prejudices are mobilized so easily by elites because it is precisely these privileged people who believe most staunchly that they are free of all superstition. It is here that one usually finds hidebound prejudices eruditely expressed in terms of common sense or else in a highly formalized vocabulary, such as when Herman Kahn, in the preceding chapter, speculated lightheartedly about waging thermonuclear war. A genuine examination of the "unthinkable" is not likely in the cards because such blithe spirits rarely venture beyond the parameters set by patrons. Regarding current genetic engineering fancies, however, it is hardly possible to improve on Muller's advice half a century ago: to call the eugenicist's bluff we first must work to organize a

cooperative society [where] inequalities due to artificial class distinction, race prejudice, inherited fortunes and privileges are done away with, which will bring us much closer to the ideal eugenic conditions in which practically every individual will have as favourable opportunities for development as every other, and thus have his potentialities recognisable for what they are . . . then for the first time we shall have an estimation of a man's intelligence from a genetic standpoint.[174]

What I emphasize is that anyone, even those with sparkling credentials and progressive motives, can fall prey to and promulgate pernicious doctrines. But keep in mind that few people embraced eugenics who thereby would affirm themselves as "inferior stock." Certain beliefs become convenient because of pervasive unquestioned norms that govern one's life. Yet even in its heyday there were scientists, doctors, socialists, and suffragettes who repudiated eugenics, which means there were real choices to be made and that they were morally accountable ones. If we are to exercise a realistic historical empathy with actors operating in culturally constrained milieus (as we all do), it makes sense to do so on the basis of an appraisal of the behavior of *all* relevant actors. Drawing out the actors' self-understanding of their own actions is valuable only insofar as it serves to alert us to self-deceptiveness regarding our own motives.[175] It may be tragic when specialists who sincerely imagine that they are performing worthy deeds are actually doing a great deal of harm. The greater tragedy, though, is replicating the attitudes and beliefs that enable their errors to be repeated.

Notes

1. In his essay "Hereditary Improvement," Francis Galton nurtured the belief that the Irish "face seemed to have become more prognathous, that is, more like the negro in the protrusion of the lower jaw; the interpretation of which is that men whom survived the starvation and other deadly accidents of that horrible time were more generally of a low or coarse disposition"; cited in Alexander Cockburn and Ken Silverstein, *Washington Babylon* (New York: Verso, 1996), p. 2. Also see L. Perry Curtis, *Apes and Angels: The Irishman in Victorian Caricature* (Washington, D.C.: Smithsonian Institution, 1971).

2. Most eugenicists hailed from white upper and middle classes. See Daniel Kevles, *In the Name of Eugenics: Genetics and the Uses of Human Heredity* (New York: Knopf, 1985), pp. 57–74. "Only white nations have a history," according to archetypal racist Count Grafen Gobineau, *Essays on the Dissimilarity of the Human Race* (Stuttgart: F. Fromans Publishers, 1922).

3. Susanne Klausen, "For the Sake of the Race: Eugenics Discourses of Feeblemindedness and Motherhood and the South African Medical Record," *Journal of South African Studies* 23, 1 (March 1997).

4. White upper-middle-class women, particularly in the South, were numbered among the fervent proponents of eugenics policies. Edward J. Larson, *Sex, Race and Science: Eugenics in the Deep South* (Baltimore: Johns Hopkins University, 1995), pp. 2, 32.

5. Dorothy Nelkin and Loraine Tancredi, *Dangerous Diagnostic: The Social Power of Genetic Information* (New York: Basic Books, 1988). See also Rae Good-

132 Technical Fouls

ell, "The Gene Craze," *Columbia Journalism Review* 4 (1980); also, U.S. Congress
Office of Technology Assessment, *Mapping Our Genes* (Washington, D.C.: Government Printing Office, 1988).

6. Leon J. Kamin, Richard C. Lewontin, and Steven Rose, *Not in Our Genes: Biology, Ideology and Human Nature* (London: Pelican, 1984), p. 18. "The essence of
the reductionist explanation is the assumption that a disorder is caused by a simple
malfunction of a body region—or a biochemical substance—or a gene" (p. 189).

7. See Reinhard Bendix, *Work and Authority in Industry: Ideologies of Management in the Course of Industrialization* (Berkeley: University of California, 1974).
Also note the metrical tyranny characterizing the industrial career of Frederick
Winslow Taylor in Robert Kanigel, *The One Best Way* (New York: Viking, 1997),
and Sudhir Kakir, *Frederick Winslow Taylor: A Study in Personality and Innovation*
(Cambridge, Mass.: MIT Press, 1970).

8. E. A. Burtt, *The Metaphysical Foundations of Modern Science* (London:
Compton, 1932, 2d ed), p. 11.

9. See Karl Mannheim, *Ideology and Utopia: An Introduction to the Sociology of
Science* (New York: Harcourt, Brace & World, 1963, originally published in 1929).

10. Burtt, *Metaphysical Foundations*, p. 3.

11. See chapter 6 in Hannah Arendt, *The Human Condition* (Chicago: University
of Chicago, 1962).

12. See H. Stuart Hughes, *Consciousness and Society* (New York: Knopf, 1958),
and Floyd Matson, *The Broken Image: Man, Science and Society* (New York: Anchor Books, 1964).

13. James Watson, *The Double Helix* (London: Weidenfeld & Nicolson, 1968).

14. Jacques Ellul, *The Technological Society* (New York: Knopf, 1964), p. 135.

15. Rose, Kamin, and Lewontin, *Not in Our Genes*, p. 29. Also see Ruth Hubbard and Elijah Wald, *Exploding the Gene Myth* (Boston: Beacon Press, 1993).

16. On cultural studies see Larry Grossberg, Cary Nelson, and Paula A. Treichler,
eds., *Cultural Studies* (New York: Routledge, 1995).

17. Burtt, *Metaphysical Foundations*, p. 3.

18. On the repercussions of physicist Alan J. Sokal's spoof Spring/Summer 1996
article in the journal *Social Text,* see Stephen Hilgartnek, "The Sokal Affair in Context," *Science, Technology and Human Values* 22, 4 (Autumn 1997); Jennifer Daryl
Slack and M. Mehdi Semati, "Intellectual and Political Hygiene: The Sokal Affair,"
Critical Studies in Mass Communication 14, 3 (September 1997); and Nick Jardine
and Marina Fraser-Spada, "Splendors and Miseries of the Science Wars," *Studies in
History and Philosophy of Science* 28, 2 (June 1997).

19. William H. Tucker, *The Science and Politics of Racial Research* (Champaign:
University of Illinois, 1994), p. 65.

20. Marouf Arif Hasian Jr., *The Rhetoric of Eugenics in Anglo-American
Thought* (Athens: University of Georgia, 1996), p. 140.

21. On the theme of moral "laziness" see Bruno Bettelheim and Alvin Rosenfeld,
The Art of the Obvious (New York: Thames and Hudson, 1993), and Hubbard and
Wald, *Exploding the Gene Myth*, p. 101.

22. Angus McLaren, *Our Own Master Race: Eugenics in Canada, 1885–1945*
(Toronto: McClelland & Stewart, 1990), p. 8. Also see Nancy L. Stepan, *In the*

Hour of Eugenics: Race, Gender and Nation in Latin America (Ithaca: Cornell University Press, 1991).

23. Tucker, *The Science and Politics of Racial Research*, pp. 3–4.

24. Richard Slotkin, *Gunfighter Nation: The Myth of the Frontier in Twentieth-Century America* (New York: Atheneum, 1992), pp. 20, 21.

25. Theodore Roosevelt, *The Winning of the West*, vol. 4 (New York: G.P. Putnam's Sons, 1900), pp. 54–56.

26. Steven Kuhl, *The Nazi Connection: Eugenics, American Racism and German National Socialism* (New York: Oxford University Press, 1994), p. 16.

27. Tucker, *The Science and Politics of Racial Research*, p. 93.

28. See Dwight Waldo, *The Administrative State* (New York: Ronald Press, 1948), and Samuel Haber, *Efficiency and Uplift: Scientific Management in the Progressive Era* (Chicago: University of Chicago, 1964).

29. Richard A. Soloway, *Demography and Degeneration: Eugenics and Declining Birthrate in Twentieth-Century Britain* (Chapel Hill: University of North Carolina, 1990), p. xi.

30. Francis Galton, *Hereditary Genius: An Inquiry into Its Laws and Consequences* (London: Macmillan & Company, 1869), p. v.

31. Ellen Brantlinger, *Sterilization of People with Mental Disabilities: Issues, Perspectives, and Causes* (Westport, Conn.: Auburn House, 1995), p. 1.

32. On the social construction of race see, for example, K. Anthony Appiah and Amy Guttman, *Color Conscious: The Political Morality of Race* (Princeton: Princeton University Press, 1996).

33. Galton, *Hereditary Genius*, pp. 2, 339.

34. Cited in Hasian, *The Rhetoric of Eugenics in Anglo-American Thought*, p. 182.

35. See Carl N. Degler, *In Search of Human Nature: The Decline and Revival of Social Darwinism in American Social Thought* (Oxford: Oxford University Press, 1991), and Cynthia E. Russett, *Darwin in America: The Intellectual Response* (San Francisco: Freeman Press, 1976).

36. Cited in Tucker, *The Science and Politics of Racial Research*, p. 58.

37. Cockburn and Silverstein, *Washington Babylon*, pp. 2–22.

38. Sander Gilman, *The Case of Sigmund Freud: Medicine and Identity at the Fin de Siecle* (Baltimore: Johns Hopkins, 1993), p. 44.

39. Sander Gilman, *Sexuality* (New York: John Wiley & Son, 1989), p. 264.

40. Gilman, *The Case of Sigmund Freud*, p. 15. He surmises, rather peculiarly, that Freud's "resistance to underlying presuppositions of the medical science of his time" led him to breakthroughs in diagnostics and treatment and "to create explanatory models that helped to free them from stigma of Jewish diseases since the ideology disqualified the subject from becoming judges of their own conditions."

41. Soloway, *Demography and Degeneration*, p. 20.

42. Larson, *Sex, Race and Science*, p. 19.

43. J.B.S. Haldane, *Heredity and Politics* (London: Macmillan, 1937), p. 124.

44. R. B. Cattell, *The Fight for Our National Intelligence* (London: P. S. King & Son, 1937), p. 84.

45. Matthew Thomson, *The Problem of Mental Deficiency: Eugenics, Democracy and Social Policy in Britain, 1870–1959* (Oxford: Clarendon Press, 1998),

p. 2. Also see Daniel Pick, *Faces of Degeneration: A European Disorder, 1848–1918* (Cambridge: Cambridge University Press, 1989).

46. Nicole Hahn Rafter, *White Trash: The Eugenics Family Studies* (Boston: Northeastern University Press, 1988), p. 2. Also see J. David Smith, *Minds Made Feeble: The Mythical Legacy of the Kallikaks* (Rockville, Md.: Aspen, 1985).

47. Larson, *Sex, Race and Science*, p. 21.

48. Henry Herbert Goddard, *The Kallikak Family: A Study in the Heredity of Feeble-Mindedness* (New York: Macmillan, 1912), p. 78. The field worker was Elizabeth Kite.

49. Thomson, *The Problem of Mental Deficiency*, p. 22.

50. Rafter, *White Trash*, pp. 1, 6.

51. *Ibid.*, p. 5.

52. Leonard Darwin, *The Need for Eugenic Reform* (London: John Murray, 1926), p. 115.

53. Nelkin and Tancredi, *Dangerous Diagnostics*, p. 134.

54. Philip R. Reilly, *The Surgical Solution: A History of Involuntary Sterilization in the United States* (Baltimore: Johns Hopkins University Press, 1991), p. 13.

55. Thomson, *The Problem of Mental Deficiency*, pp. 7, 20. Also see James Trent Jr., *Inventing the Feeble Mind: A History of Mental Retardation in the United States* (Berkeley: University of California Press, 1994).

56. Ethel Edelstein with Karl Pearson, "A First Study of the Influence of Parental Alcoholism on the Physique and Ability of the Offspring," in Francis Galton Laboratory for National Eugenics, *Selected Eugenics Laboratory Memoirs,* University of London (New York: Garland Publishing, reprinted 1985), pp. 1–2.

57. McLaren, *Our Own Master Race*, p. 19.

58. Thomson, *The Problem of Mental Deficiency*, p. 29.

59. McLaren, *Our Own Master Race*, p. 142.

60. Gilman, *The Case of Sigmund Freud*, pp. 15–16.

61. Larson, *Sex, Race and Science*, p. 29.

62. David Heron, "A First Study of the Statistics of Insanity and the Inheritance of the Insane Diagnosis," in Francis Galton Laboratory for National Eugenics, *Selected Eugenics Laboratory Memoirs*, p. 32.

63. *Ibid.*, p. 33.

64. Hobsbawm, *The Age of Empire*, p. 255; Tucker, *The Science and Politics of Race Research*, p. 303, fn 14.

65. In Ireland in the 1950s tuberculosis "hit every class, but mostly the poor. Crammed together in bad housing, whole families were wiped out. . . . You feared TB, you feared infecting your loved ones, you feared people knowing you had the disease, you feared the isolation and rejection that would follow"; Gene Kerrigan, *Another Country: Growing Up in '50s Ireland* (Dublin: Gill and Macmillan, 1998), p. 76. On the successful use of public sanitariums to eradicate TB, see Noel C. Browne, *Against the Tide* (Dublin: Gill and Macmillan, 1986).

66. McLaren, *Our Own Master Race*, p. 10.

67. Kuhl, *The Nazi Connection*, p. 67.

68. Larson, *Sex, Race and Science*, p. 30.

69. *Ibid.*, p. 20.

70. For a brief introduction see Steven Jones, *Genetics for Beginners* (London: Icon Books, 1993); William Banes, *Genetic Engineering for Almost Everybody* (London: Penguin, 1987); and British Medical Association, *Human Genetics: Choice and Responsibility* (Oxford: Oxford University Press, 1998).

71. Bryan Appleyard, *Brave New Worlds: Genetics and the Human Experience* (London: Viking, 1999), p. 62.

72. Eric J. Hobsbawm, *The Age of Empire, 1875–1914* (London: Abacus, 1987), p. 255.

73. Peter and Ginger Ross Breggin, *War Against Children* (New York: St. Martin's Press, 1994), p. 62.

74. Nils Roll-Hansen, "Something Rotten in the State of Denmark: Eugenics and the Rise of the Welfare State," in Gunnar Broberg and Nils Roll-Hansen, eds., *Eugenics and the Welfare State: Sterilization Policy in Denmark, Sweden, Norway and Finland* (East Lansing: Michigan State University Press, 1996), p. 24.

75. Reilly, *The Surgical Solution*, pp. 122–123.

76. Thomson, *The Problem of Mental Deficiency*, p. 182.

77. Roll-Hansen, "Something Rotten in the State of Denmark"; Francis Fox Piven and Richard Cloward, *Regulating the Poor* (New York: Pantheon, 1977).

78. Velyn claimed the Oneida experiment (the "society of perfectionists") as a successful experiment should be licensed or compelled to birth control so as to "avoid unions between partners exhibiting physiological defects: TB, syphilis, diabetes, goiter, feeble-mindedness, epilepsy, dementia praecox and schizophrenia"; R. G. Van Velyn, *Sex, Love and Eugenics: A Modern Guide to Sexual Health and Happiness* (London: Gerald G. Swan, 1941), p. 69.

79. *Ibid.*, p. 72.

80. See Christopher Jencks and Meredith Phillips, eds., *The Black-White Test Score Gap* (Washington, D.C.: Brookings Institution, 1998).

81. Cattell, *The Fight for Our National Intelligence*, p. 6.

82. Clive Ponting, *1940: Myth and Reality* (London: Hamish Hamilton, 1992), p. 139: "Public schoolboys were on average four inches taller than their working class counterparts, because of a better diet."

83. Officials found a 25 percent rate of illiteracy among recruits. Thomas A. Wilson, "Who Fought and Why?: The Assignment of American Soldiers in Combat," in Paul Addison and Angus Calder, eds., *Time To Kill: The Soldier's Experience of War in the West* (London: Pimlico, 1997), p. 291. On the poignant impression that these men made on some middle-class counterparts see, for example, Laura Kalman, *Abe Fortas: A Biography* (New Haven: Yale University Press, 1990).

84. Cattell, *The Fight for Our National Intelligence*, p. 37.

85. *Ibid.*, p. 88.

86. Reilly, *The Surgical Solution*, p. 12.

87. Cattell, *The Fight for Our National Intelligence*, p. vi.

88. *Ibid.*, p. 89.

89. *Ibid.*, p. 89.

90. Reilly, *The Surgical Solution*, p. 42.

91. Thomson, *The Problem of Mental Deficiency*, p. 181.

92. Larson, *Sex, Science and the South*, p. 83.

93. Reilly, *The Surgical Solution*, p. 26.

94. Roll-Hansen, "Something Rotten in the State of Denmark," pp. 14, 15.

95. Brian Easlea, *Fathering the Unthinkable: Masculinity, Scientists and the Modern Arms Race* (London: Pluto Press, 1983), p. 176.

96. John S. Haller and Robin M. Haller, *The Physician and Sexuality in Victorian America* (Champaign: University of Illinois, 1974), p. 204.

97. Larson, *Sex, Race and Science*, p. 27.

98. Roll-Hansen, "Something Rotten in the State of Denmark," p. 14.

99. Larson, *Sex, Race and Science*, p. 35.

100. Brantlinger, *Sterilization of People with Mental Disabilities*, p. 8.

101. Wilson, "Who Fought and Why?" in Addison and Calder, *Time to Kill*, p. 294.

102. Broberg and Tyder, "Eugenics in Sweden: Efficient Care," in Broberg and Roll-Hansen, *Eugenics and the Welfare State*, p. 135.

103. Nils Roll-Hansen, "Norwegian Eugenics: Sterilization as Social Reform," in Broberg and Roll-Hansen, *Eugenics and the Welfare State*, pp. 175, 180.

104. Reilly, *The Surgical Solution*, p. 69.

105. Brantlinger, *Sterilization of People with Mental Disabilities*, p. 7.

106. *Ibid.*

107. *Ibid.*

108. Reilly, *The Surgical Solution*, p. 87.

109. Herbert J. Muller, *Out of the Night: A Biologist's View of the Future* (London: Gollanz, 1936), p. 85. Also see the more favorable comments by his fellow traveling colleague J.B.S. Haldane in *Heredity and Politics* (New York: Norton, 1938).

110. Muller, *Out of the Night*, p. 10.

111. Kuhl, *The Nazi Connection*, pp. 36, 43.

112. *Ibid.*, pp. 23, 39.

113. John Weiss, *Ideology of Death: Why the Holocaust Happened in Germany* (New York: Ivan R. Dee, 1996), p. 130.

114. Catrine Clay and Michael Leapman, *Master Race: The Lebensborn Experiment in Nazi Germany* (London: Hodder & Staughton, 1995), p. 17.

115. Kevles, *In the Name of Eugenics*, pp. 209–210.

116. Kuhl, *The Nazi Connection*, p. 18.

117. Cited in Steven Rose, *Lifelines: Biology, Freedom, Determinism* (London: Penguin, 1998), p. 273.

118. Broberg and Tyder, "Something Rotten in the State of Denmark," p. 57.

119. Reilly, *The Surgical Solution,*, p. 109.

120. Benno Mullen-Hill, "Seeds of the Past," *Nature* 346, 2 August 1990, p. 422.

121. See Clay and Leapman, *Master Race;* and M. Hillel, Clarissa Henry, and Marc Hillel, *Of Pure Blood* (New York: McGraw-Hill, 1976).

122. Weiss, *Ideology of Death*, p. 357.

123. *Ibid.*

124. See Robert Proctor, *Racial Hygiene: Medicine Under the Nazis* (Cambridge, Mass.: Harvard University Press, 1988); Benno Muller-Hill, *Murderous Science: Extermination by Scientific Selection of Jews, Gypsies and Others* (New York: Oxford University Press, 1988); Henry Friedlander, *The Origins of Nazi Genocide: From Euthanasia to the Final Solution* (Chapel Hill: University of North Carolina,

1995); Robert J. Lifton, *The Nazi Doctors* (New York: Basic Books, 1986); and Alexander Mitscherlich and Fred Mielke, *Doctors of Infamy: The Story of Nazi Medical Crimes* (New York: Henry Schuman, 1949). For an eyewitness account see Walter Poller, *Medical Block, Buchenwald* (New York: Lyle Stuart, 1961).

125. On Wehrmacht complicity in war crimes see Omer Bartov, *The Eastern Front, 1941–45: German Troops and the Barbarisation of Warfare* (London: Macmillan, 1985); and Omer Bartov, *Hitler's Army: Soldiers, Nazis, and War in the Third Reich* (Oxford: Oxford University Press, 1991). Also see Theo Schulte, *The German Army and Nazi Policy in Occupied Russia* (Oxford: Berg Publishers, 1989).

126. For a simplistic and monocausal explanation of the Holocaust see Daniel Goldhagen, *Hitler's Willing Executioners: Ordinary Germans and the Holocaust* (New York: Knopf, 1991). For critiques see Stephen E. Bronner, "Making Sense of Hell: Meditations on the Holocaust," *Political Studies* 47, 2 (June 1999): 314–328; and Norman G. Finkelstein and Ruth Bettina Birn, *A Nation on Trial: The Goldhagen Thesis and Historical Truth* (New York: Henry Holt, 1998).

127. Kuhl, *The Nazi Connection*, p. 66.

128. Reilly, *The Surgical Solution*, p. 101.

129. *Ibid.*, p. 9.

130. Appleyard, *Brave New Worlds*, p. 73.

131. Reilly, *The Surgical Solution*, p. 95.

132. See, for example, John Demos, "Oedipal America: Historical Reflections on the Reception of Psychoanalysis in the United States," in Joel Pfister and Nancy Schwarz, eds., *Inventing the Psychological: Toward a Cultural History of Emotional Life in America* (New Haven: Yale University Press, 1997).

133. Gilman, *The Case of Sigmund Freud*, pp. 1–2.

134. James H. Jones, *Bad Blood: The Tuskegee Syphilis Experiment* (New York: Free Press, 1981).

135. Alison Mitchell, "Survivors of Tuskegee Study Get Apology from Clinton," *New York Times*, 17 May 1997, p. 9.

136. Anne Hollister, "Were You Born That Way?" *Life*, April 1998, p. 40.

137. Simon Wolff, "Who's Afraid of Molecular Biology?" *New Scientist* 131, 1788 (28 September 1991): 56; Abby Lippman, "Led (Astray) by Genetic Maps: The Cartography of the Human Gene and Health Care," *Social Science and Medicine* 35 (Winter 1992); and Daniel Kevles and Leroy Hood, eds., *The Code of Codes: Scientific and Social Issues in the Human Genome Project* (Cambridge, Mass.: Harvard University Press, 1993).

138. Speaker at conference on evolution, society, and genetics at ICA in London, 24 January 1998.

139. An indigenous biomedical company called deCODE signed a $200 million deal with Hoffman-La Roche for exclusive access to the database to probe the genetic origins of twelve common diseases. Paul Linehan, "They Just Want to Get into Your Genes," *Magill Magazine* (January 1999): 48.

140. John Frow, "Information as Gift and Commodity," *New Left Review* 219 (September/October 1996): 94.

141. For an argument on the influence of evangelical Christianity on bioengineering see David F. Noble, *The Religion of Technology: The Divinity of Man and the Spirit of Invention* (New York: Knopf, 1998).

142. Lori Andrews, *The Clone Age: Adventures in the New World of Reproductive Technology* (New York: Henry Holt, 1999).

143. Sally Lehrman, "Genome Ethics Chair Resigns Over Worries Over Autonomy," *Nature* 380, 14 March 1996, p. 96.

144. See Richard Dawkins, *The Selfish Gene* (New York: Oxford University Press, 1976).

145. Richard Lewontin, *The Doctrine of DNA: Biology as Ideology* (London: Penguin, 1993), p. 122: "This opposes the sociobiological view that believes that individual autonomous units determine the properties of the collectivities in which they are assembled."

146. Appleyard, *Brave New Worlds*, p. 77. Hasian sees "a historical reconstruction of genetics so as to sanitize genetic research," in Hasian, *The Rhetoric of Eugenics in Anglo-American Thought*, p. 218. Also see Troy Duster, *Backdoor to Eugenics* (New York: Routledge, 1990).

147. Nelkin and Tancredi, *Dangerous Diagnostics*, p. 225.

148. Kamin, Lewontin, and Rose, *Not in Our Genes*, p. 168.

149. Stephen Jay Gould, *The Mismeasure of Man* (London: Penguin, 1981), p. 60.

150. Breggin and Breggin, *War Against Children*, p. 62.

151. Lewontin, *The Doctrine of DNA*, p. 72.

152. See Richard Bentall, "Why There Can Never Be a Genetic Theory of Schizophrenia," in Steven Rose, ed., *From Brain to Consciousness* (London: Allan Lane, 1998), pp. 109–131.

153. Hollister, "Were You Born That Way?" p. 42; for a critique of the "gay" gene data see Rose, *Lifelines*, p. 289.

154. Peter R. Breggin, *Toxic Psychiatry* (New York: St. Martin's Press, 1991), pp. 288–231.

155. Appleyard, *Brave New Worlds*, p. 13. Also see Chapter 5 of this volume.

156. See Leon Kamin, *The Science and Politics of IQ* (Potomac, Md.: Erlbaum Publishers, 1974), pp. 35–46; and Kamin, Lewontin, and Rose, *Not In Our Genes*, who find "reexaminations of twins and schizophrenia reveal that investigators might have concluded that they had shown schizophrenia to be entirely environmental in origin" (p. 227). On the problem of estimating heritability of differences between populations, see Rose, *Lifelines*, pp. 190–191. Also see chapter 4 in Lawrence Wright, *Twins: Genes, Environment and the Mysteries of Human Identity* (London: Phoenix, 1997); and Norman J. Mackintosh, ed., *Cyril Burt: Fraud or Framed?* (Oxford: Oxford University Press, 1995).

157. Appleyard, *Brave New Worlds*, p. 86.

158. Also see Mary Jo Banes and Christopher Jencks, "Five Myths About Your IQ," in N. J. Block and Gerald Dworkin, eds., *The IQ Controversy: Critical Readings* (New York: Pantheon, 1976), pp. 325–336.

159. Robert J. Lifton, *History and Human Survival* (New York: Random House, 1970), p. 246. Also see Peter Wright and Andrew Treacher, eds., *The Problem of Medical Knowledge: Examining the Social Construction of Medicine* (Edinburgh: University of Edinburgh, 1982).

160. Lifton, pp. 248, 253. For a literary meditation on the impact of genetics in "fulfilling the Enlightenment's promise of the effecting of all things possible," see

Jon Turney, *Frankenstein's Footsteps: Science, Genetics and Popular Culture* (New Haven: Yale University Press, 1998), p. 2.

161. Gunnar Broberg and Mattias Tyden, "Eugenics in Sweden: Efficient Care," in Broberg and Roll-Hansen, *Eugenics and the Welfare State*, p. 137.

162. Edward Shorter, *A History of Psychiatry: From the Era of the Asylum to the Age of Prozac* (New York: John Wiley & Sons, 1997), p. 246.

163. Breggin and Breggin, *War Against Children*, p. 69.

164. *Ibid.*, p. 129.

165. Tucker, *The Science and Politics of Racial Research*, p. 185. On the Great Society programs, see John E. Schwarz, *America's Hidden Success* (New York: Norton, 1988).

166. Kuhl, *The Nazi Connection*, pp. 3, 6.

167. Richard Hernnstein and Charles Murray, *The Bell Curve: Intelligence and the Uses of Human Heredity* (New York: Free Press, 1994). See the exchange between Richard Herrnstein and Noam Chomsky in Block and Dworkin, *The IQ Controversy*, pp. 285–324.

168. Roll-Hansen, "Something Rotten in the State of Denmark," p. 53.

169. Interview on KCMU FM-Radio (Seattle, Washington), 11 April 1998.

170. McLaren, *Our Own Master Race*, p. 127.

171. Reilly, *The Surgical Solution*, p. 161.

172. Hilary Rose, conference on evolution, society, and genetics, the ICA, London, 24 January 1998.

173. Hubbard and Wald, *Exploding the Gene Myth*, p. 102.

174. Muller, *Out of the Night*, p. 104. Muller flirted heavily with eugenical propositions before rejecting most (not all) of them. At this point he retained a belief that high-IQ sperm donors might improve the gene pool, which today is deservedly grist for comedy.

175. Donna Haraway disclaims attribution of villainy even where well justified. Summing up a noxious historical episode, she says the perpetrators were not "evil capitalists in the sky" but men who saw themselves as "committed progressives struggling to dispel darkness through research, education and reform." She then adds: "The capitalists were not in the sky, but in the field, armed with *The Gospel of Wealth*." In other words, they were capitalist, and they were nasty. Donna Haraway, *Primate Visions: Gender, Race and Nature in Modern Science* (London: Routledge, 1989), pp. 55, 57, 68.

5

Emancipating Nature

Ecology and Ideology

And again he said 'Dom-bey and Son,' in exactly the same tone as before. Those three words conveyed the one idea of Mr. Dombey's life. The earth was made for Dombey and Son to trade in, and the sun and the moon were made to give them light. Rivers and seas were formed to float their ships; rainbows gave them promises of fair weather; winds blew for or against their enterprises; stars and planets circled in their orbits, to preserve inviolate a system of which they were the centre.
—Charles Dickens, *Dombey and Son*

Any critical inquiry into contemporary technological change confronts the unabashed clichés that (1) everything is connected to everything else, (2) the earth is a finite habitat, and (3) a prudent adjustment of social organization with nature is necessary if both are to thrive.[1] The clichés seem true enough. The thornier question is *how* societies should adjust to accommodate our needs intelligently to a natural world that we have not always acknowledged we are integrally a part of.[2] Anthropocentrism, a belief that voiceless nature exists solely for human exploitation and amusement, remains the dominant attitude. In a genuinely rational society nature ought to be heeded too.[3]

At the political core of every ecological question is the issue of externalities (costs of production hitherto excluded from balance sheets), who is to "internalize" them, and how this sensitive task is to be accomplished. A dilemma erupts regarding the added costs that stringent environmental policies would impose on producers whose managers typically threaten job losses, price rises, or relocation if they are forced to bear these costs.[4] In the larger scheme of things the policy choice is posed (very much like the microchip dilemma) as either taking action now at an affordable cost or else postponing corrective action until overwhelmed later by a greater and perhaps irreversible ecological backlash. Unrestrained industrial practices have inflicted enormous environmental damage through all stages of production from resource extraction to workplace production and, eventually, to the biosphere.[5]

The litany of dire environmental results accompanying the pursuit of profit *and* power—state-run firms are by no means immaculate exceptions—include the extinction or near-extinction of many species, radioactive and other hazardous wastes, vast oil spills, acid rain, rampant deforestation, and the controversial greenhouse effect.[6] Numbered among the more notorious incidents of the past few decades are the 1972 Buffalo Creek disaster in New York that killed 125 people and left 80 percent of the townspeople homeless, the deadly leakage of gas from a pesticide plant in Bhopal in India in 1984, nuclear facility accidents at Three Mile Island in 1979 and Chernobyl in 1986, and the sabotaging of the Kuwaiti oil wells in the Gulf War when retreating Iraqi troops vengefully filled the Gulf's water, land, and air with hundreds of millions of barrels of burning or gushing oil.[7]

The unique nature of modern risks is exemplified in the eerie fact that the casualties of the Chernobyl plant, which spewed fifty tons of radioactive poisons (at least ten times the fallout of the Hiroshima bomb) and may cost $10 billion to tidy up, are not even all born yet.[8] The full extent of health problems may not be known for another decade, allowing for the latency period for most cancers that originate from radiation exposure. As victims of Agent Orange or Gulf War syndrome readily would testify, our technical wizardry is not nearly so good at—or perhaps so interested in—detecting long-term effects as they are short-term ones.[9]

The accident at Three Mile Island was far less serious than Chernobyl but hardly was an isolated instance of slipshod practices or faultiness in technical control.[10] In India the Bhopal leak, which killed 2,000–3,000 people and injured 40,000 more, actually had been preceded by six significant accidents in six years.[11] Bhopal was one of *three* terrible industrial accidents in 1984: much less publicized were Ixuatapec, Mexico, where a Pemex explosion killed at least 452; and Cubatoa, Brazil, where a Petrobras gas leak killed nearly 500 people.[12] In Third World countries where the victims are often destitute and powerless, exact numbers are hard to come by. (Race and class play pervasive roles in environmental policies, particularly location decisions for hazardous plants and dumps.) The Mexican and Brazilian cases were state companies. The cautionary point is that the type of ownership (private/public/mixed) tells us little about the practices and impact of a specific industry. Incompatible economic systems have pursued growth in similar ways insofar as bureaucratic state socialist firms, at best, aspired to become a "more rational copy" of capitalist firms.[13]

Still, any analytical foray into the complex web of social relationships with nature must be attentive to the sometimes convergent, sometimes divergent purposes of private players, political institutions, local communities, and activist organizations. The relevant levels of analysis of conflict over policy extend from individual consumer habits to the organization of production to international rulemaking forums. The crucial battles will be waged at the level of changes in the operational codes and incentive structures of national and global institutions, not in shifts in individual consumption habits, as welcome as they doubtless are (especially in laying the cultural groundwork for political initiatives).

Beyond agreeing on tidily separating paper and glass refuse, the merits of lead-free over leaded gasoline, and resisting toxic dumping in their own backyards, the many strands of the environmental/ecology movement—ranging from neighborhood committees to nongovernmental organizations such as Greenpeace—are not all or always alert to the distributional, structural, and international implications of their varied approaches.[14] How strongly an activist group presses private firms and public agencies to internalize their externalities derives not only from where it stands in traditional right-left terms but also where it positions itself along a spectrum ranging from strictly local aims to global programmatic objectives.

Consumer consciousness of environmental problems can work as a progressive force so long as it is not cast exclusively in individualized terms. Otherwise citizens may become an easy mark for exquisitely calibrated public relations campaigns assuring them that powerful polluters really care and that there are such things as biodegradable disposable diapers and plastic bags. Yet less than a third of pollutants are traceable to careless individual consumption habits; most pollution spews out of corporate and military institutions.[15] In the United States in the 1990s

> if every person recycles 100% of what constituted their personal solid waste, 99% of the national solid waste would remain. Industry would still be dumping upwards of 4.6 million pounds of toxic chemicals a years into the air, water and soil; the military would still be producing 500,000 tons of hazardous wastes a year; plants would still be emitting 281 million tons of carcinogens into the environment. The solution does not lie with the individual consumer changing his individual habits.[16]

Recycling is appealing to business because it usually is paid for by local property taxes so that industries wriggle off the hook rather than be induced by, say, combinations of carrot-and-stick measures to produce "low-waste goods and packaging," which would exert far greater environmental benefits.[17] But the interesting question of "efficiency" arises because its definition changes in relation to levels of incorporated costs and changes in industrial practices. This new variability in the meaning of efficiency is potentially subversive because corporate players always invoke a staid definition to legitimate their every action, even myopic or destructive ones. If this textbook definition no longer goes uncontested, neither will corporate behavior. The environmental/ecological movement also raises an incendiary question regarding the legitimacy and mutability of property rights (which delineate legal privileges of ownership and exploitation of resources) both in specific cases of land or water usage and in regard to broad environmental categories.[18]

Regulation, at least initially, increases costs. As early as 1979 the chemical industry reportedly was spending 15 percent of capital investment to comply with new regulations.[19] But, after initial outlays, environmental measures often improved efficiency and profitability for companies that had fought reforms every step of the way.[20] Corporations also found that they can exploit new markets for "environmentally correct" goods. These market-friendly aspects open up important opportunities for forming new coalitions between environmental groups and economic entities, although ecology activists need to be a bit wary as to why industries embrace compatible goals and with what underlying agenda. One ought to keep in mind the facts that firms are profit-seeking entities and also that usually several strategies—some ecologically and democratically friendlier than others—can achieve their pecuniary ends. Some activists believe that the troublesome institution of the market can be restructured—integrating economic rationality within a larger schema of social priorities—to act as a useful facet of collective ecological management in the future.[21]

One must ask what is considered to be adequate feedback as to ecological consequences of technological change and what is the time frame in which feedback is evaluated? How inclusive of affected parties are environmental and regulatory procedures intended to be? Ordinary citizens often are portrayed as so bewildered or so manipulated that they are divested even of the dignity of detecting whether the shoe pinches, and still less could they deduce whether or not devices, after an intervening stage of comfort, will pinch with a vengeance. But this condescending characterization is not really borne out in the story of the rise of ecological movements and organizations.

Eco-Responsibility or Rain-Forest Chic?

The 1970 United Nations Conference on the Human Environment in Stockholm is widely regarded as the first formal global recognition of resource depletion, pollution, and overpopulation as expressed in the slogan "Only One World." That same year witnessed the first celebration of Earth Day. Grave environmental issues, however, had been percolating up the policy agenda of Western polities for at least a century. Even the freewheelingly capitalist United States, upon bumping up against the frontier's end, spawned a vigorous conservation movement.[22] In this field rife with exquisitely contradictory behavior, Teddy Roosevelt, who was credited with singlehandedly wiping out a third of the rhinos in a small African colony, became a hallowed force for conservation and for the creation of a national system of parks and preserves.[23]

Rachel Carson's 1962 best-seller *Silent Spring* became a landmark volume charting the poisonous impact of unregulated pesticides. The turbulent decade of the 1960s gave rise to often interlinked popular movements intent on remedying the baleful effects of poverty, racism, warfare, sexism, and environmental degradation. Feminist critics particularly pointed out cultural parallels between a patriarchy-based mistreatment of women and the abuse of nature.[24] In the 1970s the U.S. government responded to public pressures by creating the Environmental Protection Agency (EPA) and passing the Occupational and Safety Act, National Environmental Policy Acts, a Federal Water Pollution Act, pesticide regulation, a Noise Control Act, and an Endangered Species Act; it also brought the asbestos industry to heel and established a Superfund, funded by taxes on polluters, in 1980 for toxic clean-ups at over 1,200 sites. A reporter described one typical cesspool: "At the Douglassville Disposal site in Pennsylvania a pile of waste filtered from used oil lies like a poisonous pudding 12 feet deep over two acres, exposed to the elements and leaching toxins into the ground water. The runoff goes directly into the nearby Schuylkill River."[25] President Jimmy Carter's *Global 2000* committee report in 1980 affirmed the urgent need for dramatic policy changes in order to cope with environmental deterioration.[26]

This tidal wave of legislative reforms, which modified a deeply rooted system of property rights and of corporate prerogatives, triggered a powerful countermovement—despite research findings that new environmental controls in the United States and United Kingdom had not imposed competitive handicaps upon industries.[27] Congress "naturally" became the lobbying target for affected interest groups attempting to adjust to their own satisfaction just how clean or compliant their sites ought to be. Although the 1970 Clean Air Act's ambitious target of a 90-percent reduction in carbon emissions was steadily rolled back, strict bans on the use of DDT and PCBs went into effect. Britain's Clean Air Act of 1956 dissipated the legendary London fogs of sulfur dioxide, which in December 1952 alone had killed 4,000 people outright and some 8,000 more through assorted aftereffects. Thick fogs descended for the last lethal time in December 1962, when 136 died and over a thousand other victims were hospitalized.

There were encouraging policy successes in Western industrial societies (including, after a bit of a lag, Japan). Between 1966 and 1979 urban ground concentrations of sulfur dioxide fell 75 percent in the United States and by half in Britain; from 1958 to 1981 smoke emissions in Britain fell 94 percent and in the United States were halved; and from 1970 to 1977 the U.S. Clean Air Act provisions cut auto emissions by 67 percent.[28] The Thames River in England and Lake Erie in the United States—once pronounced dead—were almost miraculously revived. Yet any self-congratulations needed to be tempered by the fact that the biggest contributor to air quality seems to have been plant shut-downs that were in the cards anyway—and a number were "dirty" firms and products that were driven offshore to more lenient climes.[29] The indiscriminate use of toxic pesticides result in "about 375,000 cases of accidental pesticide poisoning in the Third World annually, about 10,000 of them fatal" (and about 1,000 U.S. farm workers are estimated to die each year from the cumulative impact of pesticide exposure).[30] In toting up disasters featuring more than 100 dead, 400 injured, 3,500 evacuated, or 70,000 deprived of drinking water, the number of major accidents has been rising. There were four in 1974–1978, ten in 1979–1983, and sixteen in 1984–1988. Of the sixteen accidents in the last period, thirteen were in developing countries.[31]

Third World Repercussions: China and Brazil

As industrial societies turned their moralizing attention to Third World depredations, one should keep in mind that in international relations the critical and hypocritical usually intersect. The United States and the Soviet Union, until its dissolution, were much greater producers of greenhouse gases than was Brazil, the third largest.[32] One should also appreciate that many Third World nations possess vibrant home-grown and grassroots environmental movements.[33] Today China is second to the United States in generating carbon dioxide and other greenhouse gases—although this outpour amounts to just an eighth of the U.S. rate when measured per capita.[34]

Global warming refers to the buildup in the atmosphere of heat-trapping and human-generated gases, mostly carbon dioxide and methane. In the past century the average temperature of the earth rose one degree, due, many (but not all) scientists argued, to the accumulation of these gases. And, unless changes are made, the rate is projected to quadruple in a century, according to the United Nations Intergovernmental Panel on Climate Change.[35] The potential hazards will range from tropical diseases such as malaria and dengue fever migrating northward with mosquito populations into warmer climates and the spread of cholera outbreaks stemming from algae growth in widening expanses of warm water. Melting ice caps will raise sea levels and slowly devastate coast lines everywhere. These diagnoses are scientifically controversial as to their causes and their pace, but these trends certainly seem to exist.

In 1995 the UN Intergovernmental Panel on Climate Change, made up of 2,500 scientists and experts, stated that global warming "suggested a discernible human influence." Given the incalculable adverse consequences that would follow if the diagnosis proves correct, many authorities decided that one "cannot wait for a lock-tight confirmation of climate change" and that measures must be undertaken to halt it.[36] At the Rio Earth Summit in 1992 the participating nations adopted a nonbinding pledge to cap emission levels at their 1990 levels. Presidents Bush and Clinton, however, rejected the idea of mandatory controls, and U.S. emissions increased 7 percent over the next three years.

The Kyoto Summit in 1997 brought out a mandatory protocol for emission curbs in wealthier nations but is unratified. Major business organizations such as the International Chamber of Commerce and the World Business Council for Sustainable Development were observers at both the 1992 environment convention and at the 1997 Kyoto protocol, which produced a binding document that goes into effect only when the major polluters responsible for 55 percent of emissions sign on and when 55 nations sign. NGO activities today, according to one student, "reflect a successful attempt by corporate NGOs to modify scientific research data and to provide additional time to comply with provisions."[37]

Developing nations such as China and Brazil behold developed nations with 25 percent of world population consuming 80 percent of the earth's resources but having the gall to say that only the Third World has a population problem. Every First World resident uses three times the water, ten times the energy, eighteen times the chemicals, and fourteen times as much paper as a comparatively abstemious Third Worlder. (Gandhi's comment comes to mind that an India that replicated British industrialization rapidly would "strip the world bare like locusts."[38]) Industrial countries generate 90 percent of the carbon dioxide and chlorofluorocarbons (CFCs) that stoke the greenhouse effect, so aspiring developers are not impressed by the tender profusion of Western concern for the pristineness of their environments.[39] One billion out of 5.5 billion people enjoy a consumer lifestyle and possess (however unevenly spread) 64 percent of world income. (Another 3.3 billion people take 33 percent of income, and the bottom 1.1 billion eke by on 2 percent.) Modernizing Third World elites, motivated by a mixture of personal aggrandizement and an authentic concern for raising average living standards, seek a bigger piece of the action and often at any cost (not unlike earlier waves of industrializers). At the April 1995 follow-up to the Rio Summit, held in Berlin, Chinese leaders staunchly resisted any imposition of pollution limits upon developing countries.

Four-fifths of China's rivers nonetheless are seriously polluted, and the vast middle kingdom has experienced considerable rises in air pollution and the spread of mercury and lead poisoning. Can the gradual growth of free markets and capitalist inventiveness really solve problems of over-fishing and resource depletion? Experts today estimate that China needs to spend 2–2.5 percent of its GNP (versus 0.7 percent today) in order to curb pollution. Even the cuddly and symbolic panda is nearly extinct under the breakneck pace of Chinese deforestation, although China, curiously, draws much less international attention than Brazil or Central America.

In September 1993 space shuttle *Discovery* astronauts reported that Brazil was obscured by clouds of smoke streaming from burning forests. Through the vast application of slash-and-burn techniques conducted by subsidized entrepreneurs, the rain forests around the world disappear at a rate of an acre and a half every second, according to the UN Food and Agriculture Organization.[40] Two and a half million acres—an area the size of Washington state—were vanishing every year. Half of 7.7 million square acres of world rain forests were erased in the past hundred years—most of it in the last quarter-century. The 7 percent of the earth's surface covered by rain forests contains beneath its verdant umbrella half of the world's species. In the 1990s alone between 10 and 20 percent of Brazil's forests were cleared to meet timber demand and to make way for cattle ranches to feed the First World's fast-food-franchise appetite for beef.

The infamous murder in December 1988 of rubber tappers union leader Chico Mendes—because his union's interest in preserving the forest clashed with the land-clearing barons—attracted international attention and brought a temporary halt to unchecked chainsawing and burning. Mendes worked in Acre, where 139 landowners controlled an Illinois-sized area and already had murdered about 1,600 local workers, calling this a process of "limpeza" ("cleansing" the land).[41] It remains important to remember, however, that these villainous landowners are situated both inside a state (which they influence) that determines the terms of their property rights and in a global-market context that sets the incentive structures they heed when deciding what to produce.

In Brazil just 4.5 percent of the population owned 80 percent of the land in a heavily indebted economy that the World Bank typically ushered into austerity, openness to foreign investors, and an export-led strategy encouraging ranchers to raise more beef and stirring timber companies to slice down more forest.[42] For all the rhetorical eco-friendliness, the material interests of international banks and foreign capital supersede soft-hearted words about sparing the "lungs of the world."[43] Brazil contains $3 trillion in valuable mineral resources and timber exports that are eagerly sought, so that strip-mining and burning acreage annually contribute a billion tons of carbon dioxide to greenhouse gases.[44] (The UN's financial accounting office itself has been accused of being penetrated by, and of promoting, the agenda of local industrial, mining, and timber interests.[45]) If the source of pollution is not technological, neither is the solution.

Land reform certainly would ease population pressures on rain forests—a tiny elite owns most land while 70 percent of the population go landless—but Brazil underwent a coup in 1964, which was the last time this touchy subject appeared on the political agenda.[46] After the coup the military junta sought to accelerate "development" of the Amazon basin through a panoply of road, mining, and rancher schemes. Judging by behavior rather than rhetoric, Western lenders prioritized debt repayment over the noble cause of environmental preservation, despite the emergence in the media of the notion of "sustainable development" based on the Brundtland Report in 1987.[47] This document optimistically assumed that profit-seeking was wholly reconcilable with ecological needs and with the wishes of local populations—which, by the way, may conflict with one another too.[48]

A World Bank moratorium on road building in the Amazon and the declaration of new "extractive reserve" areas followed the flap over Mendes's murder and his union/ecological cause—though only temporarily. In January 1996 Brazil "opened up 57 percent of all Indian land in Amazonia to claims from outside interests—a new invasion of loggers, ranchers and miners."[49] Since the mid-1980s in South and Central America "debt for nature" swaps were being worked out to buy a minuscule portion of the $100 billion-plus debt in exchange for expanding conservation areas under (usually) foreign auspices. The proliferation of national parks, whatever the sincere intentions, can be characterized as transfers of even more property from the poor to the rich as well as a further infringement upon the abused rights of the local people. Whatever the case, and these cases vary, these swaps make little difference except perhaps to create the illusion that remedial measures are being undertaken to greater effect than is actually the case.

Western Woes and Corporate Wiles

Ironically, American taxpayers though their forestry service dole out hundred of millions of dollars in subsidies to timber companies in, for example, the Tongass Forest, where recipients spent less than $2 per thousand feet for wood products whose market price varies from $200 to $600 per thousand feet. Other problems arise. The threat of global warming stirred interest even among some staunch opponents of nuclear energy—the National Audubon Society, the World Resources Institute, and Union of Concerned Scientists—to reconsider use of nuclear energy without first solving the problem of disposal of radioactive wastes with a half-life of 14 billion years or solving other safety issues at the root of public distrust.[50] The historical record, and common sense, indicate that corporations and corporate NGOs, like any interest group, work to insinuate their own agendas as strongly as possible in any reform program in which they participate. Despite Brundtland Report recommendations, or the democratic pieties expressed at the 1992 UN Rio meetings, local people rarely are consulted regarding these grand schemes, and they are heeded even less.[51]

Surveys in the United States and Western Europe (and in several major Third World countries) consistently report that 80 to 90 percent of the citizenry are worried about environmental degradation and that a large majority were quite willing to pay higher prices for recycled and biodegradable products, a finding that, among other things, sets up citizens for misleading advertising campaigns.[52] Especially since Reagan's presidency, many polluters used the windfalls of tax cuts, deductions, subsidies, and downsizing (wages saved or withheld) to fund public-relations campaigns to assure the citizenry that they are taking exquisitely good care of the environment. Meanwhile, moving briskly backward, the "Contract with America" 1994 Republican Congress strived to reduce corporate polluters' responsibility for clean-ups and, to boot, even tried to open the Arctic's National Wildlife Refuge and Utah's Redrock Canyon Wilderness for oil and mining companies.

The "wise use" movement exemplifies the adroit absorption and adaptation of public concerns to modern corporate purposes—serving the coal, energy, timber, and grazing interests who forked out the cash to concoct a "corporate-financed grassroots movement."[53] This heavily disguised form of corporate resistance was triggered especially by the fear that the EPA, despite the sympathetic staffing of this agency from inception, might truly hold firms accountable for their costly and deadly messes.[54] The procedure is to concoct citizens groups with "eco-friendly" names such as National Wetland Society or National Wildlife Institute, which are staffed either directly by these firms or by well-remunerated sympathizers.[55] People for the West, for example, was 96-percent funded by a band of firms angling to retain an 1872 mining law allowing them wonderfully cheap access to rich public lands.

In Oregon, prodevelopment money accounted for 14.7% of the money statewide candidates accepted in 1990; in 1994 that number grew to 16.4%, with the winners on average receiving 21% of their campaign cash from developers. Perhaps that fact helps explain why in 1995 the legislature proposed scores of bills that would weaken water quality or destroy environmental enforcement programs, passing several.[56]

In Idaho this "prodevelopment money" comprised 25 percent and in Wyoming 26 percent of all campaign contributions in 1992. Wyoming passed a takings bill—allowing private firms to be compensated for alleged public interferences—and permitted dumping of nuclear waste (despite 70- to 80-percent levels of public opposition). These states also bestowed an unusual "audit privilege" allowing any company to audit its own environmental violations—rather like delegating to speeding motorists the right to ticket themselves, or not. An ARCO lobbyist essentially wrote a bill denying citizens the right to information about pollution harmful to public health, and then limited the polluters' liability too. A "takings bill" in Washington state likewise passed. Technology alone dictated none of these trends and outcomes. We next turn to several competing, if overlapping, critiques of development.

The Politics of Ecological Logic: Bookchin, Gorz, and Beck

Murray Bookchin argues that the radical implications of ecology lie in the nonhierarchical nature of ecosystems and the importance of diversity—lessons that he carries into an anarchist study of forms of social organization. The objective is to devise a "social ecology" that transcends the orthodoxies of both left and right, although beginning with the premise that capitalism grows regardless of any negative impact outside its bottom line.[57] Development, as he beholds it, therefore results willy-nilly in despoliation of the environment and the degradation of the majority of the planet's inhabitants.[58] Bookchin contrasts a conventional politics that is professedly environmental (but highly liable to corporate capture) against a fiercer ecological sensibility that challenges the corporate ethos as well as the narrow positivist creed animating most public-policy ventures. Environmentalism and ecology, incidentally, often are distinguished in "green" literature in terms of political agendas. The former is viewed as a reformist strategy within existing institutional boundaries whereas the latter is identified with a radical vision and movement toward a "sustainable society."[59] Bookchin believes that the solution for environmental decay lies in decentralized forms of government geared to adjust local communities less wastefully to their "bioregion" (which denotes an ecologically integral area that spills beyond political boundaries).

In Andre Gorz's more orthodox Marxist (or less anarchist) critique, technology likewise is a "matrix in which the distribution of power, social relations of production, and hierarchical division of labor are embedded," and thus it is never neutral. Hence, to struggle for "different technologies is to struggle for a different society."[60] In both Gorz's and Bookchin's radical reckonings, ecology movements are not to be conceived as ends in themselves but rather as nodal points for crafting durable and progressive social coalitions that promote more localized and participatory forms of democracy—although neither in logic nor in history has "more local" necessarily meant "more democratic," or, for that matter, "more virtuous" in any respect.

Gorz squarely confronts the "ecology-versus-growth" dilemma when asking whether an increasing capital-intensity of pollution control equipment will render such a remedial course unprofitable to undertake.[61] (This problem, however, borders on the irrelevant if firms successfully resist regulatory impositions on their power.) If so, increasing capital intensity exacerbates trends toward fewer workers, lower skills, and a fall in the share of income to workers, which can generate a crisis of overaccumulation, intensified by environmental woes. The desirable path out of this plight requires that technological instruments be designed according to criteria emphasizing durability, reparability, nonpollutants, pleasantness of manufacturing modes, and democratic input.[62] To prepare the ground for such remedies— or perhaps to avoid facing the difficulties of implementing them—a host of eco-critics have focused first on establishing a robust philosophical case for altering ingrained social attitudes and lifestyle habits.

In "deep ecology," according to founder Arne Naess, the relation of human and natural worlds is reconceptualized as "a relational-total field perspective." The ecological plight, according to this diagnosis, has deep philosophical ("anthropocentric") roots that must be unearthed in order to be examined and adjusted. The upshot is that alleviating the strain that omnivorous industrial societies and profligate urban lifestyles place on the earth requires a transformation in the way we relate to the environment, so that human desires are subordinated to the goal of a restoration of ecological balance. This viewpoint seems to be a reasonable and overdue corrective to the absolute splits between mind/body and nature/society that have typified Western philosophical traditions. Yet it is one thing to argue that the nature/society distinction is an artificial or socially constructed one, and quite another to make a creed of any version of this critique.

The real quandaries arise when one slips unwittingly into an endorsement of the primacy of nature over humanity, which—harking to the previous chapter—smacks of nothing so much as a Nazi biology that imputed to nature the cold-blooded right to determine human goals, priorities, and hierarchies. Socialist and eco-anarchist scholars therefore repudiate a "green romanticism" that promotes "separation and hypsotatization of nature as separate from social practices."[63] This romantic view fails to recognize itself as a mystification whose values are a product of a particular cultural moment and historical process.[64]

Nature cannot be the ultimate arbiter because every single discourse of nature is shot through with presuppositions that lie unexamined within the cultural backgrounds of the participants. Bookchin and Gorz oppose "deep ecology" because they believe it tends to devalue or deny human individuality rather than situate it in a mutually interacting relationship with nature (though this seems to accord with Naess's original intention). One encounters members of Earth First!, for example, who approach nature "as if it were in no sense an artificial construct," so that it seems to them perfectly plain that the "difference between a large forest and parking lot is that one's natural, the other a cultural construct."[65] Yet this is only partially true, for nature is quite malleable and bends to (often unconscious) human agendas. Still, the central argument of deep ecology remains persuasive: that a correction of our "deliberate deafness" to nature is needed. Regarding distribution of environmental goods in conditions of scarcity and carrying capacity overload, Hugh Stretton points out that the way up (breakneck industrialization) is not the same as the way down (prudent use), due to different expectation levels and, moreover, that "what the poor suffer proves something about their political weakness, not their values or marginal utility."[66] Given the rancorous reality of persistent class inequalities, there is no best way—and no "neutral" method—of allocating the costs and benefits of environmental policy measures.

We reside in a risk society, according to Ulrich Beck, which is marked by a "dynamic of modernization that had made itself autonomous" and from whose deleterious effects not even the wealthiest people can shelter themselves. The risk society begins where the industrial society's principles of calculation are annulled by its own toxic products, thereby negating instrumental rationality by exceeding insurable limits regarding production of goods and "bads." The risk society arises when the conflict over distribution of the "bads" are superimposed on the patterns of institutionalized conflict over the distribution of goods. What this means politically is that formerly unseen side-effects become visible issues, and even "flash points," at a time when people are increasingly freed from adherence to the old normative expectations of social institutions—which Bell, incidentally, long before characterized as one of the "cultural contradictions of capitalism."[67]

The technocratic reflex is to convert social problems into positivist terms that "mask important cultural, social and existential dimensions" and enable policymakers to sidestep "lasting participative and deliberative institutional and proactive change."[68] This instrumental sensibility pervades not only business and government but the citizenry, who are unable to assess ecological threats that they cannot see, hear, taste, touch, or smell. In effect, they are "disempowered" of sovereignty over their senses until the noxious results grow tangible and/or activist groups demonstrate the threat and thereby contest the authorities in a process he dubs "reflexive modernization."[69] In Seattle in November 1999 tens of thousands of demonstrators—ecological activists, trade unionists, consumer organizations, and church groups—gathered to protest the antidemocratic and nontransparent practices of the World Trade Organization (WTO) at its Third Ministerial Conference. The WTO clearly functioned as a corporate-dominated star chamber by which to dilute strict national regulations, rather than to spread "best practices" of environmental protection. The haughtiness of WTO officials and the Orwellian images of police guaranteed that seemingly arcane trade issues suddenly became front-page news and a matter of lively public interest.

Beck also foresees intensifying ecological threats inducing splits among financial and business elites—pitting producers of "bads" against relatively clean industries—and enabling new political coalitions to emerge that will enable societies to undertake needed reforms.

A "risk society" is propelled by complacent routines until the cumulative liabilities rupture the physical and mental boundaries within which elites comfortably operate. The environmental crisis is a social one because the hazards that society produces are not containable within prevailing systems of prediction and control. Authoritative decisions thus escape the province of experts and become dispersed across a range of new social groups whose cumulative counteractivities will raise society "to a new level of self-critique." Again, witness Seattle. Bell and other critics have been saying something similar for decades, although they, unlike Beck and like the WTO, were confident that this "transparency of politics," and any critical energies it unleashes, could be channeled within existing institutions.

So, in its own cramped terms, the productive system is riddled with widening cracks. But what is needed is not technical fixes but, as John Dryzek writes, "a new set of terms which reflect the co-construction of nature and culture." Dryzek accordingly suggests that processes of communicative reason, described by Habermas, be extended to nonhuman entities by ascribing agency (though not self-awareness) to them so that account is taken of the "total field" of relations in a more ecologically astute democracy.[70] Thus, deep ecology accommodates critical theory. His intermediate objective, like Beck's, is to cultivate a set of "public sphere" organizations existing apart from and in continuous and mostly courteous dialogue with public authorities.[71]

Beck, Berking, and others espy a sly reflexive capacity—a rare capacity to criticize one's own cultural assumptions—literally being forced upon modern industrial peoples by technological adversities and by a "shrinking" world that is becoming ever more interdependent. Ironically, this scenario borders on a romantic Blakean stance ("if fools but follow their folly to the end they would become wise") as a shiny new teleological way to assure us of arrival at a state of enlightened self-interest.[72] These are awfully thin reeds to rely on.

The stark reality remains that symbiotic relations between government and business erodes or bypasses democratic participation. Only a day after the Seattle ruckus the European Union commissioner, despite an EU vote to the contrary, delegated regulatory power over GM food research to the tender mercies of a WTO working group. Desirable developmental and environmental options still get overlooked because they are believed to be incompatible with existing interests. Corporate and government bureaucracies are "dynamically conservative," suffused with technocratic values, emphasizing efficiency and minimizing conflict; believing in technical fixes; biased toward dominant actors and "screening out" information antagonistic to the current mindset. Lindberg writes, "policymakers, their criteria of choice, and the institutional systems they are embedded in are part of the problem."[73] So the choices pit conservation, egalitarianism, and internationalism against technical fixes, capital intensity, and short-run forecasts. Industrial societies possess production structures that require increases of energy, and these policies are dominated by private producers. This situation requires modes of political mobilization to incorporate weak or entirely excluded groups through old-fashioned unions and parties, as well as via NGOs and new activist groups, to sway the state in a different policy direction. (In Britain, astonishingly, four times as many people are members of environmental/conservation groups as they are of political parties.)

Feminist Interrogations

Investigating the roots of ecological mayhem, feminist Carolyn Merchant focused on the "pervasive animism" of pre-Renaissance conceptions of the earth and told the saga of the loss of this concept ("earth as a living organism") as a normative constraint on human activity.[74] Mumford and others covered a good deal of this thematic territory (though not always so well) and, indeed, feminist work is not always distinctively "feminist." Feminists do delineate how the historical oppression of women is connected with the abuse of nature.[75] They also form a scholarly bloc that wields an acute awareness of the "connection between all forms of domination" (which the Frankfurt School stressed) and a sharpened sense of the underlying "constructedness" of categories and institutions based on the recognition that— even when the subject is science—we are, as Donna Haraway puts it, delving into "split, fragmented and multiple subjects, identities and collectivities."[76]

Feminists accordingly promote antihierarchical values, celebrate diversity, view nature as a "partner in existence," and probe psychological as well as economic reasons behind the drive for domination (as did the Frankfurt School). It is probably true that Bookchin's social ecology, according to a chiding former student, "without feminism is incomplete"— although it may still be incomplete.[77] (Bookchin made amends by depicting the state as "the institutionalized apex of male civilization."[78]) A popular strain of "eco-feminism" tends to romanticize the intuitive ability of non-

Western women and of women in general, and to shortchange the role of science in acting as a check on irrational and culture-bound agendas.[79] But, when applied in a way that judiciously incorporates race and class factors, the acuity of feminist analyses is hard to surpass as an instrument to unmask ideologies and pry out hidden agendas.

Reconnoitering the Battlefield

Beck's risk society thesis seems to be borne out by events. Fossil fuel firms have formed highly influential coalitions that shape and/or veto the agenda for climate change. One may mandate scrubbers for chimneys and catalytic converters for autos because these devices can be affixed quickly (if not so cheaply), but a reduction in global warming probably will entail the avid targeting of carbon dioxide, which constitutes half the greenhouse gases and 80 percent of which is emitted by coal, oil, and gas.[80] This epic goal requires cutting output, not just altering it, which is likely to stoke stronger and cleverer business resistance.

The anti-chloroflourocarbon lobby formed the Alliance for Responsible CFC Policy and only relented from successful stalling tactics when the DuPont Corporation announced that a substitute for CFC would be made commercially available within five years. The fossil fuel lobby Global Coalition on Climate Control consists of fifty-five firms and trade associations (including chemical and auto firms). Greenpeace in 1994 complained that the voluntary and incremental controls had only led to a 35-percent emission since 1990. Fossil fuels firms comprise a formidable blocking coalition, but, Beck observes, they increasingly are countered by a powerful insurance industry that frets about the stiff liabilities it suffers from the meteorological consequences of global warming.[81]

The UN Environmental Program in 1996—"Implementing Environmental Control"—was sponsored by the insurance industry and garnered sixty signatories who agreed that environmental deterioration via manmade processes leads to unnecessary financial risks and losses.[82] This proenvironmental stance in certain financial realms is a strong trend, but compliant corporate behavior depends on the degree to which implicated business leaders "view environmental issues as providing market opportunities as well as threatening increased costs." It also depends on their capacities to peddle their own diagnoses and prescriptions for the ailing environment to a skeptical citizenry.

Ideas about nature are interpreted within the cultural context into which they are inserted, but this context is not an inert background even though dominant groups try to portray a favorable context as an immutable one. "None of the supposedly nonpolitical sources of authority—not religious dispensation, not the social order, not the market or technology—can be established as legitimate without a prior political operation," Charles Maier observes. "Its advocates must control the resources of politics, including influence over the media and the capacity to shape political discourse. Once stability had been achieved, the political pressures may disappear from discussion. Indeed, the objective for any strategy for stability must be to make people forget politics."[83] The point is that elites, and their challengers, play upon the material and ideational elements available in their organizational and cultural contexts to protect and advance their concerns.[84]

This kind of conflict is exemplified in the 1990s BSE ("mad cow" disease) scandal in Britain, where the practice of feeding animal protein to herbivores apparently resulted in a degenerative disease that jumped species. Scientific and government experts denied any of this was possible until the evidence overwhelmed them.[85] Public confidence in authorities eroded, and the credibility of critical "outsiders" and activist organizations increased. Even so, as Phil Macnaghten and John Urry point out, a purely technical focus obscured the wider issues concerning the feeding of animal by-products to herbivores and regarding the industrial intensification of food production.[86] Beck asks why even scientists should be ceded the right to determine these risks rather than have them debated in public forums in which people on the receiving end participate in an effective way.[87]

Europeans, at least at the outset of the 1970s, seemed to display more trust regarding relations between civil servants and interest group associations, and of the decisions they forge together.[88] In the United States, by sharp contrast, "the prescription to 'consult the experts and do as they say' has relatively little meaning in American politics," Sheila Jasonoff observes. "The existence of competing scientific voices—regulatory agencies, scientific committees and societies, industry, pubic interest groups, even the courts—permits different constructions of risk to enter the debate; which one resonates ultimately with the public depends on the political skill, credibility, resources and occasionally the plain luck of its proponents."[89] During the Love Canal disaster the EPA's dismissive report on toxicity was challenged both by the Congressional Office of Technology Assessment and by a professional journal—and the EPA finally gave in and cracked down.[90] The U.S. Food and Drug Administration has reconsidered its position since 1992 that GM foods need no labels. In 1998 a coverup scandal regarding dioxin found in animal feed brought down the Belgian government and rocked the Dutch Cabinet. Activist tactics, pressure groups, and partisan processes can be mutually interacting sources of policy change.

Beck offers a useful if incomplete list of prescriptive goals: shift the legal burden of proof onto polluters; create committees with experts from outside disciplines (because "insiders" of all professions are less critical of their own field than of others), raise liability issues (which would have stopped nuclear power dead in its tracks had it not been indemnified), exploit differences between polluters and nonpolluter industries for the sake of coalition building, and encourage a consciousness-building countermovement.[91]

The remedy of decentralization—a battle cry for conservatives too—confers no advantage to challengers because top-down devolutions often mean that hierarchy is relaxed to the degree that it incorporates and absorbs lower-level dissent in the terms laid down by authorities. Integrating dissidents through human relations ploys compensates the authorities for any lack of rigid enforcement of compliance.[92] History would indicate that, as the state removes itself from any realm, private interests are poised to fill the vacuum. Despite these caveats, it remains a point for debate that

> if one believes in the validity of participative democracy (and what other kind of democracy is there?), then it is little more than academic presumption to begin unloading a host of institutional schemes in the abstract. It is people in the process of changing their homes, neighborhoods, cities, regions, who are most apt to know best what they need and what works. And if they don't know, they will only learn from their failures. Nothing but responsibility for their own lives makes people grow up and be competent. The resourcefulness of ordinary people whose citizenly instincts have been awakened and put in touch with the real problems of their community can indeed be amazing. Their experienced judgment always counts for more than the most prestigious expert.[93]

Given such dismal homespun spectacles as the Scopes trial or the Chinese Cultural Revolution, the word "always" may be going a mite too far. Nonetheless, note the case of scientists who were unable and unwilling to heed Cumbrian sheep farmers in regard to the impact of Chernobyl fallout.[94] These experts reportedly left the frustrated villagers feeling like two-legged guinea pigs: "We were given dosimeters at work, then they took them away from us and no one told us what dose we received," said one woman.[95] Savvy local farmers knew that "predictability was intrinsically unreliable as an assumption" about their business and thus valued flexibility and adaptability while scientists ignored these unlettered masses and superimposed their own abstract estimates on the real problem.

The scientists, ignoring local input, were bound to err in how they sized up the Cumbrian plight. Yet there is nothing intrinsic to scientific work that compels investigators to denigrate the practical knowledge of people who live in the midst of the pertinent problem; this casual snobbery (and local reactions to it) arises from cultural concerns about the wielding of social power: that is, keeping, or putting, people "in their place." Genuine expertise is to be valued, but genuine expertise will not insistently wear blinders. The risk society supposedly will impel the removal of blinders, although this benign scenario, as Beck himself recognizes, must be weighed against another common and unfortunate reaction to crises—clinging to what one has or knows regardless of consequences.[96]

The "zig-when-you-zag" mode of expert-local relations (where distrustful parties confound and dodge one another while performing a task) evident in the Cumbrian case comes as no surprise because the quest of progress aimed not for efficiency per se but an efficiency of social control over a populace who, in turn, will resist. This skewed form of efficiency ruptures any possibility of a sensitive assimilation of feedback from operations.

Take the case of what British tabloids call "Frankenstein foods." Dr. Arpad Pusztai of the Aberdeen-based Rowett Research Institute advised the British Ministry of Agriculture in 1995 that tests of genetically modified (GM) food upon animal nutrition found that GM potatoes adversely affected the immunity systems in rats, whose brain, liver, and heart sizes had decreased. Denied research and testing funds by the Scottish Office and the Rowett Institute, Pusztai went to the media. In August 1998, after television appearances, he was forced to retire after a summary suspension, and his research team was disbanded. Despite his warnings, the Ministry of Agriculture approved GM maize—and failed to call for proper GM labeling practices in marketplaces. Pusztai's research soon was corroborated by international scientists.

The British Consumer Association, not the research center or the government, called for a three-year moratorium on commercialization of GM products until an overhaul of the regulatory system could be effected.[97] Hence, further research was encouraged, not forbidden. The firms did not want to risk having new scientific findings interfere with their plans for commercial release of GM foods. All the implicated organizations—Rowett, the Durham University biology department, and the Scottish Crop Research Institute—were linked with the biotech industry through their pursuit or performance of lucrative commercial research contracts.

A House of Lords select committee already had approved the sale of GM foods because the "significant environmental risks in the technology were outweighed by substantial future economic benefits to farmers, the food industry and consumers." Consumer Association representatives pointed out that nine of the twelve-member select committee either were farmers or had some financial interest in the food industry (including supermarket magnate Lord Sainsbury).[98] They had arranged to hear testimony overwhelmingly from people with a direct stake in GM technology: Only three consumer groups and two environmental groups were invited among the fifty-some witnesses.

Nothing, barring proven brain shrinkage harming company CEOs or their offspring, would have interrupted a march of these GM products into the marketplace if not for the alternative analyses raised within a divided and contentious scientific community, whose skeptical voices were amplified by concerned consumer groups. The group Friends of the Earth had got hold of a suppressed Department of the Environment report warning that GM food could be dangerous to wildlife.[99] As of January 1999 Prime Minister Tony Blair, reluctant to declare a moratorium, was facing sustained flak from organized counter-forces.

Nonetheless, the next month negotiations for a biosafety protocol regulating international shipment of GM organisms and food products were thwarted by the adamant opposition of the United States, where 25 to 45 percent of food is genetically modified, and by five other food exporting nations. This legally binding protocol would have required exporters explicitly to seek permission from nations importing their GM food products. The U.S. government, which took the food industries' interest as paramount, asserted that GM foods "were not a threat to biodiversity, especially compared with the destruction of tropical forests to create farmland."[100] The justification for blocking the protocol was not better science, as the director of an environmental NGO noted: "It was just cheap power politics." One trouble is that complexity can be easily invoked in a politicized policy arena as a warrant to examine everything—or to do nothing.[101]

Indeed, there is no remotely adequate theory—not excluding "chaos" theory—that assesses the secondary consequences of technological measures on the totality of relationships between society and nature (or, for that matter, within them). In the absence of such knowledge we may well ask whether a regulatory regime should adopt a "default position" of green, red, or caution light as to deploying new products and processes. The choice will depend on factors other than "objective" ones. Mumford aptly draws attention to the root:

> Technics and civilization as a whole are a result of human choices and attitudes and strivings, deliberate as well as unconscious, often irrational when they appear most objective and scientific; but even when they are uncontrollable they are not external. No matter how completely technics relies upon the objective procedures of the sciences, it does not form an independent system, like the universe: it exists as an element in human culture.[102]

Nature, by the same token, "builds no machines, no locomotives, railways, electric telegraphs, self-acting mules, etc.," Marx wrote. "These are products of human industry; natural material transformed into organs of the human will over nature. They are organs of the human brain, created by the human hand; the power of knowledge, objectified."[103] Contemporary Democratic Socialists—whatever Marx's own attitude—see the "common conscious control over natural and social conditions" as a legitimate goal that, however, must include mastery of environmental consequences "since no society that ignored secondary consequence of its transformative activity could be said to be in control."[104]

Conclusion

Technology is *part* of the solution, but technical fixes, purporting to be *the* solution, are part of the problem. Technology is a dialectical process arising from relationships of humankind's interaction with nature.[105] Add to this the historical fact that the market system in which technology is embedded encourages a focus on pursuit of profit as opposed to socially rational and environmentally sensitive planning criteria.

Invoking nature for guidance is a futile (or disingenuous) act because "just about every political ideology and polito-economic system has at one time or another been justified as consistent with nature."[106] Neither controversial social issues nor cultural concerns can be settled simply by scientific fiat, particularly in a world where experts usually disagree and where science can be compromised by institutional sponsors. No laboratory can dictate what industrial practices are tolerable or what degree of industrialization is permissible for "sustainable development." Should Third World nations only employ "appropriate technologies"? These questions transcend the crude categories of technical criteria and slide-rule measurement. Hence

> in response to the declining living conditions of many of the poor, national political and social movements have increasingly moved into the sphere of "political ecology" where the hope is to redefine the environmental agenda in terms that address more fundamental questions of resource distribution and access, political rights and processes; also to consider larger philosophical issues regarding the nature of property (ranging from usufruct to intellectual property rights), the nature of nature (untrammeled Eden or artifact and habitat), and technical and development alternatives. Environmental issues are but one component in a broad range of activities, and the central focus is on social justice.[107]

In industrialized nations the utilitarian thrust of technology, particularly when utilized by interests craving a quick return on investment, diminishes science. Increasingly, science is "extrinsically motivated." This process makes the interests at play within competing camps of scientific communities more visible too. Even the cost of the deployment of corrective countertechnologies operating in an artificial environment threatens to dwarf all the sums spent on war. These factors militate against a "one best way" and the notion that only credentialed experts—unanimously!—can divine it.

Eugene Schwartz anticipated Beck's risk society thesis by several decades when he argued that in light of receding resources, "the criterion of optimality reflecting an ultimate efficiency will wane as efficiency loses validity in a closed system where myriads of competing demands will have equal legitimacy."[108] Environmental struggles, in their aggregate, can be read as a widespread if uncoordinated campaign to close the disjuncture between private entrepreneurs' costs and uncounted ecological costs and to impose democratic limits on economic rationality.

For some fervent advocates ecological correctness entails retreat into self-sacrificial hermithood (if not, like the Unabomber, more violent pastimes). But the more attractive objective is to work to devise what Gorz termed "non-reform reform," that is, reform that aims to "modify the relationship of forces, the redistribution of functions and powers, new centers of democratic decision-making [and] reestablishes real priorities that conform to social needs, and which challenges the purposes of private accumulation and of the 'consumers society.'"[109] In such an ideological battleground, a part of the technical strata hopefully is enabled to act as "system-demystifiers" by employing their knowledge to show citizens the full or likely consequences of competing solutions.[110] Charles Sabel and his coauthors describe deliberative arrangements in California and Massachusetts that blend citizen participation with expert oversight so as to yield sound regulatory decisions: "expertise without local participation remains ignorant of crucial detail, while localism unprovoked by expertise remains haplessly parochial."[111] Even if participatory democracy alone cannot guarantee benign ecological behavior, the route toward progressive policy outcomes lies in opening up decisionmaking arrangements (not just science policy) to democratic scrutiny.

Notes

1. The classic statement of the plight is Garret Hardin, "The Tragedy of the Commons," reprinted in John Dryzek and David Schlosberg, eds., *The Environmental Politics Reader* (Oxford: Oxford University Press, 1998), pp. 23–34.

2. On the "dichotomization of society and nature" see Phil Macnaghten and John Urry, *Contested Natures* (London: Sage, 1998), pp. 1, 7–15. Their argument that "separating nature from society was necessary as a prerequisite for treating nature instrumentally" (p. 11) accords with the Frankfurt School scholars. See Max Horkheimer and Theodor Adorno, *The Dialectic of Enlightenment* (London: Allen Lane, 1973).

3. See the references to Dryzek and to feminists below.

4. There is a disjuncture between "direct production costs by the private investor and the social costs which his investment will bring with it: for example, expenses for education, housing, transportation, various services; in short, the entrepreneur's criteria for profitability, which measure the desirability of the investment, and the

criteria of human and collective, are not identical. As a consequence, the collective needs engendered by capitalist development are covered haphazardly or not at all; the satisfaction of these needs is neglected or subordinated to more profitable 'priorities' because these needs were not foreseen and included in advance in the total cost of the project"; Andre Gorz, *Strategy for Labor* (Boston: Beacon Press, 1964), p. 84.

5. T. Jones, "Hazards for Export: Double Standards?" in Les Levidow, *Science as Politics* (London: Free Association Books, 1986), p. 120.

6. At least one species of higher animal is reckoned to be lost every year as well as numerous other (especially tropical) animals and plants. Erik P. Eckholm, *Down to Earth: Environment and Human Needs* (New York: Norton, 1982), p. 180.

7. See T. M. Hawley, *Against the Fires of Hell: The Environmental Disaster of the Gulf War* (New York: Harcourt, Brace, Jovanovich, 1992).

8. Ulrich Beck, "Risk Society and the Provident State," in Scott Lash, Bronislaw Szerszynski, and Brian Wynne, eds., *Risk, Environment and Modernity: Towards a New Ecology* (London: Sage, 1996), p. 31. Two people died immediately in Chernobyl, and 31 more died in the first ten weeks. At least 200,000 cleanup workers were exposed to dangerous radiation levels. On the low side, an expert estimated 1,000 to 7,500 deaths in 50 years versus a high side estimate foreseeing 50,0000 to 250,000 deaths and an equal number outside the country where the doses were lower but the exposed population wider. See Felicity Barringer, "Chernobyl: The Danger Persists," *New York Times Magazine,* 14 April 1991. See also V. K. Sovchenko, *The Ecology of the Chernobyl Catastrophe* (New York: Parthenon, 1995), pp. 3, 330.

9. See Fred A. Wilcox, *Waiting for an Army to Die* (New York: Vintage, 1983), and Russell Mokhiber, *Corporate Crime and Violence: Big Business, Power, and the Abuse of the Public Trust* (San Francisco: Sierra Club Books, 1988).

10. There was a large radioactive leakage at the Windscale nuclear reprocessing plant in Britain in 1957. The United States had a near-meltdown at the Davie-Bess plant in Toledo in 1985, a shutdown of Rancho Seco plant in California because of an unlubricated valve, and a closing of the Philadelphia Peach Bottom plant after operators were found asleep at controls. Now in the Union of Concerned Scientists, Robert Pollard resigned as project manager for the NRC in 1976 after six years: "I became convinced that the NRC does not have protection of the public as its first priority. They act much as the old Atomic Energy Commission—promoting nuclear power first and worrying about safety of the public and disposal of waste somewhere down on their priority list"; Scott Mervis, "Nuke Lite," *The Chicago Reader,* 30 March 1990, p. 9. Also on the nuclear power industry see J. K. Jacobsen, *Dead Reckonings: Ideas, Interests and Politics in the "Information Age"* (Atlantic Highlands, N.J.: Humanities Press, 1997), pp. 53–81.

11. Upwards of 200,000 residents in Bhopal were affected. Union Carbide, a $5 billion company, paid $1 million in disaster relief, or about $5 per resident harmed; Mokhiber, *Corporate Crime and Violence,* pp. 1–36.

12. Jones, "Hazards for Export," p. 126.

13. Andre Gorz, *Paths to Paradise: On the Liberation from Work* (London: Pluto Press, 1985), p. 3; and Philip R. Pryde, *Environmental Management in the Soviet Union* (Cambridge: Cambridge University Press, 1991).

14. On racial and class discrimination see Daniel Faber, "Introduction," in Daniel Faber, ed., *The Struggle for Environmental Democracy: Environmental Justice Movements in the U.S.* (New York: Guilford Press, 1998), pp. ix, 3–7. Three quarters of hazardous wastes sites are located in poor communities where, when culprits are caught, the fines are a sixth of those levied in affluent white communities. Also see Robert Bullard, *Dumping in Dixie: Race, Class, and Environmental Quality* (Boulder: Westview Press, 1990).

15. Kirkpatrick Sale, "The Trouble with Earth Day," in Christopher Plant and Judith Plant, eds., *Green Business: Hope or Hoax?* (Philadelphia: New Society Publishers, 1991), p. 39.

16. Christopher Plant with David Albert, "Green Business in a Gray World: Can It be Done?" in Plant and Plant, eds., *Green Business*, p. 12.

17. Reid Lifset and Marian Chertow, "Changing the Waste Makers: Product Bans and the New Politics of Garbage," *American Prospect* 3 (Fall 1990): 87.

18. Ronnie D. Lipschutz, *Global Civil Society and Global Environmental Governance* (New York: SUNY Press, 1996), p. 264 n54.

19. Jones, "Hazards for Export," p. 120.

20. Faber cautions that the costly installation of pollution equipment or adjustments in industrial practices will not always produce a "win-win" outcome; there usually is strong resistance. See Faber, *The Struggle for Ecological Democracy*, p. 6.

21. John Barry, *Rethinking Green Politics* (London: Sage, 1999), pp. 160–163.

22. On progressive and popular branches of the American movement see Samuel P. Hays, *Conservation and the Gospel of Efficiency* (New York: Atheneum, 1954).

23. The contradiction may be purely a matter of appearance. On the affinity of Theodore Roosevelt and a bevy of American tycoons for eugenics, conservation, and rational management, see Donna Haraway, "Teddy Bear Partriarchy: Taxidermy in the Garden of Eden, New York City 1908–30," in her *Primate Visions: Gender, Race and Nature in the World of Modern Science* (New York: Routledge, 1989).

24. Ynestra King, "Toward an Ecological Feminism and a Feminist Ecology," in Joan Rothschild, ed., *Machina ex Dea: Feminist Perspectives on Technology* (New York: Pergamon, 1983), p. 119.

25. "Budget Fights Superfund Cleanups," *Chicago Tribune* 15 January 1996.

26. *Global 2000 Report to the President* (Washington, D.C.: Government Printing Office, 1980).

27. David Vogel, *National Styles of Regulation: Environmental Policy in Great Britain and the United States* (Ithaca: Cornell University Press, 1986), pp. 159, 174–175.

28. *Ibid.*, p. 22.

29. *Ibid.*, p. 147.

30. Marc Pallemaerts, "International Regulation and the Global Pesticides Market," in Sunderlal Bahuguna, Vandana Shiva, and M. N. Buch, eds., *Ecological Crisis and Sustainable Development* (Dehra Dun: Natraj Publishers, 1992), p. 728. On the United States see Faber, *The Struggle for Ecological Democracy*, p. 6.

31. Lee Davis, ed., *Environmental Disasters* (New York: Facts on File, 1998), p. 76.

32. *Ibid.*, p. 26.

33. See, for example, Ramachandra Guha, *The Unquiet Woods: Ecological Change and Peasant Resistance in India* (New Delhi: Oxford University Press, 1989).

34. Michael B. McElroy, Chris Nielson, and Peter Lydon, eds., *Energizing China: Reconciling Environmental Protection and Economic Growth* (Cambridge, Mass.: Harvard University Press, 1998), p. 20.

35. Laura Goering, "Global Warming May Bring More Epidemics," *Chicago Tribune* 13 February 1996, p. 4.

36. McElroy, Nielson, and Lydon, *Energizing China*, p. 4.

37. Richard Smith, "Creative Destruction: Capitalist Development and China's Environment," *New Left Review* 222 (March/April 1997): 11.

38. Cited in Ramachandra Guha, "Mahatma Gandhi and the Environmental Movement in India," in Arne Kalland and Gerard Persoon, eds., *Environmental Movements in Asia* (Richmond, Va.: Curzon Press, 1998), p. 69.

39. *Ibid.*, p. 28.

40. *Ibid.*, p. 6.

41. Davis, *Environmental Disasters*, p. 22.

42. Gary McCuen, ed., *Ecocide and Genocide in the Vanishing Forest* (Hudson, Wis.: Gem Publishers, 1993), p. 102.

43. Mercury poisoning stemming from gold exploration may be a bigger environmental threat than that of loss of oxygen. See Alexander Cockburn, "Interview with Susanna Hecht," *New Left Review* 173 (January/February 1989): 36. Also in the same issue see Susanna Hecht, "Chico Mendes: Chronicle of a Death Foretold."

44. McCuen, *Ecocide and Genocide in the Vanishing Forest*, p. 96.

45. Edward Goldsmith, "Economic Development: A False God," in Bahuguna et al., *Economic Crisis and Sustainable Development*, pp. 60–61.

46. See Peter Bunyard, "World Climate and Tropical Forest Destruction," in Bahuguna et al., *Economic Crisis and Sustainable Development;* and Helen Caufield, *In the Rain Forest* (Chicago: University of Chicago, rev ed 1991).

47. The Brundtland report of the World Commission on Environment and Development was published as *Our Common Future* (Oxford: Oxford University Press, 1987). Sustainable development was defined as "development which meets the needs of the present without compromising the ability of future generations to meet their own needs" (p. 43). In this vein see Albert Gore, *Earth in the Balance: Ecology and the Human Spirit* (London: Penguin, 1992). For a critique of their top-down, managerialist views, see Macnaghten and Urry, *Contested Natures*, pp. 212–216.

48. One ought not assume that premodern and/or non-Western people adore nature. "There is nothing in Asian perceptions that prepares people for a more environmentally friendly behavior" than anywhere else, write Arne Kalland and Gerard Persoon, "An Anthropological Perspective on Environmental Movements," in Kalland and Persoon, *Environmental Movements in Asia*, p. 6.

49. Elizabeth Dore, "Capitalism and Ecological Crisis: Legacy of the 1980s," in Helen Collinson, ed., *Green Guerrillas: Environmental Conflicts and Initiatives in Latin America and the Caribbean* (Nottingham: Latin American Bureau, 1996), p. 10.

50. *New York Times*, 12 May 1991, p. E4. See also Bruce Rich, *Mortgaging the Earth: The World Bank, Environmental Impoverishment and the Crisis of Development* (Boston: Beacon Press, 1994).

51. On this important theme see James C. Scott, *Seeing Like a State: How Certain Schemes to Improve the Human Condition Have Failed* (New Haven: Yale University Press, 1998).

52. Plant and Plant, *Green Business*, p. 12; Paul Wapner, "Politics Beyond the State," in Karen T. Litfin, ed., *The Greening of Sovereignty in World Politics* (Cambridge, Mass.: MIT Press, 1998), p. 516. \

53. Samantha Sanchez, "How the West Is Won: Astroturf Lobbying and the 'Wise Use' Movement," *American Prospect* 25 (March-April 1996): 37.

54. David Vogel notes that the "EPA officials appointed by the Nixon administration were certainly not particularly antagonistic to business. Indeed in 1969, the administration established the National Industrial Pollution Control Council, consisting of representatives of major companies and trade associations"; Vogel, *National Styles of Regulation*, p. 256.

55. See David Helvarg, *The War Against the Greens* (San Francisco: Sierra Club Books, 1994).

56. Sanchez, "How the West Is Won," p. 39.

57. For a poetic anarchist critique see Richard Frost, *The Social Gene: Evolution and Anarchism* (Cumbria: Cerberus Printing, 1998).

58. Andre Gorz, *Ecology as Politics* (Boston: South End Press, 1982), p. 20.

59. Barry, *Rethinking Green Politics*, p. 78.

60. Gorz, *Ecology as Politics*, p. 19.

61. *Ibid.*, p. 22.

62. *Ibid.*, p. 40. As pointed out in Chapter 2 there is the possibility of a capital savings-effect too, which is the capital-per-output ratio versus capital-intensity, which is the amount invested per worker employed. If capital cost per unit produced is lowered, the beneficial economic effect is enormous.

63. Lash et al., *Risk, Environment and Modernity*, p. 11.

64. Ted Benton, "Ecology, Socialism and the Mystery of Nature," *New Left Review* 194 (July-August 1992): 69. Also see Reiner Grundmann, "The Ecological Challenge to Marxism," *New Left Review* 187 (May-June 1991).

65. Derrick Jensen, *Listening to the Land* (San Francisco: Sierra Club Books, 1991), p. 21.

66. Hugh Stretton, *Capitalism, Socialism and the Environment* (Cambridge: Cambridge University Press, 1977), pp. 10, 11.

67. Lash et al., *Risk, Environment and Modernity*, p. 2. See also Daniel Bell, *The Cultural Contradictions of Capitalism* (New York: Basic Books, 1976).

68. Lash, Szerszynski, and Wynne, "Introduction: Ecology, Realism and Social Science," in Lash et al., *Risk, Environment and Modernity*, p. 5. Also see Scott, *Seeing Like a State*.

69. Ulrich Beck, *Ecological Enlightenment* (Atlantic Highlands, N.J.: Humanities Press, 1995), pp. 14, 66.

70. John Dryzek, "Political and Ecological Communication," in Dryzek and Schlosberg, *The Environmental Politics Reader*, p. 591. Also see John Dryzek, *Discursive Democracy* (Cambridge: Cambridge University Press, 1990), and his *Rational Ecology: Environment and Political Economy* (Oxford: Basil Blackwell, 1987).

71. Dryzek, "Political and Ecological Communication," in Dryzek and Schlosberg, *The Environmental Politics Reader*, p. 595.

72. See Beck, *The Risk Society* (London: Sage, 1992); on the modern individual's cultural impulsion to justify altruistic action in utilitarian terms, see Helmuth Berking, "Solidary Individualism: The Moral Impact of Cultural Modernization in Late Modernity," in Lash et al., *Risk, Environment and Modernity*, pp. 192–201.

73. Leon I. Lindberg, *The Energy Syndrome* (Lexington, Mass.: D. C. Heath, 1977), pp. 116–117.

74. Carolyn Merchant, *The Death of Nature: Women, Ecology and the Scientific Revolution* (New York: Harper & Row, 1980), p. 100.

75. King, "Toward a Feminist Ecology," p. 125.

76. Haraway, *Primary Visions*, p. 172.

77. King, "Toward a Feminist Ecology," p. 119.

78. Bookchin, *Remaking Society* (Montreal: Black Rose, 1990), p. 61.

79. Maria Mies and Vandan Shiva, *Ecofeminism* (London: Verso, 1993), and Irene Diamond and Gloria Fenan Orenstein, eds., *Reweaving the World: The Emergence of Ecofeminism* (San Francisco: Sierra Club Books, 1990).

80. Peter Newell and Matthew Paterson, "A Climate for Business: Global Warming, the State and Capital," *Review of International Political Economy* 5, 4 (Winter 1998): 681.

81. *Ibid.*, p. 696.

82. Arlene Broadhurst and Grant Ledgerwood, "Environmental Diplomacy of States, Corporations and Non-Governmental Organizations: The World Wide Web of Influence," *International Relations* 14, 2 (August 1998): 11.

83. Charles S. Maier, *In Search of Stability* (Cambridge: Cambridge University Press, 1987), p. 268.

84. Margaret Archer reminds us of "the quintessential reflective ability of human beings to fight back against their conditioning [which] gives them the capacity to respond with originality to the present context—either by taking advantage of inconsistencies within it and generating new forms of syncretism, or by exploring novel combinations of compatible elements"; Margaret Archer, *Culture and Agency: The Place of Culture in Social Theory* (Cambridge: Cambridge University Press, 1988), p. xxiv.

85. On the BSE case see the discussion in Macnaghten and Urry, *Contested Natures*, pp. 251–257.

86. *Ibid.*, p. 257.

87. For Bakunin's admonitions regarding scientific and technical elites see Sam Dogloff, ed., *Bakunin on Anarchy* (New York: Pantheon, 1977).

88. Sheila Jasonoff, "American Exceptionalism and the Political Acknowledgment of Risk," *Daedelus* 119, 4 (Fall 1990): 72; also see Vogel, *National Styles of Regulation*.

89. Jasonoff, "American Exceptionalism," p. 76.

90. *Ibid.*, p. 115.

91. Beck, *Ecological Enlightenment*, p. 6.

92. One recalls the stunted form of sincere praise bestowed on William Calley, the lieutenant in charge at the My Lai massacre in Vietnam, by his high school principal: "Rusty was not a brilliant boy, but he did what he was told"; quoted in Lewis Yablowsky, *Robopaths* (Indianapolis: Bobbs-Merrill, 1972), p. 126.

93. Theodore Roszak, *Where the Wasteland Ends* (Garden City, N.Y.: Doubleday, 1972), p. 400.

94. Brian Wynne, "May the Sheep Safely Graze?: A Reflexive Review of the Expert-Local Knowledge Division," in Lash et al., *Risk, Environment and Modernity*, pp. 60–67. Also see Scott, *Seeing Like a State*, pp. 309–341.

95. Barringer, "Chernobyl: The Danger Persists," p. 39.

96. Beck, *Ecological Enlightenment*, p. 124.

97. Laurie Flynn, Michael Gillard, and Andy Rowell, "Ousted Scientists and the Damning Research into Food Safety," *Guardian*, 12 February 1999, p. 6. The authors find that 77 percent of the British public favors the moratorium and 61 percent won't eat GM foods.

98. John Vidal, "Genetic Food Findings 'Biased,'" *Guardian*, 22 January 1999, p. 14. Five corporations controlled the biggest seed companies.

99. Ewan MacAskill and Tim Radford, "Blair Insist Sainsbury Stays," *Guardian*, 17 February 1999, p. 1.

100. "U.S. and Allies Block Treaty on Gene-Altered Goods," *New York Times*, 25 February 1999, p. C4.

101. Scientists worried, for instance, that "if a plant were given genes allowing it to produce a drug, insects could be exposed, with unknown results [or] a gene conferring insect resistance or drought tolerance could spread to weeds, creating super weeds"; *ibid.*

102. Lewis Mumford, *Technics and Civilization* (New York: Harcourt, Brace & World, 1934), p. 6.

103. Karl Marx, *Grundrisse* (New York: International Publishers, 1971), p. 734.

104. Grundmann, "The Ecological Challenge to Marxism," p. 111. He aptly cites Walter Benjamin's comment that technology should seek "not the mastery of nature but of the relation between nature and man."

105. *Ibid.*, pp. 10–11.

106. Dryzek, "Political and Ecological Communication," p. 588.

107. Alexander Cockburn, *The New Age Is in Us* (London: Verso, 1996), p. 279. "In Asia environmental issues are usually intimately linked to the question of social justice," Kalland and Persoon write. "For example, [a]lmost all Philippine environmental NGOs combine struggle for a better environment with social equity, cultural survival, poverty alleviation, peace and order, health and democratization. This is equally true for NGOs in countries such as Thailand and India"; Kalland and Persoon, *Environmental Movements in Asia*, p. 251.

108. Eugene S.Schwartz, *Overskill: The Decline of Technology in Civilization* (Chicago: Quadrangle Books, 1971), p. 254.

109. Gorz, *Strategy for Labor*, pp. 58, 62.

110. Norman I. Fainstein and Susan S Fainstein, "New Debates in Urban Planning: The Impact of Marxist Theory Within the United States," *International Journal of Urban and Regional Research* 3, 3 (September 1979): 399.

111. Charles Sabel, Archun Fung, and Bradley Karkkainen, "A New Environmentalism Takes Root," *Boston Review* 24, 5 (October/November 1999): 11.

Epilogue

In search of the elusive roots of the authoritarian personality Yale psychologist Stanley Milgram in the 1960s devised the so-called Eichmann experiments to identify conditions and traits that spurred the macabre compliance enabling the Nazi Holocaust. He did not have far to look: Americans turned out to be dismayingly "good Germans." His unwitting subjects frequently overruled their own consciences to inflict punitive pain on unseen subjects so long as the lab-coated authorities, who coaxed but did not coerce, took responsibility.[1] Asked what lesson he distilled from this disturbing exercise, Milgram boiled it down beautifully: If we unquestioningly accept alternatives as given to us by authorities, we are doomed.[2]

This volume emphasized that specialists cannot be counted on to act more reflectively or less fallibly than anyone else and therefore that democratic checks and balances upon (and healthy skepticism about) their claims is indispensable. Demonizing specialists for their misadventures is pointless: so too is the alibi that they were hapless victims of culturally imposed conceptions, which is another way of saying science can do no wrong. A certain degree of "historical empathy" is helpful so long as one is not lulled into accepting the actors' self-understanding of their actions. We can deduce from the Nuremberg trials, among other notorious venues, that human beings usually believe that they behave virtuously or the only way they could under the circumstances. The social mores, institutional structures, and professional codes within which people exist do condition their thoughts, attitudes, and actions, but there remains an inescapably moral dimension to the choices that they make. After all, science is supposed to be—and usually is—a disputatious, not unanimous, process of research.

Dilemmas often crumble, or else they are disclosed as tractable *problems*, when we question the legitimacy of the carefully crafted context in which they are presented. The dilemmas treated here are not fixed by nature or iron laws of economics or technological imperatives; they are transformable situations whose appearance as being fixed reflects the distribution of power and of certain animating ideas in our culture. One would not claim that these dilemmas are "all in our heads" or that they never occur. Power is not imaginary (although political power stems partly from legitimacy, which is "in our heads"). Those who wield power too often can convert even their fantastic schemes into "facts on the ground" while punishing any challengers of their legitimacy, but they cannot always do so successfully and without unforeseen consequences.[3]

Automating the Status Quo

Scarcity can be abolished, but the prospect of freedom from want is transformed in our current institutional context into a pervasive economic insecurity for the paycheck-to-paycheck majority, which occurs under the powerful guise of technical and competitive "necessities."[4] The "information revolution" rapidly is generating a two-tier economy of high-wage skilled employees versus a descending series of layers of less-skilled workers; a visible rupture is occurring between rates of GNP growth and general living standards. In the midst of the highly selective economic boom of the 1990s, selective even for middle-income earners, "if the lesser paid spouse were laid off, half the couples in the top one fourth of earners would fall into the middle half" (with incomes ranging from $20,000 to 60,000).[5] In 1996 ATT cut 40,000 jobs, and IBM cut 63,000. Sears shed 50,000 jobs since 1993 as the stock market galloped ahead on productivity generated by fewer people, more work heaped on the remainder, and by cutting muscle, not "fat."[6]

The widest gap in incomes since the Second World War did not happen by accident or by dint of technical change. Conservatives lobbied vigorously to create the very conditions and rules that business managers say they have no choice but to obey. As a consequence nearly all new wealth since Reagan's 1980 election flowed to the top one-fifth, who have 80 percent of total wealth (and the top 10 percent share rose from 61 percent in 1989 to 66.8 percent in 1994).[7] In Britain the top 10-percent share of total income rose 62 percent since 1979 while the bottom 10 percent fell 17 percent.[8] Technologies do not spontaneously appear in puffs of smoke with a "downsizing" or "ecological" impetus mystically inscribed in their innards: These impetuses get implanted at the design stage in a skewed market economy inside class societies.

The press applauds the "great American job machine," but as an increasingly typical American worker retorted, "What's so great about these jobs—I have two or three of them." Beck reminds us that only two decades ago 80 percent of German and British workers had full-time benefit-laden jobs whereas today a third of Britain's labor and only 60 percent in Germany are so well situated. The rate of creation of high-paying jobs was identical in Germany and the United States; the difference has been America's "Macwage" job creation. Differences in training yielded a German productivity rate four times that of the United States over 25 years (100 percent versus 25 percent). So firms exported jobs and income from the same society they expect to thrive in.[9] This contradiction harks back to labor leaders pointedly chiding industrialists, Who will buy your products and therefore assure your prosperity if your workers can't afford them?

The costs of economic transformation ought to be charged against those who benefit by applying some of the gains from increasing productivity to the adjustment process. A "right-to-work concept which assured employment opportunity to all without loss of accrued rights is the best preventative of resistance to necessary technological and economic change."[10] If the policy objective is only to force private firms to internalize externalities, Gorz warns, this will raise consumer costs and preserve the system as is unless it is "being challenged at all levels by alternative social practices and an alternative vision of human civilization."[11] A revived Third World dynamism also is needed to propel the growth and export rates needed to offset productivity improvements and keep the same level of jobs—which will entail more debt relief. (Between 1990 and 1993 Zambia, for instance, spent 35 times more on debt payments than on education.[12]) A carbon tax on big polluters is an option, and a "Tobin tax" to curb foreign exchange speculation might curb corporate-defined globalization.

Is there a politically viable way other than full employment, progressive tax reform, and an extension of social amenities to spread the benefits of automation? Emphatically, no. Theda Skocpol has it right that any progressive program must be couched in terms incorporating prevailing values (especially the "work ethic").[13] This guideline means that delivery of the benefits of growth should occur through proportionate reductions in work time and/or through expanded universal amenities, like health care or education. A full-employment program can be sustained and at the same time can demonstrate that "everyone could work less provided everyone worked."[14]

Arms and Influence

Why do U.S. and British governments subsidize the armaments industry (and air transport, agriculture, shipping, railroads, and oil) but not labor?[15] During the 1995–1996 election the top twenty-five arms manufacturers shelled out $6.5 million in campaign contributions—two-thirds to Republicans—that helped to thwart the Hatfield bill to restrict arms sales to human rights offenders.[16] Meanwhile, concentration continued: Lockheed Martin bought the Loral Corporation for $10 billion in January 1996; earlier, the Northrop Grumman Corporation bought the defense electronics segment of Westinghouse Electric.[17]

Long before Kosovo, President Clinton requested an additional $112 billion to feed the Pentagon during the period 1999–2005. After rebuffing Re-

publican efforts to mandate a missile defense system by 2003, Clinton relented and permitted a partial Star Wars system. His administration
chipped in $6.6 billion to a missile defense research program, which cumu-
latively consumed three times more than the Manhattan Project without
yielding a single usable weapon.[18] Two of fifteen test flights succeeded, and
every test since 1992 failed. In March 1999 the Senate, undaunted, voted
97–3 in favor of the system.

Kosovo became another expertly edited aerial display of tax dollars at
work (and diverted from health care, education, and social programs).
Newspapers dutifully printed insets of $2-billion B-2 bombers blazing
from Missouri to Serbia. The cranky perception surged among an indignant
portion of tax-payers: Why amass this lavish arsenal if we shrink from using it as we please? Afterward, reined in for years by budget deficit politics,
the Pentagon pounced on the (technical) budget surplus to put in even more
appropriations requests. "Here we go again," sighed rear Admiral (ret.) Eugene Carroll of the Center for Defense Information. We "already spend
substantially more for military forces than any other nation, with no significant threats to our national security. We're engaged in an arms race with
ourselves," he notes.[19]

Mean Genes

Genetics and warfare predictably mix in frightful ways. In 1999 the British
Medical Association (BMA) reported that genetic weapons were under development that could attack ethnic groups with diseases designed to ig-
nite—like proximity fuses—in the presence of certain groupings of genes
(e.g., sickle cell).[20] The BMA cites evidence of this customized killer disease
research conducted in Iraq, in South Africa under apartheid, and in the former Soviet Union. In a world teeming with interethnic violence, the temptations to use such a weapon are almost irresistible, and there accordingly is a
need to strengthen the 1972 Biological Weapons and Toxins regime, which
unlike the Chemical Weapons convention contains no provisions for inspection. This research represents, the BMA stated, a "threat to the existence of *Homo sapiens* and a development of biotechnology which perverts
the humanitarian nature of science: 'It is all the more frightening that medical professionals may contribute, willingly or unwittingly, to the development of new, potent weapons. This potential for malign use of biomedical
knowledge also places responsibility on doctors and scientists to protect the
integrity of their work.'"[21]

No barrier against abuse could be flimsier than that of reliance on self-
policing professions. Neither "tragically misled figures" nor aberrations,
the Nazi doctors were the "cream of their profession" and expressive of its
scientific beliefs.[22] One finds people in every field who out of opportunism

or ideology or monomania will perform morally repellent lines of research. Even the most conservative profession can swing into amoral pragmatism during economic crises such as Germany had in the 1930s. Much of this professional and moral malleability lies in a common attitude:

> Technology seduces the physician, who is continually confronted with the imperfect, unpredictable human being, to escape into the apparently safe world of laboratory parameters and computer scans. In the Weimar republic many physicians complained about the decay of modern medicine to a purely diagnostic science. Under the Nazis, it was as if an already weak dam had broken.[23]

The shrewdest bet usually is to predict the future on the basis of present trends, trends that seem far from favorable. Corporate capital strives to do what it pleases; the world's only superpower bombards whomever it likes; genetics engineers strain to clone citizens with great complexions and gutted souls. Shrewd bets fortunately have often been wrong. Ask the Russian czars or General William Westmoreland or the former leaders of Eastern bloc nations.

Predictions are projections of present trends and can exert, as Arendt noted, "a hypnotic effect; they put to sleep our common sense."[24] But participation in political contests or ecological struggles is itself a transformative condition that makes possible "changes in perspective and attitude, especially if the political struggle is well chosen and well organized."[25] In science policy today the spectacle of "dueling experts" is commonplace, and citizens accordingly are becoming savvier in picking their way through the cases that these warring authorities make in order to incorporate them into deliberative decisionmaking processes. Instrumental rationality, by contrast, smothers truly critical perspectives, which encompass our aspirations for emancipation from unnecessary toil, from rampant or rigged markets, from arbitrary or biased authorities, and from racial and gender oppression. There is no single map or blueprint. The social goal worth working for through innumerable trials and errors and setbacks remains the construction of a genuinely rational society where it will be dilemmas such as these, not utopian promises, that are made to be broken.

Notes

1. See Stanley Milgram, *Obedience to Authority* (New York: Harper & Row, 1974).

2. Interview with Stanley Milgram, *Psychology Today* 8, 1 (June 1974): 80.

3. James C. Scott, *Seeing Like a State: How Certain Schemes to Improve the Human Condition Have Failed* (New Haven: Yale University Press, 1998), p. 47.

4. Herbert Marcuse, *Negations: Essays in Critical Theory* (Boston: Beacon Press, 1968), p. xix.

5. "Squeezing a Lot into the Middle Class," *New York Times*, 18 May 1997, p. E6.

6. William Raspberry, "Technology Phases Out Job Security," *Chicago Tribune*, 9 January 1996, p. 13.

7. Keith Bradsher, "Rich Control More of US Wealth, Study Says, as Debts Grow for Poor" *New York Times*, 22 June 1996, p. B1. The top 1 percent increased their wealth from $2.7 trillion in 1982 to $6.9 trillion by 1995, or from 30 percent to 40 percent of total national assets. They improved $4.2 trillion in just thirteen years, whereas national debt rose $4.1 trillion. See Leon Friedman, "A Snare-the-Wealth Tax," *Nation*, 1 June 1997, p. 23.

8. Nicholas Timmins, "Fewer Poor—A Tall Tory Tale?" *Independent*, 30 June 1996, p. 1.

9. Ulrich Beck, "Capitalism Without Work," *Dissent* (Winter 1997): 50.

10. Gary Magnum, ed., *The Manpower Revolution: Its Policy Consequences— Excerpts from the Senate Hearings Before the Clark Subcommittee* (Garden City, N.Y.: Doubleday, 1965), p. 264.

11. Andre Gorz, *Ecology as Politics* (Boston: South End Press, 1982), p. 7.

12. *Guardian*, 1 July 1996, p. 15.

13. Theda Skocpol, "Targeting with Universalism: Politically Viable Policies to Combat Poverty in the US," in Christopher Jencks and Paul Peterson, eds., *The Urban Underclass* (Washington, D.C.: Brookings Institution, 1991).

14. Gorz, *Ecology as Politics*, p. 41.

15. Victor Keegan, *Guardian*, 19 January 1996, p. 11.

16. *Nation*, 9 December 1996, p. 7.

17. *Chicago Tribune*, 1 September 1996, Section 3, p. 1.

18. Ira Schorr, "Phantom Menace: The Pentagon Budget Shoots for the Stars," *In These Times*, 7 March 1999, p. 16.

19. *Ibid.*, p. 15.

20. Sarah Boseley, "BMA Sounds Genetic Weapons Alarm," and David Beresford, "South Africans Were Working on Blacks-Only Germ," *Guardian*, 22 January 1999, p. 2. The weapons research program at Roodeplaat laboratory was under the direction of President Botha's personal cardiologist, Wouter Basson.

21. *Ibid.*

22. Gotz Aly, Peter Chroust, and Christian Pross, *Cleansing the Fatherland: Nazi Medicine and Racial Hygiene* (Baltimore: Johns Hopkins University Press, 1994), p. 5.

23. *Ibid.*, p. 2.

24. Hannah Arendt, *On Violence* (New York: Harcourt, Brace & World, 1969), pp. 7–8.

25. Norman Diamond, "The Copernican Revolution: Social Foundations of Conceptualization in Science," in Les Levidow, *Science as Politics* (London: Free Association Books, 1986), p. 35.

Selected Bibliography

Books

Adams, Sam. *War of Numbers: An Intelligence Memoir*. South Royalton, Vt.: Steelforth Press, 1994.

Addison, Paul, and Angus Calder, eds. *Time to Kill: The Soldier's Experience of War in the West*. London: Pimlico, 1997.

Allen, Thomas B. *War Games*. New York: McGraw-Hill, 1987.

Allison, Graham. *Essence of Decision: Explaining the Cuban Missile Crisis*. Boston: Little, Brown, 1971.

Aly, Gotz, Peter Chroust, and Christian Pross. *Cleansing the Fatherland: Nazi Medicine and Racial Hygiene*. Baltimore: Johns Hopkins University Press, 1994.

Ames, Mary. *Outcome Uncertain: Science and the Political Process*. Washington, D.C.: Communications Press, 1977.

Appiah, K. Anthony, and Amy Guttman. *Color Conscious: The Political Morality of Race*. Princeton: Princeton University Press, 1996.

Appleyard, Bryan. *Brave New Worlds: Genetics and the Human Experience*. London: Viking, 1999.

Archer, Margaret. *Culture and Agency: The Place of Culture in Social Theory*. Cambridge: Cambridge University Press, 1988.

Arendt, Hannah. *The Human Condition*. Chicago: University of Chicago, 1962.

_____. *On Violence*. New York: Harcourt, Brace & World, 1969.

Aronowitz, Stanley, and William DiFazio, *The Jobless Future: Sci-Tech and the Dogma of Work*. Minneapolis: University of Minnesota Press, 1994.

Bahguna, Sunderlal, Vandana Shiva, and M. N. Buch, eds. *Ecological Crisis and Sustainable Development*. Dehra Dun: Natraj Publishers, 1992.

Bailes, Kendall. *Technology and Society Under Lenin and Stalin*. Princeton: Princeton University Press, 1978.

Bailey, Brian J. *The Luddite Rebellion*. New York: New York University Press, 1998.

Balassa, George. *The Evolution of Technology*. Cambridge: Cambridge University Press, 1988.

Barnet, Richard J. *Economy of Death*. New York: Atheneum, 1969.

Bartov, Omer. *The Eastern Front, 1941–45: German Troops and The Barbarisation of Warfare*. London: Macmillan, 1985.

_____. *Hitler's Army: Soldiers, Nazis, and War in the Third Reich*. Oxford: Oxford University Press, 1991.

Beck, Ulrich. *The Risk Society*. London: Sage, 1992.

_____. *Ecological Enlightenment*. Atlantic Highlands, N.J.: Humanities Press, 1996.

Bell, Daniel. *The End of Ideology*. Glencoe, Ill.: Free Press, 1956.

_____. *The Coming of Post-Industrial Society*. London: Penguin, 1973.

_____. *The Cultural Contradictions of Capitalism*. London: Penguin, 1976.

Ben-David, Joseph. *The Scientist's Role in Society*. New York: Prentice-Hall, 1972.

Bendix, Reinhard. *Max Weber: An Intellectual Portrait*. New York: Doubleday, 1962.

_____. *Work and Authority in Industry: Ideologies of Management in the Course of Industrialization*. Berkeley: University of California, 1974.

Beres, Louis Rene. *Apocalypse*. Chicago: University of Chicago, 1980.

Bernal, J. D. *The Social Function of Science*. London: Macmillan, 1939.

Bettelheim, Bruno. *The Empty Fortress*. New York: Free Press, 1967.

Bettelheim, Bruno, and Alvin Rosenfeld. *The Art of the Obvious*. New York: Thames and Hudson, 1993.

Bever, Martin, ed. *Resistance to New Technology: Nuclear power, Information Technology, and Biotechnology*. Cambridge: Cambridge University Press, 1995.

Block, N. J., and Gerald Dworkin, eds. *The IQ Controversy: Critical Readings*. New York: Pantheon, 1976.

Bottomore, Tom, and Maximilien Rubel, eds. *Karl Marx: Selected Writings on Sociology and Social Philosophy*. London: Penguin, 1961.

Brantlinger, Ellen. *Sterilization of People with Mental Disabilities: Issues, Perspectives, and Causes*. Westport, Conn: Auburn House, 1995.

Braverman, Harry. *Labor and Monopoly Capital: The Degradation of Work in The Twentieth Century*. New York: Monthly Review Press, 1974.

Breggin, Peter R. *Toxic Psychiatry*. New York: St. Martin's Press, 1991.

British Medical Association. *Human Genetics: Choice and Responsibility*. Oxford: Oxford University Press, 1998.

Broad, William J. *Teller's War*. New York: Simon & Schuster, 1992.

Broberg, Gunnar, and Nils Roll-Hansen, eds. *Eugenics and the Welfare State: Sterilization Policy in Denmark, Sweden, Norway and Finland*. East Lansing: Michigan State University Press, 1996.

(Brundtland report.) *Our Common Future*. Oxford: Oxford University Press, 1987.

Brzezinski, Zbigniew. *Between Two Ages: America's Role in the Technetronic Arena*. New York: Viking Press, 1970.

Buckingham, Walter. *Automation: Its Impact on Business and People*. New York: Mentor, 1965.

Bullard, Robert. *Dumping in Dixie: Race, Class, and Environmental Quality*. Boulder: Westview Press, 1990.

Burtt, E. A. *The Metaphysical Foundations of Modern Science*. London: Compton, 1932.

Bush, Vannevar. *Science: The Endless Frontier*. Washington, D.C.: National Science Foundation, 1960; first published 1945.

_____. *Modern Arms and Free Man*. Cambridge, Mass.: MIT Press, 1968; first published 1949.

Buzzance, Robert. *Masters of War: Military Dissent and Politics in the Vietnam Era.* Cambridge: Cambridge University Press, 1996.

Calder, Nigel. *Technopolis.* New York: Simon & Schuster, 1969.

Calvocoressi, Peter, Guy Wint, and John Pritchard. *Total War: The Causes and Consequences of the Second World War.* 2d ed. London: Viking, 1989.

Cattell, R. B. *The Fight for Our National Intelligence.* London: P.S. King & Son, Ltd., 1937.

Caufield, Helen. *In the Rain Forest.* Rev. Ed. Chicago: University of Chicago, 1991.

Chomsky, Noam. *American Power and the New Mandarins.* New York: Vintage, 1969.

_____. *For Reasons of State.* New York: Pantheon, 1975.

_____. *Deterring Democracy.* New York: Verso, 1992.

Clay, Catrine, and Michael Leapman. *Master Race: The Lebensborn Experiment in Nazi Germany.* London: Hodder & Stoughton, 1995.

Cockburn, Alexander. *The New Age Is in Us.* London: Verso, 1995.

Cockburn, Alexander, and Ken Silverstein. *Washington Babylon.* New York: Verso, 1996.

Cohen, Stephen S., and John Zysman. *Manufacturing Matters: The Myth of the Post-Industrial Economy.* New York: Basic Books, 1987.

Cole, Leonard A. *Politics and the Restraint of Science.* Totowa, N.J.: Rowman & Allanheld, 1983.

Collins, Harry, and Trevor Pinch. *The Golem: What You Should Know About Science.* Cambridge: Cambridge University Press, 1993.

_____. *The Golem at Large: What You Should Know About Technology.* Cambridge: Cambridge University Press, 1998.

Collinson, Helen, ed. *Green Guerrillas: Environmental Conflicts and Initiatives in Latin America and the Carribean.* Nottingham: Latin American Bureau, 1996.

Cowan, Ruth Schwartz. *More Work for Mother: The World of Household Technology from the Open Hearth to the Microwave.* New York: Basic Books, 1983.

Cox, Ronald, ed. *Business and the State in International Relations.* Boulder: Westview Press, 1996.

Crick, Bernard. *In Defence of Politics.* London: Penguin, 1962.

Crozier, Michel. *The Bureaucratic Phenomenon.* Chicago: University of Chicago Press, 1967.

Cumings, Bruce. *The Origins of the Korean War: The Roaring of the Cataract.* Vol. 2. Princeton: Princeton University Press, 1990.

Curtis, L. Perry. *Apes and Angels: The Irishman in Victorian Caricature.* Washington, D.C.: Smithsonian Institution, 1971.

Cyert, Richard, and David Mowery. *Technology and Employment: Innovation and Growth in the U.S. Economy.* Washington, D.C.: National Academy Press, 1987.

Dahrendorf, Rolf. *Class and Class Conflict in Industrial Society.* Stanford: Stanford University Press, 1959.

Darwin, Leonard. *The Need for Eugenic Reform.* London: John Murray, 1926.

Davis, Lee, ed. *Environmental Disasters.* New York: Facts on File, 1998.

Dawkins, Richard. *The Selfish Gene.* New York: Oxford Unversity Press, 1976.

Dechert, Charles. *The Social Impact of Cybernetics*. New York: Simon & Schuster, 1965.

Degler, Carl N. *In Search of Human Nature: The Decline and Revival of Social Darwinism in American Social Thought*. Oxford: Oxford University Press, 1991.

DeGrasse, Robert W. *Military Expansion, Economic Decline: The Impact of U.S. Military Spending on U.S. Economic Performance*. New York: M. E. Sharpe, 1983.

DeLanda, Manuel. *War in the Age of Intelligent Machines*. New York: Zone Books, 1991.

Del Tridici, Robert. *At Work in the Fields of the Bomb*. New York: Harper & Row, 1987.

de Tocqueville, Alexis. *Democracy in America*. New York: Doubleday, 1969.

Diebold, John. *Automation*. Princeton: Von Norstrand, 1952.

Dogloff, Sam, ed. *Bakunin on Anarchy*. New York: Knopf, 1972.

Dosi, Giovanni, Christopher Freeman, Richard Nelson, Gerald Silverberg, and Luc Soete, eds. *Technical Innovation and Economic Change*. London: Frances Pinter, 1991.

Douhet, Giulio. *The Command of the Air*. London: Faber and Faber, 1943; first published 1921.

Dower, John. *War Without Mercy: Race and War in the Pacific*. New York: Pantheon, 1986.

Dryzek, John. *Rational Ecology*. Oxford: Basil Blackwell, 1987.

_____. *Discursive Democracy*. Cambridge: Cambridge University Press, 1992.

Dryzek, John, and David Schlosberg, eds. *The Environmental Politics Reader*. Oxford: Oxford University Press, 1998.

Duster, Troy. *Backdoor to Eugenics*. New York: Routledge, 1990.

Easlea, Brian. *Fathering the Unthinkable: Masculinity, Scientists and the Modern Arms Race*. London: Pluto Press, 1983.

Eckholm, Erik P. *Down to Earth: Environment and Human Needs*. New York: Norton, 1982.

Edgerton, David H. *England and the Aeroplane: An Essay on a Militant and Technological Nation*. London: Macmillan, 1991.

Ehrenreich, Barbara. *Blood Rites*. New York: Henry Holt, 1997.

Ellis, John. *Brute Force: Allied Strategy and Tactics in the Second World War*. London: Andre Deutsch, 1990.

_____. *The Social History of the Machine Gun*. New York: Pantheon, 1976.

Ellul, Jacques. *The Technological Society*. New York: Knopf, 1964.

Erenberg, Lewis A., and Susan E. Hirsch, eds. *The War in American Culture: Society and Consciousness During World War II*. Chicago: University of Chicago, 1996.

Evangelista, Matthew. *Innovation and the Arms Race*. Ithaca: Cornell University Press, 1988.

Ewald, William R., ed. *Environment and Change: The Next Fifty Years*. Bloomington: Indiana University Press, 1968.

Ezrahi, Yaron, ed. *Technology, Pessimism and Postmodernism*. Amherst, Mass.: University of Massachusetts Press, 1995.

Faber, Dennis, ed. *The Struggle for Environmental Democracy: Environmental Justice Movements in the U.S.* New York: Guilford Press, 1998.

Falk, Richard A., Gabriel Kolko, and Robert Jay Lifton, eds. *Crimes of War*. New York: Vintage, 1971.

Fallows, James. *National Defense*. New York: Random House, 1981.

Ferkiss, Victor. *Technological Man: The Myth and the Reality*. New York: Mentor Books, 1968.

_____. *The Future of Technological Civilization*. New York: Oxford University Press, 1974.

Feyerabend, Paul. *Against Method*. London: New Left Books, 1975.

Finkelstein, Norman G., and Ruth Bettina Birn. *A Nation on Trial: The Goldhagen Thesis and Historical Truth*. New York: Henry Holt, 1998.

Fitzgerald, Frances. *Fire in the Lake*. Boston: Little, Brown, 1972.

Foerstel, Herbert N. *Secret Science: Federal Control of American Science and Technology*. Westport, Conn.: Praeger, 1997.

Forman, Paul, and Jose M. Sanchez-Ron, eds. *National Military Establishments and the Advancement of Science and Technology: Studies in 20th Century Science*. Dordrecht: Kluwer Academic Publishers, 1996.

Forsberg, Randall, ed. *The Arms Production Dilemma: Contraction and Restraint in the World Combat Aircraft Industry*. Cambridge, Mass.: MIT Press, 1994.

Foucault, Michel. *The Archeology of Knowledge*. New York: Random House, 1962.

_____. *Madness and Civilization*. New York: Random House, 1965.

Franklin, Bruce. *War Stars: The Superweapon and the American Imagination*. Oxford: Oxford University Press, 1988.

Freeman, Christopher, John Clark, and Luc Soete. *Unemployment and Technical Innovation*. London: Frances Pinter, 1982.

Friedlander, Henry. *The Origins of Nazi Genocide: From Euthanasia to the Final Solution*. Chapel Hill: University of North Carolina, 1995.

Friedman, David. *Misunderstood Miracle*. Ithaca: Cornell University Press, 1988.

Fromm, Erich. *Escape from Freedom*. New York: Rhinehart, 1941.

Frost, Richard. *The Social Gene and the Survival of the Fit Enough: Evolution and Anarchism*. Cumbria: Cerberus Printing, 1998.

Fulbrook, Mary. *The Fontana History of Germany: The Divided Nation, 1918–1990*. London: Fontana, 1991.

Fuller, J.C.F. *Armaments and History*. New York: Da Capo Press, 1945.

Galbraith, John Kenneth. *The Galbraith Reader*. London: Andre Deutsch, 1987.

_____. *Culture of Contentment*. Boston: Houghton Mifflin, 1992.

Galton, Francis. *Hereditary Genius: An Inquiry into Its Laws and Consequences*. London: Macmillan & Company, 1869.

Geertz, Clifford. *The Interpretation of Cultures*. New York: Basic Books, 1973.

Gibson, James William. *The Perfect War*. New York: Atlantic Monthly Press, 1986.

Gilman, Sander. *Sexuality*. New York: John Wiley & Son, 1989.

_____. *The Case of Sigmund Freud: Medicine and Identity at the Fin de Siecle*. Baltimore: Johns Hopkins, 1993.

Global 2000 Report to the President. Washington, D.C.: Government Printing Office, 1980.

Gobineau, Count Grafen. *Essays on the Dissimilarity of the Human Race.* Stuttgart: F. Fromans Publishers, 1922.

Goldstein, Joshua. *Long Cycles: Prosperity and War in the Modern Age.* New Haven: Yale University Press, 1988.

Gordon, David M., Michael Reich, and Richard Edwards. *Segmented Work, Divided Workers: The Historical Transformation of Labor in the United States.* Cambridge: Cambridge University Press, 1982.

Gore, Albert. *Earth in the Balance: Ecology and the Human Spirit.* London: Penguin, 1992.

Gorz, Andre. *Strategy for Labor: A Radical Proposal.* Boston: Beacon Press, 1964.

_____. *Ecology as Politics.* Boston: South End Press, 1982.

_____. *Paths to Paradise: On the Liberation from Work.* London: Pluto Press, 1985.

Gould, Stephen Jay. *The Mismeasure of Man.* London: Penguin, 1981.

Gray, Chris Hables. *Postmodern War: The New Politics of Conflict.* London: Guilford Press, 1997.

Green, Philip. *Deadly Logic: The Theory of Nuclear Deterrence.* New York: Schocken Books, 1968.

_____. *The Pursuit of Inequality.* New York: Pantheon, 1981.

Grieder, William. *One World, Ready or Not.* New York: Simon & Schuster, 1997.

Grossman, Lt. Col. Dave. *On Killing: The Psychological Cost of Learning to Kill in War and Society.* New York: Little, Brown, 1995.

Guha, Ramachandra. *The Unquiet Woods: Ecological Change and Peasant Resistance in India.* New Delhi: Oxford University Press, 1989.

Gusterson, Hugh. *Nuclear Rites: A Weapons Laboratory at the End of the Cold War.* Berkeley: University of California, 1996.

Haber, L. F. *The Poisonous Cloud: Chemical Warfare in the First World War.* Oxford: Clarendon Press, 1986.

Haber, Samuel. *Efficiency and Uplift: Scientific Mangement in the Progressive Era.* Chicago: University of Chicago, 1964.

Habermas, Jurgen. *Toward a Rational Society.* Boston: Beacon Press, 1984.

_____. *The Theory of Communicative Action.* Boston: Beacon Press, 1984.

Halberstam, David. *The Best and the Brightest.* New York: Vintage, 1975.

Haldane, J.B.S. *Heredity and Politics.* New York: Norton, 1938.

Haller, John S., and Robin M. Haller. *The Physician and Sexuality in Victorian America.* Champaign: University of Illinois, 1974.

Hansen, J. T., A. Susan Owen, and Michael Patrick Madden. *Parallels: The Soldier's Knowledge and the Oral History of Contemporary Warfare.* Hawthorne, N.Y.: Aldine De Gruyter, 1992.

Harding, Sandra. *The Science Question in Feminism.* Ithaca: Cornell University Press, 1986.

Hart, David M. *Forged Consensus: Science, Technology and Economic Policy in the United States, 1921–53.* Princeton: Princeton University Press, 1998.

Hasian, Marouf Arif Jr. *The Rhetoric of Eugenics in Anglo-American Thought.* Athens: University of Georgia, 1996.

Hawley, T. M. *Against the Fires of Hell: The Environmental Disaster of the Gulf War.* New York: Harcourt, Brace, Jovanovich, 1992.

Hays, Samuel P. *Conservation and the Gospel of Efficiency.* New York: Atheneum, 1954.

Hearne, R. P. *Aerial Warfare.* London: John Lane Cooper Publishers, 1909.

Helvarg, David. *The War Against the Greens.* San Francisco: Sierra Club, 1994.

Hendersen, Jeffery. *The Globalization of High Technology.* London: Routledge, 1989.

Henry, Clarissa, and Marc Hillel. *Of Pure Blood.* New York: McGraw-Hill, 1976.

Henry, Jules. *On Sham, Vulnerability, and Other Forms of Self-Destruction.* New York: Vintage, 1973.

Hernnstein, Richard, and Charles Murray. *The Bell Curve: Intelligence and the Uses of Human Heredity.* New York: Free Press, 1994.

Hersh, Seymour. *My Lai 4: A Report on the Massacre and Its Aftermath.* New York: Random House, 1970.

_____. *The Dark Side of Camelot.* New York: Little, Brown, 1998.

Hobsbawm, Eric J. *The Age of Capital, 1848–1877.* London: Weidenfeld and Nicolson, 1975.

_____. *The Age of Extremes: The Short Twentieth Century, 1914–1991.* London: Abacus, 1994.

Holloway, David. *Stalin and the Bomb: The Soviet Union and Atomic Energy, 1939–1956.* New Haven: Yale University Press, 1994.

Holmes, Richard. *Firing Line.* London: Jonathan Cape, 1985.

Hubbard, Ruth, and Elijah Wald. *Exploding the Gene Myth.* Boston: Beacon Press, 1993.

Hughes, H. Stuart. *Consciousness and Society.* New York: Knopf, 1958.

Inglehart, Ronald. *Culture Shift in Advanced Industrial Society.* Princeton: Princeton University Press, 1992.

Jacob, Margaret C., ed. *The Politics of Western Science, 1640–1990.* Atlantic Highlands, N.J.: Humanities Press, 1994.

Jacobsen, J. K. *Dead Reckonings: Ideas, Interests and Politics in the "Information Age."* Atlantic Highlands, N.J.: Humanities Press, 1997.

Jencks, Christopher, and Meredith Phillips, eds. *The Black-White Test Score Gap.* Washington, D.C.: Brookings Institution, 1998.

Jensen, Derrick. *Listening to the Land.* San Francisco: Sierra Club, 1991.

Jones, James H. *Bad Blood: The Tuskegee Syphilis Experiment.* New York: Free Press, 1981.

Juenger, Friedrich Georg. *The Failure of Technology.* Chicago: Henry Regnery Press, 1956.

Jungk, Robert. *Brighter Than a Thousand Suns.* Rev. Ed. New York: Penguin, 1982.

Kahn, Herman. *Thinking About the Unthinkable.* New York: Horizon, 1962.

_____. *On Escalation: Metaphors and Scenarios.* New York: Praeger, 1965.

Kakir, Sudhir. *Frederick Winslow Taylor: A Study in Personality and Innovation.* Cambridge, Mass.: MIT Press, 1970.

Kamin, Leon. *The Science and Politics of IQ.* Potomac, Md.: Erlbaum Publishers, 1974.

Kamin, Leon J., Richard C. Lewontin, and Steven Rose. *Not in Our Genes: Biology, Ideology and Human Nature.* London: Pelican, 1984.

Kanigel, Robert. *The One Best Way*. New York: Viking, 1997.
Kaplan, Fred. *Wizards of Armageddon*. New York: Simon & Schuster, 1983.
Katsiaficas, George, ed. *Vietnam Documents: American and Vietnamese Views of the War*. London: M. E. Sharpe, 1992.
Katzenstein, Peter, ed. *The Culture of National Security*. New York: Columbia University Press, 1996.
Kearny, Hugh. *Science and Change, 1500–1700*. London: Weidenfeld & Nicolson, 1971.
Keegan, John. *The First World War*. London: Hutchinson, 1998.
Kevles, Daniel. *In the Name of Eugenics: Genetics and the Uses of Human Heredity*. New York: Knopf, 1985.
Kevles, Daniel, and Leroy Hood, eds. *The Code of Codes: Scientific and Social Issues in the Human Genome Project*. Cambridge, Mass.: Harvard University Press, 1993.
Kimball, Jeffrey. *Nixon's Vietnam War*. Lawrence: University of Kansas Press, 1998.
Kolko, Gabriel. *Anatomy of a War: Vietnam, the United States and the Modern Historical Experience*. New York: Pantheon, 1985.
_____. *Century of War: Politics, Conflicts and Society Since 1914*. New York: New Press, 1994.
Kuhl, Steven. *The Nazi Connection: Eugenics, American Racism and German National Socialism*. New York: Oxford University Press, 1994.
Kuhn, Thomas S. *The Structure of Scientific Revolutions*. Chicago: University of Chicago, 1962.
Lakatos, Imre, and Alan Musgrave, eds. *Criticism and the Growth of Knowledge*. Cambridge: Cambridge University Press, 1969.
Larson, Edward J. *Sex, Race and Science: Eugenics in the Deep South*. Baltimore: Johns Hopkins University, 1995.
Lash, Scott, Bronislaw Szerszynski, and Brian Wynne, eds. *Risk, Environment and Modernity: Towards a New Ecology*. London: Sage, 1996.
Latour, Bruno. *Science in Action*. Milton Keynes: Open University Press, 1987.
Latour, Bruno, and Stephen Woolgar. *Laboratory Life: The Construction of Scientific Fact*. 2d ed. Princeton: Princeton University Press, 1986.
Levidow, Les. *Science as Politics*. London: Free Association Books, 1986.
Lewontin, Richard. *The Doctrine of DNA: Biology as Ideology*. London: Penguin, 1993.
Liepitz, Alain. *Mirages and Miracles: The Crisis of Global Fordism*. London: Verso, 1987.
Lifton, Robert J. *History and Human Survival*. New York: Random House, 1970.
_____. *The Nazi Doctors*. New York: Basic Books, 1986.
Lindberg, Leon I. *The Energy Syndrome*. Lexington, Mass: D. C. Heath, 1977.
Litfin, Karen T., ed. *The Greening of Sovereignty in World Politics*. Cambridge, Mass.: MIT Press, 1998.
Littauer, Raphael, and Norman Uphoff, eds. *The Air War in Indochina*. Boston: Beacon Press, 1971.
Lowi, Theodore. *The End of Liberalism*. New York: Norton, 1969.
MacDonald, Callum. *Korea: The War Before Vietnam*. New York: Free Press, 1986.

MacLear, Michael. *The Ten Thousand Day War*. New York: St. Martin's Press, 1981.

Macnaghten, Phil, and John Urry. *Contested Natures*. London: Sage, 1998.

Maier, Charles. *In Search of Stability*. Cambridge: Cambridge University Press, 1987.

Mandel, Ernest. *Late Capitalism*. London: New Left Books, 1975.

Mannheim, Karl. *Ideology and Utopia: An Introduction to the Sociology of Science*. New York: Harcourt, Brace & World, 1963; originally published 1929.

_____. *Man and Society in an Age of Reconstruction*. New York: Harcourt, Brace & World, 1951.

Marcuse, Herbert. *Eros and Civilization*. New York: Random House, 1955.

_____. *Reason and Revolution*. Boston: Beacon Press, 1960.

_____. *Negations*. Boston: Beacon Press, 1968.

Marglin, Stephen, and Juliet Schor, eds. *The Golden Age of Capitalism: Reinterpreting the Postwar Experience*. Oxford: Oxford University Press, 1990.

Marx, Karl. *Capital*. Vol. 1. New York: Modern Library, 1964.

_____. *Grundrisse*. Harmondsworth, Middlesex: Pelican, 1973.

Marx, Karl, and Frederick Engels. *The Communist Manifesto*. Chicago: Henry Regnery, 1950.

Marx, Leo. *The Machine in the Garden*. New York: Oxford University Press, 1964.

Maslow, Abraham. *The Psychology of Science: A Reconnaissance*. New York: Harper & Row, 1966.

Matson, Floyd. *The Broken Image: Man, Science and Society*. New York: Anchor Books, 1964.

Matthews, John. *Tools of Change*. London: Pluto Press, 1989.

Mazur, Allan. *The Dynamics of Technical Controversy*. Washington, D.C.: Communications Press, 1981.

McCuen, Gary, ed. *Ecocide and Genocide in the Vanishing Forest*. Hudson, Wis.: Gem Publishers, 1993.

McElroy, Michael B., Chris Nielson, and Peter Lydon, eds. *Energizing China: Reconciling Environmental Protection and Economic Growth*. Cambridge, Mass.: Harvard University Press, 1998.

McLaren, Angus. *Our Own Master Race: Eugenics in Canada, 1885–1945*. Toronto: McClelland & Stewart, 1990.

McNeill, William H. *The Pursuit of Power: Technology, Armed Forces and Society Since A.D. 1000*. Chicago: University of Chicago Press, 1982.

Mearsheimer, John. *Conventional Deterrence*. Ithaca: Cornell University Press, 1986.

Melman, Seymour. *The Permanent War Economy*. New York: Touchstone, 1974.

Mensch, Gerhard. *Stalemate in Technology*. Cambridge, Mass.: Ballinger Press, 1979.

Merchant, Carolyn. *The Death of Nature: Women, Ecology and the Scientific Revolution*. New York: Harper & Row, 1980.

Merton, Robert. *Science, Technology and Society in the Seventeenth Century*. New York: Howard Fertig, 1938.

Messinger, Charles. *Bomber Harris and the Strategic Bombing Offensive, 1939–45*. London: Arms and Armoury Press, 1984.

Mesthene, Emmanual. *Technological Change: Its Impact on Man and Society.* Cambridge, Mass.: Harvard University Press, 1970.

Meynaud, Jean. *Technocracy.* London: Faber & Faber, 1968.

Milgram, Stanley. *Obedience to Authority.* New York: Harper & Row, 1974.

Mills, C. Wright. *The Sociological Imagination.* New York: Oxford University Press, 1959.

Mitscherlich, Alexander, and Fred Mielke. *Doctors of Infamy: The Story of Nazi Medical Crimes.* New York: Henry Schuman, 1949.

Mitzman, Arthur. *The Iron Cage.* New York: Grosset & Dunlap, 1971.

Mokhiber, Russell. *Corporate Crime and Violence: Big Business, Power, and the Abuse of the Public Trust.* San Francisco: Sierra Club, 1988.

Mowery, David, and Nathan Rosenberg. *Technology and the Pursuit of Growth.* Cambridge: Cambridge University Press, 1989.

Muller, Herbert J. *Out of the Night: A Biologist's View of the Future.* London: Gollanz, 1936.

Muller-Hill, Benno. *Murderous Science: Extermination by Scientific Selection of Jews, Gypsies and Others.* New York: Oxford University Press, 1988.

Mumford, Lewis. *Technics and Civilization.* New York: Harcourt, Brace & World, 1934.

_____. *The Myth of the Machine: Technics and Human Development.* New York: Harcourt, Brace & World, 1967.

_____. *The Myth of the Machine: The Pentagon of Power.* New York: Harcourt Brace, 1970.

Nef, John. *War and Human Progress.* Cambridge, Mass.: Harvard University Press, 1950.

Nelkin, Dorothy, and Loraine Tancredi. *Dangerous Diagnostic: The Social Power of Genetic Information.* New York: Basic Books, 1988.

Newhouse, John. *War and Peace in the Nuclear Age.* New York: Knopf, 1989.

Noble, David. *America by Design: Science, Technology and the Rise of Corporate Capitalism.* New York: Oxford University Press, 1977.

_____. *Forces of Production: A Social History of Automation.* New York: Oxford University Press, 1985.

_____. *The Religion of Technology: The Divinity of Man and the Spirit of Invention.* New York: Knopf, 1998.

Nora, Simon, and Alain Minc. *The Computerization of Society.* Cambridge, Mass.: MIT Press, 1980.

Nye, David E. *American Technological Sublime.* Cambridge, Mass.: MIT Press, 1994.

Overy, Richard. *Why the Allies Won.* New York: Norton, 1995.

Persuading the Public. London: HMSO, 1995.

Pfister, Joel, and Nancy Schwarz, eds. *Inventing the Psychological: Toward a Cultural History of Emotional Life in America.* New Haven: Yale University Press, 1997.

Pick, Daniel. *Faces of Degeneration: A European Disorder, 1848–1918.* Cambridge: Cambridge University Press, 1989.

Piore, Michael, and Charles Sabel. *The Second Industrial Divide.* New York: Basic Books, 1987.

Plant, Christopher, and Judith Plant, eds. *Green Business: Hope or Hoax?* Philadelphia: New Society Publishers, 1991.

Polanyi, Karl. *The Great Transformation.* Boston: Beacon Press, 1944.

Polenberg, Richard. *War and Society: The United States, 1941–45.* New York: J. B. Lippincott, 1972.

Poller, Walter. *Medical Block, Buchenwald.* New York: Lyle Stuart, 1961.

Ponting, Clive. *1940: Myth and Reality.* London: Hamish Hamilton, 1990.

_____. *Armageddon: The Second World War.* London: Sinclair-Stevenson, 1995.

Proctor, Robert. *Racial Hygiene: Medicine Under the Nazis.* Cambridge, Mass.: Harvard University Press, 1988.

Rafter, Nicole Hahn. *White Trash: The Eugenics Family Studies.* Boston: Northeastern University Press, 1988.

Rasler, Karen A., and William Thompson. *War and State Making: The Shaping of the Global Powers.* Boston: Unwin Hyman, 1989.

Reilly, Philip R. *The Surgical Solution: A History of Involuntary Sterilization in the United States.* Baltimore: Johns Hopkins University Press, 1991.

Rhodes, Richard. *The Making of the Atomic Bomb.* New York: Touchstone, 1986.

Rich, Bruce. *Mortgaging the Earth: The World Bank, Environmental Impoverishment and the Crisis of Development.* Boston: Beacon Press, 1994.

Rose, Steven. *Lifelines: Biology, Freedom, Determinism.* London: Penguin, 1998.

_____, ed. *From Brain to Consciousness.* London: Allan Lane, 1998.

Rosen, Stephen Peter. *Winning the Next War: Innovation and the Modern Military.* Ithaca: Cornell University Press, 1991.

Rosenberg, Nathan. *Inside the Black Box: Technology and Economics.* Cambridge, Mass.: MIT Press, 1982.

Ross, Andrew. *Strange Weather: Culture, Society and Technology in the Age of Limits.* London: Verso, 1991.

Roszak, Theodore. *The Making of a Counter-Culture: Reflections on the Technocratic Society and Its Youthful Opposition.* New York: Anchor Books, 1969.

_____. *The Cult of Information.* London: Butterworth Press, 1986.

Rothschild, Joan, ed. *Machina Ex Dea: Feminist Perspectives on Technology.* New York: Pergamon, 1983.

Russell, Colin. *Science and Social Change in Britain and Europe, 1700–1900.* New York: St. Martin's Press, 1983.

Sagan, Scott D. *The Limits of Safety: Organizations, Accidents, and Nuclear Weapons Prevention.* Princeton: Princeton University Press, 1993.

Sale, Kirkpatrick. *Rebels Against the Future.* Reading, Mass.: Addison-Wesley, 1995.

Schell, Jonathan. *The Military Half.* New York: Knopf, 1968.

Schor, Juliet. *The Overworked American: The Unexpected Decline of Leisure.* New York: Basic Books, 1994.

Schrecker, Ellen. *Many Are the Crimes: McCarthyism in America.* Boston: Little, Brown, 1998.

Schroyer, Jo Ann. *Secret Mesa: Inside Los Alamos National Laboratories.* New York: John Wiley & Sons, 1998.

Schulte, Theo. *The German Army and Nazi Policy in Occupied Russia.* Oxford: Berg Publishers, 1989.

Schuman, Michael H. *Going Local: Creating Self-Reliant Communities in a Global Age*. New York: Free Press, 1998.

Schumpeter, Joseph. *Capitalism, Socialism and Democracy*. New York: Harper, 1942.

Schurmann, Franz. *The Logic of World Power: An Inquiry into the Origins, Currents and Contradictions of World Power*. New York: Pantheon, 1974.

Schwartz, Eugene S. *Overskill: The Decline of Technology in Civilization*. Chicago: Quadrangle Books, 1971.

Schwarz, John E. *America's Hidden Success: A Reassessment of Public Policy from Kennedy to Reagan*. New York: Norton, 1988.

Scott, James C. *Seeing Like A State: How Certain Schemes to Improve the Human Condition Have Failed*. New Haven: Yale University Press, 1998.

Segal, Harold P. *Technological Utopianism in American Thought*. Chicago: University of Chicago, 1985.

Sheehan, Neil. *The Pentagon Papers*. New York: Bantam Books, 1971.

_____. *A Bright Shining Lie*. New York: Random House, 1988.

Sherry, Michael S. *The Rise of American Air Power: The Creation of Armageddon*. New Haven: Yale University Press, 1987.

_____. *In the Shadow of War*. New Haven: Yale University Press, 1995.

Shorter, Edward. *A History of Psychiatry: From the Era of the Asylum to the Age of Prozac*. New York: John Wiley & Sons, 1997.

Simpson, Christopher. *Blowback: America's Recruitment of Nazis and Its Effect on the Cold War*. London: Weidenfeld & Nicolson, 1988.

Skocpol, Theda. *Protecting Soldiers and Mothers*. Cambridge, Mass.: Harvard University Press, 1992.

Slotkin, Richard. *Gunfighter Nation: The Myth of the Frontier in Twentieth-Century America*. New York: Atheneum, 1992.

Smith, Bradley F. *The War's Long Shadow: The Second World War and Its Consequences*. New York: Touchstone, 1986.

Smith, J. David. *Minds Made Feeble: The Mythical Legacy of the Kallikaks*. Rockville, Md.: Aspen, 1985.

Smith, Merritt Roe, ed. *Military Enterprise and Technological Change: Perspectives on the American Experience*. Cambridge, Mass.: MIT Press, 1985.

Snyder, Jack. *Myths of Empire*. Ithaca: Cornell University Press, 1989.

Soloway, Richard A. *Demography and Degeneration: Eugenics and Declining Birthrate in Twentieth Century Britain*. Chapel Hill: University of North Carolina, 1990.

Sovchenko, V. K. *The Ecology of The Chernobyl Catastrophe*. New York: Parthenon, 1995.

Speer, Albert. *Inside the Third Reich*. New York: Avon, 1970.

Speirs, Edward. *Chemical Warfare*. London: Macmillan, 1986.

Spraight, J. M. *Air Power and the Cities*. London: Longman, Green & Co., 1930.

_____. *Air Power in the Next War*. London: Geoffrey Blos, 1938.

Stacewicz, Richard. *Winter Soldiers: An Oral History of the Vietnam Veterans Against the War*. New York: Twayne Publishers, 1996.

Stepan, Nancy L. *In the Hour of Eugenics: Race, Gender and Nation in Latin America*. Ithaca: Cornell University Press, 1991.

Stretton, Hugh. *Capitalism, Socialism and the Environment*. Cambridge: Cambridge University Press, 1977.

Stone, I. F. *Polemics and Prophecies, 1967–1970*. New York: Vintage, 1973.

Talbot, Strobe. *The Master of the Game: Paul Nitze and the Nuclear Peace*. New York: Vintage, 1989.

Tenner, Edward. *Why Things Bite Back: Technology and the Revenge of Unintended Consequences*. New York: Knopf, 1996.

Terkel, Studs. *The 'Good War': An Oral History of World War Two*. New York: Pantheon, 1984.

Thompson, James Clay. *Rolling Thunder: Understanding Policy and Program Failures*. Chapel Hill: University of North Carolina Press, 1980.

Thomson, Matthew. *The Problem of Mental Deficiency: Eugenics, Democracy and Social Policy in Britain, 1870–1959*. Oxford: Clarendon Press, 1998.

Tilly, Charles. *Coercion, Capital and European States, A.D. 990–1990*. London: Basil Blackwell, 1990.

Tucker, William H. *The Science and Politics of Racial Research*. Champaign: University of Illinois, 1994.

Turney, Jon. *Frankenstein's Footsteps: Science, Genetics and Popular Culture*. New Haven: Yale University Press, 1998.

U.S. Congress Office of Technology Assessment. *Mapping Our Genes*. Washington, D.C.: Government Printing Office, 1988.

Van Crevald, Martin. *Technology and War*. New York: Free Press, 1991.

Van Velyn, R. G. *Sex, Love and Eugenics: A Modern Guide to Sexual Health and Happiness*. London: Gerald G. Swan, 1941.

Veblen, Thorstein. *The Engineers and the Price System*. New York: Viking, 1940.

Vogel, David. *National Styles of Regulation: Environmental Policy in Great Britain and the United States*. Ithaca: Cornell University Press, 1986.

Waldo, Dwight. *The Administrative State*. New York: Ronald Press, 1948.

Weiner, Tim. *Blank Check: The Pentagon's Black Budget*. New York: Warner Books, 1990.

Weizenbaum, Joseph. *Computer Power and Human Reason*. New York: Freeman, 1975.

White, Lynn T. *Medieval Technology and Social Change*. Oxford: Clarendon Press, 1962.

Wiener, Norbert. *The Human Use of Human Beings*. Boston: Houghton Mifflin, 1950.

Wilcox, Fred A. *Waiting for an Army to Die*. New York: Vintage, 1983.

Williams, Peter, and David Wallace. *Unit 751: The Japanese Army's Secret of Secrets*. London: Hodder & Stoughton, 1989.

Williams, Reese, ed. *Unwinding the Vietnam War*. Seattle: Real Comet Press, 1987.

Wilson, William Julius. *When Work Disappears: The World of the New Urban Poor*. New York: Knopf, 1996.

Winner, Langdon. *Autonomous Technology: Technology-Out-of-Control as a Theme in Political Thought*. Cambridge, Mass.: MIT Press, 1977.

188 Selected Bibliography

Winter, J. M. *War and Economic Development*. Cambridge: Cambridge University Press, 1995.

Wolferen, Karel von. *The Enigma of Japanese Power*. New York: Knopf, 1989.

Wolff, Edward N. *Top Heavy*. New York: Twentieth Century Fund, 1995.

Wright, Lawrence. *Twins: Genes, Environment and the Mysteries of Human Identity*. London: Phoenix, 1997.

Wright, Peter, and Andrew Treacher, eds. *The Problem of Medical Knowledge: Examining the Social Construction of Medicine*. Edinburgh: University of Edinburgh, 1982.

Ziegler, J. Nicholas. *Governing Ideas: Strategies for Innovation in France and Germany*. Ithaca: Cornell University Press, 1997.

Zuboff, Shoshona. *In the Age of the Smart Machine*. New York: Basic Books, 1989.

Articles

Alperowitz, Gar, and Kai Bird. "The Centrality of the Bomb." *Foreign Policy* 94 (Spring 1994).

Barringer, Felicity. "Chernobyl: The Danger Persists." *New York Times Magazine*, 14 April 1991.

Benton, Ted. "Ecology, Socialism and the Mystery of Nature." *New Left Review* 194 (July/August 1992).

Broadhurst, Arlene, and Grant Ledgerwood. "Environmental Diplomacy of States, Corporations and Non-Governmental Organizations: The World Wide Web of Influence." *International Relations* 14, 2 (August 1998).

Cerny, Philip. "Paradoxes of the Competition State: The Dynamics of Political Globalization." *Government and Opposition* (Spring 1998).

Cockburn, Alexander. "Interview with Susanna Hecht." *New Left Review* 173 (January/February 1989).

Evangelista, Matthew. "Stalin's Postwar Army: A Reappraisal." *International Security* 15, 7 (Winter 1982–1983).

Forsberg, Randall. "Force Without Reason." *Boston Review* 20, 3 (Summer 1995).

Frow, John. "Information as Gift and Commodity." *New Left Review* 219 (September/October 1996).

Galbraith, James K. "With Economic Inequality for All." *Nation*, 7–14 (September 1998).

Geyer, Roger L. "What Happened After Sputnik?: Shaping University Research in the United States." *Minerva* 35, 4 (Winter 1997).

Grundmann, Reiner. "The Ecological Challenge to Marxism." *New Left Review* 187 (May/June 1991).

Hartnung, William. "Reagan Redux: The Enduring Star Wars Myth." *World Policy Journal* 15, 3 (Fall 1998).

Haas, Peter, and Emmanuel Adler. Special issue on epistemic communities. *International Organization* 43, 2 (Autumn 1991).

Hecht, Susanna. "Chico Mendes: Chronicle of a Death Foretold." *New Left Review* 173 (January/February 1989).

Hilgartnek, Stephen. "The Sokal Affair in Context." *Science, Technology and Human Values* 22, 4 (Autumn 1997).

Jardine, Nick, and Marina Fraser-Spada. "Splendors and Miseries of the Science Wars." *Studies in History and Philosophy of Science* 28, 2 (June 1997).

Jasonoff, Sheila. "American Exceptionalism and the Political Acknowledgement of Risk." *Daedelus* 119, 4 (Fall 1990).

_____. "The Dilemma of Environmental Democracy." *Issues in Science and Technology* (Fall 1996).

Klausen, Susanne. "For the Sake of the Race: Eugenics Discourses of Feeble-mindedness and Motherhood and the South African Medical Record." *Journal of South African Studies* 23, 1 (March 1997).

Lifset, Reid, and Marian Chertow. "Changing the Waste Makers: Product Bans and the New Politics of Garbage." *American Prospect* 3 (Fall 1990).

MacKenzie, S. P. "On Target: The Air Ministry, RAF Bomber Command and Feature Film Propaganda, 1940–42." *War and Society* 15, 2 (October 1997).

Martin, Brian. "Science, Technology and Nonviolent Action: The Case for a Utopian Dimension in the Social History of Science and Technology." *Social Studies of Science* 27, 2 (June 1997).

McBride, William. "The Unstable Dynamics of a Strategic Technology: Disarmament, Unemployment and the Interwar Battleship." *Technology and Culture* 38, 2 (April 1997).

McKenzie, Donald. "Nuclear War Planning and Strategies of Nuclear Coercion." *New Left Review* 148 (November/December 1984).

Newell, Peter, and Matthew Paterson. "A Climate for Business: Global Warming, the State and Capital." *Review of International Political Economy* 5, 4 (Winter 1998).

Nolan, Jayne E. "Crunch Time for Control of Advanced Arms Exports." *Issues in Science and Technology* 12 (Fall 1996).

Olsen, Gregg M. "Remodeling Sweden: The Rise and Demise of the Compromise in a Global Economy." *Social Problems* (February 1996).

Rhodes, Richard. "The General and World War II." *New Yorker* (August 1995).

Rolfe, Heather. "In the Name of Progress: Skills and Attitudes Toward Technological Change." *New Technology, Work and Employment* 5 (1991).

Sabel, Charles, Archon Fong, and Bradley Karkainen. "A New Environmentalism Takes Root." *Boston Review* 24, 5 (October-November 1999).

Sanchez, Samantha. "How the West Is Won: Astroturf Lobbying and the 'Wise Use' Movement." *American Prospect* 25 (March-April 1996).

Sandberg, Ake. "Volvoism at the End of the Road." *Studies in Political Economy* 45 (1994).

Sapolsky, Henry M., Mike Trahan, Eugene Gholz, and David T. Burbach. "Let's Have a Parade." *Breakthroughs* 6, 1 (Spring 1997).

Shenhau, Yehonda. "Manufacturing Uncertainty and Uncertainty in Manufacturing: Managerial Discourse and the Rhetoric of Organizational Ideology." *Science in Context* 7, 2 (Summer 1994).

Slack, Jennifer Daryl, and M. Mehdi Semati. "Intellectual and Political Hygiene: The Sokal Affair." *Critical Studies in Mass Communication* 14, 3 (September 1997).

Smith, Philip, and Michael McGerry. "Don't Look Back: Science Funding for the Future." *Issues in Science and Technology* 13, 3 (Spring 1997).

Smith, Richard. "Creative Destruction: Capitalist Development and China's Environment." *New Left Review* 222 (March/April 1997).

Thompson, William R. "Long Waves, Technological Innovation, and Relative Decline." *International Organization* 44 (1990).

Index

In November 1982, Professor Charles Hapgood wrote to a young correspondent, Rand Flem-Ath, adding an amazing postscript to his life's work on ancient civilizations:

"There is evidence that the last displacement of the crust moved both American continents southward about 30 degrees, and absolutely devastated life and civilization on them. . . .
"Furthermore, in recent exciting discoveries I believe I have convincing evidence of a whole cycle of civilization in America and Antarctica, suggesting advanced levels of science that may go back 100,000 years. . . ."

Hapgood was, admittedly, a maverick, but he would not have placed his whole reputation in jeopardy with some crank theory. He evidently felt that he had found evidence of *science* dating back 100,000 years, at a time when, according to paleontology, the most advanced human being on earth was Neanderthal man.

Rand Flem-Ath replied immediately, asking for some hint of Hapgood's reasons for this amazing assertion. For weeks there was no reply, then his letter was returned, stamped "deceased."

Hapgood's last letter led Flem-Ath to his own quest for the origin of science and civilization, of which this book tells the story. . . .

Also by Rand Flem-Ath

WHEN THE SKY FELL: IN SEARCH OF ATLANTIS
(with Rose Flem-Ath)

Also by Colin Wilson

MYSTERIES: AN INVESTIGATION INTO THE OCCULT,
THE PARANORMAL AND THE SUPERNATURAL

STARSEEKERS

UNSOLVED MYSTERIES PAST AND PRESENT
(with Damon Wilson)

FROM ATLANTIS TO THE SPHINX:
RECOVERING THE LOST WISDOM OF THE ANCIENT WORLD

THE ATLAS OF HOLY PLACES AND SACRED SITES

ALIEN DAWN

THE
ATLANTIS
BLUEPRINT

Unlocking the Ancient Mysteries
of a Long-Lost Civilization

COLIN WILSON
and
RAND FLEM-ATH

Delta Trade Paperbacks

A Delta Book
Published by
Dell Publishing
a division of
Random House, Inc.
1540 Broadway
New York, New York 10036

PUBLISHING HISTORY
Little, Brown and Company Hardcover / October 2000
Delacorte Press Hardcover / March 2001
Delta Trade Paperback published June 2002

Library of Congress Card Catalog Number: 00-047449
ISBN: 0-440-50898-3

Printed in the United States of America
June 2002

10 9 8 7 6 5
BVG

For Rose, for ever . . .
Rand Flem-Ath

For my wife, Joy
Colin Wilson

CONTENTS

ANALYTICAL TABLE OF CONTENTS

the Sphinx – the golden section – *When the Sky Fell* – other books – misaligned Mesoamerican and Middle East sacred sites – linkage by latitude to the Hudson Bay Pole.

Chapter 3: Giza Prime Meridian

1884 Washington DC conference on the prime meridian – Charles Piazzi Smyth opts for Giza – conference settles on Greenwich – Tiahuanaco 100 degrees west of Giza – 10 phi sacred sites – Lubaantum and the crystal skull – Portuguese bandeiristas in the Amazon – Percy Fawcett's Amazon quest for Atlantean cities – Easter Island, Teotihuacan, Tula, Copan, Quirgua, Lubaantum and Quito on the Giza prime meridian – locating Fawcett's Atlantean cities using the blueprint – Canterbury Cathedral on a sacred site.

Chapter 4: Thoth's Holy Chamber

Herodotus and the Great Pyramid – Al-Mamum's break and entry – Christopher Dunn and the pyramid – a magical spell cast upon Thoth's Holy Chamber – *The Secrets of Alkazar* – misdirection – David Furlong and phi at Giza – a Fibonacci spiral running through the tips of the pyramids – red granite in front of the Sphinx – 28 degrees at Giza – breaking the spell that hides Thoth's Holy Chamber.

Chapter 5: 6,000 Degrees Celsius

Nine skeletons in the Libyan Desert – the mystery of tektites – bore holes and high temperatures – Lord Rennell contacts Hapgood – 6,000 degrees Celsius – powdered metallurgy – Shawn Montgomery introduces Rand to Brown's Gas – alchemy and glass – Jules Verne's prediction – Yull Brown escapes the Iron Curtain – Shawn interviews Brown – gold mining in the Americas – portable forges – Dr Oswaldo Rivera and the age of Tiahuanaco.

Chapter 6: Ancient Voyagers

Stone balls of Costa Rica – ley lines – ancient Japanese pottery

links between Baalbek and Ollantaytambu – Rosslyn as a 50/50 sacred site – Templars in America?

Chapter 10: The Legacy
Bill Denevan over the jungles of Bolivia – Thor Heyerdahl and the Canary Island pyramids – tomb robbers of the Sipan pyramid – the cocaine mummies – Robert Temple and the Hadji Ahmad map – the Yukon Pole – the X event – anatomically modern humans in South Africa – ocean currents of 100,000 years ago – the Atlantis Channel – Uriel's machine in the south – satellite over Antarctica – the location of the city of Atlantis.

Appendix 1: Blueprints from Atlantis
A fax from John Anthony West – 10,500 versus 9,600 BC – friendly debate with Bauval – Dr Anthony Aveni and the misaligned Mesoamerican sites – sacred sites linked to former poles – geological markers and time capsules.

Appendix 2: Letter to Rand Flem-Ath from Charles Hapgood, 16 October 1982
Role of earth crust displacement in evolution – catastrophe myths – origins of agriculture article – elevation not a safe bet – 100,000-year-old civilisations – a new edition of *Earth's Shifting Crust* – timescale for displacements – regions of maximum displacement.

Appendix 3: Sacred Sites Linked to the Hudson Bay Pole (60N 83W)
The half a degree (30 nautical miles) margin of error – sacred sites by latitude – sacred sites by distance to the Hudson Bay Pole.

Appendix 4: Sacred Sites Linked to the Yukon Pole (63N 135W)
Sacred sites by latitude – sacred sites by distance to the Yukon Pole.

ACKNOWLEDGEMENTS

Rand Flem-Ath

My wife, Rose, has often taken time from writing her own book to give me much invaluable help throughout the writing of *The Atlantis Blueprint*. Many thanks to Bill Hamilton of A.M. Heath for a marvellous job and for his infinite patience. A special thank you to Alan Samson for having faith in this book from the beginning. Also, grateful acknowledgement to Caroline North and Andrew Wille for their meticulous and insightful editing of our manuscript.

Thank you to my friend Martin Schnell for his help with the exciting but exhausting job of tackling Charles Hapgood's uncatalogued archives. The staff at the Yale/Beinecke Rare Book and Manuscript Library were very helpful in permitting us to explore those materials. Likewise, the staff at the Jewish National and University Library in Jerusalem allowed me the privilege of viewing the Einstein–Hapgood correspondence. Also, G. Thomas Tanselle of the John Simon Guggenheim Memorial Foundation generously sent me copies of Albert Einstein's writings about Professor Hapgood.

As always, Ray Grasse's humour and good advice continues to help keep me on an optimistic road. The friendship of Laura Lee, and her husband Paul, is a lighthouse in the sometimes stormy seas I've found myself in over the past few years. And thanks also to our mutual friends, Jo Curran and Rick Levine. Thanks also to Tony Wharrie.

Shawn Montgomery contributed his great enthusiasm and knowledge of Brown's Gas. Raymond Beaumont sent several timely articles about the peopling of America. Thanks also to Simon Cox, for getting us copies of *The Shining Ones*; Robin Pack, for his always thoughtful ideas; and Paul Stevens, for setting up and hosting our website in the early days. My introduction to Bruce and Wendy Cathie was a refreshing change when I most needed it. Bruce was the first to publish the co-ordinates of the pyramids in China. I'm especially thankful to many friends and colleagues at the Vancouver Island Regional Library who have been so supportive, including: Julie Berreth; Dave Devana; Penny Grant; Janice McLean; Kay Morley; Elizabeth Pack; and Leif Rosvold. Thanks to Lady Juliet Boobbyer for her assistance with the research of her father, Lord Rennell; and to Doug Kenyon of *Atlantis Rising* magazine, who was the first to publish the ideas that evolved into this book.

The Atlantis Blueprint wouldn't have been possible without the work of many scholars, amongst them Christian and Barbara Joy O'Brien, whose groundbreaking work in *The Genius of the Few* and *The Shining Ones* was ahead of its time. Also the marvellous books of Christopher Knight and Robert Lomas can't go unmentioned. I am also in debt to three true pioneers: John Anthony West, John Michell and Nigel Pennick.

Thanks also to Fred Hapgood and Beth Hapgood for their gracious co-operation.

None of my work would have been possible without the foundation built by Charles Hapgood and Captain Arlington Mallery.

Finally, last but never least, gratitude to Plato and his marvellous legend of Atlantis, which will continue to inspire many generations to come!

Colin Wilson

More than most of my books, this one has been a collective effort, with co-operation and feedback from many friends.

Charles Hapgood's cousin Beth Hapgood has been tireless as a facilitator and establisher of connections – it was she, for example, who put the authors in touch with Elwood and Daria Babbitt, who in turn did their best to help us track down the missing notes for what was meant to be Hapgood's revised and finalised edition of *The Path of the Pole*. Beth's friend Jim Bowles also provided some important hints and clues.

Shawn Montgomery of Toronto, whose role is described in the second and third chapters, also provided a vast amount of information on a subject that is his speciality – scientific mavericks and forgotten geniuses – in such embarrassing quantities that this volume could easily have been twice as long.

Many authors in this field of 'anomalous' historical research have also provided important information or indicated valuable lines of research. These include John Michell, Andrew Collins, Robert Bauval, John West, Robert Schoch, Christopher Dunn, Robert Lomas, Michael Baigent, Henry Lincoln, John Lash, Ivar Zapp, Lynn Picknett, Stan Gooch, Christian and Joy O'Brien, Edmund Marriage, Emilio Spedicato, Alexander Tollmann and Bill Denevan.

Eddie Campbell has earned my gratitude by introducing me to Henri Bortoft's work on Goethe.

It was the fortunate chance of meeting Gerd and Maria Walton on a Nile steamer that led to the discovery of *Our Cosmic Ancestors* by Maurice Chatelain, and of Chatelain's research into the Nineveh and Quiriga numbers which has played such an important part in this book. It was on that same Nile trip that our guide, Emil Shaker, made some highly enlightening comments on Egyptian temple ritual.

I am grateful to my friend Michael Baldwin, who has read most of this book in typescript, for sending me a copy of Jeremy Narby's *The Cosmic Serpent*.

My son Damon arrived one weekend with a copy of Stephen Oppenheimer's *Eden in the East*, thus drawing my attention to a book that was of enormous importance in our research.

Two old friends, Maurice Bassett and Ted Brown, have been indefatigable in helping me to find hard-to-trace volumes.

My thanks also to Stephen Phillips for allowing me to quote from both his published and unpublished work in Chapter 11.

Finally, my thanks to the London Library for the loan of such rare volumes as A.E. Berriman's *Historical Metrology* and Peter Fleming's *Brazilian Adventure*.

PREFACE

RAND FLEM-ATH

At a local shopping mall, a boy reaches for the coins that glisten beneath the water of a bubbling fountain. The adventurer pulls off his shoes but before he can climb over the lip of the pool to seize the sunken treasure his mother pulls him back and tucks a shiny penny into his fist. 'Make a wish,' she urges him. With dramatic flair the coin is tossed into the water and closely watched as it sinks to the blue-tiled floor of the fountain.

As I watched the child's initiation into the wishing ritual I wondered just how many coin tossers know the true origin of this romantic superstition.

In ancient times flowing water was cherished as a gift from the gods. Wherever the earth goddess allowed it to appear was considered a sacred place. To express their gratitude, people would leave a small gift at the site. This tradition was retained even after humans learned to find water by digging wells.

Then came a subtle but lasting change in our worldview. We began to control nature, to bend it to our own design. The original religious impulse to honour the gods and goddesses faded, and was transformed into acts of magic designed to appropriate their powers for our personal use.

Today, when we pause in the midst of the bustle of a shopping centre or linger at a cool fountain while on holiday to toss a coin into a fountain, most of us are unaware that we are miming an ancient ritual. A shopping mall receives its water from an elaborate system of pipes and filters, its true origin possibly miles away. And in spirit it is even further removed from the idea of the gift from a goddess. It marks no sacred place.

But in the ancient world location held tremendous significance. Certain places were so holy that only a handful of visitors were permitted entrance. A web of intricate meaning surrounded rivers, lakes and forests. In time, this significance was transferred to temples, pyramids and other monuments built upon sacred ground. There was profound meaning to where we lived and to where we worshipped, because so much depended on our relationship with the earth.

With the coming of agriculture, humanity broke that covenant with nature. No longer did we feel subject to a careful order overseen by a powerful earth goddess. As hoes broke open the soil, we realised that nature could be forced to our will. But part of the price we paid for that power was fear: fear that the gods would seek vengeance for our disruption of nature.

At Delphi, the ancient Greeks honoured a sacred rock called the 'omphalos', which marked the 'navel' or 'centre' of the earth. A myth tells the story of its origin. From the opposite ends of the earth Zeus released two eagles. One flew west and the other east. Eventually the two birds crossed flight paths at Delphi, thus designating that city as the centre of the world. But before Delphi could be occupied, the sun god, Apollo, had to sanctify its ground through battle with a gigantic serpent, 'Python', who lived beneath the earth.

Like the dragons of ancient China, Python was thought to be dangerously unpredictable, but after a valiant struggle

Apollo triumphed in taming the creature by driving a lance through its head. In celebration, a sacred rock, the *omphalos*, was placed over the spot of Apollo's victory.

In ancient Japan, a similar story was told in Hitachi Province, where a sea monster by the name of Hishin-Uwo was thought to be responsible for earthquakes. A god pinned down this creature with a river-rock called the Kaus-mi-ishi so that he could temper the fearful shaking of the earth.

And at Deli, in India, there is an iron pillar driven so deep into the ground that it was believed that it had impaled the head of the serpent king, Vasuki, thus keeping the world safe as long as this pillar remained in place.

Widespread myths testify to the ancient belief that certain places on earth are sacred and demand respect. Often, as in the case of Delphi, these sites were perceived to hold the extraordinary power of also being the centre or the navel of the earth. Cuzco in the central Andes, Nippur in ancient Sumeria, Jerusalem, Mecca, Easter Island and Deli have all at one time been held in such esteem.

Many ancient people regarded the world as a giant disc floating upon the world's ocean. The holy city lay at what its citizens believed to be the exact centre of the earth-disc. When constructing temples and monuments, the ancients aligned their buildings with great precision so as not to dishonour any gods. This was considered a practical duty, since if a sacred site was marred by improper placement then the uncontrollable forces of nature could be released, followed by disaster.

Feng shui is the Chinese art of divining the most fortuitous arrangement of space. The foundation stone of each new building was always selected with great care since it was considered the anchor of the whole edifice and its position would prevent the violent actions of underground spirits from destroying the structure. The entire surrounding environment was also carefully considered. Mountains were thought to harbour dragons that, if not appeased, might arise from their slumber and destroy the works of humans. If a peak was not perfectly balanced, it must be modified. The Chinese were terraformers, reshaping the elevations of the earth around them to ensure perfect harmony.

Numerous tactics were adopted to allow the free flow of 'chi', the positive energy believed to stream throughout the universe. Mirrors and fountains, if properly arranged, could enhance the positive flow of chi and, by avoiding a design that included straight lines, evil forces might be diverted from homes and places of work.

Around AD 1700 the Jesuits arrived in China. During their tenure they systematically destroyed any books about feng shui while hypocritically copying the writings. So it was only a matter of time before the ancient Chinese practice was finding its way into the design of such sites as Versailles. The original plans of the famous French palace built for Louis XIV were rectangular in shape, but the secret application of feng shui forced a change. Winding paths and kiosks were introduced to please the eye, and if they also warded off evil spirits, so much the better. This notion that a place holds intrinsic meaning is called geomancy.

Just as astrology evolved into astronomy, and alchemy became chemistry, so has the ancient science of geomancy found its modern equivalent in geology, the forgotten science of antiquity. Unlike astrology/astronomy, which conjures up images of a priest gazing at the stars, or alchemy/chemistry, which brings to mind Frankenstein-like laboratories filled with test tubes and foaming gases, geomancy/geology is devoid of a popular image, but it was once an esteemed science.

At the heart of geology lies another ancient science, geometry. Geometry, which means 'the measuring of the earth', is a science that was practised, as we shall see, throughout the globe, but most purposefully in ancient Egypt, where the annual flooding of the Nile drowned the boundaries between farming plots. In *Sacred Geometry: Symbolism and Purpose in Religious Structures*, Nigel Pennick explains the process undertaken by the priests to restore order each year:

Of necessity, the method of surveying had to be practical
and simple. It required but two men and a knotted rope,
and the knowledge of the so-called 'Pythagorean' triangle, centuries before Pythagoras walked this earth.

The laying out of areas required a foolproof method
for the production of the right angle. This was achieved
by marking off the rope with thirteen equal divisions.
Four units then formed one side of the triangle, three
another and five the hypotenuse opposite the right angle.
This simple method has persisted to this day, and was
used when tomb and temple building began. It was the
origin of the historic 'cording of the temple', and from
this technique it was a relatively simple task to lay out
rectangles and other more complex geometrical figures.[1]

The 'cording of the temple', using a simple rope with thirteen
knots, turns out to be an important clue about the origins of
the people who brought sacred geometry to Egypt.

Underlying the idea of geomancy is the assumption that
there is something unique about sacred sites that prompted
people to construct marvellous monuments at specific locations. Some authors have speculated that the ancients knew of
forces within the earth that emitted energy at particular points
on its surface. This energy might be psychic, as in the case of
Delphi, where the spirit of the earth goddess's serpent,
Typhon, released powers that the priests and priestesses drew
upon to devise oracles. Other authors, such as Bruce Cathie,
believe that there are sacred sites at critical points on the
earth's surface where the ancients could tap a universal energy
flowing through the planet.[2]

But perhaps there is another explanation for the placement
of the sanctified monuments? John Michell, in *City of
Revelation*, comments that 'the traditions relating to these
monuments are unanimous in claiming that they are relics of a
former elemental science, founded upon principles of which we
are now ignorant'.[3] Among Masons the search for these lost

principles has become an essential feature of their secret society. In November 1752, when George Washington became a Mason in Fredericksonburg, he heard the following words:

> The proper business of a Mason is astronomical, chemical, *geological* and moral science, and more particularly that of the ancients, with all the mysteries and fables founded upon it.
>
> Let us endeavor to *turn the stream*; to go from priest-craft to science, from mystery to knowledge, from allegory to real history.[italics added].[4]

Whatever we may think of the Masons in modern times, we can perhaps agree that the priest-craft of geomancy needs to be reborn.

Just as astrology may well be a form of degenerated astronomy and alchemy may have had its origins in the science of chemistry, so might not geomancy be a debased form of ancient geology? That was the question that ultimately sent me on the quest that would become *The Atlantis Blueprint*.

Today we assume that sacred sites such as the Egyptian, Chinese and South American pyramids were built by local people for local reasons, but *The Atlantis Blueprint* will reveal that there is a single global pattern that ties these monuments together. This in turn implies the existence of an advanced civilisation that existed before the flood and managed to communicate important geodesic, geological and geometric information to people who became ancient mariners and recharted the globe.

This knowledge was periodically lost and rediscovered: first by an unknown people who may have been centred in Lebanon, and then by the Phoenicians, and most recently by the Knights Templar. This lost civilisation preserved some of its great knowledge as a gift to future generations.

Joining me in the quest is Colin Wilson, author of scores of books, including *From Atlantis to the Sphinx*.

Our collaboration had an unexpected beginning. Colin had written an introduction to *When the Sky Fell: In Search of Atlantis*, the book that my wife, Rose, and I published in 1995. In the winter of 1997–8 he sent me a fax asking if I could verify Charles Hapgood's signature on a copy of his first important book, *Earth's Shifting Crust*. Colin knew that I was familiar with Hapgood's signature because of my correspondence with him from 1977 to 1982. I was happy to be able to tell him that the book had indeed been signed by Charles.

Colin and I stayed in touch and he sent me a copy of a documentary called *The Flood* that he'd introduced and in which I had appeared. It was around that time that I had decided to gather together the previous four years of research into a new book. Rose was occupied with working on her first novel[5] and so I was temporarily without a co-author. I wondered if Colin would be interested in joining me in this adventure? To give him an idea about where the latest work had taken me, I sent him an article called 'Blueprints from Atlantis' that was about to be published in the American magazine *Atlantis Rising* (see Appendix 1). After reading the article Colin phoned to say he was keen to join me in the quest.

We began with the death of a professor in New England.

Author's note: The text of The Atlantis Blueprint *has been jointly written by Rand Flem-Ath and Colin Wilson. However, to enable the reader to distinguish between their individual voices, Colin Wilson takes the role of first-person narrator and Rand Flem-Ath contributes in the third person.*

1

HAPGOOD'S
SECRET QUEST
FOR ATLANTIS

O N A RAINY night in December 1982, a retired New England professor of anthropology named Charles Hapgood stepped off the pavement without looking left and was hit by an oncoming car. He died in hospital three days later.[1]

Two months earlier he had sorted out his books and papers, and invited his sons to come and take what they wanted. He had been retired for sixteen years, and, at the age of seventy-eight, had the satisfaction of knowing that the last thirty years of his life had produced work of amazing originality. *Earth's Shifting Crust* (1958),[2] written with the active encouragement and co-operation of Albert Einstein, had proposed a revolutionary new theory of the great ice ages: namely, that the crust of the earth can slide,[3] like the skin on cold gravy, under the weight of polar ice caps, and move whole continents around. But perhaps his most revolutionary book was *Maps of the Ancient Sea Kings* (1966),[4] which proved beyond reasonable doubt that civilisation is far older than historians had suspected; it should have brought him worldwide celebrity, since his arguments were irrefutable. He also produced a second

1

edition of *Earth's Shifting Crust* (called *The Path of the Pole*, 1970)[5] with still more evidence for his theory of crust slippage.

Born in 1904, Hapgood had graduated from Harvard in philosophy of science, then studied at Freiburg during the 1930s, when he witnessed the rise of the Nazis. At the outbreak of the Second World War, he was inducted into the Office of Strategic Studies – the forerunner of the CIA – as an expert on Germany. When the war was over, Hapgood became a professor of anthropology at Springfield College in Massachusetts.

He was a good teacher, who believed in involving his students as much as possible. When, in 1949, a student named Henry Warrington asked him about the lost continent of Mu, the legendary civilisation that is supposed to have been engulfed by the Pacific Ocean, Hapgood told him to go away to research it, then report back to the class. As an afterthought, he told Warrington to examine the evidence for Atlantis too.[6]

Warrington had only to consult any good encyclopaedia to learn that in the 1850s an English zoologist named P. L. Sclater had observed a strange similarity between animals and plants as far apart as India and Australia, and suggested that there must have been a land bridge between the Malay archipelago and the south coast of Asia during the Eocene Age, around 55 million years ago. He called this Lemuria, because his missing continent connected places where lemurs – a primate species – were common.

The existence of Lemuria became incorporated into the teachings of the eccentric genius Madame Blavatsky, who said it was the home of what she called the 'third root race', predecessors of human beings who looked like giant apes and communicated by telepathy, who were followed by Atlantis, then our current civilisation, the fifth root race. But, since only members of the Theosophical Society took Madame Blavatsky seriously, this view of Lemuria failed to gain wide currency.

In the 1880s a brilliant but erratic French scholar called Augustus Le Plongeon claimed to be able to read texts of the ancient Maya of Mexico, where he said he had found references to a continent called Mu that had vanished beneath the waves after tremendous earthquakes. Few took him seriously. Then in 1926 a British ex-intelligence officer named James Churchward, who had been a colonel in the Bengal Lancers, wrote a book called *The Lost Continent of Mu*,[7] following it up with four sequels. Churchward had a friend called William Niven, a Scottish engineer and amateur archaeologist, who had been excavating near a village called Amantia, north of Mexico City, when he found hundreds of tablets apparently written in the Mayan script. From their depth, Niven judged them to be more than 12,000 years old. Contemporary Mayan scholars were unable to decipher the script, but when Niven showed some of the tablets to Churchward, the ex-lancer claimed to be able to read it. During his time in India, he explained, he had formed a friendship with a Hindu priest who, when he learned that the young British officer was interested in archaeology, spent two years teaching him to read inscriptions that, he claimed, were written in Naacal, which was the original tongue of mankind and also the language of the lost continent of Mu. And now Niven had demonstrated the truth of another assertion of Churchward's mentor: that the priesthood of Mu had sent emissaries to Central America to teach their secret knowledge and to prepare a place of refuge in the event of the destruction of their own civilisation. This had finally come about, according to Churchward, about 50,000 years ago.

Because Churchward made no attempt at a scholarly presentation, his books were generally dismissed as fantasy. When Henry Warrington presented his report to Charles Hapgood's class at Springfield College, everyone agreed that there was no real evidence for Mu.

Atlantis was a different matter. It had first been described by Plato in two of his dialogues, the *Timaeus* and *Critias*, and the Greek Neoplatonist philosopher Proclus had stated that Plato's student Crantor (c.340–275 BC) had visited Egypt, where he saw pillars inscribed with the legend of Atlantis.

In the *Timaeus*, Plato's uncle, Critias, describes how his ancestor Solon (639–559 BC), the great statesman, had visited Egypt about two centuries earlier. Realising that the Egyptians knew far more about history than the Greeks, he lured a group of priests to talk about the past by telling them what he knew of Greek history. The bait was successful; an old priest told him, 'Oh Solon, Solon, you Greeks are all children.' He went on to say that the earth had experienced many catastrophes that had almost destroyed mankind, some by fire, some by water, and some by other means. But 9,000 years before (i.e. about 9,600 BC), one of the greatest of these catastrophes had occurred – a destruction by water. At this time, Solon was told, Athens already existed, and out in the ocean, beyond the Pillars of Hercules (which we now know as the Straits of Gibraltar), there was an island-continent called Atlantis, 'as large as Libya and Asia combined'. (By Libya he meant all of North Africa and by Asia he meant an area equivalent to the Middle East.)

The priest then made a baffling statement. From Atlantis, he explained, it was possible to reach other islands that formed part of Atlantis, 'and from them, the whole opposite continent that surrounds what can be truly called the ocean'.

It is conceivable that, by the 'opposite continent', the priest was referring to America – for there is evidence that Europeans visited America thousands of years before Columbus – but to say that the opposite continent *surrounds* the ocean sounds odd. Sea can surround a continent, but surely a continent does not surround the sea?

On Atlantis, said the priest, a powerful dynasty of kings had succeeded in extending their empire as far as the borders of Egypt. Their next ambition was to conquer Egypt and Greece. But Greece had resisted; an alliance led by Athens succeeded in defeating the Atlanteans. After this, a tremendous catastrophe, involving earthquakes and floods, destroyed most of the Greeks, and engulfed Atlantis under the waves.

This is not the usual version of history. According to the *Oxford Classical Dictionary*, Athens probably dates from about 900 BC, possibly a few centuries earlier. Even though it admits that 'the more substantial remains of later periods have largely effaced prehistoric settlement evidence', there is still a huge gap between 900 BC and 9,000 BC. On the other hand, we know that archaeology is continually pushing back the age of civilisation. In the 1960s, Jericho – the first walled city – was believed to date from about 6,500 BC, but it is now believed to date from at least 2,000 years earlier. 'The great stone wall, some twenty feet high and nine feet thick, was joined by at least one apsidal tower which . . . would not have disgraced one of the more impressive mediaeval castles,' says one expert.[8] But early settlers do not build walls and towers like that; they build one-room huts. It took European man about 1,000 years to move from fortified wooden barricades to medieval castles. So Jericho might well be as old as 8,000 BC. And in that case, why not Athens?

In the *Critias*, Plato continues the story. Atlantis was founded by the sea god Poseidon (Neptune), who fathered five pairs of twins on a mortal woman. The god built her a home on a hill, and surrounded it with concentric rings of sea and land. The twins were each allotted a portion of the island, and over the generations extended their conquests to other islands and to the mainland of Europe.

Great engineers, the Atlanteans built a circular city, 11 miles in diameter, with a metal wall and a huge canal connecting it to the sea. Behind the city there was a plain 229 by 343 miles wide, on which farmers grew the city's food supply. Behind this were mountains with fertile meadows and every kind of livestock, including elephants. Plato spends many pages describing the magnificent buildings, with hot and cold fountains, communal dining halls and palaces of many-coloured stone, then goes on to describe the Atlantean social structure at equal length.

As time went by, the *Critias* goes on, the god-like element among the Atlanteans became diluted with human stock and they were no longer able 'to carry their prosperity with moderation'. The meaning is quite clear: undisturbed prosperity makes human beings lazy, and those who are too aggressive to allow themselves to vegetate fly from boredom by using up their energies in a struggle for power and wealth (things have not changed all that much). Although the Atlanteans regarded themselves as fortunate and contented, the gods were fully aware of their corruption. So Zeus summoned all the gods to a meeting in his palace . . .

And at that point, the *Critias* breaks off. Plato never completed it, or went on to write the third dialogue of a projected trilogy, the *Hermocrates*. The likeliest explanation is that his plans were interrupted by illness and death – he died at the age of eighty.

The story of Atlantis continued to fascinate readers for more than 2,000 years. In the nineteenth century an American congressman named Ignatius Donnelly wrote the first complete study of the legend, concluding that it is almost certainly a record of fact. *Atlantis, The Antediluvian World*,[9] which has been in print ever since it was first published in 1882, is a work of extraordinary range that argues that the colonies of Atlantis included North and South America, as well as Egypt and Spain, and is inclined to believe that the Azores, in the mid-Atlantic, are the only part of the sunken island that remains visible. Donnelly came close to persuading the British prime minister Gladstone to send a naval vessel to look for Atlantean remains.

Donnelly – described as 'the most erudite man ever to sit in Congress' – seems to have been a remarkable man. He was the author of an influential book proposing that William Shakespeare was in fact Francis Bacon, while a sequel to his text on Atlantis, *Ragnarok, The Age of Fire and Gravel* (1883),[10] set out to explain the origins of the layer of sand, gravel and clay that covers most of our earth, arguing that it was left behind after a flood caused by the impact of some great comet which vaporised oceans and caused an age of darkness. This happened, Donnelly suggests, when man had already begun to establish civilisation, and the event is reflected in many myths of catastrophe. The area where the comet struck, he thinks, may have been the mid-Atlantic – in short, Atlantis.

It is an interesting speculation, for a cometary impact is as good an explanation as any for the destruction of Plato's legendary civilisation. But Donnelly's belief that Atlantis was located in the mid-Atlantic cannot be sustained. The explanation is summarised in a popular volume on mysteries published in 1961:

> At first sight the configuration of the bed of the Atlantic between Bermuda and Spain appears to confirm the former existence of Atlantis. Depth sounders carried westwards from Spain disclose first a valley three thousand feet in depth, the sea bed then rising perpendicularly to the summits of the Azores which are in effect the tops of a high mountain range which runs under the sea north and south in the Atlantic. The ocean bed then drops to another valley two thousand feet deep and rises steeply again to the island of Bermuda, another mountain top. It appears, therefore, that the Azores represent the last remaining outposts of Atlantis. But geological surveys of the ocean bed have disclosed that, if any subsidences took place, they occurred at a date a hundred thousand years or more before the time of the supposed loss of Atlantis.[11]

This, then, would appear to rule out the existence of Atlantis in the Atlantic Ocean – at least, if it was the size of North Africa and the Middle East combined.

As Hapgood reread Plato's account, he was struck by the fact that this sounded like a description of something that had actually happened. It seemed to him that the most interesting question was not so much where Atlantis was located, but what could have caused such a catastrophe. No volcanic eruption could be great enough to wreck a whole continent and extend its destructiveness as far as Greece.

A trivial domestic incident started a new train of thought. Hapgood had put a heavy rug, rolled into a bundle, into the washing machine, and when the drum had begun to spin, the machine shook until it tore the bolts out of the kitchen floor. At roughly the same time as this incident, a friend of Hapgood, Hugh Auchinloss Brown, an engineer, suggested his own theory of how an earth catastrophe could have taken place. The earth's polar ice caps are huge, Antarctica's alone being about twice as large as the United States; the northern ice cap is almost entirely floating ice, but Antarctica, on the other hand, is a vast continent covered with ice. Since the earth is continually spinning like a washing machine, its ice cap could act like the bunched-up rug, causing an uneven distribution of mass. Auchinloss Brown even went so far as to propose that the mass of ice at the poles can cause the earth to topple on to its side every 7,000 years, a view that was used by the science fiction writer Allan Eckert in a novel called *The Hab Theory*, 'HAB', being Auchinloss Brown's initials.

Auchinloss Brown pointed out that there is a significant difference between the rotations of a washing machine and our planet. Because it spins on its axis, the earth is 'fatter' at the equator than at the poles, so in effect it is like an enormous flywheel whose spin stabilises itself. A flywheel would spin erratically if someone attached a weight to its edge, but the polar ice is not on the edge but, so to speak, at the centre of the wheel. Hapgood had to try to work out the mass of irregular ice that could cause the wheel to 'judder'. He asked a colleague to calculate the centre of gravity of the Antarctic ice cap, which has an irregular shape. He learned that the centre of gravity of Antarctica was around 340 miles to the west of the

Pole itself, which meant that when the ice reached a certain thickness, Antarctica could, in theory, cause a bunched-up-rug effect. Then he had to work out whether this irregular sheet of ice, much of it 2 miles thick, could cause the flywheel to judder. The answer, when it came, was disappointing. The flywheel-stabilising effect was thousands of times greater than the weight of ice at the South Pole. Auchinloss Brown's 'Hab theory' was also disproved.

At this low point, his friend James Hunter Campbell, an engineer and inventor and an associate of Thomas Edison's, made a suggestion that completely changed the direction of the investigation. Surely, said Campbell, there was no need for the bunched-up-rug effect to make the whole earth wobble on its axis? The earth's crust is a fairly thin layer of solid matter, between 20 and 40 miles thick, which floats on a sea of molten rock, so the mass of irregular ice would only have to make the earth's crust slip on the liquid underneath.

This was Hapgood's great breakthrough. Suddenly he had the makings of a plausible theory about what might have happened to Atlantis. Moreover, he had extremely powerful support in the theories of a German meteorologist named Alfred Lothar Wegener, who had taught at the University of Graz. Around 1910 Wegener had pointed out that we only have to look at a map of the world to see that the bulge on the coast of South America appears to fit very neatly into the hollow on the coast of Africa. Is it not possible that they were once part of the same continent, then drifted apart? Wegener labelled his hypothetical supercontinent Pangaea.

Wegener's Hypothesis, as it was known, was presented to the academic world in 1915 in a book called *The Origin of the Continents and Oceans*.[12] It encountered furious resistance, and was widely ridiculed. What, his colleagues wanted to know, had driven the continents apart? Why *should* they drift apart when the surface of the earth is obviously solid? Wegener's reply was along the same lines as Sclater's observations on Lemuria in the 1850s: there were similar rock strata and fossils in both Africa and South America. That, said his opponents, was coincidence.

Wegener struggled on, aware that he had lost the battle, and by 1930 his theory had been generally rejected. He went on a final expedition to Greenland, where he met his death from a heart attack induced by overexertion. His theory was promptly forgotten.

His critics were not entirely wrong. His theory was based on two presuppositions: that the sea bed is a smooth plane, so that continents can drift over it like immense rafts; and that it is soft and plastic. In fact the sea bed is not flat – it is often mountainous – and the rock of the sea bed is rigid. Yet Wegener's basic intuition – that the continents were once a solid land mass that has since split apart – was correct, and was recognised as such within a few decades of his death. His name can now be found in every dictionary of science.

In 1952, Hapgood was in effect re-examining the Wegener Hypothesis – with one important difference. Unlike Wegener, Hapgood had a clear idea of what might cause 'continental drift': the mass of polar ice. He decided to try to enlist the support of the most famous living scientist, Albert Einstein. Hapgood had written to him before, with some questions about the nature of the expanding universe, and Einstein had replied. Hapgood wrote again, this time asking whether Einstein thought that radioactive elements such as radium might be built up in the earth's crust from simpler elements because of the enormous pressures.

Although his reply has been lost, Einstein seems to have shown interest, for, on 15 November 1952, two weeks after his first letter, Hapgood was sending him a lengthy memorandum about the forces exerted by the earth's crust. He made one comment that would be central to his whole theory. Noting the size of the last great American ice sheet, known as the Wisconsin, Hapgood pointed out that if it had extended as far north as the present North Pole, its weight would have been so great that it would have pulled the globe sideways.

(Hapgood used the term 'careened'.) The answer, Hapgood thought, was that the North Pole was not then in its present position, but further south in Hudson Bay.

Einstein immediately grasped the essence of the rather diffuse memorandum; he replied nine days later (24 November 1952),[13] remarking that he had once read a popular article suggesting that an irregular mass of ice at the poles could cause the earth's crust to slip. And he advised Hapgood that, in his opinion, 'a careful study of this hypothesis is really desirable'.

That was exactly what Hapgood wanted – encouragement from the world's most famous scientist to go ahead and develop his theory of the earth's shifting crust. His reaction was to begin to write a book about his theory.

It was six months before he wrote to Einstein again, when he enclosed the typescript of 'The Ice Age', the first chapter of his book. A mere century ago, Hapgood pointed out, people were simply unable to accept that the earth had once been covered with vast sheets of ice, but finally, the evidence became too powerful to ignore. Not only the extreme northern and southern regions had been covered with ice, but India and Africa too. In fact, we now know that in the Pre-Cambrian Era, about 800 million years ago, the whole earth remained frozen solid almost as far as the equator, and that this ice age lasted for another 300 million years. Nothing as extreme has happened since, but the earth has passed through a succession of ice ages whose cause is still a mystery.

If ice ages occurred at regular intervals, an obvious explanation would be that the solar system passes periodically through some giant cloud of cosmic dust, but they have no perceptible pattern of frequency, so other theories must be considered.

In 1872, a Scotsman named James Croll produced a book called *Climate and Time*, arguing that the key to the ice ages lies in the tilt of the earth's axis, which causes our winter and summer; at present it is 23.4 degrees. If there were no tilt, there would be no seasons. It follows that if the tilt were increased, winter and summer would be more extreme. In fact, the tilt *does* increase, as far as 24.4 degrees, and this, Croll suggested, can produce ice ages.

In 1920 a Serbian scientist named Milutin Milankovich developed this idea further. He contended that the movement of the earth around the sun varies in three ways: the tilt of the earth's axis, which varies slightly over 41,000 years; the point when its orbit comes closest to the sun (called the perihelion), which varies every 22,000 years; and the slight changes in the orbit (known as eccentricity), which vary over a period of 100,000 years. Milankovich suggested that if these three factors coincide, they cause an ice age. For the next twenty years, Milankovich continued to produce charts and graphs, and climatologists were deeply impressed. Milankovich was only concerned with the Pleistocene, the most recent geological epoch, which ended a mere 10,000 years ago, but his graph of the Pleistocene – 'the Milankovich curve' – showed the climatic changes of the Pleistocene in remarkable detail.

The problem with the Milankovich theory is that, while it can explain small fluctuations in the earth's climate, it cannot answer the question of why vast ice sheets extended beyond the tropics. The 300-million-year-long ice age of the Pre-Cambrian seems to require something more than three orbital variations occurring at the same time.

Another interesting theory was put forward by the meteorologist Sir George Simpson in the 1950s. His notions sound totally paradoxical: that ice ages are caused by an increase in heat from the sun. Simpson pointed out that an increase in the sun's heat would cause heavier rainfall, as the sun would evaporate more water from the sea (that is why the tropics have monsoons). In the polar regions, precipitation falls as snow, and if more snow falls in winter than can evaporate in summer, the ice caps will grow larger and larger, and the result will be an ice age. But if increased solar radiation caused the ice ages, it should also have warmed the seas, until most of the ice-free ocean was as warm as the Mediterranean. A study of shell deposits on the sea bottom, carried out by Cesare Emiliani of the University of Chicago, shows no such rise in temperature, so Simpson's theory also has to be abandoned.

There is one more likely possibility: that ice ages are caused by volcanic dust in the earth's atmosphere. During the first part of the twentieth century, there was a lessening of volcanic activity, resulting in the long, hot summers that can be remembered by those born before 1950. An increase in volcanic eruptions has brought an increased variability in the weather – rainy summers, warm winters. What causes this rise in volcanic activity? One theory suggests that the earth may have been struck by large meteors or small asteroids, but there have been no such major strikes since the great Tunguska explosion which devastated hundreds of square miles of Siberian forest in 1908.

We still have no firm ideas about the causes of the ice ages, but Hapgood went on to raise an even more baffling question: why are the records of ice ages not distributed across locations where you would expect them to be found, namely showing ice spreading from the poles and working towards the equator? How can we explain the recent ice ages that left Siberia and Alaska untouched, yet froze Europe almost as far south as London and Berlin? And what about the ice sheet that covered India and moved *northwards* in the Carboniferous Period? One explanation might be that around 300 million years ago this part of India was much higher – and therefore colder – than today, but there were also vast ice sheets at *sea level* in Asia, Africa and Australia, and ice sheets in Africa and Madagascar also spread 'the wrong way', from the equator.

You might also expect that an ice age would affect the northern and southern hemispheres at the same time. Not so; there is evidence to show that there have been ice sheets in the southern hemisphere but not at the same time in the north, and vice versa.

If you assume that the earth's crust cannot move, and that

13

the land that is now at the North and South Poles has always been located at the same places, these facts cannot be supported. Instead assume that the earth's crust can move around, and all is explained: the ice that almost reached the latitude of London while Siberia remained unfrozen, the ice sheet over India, and other irregularities.

Hapgood was lucky to have a friend in the zoologist Ivan Sanderson, who was interested in what are now called 'anomalies', meaning strange and unexplained phenomena. It was Sanderson who brought to his attention the Russian scientist Immanuel Velikovsky's investigations of the Beresovka mammoth, found frozen in Siberia around 1901 in a half-standing position with buttercups in its mouth. Obviously, for such flora to have been growing, the climate had changed very suddenly, but how could even an earth crust slippage have caused the temperature to drop so rapidly? Hapgood had himself been in Canada one Indian summer; it had been hot enough for him to bathe in a lake and then dry out in the sun, until suddenly the wind had changed to north-west and the temperature had dropped so that the lake was frozen over within hours. He imagined the Beresovka mammoth chewing buttercups in a warm meadow when a storm had blown up, with a wind of 150 miles an hour. (One of the consequences of volcanic dust in the air is an increase in the temperature difference between poles and equator and more powerful winds.)

But why were other mammoths not affected? The answer is that they were – in their thousands. Twenty thousand mammoth tusks were exported from Siberia in the last decades of the nineteenth century and thousands more must have remained buried. Ivory is unusable unless it comes from freshly killed animals, or can be frozen very quickly. Many of the frozen mammoths were perfectly edible, indicating that they had been frozen to temperatures well below zero and kept like that for thousands of years. If meat is merely kept at or around freezing point, ice crystals form and 'spoil' it by disrupting the cells. Evidently, some huge catastrophe plunged Siberia from a warm day into sub-zero temperatures that lasted 15,000 years.

Hapgood then discussed the mastodon bones found in New York State around 1880, which at the time were assumed to prove that mastodons survived the Ice Age. Subsequent geological studies have proved that, like the Siberian mammoths, they were caught by a sudden drop in temperature, then in the ice sheet that subsequently formed, so the mastodons of North America – as well as bears, horses, giant beavers, deer, caribou, elk and bison – were also overtaken by catastrophe. The basic difference was that Siberia became freezing cold. Why? Because it had moved north.

Einstein read Hapgood's material and replied within five days: 'I find your arguments very impressive and have the impression that your hypothesis is correct. One can hardly doubt that significant shifts of the earth's crust have taken place repeatedly and within a short time.'[14] His encouragement led Hapgood to send him more of the typescript. In spring 1954, Einstein supported Hapgood's application for a grant or research appointment at the Institute of Advanced Studies at Princeton, where Einstein was based.[15] Unfortunately, Robert Oppenheimer, the 'father of the atom bomb', who was an influential member of the committee, opposed Hapgood, and the request was turned down. On 18 May 1954, Einstein wrote to express his sympathy, and, perhaps as a consolation prize, sent Hapgood a short introduction to the book that would become *Earth's Shifting Crust*, probably recognising that, in the long run, this would be worth more than a grant.

Again, in November 1954, Einstein supported Hapgood's request for a research grant from the Guggenheim Foundation. Once again, it was turned down. The following January, Hapgood and Campbell called on Einstein at Princeton and held a long discussion which Hapgood wrote up into an account that he later sent to Einstein, who agreed that it was accurate, although he asked not to be quoted, since his remarks had been made without preparation. Hapgood later reprinted the notes in *Earth's Shifting Crust*. Campbell was trying to work out the mathematics of how the Antarctic ice cap could cause the earth's crust to fracture. Einstein was totally convinced by Hapgood's geological evidence that the earth's crust *could* fracture and slide; what he doubted was whether the polar ice cap had anything to do with it, a view that Hapgood had come to share by the time he issued the second edition, *The Path of the Pole*, in 1970. He simply doubted whether the mass of ice – even when contained in an irregular shape like Antarctica – could cause the crust to slip.

On 16 April, at the age of seventy-six, Einstein died in hospital. Hapgood had lost his most influential champion, but at last *Earth's Shifting Crust* was now almost completed. What had once seemed a wild theory was steadily gathering support from other sources. Professor George W. Bain realised that the chemical composition of soil is altered by sunlight, and discovered that, for example, tropical soil is quite different from soil in a cool zone. His studies of very early geological periods led him to conclude that in the Carboniferous Period, the equator ran through the New Siberian Islands – or, to put it another way, that Siberia was located closer to the equator.

Bain published his results in 1953. For twenty years before that, the Chinese professor Ting Ying H. Ma, of the University of Fukien,[16] had been studying corals and had reached similar conclusions: ancient coral seas were not in the same position as at present, but in fact changed their position from age to age. At first Ma tried to explain this by Wegener's theory of drifting continents, but by 1949, when Hapgood started working on the problem, he had concluded that only shifts in the earth's crust itself could account for the patterns of change. Ma suspected that the movement went deeper than the crust, into the mantle, the layer below the crust.

For Hapgood, five years' work was drawing to a close; all

that remained now was to find a publisher. And at this junc-
ture, another fascinating investigation fell into his lap.

On 26 August 1956, a radio broadcast from Georgetown
University, in Washington, DC,[17] featured a panel discussion
in which the leading speaker was a scholar of Viking maps,
Captain Arlington H. Mallery. The panel was arguing about a
map, dating from 1513, that bore an inscription stating that it
had been pieced together from a number of other old maps by
a Turkish seafarer and one-time pirate named Piri Reis ('*piri*'
means admiral); Reis was apparently eventually beheaded
through the machinations of an enemy in 1554. His map
showed South America, a portion of West Africa and, at the
bottom, what appeared to be part of the coast of Antarctica.
Earlier that year, Mallery had been reading an article in the
Geographical Journal about discoveries made in Antarctica
during an international exploration in 1949, including sonar
soundings under the ice that surrounded the coast.[18] At that
moment his friend M.I. Walters dropped on his desk a copy of
the Piri Reis map, which had recently been presented to the
Library of Congress by a Turkish officer. A single glance
showed Mallery that there appeared to be an amazing correspondence between the bays shown on the Piri Reis map and
the bays recently revealed by the sonar. Piri Reis himself had
stated that some of the twenty maps he had used dated back to
the time of Alexander the Great, who was born in 356 BC.
Since Antarctica was undoubtedly by that time covered with a
sheet of ice – much of it 2 miles deep – these original maps
must have been made long before Alexander – at a conservative estimate, around 4,000 BC.

But a map is no use without something written on it, and
writing was not supposed to have been developed until the
Sumerians began to use it for tax demands around 3,500 BC. It
looked very much as if the Piri Reis map proved that writing
had been in use long before 4,000 BC. Furthermore, Antarctica
itself was not officially discovered until 1818. The Piri Reis
map suggested the existence of a sophisticated seafaring

civilisation at a time when, according to historians, civilisation was only just evolving in the Middle East.

Understandably, in view of his interest in Antarctica, Hapgood was tremendously excited by the new discovery. He had already concluded that, before the last great crust slippage, Lesser Antarctica – the smaller half of the divided continent, directly south of Patagonia – was located outside the Antarctic Circle, and had later moved inside it, so it would quite probably have been free of ice in 9,600 BC, when, according to Plato, Atlantis had vanished. Although Hapgood had no intention of breathing a word about it to anyone – he had no desire to be dismissed as a member of the lunatic fringe – it looked as if the Piri Reis map confirmed his suspicion that Plato had been right about an ancient civilisation that pre-dated known historical records.

Hapgood was by then an assistant professor at Keene State College, part of the University of New Hampshire. He again enlisted the aid of his students in his latest enterprise. Their business was simply to study the Piri Reis map without preconceptions and compare it with other early maps. One of the first things they discovered was that the land maps of the period were extremely crude; one showed Italy joined to Spain, another showed England shaped like a teapot. Yet the maps used by mariners – known as 'portolans', which means 'port to port' – were often incredibly accurate. According to Piri Reis, his map had been based partly on a map possessed by Columbus, although no one had succeeded in locating this. But perhaps he had used maps from the ancient library of Alexandria; Hapgood was inclined to believe that these had found their way to the great library in Constantinople, which then fell into the hands of the Turks when the city was captured in 1453.

As long ago as 1889, Adolf Erik Nordenskiold (1832–1901), another leading expert on early maps, had also been convinced that the portolans were based on maps that dated back centuries before Christ. After ten Arctic expeditions, Nordenskiold became aware of the deplorable state of polar cartography. He undertook a systematic reappraisal of all ancient maps, culminating in the *Facsimile-Atlas* (Stockholm, 1889), which is commonly regarded as an impetus for the modern study of cartography. The great geographer and astronomer Ptolemy, who had been a librarian in Alexandria around 150 BC, had made maps that were less accurate than the medieval portolans despite having the greatest library in the world at his disposal. Was it likely that ordinary seamen could surpass the work of Ptolemy, unless they had other maps to guide them?

In fact, the Piri Reis maps contained a number of errors — for example, he had allowed the twenty maps he used to overlap, so that he had shown the Amazon River twice, although he had also left out a 900-mile stretch of coastline. One error could be pinned down to the Greek astronomer Eratosthenes, who was born about 275 BC. He knew that in Syene, in Upper Egypt (close to the present Aswan), the sun was reflected in a certain deep well on the solstice, 21 June, so towers there did not cast a shadow at that time. But in Alexandria, 500 miles due north, they did. He measured the length of the shadow of a tower in Alexandria at midday on 21 June, and used this to calculate the angle of the sun's rays. This was about 7 degrees, which is approximately one-fiftieth of 360. Since he knew the distance to Syene, this meant that 500 miles represented 7 degrees of the earth's polar circumference, so it was easy to work out that 360 degrees would be represented by 25,000 miles. The actual circumference around the poles is 24,821 miles, so this was an amazingly accurate calculation for 240 BC, when most people were not even aware the earth was round.

Through a slight error, Eratosthenes had increased the diameter of the earth by 4.5 degrees. If Hapgood allowed for that 4.5 degrees error, the Piri Reis map became even more accurate, suggesting that it had been based on ancient Greek (and Egyptian) source maps.

When Piri Reis made his map, the famous mapmaker Gerardus Mercator was only one year old, so his work predated

Mercator's method of 'projecting' the earth on to a flat surface and marking it with latitude and longitude. Mapmakers used a simpler method, choosing some town as a centre, then drawing a circle round it that they divided into sixteen slices, like a cake. Then they drew squares inside the circle, and went on extending these outward, creating a kind of crude latitude and longitude – a complicated method, but one that worked well enough. When Hapgood's students studied the Piri Reis map, they soon realised that its original 'centre' lay somewhere off the chart, to the east. Most of them guessed it would be Alexandria, but careful calculation revealed that the actual centre seemed to be Syene, the sacred centre of Upper Egypt, further support that they might have been dealing with an ancient map.

When the mapmakers of Alexandria made their own maps, we may presume that they did not sail off to look at South America and Antarctica but based them on other older maps. But how old were they?

An interesting piece of evidence offers us one clue. Towards the end of the second century BC, the Greek grammarian Agatharchides of Cnidus, a tutor to one of the Ptolemy kings of Egypt, was told that, according to ancient tradition, one side of the base of the Great Pyramid was precisely one-eighth of a minute of a degree of the earth's polar circumference[19] (a minute is one-sixtieth of a degree). Each side of the Great Pyramid's base is 756 feet, or just over 230 metres, and if this is multiplied by 8, then by 60, then by 360, the result is just under 40,000 kilometres, or just under 25,000 miles (in fact, 24,933 miles) – again, an amazingly accurate assessment of the polar circumference of the earth. In fact the height of the Great Pyramid, in addition to its base, is also in exact proportion to the size of the earth – that is, its apex is where the North Pole should be.

The Great Pyramid was built by the pharaoh Cheops (Khufu) around 2,500 BC, so how can the ancient Egyptians possibly have known the size of the earth? It is possible that they might have understood that it was a sphere, for example, by noting that the shadow of the earth on the moon during eclipses is curved, or by observing that a ship gradually vanishes below the horizon as it sails away.

What impressed Hapgood so much was the astonishing accuracy of the Piri Reis map, once the 4.5-degree error had been allowed for. He noted that, in 1541, savants in Mexico City set out to decide its exact longitude by timing two eclipses of the moon, one in Mexico City and one in Toledo in Spain. Their calculations were off by miles. The ancient maps, on the other hand, were frequently accurate to within one half-degree of longitude – something Europeans didn't achieve until John Harrison invented the marine chronometer in the eighteenth century.

Hapgood was also intrigued by a large island shown off the coast of South America. Located at 5 degrees north on the Mid-Atlantic Ridge, it seems to be about 300 miles in diameter, yet it is certainly not there today. Moreover, the island is also shown on the Reinel Chart of 1510, and on a map of 1737 by the French cartographer Philip Buache.

Hapgood was naturally interested in other portolans, and in 1959 he wrote to ask the Library of Congress if they had any more. He was invited to come and see for himself – when he arrived there at Thanksgiving, he was slightly embarrassed to find hundreds of them laid out for his inspection. He spent several days looking through the maps, and then, as he describes it, 'I turned a page and sat transfixed.' What he was looking at was a map made by Oronteus Finnaeus in 1531, showing Antarctica looking much as it does on a modern map. But it depicted the bays without the ice, rivers flowing to the sea, and even mountains that are now buried under ice. Although the Oronteus map failed to show the Palmer Peninsula, which stretches between north-western Antarctica and the coast of Patagonia, in reality, there is no such peninsula – if the ice melted, there would only be an island. In short, the original map had been made by someone who knew the *whole* of Antarctica – inland, as well as the coast. That

21

could mean either that Antarctica had originally been mapped by sailors who had explored and mapped it inland, or that the original inhabitants of the continent had mapped it for themselves. Whatever the case, it suggested that Antarctica had been mapped more then 6,000 years ago.

Other portolans were equally significant. The Dulcert Portolano of 1339 shows precise knowledge of an area from Galway to the Don Basin in Russia. A Turkish Hadji Ahmad map of 1559 shows the world from a northern projection, as if hovering over the North Pole, and also seems to show Siberia and Alaska as joined. Since this is a heart-shaped map, with Siberia in one dimple and Alaska in the other, this could simply reflect the fact that the mapmaker did not have space to include the stretch of sea of the Bering Strait between the two. However, if there was no Bering Strait, the original map must have been made more than 12,000 years ago, when Siberia and Alaska were joined by a land bridge at this location. A 12,000-year-old map sounds unlikely, but everything Hapgood was uncovering seemed equally absurd. He began to understand why the portolans had remained unexamined in the Library of Congress for decades – any scholar who had taken a close look at them had probably shuddered and hastily closed the folder.

The map of Antarctica published by Philip Buache in 1737 showed the Antarctic continent divided into two islands – as we now know, it is below the ice. How did Buache know this? He must have been using maps even older than those used by Oronteus Finnaeus and the creator of the Dulcert Portolano, which had used old maps that showed the inland sea frozen over.

The map Hapgood found in Joseph Needham's *Science and Civilisation in China*,[20] dating from 1137, was carved on stone; it was drawn over a grid of squares. Hapgood had made an interesting discovery about the Piri Reis map and various others that could be traced back to the time of the library at Alexandria. Their degree of latitude was shorter than their degree of longitude, because the original mapmaker had used an oblong grid; a later mapmaker had mistakenly changed this into a square grid, causing a 'longitude error'. Since this same longitude error was also present on the Chinese map, it looked as if its original also dated from a very long time ago. Hapgood came to the conclusion: 'Perhaps we have here evidence that our lost civilisation of five or ten thousands years ago extended its mapmaking here, as well as to the Americas and Antarctica.'

Again, Hapgood noted that West Africa, as depicted by Piri Reis, seems to have an ample water supply – for example, lakes that do not now exist are depicted – and other ancient maps cited by Hapgood show lakes in the Sahara. Between 10,000 and 6,000 years ago, the mistral - the north wind – was very wet, carrying moisture from the melting glaciers of the Ice Age, so that the Sahara was green and fertile. Since the Piri Reis map shows West Africa with lakes, it would seem that the original map used by Piri Reis dated from that wet period.

In *Maps of the Ancient Sea Kings* Hapgood built up his case until it became irresistible. It is impossible to dismiss the book as a work of imaginative speculation, for every page bears the marks of wide and patient scholarship. Yet the conclusions of its final chapter, 'A Civilisation That Vanished', would be bound to shock any scholar who took it seriously, for it sounds like the raw material of a novel by H. Rider Haggard or Jules Verne:

The evidence presented by ancient maps appears to suggest the existence in remote times, before the rise of any known cultures, of a true civilisation, of an advanced kind, which either was localised in one area but had worldwide commerce, or was, in a real sense, a *worldwide* culture. This culture, at least in some respects, was more advanced than the civilisations of Greece and Rome. In geodesy, nautical science, and mapmaking, it was more advanced than any known culture before the 18th century

23

of the Christian era. It was only in the 18th century that we first developed a practical means of finding longitude. It was in the 18th century that we first accurately measured the circumference of the earth. Not until the 19th century did we begin to send out ships for exploration into the Arctic or Antarctic Seas and only then did we begin the exploration of the bottom of the Atlantic. These maps indicate that some ancient people did all these things.[21]

Asking how a great civilisation can vanish without trace, Hapgood enunciated a basic principle of exploration: *that we find what we look for.* The portolans had been known for centuries. The Piri Reis map, discovered in the Topkapi Palace in Istanbul in 1929, had been discussed in the Library of Congress as early as the 1930s, before interest suddenly revived in 1956. But no one had seen its significance – or, if anyone saw it, was courageous enough to raise the questions that Hapgood asked.

Then why did the publication of *Maps of the Ancient Sea Kings* not cause a major academic controversy in 1966? The answer must be, partly, that academia was already a little suspicious of Hapgood. In 1958, when *Earth's Shifting Crust* finally appeared in print, it was accepted for abridgement by one of America's most popular weeklies, *The Saturday Evening Post*, which alone was enough to arouse the irritation – and envy – of academics. In his foreword to the later edition, *The Path of the Pole*, in 1970, the geologist F. N. Earll tells how, after reading this abridgement, he looked for reviews in technical and academic journals but found none. When the reaction finally came, says Earll, it 'could hardly be described as rational – hysterical would be a better description'. One academic declared indignantly that Hapgood was not a geologist, while another cited an authority who disagreed with the authorities Hapgood quoted and used that as a basis for condemning the whole book. In short, Hapgood was treated with fury and contempt for daring to write about geology.

As a result, none of these professors were going to enter into discussion of a book that claimed to have discovered evidence for a civilisation predating anything known to history. It was easier to ignore Hapgood.

There was another reason that no one was prepared to take Hapgood seriously. In 1960, a book called *Le Matin des Magiciens*, by Louis Pauwels and Jacques Bergier, broke all bestseller records in France, and was translated into dozens of languages. Pauwels was a journalist, while Bergier was a physicist who was also interested in alchemy. Their book was a flamboyant and dazzling hotchpotch of alchemy, archaeology, magic, hermeticism and literary speculation, with chapters on Lovecraft, the Great Pyramid, Gurdjieff and Nazi occultism. One of its major exhibits was the Piri Reis map, among other portolans. 'Had they been traced,' asked the authors, 'from observations made on board a flying machine or space vessel of some kind? Notes taken by visitors from Beyond?' As *The Morning of the Magicians* made its triumphal progress all over the world, the Piri Reis map became more widely associated with evidence for 'ancient astronauts'.[22] Hapgood, who had spent ten years working on *Maps of the Ancient Sea Kings*, could hardly have had worse luck.

In 1966, a Swiss hotel manager named Erich von Däniken, whose passion for travel had been satisfied mainly in the world of books, devoted his nights to writing a work arguing that our earth has been visited by spacemen in the remote past. The idea had been suggested four years earlier by a Russian astronomer called Joseph Shklovkii, in a book entitled *Universe, Life, Mind*, which was issued in America in 1966, with additional material by astronomer Carl Sagan, under the title *Intelligent Life in the Universe*.[23] Däniken's book consisted mainly of assertions that monuments such as the pyramids, the statues of Easter Island and the Mayan temples of Mexico were built by – or with the aid of – ancient astronauts.

Published in Switzerland under the title *Erinnerungen an die Zukunft (Memories of the Future)* in March 1968, it quickly became a bestseller, as did the English and American editions, entitled *Chariots of the Gods?*.

Scholars pointed out that the book was full of absurdities and inaccuracies. Däniken had managed to multiply the weight of the Great Pyramid by five, and his assertion that the Egyptians did not possess ropes or wood for rollers was easily contradicted by paintings on the walls of tombs and pyramids. His claim that the statues of Easter Island could not have been carved out of 'steel-hard volcanic rock' by stone tools was also disputed – Thor Heyerdahl did it in the 1950s with a few natives of the island, using stone tools found in the quarries. Däniken asserted that Easter Island also lacked wood for rollers, apparently unaware that trees once grew there, before all the timber was used up. Of the Nazca lines in Peru, Däniken claimed they were intended as runways for spaceships, ignoring the fact that they are merely scratched in the loose rocks of the surface. Whole books – and television documentaries – have been devoted to attacks on Däniken's 'evidence', demonstrating that most of it is based on ignorance of what the inhabitants of Egypt, Easter Island, Peru and other lands could actually have achieved.

Early in the book, Däniken (like Pauwels and Bergier) introduced the Piri Reis map: 'The latest studies of Professor Charles H. Hapgood . . . give us some more shattering information. Comparisons with modern photographs of our globe taken from satellites showed that the originals of Piri Reis's maps must have been aerial photographs taken from a very great height. How can that be explained?'

Hapgood, of course, had never said anything of the sort. The fact that Piri Reis failed to feature a 900-mile stretch of South American coastline and repeated another stretch suggests that the map was not taken from an aerial photograph. Nevertheless, millions of people were left with the impression that Hapgood was a supporter of von Däniken, and that he also believed the maps had been drawn by 'ancient astronauts'.

Hapgood was less concerned than he might have been – he had more important things to occupy his mind. For several years he had been convinced that he had found the actual whereabouts of Atlantis, and that this might even lead him to abandon the academic world for the more active life of an explorer. On 5 December 1958, he had written to his friend Ivan Sanderson to announce what he termed 'the most sensational discovery of our time'.

In studying the Piri Reis map, Hapgood had, as we have seen, noted a mysterious island about 1,000 miles off the coast of Venezuela and the mouth of the Orinoco River. Hapgood had also found two more ancient maps showing the island[24] and testifying to its existence. There is no such land mass now, only two very small islands known as the Rocks of St Peter and St Paul. Each about a quarter of a mile long, they are located above the Mid-Atlantic Ridge and are the tips of mountains that are now submerged. This, Hapgood was convinced, was all that remained above the surface of Plato's Atlantis – just where Plato hinted it was, in the mid-Atlantic. The size of this mysterious island – about 350 by 250 miles – sounded about correct. Plato also claimed that Atlantis had a great central mountain, a holy mountain, which Hapgood was convinced was now the Rocks of St Peter and St Paul.

Sanderson had advised Hapgood to avoid mentioning the word 'Atlantis' in *Maps of the Ancient Sea Kings* in case he was labelled a crank, but the warning was hardly necessary – Hapgood was too aware of the hostility of his critics to lay his head on the chopping block. Besides, the evidence should soon be available for everyone to see. All that was now needed, Hapgood assured Sanderson, was a rich benefactor who would lend them a yacht and pay for underwater cameras that would survey the slopes of the mountain – where, according to Plato, there should be about $500 million worth of gold.

In *Atlantis: The Eighth Continent* (1984),[25] Charles Berlitz
says that in 1963 Hapgood approached the White House,
hoping he could persuade President Kennedy to lend him an
aircraft carrier to investigate the seabed under the Rocks of St
Peter and St Paul. He quotes from Hapgood's unpublished
memoirs: 'It was fortunate that I had had previous contacts
with the White House when I did some errands for President
Roosevelt during World War II . . . It was no problem to find
someone close to the Kennedys in Massachusetts who could
arrange a meeting for me with the President . . . We had
mutual friends in the Democratic Party in Boston.' Hapgood
worked out a scheme whereby planes would fly in increasingly wide circles over the Rocks of St Peter and St Paul; if
anything was seen on the sea bottom, it would be investigated
with underwater cameras. He recognised the danger: if the
newspapers got hold of the story, it would become front-page
news and his own reputation would suffer; he therefore suggested that the search should be disguised as 'just another
oceanographic expedition'.

By October 1963 the meeting with Kennedy was arranged –
only to be frustrated by Kennedy's assassination in
November. Undeterred, Hapgood went on to suggest that
Nelson Rockefeller – who was a friend of Sanderson – might
be interested. Since Sanderson had once met Walt Disney at a
party, he might also be worth approaching; the search for
Atlantis would have made a marvellous live-action film.

But again, Hapgood was to be disappointed. For a decade
he continued to concentrate on writing and teaching. His
friend Sanderson died in 1973, and in that year Hapgood told
a correspondent named Henriette Mertz that although he
knew that the site of Atlantis 'lay around the Rocks of St
Peter and St Paul', he was abandoning the quest and could
only hope that others would follow up the trail he had so labo-
riously laid.

In October 1982, Hapgood wrote to a young correspondent
called Rand Flem-Ath,[26] adding an amazing postscript to his

life's work on ancient civilisations. After telling him that he was now preparing a third edition of *Earth's Shifting Crust*, to be published in 1983, he went on to speak of his latest discoveries: 'Furthermore, there is evidence that the last displacement of the crust moved both American continents southward about 30 degrees, and absolutely devastated life and civilisation on them, while climatic change was much less drastic in the Old World, and more avenues of escape existed.'

A shift of 30 degrees represented about 2,000 miles, a vast distance. If there had been a great catastrophe that devastated life and civilisation, then surely it must have happened more quickly than in the 5,000 years that Hapgood had previously supposed?

The next paragraph of the letter offered an even greater revelation: 'Furthermore, in recent exciting discoveries I believe I have convincing evidence of a whole cycle of civilisation in America and in *Antarctica*, suggesting advanced levels of science that may go back 100,000 years . . .'

One hundred thousand years? Could that have been a mistake for 10,000 years? No – the rest of the long letter was typed immaculately, without even a minor error. Hapgood obviously read it through carefully before putting it in the envelope. But at that time the ancestor of modern man, Cro-Magnon man, was not believed to have appeared on earth until about 40,000 years ago (although the date has since been pushed back beyond 200,000 years). Besides, Hapgood was not talking about cavemen with clubs, but a 'whole cycle' of civilisation, which included 'advanced levels of science'.

And in the next sentence he told Rand: 'A good deal of the evidence I have on this will be included in the new edition of ESC [*Earth's Shifting Crust*].' Hapgood was, admittedly, a maverick, but he would not have placed his whole reputation in jeopardy with some crank theory. He evidently felt that he had found evidence of *science* dating back 100,000 years, at a time when, according to 1982 palaeontology,* the most advanced human being on earth was Neanderthal man.

Rand Flem-Ath replied immediately, asking for some hint of Hapgood's reasons for this amazing assertion. For weeks there was no reply, then his letter was returned, stamped 'Deceased'.

Hapgood's last letter led Rand to his own quest for the origin of science and civilisation, of which this book tells the story.

---

*In 1982 anatomically modern humans were thought to be no older than 65,000 years. Today many palaeontologists believe that modern humans may have originated 200,000 years ago.

2

THE BLUEPRINT

In the summer of 1976 a twenty-seven-year-old Canadian named Rand Flem-Ath (he had changed his name from Fleming when he married Rose De'ath and they combined their names) went for a job interview at the Greater Victoria public library in Victoria, which is at the southern tip of Vancouver Island, in British Columbia. He would not hear the result until the following Monday, so to take his mind off the waiting over the weekend he decided to sketch out a screenplay. It was about a group of aliens, marooned on the earth, who decide to hibernate. While he was thinking about a suitable location, he heard a song by Donovan on the radio called 'Hail Atlantis'. An idea came into his head, and he scrawled on his writing pad: 'Atlantis = Antarctica'. Since he knew nothing about Atlantis, he spent the rest of the day at the public library reading up on Plato's lost continent beyond the Pillars of Hercules.

By the time he heard that he had the job, he was so fascinated by his research that there was no question of giving it up. And one reason, oddly enough, was his name. When he was at school, the class had been given an assignment to write

31

an essay on a famous person who shared their name. Doing research on his famous namesake, Sir Alexander Fleming, who was awarded the Nobel Prize for medicine, he learned how in 1924 Fleming had returned to his lab after a period away. He found that an unwashed culture dish in the sink was sprouting a mould that had killed off bacteria in the area around it. He tested the mould and discovered that it would destroy most bacteria – he had stumbled upon penicillin. Reading of his namesake's breakthrough, Rand Fleming decided there and then that he would never allow a coincidence to go uninvestigated – it could be the doorway to discovery.

Soon after beginning his job with the Greater Victoria public library, Rand stumbled upon his own coincidence. In book after book about Atlantis, he came across the same map. It was drawn by the seventeenth-century Jesuit priest Athanasius Kircher, a polymath who was as famous in his own time as Albert Einstein. In his *Mundus Subterraneus* (*Subterranean World*) of 1665, Kircher stated that it showed Atlantis, and that it was based on a map stolen from ancient Egypt by Roman invaders and found in the cellars of the Vatican. For some odd reason, Kircher put north at the bottom.

Rand had been an enthusiastic map reader ever since he was seven, when his father, who was in the air force, drove him from Nova Scotia to Arizona and then on to Los Angeles to see Disneyland. Rand was assigned the task of reading the road maps; he enjoyed this job so much that, from then on, he always took over the navigation on car journeys.

The Athanasius Kircher map led him on to the study of ancient charts, and he soon found Hapgood's *Maps of the Ancient Sea Kings*, with its subtitle *Evidence of Advanced Civilisation in the Ice Age*, in the catalogue of his library. Hapgood's book took his breath away. Here was a combination of his current obsessions, ancient maps and ice.

Flipping through the pages, he suddenly stumbled upon another significant coincidence. He was looking at a map of Antarctica without the ice, and it looked remarkably similar to

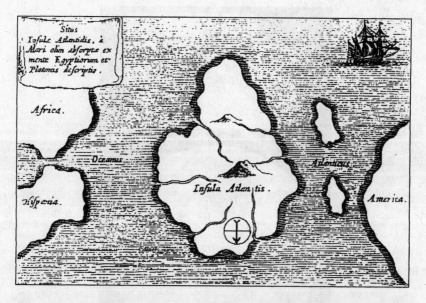

In 1665 Athanasius Kircher published a map of Atlantis which he claimed originated in Egypt. The Latin scroll reads: 'Site of Atlantis now beneath the sea according to the Egyptians and the description of Plato.'

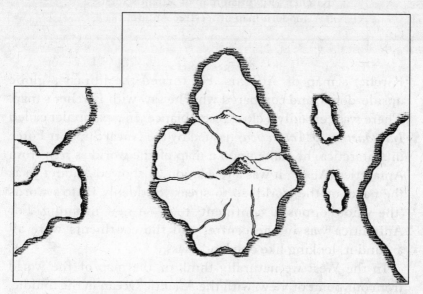

Kircher's map with his labels removed.

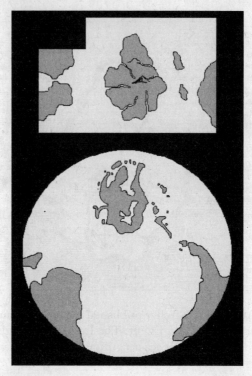

Kircher's Egyptian map of Atlantis versus a
modern map of ice-free Antarctica.

Kircher's map of Atlantis. He turned the library's globe
upside-down, and compared what he saw with Kircher's map.
There was certainly a close resemblance. In a pamphlet called
Introduction to Antarctica,[1] issued by the Naval Support Force
in Antarctica, he came upon a map of the world as *seen* from
Antarctica. Again, it was a revelation. It showed Antarctica as
the navel of the world, so to speak. Suddenly Plato's words
'the whole opposite continent' took on new meaning. For
Antarctica was in the centre, and the continents were all
around it, looking like one land mass.

In the West we naturally think of the map of the world
from our point of view, with the Atlantic Ocean in the middle,
as in the maps of our schooldays, divided off from the other

34

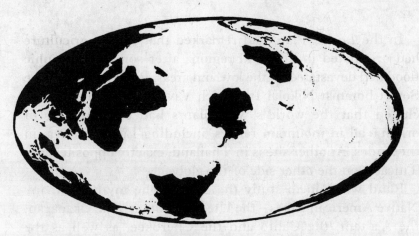

Oceanographers believe that the earth has only one ocean. The unity
of the 'World Ocean' can be seen in this US naval projection with
Antarctica in the centre. Plato's account of Atlantis tells of a lost
island continent in the 'real ocean'.

great ocean, the Pacific, by the American continent. Seen from
Antarctica, the world has only one great ocean, the 'true
ocean', just as Plato said.

Rand was so excited by his discovery that he wrote a paper
about it, entitled 'Atlantis of the True Ocean', and had it
notarised. Its opening paragraph contained the comment:
'Viewed from a satellite perspective, the Earth has but one
true ocean, and Antarctica is in its centre . . . The priest
described the location of Atlantis *from Atlantis*.'

Rand became obsessed by Atlantis; he now wonders how
Rose could tolerate him. He comments: 'I was a fanatic, as
defined by Winston Churchill as someone who can't change
his mind and won't change the subject.'

There was still one major obstacle to his identification of
Atlantis with Antarctica. Every encyclopaedia he consulted
said that Antarctica had been under the ice for millions of
years. Like Hapgood before him, Rand turned his attention to
the problem of what sort of catastrophe could destroy a whole
continent in a day and a night.

In the *Laws*,[2] Plato had remarked that world agriculture
had originated in highland regions after some catastrophic
flood had devastated all the lowland areas. Rand noted that the
Soviet botanist Nikolai Ivanovich Vavilov (1887–1943) concluded that the world's wild plants had eight centres of
origin,[3] all in mountain ranges, including Lake Titicaca, in
the Andes. Another site is in Thailand, exactly opposite Lake
Titicaca, on the other side of the globe.

Rand went on to study the catastrophe myths of many
Native American tribes – the Ute, the Kutenai, the Okanagan,
the A'a'tam, the Cahto and the Cherokee, as well as the
Araucanians of Peru. All have legends of violent earthquakes,
followed by floods. Many declare that a change in the face of
the sun made it look as if it was splitting apart; there were
dozens of flood myths too. It began to look to Rand as if their
sheer number pointed to some primeval catastrophe, 'when
the sky fell'.

In April 1977 Rose gave Rand the *National Atlas of Canada*
for his twenty-eighth birthday. Here he encountered another
anomaly that appeared to offer a clue. A map of Ice Age North
America showed that many islands in the far north, where
Rand's father had been stationed when Rand was twelve, had
been ice-free during the Ice Age. How could that be?

Rand tracked down a copy of Hapgood's *Earth's Shifting
Crust* at the University of Victoria, in fact the second edition,
retitled *The Path of the Pole*. And when Rand opened it, he
found himself looking at the end paper with a map labelled
'Path of the North Pole', showing no fewer than three different
positions of the pole over the past 80,000 years – the Yukon, the
Greenland Sea and Hudson Bay, the latter being the position it
occupied until around 9,600 BC. Hapgood's vast accumulation of
geological and geomagnetic evidence supported his views.

The geographic or what are known as the true North and
South Poles are measured by the earth's axis. However, the
magnetic North and South Poles are measured by the location
of the highest intensity of the earth's magnetic field. This is

usually within the proximity of the true pole. Using the fact of this proximity, Hapgood had been able to calculate the position of the former poles by examining their magnetic signatures written in cooling lava and rock in the past. As it flowed from the inner earth, the lava and the metals within it (especially iron) hardened into a position that pointed directly towards the magnetic pole. This provided Hapgood with the data he needed to determine the location of the previous poles.

The main piece of data was very simple. Geologists could trace the extent of the previous ice sheet by the marks it left behind, such as valleys carved by glaciers. We can picture the Arctic Circle as a circular piece of adhesive plaster, with the

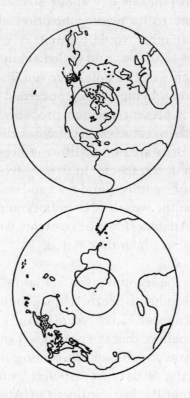

Prior to 9,600 BC, the Arctic Circle was centred on Hudson Bay (60N 83W) and the Antarctic Circle was in the South Indian Ocean (60S 97E).

North Pole as its centre. Before 10,000 BC, that plaster apparently reached further down, so that its centre was in Hudson Bay and its southernmost edge was as far south as Ohio. As Rand had noticed, the western edge of the plaster did not extend to the west coast of Canada. Hapgood concluded: 'Thus we are able to say that warm conditions of the Arctic Archipelago of Canada persisted for the entire duration of the Wisconsin glaciation, from 40,000 years ago to the establishment of modern conditions.'

Hapgood presented evidence to demonstrate, in the same way, that the North Pole moved from the Yukon district to the Greenland Sea about 80,000 years ago, then from the Greenland Sea to Hudson Bay about 50,000 years ago, and from Hudson Bay to its present position about 17,000 to 12,000 years ago. In other words, the most recent crustal movement began about 15,000 BC, and ended about 10,000 BC.

These movements of the Pole were not gentle and steady, and as far as human beings were concerned this shift from Hudson Bay to its present position probably involved many shocks, some of them cataclysmic, such as the crustal movement in the La Brea area of California around 11,000 BC, which killed off a dozen species in twenty-five years.

For the next four months, Rand read and reread *The Path of the Pole*, thrilled at the wealth of corroboration that Antarctica might have been Atlantis. Then he co-wrote with Rose a paper on his discoveries, in which they stated:

We believe that the account given in Plato's *Timaeus* is an accurate southern hemispheric 'global' view of the earth as it did in fact appear 12,000 years ago.

Further, we believe that the previous Temperate Zone of Antarctica was capable of supporting human settlements prior to the earth crust displacement.

We believe that the lost continent of Atlantis was our generally ignored lost island continent of Antarctica.

In addition, we believe that Atlantis was an advanced

civilisation (possibly a World Culture) which possessed an accurate advanced geographic view of the total planet.[4]

In July 1977, they sent this paper to Hapgood. The response they received was enthusiastic: 'I am astonished and delighted by your article which arrived here today. Believe it or not, it is the *first* truly scientific exploration of my work that has ever been done. You have found evidence for crustal displacement that I did not find.'[5]

They were thrilled, not only by Hapgood's typical warmth and generosity, but by his acknowledgement that they were doing important work. Rand's new evidence concerned the fact that in Antarctica the ice was thickest where there was least snowfall, which seemed absurd, since snow turns into ice. Equally odd was the fact that the ice was thinnest in areas with the heaviest snowfall. The most obvious explanation was that the areas with the thickest ice had been within the Antarctic Circle thousands of years longer than the areas with the thinnest ice. In other words, Antarctica had slipped lower, and a part that had once been outside the Antarctic Circle was now located inside it.

Rand had uncovered evidence of a massive floating ice sheet that once extended from the Antarctic to the southern Indian Ocean. If such an ice sheet melted quickly because it suddenly entered a warmer zone, the bottom would be severely disturbed; in fact there was evidence in the scientific literature that that was just what had happened. When the continent of Antarctica, which had once been free of ice, slipped into the Antarctic Circle, it pushed a giant ice sheet – of the type that now covers the North Pole – up towards India on the other side of the globe. Rand found references to this ice sheet in two obscure papers tucked away in the journal *Science*,[6] published since Hapgood's *Path of the Pole*.

Rand had made another important discovery that had eluded Hapgood: the work of a forgotten writer named William Fairfield Warren, the founder of Boston University, who had first conjectured that worldwide myths of a falling sky and a lost paradise were memories of a great geological upheaval, although he suggested that this original paradise was at the North Pole. *Paradise Found: The Cradle of the Human Race at the North Pole* (1885)[7] is an immensely erudite work, obviously inspired by Donnelly's *Atlantis*, citing evidence from Japanese and Chinese literature and a vast array of ancient cultures: Persian, Egyptian, Akkadian, Assyrian, Babylonian and Greek.

Rand also discovered the work of another forgotten scholar, the Indian Bal Gangadhar Tilak, who published studies of the earliest Indian sacred texts, the Vedas. Tilak, inspired by Warren, wrote *The Arctic Home in the Vedas* (1903).[8] He had found evidence for Warren's arctic paradise in the scriptures of ancient India, as well as in the Persian *Zendavesta*, especially in the fact that the ancient scriptures contain evidence of knowledge of polar conditions, including the length of the polar day and night. The unknown authors of the Vedic hymns appeared to be familiar with the geography of the polar regions.

Rand pointed out that if Tilak had not been so influenced by Warren's interpretation of Vedic literature, which placed north at the centre of the earth, he would have seen that the Antarctic was a far likelier home for his island paradise. Hapgood had pointed out, in any case, that the North Pole ice cap dated back at least 50,000 years, which was an unlikely time for the island paradise to have evolved, whereas the Antarctic ice sheet dates back only 10,000 or 15,000 years. (Rand was mildly irritated when Hapgood used his arguments about Warren and Tilak in the second edition of *Maps of the Ancient Sea Kings* in 1979 without acknowledgement.)[9]

As delighted as they were with Hapgood's warm encouragement, the Flem-Aths were puzzled that he failed to react to the suggestion that Atlantis *was* Antarctica. If someone had taken the trouble to map the interior of Antarctica when it was divided into two islands, the people most likely to be responsible were, surely, its inhabitants? It was not until 1995, when Rand was investigating the Hapgood archives at Yale, that he realised that Hapgood thought he had already discovered Atlantis much further north, in the Rocks of St Peter and St Paul. Rand's own view, however, was that Hapgood was mistaken. It was true that the mysterious island on the Piri Reis map looked about 250 by 350 miles, and that according to Plato the plain behind the city of Atlantis was about 229 by 343 miles,* but Plato also explained that the continent of Atlantis was as big as Libya and Asia (approximately North Africa and the Middle East) put together, the mountainous part of Atlantis being far greater than the plain. There is no sign of a continent as large as that beneath the Atlantic.

Encouraged by Hapgood as Hapgood had been by Einstein, Rand and Rose began work on a book called *Atlantis At Last!*, which summarised the results of his research. It was finished in 1980. They began to look for a publisher and Rand continued to develop his own theories about 'when the sky fell'.

In 1981 Rand and Rose (who had been born in England) moved to London, where Rand was able to use the facilities of the British Museum Reading Room to continue his research on Atlantis. To support themselves, Rose found work as a temp, while he found work at the Conoco oil company.

The job suited Rand; he was in daily contact with geologists and geophysicists, for it was his responsibility to provide them with maps of the North Sea bed, along with available geological evidence, in preparation for a government announcement about North Sea oil exploration. The information Rand was gathering would enable the company to decide which areas to bid for. He led a team of five people, and his skills in map-reading served him well. He also enjoyed discussing Hapgood's shifting crust theory with professional geologists,

---

*The figures Plato gives are 3,000 by 2,000 stadia (or stade), and a stadia (or stade) is roughly equivalent to an English furlong, about an eighth of a mile.

and was pleased to find that so many were open-minded about it. All his spare time was spent in the British Museum. They found a publisher for *Atlantis at Last!*, but unfortunately it went out of business before publication. However, Rand's days in the Reading Room were providing so much fascinating information that publication undoubtedly would have been premature and would have led to a sense of anticlimax. He worked on with an increasing excitement as new discoveries strengthened his certainty that Hapgood's theory of earth's shifting crust was sound.

What continued to puzzle him was why Hapgood continued to be ignored by earth scientists, even though his arguments for 'the path of the pole' were backed with such a mass of scientific evidence and scientific acceptance of the theory of plate tetonics had made his crust displacement theory far less controversial. While following up some remarks by Hapgood on the origins of agriculture, he stumbled upon a possible explanation in a book called *The Structure of Scientific Revolutions* by Thomas S. Kuhn. Its arguments had made Kuhn famous – or infamous – in the scientific community when it appeared in 1962: Kuhn had proposed that scientists are mistaken to think of the pursuit of science as a detached and unemotional activity. Once they have become comfortably settled with a certain theory – Kuhn preferred to use the word 'paradigm' – they develop an emotional attachment to it, like a mother with a baby, and if anyone challenges it they become defensive, remaining totally convinced that their irritation is the annoyance of a reasonable man in the face of time-wasting absurdities. This is why the great scientific revolutions – of Copernicus, Newton, Einstein and quantum theory – encountered such furious resistance. Even into the 1960s, the eminent British geophysicist Sir Harold Jeffreys maintained that the earth's crust is immovable in spite of the evidence of plate tetonics. Kuhn pointed out that the proof required to budge such entrenched opinion is enormous – facts stand no chance in the face of a lifetime of believing in the same theory.

Now working for a group called Business International, a consulting firm specialising in providing research for corporate executives, Rand encountered an instructive – and amusing example – of this. He became a friend of one of Kuhn's graduate students, and on many occasions the two of them discussed Hapgood's shifting crust theory, with Rand explaining how it could account for the origins of agriculture, extinctions and glaciation patterns. After several months, Kuhn's student was in total agreement that Hapgood's crust displacement was a good example of Kuhn's 'paradigm shifts' and the kind of hostility they encounter, until one day, when Rand admitted that his interest in the subject had been triggered by Plato's account of Atlantis. Suddenly Kuhn's student refused to discuss earth crust displacement any more.

Concerned that increasing commitments to their careers might prevent them from dedicating their energies to developing their ideas about Atlantis, Rand and Rose decided to return to Victoria to work on the book. The four years in London had been of immense importance to the development of Rand's theory. After Hapgood's death in 1982 – which shook Rand badly – Rand felt that he had inherited the problems that Hapgood had left unsolved.

The main one, of course, was what actually caused the crust to shift. In *The Path of the Pole* Hapgood had come to agree with Einstein that the answer was *not* the 'washing machine' effect, whereby an irregular polar ice cap caused the earth to 'judder', but he had accumulated a vast amount of other evidence that the crust does shift. Rand was inclined to believe that Milankovich's hypothesis about ice ages was right, agreeing that they occur when three factors – tilt, perihelion and eccentricity – coincide. He concluded that the main factor was the earth's 41,000-year tilt cycle.[11]

Rand and Rose wrote *When the Sky Fell*, and began to submit it to publishers. Perhaps he might have been better off retaining the old title *Atlantis at Last!*. If Rand had suggested that the ancient maps proved that the earth had been visited by extraterrestrials from another galaxy, the book would probably have been accepted by the first publisher who read it, but a sober study on earth crust displacement, with an appendix on the origins of agriculture, seemed to lack bestseller potential, even if it did argue that Atlantis was in Antarctica. Hapgood was forgotten and his works had fallen out of print; why bother to revive them? One publisher found it 'fascinating but too academic', and another 'intriguing but too academic', while a third said it left him breathless but he couldn't figure out what audience they had in mind. Finally, the Flem-Aths accepted that the book would never be published.

A decade passed, during which Rand and Rose moved to Vancouver Island. A publisher had not been found for the Atlantis book, but Rand continued to read the scientific literature on archaeology, mammal extinctions and anything else that had a bearing on his quest for Atlantis. Although he was unaware of it, the climate was gradually becoming more favourable for his book. The breakthrough came when John Anthony West read the manuscript and agreed to write an afterword.

West was an Egyptologist, although he would certainly not have been recognised as such by the archaeological establishment. To begin with, he was fascinated by the work of a man who was unmentionable in Egyptological circles: René Schwaller de Lubicz. Schwaller (the 'de Lubicz' was bestowed later by a Lithuanian prince of his acquaintance) was the son of a well-to-do Alsatian pharmacist; he went to Paris in his twenties to study painting under Matisse, but soon moved into the study of theosophy and alchemy. He founded an 'esoteric school' called Suhalia near St Moritz, in Switzerland; after it broke up in 1929, he and his wife Isha moved to a large country mansion in Grasse, in the south of France, then in 1937 to Egypt, where he became fascinated by the temple of Luxor.

Schwaller came to believe that the Egyptians possessed a mode of thought that the modern world is almost incapable of grasping. In Alexandria he visited the tomb of Rameses IX, where he was fascinated by a painting that showed a right-angled triangle in which the hypotenuse was formed by the body of the pharaoh. The sides of the triangle formed the ratio 3:4:5, in other words, the triangle with which every schoolchild is taught Pythagoras's theorem that the square on the hypotenuse is equal to the sum of the square of the other two sides. Schwaller was intrigued, since Rameses IX ruled around 1,100 BC, more than 500 years before Pythagoras. Since Schwaller had spent many years studying the architecture of the cathedrals of the Middle Ages, he was familiar with the story that the knowledge of the medieval masons came from ancient Egypt. He began a systematic study of Egyptian temples, and of Luxor in particular.

The first thing that strikes the tourist who looks at his map of Luxor is that the temple is 'bent', as if the courtyard that lies inside the entrance has been knocked slightly sideways by a blow from a giant mallet. Since the Egyptians were master builders, who could place blocks together so precisely that a razor blade cannot be inserted between them, there is obviously a reason for this anomaly. The marvellous harmony of the architecture leaves little doubt that it is part of some geometrical plan.

Schwaller set out to solve the riddle. The outcome was his masterwork, *The Temple of Man* (1957),[12] demonstrating that the Luxor temple is of immense geometrical complexity, and that it is a symbolic representation of a man – a kind of gigantic hieroglyph. Because the man is striding forward, like the striding colossus of Rameses II in its south-east corner, the courtyard representing the lower part of the leg has the shape of a square knocked sideways.

One of Schwaller's main insights was that the temple also contains many examples of the geometrical proportion known as the 'Golden Section' (and called by the Greek letter phi). It sounds like an obscure definition from a geometry book, but it is a notion of profound importance, and it also plays a central part in the precise location of sacred sites.

45

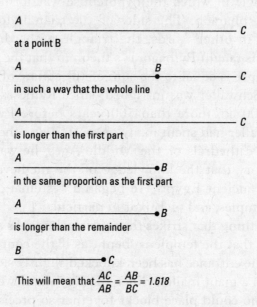

The Golden Section, or φ, is obtained by dividing a line

A ——————————————————————— C

at a point B

A ———————————————— B ————— C

in such a way that the whole line

A ——————————————————————— C

is longer than the first part

A ————————————————————• B

in the same proportion as the first part

A ————————————————————• B

is longer than the remainder

B ————————————• C

This will mean that $\frac{AC}{AB} = \frac{AB}{BC} = 1.618$

Nature uses the Golden Section all the time. Your body is an example, with your navel acting as the division between the two parts. It can be found in the spirals of leaf arrangements, petals around the edge of a flower, leaves around a stem, pine cones, seeds in a sunflower head, seashells – even in the arms of spiral nebulae. Why is nature so fond of it? Because it is the best way of packing, of minimising wasted space. Artists also discovered it at a fairly early stage, because this way of dividing a picture is oddly pleasing to the eye, in exactly the same way that musical harmonies are pleasant to the ear.

Obviously, there is something very important about this simple-looking number. It is, in fact, 0.618034 . . . , going on to infinity, non-recurring, as some decimals do.

Another form of phi is 1.618. If you wish to extend a line a phi distance, you simply multiply it by 1.618.

Another piece of mathematics is significant: a sequence of numbers discovered by the mathematician Fibonacci, in which each number is the sum of the preceding two numbers. If you begin with 0 and the next number is 1, 0 + 1 equals 1. And that 1 plus the previous 1 equals 2. And that 2 plus the preceding 1 equals 3. And so on: 0, 1, 1, 2, 3, 5, 8, 13, 21, 34, 55 . . .

If you take any two Fibonacci numbers, and divide each one by the one before it, the answer gets closer and closer to the Golden Number 0.618034 . . . the bigger the numbers concerned. No matter how big the numbers become – even billions or trillions – the number never quite reaches the Golden Number.

These Fibonacci numbers can be found in pine cones, nautilus shells and spiral nebulae.

This is what excited Schwaller so much when he detected it in the Luxor temple. He had spent his years in Switzerland studying the laws of universal harmony, as epitomised in cathedrals such as Chartres. His results had been stolen by an alchemist called Fulcanelli, who had published them as his own in 1925 in a book called *The Mystery of Cathedrals*,[13] which quickly became a classic. Schwaller had no doubt that this law of harmony was a part of a far older tradition that was already well established by the time of ancient Egypt. When his first results were published in 1949 in *The Temple in Man*, they caused an intellectual furore of the kind that the French enjoy so much, and Schwaller became briefly as famous as contemporaries like Sartre and Camus. (It did not last – the public soon tired of Egyptian geometry.)

Schwaller believed that this tradition predated ancient Egypt because during his first visit to the Sphinx he had no doubt whatever that it had not been eroded by wind-blown sand, but by water. This suggested that it dated back long before 2,500 BC, the usual date assigned to the pyramids of Giza. Schwaller was familiar with an occult tradition that the Sphinx was not built by ancient Egyptians, but by survivors from the civilisation of Atlantis, who had fled some time before the final catastrophe. In his last book, *Sacred Science*,[14] he spoke of an Atlantean race, 'ancient vestiges of which have now been determined in western Africa; a wave of these people, having crossed Saharan Africa, finally settled in the valley of the Nile'. The true date of the construction of the Sphinx must be some time around 10,000 BC.

Schwaller died at Grasse in 1961, at the age of seventy-four. Although his books soon went out of print, a copy of *Sacred Science* fell into the hands of a student of Egyptology called John Anthony West. West was convinced that it was absurd to believe that ancient Egypt had come into being about 3,100 BC – the date accepted by most Egyptologists – and that a mere five centuries later it was already building the pyramids. That, he felt, would be like asking us to believe that Europeans had no civilisation until five centuries before Chartres Cathedral. The more West learned of Egyptian science, medicine, mathematics and astronomy, the more it seemed to him obvious that Egyptian civilisation was far, far older than Egyptologists usually believe.

As he read *Sacred Science*, he realised there might be a simple way to prove this. If the Sphinx and its enclosure had been eroded by rain, not by wind-blown sand, a good geologist ought to be able to tell at a glance. He discussed the problem in a strange book called *Serpent in the Sky*[15] – strange because it spends most of its time discussing Schwaller de Lubicz, Egyptian geometry and the Golden Section. The book was sent to me for review in July 1979, and I was naturally most impressed by its final chapter, 'Egypt: Heir to Atlantis', with its photographs comparing the Sphinx enclosure with the cliff face behind the temple of Queen Hatshepsut, with erosion in both places that geologists agree to be water weathering. To me they certainly looked remarkably similar.

It took West many years to find an open-minded geologist who could command the respect of his colleagues. Eventually, accompanied by Boston University geologist Robert Schoch, West made the trip to Cairo. As they stood before the Sphinx enclosure, he was understandably nervous, half expecting

Schoch to point out that he had made some elementary error and that the erosion *was* caused by sand. To his relief, Schoch took one look and agreed that this was water weathering.

The difference is easy to explain. When a rock face is blasted by wind-blown sand, its soft layers are worn away while its hard layers continue to jut out, so the profile of the rock looks like a layer cake or a club sandwich. When a rock face is eroded by rainfall, the soft layers are still worn away horizontally, but the rain also cuts vertical channels, so the profile of the rock is a little like a series of babies' bottoms, with rounded curves. Such weathering could be seen on the Sphinx and the Sphinx enclosure.

In Schoch's opinion the Sphinx might well have been built around 7,000 BC which would make it 9,000 years old instead of 4,500. When he announced this result to fellow geologists at a conference of the Geological Society of America in October 1991, it aroused intense controversy, although – strangely enough – many of the geologists were inclined to agree. It was the Egyptologists among them who denounced Schoch's views as pure fantasy.

West also persuaded a senior forensic artist, Frank Domingo of the New York Police Department, to examine the battered face of the Sphinx, and assess whether it might be that of the pharaoh Chefren, whose bust had been found buried in the Valley Temple facing the Sphinx. Domingo went to Cairo and applied to the Sphinx the same methods he would employ in trying to identify the damaged face of a corpse from a photograph. His conclusion was that the Sphinx was emphatically *not* Chefren – the chin was more prominent, the mouth a different shape, and the cheeks sloped at a different angle.

West published an article about the findings in a glossy magazine and sent me a copy. It so happened that I had been asked to write a film outline about Atlantis for a Hollywood producer, and had used West's theory that the Sphinx had been built by survivors from Atlantis. We met in New York in

September 1993, and he showed me the rough cut of a television documentary he had made about the Sphinx. When I told him that I was thinking of writing a book about the whole question of the Sphinx and the age of civilisation, he recommended that I contact two other writers who were working along the same lines. One was an economics journalist named Graham Hancock, who had written a book called *The Sign and the Seal*,[16] about the Ark of the Covenant, and was now writing a book arguing that civilisation may be many thousands of years older than historians believe. The other was a Canadian librarian called Rand Flem-Ath, who had written a book about Atlantis that was still in typescript. I made a note of both their addresses.

How had John West come to hear about Rand and *When the Sky Fell*? By another coincidence. In March 1993, Rand read a copy of a magazine called *Saturday Night*, which contained an article about the Sphinx by Paul Roberts,[17] a writer on Eastern philosophy, telling the story of John West and Robert Schoch and describing West's suspicion that the Sphinx may have been built by survivors of Atlantis. Rand wrote to Paul Roberts, enclosing an outline of *When the Sky Fell*. To his delight, Roberts replied a few days later by fax, expressing his willingness to read the entire book. Paul Roberts sent the outline on to his old friend John West, and also suggested a Canadian publisher.

When I returned to England in late September 1993, I lost no time in writing to Rand and to Graham Hancock. Within little more than a week, I had received typescripts of *When the Sky Fell*, and of a book called *Fingerprints of the Gods*.[18]

Hancock's typescript was vast. He was not, like Däniken, arguing that space visitors were responsible for civilisation but simply proposing that our human ancestors – who built Tiahuanaco in the Andes and the pyramids of Mexico and Egypt – were far more technically accomplished than had ever been acknowledged. He cited astronomical evidence by the Bolivian scholar Arthur Posnansky, who had spent a lifetime studying the ruins of Tiahuanaco, that the 'temple' (or Kalasasiya) had been built about 15,000 BC, some 9,000 years before the latest estimates of the beginning of civilisation in the Middle East.

Hancock also drew on the work of a Belgian engineer, Robert Bauval, presented in a book called *The Orion Mystery*.[19] Bauval had seen a photograph of the three pyramids at Giza taken from the air, and had been struck by their rather odd arrangement. The first two pyramids – the Great Pyramid of Cheops (Khufu), and the pyramid of his son Chefren – were neatly arranged so that a diagonal could be drawn from the upper left-hand corner of the Great Pyramid, straight through the opposite corner, and then on through the same two corners of the Chefren pyramid. You would expect that line to continue on through the two corners of the smallest of the three pyramids, that of Menkaura. So why was the third pyramid completely out of alignment? And why was it so small, compared to the other two? Menkaura was as powerful a pharaoh as his father and grandfather.

The answer came to Bauval when he was in the desert one night, and saw the three stars of Orion's Belt – Orion looks like two triangles placed point to point, and the Belt runs across its middle. The three stars were arranged exactly like the three pyramids. Moreover, the Milky Way, stretching across the sky beside them, looked very much like the Nile running north past the pyramids. Bauval knew that the Egyptians regarded their land as a reflection of heaven. Did they mean that quite literally, building the pyramids to reflect the Belt of their sacred constellation of Orion, which represented the god Osiris?

However if the pyramids were meant as a representation of the stars of Orion's Belt, Bauval noticed that they were not quite an exact reflection. Because of a phenomenon called the precession of the equinoxes, the constellation moves up and down the sky over a period of about 26,000 years. As it does so, it twists slightly – imagine that the double-triangle is impaled on the end of the minute hand of a clock, and you can see that as it moves from twelve o'clock to half past twelve, it will turn completely upside down. Actually, precession causes the constellation to move only to about ten past twelve, but it still changes its angle. Bauval calculated that the last time Orion actually 'reflected' the pyramids of Giza, as if reflected in a vast mirror, was about 10,500 BC.

Bauval felt that this date must have had some deep significance for the ancient Egyptians – in fact, it was what their holy scriptures referred to as the 'First Time', *zep tepi*, the beginning of Egyptian history. Was the Sphinx built to commemorate that 'First Time' around 10,500 BC? If Bauval was correct, the Sphinx's construction predated Schoch's estimate of 7,000 BC.

Bauval did not think that the pyramids were also built in 10,500 BC – he thought that certain astronomical evidence concerning the 'air shaft' out of the Queen's Chamber indicated that the Great Pyramid had actually been built around 2,500 BC, just as Egyptologists believe, but he felt the whole Giza complex was almost certainly planned in 10,500 BC. In *Fingerprints of the Gods*, Graham Hancock suggests that perhaps the lower part of the Chefren pyramid had been built in 10,500 BC, since its massive blocks are quite unlike the much smaller blocks of the other two pyramids.

Graham Hancock was immensely helpful to me when I began my own book, which was eventually published as *From Atlantis to the Sphinx*.[20] Graham sent me two complete versions of the typescript of *Fingerprints of the Gods*, and the next year the typescript of the sequel on which he and Robert Bauval collaborated, *Keeper of Genesis*,[21] with an invitation to use anything I wanted.

Rand had also played his part in the success of *Fingerprints of the Gods*. Graham has described how, when he was finishing *Fingerprints of the Gods*, he was at a low ebb physically and mentally – physically because of months of travel, mentally because he was beginning to doubt his own findings about a lost civilisation that preceded ancient Egypt and Sumeria. His researcher added to his problems by resigning, explaining that there was simply no place on earth where the remains of such a lost civilisation could be concealed. It was certainly not at the bottom of the Atlantic, where there was no evidence whatever of a sunken land mass.

At that moment Graham received a letter from Rand, who had been given his address by Paul Roberts. The enclosed outline of *When the Sky Fell* solved his problem, while the various maps he had studied – those of Piri Reis, Philip Buache, Oronteus Finnaeus – now all fell into place, like the missing pieces of a jigsaw puzzle. Atlantis *had* to be situated in Antarctica. With that single recognition, Graham tied up all his loose ends.

Also in *When the Sky Fell* Rand suggested that the language of the Aymara, who live around Lake Titicaca, has a structure that is so logical that it can be written in an algebraic shorthand that computers can understand; it can therefore be used as an intermediate language in enabling computers to translate other languages. Its structure is so simple that a Bolivian mathematician, Rojas de Guzman, suggests that it did not just evolve, but was constructed from scratch.[22]

That sounds like another argument for Erich von Däniken's visitors from the stars, but neither the Flem-Aths nor Graham Hancock use it as such. They simply point out that legends of 'gods' exist all over Central and South America, and that the gods come from the east. Their chief has a beard (Native Americans do not have beards) and looks like a European; he had many names in different parts of South America – Viracocha, Quetzalcoatl, Kon Tiki, Votan, Kukulcan – and he is known as the 'god' who brought civilisation and a moral code forbidding slaughter. When he finally sailed away, he promised to return. In fact, the Aztecs of Mexico mistook the invasion of the Spaniards for the return of the gods, which is why their empire was conquered so easily. Professor Arthur

Posnansky concluded, from Aymara legends,[23] that they believe that their language was that of the gods. Neither Graham Hancock nor the Flem-Aths assume the existence of visitors from space to explain many of these ancient mysteries – the white gods from the east may have been fleeing from their own disintegrating continent when they came to Mexico and South America.

So in 1993, after years of disappointment in trying to find a publisher for *When the Sky Fell*, the Flem-Aths suddenly began to sense that things were improving. I offered to write an introduction to the book, and it appeared in 1995, a year before my own *From Atlantis to the Sphinx* and Bauval and Hancock's *Keeper of Genesis*.

Keeper of Genesis aimed to explain why, if the ancient Egyptians (or Atlanteans) had made plans for the Giza pyramids in 10,500 BC, they waited another 8,000 years to build them. The reason, according to Bauval and Hancock, was ceremonial. By 2,500 BC, the precession of the equinoxes had finally brought the constellation of Orion (which represented Osiris) to a point in the heavens that reflected the Giza plateau – the place of the 'First Time' – on the ground. The Egyptians built the Great Pyramid and enacted an elaborate ceremony in which Osiris arrived home in the pyramid, and then left for his home in the sky. It is a thesis that is bound to arouse a certain scepticism, rather like suggesting that disciples who were present at Jesus's crucifixion later planned to build the Vatican in AD 8,000 in order to perform a ceremony symbolic of the Resurrection, but it is certainly argued on the basis of immense astronomical knowledge.

When the Sky Fell was translated into nine languages. Rand soon found himself embarking on a new project, linked to his previous work.

In November 1993, shortly before *When the Sky Fell* had been accepted, John West sent Rand an article by Robert Bauval that summarised the arguments that would appear in *The Orion Mystery* and *Keeper of Genesis*. Bauval had explained his view that the pyramids of Giza exactly mirrored the stars of Orion's Belt most recently in 10,500 BC, at the beginning of the present 'precessional cycle', and he argued that the Sphinx had been built at that date. Rand had dated the last great crust shift at 9,600 BC. John West wanted to know how could Rand account for this discrepancy of 900 years?

Rand replied that all the archaeological and geological evidence pointed to 9,600 BC as the correct date. But Bauval's argument did not imply that the Sphinx *had to* have been built in 10,500 BC, simply that it memorialised that date. There is a memorial in Plymouth to the Pilgrim Fathers who sailed on the *Mayflower*, but it was not built in 1620.

The question nevertheless continued to nag at Rand, just as the Atlantis problem had nagged at him twenty years earlier, until a serendipitous event brought it into sharper focus. Rose often brought home library books that she thought might interest Rand; one was *Archaeoastronomy in Pre-Columbian America* (1975) by Dr Anthony Aveni.[24] It provided a vital clue.

The most important prehistoric monument in Mexico is undoubtedly the vast religious complex of Teotihuacan, 20 miles north-east of Mexico City. At the height of its prosperity, around AD 600, it had extended for 12 square miles, a city larger than imperial Rome. Then, around AD 750, there was a sudden and total collapse. Its cause is still unknown, although an earthquake seems probable, since large areas of the city were found to have burned to the ground.

A 2-mile avenue, known as the Way of the Dead, runs through Teotihuacan from north to south. At its northern end stands the pyramid of the moon, while the immense pyramid of the sun lies off the avenue to the west.

But, oddly enough, the Way of the Dead does not run exactly north–south – it was 15.5 degrees off true north, pointing north-east. No one knows why. One suggestion was that the avenue was aligned on the setting of the Pleiades (or Seven Sisters), a constellation that was important in Meso-American mythology.

Rand was excited to learn that there are no fewer than forty-nine other sacred sites in Mexico that are also misaligned to the north-east. As he studied the Way of the Dead, he was struck by an interesting suspicion. Was it conceivable that when the holy site of Teotihuacan was first laid out, it *did* point to true north – *at the old North Pole in Hudson Bay?*

At first sight, that seemed unlikely. The Hudson Bay Pole dated back before 9,600 BC, and even outside estimates for Teotihuacan claim that it was founded no earlier than about 4,000 BC (the most widely accepted estimate among archaeologists is a mere 150 BC).

Rand was also aware that most major religious sites are built on older religious sites, as if the ground itself is regarded as sacred. From Australia to Northern Europe, from China and Japan to Canada, a sacred place remains sacred over the millennia. Many temples are built on the site of older temples. In the early seventh century AD, Pope Gregory the Great told Augustine, who Christianised England, to build Christian churches on pagan sites. The Dome of the Rock in Jerusalem, one of Islam's holiest places, is built on a Jewish holy site. Archaeology has uncovered the remains of five different cities at Tiahuanaco in the Andes. If civilisation existed before 10,000 BC, as both Hapgood and the Flem-Aths believed, then it was likely that Teotihuacan had been a holy place for thousands of years before 4,000 BC.

Hapgood had stated that the longitude of the old North Pole in Hudson Bay was about 83 degrees west of our present Greenwich meridian (its latitude was 60 degrees north). Teotihuacan is 98 degrees, 53 minutes west. On a map of the Americas, it looked very much as if the Way of the Dead pointed straight at the Hudson Bay Pole, but as a map is a projection of the globe on a flat surface, it might therefore give the wrong impression. At all events, it *looked* as if the Way of the Dead was aligned on the old North Pole, and that was a vital first step.

What about the other forty-nine 'misaligned' Mexican sites?

Rand examined four – Tula, Tenayucan, Xochicalco and Copan – and the results were always the same. The layout of all of the sites seemed to point within a degree of the old North Pole, as if they pointed at the old North Pole like sign-posts.

Aveni made one extremely interesting comment: 'Many persist in believing that what we're really looking at are the remains of a mega-land survey undertaken by a vanished civilisation of Atlanteans.' He obviously had in mind writers such as Peter Tompkins (author of *Secrets of the Great Pyramid*[25] and *Mysteries of the Mexican Pyramids*)[26] and the British writer John Michell,[27] who popularised the concept of 'ley lines' – lines of earth-force – in the 1970s, but he had only mentioned this idea to dismiss it. Like all academics Aveni would have regarded Atlantis as purely mythical, a happy hunting ground for cranks. Since both Hapgood and Rand were fairly certain that Atlantis – or some civilisation like it – had actually existed, Aveni's comment was certainly thought-provoking.

Let us assume, for the sake of argument, that there had been some kind of sacred temple at Teotihuacan before 10,000 BC, and that it was aligned on the old North Pole. And let us also assume that the forty-nine other 'misaligned' sites in Mexico were also aligned on the Hudson Bay Pole. If Hapgood is correct, Antarctica would have been perhaps 2,000 miles further north than it is today, and would have had a pleasant, temperate climate.

The different locations under scrutiny suggest a civilisation that is spread over a fairly wide area. Professor Posnansky thought that Tiahuanaco, in the Andes, had been a flourishing city around 10,000 BC and that it had been so since 15,000 BC. We also seem to be looking at something like Hapgood's notion of a worldwide maritime civilisation (he dated this around 7,000 BC, but we also know that he believed that Atlantis was destroyed in 9,600 BC). If such a civilisation existed, then the idea of a 'mega-land survey' ceases to look absurd. Hapgood's 'maps of the ancient sea kings' implied something of the sort – maps that showed the present Antarctica when it was free of ice.

At this point, a website called 'How Far Is It?' enabled Rand to calculate the exact distance from any place on earth to any other spot. More importantly, it also showed the exact bearings from one to the other. Sadly the first result of this new tool was a major disappointment. When Rand used it to calculate the position of Teotihuacan relative to the Hudson Bay Pole, he discovered that it did not, after all, point at it like a signpost – it was at an angle of 11.6 degrees rather than the 15.5 degrees he had been assuming. Rand pressed on with his studies. The idea that the Mexican sites pointed to the old North Pole like different signposts had not been proved, even though so many *were* aligned east of north, but the website had given him another, and equally useful, tool – distance.

All over the earth, 1 degree of latitude is equal to roughly 70 miles. (Degrees of longitude, by contrast, vary from 66 miles at the equator to inches at the poles. Indeed, at the North or South Pole you can walk around all the earth's longitudes in seconds.)

Rand knew that the Great Pyramid revealed an extraordinary knowledge of mathematics and geography. Its four sides are aligned exactly to the four points of the compass, and its site is exactly 30 degrees north of the equator – precisely one-third of the distance from the equator to the pole. Evidence that the Egyptians knew the length of the equator and its distance from the poles and that the Pyramid itself is intended to represent half of the earth, from the equator to the North pole, indicates that the Egyptians of 2,500 BC had knowledge of *worldwide* geography.

Would the Great Pyramid, probably the most famous sacred site in the world, yield any evidence to support the theory that sacred sites were aligned on the old North Pole?

Rand fed the Giza co-ordinates into the website, and discovered that, at the time of the Hudson Bay Pole, Giza would have been 15 degrees further south (naturally, because the pole itself was further south). Rand now imagined drawing a line from the Great Pyramid to the old North Pole, and another from the Great Pyramid to the present pole. He discovered that the angle between the two lines was 28 degrees – the number 28 seems to play a basic part in the Giza site: there are 28 steps in the Grand Gallery that leads up to the King's Chamber, and the Sphinx Temple had 28 pillars. Moreover, in *Keeper of Genesis*, Bauval and Hancock had pointed out that, as seen from Giza, the solstice points (the positions where the sun comes up over the horizon during the longest day of the year and the shortest day of the year) are 56 degrees apart – that is, 28 degrees between each solstice* and the equinox point.

Rand's most exciting discovery was that the Sphinx Temple had a 28-degree bearing from the mortuary temple of the Great Pyramid, *and that if this bearing is extended it points literally like a signpost to the Hudson Bay Pole.*

It is worth noting that the Sphinx Temple and the Valley Temple, both standing in front of the Sphinx (and on either side), were built in a 'megalithic' style from gigantic blocks, and that West, Hancock and Bauval have all argued that they date from a more remote early period. The same is true of the mortuary temple of the Great Pyramid, which is why Rand looked for a connection.

Concerned to verify the methods of his approach and to be sure his results were not just the outcome of chance calculations, Rand looked carefully at other sites, concentrating on locations on the far side of the Atlantic, in the Middle East. Here he had no Professor Aveni to summarise the evidence conveniently, so he had to piece together the evidence from site to site. It was slow work, but proved to be worthwhile. Just

---

*Solstices occur on the dates (22 December and 21 June) when the sun stops rising further north or south every day, and turns back (at the Tropic of Cancer or Capricorn) to retrace its route.

as the Mexican sites are misaligned to the east of the present North Pole (i.e., towards the old Hudson Bay Pole), so the Middle Eastern sites were oriented to the west of it, again towards the Hudson Bay Pole. These included:

(1) Ur of the Chaldees. Its famous ziggurat and shrine to the moon goddess Nanna are oriented west of north.
(2) Nippur, south of Baghdad, where the tablets of *Gilgamesh* were found, relating how the island paradise Dilmun was destroyed in a great flood.
(3) The ziggurat and 'White Temple' of the Sumerian city of Uruk.
(4) The Wailing Wall of Herod's temple in Jerusalem, which pointed straight at the old North Pole.

As in the case of Giza, what Rand also began to look for were the latitudes of the sacred sites. He soon came to note what he called 'sacred latitudes' occurring again and again: any latitude that would divide neatly into 360 degrees – such as the 30 degrees of Giza. Quito, the northern capital of the Inca Empire, and Carthage, the Phoenician city, had both been at 30 degrees north during the Hudson Bay Pole. Others, such as Easter Island, Mohenjo-Daro and the Tibetan holy city of Lhasa, were located on the equator.

When he had identified forty sites on 'sacred latitudes' Rand was fairly certain that this was not just a game with numbers.

Sacred latitudes when the Pole was at Hudson Bay (60N/83W). All of these sites are within half a degree (30 nautical miles) of a sacred latitude. Raiatea and Tahiti, in the South Pacific, are the closest land to the sacred latitude.

50°   Rosslyn/Loanhead/Kilwinning, Tara/Newgrange/Knowth, Dunecht, Uxmal, Chichen Itza

45°	Copan/Quirigua, Canterbury
30°	Carthage, Quito
25°	Troy, Constantinople
15°	Giza Pyramids, Jericho/Jerusalem, Ashur, Nazca, Gilgal, Heliopolis
12°	Babylon, Pyongyang
10°	Ur/Uruk/Eridu, Thebes/Luxor, Susa, Ise, Nara, Kyoto Heian, Kumasi, Naqada, Lagash
5°	Byblos, Xi'an, Lalibala, Elephantine, Raiatea, Tahiti
0°	Lhasa, Aguni, Mohenjo-Daro, Easter Island

Note: Sites connected by '/' are located so close together that they yield the same results.

When the Sky Fell was published in Canada in January 1995, and was soon translated into several languages. Graham Hancock's *Fingerprints of the Gods* came out in April 1995, and its immense success made it clear that there was now a worldwide audience for seriously researched books about ancient civilisations. My own *From Atlantis to the Sphinx*, dedicated to John West, Graham Hancock and Robert Bauval, appeared in May 1996, and sold out its first impression on the day of publication. *Keeper of Genesis*, by Robert Bauval and Graham Hancock, appeared in 1996, and was soon at the top of the bestseller list. *The Hiram Key*[28] by Christopher Knight and Robert Lomas was equally successful.

In due course, the television programme I had made with Rand was shown on the Discovery Channel – it was called *The Flood*. While watching it early in 1998 I wondered if Rand and Rose had seen it. The answer proved to be no – they had not even known that it had been transmitted – so I made them a copy and airmailed it to Vancouver Island.

Its arrival was again serendipitous. Rand had written an article about his sacred alignment theory, which was being published in a magazine called *Atlantis Rising*. It concluded:

I never thought to find another adventure to compare with my eighteen-year search for Atlantis. But the unique placement of the earth's most sacred sites has emerged as a mystery that compels me with the same kind of fascination as that journey. I hope to share this quest within the pages of a new book, *Finding the Future: Blueprints from Atlantis*, which will lift the veil from these ancient sites to reveal concealed time capsules – messages, records and even blueprints – from Atlantis.[29]

But he had a problem. Rose was busy working on her second novel and, as a full-time librarian, Rand had even less free time. As they watched the tape of *The Flood*, Rand said, 'I wonder if Colin might be interested?' They both thought it unlikely, since they knew I was working on *Alien Dawn*,[30] but Rand decided to fax me anyway, also sending the article he had written for *Atlantis Rising*.

As I read it, I felt my scalp prickling. If his theory of sacred alignments was correct, then he had stumbled on the most powerful proof so far of a pre-Atlantean civilisation. I lost no time in faxing back my acceptance. After that, we transferred our correspondence to email, for it soon became clear that the vast amount of information he had accumulated would have to be sent in files of a dozen or so pages at a time. Within less than two months I had more than 200 pages.

Most of this material was about sacred alignments. However, another line of investigation produced some astonishing and almost unbelievable evidence of Hapgood's 'advanced levels of science' long before the earliest known civilisations.

3

THE GIZA PRIME
MERIDIAN

IN OCTOBER 1884, Professor Charles Piazzi Smyth, the Astronomer Royal for Scotland, was involved in a controversy on a matter dear to his heart: persuading a committee of experts from twenty-five countries of the world to make the north–south line that ran through the Great Pyramid the prime meridian of the world, 0 degrees longitude.

It may sound odd that, towards the end of the nineteenth century, when great steamships had been plying the oceans for decades, such a question should remain undecided. There had been numerous prime meridians – virtually one for every country that used the sea. Pope Alexander VI had decreed in 1493 that it should run 100 leagues west of the Azores. Louis XIII of France supported a line through Fero in the Canaries. That was enough to make Charles II of England decide to build the Greenwich Observatory, with the intention of designating Greenwich as the prime meridian. The French disagreed, and then said it should run through Paris. As other countries built observatories, most of them declared their own capital the site of the prime meridian, which is why, in

October 1884, twenty-five European countries gathered in Washington, DC, to make a final decision.

Greenwich was high on the list of candidates because so many ships used the port of London, but Smyth was passionately opposed to it. In the *Report of the Committee on Standard Time and Prime Meridian*,[1] published in Cleveland, Ohio, in June 1884, he argued that the Pyramid was the ideal choice because such a meridian would pass over more land than any other.

The Great Pyramid, he pointed out, was acknowledged to be the grandest monument ever erected. As a further argument, he drew attention to its closeness to Jerusalem, evoked the Second Coming of Christ, and asked whether every good Christian would not agree that a Giza meridian would be ideal.

The answer was no. The delegates were not at the conference as Christians but as scientists. Twenty-two of the twenty-five candidates voted for Greenwich – the French, of

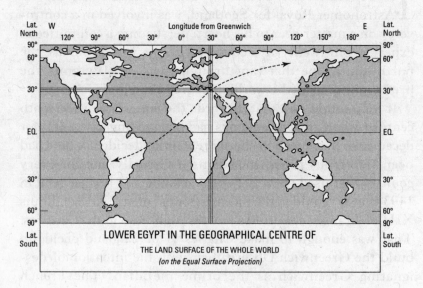

Astronomer Charles Piazzi Smyth recognised that the Great Pyramid was located at the centre of the earth's land mass.

course, abstaining. And so a thoroughly sensible and logical proposal was rejected.

In 1997, Rand was approached by a friend of John West, an airline pilot, who wanted to know if he had any information to suggest that Giza was the prime meridian – the pilot wanted to organise a Millennium rock concert at Giza, which could claim to have entered the new century two hours before London. When Rand sent him the reference to Smyth it struck him that, since he had the latitude and longitude of so many sacred sites, it would be a simple matter to add or subtract Giza's longitude (31 degrees, 8 minutes east) to see what would happen if Giza *was* the prime meridian instead of Greenwich. Suddenly dozens of sacred sites began to fit into a vast global pattern.

Quite simply, sites whose latitude and longitude looked unpromising because they seemed 'too complicated' (with too many decimals) now began to fall into simple round figures.

For example, Tiahuanaco, whose longitude is 69 degrees west of Greenwich, is also 100 degrees west of the Great Pyramid. The former Inca capital at Quito is at 110 degrees west of Giza and other very significant sites, including Teotihuacan and Easter Island, are found at 120, 130 and 140 degrees west of the Great Pyramid. This pattern also extends eastward. Ur of the Chaldees is exactly 15 degrees east of Giza and the Tibetan capital of Lhasa is 60 degrees east of the Great Pyramid.

What was even more significant was the fact that many of these round figures were phi numbers. Tiahuanaco, for example, was 10 phi; so was the ancient Polynesian spiritual centre Raiatea (this is also at 180 degrees latitude from the Giza meridian). Since I had described so many of them in my *Atlas of Sacred Sites*,[2] I was as astounded and excited as Rand when he told me of his breakthrough.

One of Rand's most startling discoveries came shortly afterwards. He had discovered that there were no fewer than eight sacred sites at the 10 phi north latitude during the Hudson Bay Pole.

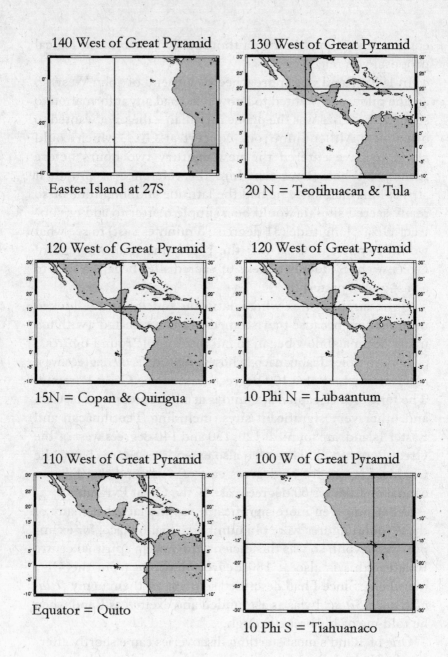

140 West of Great Pyramid

Easter Island at 27S

130 West of Great Pyramid

20 N = Teotihuacan & Tula

120 West of Great Pyramid

15N = Copan & Quirigua

120 West of Great Pyramid

10 Phi N = Lubaantum

110 West of Great Pyramid

Equator = Quito

100 W of Great Pyramid

10 Phi S = Tiahuanaco

Pyramids and megaliths in America and Easter Island
are linked to a Giza prime meridian.

10 phi sites during the Hudson Bay Pole. 10 phi is 4429.2 nautical miles from the Pole, which is equal to 16:11N.

Sacred site	Co-ordinates	Distance to HBP (nautical miles)	Former latitude
Baalbek	34:00N/36:12E	4,431	16:09N
Paracas	13:50S/76:11W	4,431	16:09N
Cuzco	13:32S/71:57W	4,433	16:07N
Sidon	33:32N/35:22E	4,437	16.03N
Machu Picchu	13:08S/72:30W	4,407	16:33N
Ehdin	34:19N/35:57E	4,408	16:32N
Ollantaytambo	13:14S/72:17W	4,414	16:26N
Nineveh	36:24N/43:08E	4,451	15:49N

Rand reasoned that there should be a current sacred site at 10 phi north to match Tiahuanaco's 10 phi south, and that it should also be linked to the Great Pyramid. He had looked in his atlas for a very specific spot: 10 phi north of the equator, and 120 degrees west. There was nothing obvious – just three little red dots, and a name that was so tiny that he had to take off his glasses to read it. He had never heard of it: Labaantum, in Belize in central America. Via the Internet he had found out that 'Lubaantum (Place of Fallen Stones)' was an ancient Mayan ceremonial centre with three pyramids and terraces made of dressed stone blocks.

It turns out I could have told Rand about Lubaantum immediately, for I had written an article about it in a book called *Unsolved Mysteries Past and Present*.[3] Lubaantum will always be associated with the famous Crystal Skull, better known as the Skull of Doom, dating to about AD 700 and discovered in a Mayan temple by the adopted daughter of the explorer F. A. 'Mike' Mitchell-Hedges, Anna Mitchell-Hedges, on her seventeenth birthday in 1927.

According to Anna, she had called her father after seeing something shining under an altar. With the help of locals (descendants of the Maya), they moved the stones and saw that the shining object was the top part of a skull. It proved to be a beautifully carved death's head. Three months later, Anna found the missing lower jaw buried in rubble. The local Maya told Mitchell-Hedges that the skull had been an object of worship, and had been used for healing and dealing death to enemies. Mitchell-Hedges gave it back to the locals, but when he finally left, at the end of the rainy season, they returned it to him as a mark of appreciation.

There are two other rock crystal skulls in existence, but the 'Skull of Doom' is by far the most beautiful and perfect. With the rise of New Age thinking in the 1960s, it became legendary, and many books have been devoted to it.

Oddly enough, Mitchell-Hedges was curiously reticent about the skull in his autobiography *Danger My Ally*.[4] After claiming that it is at least 3,600 years old and took about 150 years to be polished, Mitchell-Hedges went on to say: 'How it came into my possession I have reason for not revealing.'

Sadly, the reason was almost certainly that the Skull did not actually originate in Lubaantum. In the 1980s, an American investigator named Joe Nickell unearthed an article about crystal skulls in a journal called *Man*, which dated from 1936, including a description of a skull with a moving jaw that sounded very much like the Skull of Doom. But it stated that this skull was in the possession of an art dealer named Sidney Burney, who had put it up for auction at Sotheby's in 1943, but it had been withdrawn when the bids reached only £340. The records of the British Museum state that the skull was sold to Mitchell-Hedges for £400 in 1944. Mitchell-Hedges, who died in 1959, at the age of seventy-one, was an adventurer rather than an explorer, and his books – with titles like *Land of Wonder* and *Battles With Giant Fish* – reflect the character of a man who was in some respects an overgrown schoolboy. His character was not above reproach – in 1928 he lost a libel battle against the *Daily Express*, which had accused him of having staged a fake robbery for the sake of publicity – so the Crystal Skull was most likely not found in Lubaantum.

In spite of the uncertainty that surrounds the events of its appearance in the twentieth century, the skull is undoubtedly genuine. The rock crystal from which it is carved probably came from Calaveras County, in California. A Californian art conservator named Frank Dorland, who was allowed to examine the skull for a period of six years, concluded that it might well have been over 12,000 years old. Nickell had objected that mechanical grinding of the teeth proved that it was more recent, but a far less perfect crystal skull in the British Museum, also genuine, displays mechanical grinding of the teeth too. The laboratory of the Hewlett-Packard Company, which manufactures crystal oscillators, subjected the skull to laser-beam tests and concluded that it had been manufactured from a single large crystal and polished over about 300 years, doubling Mitchell-Hedges's estimate. It had peculiar optical qualities, as if lenses had been inserted inside it, although this is obviously impossible. Dorland claimed that, when he kept it in his house overnight instead of returning it to the bank, there were poltergeist disturbances.

If the skull was *not* found at Lubaantum, why should all this be relevant? Because Frank Dorland concluded that the skull originated in Mexico, and went on to point out that the native peoples there used a grinding wheel driven by a string stretched across a bow.

An altogether more credible figure in South American exploration was Lieutenant-Colonel Percy Harrison Fawcett, whose disappearance was one of the most widely publicised mysteries of the 1920s.

During the last decade of his life, Fawcett was searching for a lost city in the jungles of Brazil. There is strong evidence that this mysterious city really existed. In the National Library in Rio de Janeiro, Manuscript No. 512 gives an account of how, in 1753, a band of Portuguese treasure hunters spent ten years wandering in the vast interior of Brazil, an area that is almost the size of Europe.[5] Coming upon a deserted city built of huge blocks of stone, they decided to return to civilisation for reinforcements and sent an account of the city by native runner to the Viceroy in Bahia. What happened to them then is unknown, and the manuscript lay forgotten in the archives for almost eighty years.

This story actually goes back further, to 1516, twenty-four years after Columbus discovered America, when a Portuguese sailor named Diego Alvarez was the sole survivor of a shipwreck close to the place where Bahia now stands. He was taken captive by a cannibal tribe, the Tupinambas, but for some reason they spared his life and allowed him to live among them. This may have been because of the influence of a local girl named Paraguassu, who became his wife (Fawcett refers to her as 'the Pocahontas of South America'). More Portuguese arrived, and, through the good offices of Alvarez, they established a colony. Paraguassu's sister also married a Portuguese, and it was her child, Melchior Dias Moreyra, who became known to the locals as Muribeca. He discovered silver mines and became a wealthy man, but he kept their location in the interior a secret.

Regrettably his son, Roberio Dias, born to wealth, cherished an ambition to become a member of the aristocracy. In about 1610, Roberio approached the King of Portugal, Dom Pedro II, and offered to sell him the mines of Muribeca in exchange for a title of nobility – the Marquis of the Mines.[6] The king agreed, but first he wanted to lay his hands on the silver mines.

On his way back to Bahia, Dias discovered that the King had no intention of keeping his half of the bargain. When he persuaded an officer to let him see the sealed patent of nobility, he was infuriated to discover that the document would merely confer the rank of captain in the army. Dias knew that he was in a dangerous position. If he refused to hand over the silver mines, he would be imprisoned by the governor, Dom Francisco de Souza, a haughty aristocrat who disliked being frustrated. So Dias played for time, and led the governor's expedition on a wild-goose chase. The governor, finally realising he had been outwitted, threw Dias into prison, where he remained for two years until he managed to buy his freedom. He died shortly thereafter, and the location of the mines of Muribeca remained a secret.

Many adventurers set off into the wilderness in search of the lost silver mines, and the government also sponsored expeditions called bandeiras, or 'flags', the members of which were known as bandeiristas. In 1753, more than a century after the death of Roberio Dias, a group of six Portuguese bandeiristas set out on a well-equipped expedition with black slaves, native guides, and pack animals. They went inland, into the state of Minas Geraes, then made for the Central Plateau. There they vanished for many years, but Manuscript No. 512 describes their adventures in some detail. A full translation can be found in *Mysteries of Ancient South America* (1956) by Harold Wilkins.[7]

After years of wandering, the party eventually encountered a cordillera (mountain chain) largely composed of a mineral whose crystals glittered in the sun. At close quarters, the mountains were seen to consist of bare rock, with white streams plunging from the heights. They seemed to be practically impenetrable until one of the slaves saw a white deer that fled into a cleft. Pursuing it, he came across a road, which seemed to have been man-made. He fetched the others, and soon they were all ascending it, dazzled by the crystalline splendour of the mountains above them.

At the summit of the pass, they were able to look down on an open plain, and there, about 3 miles away, they saw a great city, so impressive that they assumed it must be connected with the court of Brazil. Afraid that they had been seen against the skyline and that the inhabitants might be hostile, they descended as quickly as possible to the valley then decided to wait to see what would happen. After two days of silence, they sent one of the natives on a scouting expedition. He returned saying that he had seen no one, not even a footprint. The rest of the scouts then went ahead to investigate, and came back with the same story. The city seemed to be uninhabited.

At daybreak the next day, the whole party advanced cautiously and prepared for an ambush. The road led them to three great archways; the one in the centre, the tallest, had unknown letters engraved on it far above their heads. Beyond the arches was a wide road, with great houses whose facades were 'blackened with age'. Everything was silent and deserted. There were broken pillars, with parasitic vegetation growing from the cracks, and the buildings were roofed with stone slabs. When the bandeiristas ventured inside the rooms, they found that the floors were covered with debris and bat droppings to a depth that suggested that these buildings had been abandoned many centuries ago.

In the middle of the city they came to a vast square, in the centre of which was a black stone column with a statue of a man who pointed towards the north. Carved obelisks of black stone stood at each corner of the square. On one side of the plaza was a magnificent building, whose roof had partly collapsed. Ruined steps ran up to a wide hall, and the walls showed traces of coloured frescoes. This place was also full of bats, and the smell of their droppings made them cough.

Beyond the main square, the city was a ruin, with mounds of earth and chasms in the ground. It was obvious that this place had been devastated by an earthquake. The city was bounded by a deep and wide river, on the far side of which were green fields with many flowers. They could also see lakes with flocks of geese.

They decided to follow the river downstream, and after three days came to a huge waterfall, beyond which the river spread so wide that it 'appeared to be a great ocean'. There were several tree-covered islands and an abundance of game. They also saw big anacondas and poisonous snakes.

To the east of the river they found great holes that could have been mine shafts, and one was covered with a huge flagstone with certain symbols carved into it. Near the 'mines' they found some abandoned bars of silver.

There was also a ruined temple with more of the strange letters above its portico, as well as the ruins of a 'country house'. Looking inside, they found a stairway built of coloured stone leading to a large hall, with rooms opening out from it. Each of these rooms contained the remains of a fountain.

They continued downriver, and the narrator became convinced that they were in the vicinity of rich mines – perhaps the legendary mines of Muribeca. A scouting party ventured on for nine days, and at a place where the river spread out so wide that it was like 'a great bay' they saw a canoe manned by 'two white persons with long, flowing black hair, dressed like Europeans . . .' When they fired a gunshot to attract attention, the canoers paddled off in the opposite direction.

The narrator mentioned that one of their company, a man called Joao Antonio, found a large gold coin with an image of a kneeling youth on one side. No doubt, he said, there were other such coins to be found under the rubble of the dead city.

The party decided that they had better make their way back to civilisation. At the Paraguassu River, the narrator wrote their story – and presumably sent an Indian messenger ahead with it. He concluded by begging the governor to keep its contents secret, lest someone else should mount an expedition before they could.

What happened to the group of Portuguese and their slaves and guides is unknown; all that we know is that the manuscript disappeared into the archives, became partly eaten by insects, and was found eventually by a Brazilian archivist in 1841, almost a century after it had been written.[8]

Harold Wilkins, a British author who wrote in a pleasantly old-fashioned style but whose books were excellently researched, obtained his transcript of the document in 1939 with the help of the American consul-general in Rio de

Janeiro, W. G. Burdett. Colonel Fawcett had seen it at least twenty years earlier, and concluded that it was a truthful and accurate account.

A reader's first reaction to the tale of a journey to a lost city is that it is probably fiction, but both Fawcett and Wilkins saw the manuscript, and the travel writer Peter Fleming, who tried to follow in Fawcett's footsteps (and describes it in *Brazilian Adventure*, 1933),[9] quoted its archive reference, No. 512.

Percy Harrison Fawcett, born in Devon in 1867, joined the Royal Artillery and in his twenties served at Trincomallee, in Ceylon, where he became interested in Buddhism and spent his leaves in a search for the lost treasure of the Kandyan kings. On the whole Fawcett disliked the army, so when, in 1906, the President of the Royal Geographical Society asked him how he felt about the idea of going to Bolivia to map the north-eastern frontier, Fawcett accepted eagerly on condition that the army would agree to lend him to the Bolivian government. His story of these adventurous years was told in his posthumous book *Expedition Fawcett*, edited by his son Brian.[10] He described encounters with poisonous spiders, snakes, vampire bats, even wild bulls, which they were forced to kill. Searching for the source of the River Verde, the whole party ran out of food and starved for twenty-three days. They were all close to death when a deer suddenly appeared. Fawcett was so weak he could scarcely lift his rifle, but by what he regarded as a miracle he killed it. They ate the whole deer, including the fur and skin.

It was during this expedition that Fawcett tried to take a short cut over flat-topped hills covered with forest, but he was finally forced to return to the valley. It was his story of this forest-covered plateau that inspired Sir Arthur Conan Doyle to write *The Lost World*.[11]

Fawcett returned to England to serve in Intelligence during the First World War, emerging with a Distinguished Service Order; then he went back to South America, hot on the trail of the lost city of the bandeiristas. In 1920 floods caused him to turn back from an expedition into the Matto Grosso (Great Forest) of Brazil.

Fawcett had no doubt of the existence of Atlantis. Although he accepted that the continent had sunk beneath the waves, as Plato describes, he was convinced that many of the inhabitants had escaped to South America. He wrote in *Exploration Fawcett*:

> However much romance may have coloured the tales, the fact remains that the legendary existence of a highly civilised remnant of an ancient people persisted among the indigenes of the continent . . . There is a remarkable similarity in the accounts, which makes it reasonable to conclude that there is a basis of truth in them.[12]

Fawcett stated his belief – remarkable for that time – that 'the curse of a great cataclysm'[13] fell on South America, and he seemed to accept that this was the catastrophe that destroyed Plato's Atlantis. 'There can be little doubt that a cataclysm of such dimensions produced tidal waves and minor catastrophes throughout the world.' It caused 'the rising of the Andes' and brought to South America a people who were 'expert in the arts of civilisation'. Fawcett's conclusions were remarkably similar to those we have reached in this book.

The survivors also built cities like the one discovered by the 1743 expedition. 'The existence of the old cities I do not for a moment doubt,' says Fawcett. 'How could I? I myself have seen a portion of one of them – and that is why I observed that it was imperative for me to go again. The remains seemed to be those of an outpost of one of the biggest cities . . .'[14]

This raises an interesting question. Why does he seem unsure? It seems likely that the rest of the city was completely covered by the jungle, like those lost Mayan cities discovered by Stephens and Catherwood in the 1830s. This means, in turn, that Fawcett knew where to look for a lost city, although it emerges from his book that he thought there were many of them.

He determined to go and find at least one of them, but his objective on that last expedition was not apparently the deserted city of 1753 discovered by the bandeiristas. He had heard of 'clothed natives of European appearance', who avoided all contact with the outside world. 'Our destination on the next expedition – I call it "Z" for the sake of convenience – is a city reputed to be inhabited, possibly by some of these timid people . . .' This implies three different cities: the deserted city of 1753, the city whose outskirts he observed, and 'Z'. No wonder Fawcett was determined to return to Brazil.

He left England for South America once more, spending the years from 1921 to 1924 raising the money for the expedition. When an American 'fund-raiser' squandered most of this on a six-week orgy of drunkenness, Fawcett set to work again, and finally had sufficient funds to continue.

It was not to be an elaborate expedition; there was only Fawcett, his twenty-one-year-old son Jack and a young Devon friend of Jack called Raleigh Rimell. They had to be prepared to carry their equipment on their backs.

The greatest danger would be after they had reached Cuyaba (now spelled Cuiaba), the capital of the Matto Grosso, by boat, then made their way north to the unknown region between the rivers Xingu and Araguaya. Fawcett believed 'Z' lay to the east of this. In the manuscript later published by his son, Fawcett left fairly exact directions: first of all, he explained, he wanted to visit an ancient stone tower, to solve the mystery of why its doors and windows were lit up at night, terrifying the local Indians.

Beyond the Xingu we shall take to the forest at a point midway between that river and the Araguaya, and from there cross by an existing trail to the Rio Tocantins at Porto Nacional or 'Pedro Alfonso'. Our way will lie between latitude 10 degrees 30 minutes and 11 degrees to the high ground between the states of Goyaz and Bahia, a region quite unknown and said to be infested by savages, where I expect to get some trace of uninhabited cities. The mountains there are quite high. We shall then follow the mountains between Bahia and Piauhy to the River Sao Francisco, striking it somewhere near Chique-Chique, and if we are in fit condition to do so, visit the old deserted city [that of 1753] which lies approximately 11 degrees 30 minutes south and 42 degrees 30 minutes west, thus completing the investigations and getting out at a point from which the railway will take us to Bahia City.[15]

Although Fawcett gave the precise latitude and longitude of the 'deserted city' of the bandeiristas, his son Brian, in a footnote, added: 'I have personally investigated the bearings he gives for the 1753 city, and can state authoritatively that it is not there.'[16] It would seem that, for whatever reason, Fawcett gave the wrong co-ordinates – an odd mistake for a man who was so meticulous.

By 20 May 1925 they had reached the village of the Bacairy, north of Cuiabo.[17] They were still experiencing inconvenience rather than danger – the man who had sold them mules had cheated them, and Jack's leg had swelled with a tick bite, so they had to stay at the farm of a friend to recover. The chief of the Bacairy told them that he had always hoped to make the journey to the 'great waterfall'.

Then, after staying in a village of the Nafqua – where Fawcett had in 1920 presented the chief with a uniform case[18] – they went by river to a village of the Kalapalo on the River Kuluene. And there, on 29 May 1925, their trail comes to an end. The Kalapalo later claimed that Fawcett's party had struck out across country to the east, and that the smoke of their camp fires had been visible for five days, but in 1951 the chief of the Kalapalo, Izarari, made a deathbed confession to killing Fawcett and his companions. He claimed that Fawcett had slapped his face when he had refused carriers, and that he had clubbed him to death; the other two, he said, had been killed defending Fawcett.

This story raises doubts: a man with Fawcett's self-control would not be likely to strike a tribal chief. Izarari also alleged that Jack Fawcett had seduced one of his wives, which sounds more likely. In later years, many travellers claimed to have learned the truth about Fawcett's death, and one of the more plausible stories is that Jack Fawcett had violated some tribal taboo, and that his crime had to be punished by death else Izarari's people would themselves become outcasts and killed by other tribes.

Whatever happened, it seems clear that Fawcett never reached the city he called 'Z', or the deserted city of Manuscript No. 512.

I finished *Exploration Fawcett* in an odd state of frustration. No one who reads it could doubt that Fawcett knew exactly where he was going and what he was looking for. He had talked to many people – Europeans and Indians – about lost cities, and was quite certain that they existed and knew roughly where they were.[19] The person I needed to consult was obviously Rand, whose fascination with Fawcett and Brazil had started when he found references to him in the Hapgood archive at Yale in 1995. He was also interested in South America, since he felt that if Atlantis *was* Antarctica, then it was almost certain that many of its inhabitants escaped to South America.

Rand had one site in mind as the location of the deserted city. He had already ascertained that if Giza is used as the post-Atlantis prime meridian, a whole series of sites fall on multiples of 10 degrees: Tiahuanaco is 100 degrees west of the Great Pyramid, Quito is at 110 degrees, and so on. It seemed to Rand that there *ought* to be a major sacred site at 90 degrees from Giza, not merely because it is a multiple of ten but because it is also a quarter of the distance around the world.

Tiahuanaco's latitude (16 degrees, 38 minutes) had at first seemed disappointing, until Rand realised that it is 10 phi from the pole. The perfect place for a major religious site in the Matto Grosso would be at 90 degrees west of Giza, and 10 phi south.

I looked up this site in my *Times Atlas*, but saw that this could not have been Fawcett's objective on that last journey. It was about 50 miles south of Cuiaba – Fawcett's last major halt – and on the border of Bolivia and Brazil. However, as Rand pointed out to me, it was in an area that Fawcett had explored during his surveying days (the area where he and his companions had almost starved to death). In *Mysteries of Ancient South America*, Harold Wilkins states: 'Fawcett's friends speak of other strange tales brought to the Colonel by wandering Indians, whose tribal law he had studied in the Matto Grosso and the borders of Brazil and Bolivia.'[20] It seems at least probable that this site is the location of the city that was half covered by jungle, but it was not on Fawcett's route during that final journey.

Meanwhile I had faxed to Rand Fawcett's own map of his intended route (from *Exploration Fawcett*), together with his co-ordinates for the 'city of 1753'. I was hoping, of course, that Fawcett's coordinates (11 degrees, 30 minutes south, 42 degrees, 30 minutes west) would fall on one of Rand's sacred sites, but it was not to be. It turned out to be 73 degrees, 38 minutes west of Giza, and in terms of the 'blueprint' that means nothing.

But Rand, far from being disappointed, recognised that it provided an important clue. He noted another possible sacred site within 100 miles of the 'city of 1753', at 72 degrees west of Giza, which is one-fifth of the distance around the world, and again 10 degrees south. He wrote to me:

Fawcett gave 11 degrees 30 minutes south and 42 degrees 30 minutes west for the site of the 'city of 1753', whereas the 'blueprint' location is 10 degrees south and 40 degrees 52 minutes west. When you round out the blueprint lon-gitude to the closest half degree (which seems to have been Fawcett's practice), it becomes 41 degrees west. Please note the following:

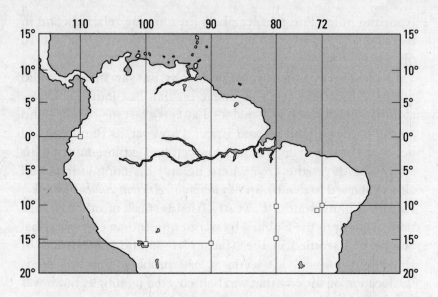

The Giza Prime Meridian links sacred sites from Easter Island (140 West of Great Pyramid) to Tiahuanaco (100WGP). This pattern can be extended into the Amazon, where other sacred sites await discovery. Each box represents a sacred site or a potential sacred site. From left to right they are: Quito (Equator 110WGP); Tiahuanaco (10Phi S 100WGP); Lost Atlantean City (10Phi S 90WGP); Fawcett disappeared here; Potential sacred sites (10S 80WGP and 15S 80WGP); Fawcett's Z location; Potential sacred site (10S 72WGP)

11 degrees 30 minutes south, 42 degrees 30 minutes west – Fawcett's location of the city of 1753
minus 10 degrees south, 41 degrees west – Atlantis blueprint location to the nearest Greenwich longitude
equals 1 degree 30 minutes, 1 degree 30 minutes.

Both are off one and a half degrees.

In short, Rand suspected that Fawcett had disguised the location by one and a half degrees east and south.

Rand made another interesting point. *If* Fawcett was disguising the location of the 'deserted city' by adding 1 degree 30 minutes to both its co-ordinates, then he was identifying a spot that is one-fifth of the way around the world from the Giza meridian. Is it possible that Fawcett had also stumbled on this notion of the Giza meridian? Fawcett was a youth of seventeen when Smyth was agitating for the prime meridian to run through Giza, arguing that the ancients probably used Giza as their central meridian. Fawcett knew Egypt well, since he was working for British Intelligence in Cairo during the war, and he was also a surveyor. Could he have been using the Giza meridian to locate possible sites for ancient cities in South America?

As I pored over the map of Brazil, I was struck by another matter. Fawcett seems to have chosen a very strange route. Cuiaba is about 1,000 miles west of the site he was aiming at (the deserted city), and 700 miles south. Bahia itself – his ultimate goal – is only about 250 miles east of 'the deserted city' (which makes sense; the lost mines of Muribeca cannot possibly have been far from the coast, or it would have taken too long to transport the silver to Bahia). It looks – as G.K. Chesterton put it in one of his poems – as if Fawcett had decided to go to Bannockburn by way of Brighton Pier. Why would Fawcett have started from Cuiaba, 1,000 miles east of the deserted city? Why not go west from Bahia to the deserted city?

A possible explanation occurred to me, and, as Rand's next email showed, it had dawned on him at the same time. If sacred longitudes run in tens, then Fawcett would be crossing yet another on his way west – the 80-degree longitude west of Giza (which is about 49 degrees west of Greenwich). Since he would be travelling along the 10th parallel – another sacred latitude – the likeliest location for the city he calls 'Z' is where the 80th and the 10th cross.

This crossing point of the two meridians – 80 degrees west of Giza, and 10 degrees south – is only about 200 miles northeast of where Fawcett vanished. If 'Z' was a sacred site, then this, according to the blueprint, is its most likely location. From 'Z', Fawcett would have to travel almost 500 miles east to reach the deserted city of 1753.

Which brings us back to the question: why would Fawcett want to disguise its location?

Perhaps Fawcett was hoping to return to England to announce his discovery of three 'lost cities'. One he already knew – the city covered by jungle. If he could also pinpoint 'Z' and the deserted city of 1753, his triumph would be complete. He would have been hailed as one of the greatest explorers of all time, the manuscript of *Exploration Fawcett*, back at his home in Devon, would certainly become a bestseller, and he would have plenty of funds for another expedition. Even if he failed, he would certainly want to return to Brazil, and if anyone had seen the manuscript in the meantime, then he might be beaten to his objective by a rival. It would be a simple, obvious precaution to disguise the location of the deserted city until he had been there.

Whether Rand is correct about the locations of the three lost cities may not be as difficult to establish as one might suppose. Nowadays it is unnecessary for an explorer to equip an expedition and plunge into the Brazilian jungle. A space satellite, using the kind of radar that was used to penetrate the clouds of Venus, would only have to overfly the site – and track it in strips – to locate ruins buried under vegetation.[21] Archaeologists have even developed a radar that can penetrate the ground and locate ruins buried under sand.

What they have not yet developed is a method for deciding where to look, and this is what Rand has provided with his Atlantis blueprint.

Rand had already discovered that if you drew a line from the Great Pyramid to the North Pole, and another line from the Great Pyramid to the *old* North Pole, in Hudson Bay, the angle between the two is 28 degrees, and that 28 plays an important part in the Giza site (see Chapter 4).

Intrigued by this discovery, Rand had begun to look for other examples of a relationship between the two poles. From Rosslyn, the site of the Templar church in Scotland, the angle

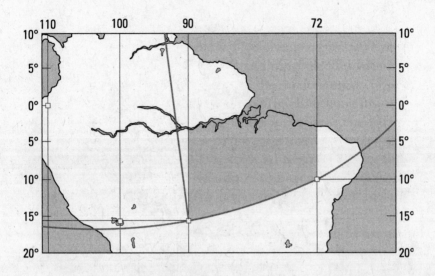

Two of the sites that Fawcett was interested in were located
at 12N during the Hudson Bay Pole. From the Lost Atlantean City
the Hudson Bay Pole is 12 degrees west of north. This is a 12/12 site.
12N latitude during Hudson Bay Pole; 12°
(the line to the left of 90)

between the two poles is 50 degrees. But its latitude is also
50 degrees north. Rand called this a 50/50 site. Again,
Stonehenge was at a latitude of 46 degrees, and the angle
between the two poles from Stonehenge was also 46 degrees –
another 'double' site, 46/46. And when he discovered many
more of these 'double' sites, he became convinced that this was
one of the basic factors that led the ancients to regard a certain
site as sacred. This is why his suggestion for the location for
one of Fawcett's lost cities (the one covered in vegetation) was
at a spot where the angle between the poles was 12 degrees and
the latitude was also 12 degrees south – a 12/12 site.

Rand then took an interesting leap in the dark. From the
Giza meridian, the only important line of longitude (i.e., a
multiple of ten) that runs through England is 30. If the blueprint theory is correct, there *ought* to be a major sacred site on

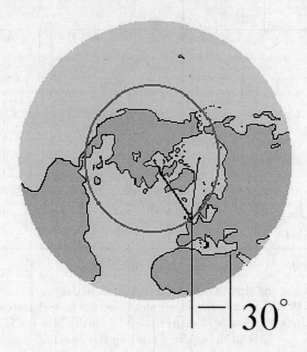

$30°$

Canterbury Cathedral may have been built on top of a much more
ancient site. During the Hudson Bay Pole it was midway between the
pole and the equator at latitude 45N. The angle between Canterbury,
the current pole and the former Hudson Bay Pole is 45 degrees.
Canterbury is a 45/45 site. It is also 30 degrees west of the Great
Pyramid and during the Hudson Bay Pole, when Giza was at 15N,
Canterbury was 30 degrees further north at 45N.

this line. Rand ran his finger down a map of England, and
found that the line ran through Canterbury, England's most
sacred site.

He drew an imaginary line to the North Pole and to the old
North Pole in Hudson Bay. The angle between them was 45
degrees, and Canterbury was at 45 degrees north during the
Hudson Bay Pole. So Canterbury is a 45/45 site, and since it
was 30 degrees north of Giza, *and also* on the 30-degree longitude, it is a 30/30 site relative to Giza.

Canterbury may be regarded as a relatively modern site. Its

first cathedral was built soon after St Augustine's arrival in England in AD 597. Before Augustine's arrival, however, it was the capital of Ethelbert, the Saxon king who became a Christian. And a little research into Dean Stanley's *Memorials of Canterbury* reveals that Ethelbert gave the site of a pagan temple to Augustine, who, following the decree of Gregory the Great to build on pagan sites, built an abbey there, and later began to build the cathedral nearby.

The pagan temple had been built on a 45/45 site – that is to say, by someone with a knowledge of the Hudson Bay Pole. England's most important religious site, Canterbury, also fits perfectly into Rand's Atlantis blueprint.

What is most significant about the line of investigation opened up by Lubaantum is that Rand had found it by applying his theory that a sacred site *ought* to be found at that location, at the 10 phi longitude north. If his theory was unsound, the odds against anything being found at that site would have been a million to one. When he located Lubaantum at a longitude of 10 phi north and latitude 120 degrees west, he had virtually confirmed Smyth's belief that the meridian used by the ancient Egyptians was the line of longitude that ran north and south through the Great Pyramid.

4

THOTH'S HOLY
CHAMBER

ACCORDING TO HERODOTUS, contemporary Egyptians had
decided on a crudely simplistic explanation of the purpose of the Great Pyramid; they said it was basically a
monument to the vainglory of the pharaoh Cheops (Khufu).
The wickedness of Cheops was unsurpassed – he closed down
all the temples during his fifty-six-year reign, and when he ran
out of money to build the Great Pyramid, sent his daughter out
to work as a harlot. She made enough not only to complete its
construction, but also to build a pyramid of her own. Herodotus
was also told that underneath the Great Pyramid there were a
series of vaults 'for the Pharaoh's own use', so that it also served
as a luxury apartment. Nile water was introduced by means of
a tunnel, forming an underground lake in the midst of which
there was an island on which Cheops was laid to rest. The Great
Pyramid, apart from being a monument to monstrous egoism,
was also a tomb then. The notion of the pyramids as tombs persists down to the present day – in his standard work on the
pyramids of Egypt, Professor Ion Edwards states that they were
intended as tombs and nothing more.

This assumption has been questioned. In *The Riddle of the Pyramids*,[1] Kurt Mendelssohn, a physicist who studied under Max Planck then turned his attention to the problem of why the pyramids were built, concluded that there was little evidence that they were tombs. Of the ten major pyramids, only one, the Step Pyramid of King Zoser (or Djoser) at Saqqara, showed unmistakable signs of being a tomb, although mummy fragments found in its granite vault proved – when subjected to radiocarbon-dating – to be dated to several centuries later than Zoser's reign. Of the other nine pyramids, only three had sarcophagi (which were empty) – it is hard to see why thieves should have gone to the trouble of stealing the other six.

Mendelssohn's own somewhat unlikely theory is that the pyramids were merely a 'work project' designed to unite Egypt's tribes into a nation state, although it could be asked why the pharaohs did not choose a more practical task, like building harbours or dams. All the same, Mendelssohn's objections to the tomb theory are certainly convincing, particularly in the case of the Great Pyramid itself. When Herodotus went there, it was covered in gleaming limestone, and was already 2,000 years old.

In AD 820, the caliph Al-Mamun, son of Haroun Al-Raschid, decided to break into it to see whether, as legend declared, it was full of fabulous treasures, but there seemed to be no way in. The position of a hidden door, high up on the north side, had long been forgotten.

Chisels failed to dent the limestone, so Al-Mamun ordered fires to be lit to crack it, then attacked it with battering rams. After months of exhausting effort, his men had only tunnelled a hundred feet or so. Just as they were about to give up, one of the workmen heard a dull thud nearby. They finally broke into a narrow tunnel, and saw that a large stone had fallen from its ceiling.

By sheer luck they had entered several courses below the original entrance, otherwise they might have tunnelled on until they came out the other side. Crawling up the sloping tunnel they found the entrance, covered with a hinged stone. Crawling back down the other way, they eventually found themselves in a small subterranean chamber with a vermin-infested pit and a short tunnel running out of the other side until it simply came to a halt. This seemed to be the disappointing reality of Herodotus's lake, island and luxury apartment.

But at the point where the stone had fallen from the ceiling, they found a passage ascending towards the heart of the pyramid. This proved to be blocked by a massive granite plug. They used their chisels to cut into the limestone around it, only to find another plug, and then yet another. Finally they were able to stand upright, and were faced with another low corridor that ran horizontally. It led to a barn-like chamber with a gabled roof and salt-encrusted walls – but it was empty. They labelled this the Queen's Chamber, since Arab tombs for women had pointed roofs. They hacked out part of a wall, but found no treasure.

Retracing their steps to the place where they could stand upright, they discovered that the ascending passage continued upward, but that a connecting part of the causeway had been removed, presumably to discourage further exploration. Suddenly the corridor turned into an awesome gallery, whose sloping walls stretched far above their heads. At the top of this smooth slope they found their way blocked by a 3-foot-tall stone. After clambering over this, they found themselves in what came to be called the Antechamber, faced with a kind of giant portcullis made of granite, which seemed designed to be lowered to block the intruders' further progress – except that the grooves at the sides terminated 4 feet above the floor, so it could never be lowered. Beyond that, the walls contained three more 'portcullis' grooves, this time down to the floor, but no portcullises.

They continued down another low passageway, finally arriving at a larger and rectangular chamber, which became known as the King's Chamber. This was also empty, except for a huge granite sarcophagus that was lacking its lid. It was so big that it must obviously have been introduced while the King's Chamber was being built, for it was too large to have been brought up the ascending passage.

So it seemed that the Great Pyramid was not a tomb, as it would have been impossible for there to have been a coffin inside the sarcophagus – there was no way that tomb robbers could have got it out.

It has been generally assumed that the granite plugs must have been slid into place from above, and had been stored in the 'Grand Gallery', but once the workmen had allowed them to slide into place, how had they escaped? There were no skeletons to suggest they had been entombed alive. The problem remained unsolved for 800 years until, in 1638, an English astronomer called John Greaves noticed a stone missing from the ramp at the west side of the Grand Gallery, just before it rejoined the narrower passage. It looked like a kind of well, but when Greaves tried to lower himself down it he found that it was blocked with sand and rubble and gave up. Two centuries later, in 1814, an Italian named Giovanni Caviglia made a more determined attempt, and found that the 'well' descended to the low passageway that led down to the subterranean chamber with the vermin-infested pit.

This route, then, must have allowed the workmen to escape after sliding the granite plugs into place – unless, of course, the top of the Pyramid was still open at that time (this latter was an obvious possibility, for someone must have blocked the well with sand and rubble, presumably from above).

So the Great Pyramid remained a mystery consisting of many small mysteries. Why, for example, had the Queen's Chamber been left unfinished, as the rough state of its floor suggested? And why were its walls covered in crystallised salt? And, if the pharaoh had changed his mind and decided that he would prefer a larger chamber built on a higher level, why did he not place the King's Chamber directly above the Queen's Chamber? The latter is placed symmetrically in the centre of

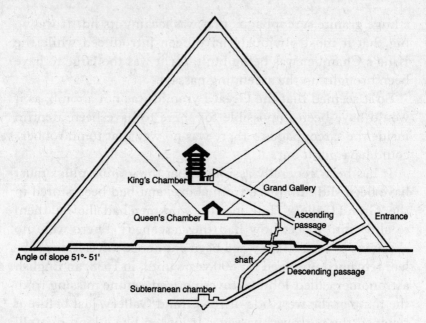

King's Chamber

Grand Gallery

Queen's Chamber

Ascending
passage

Entrance

Angle of slope 51°- 51'

shaft

Descending passage

Subterranean chamber

Cross-section of the Great Pyramid of Giza

the Pyramid, where you might expect a burial chamber to be; the King's Chamber is located slightly beyond this meridian.

One theory that seems to fit these facts is based on the speculations of Professor I. E. S. Edwards, one of the British Museum's foremost authorities on the pyramids. Around 2,500 BC, the pharaoh Cheops (Khufu) decided to build himself a tomb that should be impregnable to thieves. Having surveyed the subterranean chamber his workmen had hacked out of the rock, he felt it was too stuffy and depressing and decided to build himself a pyramid, like his father and grandfather. The Queen's Chamber was a deliberate red herring, to persuade any robbers who had penetrated that far that there was nothing for them to steal. Such robbers would only carry torches or candles, and would probably not notice that another passage ran above their heads.

At that point, his obsession about tomb robbers developed into paranoia, and he decided to have the ascending passage blocked with the granite plugs to make quite sure that no robbers could get that far. But the plugs needed to be slid into place. For that reason, the floor of the Grand Gallery was made smooth, so they could be stored there and slid down. At the top of the Grand Gallery he placed another obstacle in the form of a tall stone, and on its other side was the antechamber and the King's Chamber, which he had chosen for his tomb. He had his sarcophagus placed ready, but at this point he realised that it would be virtually impossible to carry the coffin up to the chamber – the granite plugs and the tall stone blocked the way.

The only solution was to slide the granite plugs into place there and then and to leave the Great Pyramid unfinished until after his death, when his coffin could be brought into the King's Chamber from above. But that would entail leaving the Great Pyramid open until he died. In the meantime, any number of thieves could creep in by night and explore its secrets.

At which point, I suggest, Cheops gave up in disgust. The Great Pyramid itself, he decided, should become a gigantic red herring, to divert tomb robbers from his true resting place. And to this day we have no idea of where his body lies . . ..

Why did he order the 'well' to be dug, then blocked up with rubble? Perhaps because, just before the Great Pyramid was completed, he had a sudden pang of regret at the thought that he would never again look upon his magnificent handiwork, and left this hidden entrance . . .

One objection to this theory is the matter of why he ordered his workmen to construct so many puzzling anomalies. Why are there slots cut into the walls of the antechamber, as if to hold three massive 'portcullis' stones, when no such stones are to be found? Why is there a niche in the wall of the Queen's Chamber that is slightly off-centre? Why does a 2-foot step suddenly appear in the passage to the Queen's Chamber? Why do 'air vents' out of the Queen's Chamber fail to reach the outside and were not even taken through the

walls of the Chamber? There are, of course, 'air vents' out of
the King's Chamber – but what is the purpose of air vents in
a tomb? And why did the builders decide to build the thirty-
sixth course of far larger blocks than the other courses – surely
it would have made sense to place the largest at the bottom?

Above all there is the mystery of the Grand Gallery. Why,
when most of the passages in the Great Pyramid are so low
that it is necessary to stoop (or even crawl), did the pharaoh
order his workmen to build a passageway 7 feet wide, 28 feet
high and 157 feet long? Why does it narrow to half its width by
the time it reaches the ceiling? And why is the ceiling not flat,
like most of the ceilings in the Great Pyramid, but made of
overlapping blocks, as if designed as steps for a man who could
walk upside down? And why is there a raised ramp on either
side of the upward slope, making it a sunken channel? And
why are there square holes cut on the wall side of the ramp,
making it look – from above – like a piece of cinema film?

The answer, clearly, is God only knows. Common sense
seems to afford no clues to the answers. And therein lies the
merit of J Charles Piazzi Smyth. He at least made the world
aware that the Great Pyramid is a giant enigma.

Regrettably, his efforts were in some respects too successful. A Scotsman named Robert Menzies took their theories to
a logical extreme. If God was the author of the Great
Pyramid as well as of the Bible, then it should obviously be
regarded as a book in stone; all that remained was to decipher
its message, which must be conveyed in terms of *measurements*. The way from the entrance to the three chambers must
be a symbolic journey through time, probably with pyramid
inches representing years, including all the great events of
the world's history, among them the flood, the Exodus, the
Crucifixion and the Second Coming. The beginning of the
Grand Gallery marked the birth of Christ, and, counting
back from there, it could easily be verified that the world had
been created in 4,004 BC, just as Archbishop Ussher had
declared in 1650.

Smyth had worked out that the Pole Star, which was then Alpha Draconis, had shone straight through the entrance and down the descending passage when the Great Pyramid was build in 2,100 BC (missing the actual date by about four centuries). Menzies declared that there should be some indication on the walls of the Descending Passage marking the year, and was delighted when Smyth told him of two scored lines on either side of the passage at the spot that marked 2,100 BC – and so was confirmed in his peculiar form of insanity.

Within a decade or so, the Great Pyramid became the happy hunting ground of religious cranks all over the world. In Boston, a society was formed to alter modern measuring units to those used by the Pyramid's builders, and was supported by President Garfield. In England, a book called *Miracle in Stone* (1877)[2] by Joseph Seiss became a bestseller. A preacher named Charles Taze Russell became a convert, and founded the Jehovah's Witnesses on the basis of Pyramid prophecies, in 1891 announcing that the Battle of Armageddon would occur in 1914 and that all Jehovah's Witnesses would thereafter live forever on a 'paradise earth'. When 1914 failed to bring the end of the world, thousands of Jehovah's Witnesses left the movement in disillusionment, and Russell had difficulty convincing those that remained that Christ *had* returned, but invisibly. When Russell died in 1916, his successor 'Judge' Rutherford decided to discard pyramidology; he explained that Russell had been deluded by Satan, realising the danger of setting a definite date for the end of the world when his own choice, 1925, passed without incident.

The beliefs of an early pyramidologist, John Taylor, that the British were the ten lost tribes of Israel led to another highly successful movement, the British Israelites, whose Bible was a vast work by David Davidson called *The Great Pyramid: Its Divine Message* (1924),[3] which announced that the 'final tribulation' of the Anglo-Saxon race would last from 1928 to 1936, and that Armageddon would occur in 1953.

According to the British Israelites, another date that would be of immense significance to the world was 16 September 1936. The only newsworthy item that day was that the Duke of Windsor told his prime minister that he intended to marry Mrs Simpson, an interesting but not world-shaking event.

A few 'pyramidiots' (as a modern writer has called them) were perhaps a small price to pay for the tremendous impetus given to the study of the pyramids by Taylor and Smyth. They had made a very serious point: the mathematical and technological knowledge revealed by the Great Pyramid seems far too sophisticated for 'primitives' who tilled their fields with pointed sticks. If Taylor and Smyth had lived a century later, they might well have preferred the 'ancient astronaut' alternative to the idea that the Great Pyramid's builders worked under the direct guidance of God. Anyone who finds either view unacceptable must be driven to the only other conclusion: that the Egyptians knew far more than historians supposed.

John West expressed the problem in *Serpent in the Sky*, summarising the views of Schwaller de Lubicz:

> Egyptian science, medicine, mathematics and astronomy were all of an exponentially higher order of refinement and sophistication than modern scholars will acknowledge. The whole of Egyptian civilisation was based upon a complete and precise understanding of universal laws . . . Moreover, every aspect of Egyptian knowledge seems to have been complete at the very beginning. The sciences, artistic and architectural techniques and the hieroglyphic system show virtually no sign of a period of 'development'; indeed, many of the achievements of the earlier dynasties were never surpassed or even equalled later on.[4]

West argues that it would have been virtually impossible for Egypt to have reached such a degree of sophistication in a mere 500 years – the time Egyptian civilisation is supposed to have been founded. It is rather, West says, as if the first motor car had been a modern Rolls-Royce.

Scholars in the ancient world should have realised that the builders of the Great Pyramid knew far more than 'primitives' were supposed to know – at least, after Agatharchides of Cnidus revealed that the base of the Great Pyramid is a known percentage of the earth's circumference. But at that time no one knew if this calculation was correct; in fact, no one was interested, for most people thought the earth was flat. By the time of Charles Piazzi Smyth, everyone knew the earth was round, so his revelation that the Egyptians knew the value of pi left Victorian scientists in little doubt that the Egyptians had achieved a sophisticated level of mathematics.

The Great Pyramid continues to offer unsolved mysteries. One modern student, Christopher P. Dunn, consulted a manager of the Indiana Limestone Institute about how long it would take their thirty-three quarries to cut and deliver around 2.5 million blocks, each weighing between 6 and 30 tons, and was told that, using modern rock-cutting machinery, it would take twenty-seven years. But no one has worked out how the builders moved these blocks up a 52-degree slope. Herodotus says that they had a machine made of short wooden planks to lift the blocks, but since the flat top of the 'step' is often as little as 6 inches wide this is not practicable. A better suggestion is that they built a gently sloping ramp and heaved the blocks up it with ropes, which would have worked well for the lower courses, but as the Great Pyramid got higher the ramp would have to become longer and steeper and of sufficiently solid construction not to collapse under its own weight. It would need to be about a mile long, and would require as much stone as the structure itself. A modern builder would need a crane more than 500 feet high, with a boom of 400 feet – there is no crane of that size in the world today, and one certainly did not exist in ancient Egypt.

Another problem is the time factor. Herodotus was told that the Great Pyramid took twenty years to build, which would have involved placing about 340 blocks in position every day, an impossible task without heavy lifting machinery. A more reasonable estimate would be thirty-four blocks a day, but this would mean that it took 200 years to build.

Christopher P. Dunn, the British toolmaker and engineer already mentioned, has examined the Great Pyramid from the engineering point of view. His study led him to conclude – in an article called 'Advanced Machining in Ancient Egypt' – that the Egyptian pyramids and temples 'reveal glimpses of a civilisation that was technically more advanced than is generally believed'. Examining blocks that had been hollowed out with some kind of drill in the Valley Temple, in front of the Sphinx, he noted that the marks left in the hole showed that it was cutting into the rock at a rate of one-tenth of an inch for every revolution of the drill, and he concludes that this could not be achieved by hand. A hole drilled into a rock made of quartz and feldspar provided another strange observation. The drill had cut faster through the quartz than the feldspar, even though quartz is harder than feldspar. Dunn points out that modern ultrasonic machining depends on vibration, like the chisel of a pneumatic drill, which vibrates up and down. An ultrasonic drill vibrates tens of thousands of times faster. Quartz crystals, which can be used to produce ultrasonic sound, also respond to ultrasonic vibrations, which would enable an ultrasonic drill to cut through them faster. Does this suggest that there were ultrasonic drills in ancient Egypt?

The notion sounds ridiculous, yet the mystery of the Great Pyramid led Sir Flinders Petrie, the grand old man of Egyptology, to suggest an idea almost as strange. In his standard work *The Pyramids and Temples of Gizeh* (1883),[5] he casually threw off the suggestion that the sarcophagus, whose external volume is precisely twice that of its internal volume, was cut with an 8-foot saw that was made of bronze with diamonds in the cutting edge. No such saws, of course, have ever been found; neither have the drills that Petrie thought were used to hollow out the sarcophagus.

Christopher Dunn's close study of the Pyramid made him aware that its precision seems almost superhuman. He asked an engineer who worked at stone cutting in the quarries of Indiana what tolerances they worked to (i.e., how much inaccuracy did they allow themselves). He was told 'pretty close', which was defined as 'a quarter of an inch'. When told that the blocks of the Great Pyramid were cut to 0.01 tolerance, the stonecutter was incredulous.[6]

In a TV programme Dunn produced a device used by engineers to test that a metal surface has been machined to a thousandth of an inch, and applied it to the sacred stone called the Benben, in the Cairo Museum. He shone a powerful torch on one side of the metal, and looked on the other side to see if any gleam of light showed through. There was none whatever.

Petrie's examination of the casing stones of the Great Pyramid showed that they had been cut according to highly accurate engineering tolerances. But why should the Pyramid's builders have worked to machine-shop tolerances rather than those of a construction site, as you would expect? And even more baffling: *how*? What tools were used to cut granite or limestone with such precision? This is the kind of precision we would expect of an optician, but not a builder.

In trying to fashion a theory that might explain the purpose of the Great Pyramid, Dunn was struck by a comment made by Colonel Howard-Vyse, one of the early explorers who had discovered four of the five 'relieving chambers' above the King's Chamber. Howard-Vyse had noted that when he stood in the King's Chamber, he was able to hear people speaking in the subterranean chamber, indicating that the acoustics of the Great Pyramid are as perfect as those of a concert hall.

TV producer Boris Said – who, together with John West, made the documentary *The Mystery of the Sphinx* – had said in the promotion material of another documentary:

Subsequent experiments conducted by Tom Danley in the King's Chamber of the Great Pyramid and in chambers above the King's Chamber suggest that the pyramid was constructed with a sonic purpose. Danley identifies four resident frequencies, or notes, that are enhanced by the structure of the pyramid, and by the materials used in its construction. The notes from an F sharp chord . . . according to ancient Egyptian texts were the harmonic of our planet. Moreover, Danley's tests show that these frequencies are present in the King's Chamber even when no sounds are being produced. They are there in frequencies that range from 16 Hertz down to ½ Hertz, well below the range of human hearing. According to Danley, these vibrations are caused by the wind blowing across the ends of the so-called shafts in the same way as sounds are created when one blows across the neck of a bottle.[7]

He went on to mention that a producer of Native American sacred flutes, created to 'serenade' Mother Earth, tunes them to the key of F sharp.

This notion that Egyptian pyramids – and temples – are tuned to sound has become increasingly widespread. In November 1998 I joined a trip to Egypt organised by Robert Bauval in which John West acted as tour guide. Together with a number of other writers – among them Robert Temple, Michael Baigent, Yuri Stoyanov and Ralph Ellis – we looked at many Egyptian temples, including Karnak and Luxor, Dendera, Edfu and the Oseirion at Abydos. Again and again we noted their acoustic properties as members of the group intoned notes in closed chambers, or even in doorways. It was as if the stone was a giant tuning fork.

In 1998 scientists at Southampton University discovered that the stones of Stonehenge also have acoustic properties and would have acted as gigantic amplifiers for drums during festivals, their flat surfaces accumulating and then deflecting sound over a wide area.

It was in the immense Temple of Horus, at Edfu, midway between Luxor and Aswan, that my attention was drawn to the importance of sound. An Egyptian historian named Emil Shaker showed me some hieroglyphics on the wall close to the sanctuary, pointing out how they specified the number of times the temple ritual had to be performed. In this case it was three. He explained: 'It is no use performing the ritual two or four times. It will not work. If it says three times, it means three times.' This ritual, like all religious rituals, involves chanting a hymn to the sun and presenting the god with offerings.

I asked, 'But what does the ritual actually do?'

'It *activates* the temple.'

'You mean like switching on a light?' I said, giving voice to the first image that came into my head.

'Exactly like switching on a light,' said Emil.

I found this notion fascinating – a ritual involving chanting could 'activate' a temple. Emil made it sound as if it was as automatic as switching on a light, or going through a certain sequence of actions to send an email.

According to my guidebook, John West's *Traveler's Key to Ancient Egypt*,[8] the Edfu temple was built over a period of 200 years, between 257 and 57 BC, but part of it dated back to the pyramid age. It is built, of course, on 'hallowed ground'.

The sanctuary looked rather like an immense stone box turned on its side. I decided to walk all the way around it but found the narrow passage at the back blocked by someone who was obviously meditating, with his forehead and palms pressed against the stone. I realised that it was Michael Baigent, the co-author (with Henry Lincoln and Richard Leigh) of *The Holy Blood and the Holy Grail*.[9] I backed away so as not to disturb him, and instead followed John West to look at the famous 'Building Texts' inscribed on the walls – texts that refer back to the remote age called the 'First Time', when seven sages designed the temples and pyramids.

An hour later, back on the boat, Robert Bauval told me that Michael Baigent had not returned with the rest of us on the bus, and asked me if I could give a lecture in his place that afternoon. Everyone was concerned, since Baigent could only rejoin us further down the Nile by taking a taxi, and we were in 'bandit country' – not long ago, tourists had been machine-gunned to death at the Temple of Hatshepsut. When Michael later turned up unharmed, after I had given his lecture, I asked him what had happened.

'I don't know. I was meditating for a few minutes, then I found you'd all gone.'

I told him that I had seen him behind the sanctuary. 'That wasn't a few minutes before we left – it was at least twenty minutes.'

He was incredulous. 'It only seemed a few minutes.'

He may have simply lost track of time, but I am inclined to believe that he had 'tuned in' to the vibrations of that hallowed ground, vibrations that are still powerful after more than 2,000 years.

In Bauval and Hancock's *Keeper of Genesis* I find a quotation from the scholar E. A. E. Reymond, which refers to the 'founding, building and *bringing to life* [my italics] of the historical temple of Edfu'. This 'bringing to life', this activation, is brought about by a ritual that involves sound.

The earth also has its own frequency, known as the Schumann Resonance, which results from electromagnetic activity between the earth and the upper atmosphere. It is far too low in frequency to be heard, but Christopher Dunn found himself speculating whether, if the Great Pyramid was constructed with some 'sonic' purpose, as Tom Danley suspected, and if it was deliberately built to correspond to the size of the earth, its purpose might be connected with the earth's vibrations.

Dunn had already conducted some of his own experiments. In February 1995, when visiting Egypt with Bauval and Hancock, he bribed an inspector to leave him in the King's Chamber alone for half an hour after it closed to visitors. The inspector assumed he wanted to meditate, and agreed to turn off the lights. In fact, Dunn wanted the lights turned off so that no background hum would spoil his tape recording. He was also carrying a digital frequency counter to measure the radio frequencies he thought might be generated by the King's Chamber.

When the sound of tourists had receded into the distance, he thumped the side of the sarcophagus with his fist and listened to the humming sound it made. He hummed this note to test the resonance, then hummed his way up the scale until noted that the resonance became even more powerful when he reached the note an octave higher.

Concerned that he was running out of time, he went through to the Antechamber to yell down at the guard to turn off the lights, whose humming was spoiling his recording. Then, still humming the note of the sarcophagus, he went back to the King's Chamber, where he realised that the humming of the fans in the 'air shafts' was still spoiling his recording. After a few more recordings, he left the Great Pyramid and walked back to his hotel.

Back in his room he played back his recording and realised that his time had not been wasted after all. The note he had been humming had caused overtones – sympathetic vibrations – in the Chamber. When he listened to his own voice calling for the lights to be turned off, he was astonished that it sounded as if he was still in the Chamber and not on the far side of the Antechamber, despite the fact that walls and leaves of granite and limestone stood between himself and the recorder. His humming was also clearly recorded. He also noted that the sound of his footsteps as he walked back from the Grand Gallery resonated clearly at the Chamber's natural resonance – the note of the sarcophagus.

Dunn had proved two things: that, as Howard-Vyse had said, the Great Pyramid seemed to have perfect acoustics, and that the King's Chamber was a kind of sounding box, producing the same note as the sarcophagus. In fact, it was more than a matter of perfect acoustics. The Great Pyramid was designed like the Whispering Gallery in St Paul's Cathedral in London, where a whisper at one side of the gallery is reflected around the walls.

Dunn's own observations were confirmed by the scientist Stephen Mehler, who had also made recordings in the King's Chamber. These had been analysed by a sound engineer named Robert Vawter, who agreed that the King's Chamber was designed as a resonance chamber.

Even if we agree that the Pyramid was intended to be a sounding box, this still leaves the question of why. Christopher Dunn's own conviction was that the important clue was the fact that the Great Pyramid's proportions are the same as those of the earth, suggesting that the 'sounding box' was intended to vibrate to the earth. Or, as he puts it in his book *The Giza Power Plant*,[10] '*the pyramid acts as a receiver of energy from within the earth itself*'.

Inevitably, most readers will feel that the notion of the Great Pyramid as a giant resonator is far fetched, but sceptics will also have to admit that Dunn succeeds in making sense of its anomalies and apparent absurdities, producing plausible explanations for all kinds of features, from the subterranean gallery to the iron plate with traces of gold found at the top of the southern air shaft. One of Dunn's illustrations is based upon Charles Piazzi Smyth's drawings (see page 64).

The Great Pyramid is not only located on the meridian that covers more land than any other; it is also at the centre of the earth's land masses. In addition, it is situated so accurately in the centre of the Nile Delta that a compass point placed on the Great Pyramid can neatly enclose the whole Delta in an arc. That is why Piazzi Smyth thought the Giza meridian ought to be our modern prime meridian. He also believed that, for the ancient Egyptians, it probably *was* their prime meridian.

In *The Giza Power Plant*, Christopher Dunn has produced a fascinating book about the possible technological purpose of the Great Pyramid. Rand has another, equally interesting theory of the location of what has become known as 'Thoth's Holy Chamber'.

One of Rand's major aims, in trying to understand the hidden geometry of the Giza site, was to try to locate this 'secret chamber'. The notion seems to have originated in a document called the Westcar Papyrus,[11] now in the Berlin Museum, which seems to be a New Kingdom copy of a Fifth Dynasty original (soon after the time of Cheops, or Khufu). It tells how Cheops asked a magician named Djedi the number (or precise location) of Thoth's secret chamber, and was told that it could be found in a flint chest in a building called the Inventory. But no one, Djedi added, would be able to obtain the number until the coming of three kings as yet unborn . . . The papyrus breaks off at this point.

In their book *Keeper of Genesis*, Robert Bauval and Graham Hancock make an interesting suggestion. Bauval regards the Giza pyramids as a 'reflection' on the ground of the three stars of Orion's Belt, and he and Hancock explain their belief that the secret chamber can be found reflected on the ground where the 'vernal point' – the location in the heavens of the spring equinox – was located in 10,500 BC. This was under the rear paws of the constellation of Leo, and Bauval and Hancock go on to suggest that the chamber is therefore located under the rear paws of the Sphinx.

More recently, Nigel Appleby[12] has proposed that the secret chamber will be found at a spot on the ground that is a 'reflection' of the star Sirius, which embodies the goddess Isis. This location has proved to be on someone's allotment on the outskirts of Cairo, and at the time of writing the theory has not yet been tested.

Rand, naturally, was inclined to approach this problem of Thoth's holy chamber from the angle of his own Atlantis blueprint. All our researches have led us to believe that ancient Egypt preserved the legacy of an earlier civilisation, perhaps of more than one, and that contemporary science is inclined to greatly underestimate the intelligence of the people of the remote past. It was, at least, plausible that there was a hidden cache of knowledge inside or around the Great Pyramid. The

Byzantine historian George Syncellus in the ninth century AD wrote a commentary that included a reference to a lost Egyptian text called *The Book of Sothis*,[13] which was circulating in the third century BC. This lost book, according to Syncellus, contained important 'records' brought to Egypt immediately 'after the flood'.

Robert Bauval, in *Secret Chamber*,[14] unearths another clue in a tract called the *Kore Kosmou*, from the famous 'Hermetic Writings' attributed to Hermes Trismegistos (or Thoth), of which the most famous sentence is: 'As above, so below.' Scholars had been inclined to dismiss these writings as Neoplatonist texts written by Greeks in the third century AD, but more recently it has been widely accepted that they date back to early Ptolemaic times in Egypt (i.e., from 323 BC onwards). In the *Kore Kosmou*,[15] Isis tells her son Horus that the secret knowledge of Hermes was engraved on stone and hidden away 'near the secrets of Osiris'. She also declares that a spell has been cast on these books, to ensure that they remain unseen. The fourth-century Roman historian Ammianus Marcellinus also writes of 'subterranean passages and winding retreats' built by men before the flood to house documents, 'lest the memory of all their sacred ceremonies should be lost'.[16]

Rand had read a children's book on magic called *The Secrets of Alkazar*, and had never forgotten its advice to aspiring young magicians: pay attention to the techniques of misdirection. 'The audience will always look where the magician looks. The magician must never look at what he wants to conceal. The audience will treat as important what the magician treats as important, and as unimportant what the magician treats as unimportant.'[17] Rand reflected that a hidden chamber might well be concealed according to the methods of Alkazar.

The most obvious things at Giza are the pyramids and the Sphinx, so someone who wished to conceal something would expect future generations to devote their attention to these. But supposing this is just 'misdirection'?

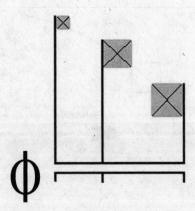

In *Keys to the Temple*, David Furlong discovered that there is a phi
relationship between the pyramids at Giza.

Rand also recalled that one of the sacred names of the
Sphinx is *neb*, which means 'the spiralling force of the universe'.[18] Why should a spiral be associated with the Sphinx? Is
it possible that the spiral was a Fibonacci spiral?

In *The Keys to the Temple*, David Furlong[19] had also
pointed out that the golden section has been used in the layout
of the three Giza pyramids:

Rand recalled that, in a book called *The Giza Necropolis
Decoded*, (1975),[20] Rocky McCollum had noted that he could
draw a Fibonacci spiral that would touch the apex of all three
Giza pyramids. It folds in on itself, as can be seen, at a spot
south-east of the pyramids, between the Sphinx and the
Nile. It is Rand's conviction that Thoth's Holy Chamber
lies at the centre of this spiral.*

In September 1980, engineers from the Egyptian Ministry
of Irrigation had been measuring the depth of the water table
under the Sphinx and set up their drilling equipment half a
football field to the east of the Sphinx. They expected to have
to penetrate about 20 feet and were puzzled when their drills
went on through the sand until, at more then 50 feet, they hit
something solid.

It proved to be red granite, of the same kind that can be

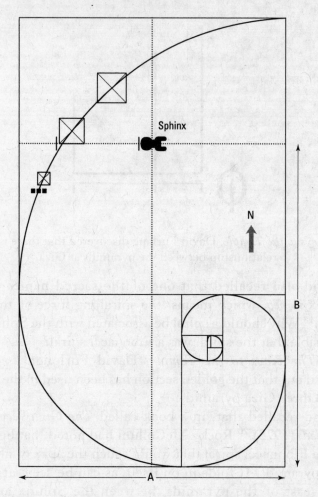

Sphinx

N

B

A

In *The Giza Necropolis Decoded*, Rocky McCollum created a phi
spiral which passed through the tips of the pyramids at Giza.

found in the antechamber to the King's Chamber of the Great
Pyramid. Such granite is not to be found in the area of Giza;
like the black granite that lines the King's Chamber, it has to
be brought from Aswan, 500 miles south. The implication
would seem to be that there is some kind of underground
chamber. The irrigation engineers also thought that the layout
of the red granite suggested an ancient harbour.

In 1990, the geologist Thomas Dobecki, who accompanied John Anthony West and Robert Schoch to Giza to check the notion that the Sphinx might have been weathered by water, sent vibrations down into the rock under the Sphinx's front paws and found evidence of a rectangular underground chamber. In October 1992 a French engineer named Jean Kerisel was in the 'descending passage' that goes down to the underground chamber of the Great Pyramid, using ground-penetrating radar. Beneath the horizontal passageway that connects the end of the descending passage to the underground chamber, Kerisel's equipment detected a 'structure' that could be a corridor crossing the horizontal passageway at an angle of about 45 degrees. It seemed to lead directly to the Sphinx.

The historian Herodotus, as we have seen, had been told of underground chambers intended to be the tomb of Cheops, but this has generally been discounted as misinformation. That may be so. What *does* seem certain is that the Giza plateau is honeycombed with underground tunnels.

This was again demonstrated in 1977, when a team from Stanford Research Institute[22] used a new technique called 'resistivity' (which involves the passing of an electric current into rods driven into the rock) to investigate the Sphinx, and concluded that behind the north-west rear paws there was an 'anomaly' that looked like a tunnel running north-west (the direction of the Great Pyramid) to south-east.

If the centre of Rocky McCollum's Fibonacci spiral is, in fact, Thoth's Holy Chamber, then presumably there is some connection with the Great Pyramid. Rand drew a line from

---

*Rand notes that the south-east corner of the Great Pyramid is highlighted in Robert Temple's *The Crystal Sun*. He has discovered that once a year, at sunset, during the winter solstice, the Middle Pyramid casts a Golden Triangle shadow upon the south-east corner of the Great Pyramid. Once again we find the geometric appearance of the Golden Section linked with the geographic direction of the south-east. Is the shadow another way of pointing towards Thoth's Holy Chamber.[21]

this centre point to the foundation stone of the Great Pyramid, and noted that it passed through the rear paws of the Sphinx, in the same direction as the Stanford researchers' hypothetical 'tunnel'.

At that point, he discovered something that intrigued him. This line, continued in a straight direction, through the foundation stone in the north-east corner of the Pyramid, pointed directly at the Hudson Bay Pole. Moreover, if a line was drawn from the foundation stone to the North Pole, and another from the Sphinx to the foundation stone, they form an angle of 28 degrees. We have noted in earlier chapters the importance of this angle on the Giza plateau. Rand comments:

> This solution to the location of the Holy Chamber breaks Thoth's magic spell by revealing that the pyramids and Sphinx are the most amazing case of misdirection ever conceived. It solves the mystery of the south-east to north-west directions that show up at Giza. This direction points at the former position of the North Pole when it was in Hudson Bay. The red granite in front of the Sphinx may prove to be a part of a roof covering a secret subterranean structure designed to house treasures from a lost world. Only a civilisation equipped with the tools of astronomy, geometry, geodesics and a knowledge of the former location of the earth's crust would be able to find the treasure so carefully hidden in the 'desert sands'. Thoth hid his treasure well.

Part of that message, he thinks, is a deliberate indication of the direction of the Hudson Bay Pole, intended as a warning of what can happen to our earth. We are not invulnerable. Echoing Hapgood, Rand writes: 'Our notion of progress is an illusion. We are deceiving ourselves if we think we are immune to the forces of nature. Civilisation, as the ancients have repeatedly told us, unfolds in cycles.'

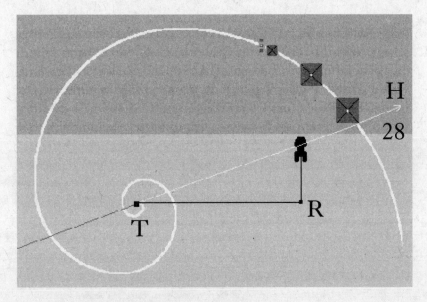

T = Thoth's Holy Chamber
R = Red granite in front of Sphinx
H = Hudson Bay Pole @ 28 degrees NW

A phi-controlled spiral running through the tips of the Giza pyramids folds in upon itself at a point in the desert. A line extending from the centre of the spiral to the Great Pyramid's foundation stone points directly towards the Hudson Bay Pole.

109

5

6,000 DEGREES CELSIUS

THE LIBYAN DESERT is one of the most godforsaken wilder-nesses on earth. Its white sand dunes tower like cliffs, often 600 feet high, and there is no sign of a living thing. Its desolate nature was underlined on 3 June 1971, when three scientists discovered an Egyptian plane in the desert near the Gilf Kebir Plateau. The plane had vanished three years earlier and aerial searches had failed to locate it. It had crash-landed for some unknown reason, and all that remained inside were the nine skeletons of the crew. The airmen had obviously died of thirst.[1]

The area in which they were found was a broad sand-free corridor of hard rock between the giant dunes. The three explorers, Virgil E. Barnes, James Underwood and Ali Sbeta, were investigating a mystery that had intrigued scientists for almost forty years: the enigma of the Libyan Desert 'glass'.

Pieces of this 'glass', found on the surface of the Libyan Desert – which, in spite of its name, is in Egypt, 500 miles south-west of Cairo – were originally identified as 'tektites'. Often very beautiful, their colour varies from pale yellow to

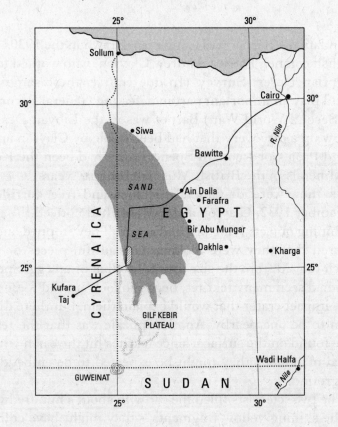

The Libyan Desert glass deposits are located in the desert near latitude 25 degrees north and the border between Egypt and Libya.

dark yellow and yellow-green, and can be worked by a jeweller into semi-precious stones. No one really knows where they come from. Most scientists are inclined to believe that they have originated in space and have melted as they came hurtling down through the atmosphere.

For Barnes and his companions, the finding of the crashed plane was a stroke of luck, for within a hundred yards or so they also found more than two dozen tektites lying on the sandstone. They lost no time in returning to their Land Rover and setting out on the long drive back to civilisation.

On his expedition – funded by the National Science

Foundation – Barnes was using maps drawn in the 1930s by an English colonel, Patrick Andrew Clayton, who worked for the Egyptian Desert Survey. (In due course, these same maps would play an important part in defeating General Rommel in the Second World War.) Barnes was in the Libyan Desert to follow up a discovery that had been made by Clayton and his friend Professor Leonard Spencer, who had been the Keeper of Minerals in the British Museum for forty years.

As they were driving along the sand-free corridor in December 1932, Clayton and Spencer had noticed the glitter of shining objects lying on the surface. They stopped and discovered that they were looking at beautiful pieces of glass, which ranged from the size of a pea to that of an egg. Spencer, who had seen many tektites, began to look around for a meteorite impact crater that would explain them, but there did not seem to be one nearby. Another puzzle was that the tektites were found on the surface; since tektites hit the earth with the speed of bullets, they might be expected to be embedded in the ground.

The two scientists filled the car with about a hundredweight of the shining yellow fragments – they might have collected many times that amount if they had had the space – and turned back towards Cairo. During the next few days, as they examined their find, Clayton and Spencer began to realise just how strange it was. To begin with, some of the pieces had fractures that looked as if they had been produced by deliberate blows; in fact, they resembled the pieces of flint found near prehistoric hand axes. But if they were flakes, not a single tektite resembled a Stone Age tool. A further oddity was their sheer quantity. Tektites are fairly rare; they are not found by the hundredweight.

Chemical analysis threw an unexpected light on the matter, but only to leave another mystery. It seemed these were not tektites after all – they were made of the same silicon as the desert sand. The only obvious solution was that they were fragments that had been instantly fused by the impact of a white-hot meteorite, and were hurled through the air like shrapnel.

Further examinations of the site in the following years failed to locate any kind of crater. Moreover, one particular piece of evidence suggested that the glass had not been created by a meteor impact. One fragment about the size of a lemon had a neat hole running right through it – it looked as if some-one had poked it with a metal rod while it was still molten. Two other 'bore holes' penetrated the glass for only a short distance. The evidence suggested that this glass had been manufactured by human beings. Further signs suggested that the glass had been handled by human hands: for example, the few bubbles in it were elongated, as if the glass had been turned or lifted while it was still molten.

In 1933, Clayton and Spencer[2] presented their evidence to the Royal Geographical Society in a paper. The audience included a distinguished member named Francis James Rennell, later Lord Rennell of Rodd, who had been a staff officer in Egypt during the First World War and had later been involved in explorations in the Sahara. Rennell, who would become President of the Royal Geographical Society in 1945, became fascinated by the mystery of the Libyan Desert glass.

Archaeologists had dated rock carvings in the area to about 5,500 BC. It had generally been assumed that they were carved by illiterate nomads, but if they were made by the producers of the glass, it suggested that a fairly sophisticated level of civilisation had been achieved in the area by the sixth millennium BC.

Whenever archaeologists stumble upon such anomalies, they are inclined to keep quiet about them, in case their colleagues accuse them of being too imaginative. Such was the case, for example, in the 1890s, when the great Flinders Petrie excavated a village called Naqada, on the Nile, and found pottery and vases of such sophistication that he assumed they must date from the Eleventh Dynasty, around 2,000 BC; he even coined the term 'the New Race' to describe this unknown people, whose artifacts seemed oddly unlike those of the Egyptians. But when he found more of their typical pottery in tombs dating from 1,000 years earlier, he decided to drop Naqada from his chronology rather than face the embarrassment of explaining how 'primitives' of an earlier civilisation could produce work of such excellence.

Equally problematic were the long-necked vases found in the Step Pyramid at Saqqara,[3] which dates from 2,650 BC. Clay vessels can be made in any shape, because the potter can mould the inside with his hand, but what can explain a vessel carved out of hard materials such as basalt, quartz or diorite? How does the potter carve out the inside of the vessel when the neck is too narrow to admit even the smallest hand? We are forced back on the improbable hypothesis that the craftsmen had some method of melting the hard rock, just as it was once melted in the furnace of the earth's interior, before they blew it into shape like glass.

Lord Rennell, who had spent many years in Egypt, was intrigued by such mysteries. He was still brooding on the Libyan Desert glass when, in the late fifties, he met Dr John R.V. Dolphin, the chief engineer of the British Atomic Energy Authority. When Rennell told Dolphin about the glass, Dolphin replied that he had also seen something similar in the Australian desert, and knew just how it had been created – by the detonation of an atomic bomb.[4]

Dolphin gave Rennell a sample of his glass from the test site, and Rennell in turn showed Dolphin some of the Libyan Desert glass. They looked amazingly similar. Like the Libyan Desert glass, Dolphin's Australian specimens contained virtually no water, because of the tremendously high temperature at which they had been formed. Dolphin's estimate was that they were produced at about 6,000 degrees Celsius.

It had the makings of a first-class mystery. Sherlock Holmes might have reasoned thus: Glass fragments are found over a fairly wide area even to parallel corridors to the east and west. Since their silicon content is the same as that of the desert sand, we know they are not tektites. We are left with the notion of a meteorite impact – yet there is no crater. The making of coloured glass was one of the preoccupations of the alchemists, and we know that alchemy was studied in Graeco-Roman Egypt as well as ancient India and China. Could this be alchemical glass? Since the glass shows signs of being handled by humans, the only possible explanation is that it is the leftover or by-product of some industrial process. But if Dolphin was correct about the temperature at which the glass was made, then we seem to be assuming that the ancient Egyptians – or other men in the region – possessed something like atomic power.

At that point Watson would have asked Holmes if he was feeling feverish, but this apparently preposterous conclusion was nevertheless proposed by Dolphin and taken seriously by Lord Rennell. After studying the Libyan Desert glass, Dolphin suggested that for the ancient Phoenicians to have worked with temperatures equivalent to 6,000 degrees Celsius they may have known the secret of atomic power. He went on to suggest that the desert glass may have been formed when the atomic power got out of hand and caused an explosion.

Another reason why Lord Rennell took the mystery seriously is that he himself was in possession of a necklace from ancient Egypt, made of virtually pure gold.[5] It is impossible to make pure gold by any normal metallurgical process, because of the problems of removing various impurities present in the ore. Nowadays, it can be done through a chemical process that was unknown in the ancient world, although another method involves heating gold until it vaporises, like liquor in a still, then allowing it to cool, leaving behind the impurities. This again requires an immensely high temperature.

If indeed the ancients had been working with some form of atomic energy, they would have been able to produce the necessary temperature, but they would have needed lots of water. The same could be true if the Libyan Desert glass was simply the by-product of some industrial process.

Had the Libyan Desert always been waterless? To answer that question, Dolphin contacted another member of the Royal Geographical Society who was an expert on the geography of the ancient world. His name was Charles Hapgood.

Dolphin wrote to Hapgood early in 1957, telling him about the Libyan Desert glass and his theory that it must have been produced by some kind of atomic fission; he asked whether there had ever been any water in the Libyan Desert. In reply, Hapgood assured him that there had been plenty of water in 6,000 BC in what is now the Sahara Desert. For several thousand years after the pole displacement the Sahara was green and there were many lakes in the area where the Libyan Desert glass was found. Some of the Saharan rock carvings and paintings depict cattle and herdsmen.

Soon Hapgood was corresponding with Lord Rennell, too, but he expressed his doubts about Dolphin's notion of atomic power. To Charles B. Hitchcock, a fellow member of the American Geographical Society, Hapgood wrote on 1 January 1959: 'These two [Rennell and Dolphin] have provided me with practically indisputable evidence that some very ancient race (before 6,000 BC perhaps) could control temperature at 6,000 degrees C in the refining of metals and silicates. The very statement is enough to blow the head off the average archaeologist, but I see no way to explain away the evidence they sent me.'[6]

Rennell and Dolphin's observations fitted very comfortably with the conclusions that Hapgood was reaching through the study of the 'maps of the ancient sea kings': that civilisation was thousands of years older than historians assume. The generally accepted view is expressed in the article on metallurgy in the most recent *Encyclopaedia Britannica* – man began to smelt ore to obtain metals around 4,000 BC. If, as Hapgood believed, man was building ocean-going ships at least 3,000 years before that, then he was certainly technically accomplished enough to have learned how to use metals.

It so happened that Hapgood himself had seen a necklace made of pure gold, but this had come from Mexico rather than Egypt. Moreover, Captain Arlington Mallery, who had been the first to study the Piri Reis map, had also made some extraordinary claims about metal technology, speaking about it in the broadcast of August 1956 that had introduced Hapgood to the study of ancient maps.

Mallery had excavated a number of furnaces in Ohio and Virginia, and was convinced that iron-smelting techniques were in use long before 4,000 BC. During the Georgetown broadcast,[7] Mallery made the even more astonishing claim that the British Museum had sent some iron tools from Egypt to a metallurgist and was 'astounded to find out that the ancient Egyptians were using powdered metallurgy', a process that involves heating the metal to a temperature where it vaporises, after which it condenses in the form of a powder. The Egyptians obtained these temperatures, Mallery contended, by 'the same processes that made our atomic bomb possible' – atomic fission – 'so 5,000 years ago the Egyptians were using the same processes that we thought we had discovered today to make the atom bomb'. Mallery added that 'the timing of the process agrees with the timing of the ancient maps' – in other words, perhaps 6,000–7,000 BC. Mallery was also convinced that he had found gold that was 100 per cent pure.

So Hapgood was already familiar with the claim, now made by Dolphin, that prehistoric men he described as 'Phoenicians' had learned to create and sustain temperatures of 6,000 degrees Celsius (which is only 2,000 degrees cooler than the surface of the sun). He was not prepared to concede that the answer lay in atomic power, though. Hapgood had his own theory, which came from a comment he found in a book called *Mysteries of Ancient South America* (1956) by Harold Wilkins, who had written:

Again, in the same country of Ecuador, on the sea-shore, close to a place called Esmeraldas, queer relics have been found which are not only pre-Incaic, but seem even to have preceded the old European stone age . . . The artifacts of this unknown nation, whose city is below the sea off Ecuador's shores, are singular. Beside fine obsidian mirrors, carved like lenses in a way to suggest that the race had a knowledge of optics, there are queer, oblong-shaped prisms, on whose facets are carved animals, hieroglyphics, or symbols . . .[8]

Concave mirrors can, of course, be used to concentrate the sun's rays – Archimedes devised huge metal mirrors to hold the Romans besieging Syracuse at bay in 211 BC, setting their ships ablaze. Hapgood told his correspondent Charles Hitchcock: 'On the other hand, I am loath to accept the explanation to which Lord Rennell finds himself pushed: that these ancient people (unidentified) had atomic power. I see another possible explanation: that they used solar power through a system of lenses like those reportedly found off the coast of Ecuador.'[9]

Rennell himself was disinclined to accept the atomic power hypothesis, but he and Dolphin had no doubt that the Libyan Desert glass demonstrated the existence of a civilisation that possessed the technology to create high temperatures in at least 6,000 BC.

In November 1958, Hapgood wrote to Ion Edwards, Professor of Egyptology at the British Museum, to check Mallery's claim that the ancient Egyptians possessed powdered metallurgy; Edwards replied that there was no evidence that the Egyptians possessed anything but the simplest forms of metallurgy. Reluctantly, Hapgood was forced to abandon his hope that he had found proof for ancient technology, but like Rennell and Dolphin he was totally convinced that it had existed. Less than a year later, his discovery of the portolans in the Library of Congress left him in no doubt of the existence of a civilisation that predated even the 'Phoenicians' of Dolphin and Rennell.

In the summer of 1995 Rand visited the Hapgood Archives at Yale University. He and his friend Martin Schnell – who had drawn Rand's attention to the article on the Sphinx by Paul Roberts – arrived on the deserted campus and took rooms in an empty hall of residence. For three weeks they made their way across to the Beinecke Rare Book and Manuscript Collection immediately after breakfast, only leaving when it closed. It was there they found and made extensive notes on the file on Lord Rennell and the Libyan Desert glass, as well as the correspondence that revealed Hapgood's 'secret quest for Atlantis'.

The following summer, another piece of the jigsaw puzzle fell into place. Rand and Rose were visited by a friend named Shawn Montgomery, whom they had met earlier in the year when they went to launch *When the Sky Fell* in Toronto. Montgomery was making a research trip across Canada and America, talking to people who shared his interest in 'scientific anomalies'.[10] As the three of them were sitting at breakfast on the day he was about to leave, he began to tell them about his visit to a scientist called Yull Brown, who was working on a new technology that certainly qualified as anomalous. Brown had learned how to make a mixture of hydrogen and oxygen whose properties had baffled every scientist who had examined it. He called it Brown's Gas. As he talked, Montgomery pulled out one of Brown's brochures and laid it on the table, and Rand glanced through it idly as his friend went on talking. Suddenly he stopped and stared. He was looking at a page with a picture of a sun emitting rays, and in the centre of the sun was the phrase '6,000 degrees Celsius'.[11] Rand was convinced that he had taken a major step towards solving the mystery of the Libyan Desert glass.

Montgomery had been working with Graham Smith, who was involved in the Marshall McLuhan Research Program at the University of Toronto, and the two had made a series of

119

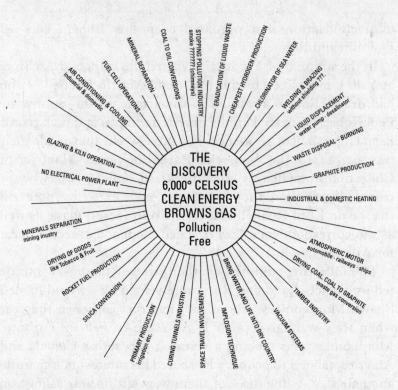

A September 1979 Sydney, Australia, press release about Brown's Gas
puts the figure 6,000 degrees Celsius at the centre of the page.

television programmes about forgotten – or suppressed – knowledge. Brown's Gas came high on the list of the things they wanted to investigate, so Montgomery rang Brown in California. He found it extremely difficult to understand his accent, which was a curious mixture of Bulgarian and Australian, but eventually he became an expert on the subject. What he learned sounded so incredible that when Brown told him that there was a Brown's Gas generator in Ottawa, he and Smith lost no time in paying a call on its owner, Professor Andrew Michrowski of the Planetary Association for Clean Energy (PACE).

Professor Michrowski led them up to the roof, where the generator stood on a table. As the generator could sublimate metals into gases, and the smell tended to linger in closed environments, open air was necessary. Michrowski used a spark to light the flame, which came from a small nozzle like a welding torch, and the demonstration began.

Brown had told Montgomery that the flame could instantaneously poke a hole in wood or metal. Montgomery held out a large wooden spoon. There was a flurry of yellow flame, and a small, clean hole appeared through half an inch of wood.

On seeing such a demonstration, most people would assume that the flame was as hot as an oxyacetylene burner, so Montgomery was startled when Professor Michrowski handed him the torch and told him to feel the temperature of the nozzle a fraction of an inch from where the flame was emanating. His instinct told him not to risk it, but he did. The nozzle was merely warm.

Montgomery picked up a rod of welder's tungsten, and applied the flame to it. It looked as if he had lit a piece of magnesium ribbon. There was a blinding white flame, and the rod proceeded to vanish. It should have become too hot to hold; instead it remained at the same temperature. Even when the white flame was within an inch and a half of his fingers, there was no heat. He tried playing the flame over his arm, moving it back and forth. It was hot, and would have burned him if he had kept it still; as it was, it merely felt warm again. The flame of a gas stove would have burned the tissue. Brown's Gas could apparently burn tungsten, at somewhere around 6,000 degrees Celsius, but did little damage to flesh.

During the next hour, Michrowski put the generator through its paces. He played the flame on a piece of brick, and the brick first of all glazed then began to melt. They welded a piece of glass to a piece of brick, then a piece of copper to the brick, then a piece of glass to the copper, then cut holes in a fire brick – designed to withstand high temperatures – and also welded copper to it. They turned a fistful of sand into a glass ball, then welded together samples of dissimilar metals, such as copper and bronze, and nickel and iron. Finally, they turned various metals into molten pools.

How could the flame do this without enough heat to burn flesh? Michrowski had no idea. Neither did anyone else. And that was why science had determinedly ignored Brown's Gas.

Back in Toronto, Montgomery and Smith bought themselves a small Brown's Gas generator from China, the only country that manufactured them. There were three sizes, and they could only afford the smallest – like the one they had seen at Dr Michrowski's. This was frustrating, because its flame was only the size of the tip of a pencil, and the operations it would carry out necessarily took place on a smaller scale. But it was obvious that it worked – even if it did seem to contradict the laws of nature.

Who was the Bulgarian magician who had created this extraordinary machine? Yull Brown's real name was Ilya Velbov, and he was born on the stroke of midnight on Easter Eve in 1922. His disposition was religious, and he became a student in a seminary, destined for the priesthood. The question that would lead to the creation of Brown's Gas occurred to him when he was reading the Bible at the age of seventeen. The Second Epistle of St Peter declares that one day the earth will be consumed by fire. How, the young Velbov found himself wondering, could a planet whose surface has far more sea than land be consumed by fire? Perhaps water could somehow be turned into flames?

The student was also fond of the works of Jules Verne. A few weeks later he happened to be reading one of his finest works, *The Mysterious Island*, written in 1874. And here Velbov again came upon the interesting suggestion that water might be used as a fuel. It is a modern version of *Robinson Crusoe*, except it has five main characters (six if you count Captain Nemo of *Twenty Thousand Leagues Under the Sea*, who appears at the end and whose death concludes volume three with a dramatic flourish). They are wrecked on a remote island when their balloon crashes into the sea. Verne's aim was to show how such a group could not only survive, but, with the help of nineteenth-century science and common sense, create themselves a small but comfortable version of civilisation.

Halfway through volume two, the castaways sit around the fire on a winter evening, sipping coffee made from elderberries and discussing the problem of what will happen when the world runs out of coal. 'What will they burn instead of coal?' asks one of the characters. Cyrus Harding – the novel's scientific genius – answers, 'Water.' He goes on to explain:

> Water decomposed into its primitive elements . . . by electricity, which will then have become a powerful and manageable force . . . Yes, my friends, I believe that water will one day be employed as a fuel, that hydrogen and oxygen, which constitute it, used singly or together, will furnish an inexhaustible source of heat and light . . . One day the engine rooms of steamers and the tenders of locomotives will be stored with these two condensed gases, which will burn with enormous calorific power . . . Water will be the coal of the future.[12]

Even the remark about electricity was an astonishing piece of prophetic anticipation. We have to remember that Verne composed his novel by gaslight. Edison did not invent the electric light bulb until 1879, five years later, and it was not until 1883 that Nicola Tesla invented alternating current and made it practicable to transmit electric current over long distances.

Any scientist who read Verne's novel would have dismissed his prophecy as nonsense. The law of the conservation of energy declares that you can only get out of a machine as much energy as you put in. If you decompose water by electrolysis – running an electric current through it – and then recombine the hydrogen and oxygen by dropping in a match, the resulting explosion only produces as much energy as you have introduced via the electrolysis. Perhaps the seminary student was unaware of this. At all events, he continued to dream of one day turning Cyrus Harding's dream into reality.

But in the spring of 1941, Bulgaria joined the Axis Powers and declared war on Britain and the United States. Ilya Velbov found himself commanding an occupying force of marines on a tiny Greek island in the Aegean. After the Nazis were defeated and the Russians had invaded Bulgaria, Brown took a degree in electrical engineering and spent some time working in Moscow. But he hated communist society, and was finally denounced to the secret police by his wife, a devout communist. He spent the next six years in a 'hard regime' concentration camp, which wrecked his health and almost killed him.

But he did not die. Perhaps he was sustained by hatred. At all events, he determined to escape the communists. He did this by swimming the river dividing Bulgaria and Turkey. As he stood shivering in his clothes on the other side of the border, he was arrested by Turkish border guards and thrown into jail as a spy. There he spent the next five years.

Finally, with the aid of the US intelligence service – and in particular a major called Brown – he was released in 1958 and allowed to emigrate to a country of his choice, which happened to be Australia. Since it seemed a good idea to take an English name, he chose Brown in honour of the American major, and Yull because he admired Yul Brynner (whose name he misspelled). He was qualified as an electrical engineer, and managed to find a job in Sydney with Australian Consolidated Industries, where he designed and built test instruments and rose to become chief instrument officer. But he found working for a boss unsatisfying, and the work unexciting; after ten years, he resigned and set up in business for himself.

This was a period when plane hijackings were in the news every day, and airports all over the world were being forced to introduce security systems. The method, of course, was a simple metal detector, whose disadvantage was that it would respond to coins or belt buckles as well as concealed weapons, obliging security guards to examine pockets and wave metal detectors over passengers' arms and legs. Brown perceived, rightly, that this was a waste of money. What about a system that would recognise guns or bombs and ignore everything else? He devised a revolving door that had three detection systems: one for objects weighing more than 14 ounces, one for objects the size of guns, and one for the high-carbon steel used in pistols. It cost about 4,000 Australian dollars to install, but neither banks nor airlines were interested, favouring the old labour-intensive method. So Brown's first invention found no takers.

Brown turned his attention back to the idea that had occupied his mind since that evening in the seminary when he had read Jules Verne: turning water into a fuel. As an electrical engineer, he must have understood all the scientific objections, yet some deep intuition drove him to persist. He learned how dangerous it can be to mix hydrogen and oxygen when an accidental explosion wrecked his laboratory and almost cost him his life, but still he carried on.

The basic problem is quite simple: when oxygen and hydrogen are mixed together, their natural tendency is to combine. So when water is subjected to electrolysis, oxygen and hydrogen are placed, so to speak, in separate locked rooms – that is, a mesh is placed between them to keep the gases apart. This raises the resistance in the vessel and means that any process depending on the electrolysis of water is extremely expensive. It explains why hydrogen, which is plentiful in nature, is not used as a fuel – it is too dangerous, as the manufacturers of airships discovered. Hydrogen on its own will merely explode with a mild plop, or burn with a gentle flame; it is only when mixed with oxygen that it becomes dangerously explosive. The same is true of coal gas, though, and millions of people have gas stoves.

After three years of experiment, Yull Brown realised his dream of making use of the hydrogen in water. His major insight, it seems, was that if hydrogen and oxygen are mixed together in the same proportion as they are found in water, they ought – so to speak – to be glad to combine quietly, without a loud bang. This proved to be the case. When the two gases are recombined with a spark, the result is not an explosion, but an implosion. That is, they combine to make water, which occupies a far smaller volume, and if the reaction takes place in a closed vessel also creates a vacuum. When Brown passed these gases through a nozzle and lit them with the end of the cigar that was permanently between his lips, the result was an almost colourless flame that burned at a temperature of around 130 degrees Celsius, slightly hotter than boiling water, so that it can be wafted up and down someone's bare arm without any discomfort. Yet when applied to tungsten, which melts at 3,000 degrees Celsius, it simply vaporises it.

Obviously, something very strange is taking place. The flame is not merely heating the material; it is reacting with it. Instead of simply heating to 130 degrees Celsius, the temperature of the tungsten is soaring until it vaporises. One suggestion offered by scientists who witnessed the reaction is that perhaps Brown's Gas keeps the oxygen and hydrogen in their atomic state, that is, as single atoms, instead of allowing them to combine into molecules of O_2 and H_2. Even if that proves to be correct, it is still hard to see why a flame made of atoms rather than molecules should make the substances to which it is applied behave so unaccountably.

Shawn Montgomery's reaction was that he was witnessing something akin to alchemy.[13] If a flame that burns at around 130 degrees Celsius can punch holes in a firebrick and vaporise tungsten, then the laws of nature are, at the very least, not as straightforward as we assumed. It looks as if the Brown's Gas flame can somehow 'take account' of the substance it is heating, which sounds more like medieval alchemy than the chemistry we were taught at school.

The same might be said of the gas's ability to detoxify nuclear waste, which Brown demonstrated repeatedly. The writer Christopher Bird describes how Brown melted a piece of radioactive Americanum 241 (made by the decay of an isotope of plutonium) along with small pieces of steel and aluminium, on a brick. 'After a couple of minutes under the flame, the molten metals sent up an instant flash, in what Brown says is the reaction that destroys the radioactivity.' The Americanum, which had originally measured 16,000 curies of radiation per minute, now showed only 100 curies per minute – about the same harmless low level as background radiation.

At the point when it began to look as if Brown's work was destined to be ignored, he received an offer from the People's Republic of China. The result was that Chinese submarines began to put to sea with Brown's Gas generators instead of huge tanks of fresh water, and Chinese scientists began disposing of their nuclear waste by heating with Brown's Gas.

It is impossible that Yull Brown could have been a swindler. The Chinese found that his gas actually worked; so did the large American corporation that built him a laboratory, and the many people like Professor Michrovski who purchased Brown's Gas generators. Over the years, hundred of people have seen the demonstrations that Shawn Montgomery witnessed, such as the gas burning a hole in a firebrick or vaporising tungsten.

One possible solution to the mystery may lie in the fact that when Brown's Gas burns it implodes. An oxyacetylene flame is, in effect, a controlled explosion. The same is true of welding torches that use hydrogen gas in place of acetylene. When oxygen and hydrogen combine in exactly the same proportions as in water, they create almost no heat, and when the flame is applied to some substance like tungsten, it looks as if the oxygen and hydrogen enter into chemical reaction with the tungsten, aided by the heat of the flame. It is also possible, as has been suggested, that the flame consists of atoms of oxygen and hydrogen rather than molecules, and that their 'combinatory capacity' is therefore increased.

An ordinary flame burns by heating the substance until its elements dissociate, which is what happens when you apply a match to a piece of paper. On the other hand, if you mix sulphur and iron filings then heat them over a flame in a metal tray, the sulphur will melt and turn brown, then begin to fizz and bubble furiously. You can remove the heat, and the reaction will continue until, instead of sulphur and iron, you have a solid lump of iron sulphide. Again, if sulphur dioxide and oxygen are passed over heated platinised asbestos, they combine to form sulphur trioxide, which, when dissolved in water, makes sulphuric acid. The platinised asbestos is a catalyst – that is, it is not changed by the reaction. This sounds like 'alchemy' – certainly the kind of alchemy that takes place when tungsten vaporises when heated with a mere 130-degree flame.

In other words, Brown's Gas may simply cause the tungsten, firebrick, gold ore or radioactive waste to react like the sulphur and iron filings, combining in an essentially chemical reaction, as straightforward as dropping a piece of zinc into hydrochloric acid and watching it dissolve. If so, the essence of Brown's Gas is simply that it causes chemical reactions. This would also explain why it is possible to hold one end of a piece of tungsten as it 'burns'. This would suggest that Yull Brown was not being accurate when he made the statement that Brown's Gas can create a temperature of 6,000 degrees Celsius. When a California company named Diversified Inspections measured what happened when Brown's Gas vaporised tungsten, the inspector handling the optical measuring device was puzzled when it read 'a measurement far lower than the boiling point of that metal'. In his four-part article on Brown's Gas in *Raum und Zeit*, Christopher Bird seems to assume that this is a mistake. He says that, when a further reading was taken, using a new measuring instrument, 6,000 degrees Celsius was recorded, although Diversified Inspections declined to offer a certificate to this effect. It seems conceivable that this is because the measuring device did *not* register 6,000 degrees Celsius.

Bird goes on to record that when the temperature of the 'implosion' inside a cylinder was taken, it was a mere 4.3 degrees Celsius. The fact that Shawn Montgomery could continue to hold the tungsten rod as it was 'burning' seems to make it highly likely that Brown's Gas reactions do not take place at high temperatures.

So perhaps the ancients knew the secret of Brown's Gas. Various clues point in this direction. In June 1936, a German archaeologist named William König, from the Iraq Museum in Baghdad, was opening a Parthian grave when he came upon a clay vase that contained a copper cylinder, inside which was an iron rod held in place by asphalt and molten lead. It looked to König like a primitive battery; fellow archaeologists disputed this, since the grave was dated to about 250 BC. But Dr Arne Eggebrecht constructed a duplicate, and poured fruit juice into it; the result was a half-volt current that lasted for eighteen days, with which he was able to coat a silver figurine in gold in half an hour. Having observed that on many gold-covered Egyptian statues the gold seemed to be too fine to have been glued or beaten on, he had become convinced that the ancient Egyptians knew the secret of electroplating.

When Colonel Howard-Vyse was exploring the Great Pyramid in 1837, he instructed one of his assistants, J. R. Hill, to unblock the end of the southern 'air shaft' from the King's Chamber with gunpowder. Hill found an iron plate, 1 foot long, 4 inches wide and an eighth of an inch thick, embedded in the masonry of the pyramid. Re-examined at the Mineral Resources Department of Imperial College, London, in 1989, it was found to be iron that had been smelted at over 1,000 degrees Celsius. The ancient Egyptians were not supposed to understand the processes of smelting iron – all their iron ore came from deposits left by meteorites. But the plate was not meteorite iron – it contained too much nickel. It would seem that the Egyptians knew about smelting iron ore two thousand years before the iron age. Oddly enough, traces of gold were found on one side of the iron plate, indicating that it had been gold-plated. Of course, the gold may have been beaten on, but if Eggebrecht was correct about his statues, the plate may have been electroplated.

No one has ever satisfactorily explained what the decorators of the walls of Egyptian tombs used as a light source as they worked. There is no sign of lampblack on the ceilings. The explanation may, of course, be simple: that they went to some trouble to clean off any carbon. On the other hand, engravings on the walls of the temple at Dendera seem to depict electric lights and insulators . . .

If the Egyptians had possessed a technology even as rudimentary as the Baghdad battery, they could have been able to dissociate the hydrogen and oxygen in water by electrolysis, and could have possessed the knowledge to create Brown's Gas.

When Shawn Montgomery interviewed Yull Brown in April 1996, Brown told him that the Aztecs had a means of producing Brown's Gas. Using a particular mixture of wet wood and dry wood, they set it alight to produce a high temperature that caused the imprisoned steam to dissociate and become Brown's Gas. It would, of course, implode, but this implosion could cause gold ore – presumably also trapped in the burning wood – to yield up ten times as much gold as in the normal separation process. According to Brown: 'They were producing a lot of gold. A lot of gold. But they couldn't have produced that much gold from the amount of ore that they were producing. I was experimenting with this matter, and I found out why. Now with Brown's Gas you can produce ten times more gold with the same amount of ore.'

Montgomery asked if Brown had done this himself.[15] Brown replied, 'Oh yes. There are even some Mayans who use this in the production of gold. They have examined it, and done the lab work, and conclude that this works. Not only gold, but platinum, silver and so on.' When we recall Lord Rennell's pure gold necklace, and the pure gold necklace from Mexico seen by Hapgood, it is natural to wonder whether these might have been produced using Brown's Gas.

Montgomery also asked if there was any way of using Brown's Gas to make tektites, and again Brown replies in the affirmative: 'I have already sent two Brown's Gas machines to Texas Instruments to purify silica to make silicon chips. If you put any gas that has a hydrocarbon product to melt the silica, carbon contaminates and destroys the pure crystalline structure of the chip . . . But with Brown's Gas it melts the silica and leaves only water, which is near to the crystallisation and creates only an ideal crystal. This gives a superior high speed chip and also a good solar cell.'

Montgomery found himself speculating on the notion of a huge sheet of purified silicon in a sunny environment – perhaps the Libyan Desert – producing vast quantities of cheap electricity, although this is different from Libyan Desert glass, which looks as if it has been made in an atomic explosion.

There are other clues. In the spring of 1997, I was in Mexico, making a television documentary based on my book *From Atlantis to the Sphinx*. We spent a day at the ancient sacred site of Tula (once called Tollan), 50 miles north of Mexico City. This was once the capital of the Toltecs, the predecessors of the Aztecs, whose empire flourished from about AD 700 to 900 (although their origins can be traced back to the pre-Christian era). According to legend, Tollan is significant as the site of the final battle between two gods, Quetzalcoatl and Tezcatlipoca, usually identified as the forces of good and evil (although the Toltecs would have felt that is an oversimplification). Quetzalcoatl, who is identified with Viracocha, Kon Tiki, Votan and other gods of Central and South America, is the white god who came from the east during some remote epoch. In *From Atlantis to the Sphinx*, I cited the views of the nineteenth-century scholar Brasseur de Bourberg, who believed that Quetzalcoatl was an Atlantis survivor who brought with him the arts of civilisation. The legend records that he was finally defeated by Tezcatlipoca, the 'Lord of the Smoking Mirror' (which, like some magic crystal, conferred visions of distant places), and sailed away on a raft with a promise that he would one day return.

I had also been greatly intrigued by a passage in Graham Hancock's *Fingerprints of the Gods*, which speaks of the curious objects held by the four great statues of Tula. These stone figures, 16 feet tall, stand on a platform at the top of a truncated pyramid, the Temple of the Morning Star, and once supported the temple's wooden roof. In 1880 the discoverer of the sacred site, the French explorer Desiré Charnay, found blocks of black basalt that he thought were the feet of giant statues, which he called Atlanteans ('*Atlantes*') The four great statues of Tula were in fact discovered sixty years later, and the name was transferred to them.

What is significant about these statues is that they hold unidentifiable objects in their hands, which are pressed flat against their sides. The object on the right-hand side looks at first like a Western gunfighter's six-shooter in its holster, but the handle by which the object is held, by two fingers, looks more like the handle of some power-tool. In the left hand there is something that scholars have described as a bunch of arrows and an incense bag, but since the parallel strands are curved it seems unlikely that they are arrows. Graham Hancock remarks that he had the feeling that the original devices were made out of metal.

On our return home further examination of photographs we took of these statues failed to yield any more clues to the purpose of these objects. It was certainly impossible to see how they might have been used as *atl-atls*, or spear-throwers, as many of the guidebooks state.

Shawn Montgomery later drew my attention to a passage about Tula in a book by Zecharia Sitchin, *The Lost Realms* (1990),[16] the fourth volume of his *Earth Chronicles* series. Among respectable scholars, Sitchin's name is not one to conjure with, for he is often associated with Erich von Däniken as someone who believes that the earth was once colonised by visitors from outer space. But Sitchin differs from Däniken in an important respect: the soundness of his scholarship. Whether or not we find his theories tenable, he is an endless mine of information. And in *The Lost Realms* he discusses the statues of Tollan and points out that one of the pilasters has a peculiar carving of a man wearing a segmented suit, with what looks like a kind of backpack. In his hands he is holding the same tool – the one that resembles a pistol in its holster – and is pointing it at the rock face in front of him; a surging flame is bursting out of the barrel of the 'pistol'. Sitchin says he 'uses it as a flame thrower to shape a stone'.

Whether or not we dismiss Sitchin's theories as too far-fetched, the fact remains that the strange objects held by the gods of Tollan are devices from which curving tongues of flame issue forth, and that Brown's Gas could have been used for this purpose. It would seem that the Toltecs must have either possessed some technology, or at least known enough about it to ascribe it to their gods. Most gods in world mythology can hurl thunderbolts, but they are not depicted holding some kind of flame-spitting welding torch in their hands.

Sitchin has further interesting observations on Tollan. The pyramid was excavated again in the 1940s by the archaeologist Jorge Acosta, who also excavated Teotihuacan. It was Acosta who found a deep trench inside the pyramid, containing the 16-foot 'Atlanteans' whose giant 'feet' had been found by Charnay in 1880. There were also four columns that had once stood in the corners of the roof.

An earlier pyramid lay under this Temple of the Morning Star. The site contained the remains of inner chambers and passages, which have still not been explored, and a carved stone pipe, made of sections that fitted together, with a diameter of about 18 inches. It was positioned at the same angle as the pyramid's walls, and ran throughout its whole height.

Acosta assumed it had been intended to drain water, but, as Sitchin asks, why carve an elaborate stone pipe when a clay pipe would do just as well? The stone pipe was obviously part of the structure of the pyramid, and had a particular purpose. Sitchin says: 'The fact that the remains of the adjoining multi-chambered and multistoreyed buildings suggest some industrial processing, and also the fact that in antiquity, water from the Tula river was channelled to flow by these buildings, raise the possibility that at this site, as at Teotihuacan, some kind of purification and refining process had taken place at a very early period.' Such observations inevitably recall the speculations of John Dolphin and Lord Rennell about the possibility that the Libyan Desert glass was a by-product of some industrial process. Sitchin goes even further: 'Was the enigmatic tool a tool not to engrave stones, but to break up stones for their ores? Was it, in other words, a sophisticated mining tool? And was the mineral sought after gold?'

Sitchin argues that the space visitors wished to mine earth for precious minerals, the most important being gold, which they needed for scientific purposes. He quotes reports of the Anglo-American Corporation, who engaged archaeologists to study ancient mines, to the effect that 'mining technology was used in southern Africa *during much of the period subsequent to 100,000 BC*', and he points out that although gold was obtained in Peru and Mexico by panning in streams, 'this could in no way account for the immense treasures' of these countries. He quotes a Spanish chronicler to the effect that the Spaniards extracted from the Incas alone 6 million ounces of gold and 20 million ounces of silver annually. He believes, as did Yull Brown, that they had some far more efficient method of extracting precious metals from the ore.

He went on to point out that the four 'Atlanteans' holding up the roof of the Temple of the Morning Star bring to mind the ancient Egyptian belief that the four sons of Horus hold up the sky at four cardinal points. These same four gods would accompany the deceased pharaoh up a 'Stairway to Heaven', depicted in hieroglyphs as a kind of step pyramid. This same step pyramid symbol, which decorates the walls around the Tollan pyramid, also became a major symbol for the Aztecs, who came after the Toltecs. Sitchin also suggests a connection between the 'feathered serpent', Quetzalcoatl, and the Egyptian winged serpent that helps transport the deceased pharaoh heavenward. One of Sitchin's basic theses is that there is a close connection between the gods of ancient Egypt and the gods of Mexico.

On checking with Rand, I learned that Tula is located on exactly the same longitude as the more ancient site of Teotihuacan, emphasising again that the sites of sacred places seemed to be carefully selected, not chosen at random.

I was offered another clue to a possible connection between Egypt and Mexico as we made the same television programme. We drove from La Paz, Bolivia, across the immense plain called the Altiplano, to the ancient city of Tiahuanaco in the Andes. The sacred ruins are 2.5 miles above sea level although Tiahuanaco was once a port on nearby Lake Titicaca before some geological upheaval tilted the ground and caused the lake to move a dozen miles away.

Little remains of the great port now, except for the ruins of the port area, the Puma Punku (Puma Gate), where giant blocks lay scattered like ninepins; one has a long incision cut by a blade that seems to have been made with a diamond-tipped saw.

A few hundred yards away are the remains of a large temple enclosure called the Kalasasaya. In its north-western corner stands the most famous feature of Tiahuanaco, the Gateway of the Sun, which looks like a miniature Arc de Triomphe. The lintel of the gateway has a crack that runs down to the 'doorway' in its centre, but before the twentieth century it was more than just a crack: photographs in Professor Arthur Posnansky's classic work *Tiahauanacu: The Cradle of American Man* (1915) show it literally torn in two, most probably by some convulsion of the earth.

As I wandered around Tiahuanaco, I was struck by the precision of the workmanship. Massive blocks of stone, many weighing more than 100 tons, were carved with such exactitude that a knife could not be inserted between the blocks. Where blocks had been separated, as in the Puma Punku, it could be seen that they were often joined by metal clamps, obviously to prevent them coming apart in an earthquake. The archaeo-astronomer Professor Neil Steede, who was involved with the same TV programme, examined one of these clamps, roughly 6 inches long and shaped like a capital I, and remarked that the builders must have possessed some kind of portable forge – microscopic examination has shown that the metal was poured into position when hot. No signs of any such portable forge have ever been found, and an open fire would not have been hot enough to melt the metal for these clamps. Also, there are few trees on the Altiplano to provide the fuel.

Shawn Montgomery's account of the Brown's Gas flame creating a pool of molten metal within seconds reminded me of the metal clamps of Tiahuanaco. Rand and Shawn had, early in their discussions, wondered whether they had been melted in a 'portable forge', as Steede suggested, or by some device more like the 'blowtorch' seen on the pilaster at Tula.

The next sequence of the programme took me to Egypt, at the Giza site. Fifty yards from the Menkaura pyramid I was filmed examining a wall of precisely carved blocks and pointing out that in Egypt such blocks have been found to be joined by metal clamps. As Graham Hancock has pointed out, they are also found in Angkor Wat, in Cambodia.

Tiahuanaco has one more feature that raises some of the same questions as Tula: a pyramid known as the Akapana, which was once a vast step pyramid with seven terraces and a flat top, looking rather like some industrial complex or perhaps a modernist building. It had once dominated the temple area, but 90 per cent of its flat facing stones have been removed over the years by builders, so that what remains looks at first glance like a natural hill. Anyone who clambers to the top finds that it contains a kind of lake.

But it was not a hill. Inside, as in the Tollan pyramid, there are tunnels and a chamber of unknown purpose, which a Bolivian archaeologist, Oswaldo Rivera, has described as its 'King's Chamber'. Jointed stone channels had carried water, and it had been surrounded by a moat. The large quantities of water that would have fallen on top of the pyramid ran into the central court – what now looks like a lake – then into a drainage system that probably ran around all four sides of the first terrace, to be allowed to emerge into the open, then conducted back inside again, then out, all the way to the moat. The top was covered with green pebbles looking like the water of the 'lake'. The whole building was a monument to water. We are reminded of Sitchin's words about Tula, and 'the remains of the adjoining multichambered and multistoried buildings' that 'suggest some industrial processing, and . . . raise the possibility that at this site, as at Teotihuacan, some kind of purification and refining process had taken place at a very early period'.

As I stood on top of the Akapana pyramid, looking south towards the Quimsachata Mountains, then at the vast plain that extended all around me, I found myself trying to imagine what this place had looked like when Tiahuanaco was at the height of its prosperity. It was difficult to imagine a huge city with a port area and buildings constructed of immense blocks, some weighing nearly 200 tons. How did they get them here? And what was a city doing in the middle of this rather soggy plain? Then what had happened? It seemed that some great catastrophe had turned it into this barren plain. And when had it occurred? According to the museum opposite the Kalasasaya, and to Alan L. Kolata's book *The Tiwanaku*[17] (the spelling of the city's name varies), Tiahuanaco rose to power around AD 100, reached its peak around AD 500, then went into steady decline until about AD 1000. What was the tremendous cataclysm that snapped the Gateway of the Sun in two, and hurled the huge stones of the port all over the place? It was obviously more than a local earthquake, but there is no record of such a cataclysm around 500 AD.

Around the turn of the twentieth century Professor Arthur Posnansky, who spent his life studying the ruins, concluded that Tiahuanaco was founded about 15,000 BC. His reasoning was based on two observation points in the enclosure, which marked the summer and winter solstices. At the moment, the two tropics are located 23 degrees, 30 minutes on either side of the equator, but when the Kalasasaya was built, the tropics were slightly closer to the equator – to be exact, at 23 degrees, 8 minutes and 48 seconds. This change in the width of the tropics results from a slight rolling motion of the earth known as the obliquity of the ecliptic, and it enabled Posnansky to calculate when the Kalasasaya was built.

Posnansky's dating upset scholars, who felt it was thousands of years too early, but between 1927 and 1930 a team of German scientists, led by Dr Hans Ludendorff of Potsdam, checked Posnansky's results and were inclined to agree with him. The academic furore led them to revise their figure downward, and they ended by suggesting that Tiahuanaco might date from 9,300 BC, but even this struck archaeologists and historians as 9,000 years too early. This view, as we have seen, prevails today.

Yet not entirely. The archaeologist Professor Neil Steede, who studied Tiahuanaco for many years, concluded the sacred city was built about 12,000 years ago.* And, more surprisingly, so does Dr Oswaldo Rivera, the Director of the Bolivian National Institute of Archaeology, who conducted excavations at Tiahuanaco for twenty-one years. In a television programme called *The Mysterious Origins of Man*,[18] made in 1996, Rivera had gone on record as disagreeing with Steede's estimate. His own view was that the builders of Tiahuanaco had simply made a slight mistake – after all, we are only speaking of about 21 seconds of a degree. Steede disagreed emphatically; he felt that builders as accurate as the founders of Tiahuanaco would not have made even such a minor error.

---

*Using Posnansky's methodology but armed with better instruments, Steede established a more reliable date.

During the remainder of 1996, Rivera went on to observe the sunsets over Tiahuanaco, which involved the taking of measurements from the other end of the Kalasasaya. His calculations finally convinced him that Steede was right – there was no 'minor error'. The measurements of the sunsets gave precisely the same reading as the sunrises. Rivera came to agree that the Kalasasaya was built approximately 12,000 years ago, near the time Atlantis fell.

6

ANCIENT VOYAGERS

IN THE EARLY 1930s, the United Fruit Company began clearing the jungles of south-western Costa Rica, in Central
America, to make a banana plantation in the area called the
Diquis Delta. The workers hacking and burning their way
through jungle began to find huge stone hemispheres sticking
up out of the earth, and some hard digging revealed that they
were spheres, like giant beachballs – except that they were
made of granite. The largest was over 9 feet in diameter, the
smallest the size of a tennis ball. It seemed that the spheres
had once formed part of various religious sites: they had been
supported on top of mounds, and were surrounded by stelae
and statues. What was so astonishing was the perfect workmanship; many were exact spheres, and their surface was as
smooth as paper.

While giant stone balls are certainly an oddity, something
about them quickly exhausts one's curiosity. Some of the
wealthier inhabitants of San José and Limon, Costa Rica's
major cities, had them transported on to their front lawns, and
learned in the process that the largest weighed 20 tons. A few

archaeologists looked at them, shook their heads, and opined that they probably represented either the sun or the moon, or perhaps both, and turned their attention elsewhere.

About a decade later, an American archaeologist called Samuel K. Lothrop was spending a brief vacation in the Diquis area with his wife when he saw one of the balls on a lawn in Palmar Sur; he was told that there were hundreds of them, and that no one had any idea of what they were. Here was a puzzle worth solving. Since Lothrop happened to have time on his hands – bandits were making it difficult to continue his current task of excavating the pottery of the Chortega – he decided to devote some time to this intriguing problem.

He made little headway, for a smooth stone ball is devoid of clues, but at least he visited the site where some of the balls had been left in place and noted that they often seemed to be found in threes, in the form of a triangle. Others occurred in straight lines consisting of as many as forty-five spheres. But the triangles were oddly irregular, and were often made of balls of differing sizes, which suggested a special purpose in their arrangement, some hidden code that remained impossible to fathom. Lothrop wrote a paper on the stone balls, which was published under the auspices of the Peabody Institute at Harvard, and returned to less impenetrable mysteries. No other archaeologist pursued the subject, for Lothrop seemed to have exhausted it in his brief paper.

Three decades passed, and the stone spheres seemed to have been forgotten. Then, in 1981, Ivar Zapp, a young Professor of Architecture at the University of Costa Rica, thought he saw a new approach to the mystery. His inspiration came from the work of an English scholar, John Michell, whose name had become associated with 'ley lines' – long, straight tracks that run like canals across the English countryside. Zapp recalled the long, straight lines of stone spheres in the Diquis Delta, and began to speculate . . .[1]

Ley lines had been 'discovered' in 1921 by an English businessman named Alfred Watkins, who was riding his horse across the hills near Bredwardine, in Herefordshire, when he noticed that ancient footpaths ran straight as an arrow for mile after mile, often towards hilltops. It suddenly struck him that England seems to be criss-crossed with hundreds of these 'old straight tracks'. He called them 'leys' or 'leas', and concluded that they were ancient trade routes used by the earliest inhabitants of Britain.[2]

When John Michell approached the problem in the mid-1960s, it was largely because he was fascinated by the mystery of flying saucers, which had been causing excitement ever since a businessman named Kenneth Arnold had seen a formation of them flying at tremendous speed near Mount Rainier in Washington State in 1947. Subsequently there had been thousands of sightings.

Michell noted the curious fact that many flying saucers were seen close to ley lines, which are obviously more easily seen from the air than the ground, and especially at the crossing points of several leys. Learning that the Chinese have similar lines called *lung mei*, or dragon paths, which are designed to channel the 'magic energies of heaven and earth', Michell speculated that ley lines may mark some current of 'earth-force'. He learned that dowsers, for example, can detect ley lines by the response of their dowsing rods or pendulums, and noted that ley lines often pass through 'holy' sites, such as burial mounds, old churches, and ancient monuments like Stonehenge.

Ivar Zapp could see that the stone balls of the Diquis Delta seemed to pose some of the same questions as the megaliths of Stonehenge – or, for that matter, the huge stones of the Great Pyramid. How were they carved so perfectly? How were they moved? Some of them were even found high in the mountains along the coast of Costa Rica, and it was impossible to imagine even a large team of men rolling them uphill – it would be too difficult and dangerous.

Zapp took a party of students to the Diquis Delta to try to fathom the mystery of the spheres. They were baffled, but he began to see a gleam of light. Lothrop had left diagrams of what many of the original stones had looked like before they were moved to museums and front lawns, and Zapp noted that two groups seemed to be arranged on either side of a straight line that pointed directly at the magnetic North Pole. In that case, he wondered, was it possible that the other sides of the triangles were directed towards points on the earth?

When he tried out this theory on a map, extending the lines with a ruler, the result was disappointing. The lines seemed to point at nothing in particular, although that could be explained by the fact that a map is a flat projection of the curved surface of the earth. Zapp tried again, this time with a tape measure and a globe. One line, projected from Palmar Sur, where spheres had been found, went straight through Cocos Island, then through the Galapagos Islands, then to Easter Island. He recalled that similar spheres had been discovered on Easter Island, although they were smaller than the giant balls of Costa Rica.

When he looked more closely at this 'sight line' from Palmar Sur to Easter Island, he saw that the line actually missed Easter Island by 42 miles. Then he remembered that Polynesian sailors can detect the presence of an island up to 70 miles away by studying the waves and the clouds, for both are disturbed by the presence of land; sailors also note the presence of land-based birds such as the tern and the noddy. A 7,000-mile-long sight line, passing through two other islands, that missed Easter Island by only 42 miles would be regarded as a hit.

His observations received confirmation as he studied other sight lines. Another side of the same triangle extended across the Atlantic and led to the Straits of Gibraltar. In another group of stones the line led to the Great Pyramid. And in yet another, it not only pointed to southern England, but ran right through Stonehenge. That could hardly be chance.

It seemed that Ivar Zapp had discovered the purpose of the stone balls of Costa Rica: they were navigational aids. That explained why some were in straight lines, and some were in the mountains overlooking the sea, and also why more of the stone balls had been found on the island of Cano, off the south coast of Costa Rica, looking across the Pacific.

Lothrop had also noted that the balls were often found in association with native cemeteries, which led to the speculation that they might be some kind of homage to the dead, although it makes sense for direction markers to be found in such locations, since the sailors would hope for guidance from the spirits of dead navigators.

The question of when the spheres were carved remains a matter for debate. Archaeological finds in the Diquis Delta date from 12,000 BC to AD 500. Some archaeologists date the stone balls to the most recent period, between a few centuries BC and AD 500. Archaeologists tend to be conservative, and extreme caution in dating a new find is a way of showing that you are a sober and respectable member of the academic community, not likely to leap to wild conclusions. This can be a mistake. In the 1920s, when the Meso-American archaeologist Matthew W. Stirling found an immense negroid head at Tres Zapotes in Mexico, he suggested that the Olmec culture that carved it might be dated as early as 600 BC, and was greeted with hoots of derision from his academic colleagues. Stirling was, in fact, *too* conservative, and the Zapotec culture is now known to date from 1,200 BC. So it is also possible that the giant stone balls are another proof of Hapgood's 'worldwide maritime civilisation' of 7,000 BC.

Zapp knew Hapgood's *Maps of the Ancient Sea Kings*, and was perfectly aware of his hypothesis. A student named Humberto Carro noted that the story of Sinbad the Sailor in *The Arabian Nights* had a description of a steering device called a kamal, a long knotted cord with wooden squares at either end, the knots representing the latitudes of various ports. The Arab navigator would hold a certain knot between his teeth and point the string at the Pole Star to determine the ship's position.

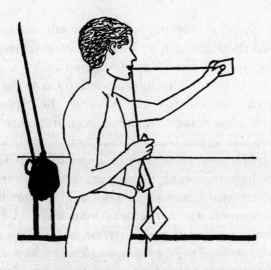

The kamal, a steering device consisting of a long, knotted cord
with wooden squares at either end.

Zapp had seen this knotted string before, on a small figure
Lothrop had found near a group of stone balls. It was holding
the ends of the string in either hand and its centre was in its
mouth, creating a V shape. Zapp had seen similar figures from
places all over the world, from pottery designs in pre-Inca
burial sites in Peru to depictions in the Indus Valley in India.

Costa Rica is, of course, a navigator's culture, since it is on
one of the narrowest parts of Central America, with two vast
oceans on either side. Humberto Carro came upon another
interesting piece of evidence, an article by Thor Heyerdahl
that explained the techniques of sailing balsa rafts against the
wind and current. Thousands of years before the keel was
invented, Peruvians used removable centre-boards that served
as keels and enabled them to tack. In the sixteenth century,
Francisco Pizarro had encountered a whole flotilla of such
rafts off the coast of Peru. They were of enormous size and
moving towards them against the wind and current. Pizarro
learned that they made journeys on these rafts along the whole
coast of South America. Heyerdahl, we recall, used a similar

145

raft called *Kon-Tiki*[3] to prove that ancient mariners could have crossed the Pacific; later on, he reinforced the point by crossing the Atlantic from Egypt to America.

When Christopher Columbus landed in Costa Rica in 1502, on his fourth voyage across the Atlantic, the explorers were received with great respect by the natives, and taken on a two-hour trek to the grave of an important person, which was decorated with the prow of a ship. The natives of Costa Rica appeared to be introducing these great navigators from Spain to one of their own famous navigators. The stone lapidas, or funeral slabs, upon which the dead man was laid out looked like the centre-boards of the Peruvian balsa rafts, and other figures – who seemed to be priests and kings – were laid out on identical centre-boards, stone replicas of the boards that played such an important part in their lives.

Could primitive navigators have sailed such enormous distances? Heyerdahl seemed to have proved the point, but he knew Easter Island was there when he set off. Would central American sailors of – let us say – 5,000 BC even have known of its existence? And even if they had, would they have dared to launch a balsa raft into the vast and empty Pacific Ocean?

Zapp came upon a book that answered his question: *We, The Navigators* by David Lewis, published in 1972,[4] in which Lewis described sailing with native islanders on native craft all over the Pacific, over 13,000 nautical miles. The islanders used the ocean lore they had learned from their forefathers. Lewis also described 'sighting stones' throughout the Pacific – he personally saw the sighting stones of Tonga and the Gilbert Islands. Unlike the stone balls of Costa Rica, these were flat slabs of coral (which you might expect from islands with plenty of coral), and they were also set in groups of three, which Lewis said were intended to 'indicate the bearings of islands'. The stones had another use. The eldest child of each family was taught to use them to learn star patterns. They learned by heart the various stars that aligned themselves with the 'stones' at various times of the year, and continued to do this over a lifetime, passing the knowledge on to their own children. Navigation came as naturally to these seafaring peoples as reading a road atlas does to a modern motorist.

Zapp noted the similarities between Meso-American, Polynesian and Greek astronomy. Zapp knew that 'atl' is not a Greek syllable, but that it comes from the Mayan and Nahuatl languages of Central America and means 'water'. Atlahuac was the patron god of Tenochtitlan, the city the Aztecs built on a lake – now called Mexico City. Plato's sunken civilisation was called Atlantis, and its major city was circular and ringed with canals, like some of the ancient cities of Central America. Was it possible that Atlantis was actually America? This is the startling argument that Ivar Zapp and his co-author George Erikson present in their book *Atlantis in America* (1998).[5]

They point out that there have been many theories about the location of Atlantis: in the Mediterranean, in the North Sea, in the Atlantic near the Canaries, and in Antarctica. The latter, they argue, is the likeliest among these candidates, for the others are too small to fit Plato's description. But it cannot be Antarctica, they insist, because Plato described Atlantis as 'favoured by the sun' – semi-tropical – and this hardly fits Antarctica. (They had not taken into account Hapgood's hypothesis that Antarctica was once much further north.)

Zapp and Erikson also believe that the Atlantis catastrophe was caused by a comet or asteroid, about 5 miles across, which landed in the Caribbean in 10,513 BC and sent a great tidal wave thundering across Central America – the heart of their 'Atlantis' – from ocean to ocean, leaving behind folk memories of catastrophe. (In *Uriel's Machine*, Robert Lomas and Christopher Knight point out that the vast salt plains of Utah are made of sea salt, as is the lake after which Salt Lake City is named, which suggests that an immense tidal wave from the Pacific, perhaps 3 miles high, was responsible.)[6]

At the beginning of the twentieth century, American archaeologists would have dismissed the idea of folk memories on the grounds that there were no human beings in America at that time. The most influential anthropologist, Ales Hrdlicka of the National Museum, was totally convinced that man had arrived in America about 3,000 BC. The general idea that hunters came across the land bridge that once existed between Russia and Alaska across the Bering Strait is still the main theory of modern anthropology, but modern geological studies, Zapp points out, have revealed that 'Beringia' was a desert, devoid of vegetation. Since it was also 600 miles wide, there is no possible reason to assume that Asian hunters decided to cross it to reach an equally barren Alaska.

In 1927, the skeleton of a long-haired bison with a spear point lodged between its ribs was found in New Mexico. Since these bison became extinct more than 10,000 years ago, Hrdlicka's theory was placed under question. In 1932, archaeologists found more spear tips lodged in mammoth bones near Clovis, New Mexico, after which 'Clovis man' was regarded as the first human being in America, dated to around 10,000 BC.[7]

There is an immense amount of evidence for contact between America and civilisations of the Far East. Joseph Needham, the author of the monumental *Science and Civilisation in China*,[8] describing a visit to Mexico City in 1947, noted the 'palpable similarities between many features of the high Central American civilisations and those of East and South-east Asia'. He then offered two dozen or so particular points of resemblance, including pyramids, double-headed serpents, dresses made of feathers and jade beads placed in the mouths of the dead. Needham claims that a mountain of evidence has accumulated of visits by Asian people to America from the seventh century BC, although Grant Keddie, a curator of the Royal British Columbia Museum in Canada, believes that Asians established trading posts around the North Pacific rim 5,000 years ago.[9]

In the early 1960s, Emilio Estrada, an Ecuadorian businessman who was also an amateur archaeologist, read a book on Japanese archaeology and was impressed by similarities between Japanese pottery from the Jomon period (about 3,000 BC) and ancient potsherds he had dug up near Valdivia, on the coast of Ecuador. He passed on his observation to Betty Meggars, of the Smithsonian Institution, but she was unimpressed – until she went to Japan in 1963 and saw 5,000-year-old Japanese pottery found on the island of Kyushu. She became convinced that the similarities of design could not be coincidence.

Her own explanation was that a fishing boat from Kyushu had been blown across to Ecuador by a typhoon, and that the Japanese had taught the native Indians to make ceramics. She was upset that most archaeologists rejected her theory on the grounds that the fishermen would have starved to death on a voyage of more than 8,000 miles. The archaeologists were right, of course – the voyagers would have needed supplies on board, probably more than Columbus needed to cross the Atlantic. It is unlikely that such a journey was made by chance. Ivar Zapp's Costa Rican mariners could have managed it, though.

One of the most remarkable of the advocates of the spread of Asian culture to America is David Kelley, an archaeologist who, before his retirement, was on the faculty of the University of Calgary. Kelley is an expert on the Maya, who – as we have seen – are still revered for the incredible precision of their calendar.

The first calendar in general use was the moon itself. In 1962, a scholar from the Peabody Museum named Alexander Marshack studied under a magnifying glass a bone about 35,000 years old. It had a curious series of markings made by our ancestor – small holes engraved in the bone with a point. It looked like a decorative pattern, except the holes had been made at different times. Marshack realised that he was looking at the earliest known calendar, and that it showed the phases of the moon.[10]

The Greeks had based their calendar on the moon, which takes approximately 29.5 days to revolve around the earth.

They had soon encountered a major problem: 12 times 19.5 only equals 354 days, which is 11.25 days short of the year. With a calendar running as fast as this, it only took sixteen years for Midsummer Day to arrive in the middle of winter. Any Greek farmer who tried to regulate his planting by the famous *Works and Days* of the farmer-poet Hesiod, who lived around 800 BC, would soon have found himself hopelessly confused.

Even the Sumerians had been unable to solve the problem. Although they divided the day into 24 hours, and the hours into 60 minutes, they were still unable to get the year right. They added half a day to each lunar month, making it 30 days, bringing the year to 360 days.

For the average person, living in a small town or village, the number of days in a year didn't really matter. The seasons came and went, whether you counted them or not, so a calendar that was a few days out made no real difference.

It was the ancient Egyptians who finally came close to measuring the actual length of the year by adding five days that were supposed to be the birthdays of Osiris, Isis, Horus, Nephtys and Set. Some scholars believe that the Nile acted as a calendar, flooding at the same time every year, but Egypt was – as we have seen – green until a few thousand years ago. According to Egyptologist Henry Lhote, the Sahara region was green between 7,000 and 2,000 BC[11] – when the Great Pyramid was built, the surrounding landscape was probably a savannah. The Neolithic Egyptians had no reason to pay close attention to the flooding of the Nile. They were not dependent on it, as they are now. Why should these farmers have wanted a calendar of such accuracy? Schwaller de Lubicz would have said that it was a legacy from a far older civilisation – Atlantis.

The people who developed a more precise calendar than anyone else – even more exact than the Romans, whose Julian calendar was 365.25 days long – were the Maya, whose year was 365.242 days long. Why did the early Maya – the so-called 'classic Maya' who built cities in the jungle before they mysteriously abandoned them around AD 890 – want a calendar as accurate as that? Our own modern measurement, based on the caesium clock, is 365.2422, only 0.0002 seconds longer.

Moreover, the Maya had invented a symbol for zero, which is now regarded as a basic essential in mathematics (neither the Greeks nor Romans had a zero).

Mayan astronomy is also awe-inspiring in its complexity and precision. We calculate the year by the sun; so did the Maya, but they also calculated it by the planet Venus, and by Jupiter–Saturn cycles. As to the length of our earthly year, they solved the problem that the Egyptians, the Greeks and even the Romans had failed to solve by having no fewer than three distinct calendars based on different years: a solar year of 360 days, to which they added 5 supernumary days (although, as already noted, they knew its exact length); a lunar year of 354 days; and a tzolkin, a special 'sacred' calendar of 260 days divided into 13 months of 20 days each, which was used for magical and ritual purposes.

These three cycles ran concurrently. Since the tzolkin was well into its second year when the ordinary year had only just come to an end, their 'century' was a total cycle in which the three lesser cycles had finally caught up with one another, which was every 52 years. The 'Venus year' (584 days long) caught up with the other cycle every two Mayan centuries (104 years).

A further calendar, called the Long Count, was used to calculate long periods of time. Its unit, as we have noted, was 20 days; 360 days (or 18 units) was a 'tun', 20 tuns was a 'katun', 20 katuns was a 'baktun', which is 144,000 days, and 13 baktuns equalled a 'Great Cycle', or an 'earth age', at the end of which everything would be destroyed and start all over again. The end of the present earth cycle will occur in the year AD 2012.

The Mayan specialist David Kelley was interested in the Aztec calendar, which is closely related to the Mayan calendar (the Aztecs ruled a few centuries after the Maya).[12] He had noted similarities between the 20 days of the Aztec calendar and those of an ancient Hindu lunar zodiac, which divided the sky into 28 mansions, corresponding to constellations. He noticed the storm god Rudra ruling a lunar mansion exactly halfway around the cycle from Apah, the water goddess; the Aztec calendar showed rain halfway around the cycle from the water goddess. And when Kelley set the two zodiacs side by side, he noted that the Aztec Death appeared opposite Yama, the Hindu god of death. The next Aztec day, Deer, corresponded to the Hindu deer god, Prajapati.

The next day in the cycle at first seemed less similar, with the Aztec Rabbit appearing next to the Hindu soma, an intoxicating drink – until Kelley recalled that the Aztec rabbit goddess represents drunkenness. Moreover, she is also the moon goddess. Soma also rules the moon – in both Aztec and Hindu mythology, a rabbit instead of a man lives in the moon. And in Mexico, they do not say that someone is 'as drunk as a skunk', but 'as drunk as 400 rabbits'.

Kelley now had no doubt that the Aztec zodiac and the Hindu zodiac had the same source, and that there must have been trans-Pacific contact. He also comments on the similarities of the lunar zodiacs in the Middle East and the Far East, and this connection between the Hindu and Aztec zodiacs brings to mind Robert Graves's *The White Goddess*,[13] whose central argument is that the religion of the moon goddess is far older than the religion of the sun god that eventually replaced, or at least suppressed it.

Kelley has an even more conclusive piece of evidence for trans-Pacific voyagers. He was intrigued by a speculation of the American sinologist Hugh Moran that the Hebrew and Greek alphabets were derived from the Chinese lunar zodiac. This time the link is with the Mayan rather than the Aztec calendar. Again, there are obvious correspondences. The Greek kappa and the Hebrew kaph correspond to the letter k; 'kaph' also means the palm of the hand, and Kelley notes that the Mayan day Manik is represented as a hand and probably pronounced 'keh'. The following letter in the Greek alphabet is lambda, which in Hebrew is lamed; in the Mayan calendar it is lamat (another Mayan language calls it lambat, even closer to lambda). Next in Hebrew comes mem, and in Greek mu, which means water not only in Hebrew but also in the Semitic language from which the Greeks borrowed it; in Mayan, the next sign is mulu, which is ruled by the shark god and also corresponds to the Aztec day water. To Kelley this K–L–M sequence seems too close to be coincidence.

Kelley believes that the Mayan calendar originated in a Hindu city called Taxila, which was a great Indian trading post on the Silk Road to China and is now in Pakistan. He points out that, after its conquest by Alexander the Great in 323 BC, Taxila became a centre of learning like Alexandria, with scholars coming from as far away as China and Egypt. These people, Kelley thinks, undertook the long voyage to Mexico.

Kelley notes that Eastern rulers were deeply interested in eclipses because of their 'occult' significance: 'To chart future eclipses, Taxilian scholars had to know the earth's circumference. Far more advanced scientifically than the Europeans of Columbus's day, the Taxilians already knew the earth was a sphere.' So the scholars of Taxila may have mounted an expedition to 'do better astrology'.

When John Barber asked Kelley what kinds of ships could have been used by primitive man, he indicated that he felt this was the wrong question. 'The shipping problem is a straw man. People can have made the trip any time in the last 40,000 years. They could have made it intentionally and got back any time in the last 5,000 years.' In short, Kelley agrees with Zapp and Erikson that man has been a navigator for thousands of years.

In fact, this view had been stated more than twenty years earlier. *The God-Kings and the Titans* (1973)[14] by James Bailey, and *Gods of the Cataclysm* (1976)[15] by Hugh Fox, both argued that there had been a worldwide seagoing civilisation long before the Greeks and Romans. In *The God-Kings and the Titans*, Bailey asserts that the main force that drove the civilisations of the Bronze Age to the seas was the quest for copper and tin, whose alloy bronze was the hardest metal known to man. Much of the book is taken up with detailed comparisons of Meso-American culture and that of Asia and Europe, and a map shows Bronze Age trade routes following the ocean currents and trade winds all over the Atlantic and Pacific. Bailey cites a Phoenician inscription discovered at Parahyba, Brazil, describing how a ship from Sidon had been separated from a fleet of ten ships by a storm before it was cast up on those distant shores. Another Phoenician inscription at Rio, 3,000 feet up on a vertical cliff face, states simply: 'Tyre, Phoenicia, Badezir, firstborn of Jethbal.' Whether or not the Phoenicians of the Rio inscription were in search of minerals, Bailey has no doubt that the American continent was one of the old world's main sources of tin and copper. In a sequel to *The God-Kings and the Titans*, called *Sailing to Paradise* (1994), he quotes the technological historian R. J. Forbes: 'Much of ancient history could be rewritten as a struggle for the domination of quarries and ore-deposits or metal-supplies', adding: 'This is the center of our argument in this book.'[16]

In his foreword to *The God-Kings and the Titans*, palaeontologist Raymond Dart points out that historians of science took it for granted that mining began about 4,000 BC until the 1960s, when carbon-dating from the Ngwenya iron mine in Swaziland showed that mining for red iron ore (haematite) had been carried out there as long ago as 7,690 BC. By 1969, it had been established that our ancestors had been mining in 41,250 BC. Dart concludes by mentioning Thor Heyerdahl's *Kon-Tiki* expedition, saying that he 'has opened the eyes of the whole world to the grandeur of the maritime experience of mankind'.

Gods of the Cataclysm (1976) by Hugh Fox was equally original and challenging. Fox's wife was Peruvian, and Fox had spent many years studying the ancient cultures of Meso-America and South America. One of these was in Chavin, on the Peruvian coast, whose ruins were discovered in 1919. The archaeologist who had excavated Chavin had remarked that the ruins were covered by a huge amount of dirt and rocks, as if the town had been inundated by waves.

Fox had read a book called *The Biblical Flood and the Ice Epoch* (1966) by Donald Patten,[17] which argued that 'the Great Flood was the pivotal point in human history', dividing prehistory from history. Patten believed that 'an astral visitor of some sort' had swept close by the earth in 2,800 BC, destroying most of mankind. There is considerable evidence for a flood in the Mediterranean area around 2,200 BC. In *Uriel's Machine*, Christopher Knight and Robert Lomas have preferred the later date of 3,200 BC for this flood, but this was certainly not Patten's 'world flood', which almost wiped out mankind. And the date of the great flood 'when the sky fell' seems to have been about 9,600 BC.

Fox points out that Patten's notion that civilisation had almost been destroyed by a great flood seemed to have been confirmed in the silt-covered ruins of Chavin. He also noted that a stone cat he had brought from Chavin, every millimetre of which was covered in designs, strongly resembled a Chinese bronze elephant from the late Shang dynasty (2,000 BC) that he had seen in the Freer Gallery in Washington. He became convinced of a connection between China and Peru.

In Chavin excavators had also found stone heads with flat noses, exaggerated nostrils and protruding eyes. Fox had seen a piece of pottery in Taipei, in Taiwan, that had exactly the same features. His first theory was that Chinese fishermen had been swept across the Pacific, landing in Peru. Could they have been swept away by the great flood? This, he decided, was unlikely. What was far more likely was that they had come to Peru before the flood. Then he began to experience doubt:

the Chavin heads did not *look* very Chinese. To begin with, the eyes were the wrong shape. Could it be that the seafarers were not Chinese, but people who had come from elsewhere through China and also been represented on the Taipei pottery? He began to note similarities between the cultures of ancient India and Meso-America, for example, the phallic imagery in India and in Uxmal in Mexico.

What if these ancient voyagers were Dravidians, the original inhabitants of India? These were a dark-skinned, phallus-worshipping people, who were conquered and driven south by the invading Aryans. Their religion seems to have been matriarchal and they possibly worshipped the moon goddess.

Fox's comparative study of art from America, Asia and Europe led him to conclude that there was a time – which he calls Phase 1 – when there was a single world culture. Then came the Great Cataclysm – the giant asteroid that swept past the earth and caused the flood. After that, the Andes continued to rise and the green Sahara began to change into a desert, and in this new period of history, the older worldwide culture was replaced by the Mediterranean culture (Phase 2) of the Greeks and the Phoenicians. Matriarchal culture disappeared, and a more brutal patriarchal culture took its place. The Phoenicians (who had also been active in Phase 1) returned to Brazil and Mexico, but this time in search of minerals and precious stones.

As a picture of ancient history, *Gods of the Cataclysm* is powerfully argued, and its comparison of American, Asian and Mediterranean art is convincing. Two observations made earlier in this chapter seem to support its thesis: Zapp's comment that 'atl' (as in 'Atlantis') is not Greek but Mayan, and Kelley's arguments about the similarity between the Hindu and the Aztec calendars. Its central argument, that history is divided into two phases, before and after the great flood, obviously accords with that of this book, except that Fox places the flood about 7,000 years later, in 2,800 BC instead of 9,600 BC.

156

At first sight, Jim Bailey's arguments seem less compelling, since they seem to refer mainly to the Bronze Age, which in Egypt began about 2,500 BC and in Britain about 2,000 BC, but he also argues that, before the beginning of the Bronze Age, copper was equally sought after by 'ancient voyagers', and that the Copper Age began as early as 7,000 BC. (He also observes that among the thousands of clay tablets in Ashurbanipal's library in Nineveh, no less than 8 per cent were lists of minerals such as copper.) Certainly, the discovery that man has been mining in South Africa for more than 40,000 years provides powerful support for his thesis that mining has played a central part in the evolution of civilisation.

In fact, he might have cited an even more remarkable discovery: that one iron mine in Africa dated from 100,000 years ago. And since Cro-Magnon man did not appear on earth until later than 100,000 years ago, then this mining must have been carried out by his predecessor, Neanderthal man. He seems to have used the red ochre (haematite) for ritualistic purposes, including burial. And it suggests something that is directly linked to the blueprint: that the science of geology is much more ancient than we commonly assume. Mining is, after all, the technological application of the science of geology. Rand believes that, like astronomy, geology is a very ancient science.

What is beginning to emerge in all these different areas of research is a picture that has more in common with Hapgood's worldwide maritime civilisation than with the cautious views of scholars who believe that civilisation began at Sumer round about 4,000 BC. This 'Asian diffusionist' view has been gathering strength for a long time. In the 1940s, Gordon Eckholm drew up a long list of correspondences between Asia and Meso-America. One of his students, Paul Tolstoy of the University of Montreal, has virtually proved his old professor's thesis with a study of bark cloth, a cloth made from the inner bark of trees that is turned into products such as felt and paper. Mexicans were making it when Cortés and his Spanish invaders arrived, but so were natives of Sulawesi, in Indonesia. Tolstoy has spent thirty years studying bark cloth manufacture from all around the world, as well as examining the tools used in making it. Among hundreds of examples of bark cloths around the world, similarities of style between those of Indonesia and Meso-America left Tolstoy in no doubt that they were closely related. His conclusion was that Indonesians crossed the Pacific 1,000 years before Columbus. No modern scholars dispute the notion that the production and use of bark cloth moved in the opposite direction: from Java and Borneo to Africa, where it spread across the continent. This bark cloth was made with a quite different technique from that of Sulawesi – and Mexico.

The powerful case for the argument that Mayan culture came from further west, across the ocean, has further support.

Now we must consider another reason that is even more startling.

Early nineteenth-century travellers to Mesopotamia, the Biblical 'Land of the Two Rivers', must have been disappointed to find it so bare and unromantic: no pyramids or temples or obelisks, just an arid country of desert and dust storms, with odd-looking mounds that rose out of the brown plain like miniature volcanoes.

In 1840, the French Consul at Mosul, on the west bank of the Tigris, was a doctor named Paul Emile Botta. A linguist and a scholar, he took a lively interest in those academic and philosophical disputes that, then as now, divided French intellectuals into warring camps. Ever since Napoleon had taken archaeologists with him to Egypt to study its pyramids and temples, the French had displayed an interest in archaeology, particularly since a young genius named Champollion had succeeded in deciphering Egyptian hieroglyphics by means of the Rosetta Stone.

Botta had been following a dispute about the whereabouts of the ancient city of Nineveh, the capital of the Assyrians, where Sennacherib and Ashurbanipal had struck terror into the hearts of their neighbours. It seemed to have vanished into antiquity without a trace. One suggestion was that it had been located in the region of Mosul.

Botta found his consular duties less than absorbing, and Mosul full of dust and noise, so he began to make a habit of riding out in the evening, to enjoy the breeze along the river and the desert with its mysterious mounds. He also bought pieces of ancient pottery and inscribed fragments of clay tablets from local Arabs. He decided to start digging at a village called Kuyunjik, where there was a promising-looking mound. As month after month went by without any find more significant than broken pottery and clay tablets, Botta began to feel he was wasting his time and money. The local Turkish pasha – Mesopotamia was then ruled by the Turks – also made life difficult by spying on the excavation and intimidating the workmen, convinced that the French consul was in search of treasure. Botta was about to abandon archaeology when a persuasive Arab told him that he would find plenty of ancient bricks and pottery in his village. Botta needed little persuasion to take his workmen to a village called Khorsabad, 7 miles to the north, where his men sank a shaft and soon came upon a wall lined with slabs of stone, on which there were drawings of animals. Botta had no doubt that he had found Nineveh. He was wrong – he had discovered the palace of a king called Sargon II, who ruled around 700 BC. It proved to be immense, with about 200 rooms, whose walls displayed friezes of bearded men, warriors on horseback and winged animals. Botta might not have discovered Nineveh, but he had rediscovered ancient Assyria.

For three centuries, from 911 BC until 610 BC, the Assyrians had hacked and slaughtered their way to power with such ferocity that their enemies finally banded against them and killed them like vermin, reducing their cities to charred rubble.

Two centuries later, the Greek mercenaries of King Cyrus passed the vast ruins of Nineveh and Nimrud – the story is told by the historian Xenophon – and marvelled at these gigantic empty ruins, but the local inhabitants could tell them nothing about the devastated cities – even the memory of the Assyrians had been destroyed.

In 1842, Botta met a young Englishman named Henry Layard, who had been dreaming about the Middle East ever since he read, *The Arabian Nights* as a boy. The two often shared a pipe together – sometimes of opium – and when Botta showed him the mound of Kuyunjik, Layard seems to have been bitten by the bug of archaeological research, which has something in common with the gambler's love of backing long odds.

Layard had no money, but he had a persuasive tongue, and three years later succeeded in inducing the British ambassador in Constantinople to give him £60, which he used to begin excavating yet another mysterious mound, that of Nimrud (Calah). He unearthed finds even more spectacular than Botta's – huge winged lions and bulls that were soon on their way back to the British Museum. Now famous, and financed (parsimoniously) by the British treasury, Layard turned his attention to Kuyunjik, which had defeated Botta a few years earlier. Within hours, he realised how close the Frenchman had come to making one of the most momentous finds in archaeology, for this indeed *was* Nineveh, the great city of the Bible. Layard found himself digging into the burned-out palace of Ashurbanipal (669–626 BC), one of its mightiest and most ruthless kings.

The French also returned to the race, and the mound of Kuyunjik was divided between them. One day in 1852, when the French were absent, Layard's assistant Hormuzd Rassam decided to do a little poaching, and ordered his workmen to tunnel into the French territory on the other side of the dividing line. The God of Archaeology was with him, and he cut through a wall and found himself in the library of

Ashurbanipal, full of clay tablets inscribed with wedge-like cuneiform.

Ashurbanipal, in spite of being one of the cruellest tyrants in history, was an enthusiastic collector of written records. Whenever he conquered a city, he had its library transported to Nineveh, and as a result had collected some 30,000 clay tablets, mostly concerned with magic, exorcism and divination. After their recovery, they were sent back to the British Museum.

At this time no one could read cuneiform writing, although a British officer named Henry Rawlinson had made an important start by copying an inscription on a cliff near Behistun, in Persia; it had been carved there by the Persian king Darius, and was in Old Persian, Elamite and Babylonian (which was, more or less, a form of Assyrian). In 1857 Rawlinson published his first translation from the Assyrian language. By this time he had returned to England and was employed by the British Museum, with a young man named George Smith, a banknote engraver who was interested in archaeology, working for him.

Among the tablets that Smith brought back from Nineveh was one containing huge, preposterously large numbers. No mathematician, Smith did not attempt to find out what they meant, but eventually French scholars translated them into decimals. One Babylonian number contained fifteen digits: 195,955,200,000,000. It fascinated a French communications scientist named Maurice Chatelain,[18] who in the 1950s had moved to California after Morocco was plunged into chaos following independence. Chatelain worked for the United States government as an aeronautics engineer, and in due course was drafted into the attempt to reach the moon – the Apollo project.

In 1963 Chatelain had learned about the incredibly complex Mayan calendar, which is far more accurate than the European calendar. Impressed by the mathematical abilities of the Maya, Chatelain suddenly found himself wondering if there could have been any connection between the Assyrians of Nineveh and the Maya.

He soon discovered that the Nineveh number was not as arbitrary as it looked; it was 70 multiplied by 60 to the power of seven.

What would such an ancient civilisation be doing with such enormous numbers and the mathematical sophistication they imply? We think of these early peoples as farmers and artisans, rather than mathematicians. Chatelain recalled an obscure piece of information: the Sumerians, the inventors of writing, did their calculations in sixties, rather than in tens, as we do. And the Babylonians took their culture wholesale from the Sumerians. And the Assyrians, in turn, conquered the Babylonians.

The Sumerians were great astronomers, who knew how long it took each of the planets to revolve in its orbit – not just our close neighbours, such as Venus, Mars and Jupiter, but also Uranus and Neptune. The Sumerians also divided the day into 24 hours of 60 minutes each, with each minute containing 60 seconds.

With a flash of inspiration, Chatelain wondered if the Nineveh number could express time in seconds. On this assumption, he worked it out to 2,268 million days, or something over 6 million years.

The indefatigable engineer now recalled the precession of the equinoxes, that wobble on the earth's axis that takes just under 26,000 years to complete its cycle. (also known as a Big Year). He tried dividing this into the Nineveh constant (as he called it), and immediately knew he was on the right track: it proved to be an exact number of precessional cycles: in fact, exactly 240 Big Years.

Chatelain found himself wondering if the Nineveh constant was what astrologers and occultists had called 'the great constant of the solar system', a number that would apply to the revolution of all the bodies in the solar system, including moons. He proceeded to calculate the cycles of the planets in seconds (no doubt using the NASA computer), and found that each was an *exact fraction* of the Nineveh constant.

If Chatelain was correct, he had made an awe-inspiring discovery. Our patronising modern view is that these ancient astronomers were only interested in the heavens because of some absurd superstition about human fate being written in the stars, the same belief that makes modern newspaper readers turn to their astrological forecast. In fact, the 'Chaldean' astronomers apparently understood our solar system as well as Isaac Newton did, and would have found nothing beyond their comprehension in his *Principia*.

If this proposition could be proved, it would offer overwhelming support for the idea that civilisation is many thousands of years older than we assume. If the Sumerians knew the Nineveh constant over 5,000 years ago, their scientific knowledge had to have even earlier origins. Such a high level of intellectual sophistication could not have been achieved overnight.

Chatelain went a step further. When he divided the Nineveh constant into solar years, then compared this with a modern astronomical table based on a caesium clock (which gives the most accurate estimation of the length of a second), he found a slight discrepancy in the sixth decimal place. It was only a twelve-millionth of a day per year, but it puzzled him. Then he saw the solution. Modern astronomical measurements tell us that the rotation of the earth is slowing down very slightly, so every year is getting shorter by sixteen-millionths of a second.

The Nineveh constant proved to be totally accurate 64,800 years ago, and that suggested to Chatelain that it was first calculated 64,800 years ago – at a time when, according to anthropologists, our ancestor Cro-Magnon man had only recently appeared in Europe.

How does Chatelain explain a notion that seems so outrageous? The answer can be found in the title of his book *Our Cosmic Ancestors* (1987). Like von Däniken, he believes that our earth has been visited by beings from outer space. As a space scientist, he learned that 'all Apollo and Gemini flights were followed, both at a distance and also sometimes quite closely, by space vehicles of extraterrestrial origin . . . Every time it occurred, the astronauts informed Mission Control, who then ordered absolute silence.' Anyone who is interested in 'flying saucers' has heard that claim many times before. But this time it is made by a man who designed the communications system of the moon rockets.

However his explanations are viewed, it is hard to fault the logic of his deductions about the date the Nineveh constant was first calculated. If Chatelain is correct, it would seem that our distant ancestors possessed a far more sophisticated knowledge than we can explain in terms of conventional history.

When Chatelain initially heard of the immense Mayan numbers, he at first failed to attach any great significance to them. Years later he came across the notes he had made, and was intrigued by two huge numbers that had been found on steles at Quiriga, in Guatemala, the intellectual centre of the Mayan culture. Both were given (presumably) in days, which was the measure the Maya used. He translated these into years, and found that one number was just under 93 million years, while the other was 403 million years. His work with the Nineveh constant had made him curious, and he tried dividing the numbers by the Nineveh constant. He felt stunned when he realised that 93 million years is exactly 15 times larger than the Nineveh constant, while 403 million is 65 times larger.

Chatelain published this incredible discovery in a book called *Nos Ancêtres Venus du comos* (*Our Venusian Cosmic Ancestors*), published in Paris in 1975. Predictably it failed to make any impact, even when it was discussed by Peter Tompkins in his bestselling *Mysteries of the Mexican Pyramids* (1976). In November 1998 I read a much later version, *Our Cosmic Ancestors*, published by a small press in Arizona ten years before. The chapter on the Nineveh number contained a vital piece of information for the book I was about to write with Rand Flem-Ath, and Chatelain's demonstration of the connection between the Maya and the Sumerians staggered me.

Consider its implications. The Maya, we believe, date from about 1,000 BC. There seems a general agreement that they received their knowledge from the Olmecs, the creators of those giant stone heads, first discovered in the 1860s, which appear to be African, although there are authorities who believe the faces are Chinese – a notion that certainly fits in with the 'Asian diffusion' theory.

But even the Olmecs came thousands of years later than the Sumerians, who may have appeared in Mesopotamia in 4,000 BC or earlier. So how *can* there have been any contact between them?

We do not know where the Sumerians originated. In *Eden in the East* Stephen Oppenheimer theorised that they may have been driven from 'Sundaland' during the great flood of 6,000 BC and that they made their home in the Indus Valley before moving north to Egypt and Sumer. In *From Atlantis to the Sphinx* (1996) I pointed out that there is evidence that one of the Vedic hymns, the world's oldest known scriptures, seems to point to a date of 6,000 BC:

In the 1980s, a Vedic scholar, David Frawley, observed that the hymns of the *Rig-Veda* are full of oceanic symbolism that seems to argue that they sprang from a maritime culture – which certainly contradicted the assumption that the Aryans came from somewhere in central Europe. He also noted hymns that spoke of the 'ancestors' as coming from across the sea, having been saved from a great flood.

Studying the astronomical references in the Vedic hymns, Frawley concluded that one reference to a summer solstice in Virgo indicates a date of about 4,000 BC, while a reference to a summer solstice in Libra pointed to about 6,000 BC. He also concluded that the

165

authors of the Vedas were familiar with the precession of the equinoxes. These revolutionary idea were set out in a book called *Gods, Sages and Kings* (1991).[19]

I also mentioned other evidence from the Vedic hymns that they refer to an extremely early period, and concluded: 'Frawley points out that the Hindu Varuna, the Egyptian Osiris and the Greek Ouranos, are all symbolised by [the constellation of] Orion, and that their myths seem to refer to the vernal equinox in Orion around 6,000 BC.'[20]

In *From Atlantis to the Sphinx* I had also spoken at some length about *Hamlet's Mill* by George Santillana and Hertha von Dechend, a study that sets out to demonstrate that the common denominator of all early myths is the idea of a great grinding-mill of the stars (sometimes it is described as churning a sea of milk, the Milky Way). This grinding-mill represents the precession of the equinoxes – which, as we have seen, is the apparent backward movement of the vernal point (the constellation in which the sun rises at the spring equinox) through the constellations. At present the sun rises in Pisces at the spring equinox, so we live in the Age of Pisces, but in about eight centuries' time it will rise in Aquarius, and our descendants of AD 2,600 will live in the Age of Aquarius. In the normal zodiac of astrology, Aquarius comes *before* Pisces. Hence 'precession' of the equinoxes – they move backwards, in a slow circle in the heavens. This in itself offers proof that civilisation could be thousands of years older than historians and archaeologists believe: it takes 2,160 years for the vernal point to move from one constellation to the next, and 25,920 years for the whole precessional cycle to come around again to the beginning. Santillana and von Dechend make it clear that the Inuit, Icelanders, Norsemen, Native Americans, Finns, Hawaiians, Japanese, Chinese, Persians, Romans, ancient Greeks, ancient Hindus, ancient Egyptians and many others were familiar with the whole cycle of 'Hamlet's mill', the precession of the equinoxes (the book takes its title from the corn grinding-mill of Amlodhi, an Icelandic hero, whose name has come down to us as Hamlet). These ancient peoples, unaware that precession arises from a mere wobble on the axis, regarded the precession of the equinoxes as of tremendous religious significance, largely because they believed that the end of each age brings some immense catastrophe.

Another book about precession is *The Death of Gods in Ancient Egypt*, by Jane B. Sellers.[21] She has been kind enough to send us a summary of her thinking.[22]

> It is possible that as early as the first use of diagonal calendars in 2100 BC, or their apparent 'misuse' in the tombs of Seti 1 (c. 1304 BC) and Ramesses IV (c. 1115 BC), the Egyptians had calculated the necessary number of years for the 'marker stars' to rise once again on their original dates. This of course involves reading the star calendars in a different way . . . and giving them a different purpose. This 'Eternal Return' would have been far more important for the deceased king than the tracking of the hours of the night, or the days of one year. Certainly by the time of Plutarch, who, after consulting Egyptian priests wrote the first complete telling of the Osiris myth, it would appear that a numerical formula for this return of the sky had been conceived. It is in Plutarch's story of Osiris that we find all the numbers needed to announce the time of a complete precessional cycle, adding support to the argument that not only was the story of Osiris' death and rebirth grounded in the observable results of the precession, but at some time in their history the Egyptians had attempted to understand and measure this mysterious complication of the heavens.

By contrast, John Lash believes that he has found very ancient evidence of precession in a zodiac engraved on the ceiling of the temple of Hanthor at Dendera. This zodiac, dating to about 100 BC, had always fascinated me – I wrote about it for the first time in a book called *Starseekers*[23] in 1980–1 because Schwaller de Lubicz had argued in his *Sacred Science*[24] that it seemed to prove that the ancient Egyptians knew about the precession of the equinoxes in the Age of Taurus, more than 6,000 years ago.

John West was unconvinced by this particular argument. In his *Serpent in the Sky* (1979), he comments that the two superimposed circles are too irregular to prove anything. Studying the Dendera zodiac, I could see his point. However in November 1999, when I was a speaker at Andrew Collins's Questing Conference at the University of London, I heard the author John Lash talking about his work in progress, *The Skies of Memory*;[25] he offered some highly convincing new proofs that the Egyptians indeed understood about precession.

A zodiac has, of course, two axes, one running from north to south, the other from east to west, so the two superimposed zodiacs of Schwaller had four axes, which he called A,B,C and D. To my delight, John Lash had discovered a fifth axis, which he called E, and which points to our own age.

I asked him to summarise his results for this book, and he sent me the following:

The main east–west axis of the Dendera zodiac passes through the middle of the constellation of Aries, corresponding to a date circa 700 BC in precessional terms.

Dendera was restored for the last time under Augustus (30 BC–AD 14), though the work required is likely to have been ongoing for several centuries. The current temple is a make-over of a far more ancient structure. In fact the French archaeologist, Auguste Mariette, observed with some surprise that the foundations of Dendera were deeper than usual. While Luxor, Karnac and most other Egyptian temples seem to be set right on the surface of the ground (so Mariette noted), Dendera is sunk 20 feet into the earth! The date of 700 BC, attested by Schwaller de Lubicz on the authority of the French astronomer, Jean-Baptiste Biot, is roughly the midpoint of the Arien Age.

Was the Dendera zodiac originally planned at the time, hence the alignment to the east, traditional point of origin? Whatever the case, at the transition from Aries to Pisces, around 120 BC, the temple was still being renovated.

The zodiac has two North Poles: one located in the Jackal, known to us as the Little Bear, and the other in Tu-art, the Hippopotamus, known to us as Draco, the celestial Dragon.

There are two poles because, as we know, the earth's axis is tilted at 23.5 degrees relative to its plane of motion around the sun. The North Pole points currently to the Jackal, as at Dendera, but not to precisely the same place in the Jackal. This is because the terrestrial axis slowly rotates around the axis of the earth's orbital plane, centred eternally in Draco. This long-term 'wobble' marks the precessional cycle of 25,920 years. The inclusion of both poles in the Dendera zodiac may be plain evidence that precession was known to the ancient Egyptians.

Precession of the equinoxes is supposed to have been discovered around 134 BC by the Greek astronomer Hipparchus. He was looking at a star map made by his predecessor Timocharis about 150 years before, and noted that a certain bright star he was studying was positioned incorrectly, 2 degrees away from what should have been its present position. He concluded that the star was moving at a rate of about 1 degree every seventy-five years. (In fact, precession causes a movement of 1 degree every seventy-two years.)

Schwaller de Lubicz had argued that two hieroglyphs outside the circular zodiac mark a line between Gemini and Taurus, indicating a precessional date about 4,000 BC, which further demonstrates how the Egyptians intended the Dendera artifact to show the shift in precessional Ages. John Anthony West is on record as being unconvinced.

However in 1999 I was working on a book about the World Ages when I was struck by an arresting observation. Any zodiac modelled on the four seasons naturally has two axes interlocked at right angles: the line of the equinoxes (east–west) and the line of the solstices (north–south). Clearly evident at Dendera, this 'axial cross' has been noted by all scholars.

The eastern end of axis A, passing through Aries, probably identifies the epoch when the restoration of the temple was inaugurated, circa 700 BC, as noted above. The design of the zodiac also clearly incorporates two other axes, C and D.

But as I studied the overall design of the zodiac, I realised there was a fifth, as yet undetected axis. My attention was first drawn to its presence by the figure of Virgo, the grain goddess identified with Isis, who holds up a stalk of wheat in a gesture known from Sumerian sources as early as the third millennium BC.

I knew that the Dendera zodiac is an accurate astronomical model with axes that can be precisely dated according to precession – in short, a working star-clock. However, only two stars have been specifically indicated on it: Sirius, placed between the horns of the sacred cow on axis B, and Spica, the star traditionally identified with Virgo's sheaf of wheat. This led me to wonder what an axis inscribed from Spica through the Jackal pole would look like.

At the time Dendera was being restored, Spica had a special significance for astronomers. It so happened that Spica was the bright star initially observed by Timochares, the same one that later led Hipparchus to discover the precessional of the equinoxes.

Historians confirm that from 600 BC onward there was close contact between Greek and Egyptian astronomers, so we would be justified in assuming that Spica, known as

Mena to the Egyptians, was an item in their dialogue. Surely, then, there may have been a specific intention in highlighting Spica at Dendera.

When I inscribed the fifth axis (E in the figure above), I noted three remarkable features that could not, I imagined, be accidental. First, the axis culminates by bisecting the altar mounted by four ram's heads, situated on the periphery of the zodiac. This seems to interlock its internal features, represented by the solar zodiac of ecliptic constellations, with the lunar pattern of the decans, 10-degree divisions of the moon's orbit, running around the periphery.

Second, axis E crosses Pisces at the tail of the lower or foremost fish exactly where the spring equinox occurs today.

Third, axis E extended to Virgo's feet marks the tail of Leo at a point that corresponds by precession to 10,500 BC. All in all, axis E marks the moment of precession when one full cycle ends and a new one begins.

We are currently living through the last two centuries of the full 26,000-year cycle.

As the total pattern came into focus, I recognised that axis E signals this moment of epochal transition in a vivid, intentional way. Whoever designed Dendera was looking ahead in time to our age, when the spring equinox occurs under the tail of the western fish, because this is the time when the entire cycle culminates. With the spring equinox at just that position in Pisces, the axial cross locks into unique alignment with the galaxy.

In the last thirty years, astronomers have determined that the centre of our galaxy lies in line with the tip of the arrow of Sagittarius. Axis E stands at precise right angles to this point.

The half cycle, 12,960 years back from now, gives the date of 10,500 BC so hotly debated in current investigations of prehistory. The half cycle is indicated by the way that Spica, actually positioned 24 degrees from the lion's tail, is aligned with it by the lie of the axis.

Since the Egyptians were totally capable of representing the star patterns with high accuracy, I assumed that this anomaly was intended. Spica, which I call the precessional star, seems to be the master key to the Dendera zodiac. Axis E reveals an infrastructure based on galactic features *only thought to have been known in recent times*.

If my inferences are correct, Dendera proves not only that precession was known and applied to a scheme of World Ages, but that the entire cycle of 26,000 years was understood in its formal organisation.

In other words, Lash has shown that precession had been known for thousands of years before the Dendera temple was rebuilt.

Moreover, if Chatelain is correct, then both the Sumerians and the Maya also knew the exact length of the precessional cycle (the Nineveh constant is exactly 240 times this cycle) and the two vast Maya numbers discovered at Quiriga can be divided by the Nineveh constant.

As to the Mayan knowledge of astronomy, Peter Tompkins writes:

The Mayan cycle of 942,890 days, or 2,582 years, turned out to be 130 Saturn–Jupiter conjunctions. (It also covers other cycles: 15 Neptune–Uranus, 1,555 Jupiter–Mars, 2,284 Mars–Venus, 6,522 Venus–Mercury, and 2,720 Saturn–Mars.) Twice this cycle, or 5,163 years, is 260 Saturn–Jupiter conjunctions, which gives a grand cycle with the same number as there are days in the Mayan sacred year.

Furthermore, the Mesopotamians had linked their measures of time and space – in seconds of time and seconds of arc. 34,020 million days is not only the number of days in 3,600 Sumerian precessions of the equinox, but

3,600 tenths of a degree – consisting of 36,000 Egyptian feet of 0.308 meters – is the circumference of the world . . . The Mesopotamians had not only chosen as a unit of measure a foot that was earth-commensurate, it was also commensurate with the great Platonic year [the precessional cycle] of 25,920 years. Odd would it be if the unit dispensed by Hunab Ku [the Mayan Creator] to the Maya were not equally earth-commeasurable. At Teotihuacan and at Palenque this ancient Middle-Eastern foot fits Cinderella's shoe as neatly as it did at Cheops.[26]

We are being asked to accept that the same measurement – based upon the circumference of the earth – was used in ancient Egypt, Sumer, Teotihuacan and Palenque. But, even more incredible, that fairly primitive Indian people, who thought the sun might disappear permanently at the end of every 52 years, had a knowledge of the heavens that would not shame a modern Astronomer Royal. Chatelain says: 'The Mayas also knew of the precession of the equinoxes and the existence of Uranus and Neptune.' How did they know about Uranus and Neptune without telescopes, thousands of years before Western astronomers discovered them?

They had calculated the periods of revolution and conjunction of different planets, and discovered . . . some equivalent astronomical cycles, such as 65 revolutions of Venus, which are equal to 104 solar years, or 327 revolutions of Mercury. They also used the cycle of 33,968 days to predict eclipses, and this cycle was equal to 5 lunar precessions, 93 solar years, 196 eclipses, 150 lunar months . . . Meanwhile, the Mayas had also discovered a cycle of 1,886,040 days that represented exactly 260 conjunctions of Jupiter and Saturn, 2,310 of Mars and Jupiter, 2,418 of earth and Mars, and 3,230 of Earth and Venus.[27]

The great Mayan specialist Sylvanus Griswold Morley observed:

> When the material achievement of the ancient Maya in architecture, sculpture, ceramics, the lapidary arts, feather-work, cotton-weaving and dyeing are added to their intellectual achievements – invention of positional mathematics with its concomitant development of zero, construction of an elaborate chronology with a fixed starting point, use of a time-count as accurate as our own Gregorian Calendar, knowledge of astronomy superior to that of the ancient Egyptians and Babylonians – *and the whole judged in the light of their known cultural limitations which were on a par with those of the early Neolithic Age in the Old World* [my italics], we may acclaim them, without fear of successful contradiction, the most brilliant aboriginal people on this planet.[28]

The passage I have italicised underlines the problem. Graham Hancock has an interesting remark about the Maya in *Fingerprints of the Gods*, in which he talks about their amazing knowledge of astronomy, quoting the Mayan archaeologist Eric Thompson, who in 1954 asked how the Maya had come to chart the heavens yet failed to grasp the principle of the wheel, to count in millions yet never learned to weigh a sack of corn. Perhaps, Hancock suggests, the answer is quite simple: the Maya received their astronomical knowledge from 'elsewhere' – from a much older civilisation.

Gordon Eckholm found an intriguing piece of evidence that the Maya did know about the wheel. In an archaeological dig in the 1940s, Eckholm unearthed a Mayan toy – a dog on four wheels, such as Western children have been pulling about the nursery on a string for centuries. Eckholm pointed out the similarity between this toy and a Chinese wheeled toy of the same period (he dates them both about 2,000 years ago). The

Maya had a wheeled toy, yet did not see that wheels could be used on carts or other vehicles. Apparently no one looked at the wheel and had a 'Eureka' experience, which seems to suggest that the Maya were indeed, as Thompson said, 'unremarkable'. This hardly seems to be borne out by their astronomy or by their amazing calendar, with its 'Long Count'.

Chatelain makes the same point:

It is surely beyond imagination to think that thousands of years ago the Mayas could have, all by themselves, calculated a constant of 147,420 millions of days – a number that had twelve digits. But it is even more surprising to see the same number, only 65 times smaller, and expressed in seconds instead of days, has been used by Sumerians, a nation on the opposite side of the globe. *This fact seems to indicate that the Mayas and the Sumerians must have had direct connections with each other, or that they shared a common origin* [my italics].[29]

Since the Sumerians were at the height of their achievement 3,000 years before the Maya, we can probably rule out a 'direct connection', even if Hapgood is correct in believing that there was a worldwide maritime civilisation in 7,000 BC. What seems far more likely is that we are dealing with an ancient culture that had been studying the heavens for thousands of years, a culture based on seafaring.

Chatelain, like von Däniken, believes that this knowledge came from space visitors but surely it is far more likely that it was observed by astronomers who had studied the sky for thousands of years. It seems a reasonable speculation that one reason the ancients were so interested in the sky was that they made use of their knowledge of the stars in navigation.

A discovery made in 1997 adds powerful support to this argument. Exploring an ancient lake bed at Mata Menge, on the island of Flores (which is east of Java and Bali), a group of palaeoanthropologists from Australia found stone tools. The bed of volcanic ash in which the tools were found by Mike Morwood and colleagues from the University of New England (New South Wales) dated from more than 800,000 years ago, the time of *Homo erectus*. Animal bones from nearby gave the same date. What was unusual is that Flores is a relatively small island, not known to be a site of ancient man. The nearest such location is the far larger island of Java, the home of Java man, who also belongs to our earliest ancestor, *Homo erectus*.

To reach Flores, these primitive men would have had to sail from island to island, making crossings of around a dozen miles. Moreover, Morwood argues, the organising ability required by a fairly large group to cross the sea suggests that *Homo erectus* possessed some kind of linguistic ability.

This was a conclusion that I had reached when, in *A Criminal History of Mankind* (1983), I discussed the finds made in caves near Chou-kou-tien, in China, in 1929: fourteen skulls of *Homo erectus*, which had a sloping forehead and receding chin. All the skulls were mutilated at the base, as if the brain had been scooped out. Peking man, as he came to be labelled, was a cannibal – for we presume that he was killed (and roasted and eaten) by other Peking men, approximately half a million years ago.

Cannibalism is seldom a matter of nourishment; even as practised in recent times, it is mainly ritualistic, based upon the belief that the strength and vitality of a dead enemy can be absorbed by eating him. Peking man apparently had plenty of other meat, as suggested by the many animal bones in his caves. If he practised ritualistic cannibalism, then we must assume he had some kind of language, since it is hard to imagine a ritual without language.

Homo erectus was the first man we recognise as our ancestor, the first to walk upright all the time. His heart had to work harder to increase the supply of blood to his brain, which increased the size of his brain and also his intelligence. It seems at least a reasonable assumption that his brain had a 'language matrix', just as a bird's has a flight matrix.

This, at all events, seems to be one important implication of the traces of *Homo erectus* found on Flores. We cannot imagine even a chimpanzee building a raft, because it cannot communicate linguistically.

Why should *Homo erectus* want to move to Flores from Java? Presumably in search of that basic instinctive requirement of all animals – territory. He would have been able to see other islands from Java mountain tops, and if the competition for food or aggressive neighbours were making life hard, then he may have decided to move on, taking his family with him. But if he was able to build a raft, then he must have been far more intelligent than his predecessors.

Another recent discovery, described by science writer John McCrone,[30] adds weight to this notion that *Homo erectus* was possibly more intelligent than we give him credit for, in that he was using fire as long ago as 1.6 million years. From the 1970s onwards, many anthropologists have supported the view held by Louis Leakey that man learned to make fire a mere 40,000 years ago. In Leakey's view, man became a warlike creature as a result of sitting around a fire at night, telling stories of battle and heroism. So fire was responsible for the 'cultural explosion' that created *Homo sapiens*.

But in the 1970s and 1980s, evidence of campfires was uncovered at Koobi Fora and Chesowanja in Kenya. 'Lenses' of orange earth were found in association with the bones and stone tools of *Homo erectus*, and similar lenses – about 18 inches across – were found beneath the campfires of local people. In 1999, a study by Ralph Rowlett of the University of Missouri–Columbia established beyond doubt that these lenses were made by campfires, not bush fires caused by lightning.

Rowlett's colleague Randy Bellomo made an interesting use of earth magnetism to demonstrate that such fires had been made over many years. As Hapgood had noted, iron in the soil aligns with the magnetic pole, and heating 'perman-ises' this alignment like a compass. Bellomo found that the Koobi Fora iron sediments had several slightly different magnetic alignments, implying repeated visits of a nomadic tribe over a long period.

Brian Ludwig of Rutgers University studied 40,000 or so flint artifacts and the debris of tool-making, trying to deter-mine if tool-making methods had remained static. He found dimples known as potlid fractures – fractures due to exposure to fire – on tools from 1.6 million years ago.

So again, we have evidence that *Homo erectus* was a more intelligent being than any anthropologist had dared to suggest. And this again suggests that he possessed some form of lan-guage.

And if he could communicate in language and build a raft, then the next question becomes self-evident: could it be that *Homo erectus* was not only the first man but the first long-distance sailor? The upright posture is ideal for scanning the horizon at sea. And he had plenty of time – half a million years or more – to develop from island-hopping to sailing the open sea. He also had plenty of time to develop his obsession with the stars.

All this raises another pertinent question. If our ancestors were sailing the seas 800,000 years ago, why did it take man another 792,000 years (the first recognised civilisation, Jericho, is dated at 8,000 BC) to start building civilisation? The answer must be that it didn't take so long. Our problem is that we do not recognise the signs of civilisation when we see them – such as the stone balls of Costa Rica that suggest that man was navigating thousands of miles of ocean 'before civil-isation'. But if there was no civilisation, why should he bother? Men sail the ocean largely for trading purposes. Surely it is more likely that Hapgood is correct, and that a worldwide maritime civilisation existed in 100,000 BC?

Again, there is evidence that our ancestors of 400,000 years ago – by then *Homo sapiens* – were more intelligent than we give them credit for. In *Timescale*, Nigel Calder states: 'Piagetian tests applied to stone tools from Isimila, Tanzania, which may be as much as 330,000 years old [by uranium-series dating] are said to indicate that the makers were as intelligent as modern humans.'[31] Raising this question in *From Atlantis to the Sphinx*, I commented that the reason civilisation had not developed much sooner was because human beings tend to live mechanically, doing today what they did yesterday and last year. There are probably millions of human beings in the world today whose intelligence is as great as the famous scientists, artists and intellectuals in our history books, yet they remain unknown because they fail to make any determined attempt to pull themselves out of their daily routine.

When I wrote these comments, Mike Morwood and his team from New South Wales had not yet discovered the tools in the lake bed in Flores that indicated that *Homo erectus* was sailing the seas 800,000 years ago. This, in turn, altered my view about human language. Like most people, I had begun by assuming that man developed language in the past 30,000 years or so. The discovery that Peking man was a cannibal had made me revise that opinion to the extent of believing that he was intelligent enough to possess some kind of ritual, and therefore language. I was inclined to believe that the 'brain explosion' that has occurred in the past 500,000 years – the sudden increase in man's brain size – was the result of the development of language.

But the Flores discovery throws doubt on my assumption. It suggests that man had enough language 800,000 years ago to co-operate in raft-building and sailing. That in turn led me to wonder whether language may not be as natural to man as the upright posture, and that men may have been talking to one another for perhaps a million years. In which case, it seems inconceivable that he developed civilisation only in the past 10,000 years. The Mayan knowledge of mathematics and astronomy alone makes the idea seem absurd. Even if we have our doubts about Chatelain's evidence on the Nineveh constant and the two gigantic numbers discovered at Quiriga, we are still left with an achievement that seems utterly beyond what we regard as the normal human capabilities.

I would suggest that there is only one logical solution: civilisation is thousands, perhaps tens of thousands, of years older than we think. But in that case, where is the proof? Where are the ruins of this older civilisation?

This was the challenge thrown down by the Giza plateau authority when John West and Robert Schoch suggested that the Sphinx may be at least twice as old as Egyptologists believe. 'Show us the intervening civilisation.' But any evidence of such a civilisation may be buried beneath the desert sand, as that strange, monolithic structure called the Oseirion was buried under the sand below the temple of Seti I – a structure whose bleak, massive blocks and lack of ornamentation suggest some older stage of Egyptian civilisation.[32] Other evidence may lie beneath the sea, or beneath the ice of Antarctica. When we consider such evidence as Hapgood's 'ancient sea kings', or the Nineveh constant and the Quiriga numbers, it becomes hard not to acknowledge that there is something oddly wrong with our present limited view of human history.

Equally convincing, I would suggest, is the evidence that Rand Flem-Ath has amassed in his study of ancient religious sites and their curiously precise placing on the face of the earth.

7

FALLEN ANGELS

'AND THEIR FACES shone like the sun, and their eyes were like burning lamps; and fire came forth from their lips. Their dress had the appearance of feathers: their feet were purple, their wings were brighter than gold; their hands whiter than snow.'[1]

This was the sight that greeted Enoch, Noah's great-grandfather, when he was awakened one night by two tall, shining creatures. The strangers flew Enoch to the sky, from where, he tells us, 'they showed me a very great sea, much bigger than the inland sea where I lived'.[2] Since Enoch lived somewhere in the Middle East, this inland sea is probably the Mediterranean and the 'much bigger sea' may have been the Atlantic Ocean, or 'real ocean' referred to in Plato's account of Atlantis.

Before leaving with these two strange visitors, Enoch had instructed his sons not to try to find him, which suggests that his destination was on earth, not in heaven. He was transported to a place full of 'light without any darkness' which was covered in 'snow and ice' that was 'at the ends of the earth'.

Enoch lived centuries before the flood, so this is a rare description of the home of the gods before it was destroyed. He was told that he'd reached 'heaven'. Christian and Barbara O'Brien, who have studied this material in detail, are inclined to translate 'heaven' as 'highlands'.

We don't have to travel far to recognise a very real place here on our planet that fits this description; a high place of endless days and polar conditions which lies at the end of the earth. Antarctica is the highest continent on the planet, having an average altitude more than twice that of the second-highest (Asia). Was the 'heaven' that the two strangers showed Enoch another name for Atlantis? Another name for Antarctica?

All of these fascinating details are found within the Book of Enoch. Revealed within its colourful pages are the methods of ancient scientists determined to measure and survey their planet. In doing so they left a record of their findings for us in the location of sacred sites around the globe.

This important book would have been lost for ever had it not been for the wanderings of one of the most eccentric characters of the eighteenth century, a Scotsman named James Bruce, who was born in 1730 and spent twelve years of his life in a mysterious quest in the unknown heart of Africa. One of the most interesting things he brought back was a forgotten book called the Book of Enoch, regarded as so sinister and blasphemous that a Christian could endanger his soul just by reading it.

Bruce was a Scottish aristocrat, descended from a line of kings that included Robert the Bruce, who defeated the English at the Battle of Bannockburn in 1314. James Bruce would have made a formidable opponent in battle, being 6 feet, 4 inches tall and powerfully built, with red hair and a loud voice. He was also an egoist of monstrous proportions, so it becomes possible to see why he inspired more than his due share of dislike and died a thoroughly embittered man.

As a schoolboy at Harrow, Bruce wanted to be a clergyman;

his father wanted him to become a lawyer. Both were disappointed. Bruce's attempt to study law so bored him that he had a nervous breakdown, and his father let him go his own way. His ambition was to travel to distant places and explore the unknown. He applied for permission to become a trader in India, then his attention was diverted by falling in love. Unfortunately, the girl – the orphaned daughter of a wealthy wine merchant, with vineyards in Spain and Portugal – was consumptive. Bruce and his new wife were on their way to Provence when she suddenly fell ill in Paris and died within days. Sick with grief, Bruce had her buried at midnight then rode through a storm to Boulogne, where he collapsed.

Back in Scotland he flung himself into the study of languages and history – he was particularly fascinated by the Freemasons and the Knights Templar – and went off on a trip to visit Templar sites in Europe. He had to return when his father died. At twenty-eight, Bruce had become the heir to the estates.

The Age of Steam was about to arrive, and the Industrial Revolution had already started. Bruce, of course, had no interest in such matters – his mind was in the Middle Ages, dreaming of knights and crusaders – but fortunately for him coal was discovered on his land at Kinnaird, and he leased it to a mining company, who paid him a generous royalty. Now he was able to indulge his passion for faraway places. He went to Spain and studied Arabic manuscripts in the Escurial, travelled down the Rhine by boat and studied antiquities in Italy.

Bruce was a Freemason, of the Canongate Lodge of Kilwinning. Through the offices of another Freemason, Lord Halifax, he was offered the post of consul at Algiers, which appealed strongly to his romanticism and promised spare time for archaeology. It proved harder work than he expected. The Bey of Algiers was capricious, difficult and occasionally violent, and on one occasion had a court official strangled in the consul's presence. Bruce needed all his stubbornness and determination to avoid being tied up in a sack and thrown into the Mediterranean. After two years it was a relief to resign his post.

Then, at the age of thirty-five, he prepared to embark on the adventure of a lifetime. His precise goal is still not entirely known. In *The Blue Nile* (1962),[3] Alan Moorehead has no doubt that he was obsessed by finding the source of the Nile, which would certainly have brought him worldwide celebrity, since it was at that time still undiscovered. But he is also known to have been fascinated by the black Jews of Abyssinia (now Ethiopia), the Falashas, perhaps because their presence suggested that the Ark of the Covenant might have been brought there by them from Jerusalem. As a man with a deep interest in scripture, James Bruce certainly wanted to find out more about the peculiar mystery of the Book of Enoch. The apocryphal book of the Old Testament had been held in veneration by early Christian theologians such as Origen and Clement of Alexandria, then it had disappeared. Rumour suggested that it contained scandalous information about angels and their sexual behaviour, perhaps explaining why the early Church decided to suppress it (if indeed that was the case).

Encountering many perils and adventures – such as shipwreck and brigands – Bruce made his way to Cairo, and from there travelled up the Nile. His aim was to go to Abyssinia, a country virtually unknown to Europeans – only two Catholic missionaries were known to have visited there, although Bruce had a low regard for Catholics, being fiercely Protestant.

The first part of his journey was pleasant enough – up the Nile by boat as far as Aswan. It was not the first cataract that deterred him there, but a local war. He decided to continue by the Red Sea. In a few weeks, he was facing unknown territory. Eventually, Bruce and his party found their way to the town of Gondar, which was then the capital of Abyssinia and consisted of about 10,000 clay huts with conical roofs, overlooked by the king's palace, with its view down across the vast inland sea, Lake Tana.

The name Abyssinia means 'confusion', and Bruce found the country in turmoil – apparently its usual state – with the king and his vizier away on a punitive expedition. It was soon clear that an exceptionally high level of violence was regarded as quite normal. Soldiers rode around with the testicles of their enemies dangling on their lances. Their favourite meal was steak, which they ate raw, simply slicing it off the buttock of a living cow, after which the raw patch was covered in clay and the animal turned loose again. When Bruce first met the king, Tecla Haimanout, and his vizier, Ras Michael, on their return they were amusing themselves by putting out the eyes of a dozen captives.

Bruce was lucky; he might well have been castrated or beheaded. But Ras Michael took a liking to him, and gave him command of a troop of the King's Horse. Bruce, never averse to showing off, dressed up in chainmail, stuck pistols in his wide cummerbund and impressed his hosts with his ability to shoot mountain kites while galloping on a black charger.

In due course, Bruce managed to do a little exploring. He was taken to a mountain top that was the source of a river called the Little Abbai, which his guide assured him was the source of the Nile. Bruce was suitably impressed, but his guide was quite wrong – the source of the White Nile is 1,000 miles further south in Lake Victoria, while the source of the tributary Blue Nile is actually in Lake Tana, several miles to the north of the mountain where they stood. Bruce was an enthusiast rather than a conscientious geographer. But in the Gondar monastery, on the shores of Lake Tana, he came upon a discovery that made up for his misidentification of the source of the Nile.

Abyssinia had been a Christian country since AD 320, but since it was so far from the great northern centres of Christianity it had maintained its own tradition. One of the most interesting parts of that tradition is contained in an epic called the *Kebra Nagast*, or the Book of the Glory of Kings. When Bruce went to Gondar, no one in Europe had ever heard of the epic. Its narrative tells how the Ark of the Covenant was brought to Ethiopia from Jerusalem in the ninth century BC. It seemed that the Queen of Sheba had her capital in Abyssinia. She was a beautiful young virgin, who had been on the throne for six years when she heard about Solomon and his wisdom and made the trip to Jerusalem to meet him. Both were impressed, and on the night before she left Jerusalem, he begged her to spend the night with him. She agreed on condition that she should retain her virginity. Solomon gave his word, with the unusual condition that it depended upon her taking nothing from him. Since she had no intention of taking anything, she agreed.

In the middle of the night, the queen got out of bed to drink from a bowl of water. Solomon woke up and pointed out that she had broken her promise. 'But it's only water,' she protested. 'What is more precious than water?' asked Solomon. And since the queen had to agree with him, she yielded her virginity.

Nine months later, back in Abyssinia, she bore a son. After twenty years, the young man returned to Jerusalem to see his father. Solomon became so fond of him that he anointed him king, and when the youth departed for Abyssinia the eldest sons of all Solomon's courtiers went as his escort. They were dismayed and depressed at the thought of leaving behind the Ark of the Covenant, the most sacred symbol of the Hebrews, which contained the Tables of the Law brought down from Mount Sinai by Moses, so the son of the high priest suggested that they take the Ark with them. This was accomplished, with the aid of the Angel of the Lord, who declared that the Ark itself had decided it was time to leave Jerusalem.

And that, according to the *Kebra Nagast*, was how the Ark came to Abyssinia.

When Bruce read this account he must have been immensely excited. It seemed to show that not only was the Abyssinian Church the oldest in the world, but that it could trace its roots back to King Solomon. And perhaps – who knows? – this might also have been true of the Freemasons. As to the Falashas, the black Jews of Abyssinia, perhaps they traced their descent from the courtiers who had accompanied the young king to Abyssinia. Had Bruce, in fact, heard of the *Kebra Nagast* in his Arabic researches – perhaps in the Escurial – and is it possible that his motive in coming to Abyssinia was not to find the source of the Nile, but to find the Ark of the Covenant?

Bruce's next discovery was, if anything, even more exciting. In this same monastery, he was also allowed to read a copy of the long-lost Book of Enoch. It had aroused so much curiosity that Queen Elizabeth's astrologer Dr John Dee had tried to obtain a copy by supernatural means. He and his magician assistant Edward Kelley had taken part in seances in which 'angels' (or spirits) had dictated the Book of Enoch – or at least, *a* Book of Enoch – to Kelley. (Whether the text was the same one discovered by Bruce will never be known, since it has vanished.)

A glance at this strange manuscript must have told Bruce why early Christian scholars had regarded it as so important – it claimed to be a vital missing portion of the history of the world. Enoch was the grandson of Adam and the son of Cain, and was also, in turn, the father of Methuselah, who was in turn the grandfather of Noah. Bruce may have considered it merely as an interesting extension of the Biblical canon; he was a highly educated Scot, living in the age of Voltaire and Gibbon, who may have regarded the contents of the Book of Enoch as so much quaint and absurd myth. On the other hand, as a Freemason it is equally possible that he read Enoch with intense personal interest because of the Masons' ancient tradition that Enoch had foreseen the destruction of the world by the great flood.

This was in 1770, a year after he had arrived in Abyssinia. When he returned from Gondar, a civil war was taking place. Bruce decided to join in, since he was an army commander, but it ended in the defeat and flight of Ras Michael and the slaughter of his followers.

Bruce survived and was able to leave the country he had come to detest. It was a long and exhausting trip back to civilisation – about eighteen months – and he spent some time recuperating in Italy and Paris before finally returning to London in June 1774.

This exotic story had no happy ending. We might expect that Bruce's travels would have brought him fame, for the eighteenth century dearly loved travellers' tales – James Boswell had become a celebrity on the strength of visiting Corsica, while an impostor named George Psalmanazar who claimed to be a native of Formosa (now Taiwan) acquired fame and became a close friend of Dr Johnson. Bruce's reception was more like that of Marco Polo on his return from China; those who had read Marco's travels took them for fiction. James Bruce suffered a similar reception when he told his stories of men eating steaks off live cattle and chopping off parts of their fellow human beings with the same ferocity. People listened politely, hiding a smile of disbelief, which may have been partly because of the manner in which Bruce told the story, for he was unable to conceal his high opinion of himself.

He went to London, found a needy clergyman called Latrobe, and spent a year dictating his *Travels to Discover the Source of the Nile*. He promised to pay his amanuensis when the five volumes were finished, although it is typical of his mean and ungenerous nature that he delayed payment then tried to fob Latrobe off with five guineas. It is almost satisfying to record that the book was received with malice and derision. He died five years later after tripping on the stairs and falling on his head.

It has to be admitted that, for all his character defects, Bruce produced one of the great travel books. He had also performed another important service to literature by bringing back the Book of Enoch – no fewer than three copies, in fact, one of which he presented to the Bodleian Library in Oxford and another to the Bibliothèque Nationale in Paris (he kept the third himself, next to the Book of Job, where he claimed it belonged). Once again, his timing was poor. In the midst of the Age of Enlightenment, interest in religion was at a low ebb and churches were half empty. Nobody was interested in an obscure apocryphal book of the Bible, and it remained untranslated.

The Book of Enoch finally appeared in English in 1821, more than a quarter of a century after Bruce's death, translated by a Hebrew scholar named Richard Laurence. At least the world was now ready for it – the age of Romanticism had arrived, with its interest in ghosts, demons and the supernatural. This story of libidinous fallen angels thrilled a wide audience.

We might say that the Book of Enoch takes its origin from the passage in Genesis 6 that tells how the sons of God – angels – took note of the fact that the daughters of men were fair and decided to take them as wives. And then 'there were giants in the earth in those days . . . when the sons of God came in unto the daughters of men, and they bare children to them, and the same became mighty men which were of old, men of renown'.

The Book of Enoch elaborates this story. It seems that in the days of Jared, Enoch's father, 200 rebel 'angels', who are called the Watchers, descended on the top of Mount Hermon, over 9,000 feet high, and prepared to go down to the plains with the intention of having sexual intercourse with mortal women.

According to Enoch, it would seem that the rebel Watchers took mortal women into their beds, and their mistresses gave birth to 'giants' who were virtually ungovernable. They began to 'devour' human beings and developed a taste for blood. The simplest way to make sense of this passage is to assume that the offspring of the Watchers became violent and warlike, rather like the Abyssinians of Bruce's day, whose endless brutality caused him to flee the country. It seems that the rebel angels also taught men the art of making weapons by smelting metal, and that they encouraged sexual licence by teaching women how to wear ornaments and use make-up. They also instructed them in sorcery and ritual magic. The picture that emerges is that of an early tribal civilisation, where the women had so far been accustomed to bearing children and doing the hard work. The Watchers taught them that life could be more enjoyable if they treated sex as a means of pleasure. They also taught them how to abort any unwanted results of their promiscuity.

Modern readers might view this without disapproval, feeling that the women of that time probably needed encouragement towards liberation, which was, in fact, the view taken by Romantics such as Lord Byron and his friend Thomas Moore. Byron's play *Heaven and Earth* appeared in the same year as the translation of the Book of Enoch, and is based on the passage in Genesis about the sons of God taking the daughters of men for wives. It ends with a spectacular evocation of the flood, and the notes mention that 'the Book of Enoch, preserved by the Ethiopians, is said by them to be anterior to the flood'. In 1823, Moore published a poem, 'The Loves of the Angels', based on the same subject.

The rebel Watchers were not simply instructors in debauchery; one taught astronomy, another astrology, another knowledge of the clouds, another how to counter magic spells, and others knowledge of the sun, moon and earth. Despite their intentions, God decided they had to be punished, and sent off his own Watchers, including Gabriel, Raphael and Uriel, to enforce his will. (These servants of God are also called Watchers, suggesting that not all the Watchers were rebel spirits.) The rebel Watchers were rounded up and imprisoned. (The God of the Old Testament seems to be as merciless as any human tyrant.) According to Andrew Collins, whose book *From the Ashes of Angels* (1996)[4] is perhaps the best introduction to this topic, the location of the imprisonment of the rebel Watchers was close to the place where they descended, on Mount Hermon.

And so God decided to cleanse the earth with a great flood, of which the only survivor was Noah. But before that, Enoch has a further story to tell. It seems that his son Methuselah had a son named Lamech, whose wife bore a child, Noah. His appearance came as a shock to his father: the baby's skin was not the same colour as that of other natives of the Middle East, that is to say, brown, but pure white and rosy red, like that of some native of a northern country. His hair was also white and his eyes were so beautiful that they seemed to light up the room.

Lamech went to Methuselah, and told his father, 'I have begotten a strange son, not like a human being, but more like the children of the angels . . .' Lamech suspected that his son had been fathered by one of the Watchers. Methuselah was unable to reassure him, but went off in search of his father, Enoch, who had retired to a far-off land (called Paradise in a fragment of the same story found among the Dead Sea Scrolls). Enoch told Methuselah to reassure his son. The new-born child was indeed his own, and he was to be named Noah. Enoch had foreseen in a vision that the world was going to be destroyed by a deluge, but that Noah and his children would 'be saved from the corruption' that would engulf the earth. (It is apparent these events take place before the rebel Watchers arrived on earth.) So it seemed that God had chosen Noah as the father of the new race of humanity.

Still, one cannot help feeling a mild suspicion that Enoch may not have been entirely truthful with Methuselah, and that perhaps this future race would have a touch of the fallen angel in its composition . . .

The Book of Enoch that Bruce brought back from Abyssinia was not the only version. In fact, many later fragments were found, even in Greek and Latin; yet another, in the Slavonic language, contained some interesting additions to the story.

We should note that the Book of Enoch was not written down until about 200 BC, almost certainly by some member of the Essene community at Qumran on the Dead Sea, but the oral tradition was much older. The Slavonic version, known as *The Secrets of Enoch*,[5] was probably compiled by a Jewish writer living in Alexandria around the time of Jesus.

It contains the account which opens this chapter of Enoch's abduction by tall beings to a place of continuous light which was covered in snow and ice.

After they reach their destination Enoch is then taken on a tour that includes a hideous pit which became the prototype for the Christian hell:

> And the men then led me to the Northern region, and showed me there a very terrible place. And there are all sorts of tortures in that place. Savage darkness and impenetrable gloom; and there is not light there, but a gloomy fire is always burning, and a fiery river goes forth. And all that place has fire on all sides, and on all sides cold and ice, thus it burns and freezes. And the prisoners are very savage, and the angels terrible and without pity, carrying savage weapons, and their torture was unmerciful.
>
> And I said: 'Woe, woe! How terrible is this place!' And the men said to me: 'This place, Enoch, is prepared for those who do not honour God; who commit evil deeds on earth.'[6]

Hell was a Christian concept that – like the Devil – was unknown to the Jews. 'Sheol', sometimes translated as 'hell', simply meant a place where rubbish was destroyed, and this passage, which seems to prefigure Dante's Inferno, was probably a major reason that the Book of Enoch 'vanished'. The idea that 'heaven' might include a place of torment would have been unacceptable to the Church Fathers.

After his glimpse of 'hell', Enoch was taken on a tour – this time by the angel Raphael – around Paradise, or the 'Garden of Righteousness'. This seems to be the Garden of Eden, for when he commented on a particularly beautiful tree with a delicious fragrance, he was told that this was the Tree of Knowledge from which Eve plucked one of the fruits (apparently these fruits hung in clusters like grapes, so they cannot be apples). What seemed to be worrying the Lord – who is referred to as Yahweh-Elohim – is a second tree called the Tree of Life. If man ate the fruits of this tree, his life would be immensely extended.

Now comes one of the most interesting passages in the Book of Enoch: 'And I saw in those days how long cords were given to the Angels, and they took themselves wings and flew, and went towards the north. And I asked an Angel, saying unto him: "Why have they taken cords and gone off?" and he replied: "They have gone to measure."'

Knotted 'cords' were used by Egyptian priests to plan their temples. These cords were nothing less than practical geometric survey tools. Christian O'Brien, an engineer with surveying experience, translates this passage into secular terms: 'Then I saw how long measuring "tapes" were given to some of the angels and they hurried off towards the north. So I asked the angel with me why the others had taken tapes and gone away, and he replied, "They have gone to make a survey."'[7]

Angels undertaking a survey? It doesn't make sense within the Christian concept of angels. But what if these beings were ancient scientists pursuing a geological and geographic survey?

For the Book of Enoch also reveals the all-important purpose of the survey with the words: 'And these measures shall reveal all the secrets of the depths of the earth . . .'[8] *The survey was geological.*

Rand was familiar with Andrew Collins's book *From the Ashes of Angels*, which recounts the story of Enoch. Collins describes how, in the late nineteenth century, the Babylonian Expedition from the University of Pennsylvania discovered fragments of a broken clay cylinder at Nippur, in what was still called Mesopotamia. They were found in the temple of

Enlil, the supreme god of the Sumerians, less important only than Anu, Lord of the Universe, and were written in cuneiform wedge script. We may recall the tablets found in the mound of Kuyunjik in 1852, which proved to contain the epic of *Gilgamesh*, and might be forgiven for assuming that the translation of this cylinder became a matter of prime importance, but it was taken back to the University of Philadelphia by Professor Herman V. Hilprecht, where it was left in the basement of the museum, still in its packing case.

Hilprecht is known to the history of psychical research through another curious incident involving Nippur. In 1893, he was trying to decipher the inscription on what he believed was a ring from the temple of Bel. Exhausted by the fruitless effort, he fell asleep and dreamed that the priest of the temple of Bel showed him the treasure chamber and explained that the 'ring' was part of a votive cylinder that had been cut into three. Ordered suddenly to make earrings for Bel's son Ninib, the priest had decided to carve up the cylinder. The third part, said the priest, would never be found, but the second part was still in existence.

The next day, armed with the new information, Hilprecht found that his dream had been correct. The second ring did exist among the catalogued items, and when the two parts were fitted together an inscription to the god Ninib could be read. It was later verified that the two rings had come from the treasure chamber of the temple of Bel. As the priest in the dream said, the third part was never located.

Another twenty years would pass before a professor from Bryn Mawr named George Aaron Barton assembled the fragments, scattered in three boxes. His discovery initially filled him with excitement. This was not a list of temple treasures, or even a hymn to Enlil, but a long, continuous narrative that deserved comparison with *Gilgamesh*. It was, Barton thought, possibly the oldest text in the world, and was nine tablets long. Barton ultimately concluded, though, that this was simply a version of the Sumerian creation myth. His translation of it, in a volume called *Miscellaneous Babylonian Inscriptions* (1918),[9] failed to excite even his colleagues, still less the general public, which was more concerned with the end of the Great War.

More than half a century passed before, in the 1970s, a copy of Barton's book fell into the hands of a geologist named Christian O'Brien, who had spent much of his life working for British Petroleum in the Middle East. O'Brien had taught himself to read cuneiform script, and as he looked at Barton's translation and the reproductions of the original texts, he concluded that Barton's understanding left much to be desired. He set out to translate it himself.

O'Brien discovered that, far from being a 'creation myth' featuring Sumerian gods, the text seemed to be a down-to-earth account of how a group called the Anunnaki, or Anannage, built an agricultural community called Kharsag on a plateau in a mountain region. This settlement was also known as Ehdin – which, as O'Brien points out, reminds us of Eden. Readers of Sitchin's *Earth Chronicles* will immediately recognise the Anunnaki as the beings from 'the twelfth planet' Niburu, who, the author claims, came to earth nearly half a million years ago in search of gold to be used (in some mysterious way) to protect their atmosphere from deterioration. Sitchin finds the evidence for these space visitors in the Old Testament, and in various ancient Sumerian texts (although not the Kharsag fragments). He believes that they actually created man as a slave to do the hard work of gold mining.

Christian O'Brien and his wife and co-writer Barbara Joy rejected the spacemen hypothesis. They are students of Eastern religion, and are inclined to accept the existence of 'astral planes', realms of existence beyond solid matter, so although they never commit themselves to where the Anannage came from, their belief seems to be that it is something more like a 'parallel dimension'.[10] (A similar division of opinion exists in the world of those who study UFO phenomena. At the time they first excited attention, in the late 1940s, most writers on the subject thought that flying saucers were visitors from other planets; more recently, there is an increased acceptance of the view that 'they' may be literally 'extra-terrestrial' in the sense of being able to control a 'higher vibration rate' and should not be thought of as purely material.)

In 1986, the O'Briens brought out their account of the Kharsag inscriptions in *The Genius of the Few: The Story of Those Who Founded the Garden of Eden*.[11] It is hardly surprising that, with its careful, scholarly and unsensational approach, it should have failed to make the impact of Sitchin or Velikovsky. Too controversial for the academics, it was too sober and erudite for the popular audience who devoured ancient mysteries, but since that time it has attracted an increasing number of readers.

The title *The Genius of the Few* is a quotation from André Parrot, O'Brien's mentor in archaeology, who pointed out that the flame of Middle Eastern civilisation blazed up simultaneously in a number of places: Susa, Lagash, Ur, Uruk, Ashnunnak, Nineveh and Mari, 'until, at last, thanks to the genius of the few . . . there was wrought forth, as in an alchemist's crucible, a prodigious, many-sided art'.

What, ask the O'Briens, caused this simultaneous seeding of civilisation in so many places? They believe that the answer lies in the Anannage, or (as they prefer to call them) the Shining Ones, whose name is explained in the second chapter of *The Genius of the Few*. Why, O'Brien asks, does the Bible start with the sentence 'In the Beginning, God created the heavens and the earth', when it says that the Elohim created the heaven and earth? Elohim is plural, not singular, so it should read 'the *gods* created the heavens and the earth'. If the Bible had meant God, it would have used the singular form '*el*', which actually means 'shining'. It can be found in many ancient languages. In Sumerian it means 'brightness'. In Babylonian, '*ellu*' means 'Shining Ones'. Even our English word 'elf' means a shining being, while in Cornwall – where I live – '*el*' means an 'angel' (in old Cornish).

So the Bible is saying that 'the Shining Ones' who created heaven and earth said, 'Let us make a man in our image.' Yahweh, the leader of the Shining Ones, 'planted a garden in Eden', and the prophet Enoch did not 'walk with God' but with the Shining Ones.

O'Brien makes another important point. The word 'heavens' – *'ha'shemin'* – originally meant 'the highlands'. And 'earth' – *'ha'ares'* – means 'the ground' or (in this context) the lowlands. So the Bible is actually saying that these Shining Ones (or angels) made the highlands and the lowlands, and the highlands included the Garden of Eden.

O'Brien also relates the story of the finding of the Kharsag material in Nippur, describing how it was unearthed from the Philadelphia museum basement by George Barton and translated as religious fragments, explaining why he found the Barton translation so unsatisfactory with lengthy quotations from the original text in Akkadian. O'Brien then tells the story of Kharsag after the Shining Ones had descended to earth. And he makes it clear that he regards these Shining Ones as more or less identical with the Watchers of the Book of Enoch.

Since talking about 'Shining Ones' or 'Watchers' may confuse, I suggest that here we refer to them simply as the civilisers, the 'few' whose genius created civilisation. The Kharsag epic makes it clear that they were not angels – otherwise they would surely have been immune to a plague that devastated Eden – but flesh and blood beings whose powers and talents were far beyond those of the human beings of the time.

The leader of the civilisers was called Enlil – the name of the god in whose temple the Kharsag cylinder was found. His wife, the Lady of Kharsag, was called Ninlil. They decided to name the settlement Edin, the Akkadian for 'plateau'. Its other name, Kharsag, means 'the lofty fenced enclosure'.

In other words, the Shining Ones built the first agricultural settlement in a world where human beings were primitive hunters. The spot they chose was surrounded by mountains – O'Brien believes it was at the point where modern Lebanon, Syria and Israel join. The time, the O'Briens believe, was about 8,200 BC. On the plateau of Eden the civilisers built houses of cedar wood, made a reservoir, and dug irrigation ditches. Enlil and other leaders among them had Great Houses, and there was even a maternity hospital. The surrounding hills were covered with orchards, they planted grain, and harvests were so plentiful that they allowed their neighbours to join the settlement and share the bounty.

Although Enlil was recognised as the leader, Eden was run on democratic lines, with a council of seven. If we suppose that the civilisers were mortal, then we must also assume that, over the 2,000 or so years that Kharsag existed, there were many Enlils, and that it became a title like 'king'.

The Lady of Kharsag, Ninlil, is also referred to as the Serpent Lady, which led George Barton to assume that she was some kind of snake goddess. In fact, Andrew Collins cites another ancient fragment of text about the Watchers, which describes one of them as having a 'visage like a viper'. Collins is inclined to feel that this suggests a hollow, gaunt face with slit-like eyes.

This use of another ancient fragment of text offers an opportunity of raising a question that may be troubling some readers: why should anyone take seriously these strange tales and legends about lustful fallen angels and Shining Ones who planted the Garden of Eden? We recognise the stories about the Greek gods as no more than myth; no one believes that Zeus really lived on Mount Olympus with his wife Hera and spent half his time turning himself into a bull or a swan to seduce mortal maidens.

One explanation is that the many different texts about – for example – Enoch or the Watchers suggests that these stories were passed down by word of mouth through many genera-tions before they were written down. When we read the *Iliad*, we soon come to feel that this is not just an idle tale invented

Charles Hapgood, 1904–82.
Beth Hapgood

Seventh- to ninth-century stone warrior figures at Tula, Mexico.
Werner Forman Archive

Lhasa, the spiritual capital of Tibet, pictured here in the eighteenth century, is 60 degrees east of the Giza prime meridian and was once located at the equator.
Mary Evans Picture Library

Alone in the Pacific, Easter Island lies 140 degrees west of the Giza prime meridian and was once located at the equator.
Mary Evans Picture Library

View across the 'semi-subterranean temple' to the monolithic doorway
to the Kalasasaya enclosure at Tiahuanaco, Bolivia.
N.J. Saunders/Werner Forman Archive

Mystery spheres at Costa Rica.
Dr Elmar R. Gruber/Fortean Picture Library

Andean mythology tells of how a golden wand was used
by the people to locate their capital at Cuzco.
De L'Amerique/Mary Evans Picture Library

Canterbury Cathedral lies 30 degrees west of the Giza prime meridian and was formerly midway between the equator and the pole at latitude 45N.
W. Wiscombe Gardner/Mary Evans Picture Library

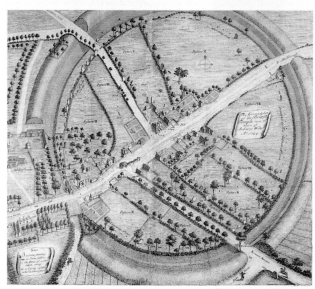

Libyan desert glass with a hole bore through it.
courtesy the Mineralogical Society

An overhead plan of the stone circles and embankment ditches at Avebury, drawn in 1743. 100,000 years ago Avebury was at latitude 29:59N. Today the Great Pyramid in Egypt lies at latitude 29:59N
Mary Evans Picture Library

Arcadian Shepherds, by
Nicolas Poussin, 1594–1665.
The Bridgeman Art Library

Apprentice Pillar, Rosslyn
Chapel, Midlothian, Scotland.
*Andreas Trottman/Fortean
Picture Library*

The drawing of 'Heavenly Jerusalem' which Lomas and Knight believed to be a copy of the picture found in the Temple.
Lambert of St. Omer, Library of University of Ghent

Lt-Col Percy Fawcett, who disappeared in the Amazon
while searching for lost Atlantean cities.
Fortean Picture Library

by a minstrel or bard: it is based on real events. And archaeological research leaves no doubt that they occurred. The sheer number of ancient texts leaves little doubt that there were about a dozen different works about Enoch and the Watchers. As with the *Iliad*, they have the ring of folk memory.

As to the epic of Kharsag, it seems to tell a lengthy and detailed story that also has the ring of fact. For example, the story continues to tell how, after centuries of prosperity, harsh weather came to Eden, with storms, floods and bitter cold. Considered in the light of what we know happened at the end of the last Ice Age, after 14,000 BC, when the climate fluctuated wildly and periods of warming were suddenly replaced again with much colder conditions, it seems likely that Kharsag would find itself under siege to the weather.

But it was more than just bad weather. There were tremendous storms, one of which O'Brien describes as the thousand-year storm, and the House of Enlil was destroyed by fire. Perpetual darkness fell, and heavy, non-stop rain caused flooding. Enlil said, 'My settlement is shattered . . . By water alone it has been destroyed.' But the final words of the lady Ninlil are perhaps the most significant: 'The Building of Learning is cut off . . . the creation of Knowledge is ruined.' Clearly, one of the major purposes of the settlement of Kharsag was to create knowledge. For the O'Briens, the Shining Ones were bringers of knowledge to the human race.

At this point, at the end of Tablet 9, the Kharsag epic breaks off. We do not know how many more tablets remain undiscovered, but the O'Briens believe that the Shining Ones went on to become the civilisers of humanity and the founders of Middle Eastern civilisation. In a later compilation called *The Shining Ones*,[12] which includes *The Genius of the Few*, they even suggested that the civilisers played some part in the civilisation of Central and South America and Atlantis. It also states that 'unquestionably, the most rewarding descriptions of the Garden of Eden . . . occur in the Book of Enoch'. They speak at some length of Enoch, suggesting that when he was taken by the angels to see the seven heavens, he actually visited Kharsag – the Garden of Eden. They point out that Enoch visited a Great House, that he described magnificent trees, and even the great reservoir.

We have already noted the passage from the Book of Enoch in which the angels are given long cords and sent off to 'measure'. It is O'Brien's view that the 'angels' were laying out part of the Garden of Eden, perhaps the irrigation system, but for Rand the passage could bear a completely different interpretation. The angels hurried off to the north, and from the South Pole all directions are north.

As to why the angels should be making a survey, Rand thought he already knew one possible answer. Having already concluded that a great number of the world's sacred sites, such as Giza and Lhasa, were arranged on a symmetrical grid of 'sacred latitudes', it seems likely that there had been some kind of worldwide survey. The same thing is suggested by Hapgood's ancient maps, ranging from China to an Antarctica free of ice. It looks as if ancient peoples who existed 'before civilisation' had an extraordinarily comprehensive knowledge of the surface of our globe.

Rand's theory was that this survey was conducted by what was then the world's most technically advanced civilisation, Atlantis, which was prompted by the recognition that some catastrophe was going to occur – almost certainly involving a movement of the earth's crust – and that its purpose was to find out how far the crust mantle had already shifted. This, Rand felt, was why surveyors would set out to 'make a survey'.

Hapgood believed that the crust movements that resulted in the shift of the North Pole from Hudson Bay to its present position began about 15,000 BC. He seemed to feel that it had occurred slowly and, as it were, almost unnoticeably, although that is unlikely. The San Andreas Fault in California moves slowly, but the occasional earthquakes it produces can be dramatically noticeable.

Rand's strong belief that the Atlanteans possessed a considerable knowledge of geology suggests that they must have studied the subject for a long time before the final catastrophe – perhaps for more than 2,000 years. In 9,600 BC, the tilt of the earth's axis was far greater than it is today, and the end of the Ice Age was marked by a great deal of flooding, so they would have had good reason to pay attention to geology.

Their efforts, as we know, proved to be a waste of time, at least if we accept that the final catastrophe destroyed their civilisation. But, Rand suggests, later generations, who came long after the catastrophe, saw the 'markers' laid down by the 'surveyors', which they took for sacred sites, and went on to build their own temples on these sites.

It seemed to me that the evidence cited by Hapgood in *Maps of the Ancient Sea Kings*, along with Rand's own researches, pointed conclusively to some former worldwide geographical knowledge.

Uriel's Machine, by Christopher Knight and Robert Lomas, lends a certain support to Rand's (and the O'Briens') 'survey' hypothesis, suggesting that Enoch knew all about the danger from the heavens. Uriel is one of the Watchers in the Book of Enoch – not one of the rebels, but one of those sent to earth to punish them. A part of the Book of Enoch called the Book of the Heavenly Luminaries is basically an astronomical treatise. At a certain point, Enoch is transported towards a mountain of 'hard flint rock' in the west: 'And I saw six portals in which the sun rises, and six portals in which the sun sets and the moon rises and sets . . . also many windows to the right and left of these portals.'[13] Lomas and Knight were reminded of Stonehenge, with its 'portals' between the stone uprights of the trilithons.

In the early 1960s, the British astronomer Gerald Hawkins had started to investigate the possibility that Stonehenge might be a kind of Stone Age computer, constructed to calculate the moment of sunrise and moonrise over an 18.6-year cycle. His *Stonehenge Decoded* (1965)[14] became an immediate bestseller, although most astronomers were unconvinced. In fact, its ideas are now generally accepted, and in the 1970s the work of Professor Alexander Thom on ancient stone circles lent support to Hawkins's theory.

The basic notion is that by standing in the centre of the circle you can face the sunrise (or moonrise) and foretell the season according to its position behind the 'markers'. Lomas and Knight decided to try and construct a 'Uriel machine' on a Yorkshire hilltop in what amounted to a simple observatory. They returned repeatedly to take their observations of sunrise or sunset from the centre of the ring to the horizon, and stuck markers in place. Persisting for a year, they ended up with two curved rows of posts facing one another. And they learned – as ancient 'henge' builders had learned – that the year is not neatly divided into four by solstices and equinoxes. Because the earth's orbit around the sun is an ellipse, there are 182 sunrises from the winter to the summer solstice, but 183 from the summer to the winter solstice. The same disparity is found between the spring and autumn equinoxes.

Their observations enabled them to learn why the ancient monument builders – these 'Stone Age Einsteins' – had chosen as their unit of length what Thom called the 'megalithic yard' – 32.64 inches. (Thom admitted he had doubled the basic unit that he found in all the megalithic sites – 16.32 inches – in order to bring it closer to our modern yard.) Lomas and Knight found that their 'machine' registered the length of the year as 366 days (between one winter solstice and another), which led them to fix a 'megalithic degree', one-366th portion of the earth's revolution. They set their posts a megalithic degree apart, and found that a star took 3.93 minutes to move from one upright to the next.

The megalith builders almost certainly used a pendulum as their clock. The time a pendulum takes to complete one swing is determined by its length, and Lomas and Knight discovered that for the pendulum to swing 366 times in 3.93 minutes it had to be exactly 16.32 inches long, which is why the 'Stone

Age Einsteins' chose 16.32 inches as their basic unit. Lomas and Knight had solved the problem that baffled Thom.

Uriel's 'machine' (amounting, in effect, to a primitive Woodhenge of posts) could not only be used as a calculator of sunrises and moonrises, but also as an observatory for measuring comets. It could determine, quite simply, whether a comet was on course to hit the earth. In other words, Uriel's 'machine' could have been used by the ancients as a catastrophe predictor.

Rand certainly thought so, although his own view was that, rather than using the earth to measure the sky, Uriel's machine had been designed to use the position of the stars to monitor the movements of the *inner* earth, a kind of ancient seismic device that could be used to anticipate crust displacements.

According to Rand's theory, in Chapter 65 of the Book of Enoch, significant geological events take place before the flood: 'And in those days Noah saw the earth, that it had sunk down and its destruction was nigh.' At this point Enoch sends an angel to warn Noah specifically about a coming global catastrophe: 'Go to Noah and . . . reveal to him the end that is approaching: that the whole earth will be destroyed, and a deluge is about to come upon the whole earth, and will destroy all that is on it.'

He began to suspect that the position of the sacred sites, scattered across the northern hemisphere at 5- and 10-degree intervals, would be an ideal way of keeping track of any geological changes within the Earth. We know that before the flood, Enoch observed the angels flying north to undertake measurements with cords.

We recall that every year after the Nile flooded the Egyptian plains the priests used knotted 'cords' to recalibrate boundaries. They also used cords as geometric survey tools to design their temples. These 'cords' were nothing less than practical survey tools.

Rand concluded that the survey was geological and that Uriel's machine was a tool used to anticipate the geological changes that were already building to a crisis when Noah pleaded for help from Enoch.

If there were dozens of astronomical observatories located at known latitudes, such as the equator, 15 degrees north, 30 degrees north, and so on, then the collated information from these 'observatories' would permit the people of Atlantis to make an appraisal of the direction of the displacement. For instance, Giza, which was formerly at 15 degrees north and ended up at 30 degrees north, would first pass through latitude 16 degrees north. Likewise, Easter Island, formerly on the equator, moved south until it reached its present location at 27 degrees south by first passing through 1 degree south. And Lhasa, the spiritual capital of Tibet, passed through 1 degree north as it slid from the equator to its current latitude of 30 degrees north.

Lomas and Knight's 'sophisticated horizon declinometer' would also make an ideal seismic monitor to detect any change in the earth's crust or mantle. If the earth's mantle began to move then the stars would appear out of place and Uriel's machine would spot the discrepancy. Our priest-scientist observers would know that something was terribly amiss.

When I checked with Robert Lomas, he replied that yes, indeed, Uriel's machine could be used to monitor changes within the earth. Although he noted that only the twelve first-magnitude stars (the brightest stars) would be useful, those would still be enough to accomplish the geological task.

Based upon their studies of Freemasonry, Lomas and Knight had argued that geology was an ancient science like astronomy and geometry, so Rand's notion of Atlantean astronomers observing the heavens to determine the timing of the next catastrophe was a plausible one.

It should be mentioned that Lomas and Knight also accept the idea of catastrophes resulting from cometary impact. For the impact that produced so much damage in the Mediterranean area, which they believe to be the Biblical flood, they prefer the date of 3,200 BC rather than 2,200 BC.

For the 'Atlantis flood', they prefer 7,640 BC rather than the 9,600 BC that Rand and I have been suggesting in this book.

An article on *Uriel's Machine* by Damian Thompson[15] quotes archaeologist Tim Schadler-Hall as saying that in East Yorkshire there is an unbroken geological record of centuries before and after 7,460 BC but there is no sign of the giant tidal wave that is supposed to have swept Britain clear of all life and produced the great salt lake of Salt Lake City.

Uriel's Machine leaves little doubt that a cometary impact could be calculated weeks or even months before it happened. For example, Donati's comet, named after the Italian astronomer Giovanni Battista Donati, was visible from June 1858 to April 1859, which seems to support the 'surveyor' theory. In any case, if the Atlanteans had studied geology because of earthquakes and floods, then their 'markers' could have been in place for decades or centuries.

As we read in the Kharsag tablets of the catastrophe that dispersed the 'civilisers', we find ourselves wondering what might have caused it. Could it have been one of these unexpected returns to ice age conditions that we have been discussing? That is possible, but human beings had survived ice age conditions for more than 100,000 years, and there seems no good reason why they should not have simply 'dug in' and waited for things to improve.

But what if these conditions were caused by a catastrophe such as a comet impact? In that case, we have to date it to the time of Plato's Atlantis, for the later catastrophe suggested by astronomer Bill Napier (2,200 BC) would have taken place well after the time of ancient Sumer and would postdate the Kharsag tablets. A 9,500 BC catastrophe would suggest that the whole 'Garden of Eden' period occurred a great deal earlier.

In *From the Ashes of Angels*, Andrew Collins has some interesting and important speculations. Collins was not entirely happy with O'Brien's assumption that Eden was in 'the mountain-girt valleys where modern Lebanon, Syria and Israel now adjoin'. O'Brien seems to have reached this conclusion because the Book of Enoch says that the rebel Watchers descended on Mount Hermon, near Damascus, but there is no definite indication of the whereabouts of Enoch's Garden of Eden. Collins discovered other Mesopotamian texts that spoke of an abode of the gods to the north. One Akkadian text of the third millennium BC said that 'Karsag Kurra' was a sacred mountain located immediately outside the northern limits of their country, Mesopotamia, which would seem to place it in Kurdistan. Collins went there to investigate.

One reason that O'Brien chose the vicinity of Mount Hermon was that it had cedar forests (the famous 'cedars of Lebanon'), with whose wood the civilisers built their settlement. Elsewhere in *The Genius of the Few*, O'Brien admits that the high mountain country where Kharsag was situated sounds like the Zagros Mountains of Luristan and Kurdistan. But he declares that the Zagros Mountains are covered with oak trees, and have no history of cedars – which seems to leave only Lebanon as the site of Kharsag.

In this, however, he was mistaken. Collins soon established that there *had* been cedar forests in the Zagros Mountains, and that they may have existed since the end of the Ice Age. Moreover, Collins pointed out that Genesis describes God planting a garden 'eastward, in Eden'. East of what? Mount Hermon is not east of anything except Lebanon and the Mediterranean. On the other hand, the whole area around Lake Van and Lake Urmia, where Kurdish and Armenian legends place both the Garden of Eden and the landing place of Noah's Ark, is to the east of Turkey. The earliest version of *Gilgamesh*, written in Sumerian, places a great cedar forest in the Zagros Mountains of Kurdistan.

Moreover, Collins learned about an ancient Anatolian (Turkish) city named Nevali Cori, whose carved columns at first sight looked like those of the vast courtyard called the Kalasasiya, at Tiahuanaco, in the Andes. They were the remains of a monolithic temple that seemed to be a ritual centre, parts of which were carbon-dated back to 8,400 BC. He would later come to suspect a connection between the Watchers of Enoch and the stories of Viracocha, the god who brought civilisation to Central and South America, and the cult of the plumed serpent Quetzalcoatl (the other name for Viracocha).

Collins went to the Kurdistan plateau in eastern Turkey in search of the Garden of Eden, and soon had no doubt that all the information about it in the Kharsag epic pointed to the Zagros Mountains. Rand disagreed. The blueprint suggests that the O'Briens got it right when they associated Kharsag with the Lebanese village of Ehdin, near Mount Hermon and Baalbek (see Chapter 8).

In his quest, Collins and a friend visited Cappadocia, in eastern Turkey, and discovered a kind of lunar landscape of hardened lava, mostly from the volcano of Erciyas Dag. The landscape is full of towers created by wind erosion. Early Christians tunnelled into them to make hermits' cells and chapels. This area was also where Catal Huyuk, one of the earliest cities in the world, flourished about 8,000 years ago.

After they looked at many of these early 'churches', the guide suggested that they might like to see the 'underground cities'. 'What underground cities?' Collins asked. The guide explained that they were made by Christians who were trying to escape persecution by Muslims in the time of Mohammed. He drove them to a village called Kaymakli, where a subterranean city had been discovered in 1964. It was a kind of underground tenement, with several levels and corridors 10 feet wide and 6.5 feet high. Doorways were closed by huge round stones that could be 'locked' from the inside. It seemed that the builders of these high-ceilinged rooms were (for that time) exceptionally tall. Another underground city had been discovered beneath the town of Derinkuyu, it had no fewer than eight 'storeys', although, in spite of ventilation shafts, it was completely invisible from the ground above. It was big enough to hold a population of 20,000.

As I read Collins's account, I recalled that I had seen something about these cities – there are thirty-six of them – in a book by Erich von Däniken called *According to the Evidence*. Predictably, von Däniken's theory was that the local inhabitants had been visited by extraterrestrials, who departed after threatening that they would return and punish those who did not continue to obey their orders, so the locals had retreated underground.

Even if the notion of extraterrestrials was accepted, this idea does not seem credible, since the inhabitants would have needed food, which had to be grown above ground, and cultivated fields – with cattle – would have revealed their whereabouts. The same applies to the guide's explanation that Christians had taken refuge in these cities to hide from Muslims. To 'hide' in such places would be simply to be caught like rats in a trap.

In fact, there could only be one purpose in building such a city underground: to escape the temperature of the air above ground. In stiflingly hot summers and freezing winters, the temperature in the underground cities remained around 8 degrees celsius.

Collins says there is geological evidence that Turkey was plunged into a mini-ice age for about 500 years in the middle of the ninth millennium BC. This made more sense. If the landscape was covered with snow and ice and scoured by freezing winds, an underground city would be as comfortable as a Hobbit hole.

The local archaeologist, Omer Demir, told Collins that he believed that the oldest parts of the 'city' dated to the late Palaeolithic Era, perhaps 8,500 BC. Older parts were hewn out with stone tools, not metal. Moreover, it had been made by two types of human being, and those who carved the oldest part were much taller than the others – again, they had made their ceilings higher.

We have seen that it is conceivable that the break-up of the Kharsag community through a return of ice age conditions could have occurred earlier than the O'Briens believed – that is, before 10,000 BC. O'Brien had worked out his date for the founding of Kharsag, about 8,200 BC, from the fact that the cedars of Lebanon had existed from about that time. If he was wrong about Kharsag being situated in Lebanon, then that date was purely arbitrary. If Kharsag was affected by the 9,600 BC catastrophe, and it had flourished for over 2,000 years (as O'Brien believes), that would push its foundation back to perhaps 11,500 BC.

Is it not possible that work began on the subterranean cities at that time? Collins cites a Persian legend in which a shepherd called Yima is told by God to build a 'var' – an underground city or fortress – to protect men and animals from freezing conditions brought about by an evil demon. Nearly 2,000 human beings are to be taken into the city for their protection.

Could this legend also be referring to the underground cities of Cappadocia? There was a strong connection between Cappadocia and Kurdistan, and also between Kurdistan and its neighbour Persia, in which case there is an arguable connection between these subterranean cities and the end of the last ice age.

Subsequently, the earth then had to contend with yet another catastrophe in a comet that split into 'seven burning mountains' and caused a disastrous flood, accompanied by worldwide volcanic activity. Collins argues that this catastrophe could be reflected in the words of a version of the Book of Enoch found among the Dead Sea Scrolls, which states that the rebel Watchers were finally destroyed by 'fire, naphtha and brimstone'.

There seems to be an obvious objection to this notion: surely the Kharsag epic would have mentioned the 'seven mountains'? But the Kharsag epic is an unfinished fragment, which ends (on tablets 8 and 9) with the long winter and the great storm. We do not know what might have been described on other tablets. Perhaps tablets 10 and 11 now lie in the basement of some Iraqi museum, or even underground, like the missing tablets of *Gilgamesh*, waiting for discovery by another George Smith.

I have already noted that Andrew Collins is inclined to suspect a connection between the 'civilisers' of Eden and the 'god' Viracocha, who brought knowledge to Central and South America. He also links them with ancient Egypt. Collins accepts – as I do myself – that Egyptian civilisation probably dates back thousands of years before the pharaohs.

Collins notes that among the Anannage who built Kharsag there is a council of seven, and that in the Edfu 'building texts' the Seven Sages are divine beings who organise the building of the temples and sacred places. Graham Hancock writes of them:

> This context [describing the sages] is marked by a preponderance of 'Flood' imagery in which the 'primeval waters' (out of which the Great Primeval Mound emerged) are depicted as gradually receding. We are reminded of Noah's mountaintop on which the Ark settled after the Biblical Deluge, and of the 'Seven Sages' (Apkallu) of ancient Babylonian tradition who were said to have 'lived before the Flood' and to have built the walls of the sacred city of Uruk. Likewise is it an accident that in Indian tradition 'Seven Sages' (rishis) are remembered to have survived the Flood, their purpose being to pass down to future generations the wisdom of the antediluvian world? In all cases the sages appear as the enlightened survivors of a cataclysm that wiped the earth clean . . .[17]

Hancock says that the Seven Sages come from an island that was destroyed by a flood, and that the majority of its divine inhabitants were drowned. The Seven Sages then moved on to Egypt. We might bear in mind that the island called Dilmun, which appears in Sumerian and Akkadian mythology, is a paradise that sounds remarkably like a variant of the Garden of Eden.

The Edfu texts and Pyramid texts tell us that these Seven Sages were also known as the 'followers of Horus' (*Shemsu Hor*) and that they rebuilt the world after the great catastrophe. Since we are dealing with the relatively small area of the Middle East, it seems, to say the least, not unlikely that the Seven Sages of Egypt are the seven councillors of Kharsag.

These speculations are related to Rand's observations on the geography of sacred sites (see Appendix 5). He notes that the O'Briens and Andrew Collins are in agreement that several sites in the Middle East were linked with the Shining Ones – Baalbek, Byblos and Ehdin in Lebanon, Jericho near Jerusalem, Catal Huyuk in Turkey, Edfu in Egypt and finally Nippur, the religious capital of ancient Sumer. He commented in an email to me:

> If the Shining Ones were undertaking geological surveys at these sites before the Flood then they should fit into the Atlantis Blueprint.
>
> Baalbek is perhaps the most impressive site in the Middle East because of the gigantic blocks of stone used in the construction of a platform that was later to become a temple dedicated to the Roman god, Jupiter. In John Anthony West's award-winning documentary *The Mystery of the Sphinx*, he showed just how difficult it was even for modern engineers using the largest cranes in the world to move objects weighing 200 tons. The blocks used in construction at Baalbek are much larger than those found in Egypt.
>
> Andrew Collins comments on their sheer weight: 'An outer podium wall, popularly known as the Great Platform, is seen by scholars as contemporary to the Roman temples. Yet incorporated into one of its courses are the three largest building blocks ever used in a man-made structure. Each one weighs an estimated 1,000 tonnes apiece. They sit side-by-side on the fifth level of a truly cyclopean wall located beyond the western limits

of the Temple of Jupiter. These three stones are called the Trilithon. Even if they did not exist and we were left with the six blocks of stone that lie beneath them, we would still be looking at blocks weighing in excess of 450 tonnes. The course beneath the Trilithon is almost as bewildering. It consists of six mammoth stones thirty to thirty-three feet in length, fourteen feet in height and ten feet in depth, each an estimated 450 tonnes in weight.'

Collins is highly sceptical of the claim by some scholars that the Romans were responsible for the Great Platform and remarks: 'Nowhere in extant Roman records does it mention anything at all about the architects and engineers involved in the construction of the Great Platform. No contemporary Roman historian or scholar comments on how it was constructed, and there are no tales that preserve the means by which the Roman builders achieved such marvellous feats of engineering.'

Instead, Andrew Collins looks to the mythology of the people who live in the Bequa'a Valley. Theirs is a very different tale: 'They say that Baalbek's first city was built before the Great Flood by Cain, the son of Adam, whom God banished to the "land of Nod" that lay "east of Eden", for murdering his brother Abel, and he called it after his son Enoch. The citadel, they say, fell into ruins at the time of the deluge and was much later re-built by a race of giants.'[18]

So, says Rand, according to local traditions there have been at least two ancient periods of construction at Baalbek: one well before the flood (since it was undertaken by Cain who flourished before Enoch who was in turn the great-grandfather of Noah), the second long after the flood, when a race of giants occupied the site. Rand, like Collins, believes that, like so many sacred places around the world, Baalbek was simply appropriated by later generations, in this case Roman.

Rand's next thought was to compare Baalbek's location to the Hudson Bay Pole:

> I discovered that it was situated at 10 phi distance from the equator. I knew that the largest stones used in construction in the New World were in and around Cuzco, which also had been at a 10 phi latitude before the flood. Sitchin had commented upon the similarities between Baalbek and Cuzco and now we knew that both sites shared the same sacred latitude.
>
> I was intrigued by this development and it occurred to me that the geological survey of Enoch's 'angels' might have marked off the distance to earlier positions of the earth's crust/mantle. I decided to see how Baalbek related to the Greenland Sea Pole (before 50,600 BC) and the Yukon Pole (before 91,600 BC) (see Appendix 4).

Rand's theory of sacred sites is based on the notion that, as Hapgood himself implies, the Atlanteans were a central part – perhaps the central part – of a worldwide maritime civilisation that extended as far as China, so it is highly probable that they had conducted a worldwide survey decades or centuries before the catastrophe of 9,600 BC. Rand suggests they were trying to understand the periodic earthquakes and volcanic activity that had been devastating their country for a long time (there is a persistent tradition that Atlantis suffered three catastrophes, and was destroyed by the third).

We have to suppose that the Atlanteans knew the earth's crust had been moving for a considerable time – Hapgood thinks 15,000 BC – and were aware of its rate of movement and direction. (O'Brien's suggestion that the 'civilisers' had carried their knowledge to Atlantis would certainly lend plausibility to this notion.) They also, if this theory is correct, knew the position of the North Pole before it began to move, and we have to suppose that they had built certain 'markers' – perhaps stone circles, Uriel's machines – to measure this movement.

What Rand discovered, when he measured the position of Baalbek against previous poles, was unequivocal. The position of the Yukon Pole and the Greenland Sea Pole also gave significant figures.

This was when the mystical number seven showed up. During the Greenland Sea Pole Baalbek was located at 49 degrees north (7 × 7). But the real surprise came when Rand compared Baalbek to the Yukon Pole. When the North Pole was situated in the Yukon, a time that reached back almost 100,000 years, Baalbek was located at exactly 7 degrees north.

8

GOLDEN SECTION SITES

W HEN I FIRST read Rand's original outline of his theory, only one part caused me twinges of doubt: the section on Rennes-le-Château, the tiny French village in Languedoc where a poor village priest had discovered coded documents in a hollow pillar in his church and had suddenly become wealthy.

A year earlier, my friend Lynn Picknett had sent me the typescript of her book *The Templar Revelation* (1997) (co-authored with Clive Prince).[1] She seemed to feel that part of the modern 'evidence' was little more than a hoax.

The previous autumn, I had been sent for review a book called *The Tomb of God* (1996),[2] whose authors, Richard Andrews and Paul Schellenberger, had no doubts about the truth of the Rennes-le-Château saga and believed that their researches had revealed the burial site of Jesus Christ in the Pyrenees. A BBC programme on the book exploded their theory so savagely that the authors (who had taken part in it apparently under the belief that their book was being taken seriously) must have felt as if they had stood on a landmine.

About this time I also read a book called *The Key to the Sacred Pattern* (1997)[3] by Henry Lincoln – the man who had started the avalanche of interest in Rennes-le-Château nearly thirty years before – and I realised that I was wrong: the mystery had not been exploded. Not only was the story of Rennes-le-Château as baffling as ever, but the geometry of the area provided some of the most convincing proof so far of Rand's 'geodetic' theory of sacred sites and his view that ancient people possessed sophisticated surveying skills.

In 1969, the name of Rennes-le-Château was unknown, even to most of the tourists who love Languedoc and its ancient historical sites. Most of those who went there made for the walled town of Carcassonne, the breeding ground of a medieval heresy called Catharism, which preached that 'this world' was created by the Devil and that everything to do with matter is evil (a creed also known as Manicheeism). The Cathars were bloodily suppressed when a huge army invaded the region in 1209, murdering them by the thousand. In 1244, they made their last stand in the citadel of Montségur, situated on a mountain top, and 200 of them were finally burned alive on a huge pyre.

In the last days of the siege, four men had escaped from the citadel by night, carrying the 'treasure' of the Cathars – two months earlier, another two Cathars had escaped with even more treasure. I had visited the citadel years ago, and can still recall that precipitous and exhausting climb. Was it possible that the parchment discovered in the church pillar had led the priest to the treasure of the Cathars, and that this had made him a wealthy man?

Henry Lincoln was a writer of television drama scripts when he first stumbled on the mystery in 1969. On holiday with his wife and children in a French farmhouse in the Cevennes, he picked up a paperback called *Le Trésor Maudit*[4] – *The Cursed Treasure* – by a man called Gérard de Sède. It told the story of the simple village priest called Bérenger Saunière, who was thirty-three years old when he

216

came to Rennes-le-Château in 1885. He was very poor – the income on which he supported himself and a housekeeper was about six pounds sterling a year.

Some time thereafter, a wealthy female parishioner, the Countess de Chambord, gave Saunière 3,000 francs to repair the church – the date may have been 1886 or 1891, according to different accounts. It was during the repairs that a workman found four wooden cylinders containing rolls of paper inside a square Visigothic pillar that held up the altar stone. Two of the papers proved to be genealogies of local families, allegedly linking them with the Merovingians, a dynasty of kings that had ruled France – less than successfully – from the fifth to the eighth centuries AD. The other two were Latin texts from the New Testament, but written without spaces between the words.

They were fairly obviously in code – in fact, the code of the shorter text was so straightforward that Henry Lincoln worked it out at a glance as he looked at the reproduction in de Sède's book. Some letters were raised above the others, and when these were written down consecutively they read: '*A Dagobert II roi et à Sion est ce tresor et il est là mort*' – 'This treasure belongs to King Dagobert II and to Sion, and he is there dead'. Sion was Jerusalem, and the last phrase could also mean 'and it is death'. Dagobert was a seventh-century French king of the Merovingian dynasty who had lived at Rennes-le-Château in the far-off days when it was a flourishing town. The author of these parchments was probably a predecessor of Saunière named Antoine Bigou, who had been curé of Rennes-le-Château at the time of the French Revolution.

Saunière took the parchments to his bishop, who was intrigued enough to send him to Paris to consult with various scholars. There he went along to the church of St Sulpice, and talked with its director, Abbé Bieil. He also met Bieil's nephew, a young trainee priest named Emile Hoffet, who was involved in a circle of 'occultists' who flourished in Paris in the 1890s (some of whom Huysmans portrayed in his 'Satanist' novel *Là Bas*). Hoffet introduced Saunière to a circle of writers and artists that included the poet Stéphane Mallarmé, the dramatist Maurice Maeterlinck, and the composer Claude Debussy. Saunière also – probably through Debussy – met the famous soprano Emma Calvé, and probably became her lover (he was far from ascetic).

Before leaving Paris, Saunière visited the Louvre and bought reproductions of three paintings, one of which was Nicholas Poussin's *Les Bergers d'Arcadie* – '*The Shepherds of Arcadia*' – which shows three shepherds and a shepherdess standing in front of a tomb on which are carved the words 'Et in Arcadia Ego', usually translated 'I (death) am also in Arcadia'.

Back in Rennes-le-Château, three weeks later, he hired workmen to raise a stone slab set in the floor in front of the altar – it dated from around the time of Dagobert II. They discovered two skeletons and 'a pot of worthless medallions'. Saunière sent his helpers away, and spent the evening in the church alone. He then committed an odd piece of vandalism on a grave in the churchyard – that of a distinguished lady named Marie de Blanchefort – and obliterated its two inscriptions.

He was unaware that the inscriptions had already been published in a little book by a local antiquary. One contains the words 'Et in Arcadia Ego' (in a mixture of Greek and Latin letters) on either side. The other is curious in that it contains four unexplained lower-case letters, three e's, two p's and four capitals, TMRO. From the small letters only one word can be formed – *épée*, 'sword' – while from the capitals the only word that emerges is *MORT*, 'death'. *Epée* proved to be the 'key word' to decipher the second parchment Saunière had found in the column.

And suddenly Saunière was rich. He constructed a public road to replace the dirt road to the village, as well as a water tower. And he built himself a villa with a garden, and a Gothic

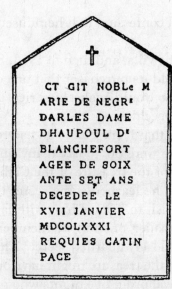

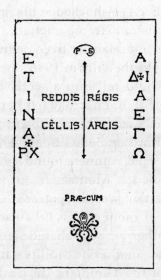

The 'obliterated' tombstone.

tower to house his library. Distinguished visitors came regularly, including Emma Calvé and the Austrian Archduke Johann von Habsburg, the cousin of Emperor Franz-Josef. His many guests were superbly fed and wined by his young peasant housekeeper, Marie Denarnaud.

A new – and less friendly – bishop became curious about the source of Saunière's wealth. When Saunière refused to divulge its source – saying merely that it was from a wealthy penitent who insisted on anonymity – the bishop ordered Saunière's transfer to another parish. Saunière refused to be transferred, and another priest was appointed in his place. (Oddly enough, when the bishop took his complaint to Rome, the Pope found in Saunière's favour . . .) In 1905 the French government – which was anticlerical – began to make his life uncomfortable by accusing him of being an Austrian spy. It seems that part of his regular income came from Austria.

In 1917, Saunière died of cirrhosis of the liver; he was sixty-five. The priest who attended his deathbed is said to have been so shocked at his final confession that he refused to administer extreme unction.

His housekeeper lived on in the villa, and died in 1953. She had sold the villa in 1946; she told its purchaser that one day she would tell him a secret that would make him rich and powerful, but a stroke left her speechless.

This was the remarkable story that Henry Lincoln had read in Gérard de Sède's book. There were obviously many questions. Had Saunière found some of the treasure of the Cathars who died at Montségur? Or had he learned some secret that led certain wealthy patrons to wish to silence him with large sums of money? Was he a blackmailer, or simply a member of a small group who shared some closely guarded secret? There was yet another possibility – that the treasure might have been that of the Templars, the medieval order of knights who possessed immense wealth and influence during the twelfth and thirteenth centuries, and was destroyed virtually overnight.

The Templars are so called because their original headquarters was in the basement of Solomon's Temple in Jerusalem (or rather, the remains of the Temple, which was destroyed by the Romans in AD 70, only four years after Herod had rebuilt it). Jerusalem fell to Christian knights in 1099, as a result of the First Crusade. Twenty years later, nine French knights from the area of Troyes approached King Baldwin II of Jerusalem, and told him they had sworn to protect the roads and make them safe for Christian pilgrims; they asked if they could establish a home on the Temple Mount, and Baldwin gave them a plot of land that included the Temple's 'basement', which they turned into a stable.

Oddly enough, the nine knights showed no sign of organising themselves to protect pilgrims (and in any case nine men would hardly have formed an effective patrol). Instead they spent the next seven years excavating their 'stable', and scarcely ever ventured outside. They were obviously looking for something. One of their tunnels was found by Israeli archaeologists in the 1970s.

But searching for what? When the Romans destroyed the Temple in AD 70, they had carried off its treasures. Could the remains of that treasure have been concealed under the Temple? Or were they looking for something else?

In *The Sign and the Seal* (1992),[5] Graham Hancock has an interesting speculation. As we saw in the last chapter, the Ethiopians claimed that the Ark of the Covenant had been taken to their country in the time of King Solomon, in the tenth century BC, but the truth is probably that it vanished from the Temple in the reign of a king named Manasseh (687–642 BC), who, according to the Bible, 'did evil in the sight of the Lord' and introduced a graven image into the Temple.

With remarkable detective work, Hancock traced the purported route of the Ark from Jerusalem to a church in Axum, in Ethiopia. The priests in charge of the 'Ark' have consistently refused to allow it to be examined, but a recent book alleges that they have admitted that what they guard is actually a box that houses post-Christian copies of the Tables of the Law brought down by Moses from Sinai.[6]

Hancock's suggestion is that the Templars were searching for the Ark, which legend declared had been hidden in a secret room below its sacred chamber when Babylonians burst into Solomon's Temple in 587 BC to destroy it and drag the Jews into their Babylonian captivity.

Why would the nine knights have wanted the Ark? Presumably because, in that age of faith, when holy relics were venerated (and brought immense wealth to the church or abbey that possessed them), the ownership of the world's holiest object would make the order that possessed it the most powerful in the world.

Whatever they were searching for, the knights do not seem to have found it. In 1126, seven years after starting their excavations, Hugh de Payens, their leader, returned to France. It looked as if the attempt to found an order had been a failure.

Then a rescuer appeared. Bernard of Clairvaux, later St Bernard, was a Cistercian and one of France's most powerful churchmen, even though he firmly refused to be promoted above the rank of abbot. He was also the nephew of one of the knights, André de Montbard, who had accompanied Payens back to France. Two years later, a synod was convened in the town of Troyes, whose purpose was to persuade the Church to back the founding of the Order of Knights Templar. This came about in 1128, when the 'Order of the Poor Soldiers of Christ and the Temple of Solomon' was founded and made answerable only to the Pope. And with the support of St Bernard, recruits and money poured in, until the Templars became the richest order in Europe.

What happened? An association that is about to dissolve itself in 1126 becomes rich and powerful in a few years. What did Hugh de Payens and André de Montbard say to St Bernard to enlist such support? Was it simply a friendly act on behalf of his uncle? Or did the knights tell Bernard of important and fascinating discoveries they had made under the Temple?

Hancock hazards the interesting guess that the knights had something to offer Bernard in return for his support: Gothic architecture. Before that time, the major style of church architecture was Romanesque, a style with rounded arches supported on short, thick pillars. This was for purely practical reasons. The sheer weight of the ceilings and upper levels of a church meant that the weight pushed downward on the pillars and tended to make the walls bulge outward so that they often collapsed. Then architects solved the problem. Ceilings were made thinner and supported on 'ribs', and the arches were made narrower and higher – typically Gothic. The first abbey to use this new Gothic style was St Denis in Paris, under a great innovator, Abbot Suger. The thinner walls – supported by flying buttresses – allowed more space for windows, one of the most famous examples being the stained glass of Chartres, built later in the century (with the active encouragement of St Bernard).

Hancock wonders if it is possible that the Templars learned the secret of Gothic architecture in the vaults of Solomon's

Temple. This is not, of course, to suggest that Solomon's Temple was built in the Gothic style, but the Temple was famous for its beauty and harmony, and the knights may have stumbled upon some of the essential principles of Gothic architecture while they were there.

However, there is a problem of dating. According to *Encyclopaedia Britannica*, architects began to solve the problem of the arches in 1120, when the nine knights had been excavating for only two years. This does not invalidate the theory – St Denis, the first Gothic abbey, was not started until 1140. And as Rand pointed out, the decline of Gothic architecture in the next few centuries was as obvious and inexplicable as the decline of pyramid building in the centuries immediately after the Giza pyramids had been built. The implication would be that in both cases, some tremendous injection of energy and inspiration created almost superhuman works of architecture and then ran out of steam.

Hancock has another, equally fascinating theory. The town of Troyes, in which the Templars received the support of the Church, was the home of the author Chrétien de Troyes, the poet who, between 1165 and 1182, was responsible for the first great literary treatments of the legend of King Arthur. He was the first to write about the Holy Grail – Hancock goes as far as to say that he invented the Holy Grail. Hancock suggests that the idea arose from the stories of the Ark of the Covenant, which Chrétien may have heard direct from Templar knights, and he cites the scholar Helen Adolf, who thought that another early Grail chronicler, Wolfram von Eschenbach, who wrote *Parzifal*, derived his version of the Grail – a stone – from the *Kebra Nagast* of Abyssinia. It is a fascinating idea, but seems to be contradicted by the opinion of various scholars, to the effect that stories of the Grail had been sung by minstrels long before Chrétien wrote them down.[7]

Why does this matter? It is important to bear in mind that the Templars were not simply seeking power – they soon acquired it in abundance – but that they began with a search for some mystery object, possibly the Ark, and that the Templar order was thereafter associated with the notion of a mystery, a belief that has persisted down to modern times.

The Second Crusade was initiated by Bernard of Clairvaux after the fall of Edessa in 1144, but it ended in failure; the Moslems under Saladin were to recapture Jerusalem in 1187. During the next century, seven more crusades failed to restore power to the Christians. The fall of Acre in 1291 completed their defeat, and the Knights Templar lost their raison d'être.

But they did not lose their power – or their wealth (based partly on exemption from taxes). With a new Grand Master, Jacques de Molay, they licked their wounds on the island of Cyprus and wondered what to do next. The problem was that Cyprus was insecure, with the Moslems raiding Limassol and taking captives who had to be ransomed. The Templars considered returning to France, but there were problems. King Philip the Fair (1265–1314) was in conflict with Pope Boniface VIII, and since the Templars regarded the Pope as their master, their return to France would be unwelcome to the king.

In fact, the whole order was unwelcome to the king, who felt they were – like their papal master – arrogant nuisances (this may have been because he had once applied to join them, and been rejected). When the Pope threatened to depose Philip, the king denounced Boniface as a heretic, and finally had him taken prisoner in his own house; Boniface died soon after being rescued.

When his successor, Boniface IX, showed signs of taking up the struggle where Boniface VIII left off, Philip arranged to have him poisoned, then had his own candidate, Archbishop Bertrand de Gotte of Bordeaux, placed on the papal throne. Philip laid down a number of preconditions for supporting Bertrand's candidacy, one being that the new Pope should move the seat of the papacy to France. Another precondition was held in reserve and has never been revealed. Most scholars have concluded that the secret clause included a stipulation that the Pope should not oppose his plan to arrest the Templars and seize their money.

Bertrand became Pope Clement V in 1305, and the king immediately began to plan one of the most amazing coups in history. It was to arrest all the Templars – 15,000 of them – and accuse them of heresy. It could be compared to a modern king plotting to arrest all the officers in the army, navy and air force.

Incredibly, it succeeded. Sealed orders went out about four weeks before the swoop, and the Templars were arrested on Friday 13 October 1307.*

The Templars were accused of homosexuality, worshipping a demon called Baphomet and spitting on the cross. Under appalling tortures – such as being held over red hot braziers – many confessed, including the Grand Master Jacques de Molay himself. But at their sentencing on 18 March 1314, Molay withdrew his confession, declaring that it had been forced from him by torture. The king was so enraged at having his plans thwarted that he immediately ordered Molay and his friend Geoffrey de Charney, who also withdrew his confession, to be roasted alive over a slow fire.

This took place on the following day, on an island in the Seine called the Ile de Palais. It is said that Molay summoned the king and the Pope to meet him before the throne of God within a year. Whether this is true or not, he certainly called upon God to avenge his death. Within three months, both were dead – Philip gored by a boar during hunting, Clement of a fever.

The irony is that, in a sense, Philip had committed this act of savagery for nothing. He had been hoping to replenish his treasury – depleted by war – with the wealth of the Templars,

---

*It has been stated that this is the reason that Friday the 13th is an unlucky day, but there is no evidence for this – Friday was considered an unlucky day by Christians because Jesus was said to have been crucified on a Friday, while the unlucky number 13 was the number present at the Last Supper.

but that wealth seems to have mysteriously disappeared. For example, the knights of Bezu (near Rennes-le-Château) avoided the trap and escaped with vast amounts of treasure. Could it be coincidence that the commander of these knights was called the Signeur de Gotte, and that he was related to the Pope, the former Bertrand de Gotte? Or, moreover, that the Pope's mother was a member of the Blanchefort family, who owned a château on the next hilltop to Bezu?

It is also known that on the day before the Templars were arrested, 12 October 1307, eighteen ships sailed out of La Rochelle, the Templars' port. No one knows what became of them; they vanished from history. But at least one of these ships seems to have made its way to Scotland, where part of the wealth it carried went into the building of a remarkable chapel called Rosslyn, near Edinburgh. (It is also worth bearing in mind that Hugh de Payens was married to a Scotswoman called Catherine de St Clair, whose descendants later built Rosslyn.)

Whether or not the wealth of Bérenger Saunière was part of a Templar treasure will never be known for certain, although Henry Lincoln is fairly sure he knows. What is certain is that there were two major Templar strongholds close to Rennes-le-Château – Bezu and Blanchefort – and that Philip the Fair failed to seize the wealth of either of them.

Back in 1969, after Henry Lincoln discovered Gérard de Sède's book on his holiday in the Cevennes, he returned to London and succeeded in interesting a friend at the BBC in the story. The two of them went to Rennes-le-Château, and even on that first visit it began to look as if they were being observed. For example, in the neighbouring village of Rennes-les-Bains Lincoln found a spring called the Lover's Fountain; close by was a rock bearing a heart pierced by an arrow, and underneath it were the words E. Calvé, 1891. Emma Calvé was the beautiful soprano who allegedly counted Saunière among her many lovers, and 1891 was the year he is supposed to have discovered the parchments. Lincoln photographed the inscription, but when he returned on the morrow, to photograph it by better light, the inscription had been hacked from the rock.

Gérard de Sède had agreed to act as a consultant on the programme, and was able to provide the key to decoding the second mystery parchment. It was an incredibly complex code, which involved a technique known to cipher experts as the Vigenère process. The alphabet is written twenty-six times, the first beginning with A, the second B, the third C, and so on. The key words MORT EPEE are placed over the parchment, and the letters are transformed using the Vigenère table.

The 'noble Marie de Blanchefort' text (which Saunière had tried to destroy) is then used as another key phrase, and finally the letters are placed on a chess board and a series of knight's moves produces a message that may be translated: SHEPHERDESS WITHOUT TEMPTATION TO WHICH POUSSIN AND TENIERS HOLD THE KEY PEACE 681 WITH THE CROSS AND THIS HORSE OF GOD I REACH THIS DEMON GUARDIAN AT MIDDAY BLUE APPLES.

This, presumably, is what led Saunière to the treasure, although it is hard to see how.

The Marie inscription ends with the letters P.S. This, Lincoln learned from de Sède, stood for an organisation called the Priory of Sion. In the Bibliothèque Nationale in Paris, Lincoln found that a number of pamphlets and documents had been deposited since 1956, many written under pseudonyms such as 'Anthony the Hermit'. One spoke about a secret order called the Priory of Sion, giving a list of its Grand Masters, which included the alchemist Nicolas Flamel (reputed to have made gold), Leonardo da Vinci, Isaac Newton, Claude Debussy and, more recently, Jean Cocteau. Saunière, we recall, had met Debussy on the trip to Paris. And according to these documents – collectively known as the *Secret Dossier* – the Priory of Sion was the inner hierarchy of the Knights Templar. And, the *Secret Dossier* claimed, the

Priory continued to exist even after the Templars were destroyed.

This suggested a new possibility, noted by another investigator, Lionel Fanthorpe, as well as by Henry Lincoln: perhaps Saunière had not found a treasure, only a secret – a secret worth a great deal of money.

Many known facts support this conclusion. According to Henry Buthion, who owned the hotel that was once Saunière's Villa Bethanie, Saunière was often short of cash, and failed to pay 5,000 francs that he owed the makers of some expensive furniture he had ordered. He certainly died penniless, but that may have been because he simply allowed large sums of money to be paid direct to his housekeeper, Marie Denardaud. Still, a man with a hidden treasure does not run short of cash, even if he banks it.

Eventually, Lincoln's television programme was made and broadcast under the title *The Lost Treasure of Jerusalem*.[8] By then, so much material had come to light that it was clear that a second programme was going to be required.

Perhaps the most intriguing clue of all came soon after the programme was transmitted. A retired Church of England vicar wrote to tell Lincoln that the 'treasure' was not gold or jewels, but a document proving that Jesus was not crucified in AD 33, but had still been alive in AD 45.

Lincoln went to visit him. The clergyman obviously wished he had kept his mouth shut, but he finally admitted that his information had come from an Anglican scholar named Canon Alfred Lilley. And – Lincoln's heart must have leaped as he heard this – Lilley had maintained close contact with scholars based at St Sulpice, and had known Emile Hoffet, who had introduced Saunière to Debussy. This obviously raised a fascinating possibility. If Debussy was, indeed, a Grand Master of the Priory of Sion, could he have shared the belief that Jesus did not die on the cross? And was *that* Saunière's secret, which so shocked the priest who listened to his final confession?

It certainly began to look more and more as if this was the answer. We may recall that when Saunière left Paris, he purchased some copies of paintings from the Louvre, among them *Les Bergers d'Arcadie*, which shows three shepherds and a shepherdess standing by a tomb bearing the words 'Et in Arcadia Ego'.

While they were filming the first programme, de Sède told Lincoln that the actual tomb used in the painting had been discovered at Arques, not far from Rennes-le-Château. In fact, the tomb, although it had no Latin inscription, was otherwise identical, even to the stone on which the shepherd is resting his foot in the painting.

Nicolas Poussin (1594–1665) was one of the most distinguished painters of his time; although born in Normandy it was in Rome that he won fame and spent most of his life. For a short time he had served Louis XIII and Richelieu. Poussin's *Les Bergers d'Arcadie* came into the possession of Louis XIV after his agents had been trying, with great tenacity, to lay their hands on it for some time, yet when the king finally obtained it, he kept it locked away in his private chambers; rumour has it that he was afraid that it might reveal some secret if it was displayed more publicly. The painting itself seems to offer no clues as to why the king wanted it so badly, or why he subsequently kept it from the eyes of the world.

What we do know, however, is that in 1656 the king's finance minister, Nicolas Fouquet, sent his own younger brother Louis to Rome to see Poussin, and that Louis then wrote to Fouquet:

He and I have planned certain things of which in a little while I shall be able to inform you fully; things which will give you, through M. Poussin, advantages which kings would have great difficulty in obtaining from him, and which, according to what he says, no one in the world will ever retrieve in centuries to come; and furthermore, it would be achieved without much expense and could even turn to profit, and they are matters so difficult to enquire into that nothing on earth at the present time could bring a greater fortune nor perhaps ever its equal . . .[9]

What can he have been talking about? 'Nothing on earth could ever bring a greater fortune' sounds like a treasure, except that he also says it could 'even turn to profit', which suggests that he means something else after all. What is certain is that the king, who was only five years old when he came to the throne, nursed an increasing dislike of his brilliant and ambitious finance minister. Fouquet became immensely wealthy and, according to his assistant Colbert, managed this by cooking the books every afternoon. In 1661, Louis had him arrested, and he was eventually imprisoned. (Some historians have suggested that he was the famous Man in the Iron Mask, but he died twenty-three years before the mysterious prisoner.)

Is it possible that when Fouquet sent his brother Louis to see Poussin it was with treasonous intent?

The Merovingian king Dagobert II, born in AD 651, was kidnapped as a child and taken to Ireland, while a usurping major-domo took his place. He returned to France – in fact, to Rennes-le-Château – married to a Visigoth princess named Giselle, and reclaimed the throne, but was murdered in 679 as he lay asleep under a tree. The Church certainly played some part in the assassination, but his major-domo, Pepin the Fat, was also involved. Pepin was the grandfather of the famous warrior Charles Martel, who turned back the Moslem invasion of France at the Battle of Poitiers. Martel's son, Pepin the Short, seized the throne and inaugurated the Carolingian dynasty, fathering its most famous member, the great Charlemagne.

The descendants of Dagobert were understandably resentful about being deprived of the throne, and there was always a movement in favour of their restoration, rather like that of the Jacobites in England. Similar to the Jacobites, they were a lost cause, but one Merovingian descendant achieved a fame that rivalled that of Charles Martel or Charlemagne. He was Godfrey de Bouillon (1058–1100), Duke of Lorraine, the man who led the First Crusade and recaptured Jerusalem – the knight who became the first King of Jerusalem.

There can also be little doubt that he was the founder – or one of the founders – of another dynasty, the Priory of Sion, or, as it was first known, the 'Order of Our Lady of Sion'. Sion is another name for Jerusalem, and soon after the capture of Jerusalem an Abbey of Sion was built on the Temple Mount and its occupants were known as the Order of Our Lady of Sion. According to the *Secret Dossier*, the Order was founded in 1090, nine years before the fall of Jerusalem. Five of the nine original Templars were members. It seems probable that the Templar order sprang out of the Order of Sion.

Lincoln cites evidence to show that the two orders soon grew apart. It seems that the fabulous power and wealth of the Templars made them headstrong, 'like unruly children'. Matters came to a head in 1187, when a Templar named Gerard de Ridefort led the knights into a rash encounter with the Saracens and lost Jerusalem – this time forever. At this point, it seems, the Order of Sion lost patience with the Templars, and broke with them. The Order now changed its name to the Priory of Sion. One of the major aims of the Priory was the restoration of the Merovingians to the throne of France. When the Templars were destroyed in 1307, the Priory continued to exist, no doubt because it was such a well-kept secret.

This could well explain why Louis XIV was anxious to get rid of Fouquet and to acquire Poussin's painting. If the 'secret that kings could not draw from him' was the secret of the Priory of Sion, Louis may well have been worried. His uncle, Gaston d'Orléans, had been married to the Duke of Lorraine's sister, and there was an attempt to depose Gaston's elder brother, Louis XIII, in favour of Gaston, which would have meant that Merovingian blood would once again have flowed in the veins of the kings of France.

The attempt failed. But since Louis XIII was childless, it looked very much as if Gaston would nevertheless inherit the throne. Then, to everyone's amazement, Louis XIII produced a son – at least his wife, Anne of Austria, did. Many people believed that Cardinal Richelieu was the true father, or perhaps that he employed a 'stud', who some suggest was Richelieu's captain of musketeers, François Dauger, thus frustrating the designs of the Merovingians and the Priory of Sion.

François Dauger had two sons, called Louis and Eustache, and many people commented on their resemblance to Louis XIV, which would be understandable if, in fact, they were his half-brothers. Eustache was a ne'er-do-well, always in trouble. Both Louis and Eustache were eventually arrested, Louis for an affair of the heart, Eustache for general hellraising, but Louis was released and continued to rise in the world. Eustache disappeared, and may well have been the Man in the Iron Mask. (It was actually a velvet mask, and if indeed Eustache was the mystery prisoner, he may have been forced to wear it because of his resemblance to the king.) His offence may have been an attempt to blackmail the king – 'Release my brother or else . . .' – or he may have got involved with the Priory of Sion and the Merovingians, who would have been delighted to learn that Louis XIV had no right to be on the throne.

The Habsburgs were also members of the House of Lorraine, and therefore prime candidates for membership of the Priory of Sion, which sheds further light on the facts that one of Saunière's guests was Johann von Habsburg and that Saunière received money from Austria. It sounds as if his visit to St Sulpice introduced him to people who were willing to share their secret and give him generous financial support as the present incumbent of Dagobert's ancient stronghold . . .

This complex and fascinating story has another twist. Lincoln learned from the retired clergyman that the 'real treasure' was the knowledge that Jesus did not die on the cross, and this knowledge came from St Sulpice. If St Sulpice was the Paris headquarters of the Priory of Sion, then it may well be that Saunière's secret – the secret that shocked the priest who attended his deathbed – was that Jesus had not died on the cross, and therefore the Christian Church had been built on foundations of sand, since it was based on the notion that Jesus died to save man from the burden of original sin.

When Lincoln was working on the BBC programme *The Shadow of the Templars*, he was suddenly struck by a startling thought. He and two researchers, Richard Leigh and Michael Baigent, were joking about a legend that the mother of King Merovec, the founder of the Merovingian line, had been impregnated by a sea creature, and one of them joked that the story sounded 'fishy'. Suddenly Lincoln and Leigh looked at one another as they were seized with the same suspicion. Fish – the symbol of Christianity. Could the legend mean that the lady had been impregnated by . . . a symbol of Christianity, a direct descendant of Jesus?

The Merovingian kings claimed that they reigned 'by right of blood' – royal blood – not by being anointed by the Church. Was the bloodline that they were so proud of that of Jesus himself? In which case, who was Jesus's wife? In the village of Les Saintes Maries de la Mer, a yearly ceremony celebrates the arrival of Mary Magdalen in France, bearing the True Cross and the Holy Grail. The church in Rennes-le-Château is dedicated to her and has two statues of her carrying the cross and the Grail. Saunière built a library called the Tour Magdala – the Magdalen Tower. Mystics of the Middle Ages identified her with the planet Venus – the goddess of love.

Lincoln and Leigh were led to speculate that Jesus and Mary Magdalen had come to France and founded the bloodline of the Merovingians. Perhaps the tomb that Poussin painted was, in fact, the tomb of Jesus? It was this extraordinary speculation – and Lincoln insists that it is merely a speculation – that made *The Holy Blood and the Grail* (1982)[10] by Lincoln, Leigh and Baigent an instant bestseller.

By now Lincoln had learned, through the detective work of a BBC researcher, that the most important living member of the Priory of Sion was a man called Pierre Plantard. Plantard was indeed the name of a noble family of the Merovingian line. A meeting was arranged, and Lincoln invited Plantard to view the second Rennes-le-Château film, *The Priest, the Painter and the Devil*. He proved to be a kindly and courteous gentleman – born in 1920 – and a group of his followers were present. The closest seemed to be a marquis named Philip de Cherisey. Lincoln was to learn that de Cherisey was responsible for much of the *Secret Dossier* deposited in the Louvre.

Sitting behind them, Lincoln was pleased to observe that they became suddenly attentive when the film showed an image of one of the parchments, in which Lincoln had detected the form of a pentagram, a figure made by joining the points of a five-pointed star.

The pentagram is, of course, one of the most ancient magical symbols. I was once advised to draw one (mentally) on my gatepost if I wanted to deter unwelcome visitors – it had to be upside-down. Upright it is supposed to keep evil at bay; upside-down (like a man standing on his head) it is supposed to attract sinister forces.

What is its origin? No one is sure, although it played an important part in the geometry of Pythagoras. One of the most convincing explanations involves the planet Venus. If we imagine the earth as the centre of the solar system (as the ancients believed), it becomes obvious that there will be moments when every planet will be 'eclipsed' by the sun as it comes between the planet and the earth. Mercury, for example, is 'eclipsed' three times a year, and if we draw lines between these three points in the heavens they form an irregular triangle. Mars is 'eclipsed' four times, and the figure is an irregular rectangle. In fact, all the planets make irregular figures, except Venus, which makes a regular pentacle. If, as we have argued in this book, the ancients were studying the heavens much earlier than anyone supposed, it seems probable that Venus was associated with the pentagram at a very early date.[11]

In addition to the hidden pentagram (which was not a

234

regular one) in one of the parchments, Lincoln also noticed something odd about the geometry of Poussin's *Les Bergers d'Arcadie*. Looking for the 'secret' that seems to have alarmed Louis XIV, he noticed that the staff of the shepherd on the right is neatly cut in two by the shepherd's arm, and the distance from the top of the staff to the shepherd's pointed finger is precisely this same 'half measure'. He soon noticed other 'half measures' throughout the painting. The picture had obviously been designed geometrically. He showed the painting to Professor Christopher Cornford, of the Royal College of Art, who found something even more fascinating.

When Cornford reported to Henry Lincoln on *Les Bergers d'Arcadie*, he explained that he began by looking for one of two 'systems' in constant use by classical painters. One is a number system, based on Plato's *Timaeus* (a dialogue about the creation of the universe), which became highly influential in the Renaissance. The other is a far older system, a geometry based on the Golden Section. Cornford expected to find the *Timaeus* system in Poussin's painting, because the Golden Section system was then regarded as extremely old-fashioned, and in fact he did find traces of it. But the basic system used in *Les Bergers d'Arcadie* is the Golden Section. The painting is also full of pentagonal geometry.

Consider the following pentagram drawn in a circle:

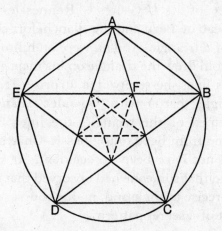

A pentagram is the quintessential golden section geometric figure. In the diagram EF is a phi ratio of EB, and CF is a phi ratio of CA.

When Cornford looked more closely, he could draw a pentagram that *went outside* the painting.

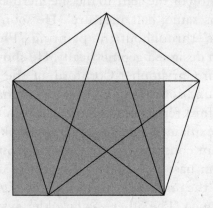

In short, the pentacle was encoded into Poussin's painting.

That led Cornford to make an interesting suggestion. Could the phrase 'Poussin holds the key . . .' be anything to do with the landscape around Rennes-le-Château, which is where Saunière searched for the treasure? This led Lincoln to one of his most important discoveries. When he looked at a map of the Rennes-le-Château region, one thing was immediately obvious: three of its key sites – Rennes-le-Château, the Templar château of Bezu and the Blanchefort château – were three points of a triangle. And all were on hilltops.

When Lincoln drew the triangle on his map, and proceeded to measure its lines, he received a surprise. It was a precise isosceles triangle, that is, with two sides *exactly equal*. With Bezu at the apex of the triangle, the lines from Bezu to Blanchefort and from Bezu to Rennes-le-Château were equal.

This could not have been an accident. At some point in time, it seemed that someone had observed that the three hilltops made a precise triangle and, in due course, they had been chosen as part of a secret pattern.

236

Lincoln found himself wondering if, by any remote chance, there were two more hilltops that would form the rest of a pentagram. Of course, he felt, that would be asking too much . . . yet when he studied the map, he was staggered to find that there *were* two such hilltops, in precisely the right places. The eastern one was called La Soulane, and the western one Serre de Lauzet. When the five hilltops were joined up, they formed an exact pentacle.

There was one more surprise to come. When Lincoln looked for the centre of the map, he found that it was marked by another hill, called La Pique. Although its summit looked on the map like the dead centre, it was actually 250 yards to the south-east of centre, but that was to be expected – after all, this was not a man-made landscape.

So this was the basic secret of Rennes-la-Château: that it was part of a sacred landscape. Perhaps this is why Rennes-le-Château was chosen by Dagobert as his home and why his son Sigisbert fled there after his father's murder. The royal blood of the Merovingians was associated with a *magic landscape*.

Rand had first become intrigued by Rennes after reading *The Holy Blood and the Holy Grail*. It states that a few miles east of Rennes-le-Château lie the ruins of the Château of Blanchefort, ancestral home of Bertrand de Blanchefort, fourth Grand Master of the Knights Templar, who presided over the order in the mid-twelfth century.

It seems that Blanchefort 'commissioned certain mysterious excavations' in the mountain where his château stood, all under conditions of the greatest secrecy. In 1156 a contingent of German miners arrived to work the mountain, apparently for gold, but there couldn't possibly have been any gold left in the mountain of Blanchefort, as the Romans had exhausted the mines centuries earlier.[12] And they were 'forbidden to fraternise in any way with the local population and were kept strictly segregated from the surrounding community'. Lincoln hints that something else in the area had attracted the Grand

Master. Rand naturally wondered if it might have anything to do with his blueprint of sacred sites.

He wrote: 'I agree with Lincoln's conclusion that the complexity of Rennes-le-Château is evidence that ". . . the ancient surveyors . . . have left us the empirical reality of their amazing labours. They have left us the evidence of their skills and knowledge which, through many long centuries, has been lost and forgotten."[13] This dovetails with everything we've discovered about the Atlantis Blueprint.'

Lincoln also notes the importance of the Golden Section in the whole Rennes complex and links it to the planet Venus. He argues that the reason Venus is so widely worshipped in world mythology is because its orbit appears pentagonal to us on earth. The pentagon is the geometric figure that most conclusively registers the Golden Section. 100,000 years ago, during the Yukon Pole, Rennes was located at a Golden Section division of a line drawn from pole to pole.

It was not alone. Nanking, China, also fits this pattern exactly. The surprising fact is that both linkages occur only during the Yukon Pole. Nor is this the only connection between ancient Celts and China. In *Uriel's Machine*, Lomas and Knight examine the research of archaeologist Dr Elizabeth Wayland Barber, whose book *The Mummies of Urumchi* is a study of the mummified remains of several Caucasians found in the Chinese region of Xinjiang. Barber discovered plaid material with the mummies. She wrote: 'Not only does this woollen plaid look like Scottish tartans but it also has the same weight, feel and initial thickness as a kilt cloth.'[14]

Lomas and Knight comment:

Barber acknowledges that two unrelated people could come up with the same twill weave, plaids and tartans, but when she considered all the factors which had coincided, she was quite firm in her conclusion: It rules out coincidence. It seems certain, then, that these people had a direct connection with the population of the British Isles who also wove plaid and tartans, the people we now call the Celts.[15]

In *The New View Over Atlantis*, John Michell also makes the connection between the ancient Celts and China:

In China until recently, as long ago in Britain, every building, every stone and wood, was placed in the landscape in accordance with a magic system by which the laws of mathematics and music were expressed in the geometry of the earth's surface. The striking beauty and harmony of every part of China, which all travellers have remarked, was not produced by chance. Every feature was contrived. Where nature had placed two hills in discord, Chinese geomancers had the shape of one altered.[16]

The fact that Rennes-le-Château and Nanking are both located at a Golden Section division of the pole-to-pole distance is further support that either the Celts and Chinese shared knowledge, or, more likely, that their separate traditions are derived from a common source.

My own favourite story about Rand's researches concerns a pyramid, not in Egypt or Mexico, but in China.

In the summer of 1997, Rand was thinking about the Hudson Bay Pole and the orientation of Mexican religious sites to it. At this time, he heard from Laura Lee, friend and radio interviewer whose Seattle-based show is broadcast internationally, that the German writer Hartwig Hausdorf was going to appear on her programme to talk about ancient pyramids in China. Rand had no idea that there were pyramids in China.

Hausdorf, the author of *The Chinese Roswell*, had been influenced by Erich von Däniken's 'ancient astronaut' theory, and had travelled in China, Tibet and Mongolia searching for evidence of aliens visiting earth in the remote past. Hausdorf explained on the radio programme how, in the spring of 1945, an American air force pilot named James Gaussman was returning from Chungking when engine trouble forced him to a low altitude near Xian, in Shansi province. Directly below him he saw a white pyramid of 'colossal size'. He took some photographs, although these would not be published for another forty-five years. Two years later, in 1947, a pilot named Maurice Sheahan caught a glimpse of another enormous pyramid when he was flying over Shansi province, and again took pictures. Although these were published in the *New York Times* and other newspapers in March 1947, Chinese archaeologists denied that China had any pyramids.[17]

In 1962, a New Zealand airline pilot named Bruce Cathie was also informed by the Chinese that there were no pyramids in China. He was nevertheless able to confirm the existence of several of them, and in a book called *The Bridge of Infinity*[18] suggested that there are a network of pyramids over the surface of the earth whose purpose is connected with ley lines and earth energies. (His views have something in common with those of Christopher Dunn.)

In March 1994, Hausdorf succeeded in getting permission to visit Xian, a former imperial capital that is regarded as the cradle of Chinese civilisation. (Emperor Qin Shihuang, who built the Great Wall, has a tomb there, surrounded by 10,000 life-size terracotta soldiers.) He saw a number of pyramids on the plain, but they were not 1,000 feet high, as Gaussman had reported, only about 200 feet high, less than half the height of the Great Pyramid. They were flat-topped, and made of clay baked to the consistency of stone. Trees and other vegetation had been planted on them. Hausdorf realised that he was standing in a kind of crater at the top, suggesting that a chamber had collapsed.

On two subsequent visits, Hausdorf examined sixteen pyramids, and he claims to have counted a hundred. Professor Wang Zhijun, director of the Banpo Museum, who discussed

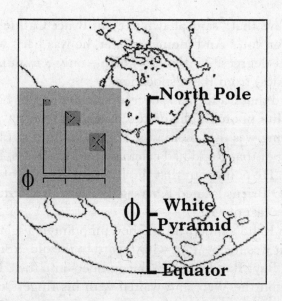

The so-called 'White Pyramid' of China is located at a Golden
Section division of the North Pole and equator distance.

them with him, seemed to feel that they might be part of a
sacred system of feng shui lines, a Chinese variation of leys.
The professor estimated that they dated from about 2,500 BC –
the time of the pyramids of Giza. Hausdorf was unable to
visit the White Pyramid of Xian himself, and admitted that he
was not sure of its existence.

Rand was investigating phi sites when he heard about the
White Pyramid. He found the city of Xian, in Shansi
province, in his *Times Atlas*, but had no idea how far away the
White Pyramid might be. As a speculation, he wondered if it
might be a phi distance from the pole, and worked out that this
should be 3,337.2 nautical miles, which would be 34 degrees,
23 minutes north.

A few days later, he rang Shawn Montgomery in Toronto to
talk about his latest investigations. He mentioned the White
Pyramid, and his difficulty finding its precise coordinates.

'Oh, I have that,' said Shawn. 'It's in Bruce Cathie's book. I'll get it for you.' And moments later, he was back with the location: 34 degrees, 26 minutes north – only 3 minutes (or 3 nautical miles) from Rand's location.

It seemed that Cathie had succeeded in getting his hands on some satellite photographs of the pyramids. What was even more exciting was that there was, in fact, another pyramid on the exact spot that Rand had calculated – 34 degrees, 23 minutes north. He points out that the Lebanese village of Ehdin, where the O'Briens located Kharsag, is also at this latitude and is 5 degrees east of Giza.

So again Rand's blueprint method pinpointed a sacred site.

But what was its location with regard to the old North Pole in Hudson Bay? Rand plugged the numbers into the 'How Far Is It?' site on the Web, and waited with his fingers crossed. When the answer appeared on the screen, he gave a chortle of delight. During the Hudson Bay Pole, the White Pyramid was at 5 degrees north, precisely the same latitude as Byblos, a city sacred to both the Egyptians and the Phoenicians.

Rand's email describing his find ended: 'It seems to me that the very position of the Chinese pyramids suggests an advanced knowledge of the earth's dimensions, coupled with an ability to determine these distances within very small margins of error.'

What is even more significant is that people in China had possessed this knowledge of the surface of the globe at a time when, according to historians, it was completely isolated from the rest of the world.

Rand told me his reason for searching for Golden Section sites:

The Golden Section is something that is consistent anywhere in the universe no matter what the number system (base 10, 12, 60 etc.). If an advanced civilisation was trying to make contact with future peoples they could never be sure that their weights and measures would be exactly the same as the ones that evolved long after they had perished.

Two things, however, would never change: the dimensions of the earth and the geometry of the Golden Section. The distance from the equator to the pole will always be the same no matter what number system you use and you will always be able to divide this distance by the Golden Section.

The geometry of Rennes-le-Château is, as we have seen, pentagonal, and pentagonal geometry is, as Lincoln points out, linked with phi, the Golden Section. Did this mean that the Rennes-le-Château site was 100,000 years old? Almost certainly not, since its pentagonal geometry is natural, not man-made. But Rand's blueprint theory suggests that Enoch's 'angels' (i.e., geologists), making their survey at the time of the Hudson Bay Pole, recognised that Rennes-le-Château was one of the most unusual sites in the world, not only because its geometry was pentagonal, reflecting the Golden Section, but also because it had been at a Golden Section site at the time of the Yukon Pole. It would certainly have deserved one of their 'markers', upon which later generations would build their sacred sites.

Other sacred sites match this pattern. Abydos, the 'birthplace of Osiris', Cuzco, in the Andes, and Nippur, the holiest Sumerian city, were all located at the equator during the Yukon Pole but must have been constructed only a few thousand years ago. Rennes-le-Château is in good company, but differs in one critical respect: being centred on a natural pentacle, it would inevitably be regarded as sacred.

This, then, was Rand's reason for including Rennes-le-Château in the blueprint; Lincoln's *Key to the Sacred Pattern* confirmed that it is one of the most remarkable sites in our book, a natural 'magic landscape'.

Oddly enough, M. Plantard refused to confirm Lincoln's insight. Although it was obvious that he and Cherisey were startled that Lincoln had discovered the pentagonal geometry in the Saunière parchments, Plantard would simply not enlarge. On the contrary, when Lincoln asked him about the hidden codes, Plantard made the incredible remark that the parchments were 'confections' concocted by his friend Cherisey for a ten-minute television film made some years previously.[19] Quite rightly, Lincoln refused to swallow this. The incredible complexity of the code left no doubt that it had taken a very long time and a great deal of skill to prepare.

There seems little doubt that it was the original aim of Plantard – and the 'Priory' – to bring this mystery to public attention. De Sède originally told Lincoln: 'We hoped it might interest someone like you.'[20] Yet now Lincoln had got his teeth into the subject, and had discovered the pentagonal geometry, Plantard seemed to feel he had been *too* successful and wanted to backtrack.

If so, he must have been delighted with the reaction to Andrews and Schellenberger's book *The Tomb of God*. The thesis of that book was that the real secret of Rennes-le-Château was the location of the tomb of Jesus, at the foot of a mountain called Pech Cardou, 3 miles east of Rennes-le-Château. The BBC programme about the book was, to put it mildly, somewhat sceptical, and took the view that Plantard was an impostor, and that the whole Rennes-le-Château mystery was a hoax – a major change of viewpoint since Lincoln's original programmes.

After I had watched the merciless debunking on television, I commented to my wife: 'Well, that looks like the end of the Rennes-le-Château mystery.' But on reflection, I saw that this is not so. The programme might have shown – or set out to show – that the Priory of Sion was a recent invention, that the parchments were probably forgeries of de Cherisey, and that Plantard was probably an impostor, but that still left the mystery untouched. How had Saunière become rich overnight? What had he discovered in the Visigothic pillar? The more I thought of it, the more I saw that the essence of the mystery remained, whether M. Plantard was an impostor or not.

But was he an impostor? Lynn Picknett and Clive Prince

laid out the case against him in *The Templar Revelation*. He came to prominence in occupied Paris in 1942, as the Grand Master of a quasi-Masonic order called the Order Alpha-Galates, which was 'markedly uncritical' of the Nazis – in fact, the Nazis seemed to approve of it. But then, they would have; part of Himmler's job was to establish that the Germans had a noble origin in the remote days of the Norse sagas and to create a modern mystical order with its roots in the Aryan past. Pierre Plantard, whom Picknett and Prince describe as 'a one-time draughtsman for a stove-fitting firm, who allegedly had difficulty paying the rent from time to time', then changed his name to Pierre Plantard de Saint-Clair. He played an important part in bringing about the return to power of General de Gaulle in 1958. In 1956, the Priory of Sion had begun depositing 'enigmatic documents' in the Bibliothèque Nationale. The implication was that these documents had been concocted as part of the 'hoax'.

In writing this chapter, I have reread Lincoln's four books – *The Holy Blood and the Holy Grail*, *The Messianic Legacy* (both with Leigh and Baigent), *The Holy Place* and *Key to the Sacred Pattern* – have studied again his television programmes on Saunière and the Priory, and reread such books as Picknett and Prince's *The Templar Relevation*, David Wood's *Genisis*[21] and Lionel and Patricia Fanthorpe's *The Holy Grail Revealed*.[22] And I can see no reason whatever for believing that the Priory of Sion is some kind of hoax, or that Pierre Plantard is not exactly who he says he is.

Lincoln himself certainly felt doubts; he describes, in *The Messianic Legacy*,[23] how he and his co-authors went along to see Plantard in Paris with the specific intention of confronting him with some major contradictions, including two apparently discrepant birth certificates, one of which named him as 'Plantard' and the other as 'Plantard de Saint-Clair'. Plantard, far from being embarrassed, answered each point with precise explanations: the birth certificate that gave his name simply as Plantard and also the profession of his father as a '*valet de chambre*' was explained as the substitution of falsified information to deceive the Gestapo, which was common during the war. When Lincoln and his friends went to the Mairie to confront officials with this explanation, they readily agreed with Plantard.

Lincoln – and I in turn – concluded that Plantard really was Plantard de Saint-Clair, and that there is every probability that the story of the Priory of Sion is true, from its inception in 1090 to Jean Cocteau and Plantard. (In *The Shadow of the Templars*, Lincoln filmed inside the church of Nôtre Dame de France, near Leicester Square in London, which has a mural of the crucifixion by Cocteau, pointing out the irrelevant rose at the foot of the cross – symbol of the Templars – and other evidence that Cocteau was indeed a member of the Priory of Sion.)

Lincoln himself writes an introduction to one of the oddest, but most interesting, books about Rennes-le-Château, *Genisis*, by David Wood, who had made another curious discovery in the area: five churches (including Rennes-le-Château) fell on an exact circle. Wood found that these were connected by a pentacle geometry. Lincoln writes (in *Key to the Sacred Pattern*): 'It was now clear that my discovery of the Pentacle of Mountains was but the first glimpse of something much more complex. Here was proof that there had been a conscious and highly skilled geometric plan . . .' Oddly enough, Wood ignored the pentacle of mountains discovered by Lincoln.

Wood's book – and its sequel *Geneset*[24] – are certainly impressive and ingenious, but his solution of the 'mystery' has more in common with Zechariah Sitchin than with Lincoln's painfully precise investigations. He finds a number code that points to the gods of ancient Egypt, and in a 'fairy story' printed as an epilogue to *Genisis* outlines his conclusions: 200,000 years ago, a super-race from the Sirius system came to our solar system in three huge space ships and colonised Mars. This super-race was called – the Elohim.

Since water was scarce on Mars, they used earth as their 'farm', although its gravity was too high for their comfort. They created humanoid beings called Set, Osiris, Isis and Nephtys and an undersized 'runt' called Horus, and also a less intelligent type of creature called 'Watchers'. The base they made on earth was an island called Atlantis. They also created two subordinate (and even less intelligent) species called the Cains and the Seths, and cloned animals for their food. The supervisors – Osiris, Isis, etc. – were naturally regarded by these subordinates as gods.

Against the specific instructions of the Elohim, Isis created more of these subordinate creatures to reduce the workload of the Seths and Cains, and the experiment soon got out of hand. The Nephilim, who had been chosen to do the work of impregnating the female 'apes', found that they so enjoyed it that they began to do it on the sly, producing hideous malformed hybrids. At this point, the Elohim decided to wipe out most of the population of the earth with a comet, which caused havoc and destroyed Atlantis. Finally, with the help of the Egyptian 'gods', the survivors created the beginnings of the civilisation we know today . . .

Understandably, Lincoln wanted nothing to do with this speculative mythology, and decided not to endorse it, yet he had no doubt that some of Wood's geometrical discoveries were valid. Moreover, he was fascinated by Wood's discovery that the English mile, not the kilometre (as one would expect), had been used as the unit of measurement by whoever originally designed the gigantic pentagram connecting the French churches. When he checked this against his own geometry, he discovered that Wood seemed to be correct.

In 1991, Lincoln had been contacted by a Danish television producer who had been born on the island of Bornholm. Erling Haagensen had become fascinated by Bornholm's fifteen churches, which dated from the thirteenth century (the time of the Knights Templar); they often seemed to be associated with ancient megaliths – in fact, some megaliths were actually built into the church walls. Lincoln had been toying with the idea that perhaps some of the Rennes-le-Château pattern had been laid out in megalithic times, and when Haagensen told him that the geometry he had identified on Bornholm was pentacular, Lincoln became convinced that they were each 'uncovering a different portion of the same mystery'.

Moreover, Haagensen had found the English mile present in the Bornholm geometry. For example, if Haagensen's geometry was correct, the distance between two of the churches, Ibsker and Povlsker, should be exactly 7 miles. And it was.

Why the mile? In a chapter called 'The Measure', Lincoln lays out some curious but highly convincing facts. The French metre, which came into use in 1791, was one-10,000,000th of the distance from the North Pole to the equator. Lincoln shows that an old English measure called the rod, pole or perch (which is one-320th of a mile) is also, in a more primitive version which Lincoln calls the Cromlech Pole (198.41874 inches) a precise measure of the earth's surface: 1 Cromlech Pole multiplied by itself (i.e., squared) is 1 kilometre (39,370 inches), When this ancient pole (198 inches) is multiplied by 1.618, phi, using the Golden Section, the result is 320, the number of poles in 1 mile. So there is a mathematical connection between the British pole and the kilometre, and between the pole, multiplied by phi, and the mile.

Rand had emphasised again and again that the Golden Section is one of the most important keys to his geometry of sacred sites. He notes: 'I found that one of the Bornhold churches was 16:18 west of the Great Pyramid. This church (at Vestermarie) is supposed to have been built on top of a megalithic monument. During the Yukon Pole it joined Avebury, Stonehenge, London and others at latitude 30N.'

If the blueprint theory is correct, Rennes-le-Château and the pyramids of China were part of a worldwide web of religious sites. It also seems that whoever arranged the specific positioning of the sites was aware of the earlier crust movements that preceded the Hudson Bay Pole.

Rand was also intrigued by an underwater site off the most westerly point of Japan. He writes:

> In 1987, a scuba-diving instructor named Kihachiro Aratake was exploring the southern waters off the island of Yonaguni when he encountered a sight that left him breathless. Beneath the waters of the island lay a structure that seemed man-made. The ramifications of this discovery, if true, would force us to rewrite Asian prehistory. This is precisely what Professor Masaaki Kimura, a marine seismologist from the University of Ryukyus in Okinawa, believes must be done. He took up the case of the Yonaguni 'pyramid' in 1990 and has been a champion of its authenticity ever since. Joining him, and enthusiastically endorsing his views, are Graham Hancock and Santha Faiia.[25]
>
> On the other side of the fence are those researchers such as John Anthony West and Robert Schoch, who believe that the structure beneath the water is a freak of nature, a natural formation. Professor Kimura counters these arguments by pointing to a 'wall' at the western edge of the monument which contains limestone blocks that aren't indigenous to the island.
>
> Although he continues to believe that this is a natural anomaly, Schoch notes: 'Yonaguni Island contains a number of old tombs whose exact age is uncertain, but that are clearly very old. Curiously, the architecture of those tombs is much like that of the monument.'[26]

Rand's blueprint makes him think that Yonaguni is a significant sacred site because it was located at the all important 10 phi latitude during the Yukon Pole, thus joining, Nanking, Rennes-le-Château and Rosslyn Chapel at a golden section division of the Yukon Pole.

But, as we will see, the 'blueprint' shows that many sites can be aligned not only to the Hudson Bay Pole but also to the much older Yukon Pole. This might suggest a tradition that extends back at least 100,000 years.

Although Rand believes that, since modern humans have been around for more than 100,000 years, the idea of a 100,000-year-old civilisation is a possibility, he thinks it far more possible that the links to the Yukon Pole were established by scientists using geological evidence before the flood, about 12,000 years ago.

In other words, just as Charles Hapgood had used applied geology in the 1950s to determine the position of earlier poles, so also might the Atlantean 'surveyors' have discovered the former latitudes of the Yukon Pole and placed their bases where these intersected with the Hudson Bay Pole (which was 'their' pole immediately before the flood).

Henry Lincoln cites a remarkable book called *Historical Metrology* (1953)[27] by a master engineer named A.E. Berriman, an erudite volume covering ancient Egypt, Babylon, Sumer, China, India, Persia and many other cultures. It begins with the question 'Was the earth measured in remote antiquity?' and sets out to demonstrate that indeed it was. It argues that ancient weights and measures were derived from measuring the earth – which, of course, means in turn that ancient people had already measured the earth.

The book must have struck Berriman's contemporaries as hopelessly eccentric. He says that one measure was a fraction of the earth's circumference, that a measure of land area (the acre) was based on a decimal fraction of the square of the earth's radius, and that certain weights were based on the density of water and of gold. It sounds almost as if Berriman is positing the existence of some ancient civilisation that vanished without a trace, except for these ancient measures.

This, of course, is consistent with Hapgood's comment that history does not necessarily proceed steadily in a forward direction; it might pause, or even backtrack. This might also be the basis of his strange assertion about a science that dates back 100,000 years.

Henry Lincoln had established contact with a Norwegian, Harald Boehlke, who had also made some strange discoveries about Norwegian distances. Norway was pagan until 1,000 years ago. With the coming of Christianity, scattered trading posts disappeared and gave way to larger centres which became cities. Boehlke's researches seemed to establish that these new cities – Oslo, Trondheim, Bergen, Stavangar, Hamar, Tonsberg – were placed in what looked like quite arbitrarily chosen spots, for example, Oslo is in what was simply a backwater, while no one has the slightest idea why Stavangar was chosen as a cathedral town. But distances seem chosen for some mathematical reason: Oslo to Stavangar, 190 miles; Oslo to Bergen, 190 miles; Tonsberg to Stavangar, 170 miles; Tonsberg to Halsnoy, 170 miles; and so on. Moreover, the position of the old monasteries again shows a pentagonal geometry. It looks as if the Church was using some secret geometrical knowledge in creating the new Christian Norway.

Lincoln also identified a 'church measure' of 188 metres, and appealed in a French magazine for further examples of it, as well as of pentagonal geodesics. A mathematics teacher named Patricia Hawkins, who lived in France, was able to find no fewer than 162 'church measures' linking churches, hilltops and the roadside crucifixes called calvaries in the Quimper area of Brittany.

Lincoln begins the last chapter of *Key to the Sacred Pattern*:

We are confronting a mystery. The structured landscape of Rennes-le-Château and its association with the English mile (as well as the mile's apparent link with the dimensions of the Earth) are easily demonstrated, with a multitude of confirming instances. The measure and the geometry are evident. The patterns are repeatable. The designs are meaningful. All this was created in a remote past, upon which the phenomenon is shedding a new light.[28]

He pleads for historians and archaeologists to turn their attention to the evidence.

By 'patterns', Lincoln is not simply talking about the pentacle of mountains or the circle of churches. His own study of the Rennes-le-Château area revealed many patterns that could only have been created by deliberate intent. The 'holy place' of his title is 'the natural pentagon of mountains, and the artificial, structured Temple that was built to enclose it.'

I must admit that I only have to see a map covered with lines drawn all over it to groan and close the book, but Lincoln soon had me convinced. For example, he has a diagram centred on the church at Rennes-le-Château, with lines drawn from it to surrounding villages, churches and castles. Straight lines ran from some distant church or château, straight through the church at Rennes-le-Château and out the other side to another château or church.

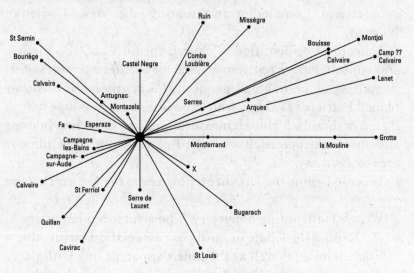

One of his most convincing discoveries is of a grid pattern. When lines were drawn connecting various sites, they were found to run parallel to one another – not only from left to right, but up and down. The lines were the same distance apart:

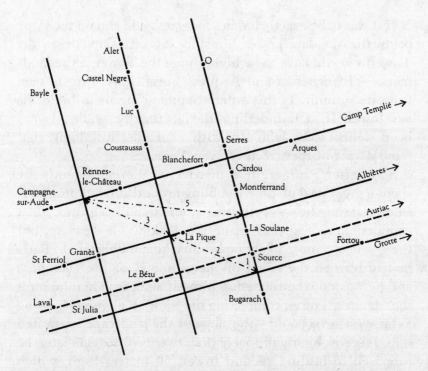

Moreover, the unit measure on this grid is the English mile – the point David Wood had also made about the geometry of the area. (Lincoln prints lists of distances that are in miles: for example, Rennes-le-Château to Bezu, precisely 4 miles; Rennes-le-Château to Soulane, precisely 4 miles.)

He also made a discovery that may throw a new light on Saunière's unexplained fortune. Many of his alignments went through the tower Saunière had built as his library, the Magdala Tower, which was placed as far to the west as Saunière could go – he built it on the edge of a sheer drop.

Furthermore, not long before his death in 1917, Saunière had commissioned another tower, 60 metres high. We do not know where it was to be located, but Lincoln points out that one of the most important alignments of the area is the 'sunrise line', which runs from Arques church, through Blanchefort, to Rennes-le-Château. This line was the one that first got Lincoln looking for English miles. It was *almost* 6 miles long.

253

If it was to be exactly 6 miles long, it would end on the slope below the Magdala Tower, but since it is on a slope below the Tower it would have to be higher than the Tower if the landmarks – Blanchefort and Arques church – were to be seen from its summit. Is this where Saunière meant to build his new tower? If so, it underlines the fact that the whole area has been deliberately laid out with a geometrical logic that reminds one of the streets of New York.

Soon after Saunière had discovered the parchments, he spent a great deal of time rambling around surrounding hillsides, claiming he was collecting stones to built a grotto. Most commentators suspect that he was looking for treasure, but there is now a more likely possibility: that on his trip to Paris he had learned the secret of the geometry of the 'Temple', and he was now familiarising himself with it. Then he built the Magdala Tower, completing the 'sunrise' alignment, going as far west as he could – the slope of the landscape frustrated him. It seems highly probable that, twenty-five years later, he prepared to build a second tower, 60 metres high, which would complete the 'sunrise line'. It sounds as if Saunière's discovery of the parchments led to his being appointed custodian of the 'Temple', with the money that went with that role.

What Lincoln has done, with his thirty-year investigation of Rennes-le-Château, is to demonstrate the existence of some ancient science of earth measurement. Since medieval times, this science seems to have been in the custody of the Church (and we must naturally suspect the involvement of the Templars), but Lincoln is inclined to believe that it may be far older – dating back to the age of the megaliths. This immediately reminds us of Alexander Thom and his 'Stone Age Einsteins', while Rand's evidence suggests that we may be looking at dates thousands of years before Stonehenge or Carnac.

Berriman seems to be making the same point in *Historical Metrology*. His argument that prehistoric measurement was geodetic in origin – that is, was derived from the size of the earth – is powerfully expanded at the very beginning of Chapter 1.

He points out that although the Greeks did not know the size of the earth, the earth's circumference happens to be precisely 216,000 Greek stade (the Greek stade is 600 Greek feet, and the Greek foot is 1.0125 times as long as the English foot).

If we want to find out how many Greek stades there are to one degree of the earth's circumference, we divide 216,000 stade by the 360 degrees in a circle, and the answer, significantly, turns out to be 600 – the same as the number of feet in a stade.

If we then divide by 60 – to get the number of stade in 1 minute of the circumference – we get 10 stade. Change this to Greek feet – 6,000 – and divide again by 60, to find the number of Greek feet in 1 second, and we see that it is precisely 100.

This simply cannot be chance. Distances do not normally work out in neat round figures. It is obvious that (a) the Greeks took their stade from someone else, and (b) that someone else knew the exact size of the earth. Berriman is full of these puzzling facts – for example, the area of the great bath of Mohenjo Daro, in the Indus Valley, is 100 square yards.

Here is another curiosity: the Romans had a land measure called a jugerum, which is five-eighths of an English acre (as the French metre is five-eighths of an English mile) and exactly 100 square English 'poles'. Again, we are faced with the idea that ancient measures are not dependent on the whim of some ancient king's land surveyor, but on a tradition stretching back into the dim past, *and based on an exact knowledge of the size of the earth.*

Lincoln has an amusing but fascinating speculation about this 'English connection'. Early in his investigation into Rennes-le-Château, he went to the Bibliothèque Nationale with Gérard de Sède, who suggested he should request a book called *Le Vraie Langue Celtique* (*The True Celtic Tongue*)[27] by the Abbé Henri Boudet, priest of nearby Rennes-le-Bains and a close friend of Saunière.

255

In fact, there is strong evidence that Boudet was Saunière's paymaster. Plantard's grandfather visited Boudet in 1892, and Boudet not only passed on more than 3.5 million gold francs to Saunière (or rather, to Saunière's housekeeper, Marie Denardaud), but more than 7.5 million gold francs to Bishop Billard, the man who appointed Saunière and who was obviously in on the secret. Since a gold franc was worth thirty-five modern francs and there are about nine francs to the pound sterling, Saunière received more than the equivalent of £13 million (over $20 million) and his bishop more than twice that amount.

Lincoln was able to obtain Boudet's book, and found it baffling as well as funny. Boudet seemed to think that the original language of mankind before the Tower of Babel was English – or rather, Celtic. This part of Boudet's book Lincoln describes as 'linguistic tomfoolery', and since Boudet was known to be an intelligent man Lincoln suspects he had his tongue in his cheek. But the volume developed into something far more interesting as he went on to discuss the complex megalithic structures of the area. The subtitle of the book is *The Cromlech of Reines-les-Bains* – a cromlech is a megalith made up of a large flat stone resting on two upright stones, rather like a huge dining table.

It looks as if Boudet's job was simply to hint at the mystery of the whole area, and imply that it dated back to megalithic times, but Lincoln is also inclined to suspect that his intention was also to tell his reader that one major key to the secret of the area lies in English – perhaps in English measures, such as the English mile. Was Boudet hinting that the original measures of mankind are English – such as the mile?

In summary, the Rennes-le-Château area certainly qualifies as one of Rand's sacred sites. It differs from all the others in being centred on a natural pentacle. Lincoln is certain that it has been sacred for at least 1,000 years, for the 'temple' – consisting of churches, castles and villages – must have been designed at least 1,000 years ago. (Rand, of course, believes it was recognised as a sacred site during the Hudson Bay Pole.)

That raises an obvious question. The pentacular structure of the mountains of the area can only be seen from the air or on a good map, but we know that there were no good maps 1,000 years ago, except portolans, which covered the sea. Land maps were crude in the extreme. We have also seen Hapgood's evidence that there were maps – even of Antarctica before the ice – that dated from thousands of years before Christianity.

9

WHAT THE
TEMPLARS FOUND

IN MAY 1996, I was in Edinburgh with my wife; we had been invited to lunch by Graham Hancock's uncle, Jim Macaulay. In the bar of his golf club, he said, 'I'd like to take you to a special place this afternoon.'

'What is it?'

'It's called Rosslyn Chapel. It was built by a Templar in the mid-fifteenth century.' He reminded me that this date was more than a century after the Templars had been arrested by Philip the Fair. 'The French Templars were arrested in 1307. Many escaped to Scotland.'

My wife Joy is the historian in our family, and she asked Jim what was special about the place.

'Well, there's a sculpture of a corncob – about half a century before Columbus discovered America.'

By the time we arrived at the chapel we were expecting something quite unusual. We were not disappointed. To begin with, the style of Rosslyn was impressively Gothic. The ticket office was also a bookshop, and I bought a couple of pamphlets about Rosslyn, including Robert Brydon's *The*

Guilds, the Masons and the Rosy Cross.[1] I noticed that they also had for sale a book called *The Hiram Key*, by Christopher Knight and Robert Lomas. I had heard about it already – in fact, had been warned about it. My own book *From Atlantis to the Sphinx* was due to be published that weekend, but *Keeper of Genesis* by Robert Bauval and Graham Hancock had already appeared, and I had been told that *The Hiram Key*, on a related theme, was due out about the same time. Literary editors of newspapers might decide to review all three in the same article, and so cut down the amount of space available to each, so I considered *The Hiram Key* as a potential rival. But that didn't prevent me from buying a copy for Joy to read on the train.

Rosslyn turned out to be a very strange place, and Jim Macaulay was an excellent guide. This Christian chapel seemed to be half pagan. To begin with, its decoration seemed to be devoted to various kinds of vegetation, a riot of carved flowers and fruits, and, as Jim pointed out, the pagan figure known as the Green Man seemed to be everywhere. In mythology he represents the rebirth of vegetation every spring, and pagan festivals revolved around him. What was he doing in a Christian church?

In my book *Mysteries*,[2] written twenty years earlier, I had discussed the ancient religion of the moon goddess Diana, which had been driven out by Christianity yet had refused to die. An eccentric scholar named Margaret Murray had even suggested that witchcraft was really a religion based on this ancient worship of Diana, and that witch trials in which the Devil is described as having presided over a Witches' Sabbat were really pagan fertility rituals, presided over by a high priest dressed as the god Pan, with a goat's feet and horns.

I found myself wondering if William St Clair (or Sinclair, as it was spelled later), the man who had built Rosslyn, was as pious a Christian as he was supposed to be. There was obviously some mystery attached to the place. There could be no possible doubt about the representation of sweetcorn, or of the plant called aloes cactus, also a native of America, which looks rather like a lily and has a bitter flavour.

We left Rosslyn after a couple of hours, feeling oddly disturbed; there was definitely something peculiar about the place. Jim dropped us off at the train back to Glasgow, where I was lecturing that evening. On the journey, I began to read a book that Jim had lent me called *Time Stands Still*, by Keith Critchlow,[3] while Joy read *The Hiram Key*. I could see immediately why Jim had lent me the book. In *From Atlantis to the Sphinx*, I speculated about a civilisation that predated the 'Atlantis catastrophe', and at the beginning of *Time Stands Still* Critchlow speaks about Alexander Thom's investigations into ancient megaliths then goes on to talk about certain Babylonian clay tablets that had been consigned to a dusty shelf in the Plimpton Library in New York. Labelled 'Commercial Tablets', they had recently proved to contain some extremely interesting numbers: pairs of Pythagorean triplets, that is, numbers referring to Pythagorean triangles.

The simplest Pythagorean triangle, where the square on the hypotenuse equals the sum of the square on the other two sides, has sides of 3, 4 and 5 units. When squared, these numbers turn into 9, 16 and 25 – and, of course, 9 plus 16 equals 25. On these Babylonian tablets, only two of the three numbers were given. But these were enormous numbers, such as 12,709, 13,500 and 18,541. How did the Babylonians – or the Sumerians, who probably originated the numbers – manage to square numbers such as 18,541? Their number system was particularly crude, as complicated as Roman numerals. Critchlow concludes that 'actual numbers conveyed some sort of immediate perception of the general relationships existing between these numbers'.[4]

Some people – known as calculating prodigies – have this odd ability to do enormous sums in their heads. A five-year-old child named Benjamin Blyth, out walking with his father one morning, asked him what time it was and his father told him, 'Ten minutes to eight.' A hundred yards later, Benjamin said, 'In that case I have been alive . . .' and named the number of seconds, about 158 million. Back at home, his father did the calculation on paper, and said, 'No, you were wrong by 172,800 seconds.' 'No I wasn't,' said the child, 'you've forgotten two leap years.'[5]

Many of these calculating prodigies are very young, and their powers disappear as they grow up (Benjamin Blyth became a perfectly normal – that is, non-prodigious – adult). We cannot imagine such odd powers, but they obviously come naturally. Is it possible that our Sumerian – or even remoter – ancestors could somehow see these immense numbers in their heads as if they were in front of their noses? The psychiatrist Oliver Sacks mentions two mentally subnormal calculating twins in a New York psychiatric hospital, who saw a box of matches fall off a table, *and had counted them before they hit the floor*. Could the ancient people who created the Nineveh constant have been like that?

The Hiram Key is equally fascinating, and nothing if not controversial. It reinforced the suspicion in my mind that William St Clair may have been the guardian of some curious – and non-Christian – mystery.

Robert Lomas and Christopher Knight are both Freemasons, and I knew little about Freemasonry. I knew that Masons are believed to have started in the guilds of the Middle Ages, such as the stonemasons who built Chartres. With so much cathedral building going on, there was plenty of work for everybody, and stonemasons travelled from place to place, having a secret handshake by which they recognised one another.

Masonry began to reach the general consciousness in the mid-seventeenth century, when it seems to have been involved with the strange affair of the Rosicrucians. This began in 1614 with the publication of a pamphlet called *Fama Fraternitas* (or 'Fraternal Declaration') *of the Meritorious Order of the Rosy Cross*. This purported to describe the life of a fifteenth-century mystic-magician called Christian Rosenkreuz, who lived to be 106 and whose body was preserved – undecayed – in a mysterious tomb for the next 120 years. The pamphlet went on to invite all interested parties to join the Brotherhood, and told them that they only had to make their interest known (by word of mouth or in writing) and they would be 'contacted'. Hundreds of people published their willingness to join, but, as far as is known, no one ever received a reply.

The *Fama* was followed by two more 'Rosicrucian' works, the *Confessio* (1615), and a larger work called *The Chemical Wedding* (1616), which both increased the Rosicrucian fever. The author is believed to have been a Protestant theologian named Johann Valentin Andrae, who is most certainly the author of *The Chemical Wedding* although he denied writing the other two. He seems to have started as an idealistic young man who hoped to launch a new spiritual movement, since – like so many other people at that period – he felt that it was time for a new beginning.

It seems that in Scotland and in England an organisation that called itself the Freemasons came into being around 1640. The Catholic Church came to detest it, but in the early days – particularly in Scotland – there seemed to have been as many Catholics as Protestants in the organisation. Freemasonry was basically about the brotherhood of man. In *War and Peace* the hero, Peter Bezukhov, feels spiritually and emotionally drained, until he meets a Freemason who renews his faith in life. The Mason tells him: 'No one can attain to truth by himself. Only by laying stone on stone, with the cooperation of all, by the millions of generations from our forefather Adam to our own times, is that temple reared which will be a worthy dwelling place of the Great God.' He goes on to explain that the chief object of the order is the 'handing down of a great mystery, which has come down from the remotest ages'. Peter becomes a Mason by going through incredibly strange and complicated rituals that involve a symbolic death and rebirth, and he ends up feeling completely refreshed, 'as if he had come back from a long journey'. Mozart, of course, underwent the same rituals, and put them into *The Magic Flute*.

The implication of all this is that Freemasonry was a secret society whose purpose was to produce in its members the sense of a great religious conversion. It can be seen that it involves a certain paradox. Andrae wrote the Rosicrucian pamphlets as a kind of 'hoax' (as he himself later put it), yet he also intended to cause a spiritual revolution. Nietzsche said, 'The great man is the play actor of his own ideals.' Andrae hoped to create greatness by creating high ideals. Nevertheless, a cynic might say that Freemasonry was the unintended outcome of a hoax.

Knight and Lomas had a far more interesting and exciting view of Freemasonry. Modern Freemasons are inclined to believe that the curious ceremony of initiation – with a noose round the neck, a slipper on one foot and the other trouser-leg rolled up to the knee – and the incomprehensible questions and answers are pure invention. As Lomas and Knight studied the ceremonies involved in the thirty-three degrees of Masonry, they increasingly began to feel that its roots lie in the remote past – and not merely two or three centuries ago, but a thousand years or more. As their research project progressed, they quickly concluded that Freemasonry can trace its origins at least to the Knights Templar, and that the most interesting mystery is precisely what those original nine knights discovered below the Temple in Jerusalem.

Although the Templars were on the surface an organisation created by a few Crusaders in the hope of achieving power and influence, behind them lies a strong sense of particular knowledge, of possession of some secret tradition. Did Philip the Fair really destroy them simply because he wanted their wealth? Or did this motive happen to fit in with some other motive shared by the Church?

Again, if the Church persecuted the Templars simply because Philip persuaded Pope Clement V to help him seize their wealth, why did its hostility persist for so long? After all,

Philip had been regarded as an enemy of the Church (which excommunicated him) and that feeling must have been strengthened by his later demand that its centre of power should be moved from Rome to Avignon. The Templars, in fact, had been servants of the Pope. After Philip's death, you might expect a back-swing of sympathy for them, so why did the Church genuinely seem to detest them and to want to stamp them out like plague rats?

Lomas and Knight set out to try and uncover the origin of Freemasonry and began by rejecting the stonemason theory, on the grounds that there were no stonemasons' guilds in England. They mention the interesting fact that Solomon's Temple was not, as most of us naturally assume, some huge building covering many acres, but smaller than Solomon's harem, about the size of an ordinary church, say the size of Rosslyn Chapel. Turning their attention to the Templars, they conclude – as we did in the last chapter – that Hugh de Payens and his knights spent years excavating beneath the remains of the Temple, searching for something specific, something whose presence they suspected in advance.

For what? Lomas and Knight believe the knights found a treasury of ancient scrolls that had been deposited there before the destruction of the Temple by the Romans in AD 70. The scrolls were the scriptures and secret rituals of a Jewish religious community called the Essenes. When the Jewish revolt against the Romans broke out in AD 66, their books were hidden away in the Temple and in caves by the Dead Sea. The latter were discovered by an Arab shepherd in 1947, who took them home with him, and fortunately decided against using them as fire-lighters. They became famous worldwide as the Dead Sea Scrolls.

Lomas and Knight believe that the scrolls hidden in the Temple were even more important. Lomas speculates: 'They knew that they had found something of immense significance that was probably very holy, so they decided to get them translated . . . The man with the solution was Geoffrey

de St Omer, the second in charge to Huges de Payen . . .'
Geoffrey took some of the scrolls back to an old priest called
Lambert, now known as Lambert of St Omer. 'Today, one of
the most famous of all Lambert of St Omer's works is his
hasty copy of a drawing that depicts the Heavenly
Jerusalem.'

This drawing, made around 1120, shows the basic symbols
of Freemasonry five centuries before Freemasonry is supposed to have been founded. Moreover, the symbolism also
leaves Lomas and Knight in no doubt that the drawing originated in the Temple, and that it was one of the things found
by the Templars.

The notion of a Heavenly Jerusalem (or New Jerusalem),
they point out, was found in the Dead Sea Scrolls, based on
Ezekiel's vision. They conclude: 'With the discovery of the
Heavenly Jerusalem Scroll . . . we were now certain that the
Templars did find the secrets of their Order inscribed upon
the scrolls buried by the Nasoreans (or Essenes of
Qumran . . .)'

Unlike Graham Hancock, Lomas and Knight do not suggest that the scrolls contain the secret of Gothic architecture,
but they do argue that the tremendous explosion of cathedral
building all over Europe, and particularly in France (80 cathedrals and 500 abbeys), was the direct result of that vision of
the Heavenly Jerusalem the Templars brought back with them
from the remains of Solomon's Temple.

Lomas and Knight researched Palestine in the time of
Jesus, and their conclusions make it clear why the Templars
were later persecuted as heretics. Jesus was a member of the
sect known as the Essenes, whose 'lost scriptures' we know as
the Dead Sea Scrolls. The original Essenes were orthodox
Jews who disagreed with the teachings of the priests in control
of the Temple. In protest they withdrew to Qumran where
they lived strictly ascetic lives. Their leader was Jesus's
younger brother James, also known as the 'Teacher of
Righteousness.'

Both Jesus and his cousin John the Baptist were regarded by the Essenes as messiahs who were expected to lead the people in revolt against the Romans and establish the Kingdom of God. After the death of John the Baptist, Jesus became more radical, and spent the period of his year of ministry gathering followers. Convinced that the time for action had finally come, and that God would support the revolt, Jesus rode into Jerusalem on an ass, fulfilling the prophecy of Zachariah that the king would arrive on a donkey. He caused a riot in the Temple by attacking the money-lenders, then withdrew to the nearby village of Bethany to await the revolt that he believed would soon follow.

But there was to be no uprising, at least not yet. The Romans arrested Jesus and his brother James. Lomas and Knight believe that James was actually the character known as Barabbas (which is not a proper name, but a title meaning 'son of the father'). James was released; Jesus was crucified.

Afterwards, when the body of Jesus disappeared from his tomb, it gave rise to the story that Jesus had risen from the dead. The Essenes believed that this was a sign of the fulfil-ment of Jesus's mission as the Messiah. So Christianity was born.

The new religion was further transformed with the coming of Paul who, around AD 60, had a vision on the road to Damascus, and as a result became the chief exponent of a new kind of Christianity. It is important to note, Lomas and Knight point out, that this Damascus would not have been the Damascus in Syria, where Paul would have had no authority, but rather Qumran, which was also known as Damascus.

James and his followers must have been incredulous when their chief persecutor arrived at Qumran, declared himself a Christian, and began asking questions about James's brother Jesus. But their relief would later turn to rage when they heard the kind of 'Christianity' Paul was preaching – that Jesus had died on the cross as a scapegoat for the sins of mankind, and that anyone could become free of original sin by accepting

Jesus as the Son of God. The Qumran Christians began to refer to Paul as 'the spouter of lies'.

By a historical accident, it was Paul's version of Christianity that survived. The reason for the triumph of Christianity was entirely political. In AD 66 there was another Jewish revolt, prompted partly by the murder of James, who was thrown from the top of the Temple by the priests. It was at that point, Lomas and Knight believe, that the Qumranians decided to hide their scriptures until peace was restored. The less important ones were hidden in the Dead Sea caves. The more important ones were hidden in the Temple, where the Templars would find them eleven centuries later.

The revolt failed. The Roman general Vespasian stamped it out with incredible brutality, also destroying most of the 'Christians'. But by that time, Paul was abroad, preaching his own version of Christianity to the gentiles. And this, ironically, was the version that went on to conquer the world.

By AD 300 the Roman empire was falling to pieces, over-stretched by its conquests and its need for huge armies. The emperor Constantine had an inspiration. About one in ten of his subjects were Christians. If he made Christianity the religion of the Roman empire, he would have a supporter in every town and village, and a fellow emperor in every city large enough to have a bishop. (Constantine himself never became a Christian – he remained a worshipper of the sun god Sol Invictus.)

His solution worked, and Christianity held together the Roman empire for another two centuries. But by now the Christian Church had taken over the reins of power. Lomas and Knight quote Pope Leo X, a contemporary of Henry VIII, as saying: 'It has served us well, this myth of Christ'.

And now we can see the possible religious reasons why the Church was so anxious to destroy the Templars. They were the direct descendants of the Jerusalem Church of Qumran. They knew the truth about the original Christianity of the Essenes, how this had been hijacked by St Paul, and how this new version of Christianity had become the religion of the Roman Empire.

It is, perhaps, this horrible secret that was part of the deathbed confession that Beranger Saunière passed onto his priest. If so, then it is not surprising that the priest was so deeply shocked by what he heard.

Rand believes that the sensational find beneath the Temple had little to do with Jesus. He thinks that King Philip and his puppet, Pope Clement V, tried to destroy the Templars for strictly secular reasons. The King was jealous of their power and deeply in debt to the order. He used the charge of heresy as a ploy to cancel his debts and seize the Templar gold. He was not one to worry over theological issues but rather a passionate egoist who only wanted to fan the flames of his own glory. Religion was simply a weapon he wielded like a club to strike down those who did not bow before him.

Rand believes the Templars discovered ancient maps beneath Solomon's Temple which they used to position their important bases at locations that mirror the geography of the Yukon Pole. It seems that Rennes-le-Château is not the only site associated with the Templars and the pole of nearly 100,000 years ago. Rand explains that it wasn't until 1127, after the original members of the order had returned to France, that Hugh de Payens began his search for new recruits for a new order. In January 1128, he acquired official recognition for the Templar Order from the Church and he became the first Grand Master. That same year de Payens visited Henry I of England, and was given a royal welcome. The following year, 1129, the first Templar site in England was founded in London on the site of what is now Holborn Underground station.[6]

When Rand compared London's co-ordinates to the Yukon Pole he discovered that it was within half a degree of 30 degrees north during the Yukon Pole. This is, of course, the latitude of the Great Pyramid today. And London wasn't the only British sacred site associated with the Templars to share this latitude. Among them were Glastonbury, Stonehenge, Bath, Avebury, Old Sarum and Tintagel.[7]

Tintagel is, of course, associated with King Arthur, his Knights of the Round Table and the quest for the Holy Grail. Rand noted that it is 36 degrees west of the Great Pyramid, one tenth of the distance around the globe. During the Yukon Pole, Tintagel was located at 29 degrees, 59 minutes north, precisely the latitude of the Great Pyramid today.

Moving east from Tintagel we encounter Glastonbury. John Michell writes: 'Glastonbury has been described as Britain's only true national shrine, the omphalos or Temple of Britain and the English Jerusalem.'[8] Like Tintagel, Glastonbury was located at 30 degrees north during the Yukon Pole.

Avebury and Stonehenge are so close to each other that for the purpose of the blueprint they, along with Old Sarum, con-stitute a single cluster of sacred sites at 30 degrees north during the Yukon Pole. Avebury, like Tintagel, was located at 29 degrees, 59 minutes north, suggesting an ancient link between the two sites. Nigel Pennick notes: 'Several researchers, includ-ing Keith Critchlow and John Michell, have drawn attention to another curious coincidence at Stonehenge. According to their calculations, the underlying geometry and dimensions of the henge have an exact parallel in St Mary's Chapel at Glastonbury, which is the reputed site of the earliest Christian chapel.'[9]

Between 1199 and 1254 the Templars had their English head-quarters at Baldock, now in Hertfordshire.[10] When Rand compared this site to other sacred places he noted that its rela-tionship to the Yukon Pole was precisely the same as a particular Asian site. Once again, as with the case of Rennes-le-Château and Nanking covered in the last chapter, there was a geodetic con-nection between a European sacred site and an Asian site, and in this case between the ancient city of Pyongyang in North Korea and the Templar's English headquarters at Baldock.[11]

Korea has many ancient monuments that are falling into ruin.[12] Pyongyang, the capital of North Korea, is now a busy industrial city but at one time contained pyramids. Korean history is divided into three periods or kingdoms. The earliest was associated with the gods and was called Koguryo. Sarah Milledge Nelson writes of this period:

> At least two social classes existed in Koguryo from the beginning; a noble class that lived well and an underclass which may have been made up of conquered peoples. The upper class were 'fond of constructing palatial build-ings'[13] lived luxuriously with clothes of embroidered silk and gold and silver ornaments, and were buried in large lavish tombs. Huge Koguryo palaces and tombs have been unearthed in both China and Korea.[14]

The kingdom known as Choson in Pyongyang dates to 2,333 BC, a time very close to the building of the Great Pyramid of Egypt. Korean legend tells how Prince Hwanung descended upon Mount Taebaeksan with 3,000 servants, bringing the gifts of civilisation and building a great city.[15]

Pyongyang's co-ordinates are 39 degrees north, 125 degrees, 47 minutes east. During the Hudson Bay Pole, Pyongyang was located at 12 degrees north (along with Babylon in the Middle East and Nikko in Japan). During the Greenland Sea Pole the city was located at 30 degrees north along with the Xi'an pyramids. And finally, and most remarkably, Pyongyang was also at 30 degrees north during the Yukon Pole. Pyongyang's latitudes through time went from 30 degrees north to 30 degrees north to 12 degrees north. This made the North Korean capital what Rand calls a 'geological marker', of which there are only a few others in the world: Aguni, Byblos, Cuzco, Jericho, Nazca, Pyongyang and Xi'an. These cities were all built at the intersection of sacred latitudes. It seems that ancient surveyors of Europe, Asia and South America used their knowledge of the earth's geological past and their ability to calculate vast distances with extreme accuracy to position geological markers that in time became sacred sites.

Rand found other Templar sites that seemed to demonstrate knowledge of the former position of the poles. La
Rochelle, the main port for the Templars in France – the place
where the famous fleet was said to have disappeared – and
Montségur were both located on the Tropic of Cancer during
the Yukon Pole. The Templars operated out of Rhodes which
had been at 10 degrees north during the Yukon Pole while
Jerusalem had been 5 degrees north. The more he studied
their past, the more he became convinced that the Templars
had obtained maps of the world of nearly 100,000 years ago
from beneath King Solomon's Temple.

But the most startling site turned out to be a tiny chapel in
Scotland south of Edinburgh: Rosslyn.

William St Clair built Rosslyn two centuries before the first
Templars are recorded in England. How do we know that St
Clair was a Templar? Lomas and Knight uncovered much
evidence at Rosslyn, which they describe in their books *The
Hiram Key* and *The Second Messiah*.[16] One of the most convincing pieces of evidence is a carving they found on the wall
outside Rosslyn.

It depicts a freemason ceremony, with the candidate blind-
folded and with a noose round his neck. The man who holds
the rope is a Templar, with the cross on his tunic, leaving no
doubt that St Clair was a Templar, and that the Templars
were also Freemasons. In fact, Lomas and Knight believe that
the building of Rosslyn marks the first appearance of
Freemasonry in the UK.

Lomas and Knight began to look into the history of the St
Clairs of Rosslyn. It seemed that William de St Clair was a
Norman who came over at around the same time as William the
Conqueror in 1066. He was known as William the Seemly. His
son Henri went off on the First Crusade in 1095, and fought
alongside Hugh de Payens, marching into Jerusalem with him,
while Hugh married Henri's niece, Catherine St Clair. The
connection of the St Clairs with the Templars was very close
indeed.

An outline of the carving at Rosslyn showing a Knight Templar
initiating a candidate into Freemasonry.

Why did the St Clairs call their home Rosslyn? A little
research revealed that they didn't. The chapel, like the castle,
was then called Roslin (as the village is today). In the 1950s
the name had been changed to Rosslyn to pull in the tourists
because it sounded more 'olde worlde'. Village names usually
have meanings. Lomas and Knight checked a Scottish Gaelic
dictionary and found that 'Ros' meant knowledge, and 'linn'
meant generation. They consulted modern Gaelic speakers
and learned that a better translation would be 'ancient knowledge passed down the generations', which sounded exactly
what they were hoping for – the place had been specifically
named by the Gaelic-speaking Henri St Clair to hint at the
Templars' secret.

The dates did not fit, though. Henri had returned from the
First Crusade about 1100, eighteen years before Hugh de Payens
and his knights moved into the Temple and began their search.

Yet surely the name Roslin, with its implication of ancient knowledge, could not be coincidence? The two authors had already wondered precisely why the nine knights went to Jerusalem. Were they merely seeking treasure? Or did they already have an idea of what they were looking for? The name Roslin suggested that the answer was yes. Studying the chapel more closely, the authors found something even more exciting. One of the pillars had a tableau that showed a figure – presumably a knight – holding up a cloth in both hands. On the cloth there was a bearded face. The head of the figure holding the cloth had been hacked off, presumably to disguise his identity. Nearby was a frieze showing the crucifixion, yet it did not seem to be Jesus's crucifixion. To begin with, the people shown were in medieval garb, and some were hooded – members of the Inquisition. Another frieze showed Templars with an executioner next to them.

The face on the cloth, the authors felt, bore a resemblance to that of Jacques Molay, the Grand Master of the Templars. Molay had not been tortured in the torture chamber of the Inquisition, but in the Paris headquarters of the Templars. The rack and suspension chains would not have been available. Lomas and Knight argue that Molay was, in fact, tortured by being crucified.

The inquisitor William Imbert, a devout Catholic, would have been horrified to learn that the Templars denied that Christ was the son of God. And he would have felt that the Templars' use of a ceremony of resurrection in their rituals was simply blasphemous. It would have been highly appropriate to torture Molay by nailing him to a door. Lomas and Knight believe that Rosslyn provides the evidence that this is what happened.

After Molay had confessed to whatever the Inquisitors had accused him of, he was taken down and wrapped in a piece of cloth. He was laid on his bed in this 'shroud', his body streaming with perspiration and blood containing a high lactic acid content. The authors suggest that the blood and perspiration 'fixed' Molay's image on the cloth, in a process similar to that which creates the image of flowers pressed between the pages of a book. (In *The Second Messiah*, they include an appendix by an expert on photography, Dr Alan Mills, on the chemistry of this process.) The piece of cloth, they believe, is now known as the Holy Shroud of Turin, the shroud that is supposed to contain the image of Jesus.

What evidence is there that the figure on the Shroud of Turin is Jacques Molay? To begin with, there is the interesting fact that in 1988 carbon-14 dating revealed that the fabric of the shroud was woven between AD 1260 and 1390, which conclusively rules out the possibility that the shroud was used to wrap the body of Jesus. But these dates do cover the arrest and torture of Jacques Molay.

There is an even more powerful piece of circumstantial evidence. The shroud belonged to the family of Geoffrey de Charney, who was roasted to death with Jacques Molay in 1314. In 1356, England's Black Prince routed France's John II, son of Louis X, at Poitiers. And another Geoffrey de Charney, probably the grandson of Geoffrey's brother Jean, died beside his king. Later, when Geoffrey's widow Jeanne de Vergy was searching through her husband's effects, she found a piece of cloth, about 14 feet long, with the brown image of a man on it – a man with a bearded face. Both his front and his back were visible, and bloodstains indicated that he had been crucified with nails through the wrists.

The Romans carried out most crucifixions with nails through the wrists, for the palm is not strong enough to support the weight of a body and tends to tear open via the fingers. Jesus must have been crucified in this way.

Not unnaturally, Jeanne was inclined to believe she was looking at an image of Jesus, and since she had been left penniless by her husband's death she decided to put the 'Holy Shroud' on display in the church at Lirey, built by her husband. It drew an unending stream of pilgrims and – presumably – solved Jeanne's financial problems.

Henry of Poitiers, the Bishop of Troyes, declared it to be a fake that had been 'made by human hands', and tried to seize it. He was unsuccessful, but in 1532 the shroud was almost destroyed in a fire, and molten silver burned a number of holes into it. Luckily, they missed the central image, and when the cloth had been repaired by nuns it looked as good as new. It was moved to Turin Cathedral in 1578.

More than five centuries later, on 25 May 1898, it was again put on public display, and a photographer named Sendono Pia was commissioned to photograph it. And when he looked at the negative, he was amazed to see that he was now looking at a real face, which could only mean that the brown image itself must have been a negative that had now become positive.

Clearly, the Bishop of Troyes was wrong; this was not a forgery, for it had not been painted. The 'miraculous' reversal of a negative left most pious Catholics in no doubt that this was an image of Christ himself. A majority of believers still hold this view.

Lynn Picknett and Clive Prince have even developed a highly original theory that the image in the shroud *is* a photographic negative, and that the photographer was Leonardo da Vinci himself, who filmed his own image on the shroud by a process he had invented.[17] The dates, of course, are all wrong, since Leonardo was not born until 1452, almost a century after the shroud had first been exhibited, but they argue that Leonardo swapped his self-portrait for the original shroud.

Alan Mills, the photographic expert, believes that immense physical stress caused the release of oxygen-free radicals in Molay, arguing that these 'photographed' the image on the shroud, which then developed during the fifty years the cloth was stored. Lomas and Knight theorise that after the torture of Jacques Molay and Geoffrey de Charney, the two men were sent back to Charney's family to be nursed back to health, but it seems equally possible that the shroud was simply taken back to Charney's home by relatives who came to visit him – and Molay – during their next seven years in prison.

Lomas and Knight argue that, as the shroud became a famous relic, the Bishop of Troyes did his best to suppress it, afraid that enough people knew it to be an image of the murdered Jacques Molay to create the danger of a cult of 'the second messiah', which might cause serious embarrassment to the Church. So the Bishop of Troyes announced that it was a forgery, and that the forger had been caught and the shroud destroyed. In fact, the shroud was hidden and put on exhibition again in 1389, when the fuss had died down.

The Rosslyn image of the headless man holding a cloth that contains a representation of a bearded head certainly supports the theory that the shroud contained an image of Jacques Molay. Lomas and Knight found an extremely interesting piece of evidence in the twenty-seventh degree of Freemasonry, a ritual concerning the false condemnation of the Templars and their denial of the cross. The nineteenth-century occultist A. E. Waite had written a book about the Templars, but expressed distaste at this ritual, on the grounds that the cross used in it – a cross of Lorraine – had two sets of initials on it, JN and JBM. Waite had been told that these stood for Jesus of Nazareth and Jacques Burgundus Molay. So the Freemason tradition appears to suggest that Molay was crucified. That there was some kind of cult of the Master of the Templars is evidenced by an event that happened in 1793, during the French Revolution; as Louis XIV was about to be guillotined, a member of the crowd shouted, 'Jacques Molay is avenged!'

One major mystery of Freemasonry still intrigued Lomas and Knight: why did the murder of Hiram Abif, the architect of Solomon's Temple, play such an important part? In fact, it is the central legend of Freemasonry, and every Mason 'becomes' Hiram Abif as he undergoes a ritual murder and resurrection in his initiation ceremony. As Hiram Abif is resurrected, certain words are spoken aloud. They sound like gibberish: '*Ma'at-beb-men-aa, Ma'at-ba-aa.*'

But Christopher Knight happened to know that '*ma'at*' is an ancient Egyptian word. It meant originally 'ordered and symmetrical', like the base of a temple. Then it came to mean righteousness, truth and justice, concepts that play such a central role in Freemasonry. Knight realised that the 'gibberish' is ancient Egyptian, meaning 'Great is the Master of Ma'at, great is the spirit of Ma'at.'

In the Old Testament Hiram is referred to as 'Hiram the King of Tyre' (I Kings), and also as 'Hiram of Tyre', son of a Tyrian bronzeworker (II Chronicles). It seems that he was not just the architect of the Temple, but the master builder who directed operations. He was attacked and killed by three of his own workers, who struck him three blows, apparently because he refused to divulge the secret signal that would have enabled them to claim a higher rank than they actually possessed (and thus higher wages). It all sounds highly unlikely – surely workers on the Temple could not get away with such a crudely conceived swindle? Lomas and Knight suspected that the story of Hiram Abif concealed some important historical truth.

Why is the ritual of Freemasonry so full of hints that its origin lies in ancient Egypt, and why is the Great Pyramid one of its central symbols? The forefathers of modern America, all Freemasons, were responsible for placing the pyramid symbol on dollar bills. Since there are so many connections between Jews and Egyptians in the Old Testament, Lomas and Knight felt that the answer probably lay in historical events involving both nations, which would have occurred long before Solomon built the Temple. According to the Book of Genesis, the Jews came into existence after Jacob had wrestled with the angel and his name was changed to Israel. His twelve sons gave their names to the twelve tribes of Israel. The date seems to have been some time in the middle of the sixteenth century BC.

The Jewish historian Josephus had identified the so-called Hyksos, or Shepherd Kings, with the Hebrews of the Old Testament. The Hyksos were, in fact, a mixed group of

Semitics and Asiatics who moved into Egypt around 1,750 BC – not as warriors, but as refugees from drought. They seized power around 1,630 BC and ruled until they were thrown out 108 years later, as a result of a revolt that began at Thebes (now Luxor). Although modern scholars do not feel that Josephus was completely accurate, there seems little doubt that the ancestry of the Jews includes the Hyksos. The Hyksos kings ruled northern Egypt (Lower Egypt), but Thebes was ruled by a traditional pharaoh, Sequenenre, whose eldest son inaugurated the revolt.

Lomas and Knight were inclined to wonder: was there an Egyptian pharaoh to whom the story of Hiram Abif might apply?

Indeed, there was – and only one. It was Sequenenre himself. It seemed that the Hyksos pharaoh of this time was called Apophis or Apopi. Knight remembered a book of Egyptian liturgies called *The Book of Overthrowing Apopi*, which is full of magic spells to get rid of him. Moreover, the Hyksos kings increased their unpopularity by worshipping the storm god Set, whom most Egyptians regarded as the god of evil.

When a pharaoh ascended the throne, he went through a ceremony whose purpose was to make him into a god – specifically, into Horus, son of Osiris. When he died, he became Osiris, and there was an important ceremony called 'the Opening of the Mouth', when his mouth was levered open with an adze so that his soul could rejoin his fellow gods in heaven and take on the task of interceding for his people. Apopi would have wanted to know the secret ceremony because after two centuries the Hyksos had been thoroughly 'Egyptianised'; they believed that the ritual would turn the pharaoh into a god. They saw themselves as upstarts, but they wanted to become truly Egyptian, and the pharaoh Apopi naturally wanted to become a god.

Sequenenre was murdered with blows on the head; we know that from his mummy. Lomas and Knight include a gruesome photograph of it with gashes on the skull and one eye missing.

The person with the most obvious motive for murdering him would be the Hyksos pharaoh Apopi.

If Sequenenre was the original of Hiram Abif, then the secret that the three murderers tried to force from him would be the ritual to make a newly crowned pharaoh into Horus.

In the scenario of Lomas and Knight – based on Masonic ritual – Sequenenre was approached by three men, called Jubela, Jubelo and Jubelum, whose task was to make him divulge the secret ritual. He refused, probably with some angry and contemptuous words – kings do not like being threatened – whereupon the three ruffians went beyond their instructions and killed him with three blows. (This is also a basic part of the Masonic tradition – they were not instructed to kill Hiram Abif, but only to force the secret from him.)

Lomas and Knight even add the fascinating speculation – based on Sequenenre's dates – that Apopi's 'grand vizier', who was behind the plot to force Sequenenre to divulge the secret ritual, was Joseph, son of Jacob, whose brothers sold him into slavery. They go further and speculate that two of the murderers were Joseph's brothers Simeon and Levi. The third murderer, they believe, was a young priest of Sequenenre's temple, dragged into the plot with the threat that Apopi meant to destroy Thebes and that the only way of averting this would be to divulge the 'god-making' ritual.

Lomas and Knight discovered some extraordinary physical evidence to support their theory. As well as the proof of violent blows on the mummified head of Sequenenre, entombed beside the pharaoh was another mummy whose state had baffled Egyptologists. Although the flesh had been mummified by the dry air of the tomb, the inner organs had not – as was usual – been embalmed. He had been castrated, and his face bore an expression of agony. He had clearly been wrapped in bandages while still alive, and died of suffocation.

There could be little doubt that this was one of the murderers of the pharaoh. The fact that he was killed so horribly and buried beside Sequenenre suggested that he was not a Hyksos but some member of the pharaoh's entourage who was being punished for treachery. The other two murderers – foreigners – would simply have been executed.

But why the castration? Because when the god Horus avenged the murder of his father Osiris in a battle with Set, Horus lost an eye and Set lost his testicles. So to punish a treacherous priest in this way would be oddly appropriate, particularly since Sequenenre had lost his eye.

Sequenenre's son Kamose avenged his father's murder by fomenting the rebellion that drove the Hyksos out of Egypt. Kamose became the founder of a new Egyptian dynasty, and the ritual of the murder and resurrection of Osiris, which would be used at his coronation, would be enriched by a new level of meaning – the death and resurrection of Sequenenre.

If Lomas and Knight are correct in believing that the pharaoh who made Joseph the governor of Egypt was Apopi – and the dates seem to support it – then the murder of Sequenenre was of even deeper significance, for Joseph's father Jacob became Israel, the founder of the Jewish people. If Joseph and his family were among the Hyksos who were driven out of Egypt, then the murder of Sequenenre also led to the creation of the Jewish nation, which would help to explain why it was regarded as so important by the Jews that it was transformed into the murder of Hiram Abif, the architect of Solomon's Temple.

In researching the history of Freemasonry, Lomas and Knight seem to have made a string of extraordinary discoveries. The claim that Freemasonry originated in Egypt would seem to have a sound factual foundation. With the murder of Hiram Abif six centuries later, Egyptian mythology was metamorphosed into Jewish mythology, implying that some form of Freemasonry had survived from the time of Sequenenre and involved a ritual death and resurrection. Lomas and Knight produce compelling evidence to suggest that the ritual was one of the secrets of the Essenes that was hidden beneath the Temple after the crucifixion of Jesus, in whose story resurrection also plays a central part. The Essenes, who guarded the secret, were wiped out by Titus, and the Temple was destroyed. Lomas writes of a ritual of Freemasonry that 'has a retrospect that tells of the fall of the Nasoreans in AD 70, and how the progenitors of Freemasonry left Jerusalem at that time to spread across Europe'. He also says that these survivors 'believed they were preserving the bloodlines of the two Messiahs of David and Aaron, who would one day arrive and establish the kingdom of God on earth'. Jesus, whom the Baptist Mandaeans (descendants of the Essenes) regard as an impostor, was raised to the status of a god by St Paul, and when Constantine used Christianity to bind his collapsing empire together, the resurrection became the Church's most powerful claim to supernatural authority.

As to the Templars, we can make one of two assumptions: either the nine original Templars were among the descendants of the 'progenitors' who left Jerusalem after the destruction of the Temple and went back with the specific intention of finding the Essene documents, or they were looking for treasure and found instead the Essene scrolls.

Lomas and Knight have no doubt that the former is the correct version of events. In fact, they believe that the First Crusade was deliberately planned to retake Jerusalem so that the knights could undertake the search for the Essene scrolls. When they were found, the illustration of the 'Heavenly Jerusalem', identified by the old scholar, Lambert of St Omer, revealed that the knights had found what they were looking for, and the scrolls became the foundation of the power and wealth of the Knights Templar. Somehow, though, the Church and the King of France learned the Templars' most carefully guarded secret – they were not Christians, in that they believed Jesus to be a man, not the son of God. This served Philip the Fair as an excuse to arrest the Templars and seize their wealth. But he failed because someone – probably Pope Clement – tipped off his relative at Blanchefort, and the

Templar fleet – of eighteen ships – escaped from La Rochelle with the Templar treasure.

Where did they go? The corncobs and aloes in Rosslyn suggests that some of them sailed for America. Other Templars went to Scotland, where an abbey named Kilwinning had been built in the first great days of Templar power, around 1140.[18] It was just south of Glasgow, and was the Templars' major centre. This would be a natural refuge, particularly since the St Clair family lived not far away, in Roslin. Robert the Bruce, King of Scotland, had been excommunicated by the Pope, so Templars had nothing to fear in Scotland.

One of the main arguments of *The Hiram Key* is that Rosslyn Chapel was built in deliberate imitation of Herod's Temple and as the home of the precious scrolls, which were the most important 'treasure' of the Templars. They argue that even the unfinished outer wall at Rosslyn, which looks as if the building was simply abandoned at that point, was a replica of an unfinished wall in Herod's rebuilding of Solomon's Temple.

In 1447, while Rosslyn Chapel was being built, there was a fire in the keep of Roslin Castle. William St Clair was frantic until he learned that his chaplain had managed to salvage four great trunks full of charters, whereupon, says the record, 'he became cheerful'. Lomas and Knight point out that it sounds odd to value four trunks of 'charters' more than his castle keep – not to mention his wife and daughter, who were also inside. If these trunks contained the secret scrolls from Jerusalem, which would have been buried in Rosslyn Chapel, his curious priorities become understandable.

We should now be able to see the connection between the Templars and the mystery of Rennes-le-Château. If Pierre Plantard de St Clair is a descendent of the man who built Rosslyn, then he is also a Templar. The confession that so shocked the local priest who attended Sauniére's death bed was certainly that Sauniére did not believe that Jesus was the son of God, but was simply a man. And this would be consistent with Henry Lincoln's suggestion that Jesus came to France with Mary Magdalene, and that his descendents were the Merovingian kings.

But this, as Lincoln admits, is pure supposition. The truth may be simpler: that the Merovingian kings were, in fact, also heirs to the secret known to the Templars, the secret contained in the Essene scrolls. If this Merovingian connection is not an invention of Plantard and the Priory of Sion, then it seems to follow that the Merovingians were an important 'missing link' between the Essenes and the Templars.

We can see why Nicolas Poussin talked about a great secret that kings would have difficulty drawing from him. He must have felt that this knowledge – that Jesus was a man, and that therefore the power of the Church was based upon completely false claims – was dynamite that could cost him, and others privy to the secret, their lives.

As I read Lomas and Knight on Hiram Abif, I found myself thinking about another interesting connection. Hiram came from Tyre. And having visited Tyre on a trip to the Lebanon, I knew that it was a Phoenician city, and that the Phoenicians were not worshippers of Yahweh. Why should Solomon want a Phoenician architect? Presumably because Hiram of Tyre was the best man for the job. But the chief Phoenician god was Baal or Bel, whom the authors of the Old Testament regard with suspicion and dislike, and their leading female deity was Astarte, also called Ashtoreth and Ishtar.

Rand's research led him to believe that the Templars were the heirs to ancient geographic knowledge once possessed by the Phoenicians. He writes:

It was their colony in Carthage that indicated that the Phoenicians had once possessed ancient maps that depicted the earlier poles. During the Hudson Bay Pole latitude 30 degrees north crossed Tunisia at Carthage. This city is presumed to have been established in the ninth century BC but may be much older. The

Phoenicians, the ancient world's most advanced sea power, may have had access to ancient maps that revealed an ancient site beneath Carthage. They may have selected this place for reasons that may go back to the time of Atlantis. Its location on the east coast of a tiny peninsula on the Tunisian coast would have presented ancient astronomers with an ideal view of the northern sky from latitude 30 degrees. The Mediterranean Sea would have acted as a perfect reflection of the heavens and the horizon would be undisturbed by mountains.

On the west coast of Africa there is another Phoenician city which the Romans regarded as the oldest city in the world. Little remains of Lixus, but it was once a Phoenician colony on the Atlantic coast of Africa. Certainly the most amazing Phoenician city was Byblos which, like Pyongyang in Korea and Cuzco in the central Andes, was linked by sacred latitudes to both the Hudson Bay and Yukon Poles. Byblos was sacred to both the Phoenicians and the Egyptians. For the Phoenicians it was the oldest city in the world and for the Egyptians it was the place that the god Osiris came to rest after his evil brother Seth locked him in a casket and set him adrift upon the waters of the Mediterranean Sea.

Byblos, along with the megalithic structures at nearby Baalbek, made Rand suspect that there had been an ancient maritime power operating worldwide out of this ancient port in Lebanon. Baalbek, as we have seen, may well have been a site constructed by the Fallen Angels that we met in Chapter 7.

Rand knew that the largest stones used in construction in the New World were in and around Cuzco, which also had been at a 10 phi latitude before the flood. Sitchin in *Lost Realms* had commented upon the similarities between Baalbek and Cuzco.[19] We know now that both sites shared the same sacred latitude (10 phi) before the flood. And it was this latitude where the city of Tiahuanaco at Lake Titicaca was founded. One of the myths associated with Tiahuanaco and Lake Titicaca concerns the god who came from the south after a flood and gave his children a device that led them to Cuzco.

In *When the Sky Fell*, Rand and Rose were fascinated by the myths of the people of the central Andes. They wrote:

> The famous Peruvian historian, Garcilasso de la Vega, son of a Spanish conquistador and an Inca princess, asked his Inca uncle to tell him the story of his people's origins. How had Lake Titicaca become the source of their civilisation? The uncle explained: 'In ancient times all this region which you see was covered with forests and thickets, and the people lived like brute beasts without religion nor government, nor towns, nor horses, without cultivating the land nor covering their bodies . . . [the sun-god sent a son and daughter to] . . . give them precepts and laws by which to live as reasonable and civilised men, and to teach them to dwell in houses and towns, to cultivate maize and other crops, to breed flocks, and to use the fruits of the earth as rational beings.'
>
> The 'gods' who brought agriculture to the vicinity of Lake Titicaca were said to have come 'out of the regions of the south' immediately 'after the deluge'. In other words, agriculture was introduced to Lake Titicaca by people who already possessed the skills and who had been forced to leave their homeland when a flood destroyed their southern land.[20]

In his classic work *History of the Conquest of Peru*, William Hickling Prescott told the legend of how Cuzco evolved into one of the most sacred cities of the Andes. This is a tale that tantalises us with the suggestion that some sort of time or survival capsule was planted at Cuzco before the flood. Prescott relates how Cuzco became a sacred city after the flood had subsided.

The Sun, the great luminary and parent of mankind, taking compassion on their degraded condition, sent two of his children, Manco Capac and Mama Oello Huaco, to gather the natives into communities, and teach them the arts of civilised life. The celestial pair, brother and sister, husband and wife, advanced along the high plains in the neighbourhood of Lake Titicaca, to about the sixteenth degree south. They bore with them a golden wedge, and were directed to take up their residence on the spot where the sacred emblem should without effort sink into the ground. They proceeded accordingly but a short distance, as far as the valley of Cuzco, the spot indicated by the performance of the miracle, since there the wedge speedily sank into the earth and disappeared for ever. Here the children of the Sun established their residence.[21]

Lost Realms also drew attention to an amazing geometric fact: 'Maria Schulten de D'Ebneth . . . in her book *La Ruta de Wirakocha* . . . drew lines showing that a 45-degree line originating at Tiahuanacu, combined with squares and circles of definite measurements, embraced all the key ancient sites between Tiahuanacu, Cuzco, and Quito in Ecuador including the all-important Ollantaytambu.'[22]

Why would the builders of these ancient sacred sites want to connect these four cities geometrically? What do Tiahuanaco, Cuzco, Ollantaytambo and Quito have in common?

Charles Piazzi Smyth believed that the Great Pyramid should be the site of the prime meridian. As we have seen, Tiahuanaco lies 100 degrees west of the Great Pyramid. And Quito, at the equator, lies 110 degrees west of Giza. This would seem to indicate that Tiahuanaco and Quito were constructed after the Giza Prime Meridian was established.

So it seemed that ancient Egypt and Peru had a powerful geodetic link. Several authors had speculated upon the mythological connection between the Egyptian god, Osiris, and the god, Viracocha, of the people of the central Andes.[23] Osiris was believed to have travelled around the globe bringing civilisation to many nations.

Viracocha was the 'god' who brought agriculture and civilisation to the Andes. He was tall, of pale complexion, bearded and dressed in a long white robe. The myths tell us that this stranger came from the south and settled among the native people of Lake Titicaca some time after the flood. He brought instruction in the arts of agriculture, animal husbandry, medicine, metallurgy and even writing, which the Inca claim was later forgotten. Two groups of men accompanied him on his mission. One group were huaminca, 'faithful soldiers', and another hayuaypanti, meaning 'shining ones', who spread the word of Viracocha throughout the world.[24]

The 'golden wedge', which Sitchin calls a 'golden wand', seems to be a kind of homing device that led the Children of the Sun directly to Cuzco as if towards a beacon situated beneath the ground. In 1575, Cristobal de Molina offered the following Andean prayer to the sun-god Viracocha:

> Oh! Day-King, Sun, my Father!
> May there be a Cuzco:
> may the Capable One be he who measures.[25]

Shining ones appeared in the Andes and in the mountains of the Middle East after the flood. And in both cases, their great concern was with measurement. Did ancient Andean mythology point to Cuzco as a sacred site? Is there a rational explanation beneath the mythological record? Was there some sort of technological or scientific reason for the 'golden wedge'? And what does it all have to do with 'measures'? The 'golden wedge' of Cuzco, the 'omphalos' of Delphi and the 'cording of the Temple' in ancient Egypt are all part of a mysterious web which spans the globe, a pattern that tempts us to believe that the sacred sites that haunt our landscape are not scattered across the earth at random but are rather part of a deliberate design.

The significant line discovered by Maria D'Ebneth that connected Tiahuanaco and Cuzco extended all the way to the equator where it intercepted Quito, the northern capital of the Inca empire. Before the Earth's mantle/crust shifted position, Quito was located at 30 degrees north. The Inca Trail, which is one of the great wonders of the ancient world, ran from Cuzco in the south to Quito in the north. This link between Cuzco and Quito is quite literal. One can still walk the Inca Trail from Cuzco to Quito today.

Prescott's *History of the Conquest of Peru* records that the Inca were desperate to maintain the Cuzco–Quito connection. Huayana Capac, the father of the last Inca, Atahuallpa, died around 1525, some seven years before Pizarro's arrival brought an end to that great empire. When Huayana Capac died 'his heart was retained in Quito, and his body, embalmed after the fashion of the country, was transported to Cuzco, to take its place in the great temple of the Sun, by the side of the remains of his royal ancestors'.[26]

Atahuallpa was eventually murdered by Pizarro, but before he died he 'expressed a desire that his remains might be transported to Quito, the place of his birth, to be preserved with those of his maternal ancestors'.[27] Pizarro refused this request and instead buried the remains of the last Inca in a Christian cemetery. 'But from thence, as is reported, after the Spaniards left Caxamalca, they were secretly removed, and carried, as he had desired, to Quito.'[28]

Prescott tells us that

the royal edifices of Quito, we are assured by the Spanish conquerors, were constructed of huge masses of stone, many of which were carried all the way along the mountain roads from Cuzco, a distance of several hundred leagues.

And while the capitals of Christendom, but a few

288

hundred miles apart, remained as far asunder as if seas had rolled between them, the great capitals of Cuzco and Quito were placed by the high roads of the Incas in immediate correspondence.

Quito, which lay immediately under the equator, where the vertical rays of the sun threw no shadow at noon, was held in especial veneration as the favoured abode of the great deity.[29]

It would seem that information buried at Cuzco before the displacement may have provided the people of ancient America with a blueprint for laying out their post-flood sacred sites. This blueprint linked Cuzco to Tiahuanaco and Cuzco to Quito and so the 45-degree 'ley line' that connects these ancient sacred sites begins to make geodetic sense. Ollantaytambo and Machu Picchu are so close to Cuzco that they should be considered a group, with Cuzco at the centre being the 'navel of the world'. The monuments at Ollantaytambo were constructed with the largest stones used in the New World. Sitchin links Ollantaytambo with ancient Baalbek in Lebanon:

> The many similarities we find between Ollantaytambu and Baalbek include the origin of the megaliths. The colossal stone blocks of Baalbek were quarried miles away in a valley, then incredibly lifted, transported, and put in place to fit with other stones of the platform. At Ollantaytambu too the giant stone blocks were quarried on the mountainside on the opposite side of the valley. The heavy blocks of red granite, after they had been quarried, hewed, and shaped, were then transported from the mountainside, across two streams, and up the Ollantaytambu site; then carefully raised, put precisely in place, and finally fused together.[30]

Little could Sitchin suspect that Ollantaytambo and Baalbek are the same distance from the Hudson Bay Pole and share the

10 phi latitude. The fact is that the largest stones used in construction in both the Old and New World are found at the same distance to the Hudson Bay Pole. This worldwide geodesic pattern repeatedly emphasises the importance of the geometric notion of the Golden Section married to the number 10.

When the people of ancient Israel conquered 'Canaan' they were occupying the homeland of the Phoenicians, who regarded themselves as the heirs of the much earlier maritime Byblos culture. The Phoenicians had drawn upon the Byblos for their art, culture and architecture. The Israelites respected the achievements of the Phoenicians and drew upon their architecture in the building of King Solomon's Temple.

In *The Temple and the Lodge*[31] Michael Baigent and Richard Leigh assert that 'modern archaeological research confirms that Solomon's Temple . . . bears an unmistakable resemblance to the actual temples built by the Phoenicians . . . It is even possible to go a step further. Tyrian temples were erected to the Phoenician mother goddess Astarte . . . hilltops and mountains – Mount Hermon for example – abounded with her shrines.' And they point out that King Solomon is also described (I Kings 3) as offering 'sacrifice and incense on the high places'.

They draw attention to the fact that Solomon's religion was not strictly orthodox. When he grew old 'his wives swayed his heart to other gods . . . Solomon became a follower of Astarte' (I Kings 11). They even state that the famous Song of Songs is a hymn to Astarte. They then ask the question: 'Was [the Temple] dedicated to the God of Israel, or was it dedicated to Astarte?'

This may seem academic until we recall that Astarte was known to the Greeks as Aphrodite, the goddess of love (from which we get the term aphrodisiac), and to the Romans as Venus. And Henry Lincoln, for one, believes that the planet Venus was the reason that the pentacle is perhaps the most important of magic symbols.

So the man who built Solomon's Temple was a worshipper of Venus, and his employer also had leanings in that direction.

When we recall that the geometry of Rennes-le-Château is pentacular, we can suddenly see another connection with Solomon's Temple and the Templars. The whole area has connections with Merovingians and Templars and the religion of gnosticism. The kind of gnosticism that led to the extermination of the Cathars was a belief that matter is created by the Devil and spirit by God, so 'this world' is evil. But according to Lomas and Knight the Essenes had a different version of gnosticism. 'Gnosis' means knowledge, and the Essenes held that when a man awakens to 'gnosis', he is 'resurrected'. Priests and saviours become unnecessary, because he now possesses the 'knowledge' himself. Such a position is, of course, anathema to all forms of established religion that depend on priestly authority, for it makes them unnecessary. It could be compared to Quakerism, with its belief in the 'inner light', and also to Buddhism, with its concept of enlightenment.

In reading Lomas and Knight, I had been particularly interested in Kilwinning, the original Templar abbey built in Scotland, for Rand had included it among his sacred sites. Recognising the importance of the Golden Section in their positioning, he had tried measuring the Golden Section from the North Pole (34 degrees, 23 minutes north), and had discovered two other important sacred sites at this latitude, the Chinese pyramids and Ehdin (the O'Briens' Eden). Measuring the Golden Section from the equator (55 degrees, 37 minutes north), he could find nothing in North America or Asia, but he found Kilwinning only 3 minutes of a degree away, at 55 degrees, 40 minutes north. And when he learned (from *The Holy Blood and the Holy Grail*) about Kilwinning, he checked its position compared to the Great Pyramid, and found that it was 36 degrees – one-tenth of 360 degrees, the total distance around the earth. When he learned that Kilwinning was reputed to be built on an ancient pagan site, he was further encouraged.

He checked Rosslyn's latitude; it was 55 degrees, 52 minutes north, only 15 minutes out – not bad, but still 17 miles too many. Then he checked its location with regard to the Hudson Bay Pole. It was precisely 50 degrees north. In an email telling me of this discovery, Rand wrote:

What made Rosslyn so special was its position relative to today's North Pole and the North Pole during the Hudson Bay Pole. Stand outside Rosslyn Chapel facing north-west and raise your right arm so the tip of your index finger is pointing to the North Pole. Now raise your left arm and point at the Hudson Bay Pole. An angle is formed by the tips of your fingers and your nose This angle is precisely 50 degrees. Rosslyn was formerly at 50 degrees north and the angle difference between it, the North Pole and the Hudson Bay Pole is exactly 50 degrees. This made it a 50/50 site, and indicates that accurate geodetic and geo-logical information was used in its location.

If the Templars deliberately sited Rosslyn on a phi latitude that was also a '50/50 site', then it looked as if they must also have had knowledge of this worldwide grid of sacred sites.

For me, this was further confirmed by Lomas and Knight's reference to the prophet Enoch. In *The Hiram Key* there are merely three brief references to him. Towards the end of *The Second Messiah*, there is a passage about the thirteenth degree of Scottish Freemasonry, which

tells how, in times long before Moses and Abraham, the ancient figure of Enoch foresaw that the world would be overwhelmed by an apocalyptic disaster through flood or fire, and he determined to preserve at least some of the knowledge then available to man, that it might be passed on to future civilisations of survivors. He therefore engraves in hieroglyphics the great secrets of science and building on to two pillars: one made of brick and the other of stone.

The Masonic legend then goes on to tell how these pil-
lars were almost destroyed, but sections survived the
Flood and were subsequently discovered – one by the
Jews, the other by the Egyptians . . .

So, according to the Masons, the origins of Freemasonry – the
two pillars that play a central part in its rituals – can be traced
back to Enoch.

When I first read *The Hiram Key* I assumed that this was
simply another more or less fictional attempt to establish the
ancient origins of Freemasonry, but by the time I finished
The Second Messiah, it seemed to me that Lomas and Knight
had made an extremely plausible case for the Egyptian origin
of Freemasonry and for secret knowledge that could be traced
through Solomon's Temple, the Essenes and the Templars.
The notion that the Book of Enoch might be involved came as
no surprise. Rand's *When the Sky Fell* had already left me in
no doubt that ancient memories of the Great Flood have survived down the millennia.

Lomas and Knight emphasise that the tradition of Enoch
and the flood is of central importance to Freemasonry, and in
their third volume, *Uriel's Machine*, Enoch is virtually the
central figure. As already noted, Lomas and Knight believe
that the flood was caused by the impact of a comet in 7,640 BC,
and that the ancients were able to anticipate this impact by
using 'Uriel's machine'. There are also no fewer than thirty-
two references to the planet Venus, which, they explain,
'symbolises rebirth in Judaism, Freemasonry and many other
ancient traditions'.

There is, then, a convergence of Masonic tradition and
other arguments about ancient civilisation. It was Rand who
pointed out one of the most fascinating implications of the
Templar tradition of an important discovery in the remains of
Solomon's Temple: the evidence that part of the Templar
fleet that left La Rochelle in 1307 made its way to America.
(Of course it is believed that the Vikings had found their way

to America centuries before Columbus, but they did not cross the Atlantic, but stuck to the coast of Greenland.) Before Columbus 'discovered' America, did one of the Templar ships that had sailed to America later return to Scotland?

The corncobs in Rosslyn suggest that some of the Templars sailed for America. Lomas and Knight mention that Westford, Massachusetts, has an image of a Templar knight carved on a slab of rock, while at Newport, Rhode Island, there is a curious tower constructed in the manner of Templar round churches.

But it is unlikely that Templars fleeing from imminent arrest and torture would set sail across the Atlantic unless they knew where they were going. How could they have known about America? The only answer can be that they had a map or maps. Could they have obtained such maps from the 'treasure' that Hugh de Payens and the knights discovered in 1126 in the basement of the Temple in Jerusalem?

In *The Hiram Key*, Lomas and Knight comment: 'Josephus . . . observed that the Essenes believed that good souls have their habitation beyond the ocean . . . across the seas to the west.' This land is marked by the star that the Mandaeans of Iraq called 'Merica', and which Lomas and Knight suggest is Venus. They believe that it was from this star that America took its name – not from the explorer Amerigo Vespucci.

In short, what the Templars discovered in Jerusalem included the knowledge contained in Hapgood's 'maps of the ancient sea kings'.

10

THE LEGACY

As you fly east from La Paz in the Bolivian Andes, the dense green of the jungle suddenly gives way to open grasslands that extend as far as the eye can see. This is the swampy flood plain of the Mamoré River, a tributary of the Amazon, which is underwater one half of the year and bone dry the other half. The few inhabitants simply have to move to higher land during the flood season.

In 1962, an American student at the University of California, Berkeley, Bill Denevan, who realised that many areas of this immense land are virtually unknown, persuaded the pilot of a Bolivian airliner to divert north over the Moxos Plain, an area called Beni. Suddenly he was goggling with excitement, rushing from side to side of the plane with his camera. What he saw below him was a landscape in two shades of green, the lighter green lying on the surrounding darker green in short, broad strokes, as if an abstract painter had taken a whitewash brush and slapped a green-tinted wash over the flat landscape in V-shaped patterns. The lighter green, he realised later, was raised fields, in effect platforms of earth that had once been surrounded by flood-filled ditches. Looking ahead, a distance of perhaps 50 miles, he could see another light green patch of landscape about the size of a fairly large village. It was all around him – a landscape with circular fields and raised mounds of tree-covered earth, and straight lines that ran towards the horizon for hundreds of miles. There were also square lakes, obviously man-made.

What excited Denevan was its sheer scale. Whoever had civilised this vast landscape had spread their raised fields, ditches and reservoirs over thousands of acres. Yet no one had ever heard of a great civilisation in the Amazon. Columbus, of course, had not penetrated this far, and when the Spanish Conquistadores arrived in the late 1600s they had found nothing to indicate the presence of an ancient people – just a few thousand Indians who were forcibly converted to Christianity.

When Denevan returned to the United States, he tried to interest archaeologists in this vanished people but failed completely. No one believed him. Eventually, an archaeologist named Oscar Saavedra, from the region's largest town, Trinidad, began to explore the ancient landscape. He soon realised that the fields ran to hundreds of thousands, that there were thousands of forest-covered mounds to which the inhabitants retreated during floods, and that there were over a thousand miles of causeways. As Saavedra penetrated the waterways with their overhanging trees in a motor-driven boat, he was actually travelling through a man-made waterscape that extended for hundred of thousands of square miles, as far as the borders of Bolivia and Brazil. These canals often connected rivers on the great swampy plain, so that the whole area might be compared to Venice, but thousands of times larger.

There are also earthworks that depict people and animals that have been compared to the Nazca lines, one anthropomorphic figure being 2 kilometres from head to toe. It is believed that these various structures were built by the Paititi tribe 5,500 years ago,[1] but Denevan dismisses this estimate as grossly exaggerated.

Then how old is it? Ceramic heads and utensils that farmers found in their fields could not be dated, but other artifacts could be carbon-dated to 5,000 BC. Denevan's own feeling is that an age of a couple of thousand years is closer to the truth. Even so, it would be as old as anything then known in South America. (No one believed that Tiahuanaco, that other great Bolivian civilisation, could be dated any further back than a few centuries BC.)

What had happened to the builders? Some pieces of evidence suggested that their descendants had still been around in large numbers when Columbus crossed the Atlantic in 1492, but by the time the Spaniards arrived two centuries later they had all but vanished. It was easy to see why no one had noticed them. Their lives appeared to be a continuous battle against nature, although their agriculture must have been capable of supporting a population that could easily have run to millions. (Historians have calculated that North and South America before 1492 might have contained 100 million people.)[2] When they vanished, the land quickly returned to nature.

Denevan's theory is that they may have been killed off by diseases brought by the white man, such as smallpox, measles and influenza, which swept across the continent like the Black Death, wiping out 90 per cent of the population.

What particularly interested me about the agricultural and forest-covered mounds in the Amazon was that this settlement answered a question that Rand and I had been asked repeatedly: if there *are* vanished civilisations, then where are the traces of their existence?

Rand always made the same reply. They might be lost under the sea, or the ice of Antarctica. Or they might by lying unnoticed under our noses, as the Moxos civilisation of the Amazon went unnoticed before Denevan persuaded the pilot to fly over it. Even around Tiahuanaco, which has been known since the time of the Conquistadores, no one suspected the sheer size of the civilisation that surrounded the present ruins, though the immense stone blocks of its port area – some weighing over 400 tons – which once looked out across Lake Titicaca, ought to have alerted scholars to the possibility that this was once a city on the scale of ancient Rome or the sacred Mexican city of Teotihuacan rather than an isolated town in the middle of a plain.

Not only were such sites found all over the world, but Rand's theory offered him a means of locating them. His method had led him to pinpoint Lubaantum, the Maya sacred centre in Belize, by looking for a specific spot 120 degrees west of the Great Pyramid and at a 10 phi longitude north of the equator. He had also discovered three immensely important sites at polar Golden Section latitudes (i.e., the Golden Section measured from the poles rather than from the equator). They were Baalbek, Ehdin (the O'Briens' Garden of Eden), and the Chinese pyramids. Tracing this line on to the east of China, he found that it passed through another sacred site of immense importance: Isé, in Japan (to which I had dedicated a page in my *Atlas of Sacred Sites*). He continued along the line and found a group of islands located on his 'sacred latitude': the Canary Islands, 700 miles off the coast of Spain, at 45 degrees west of the Great Pyramid – that is, one-eighth of the distance around the world. And they were, of course, 'phi sites'.

The Canaries are most commonly regarded as a holiday destination, but not as the location of any sacred temples or pyramids. Rand, though, recollected reading something about them in a book by the Norwegian explorer Thor Heyerdahl.

In 1969, twenty years after *The Kon-Tiki Expedition*[3] had become an international bestseller, Heyerdahl again set out to prove that ancient seamen could have crossed vast oceans – this time, from Egypt to America. He succeeded – at the second attempt – in a boat built of papyrus reeds. In his book *The Ra Expeditions*,[4] describing these ocean voyages, he pauses to speak about the mystery of the natives of the Canary Islands, the Guanches.

The Guanches were discovered by the Spaniards who sailed in the wake of Columbus, and who, in the typical manner of the Conquistadores, virtually exterminated them. They were tall, blue-eyed and blond, and are described by *Encyclopaedia Britannica* as of the Cro-Magnon type. One authority compares them to the natives of Muges, in Portugal, whose origins can be traced to about 8,000 BC.[5]

How did they get there? They must have come by sea, yet they were farmers and sheep breeders and possessed no boats. In fact, they detested the sea. Heyerdahl's suggestion is that the Guanches arrived on boats of papyrus reeds, like the *Ra*, and never mastered the technique of making wooden craft with joined planks. Another oddity was that they practised mummification and cranial trepanning, as in ancient Egypt and Peru. Were they, as Heyerdahl suggests, sailing across the Atlantic, on their way to America, when they discovered the Canaries, and decided to settle there?

Another authority on the Guanches, the Brazilian Dr Arysio Nunes dos Santos, has pointed out that their language is related to the 'Dravidian' family of languages from India,[6] but what would Aryan types from India be doing in the Canaries? Santos advances the theory that they were natives of Atlantis, escaping after the great catastrophe, and that Atlantis was somewhere in the region of Indonesia. Santos may, of course, be mistaken in calling the homeland of the Guanches 'Atlantis', but he could still be correct about where they came from, and when. At all events, Heyerdahl bore in mind the mystery of the Guanches. And when, in 1998, a native of the Canaries told him about black stone pyramids, he hastened to go and see for himself.

The pyramids – eight of them – were discovered near the town of Guimar, on Tenerife. They had six steps, and bore a distinct resemblance to the step pyramids of South America. One was even in the centre of the town, but no one had paid it much attention because it looked like a series of terraces with a flat top. Heyerdahl recognised it for what it was, persuading a Norwegian businessman to buy the pyramids and set up a museum.

If Rand is correct, some of the Guanches preferred to remain on the Canaries because they are at a sacred latitude and longitude, a suitable spot for settling and for building temples to the sun.

The Moxos Plain of Bolivia and the Guimar pyramids on Tenerife are two examples of civilisations that vanished – or at least, retreated into unrecognisability. Heyerdahl had found yet another in northern Peru, when he was looking for evidence of ancient seafaring that might prove his theory that natives of South America sailed across the Pacific.[7]

One day in March 1987 Heyerdahl was driving north from the ruins of Chan Chan, the former capital of the Chimu Indians, which is near the coastal city of Trujillo. Driving along the Pan-American Highway, he was looking for a solitary pyramid that he had once seen in the middle of the desert. He was unsuccessful, but he bumped into an old friend, the museum director Christopher Donnan, who was excavating a pre-Inca city called Pacatnamu, and told him a curious tale about robbery and violence.

A month earlier, on 6 February 1987, a group of tomb robbers dug their way into a small pyramid near a village called Sipan, near Chiclayo. To call it a pyramid would strike the visitor to Sipan as an exaggeration, for the three pyramids of Sipan look more like weathered hills scored with hundreds of water channels. The people of the area, however, know they are ancient tombs, and that small artifacts they find there, such as beads, can be sold to foreign tourists for a few pesos. Some of these amateur tomb robbers had sunk a shaft from the top of one of the pyramids, called Huaca Rajada, then dug outwards from it.

The looters often spent all night searching the tunnels made of adobe bricks and found nothing, but on this occasion they were in luck. In a groove between two bricks, their leader – an unemployed lorry driver named Ernil – found eight hammered gold beads. On the black market they were worth around $17 each. Eagerly, Ernil drove a tyre-iron into the ceiling – and was knocked to the floor by a landslide of rubble and sand. When ten fellow thieves rushed up to see what had happened, they found that the prone Ernil was covered with golden artifacts, obviously worth a fortune. Ernil had punctured the floor of a burial chamber, and it proved to be full of gold and silver knives, gold masks, chains of beads and statuettes of jaguars and horned monsters.

The looters carried off eleven rice sacks filled with treasure. There was enough gold to make them all rich. Unfortunately, they quarrelled during the division of the spoils. One man was killed with three gunshots to the chest. Another of the looters took to his heels and called the police. Not long afterwards, Ernil was killed when the police came to try and arrest him.

The local museum curator, Walter Alva, was called in to examine the captured loot. He realised immediately that the robbers had found the Peruvian equivalent of Tutankhamen's tomb, although these magnificent artifacts were not as old as those of the boy pharaoh. They had been created by a civilisation of Indians called the Moche, who flourished from about AD 100 to AD 700. Then they abruptly vanished. The reason for their disappearance was a mystery until the late 1990s, when it was realised that there had been a forty-year drought in Peru in the sixth century AD. The heavy rains caused by El Niño ceased, and the Moche starved. This was the same drought that, archaeologists speculate, led the Indians of the Nazca Plains of Peru to create their vast menagerie of animals – monkeys, whales, spiders, birds – visible only from the air, in a vain attempt to persuade the gods to send back the rain.

Regrettably most of the treasure of the Huaca Rajada had already been sold by the time the police went to arrest Ernil. Walter Alva told the story to Thor Heyerdahl as the two stood at the bottom of the robbers' shaft, and he permitted

Heyerdahl to examine a superb gold mask, with eyes made of blue lapis lazuli. As Heyerdahl looked at it, he thought again about the legends of the gods who came to South America, bringing civilisation with them.

While the Mexicans believe that the god Quetzalcoatl came from the east, the Peruvians in the Lambayeque Valley, where the pyramids are situated, have a legend of a king called Naymlap, who arrived from the west on a balsa wood raft and led his followers inland for a mile, where he built palaces at a place called Chot. Like Quetzalcoatl and Kon Tiki, he was worshipped as a god, and when he died his followers buried him in a pyramid and announced that he had flown away. A Jesuit priest named Cabello, who recorded the ancient tradition, declared that Naymlap was succeeded by eleven generations of kings, who were also buried in pyramids.

This all came to an end when the last of the kings, Fempellec, was seduced by a demon in the guise of a beautiful woman. After that, the gods sent storms, followed by the Great Drought. To propitiate them, Fempellec was tied up and thrown into the sea, but it was too late to avert catastrophe.

After the Moche came conquerors called the Chimu, who built Chan Chan, and were in turn conquered by the Incas, whose civilisation was so vast that it needed two capital cities. But the Inca empire lasted for a mere century before the arrival of the Spaniards, who brought this cycle of great civilisations to an end.

As Heyerdahl stared at the blue-eyed mask, Alva told him of more pyramids, about 130 miles north, at a place called Túcume, and offered to take him there. And so, at dusk on that March day, Heyerdahl found himself looking at seventeen pyramids that might have been mistaken for natural hills, scored into runnels by El Niño. In fact, photographs make them look rather like the giant hills of china clay waste in the St Austell area of Cornwall where I live.

As far as archaeology was concerned, these were virgin territory. Heyerdahl decided there and then that, for the next year or so, Túcume would be his home, until the pyramids had given up their secrets.

It was a risky venture for the seventy-three-year-old Norwegian. To begin with, Peru was full of terrorist guerrillas who called themselves the Shining Path; they had even stolen the telephone lines connecting Túcume to civilisation. And then the villagers of Túcume regarded the pyramids as their own property; Heyerdahl was an intruder, and a naked dead man, found shot in the head at the foot of one of the pyramids, may have been intended as a warning. They also accused this foreign intruder of being a thief – they were soon telling a story about how Heyerdahl had found a duck and twelve ducklings in pure gold and sold them. As soon as it became clear that Heyerdahl was providing the villagers with the employment they so badly needed, though, hostility turned to friendliness and they even ceased to steal from him.

Heyerdahl and his team found no treasure comparable to that uncovered at Sipan by Ernil and his fellow thieves, but early in 1992 he found something that meant even more to the explorer. One of the archaeologists, Alfredo Narvaez, was told about a small pyramid that had been penetrated by looters. Narvaez found a looters' pit with two spiny trees growing in its centre. As a workman was clearing these away, he saw that one tree had the form of a cross, which is regarded as sacred by the locals. The workman made an offering to the tree, and asked it to help them find 'beautiful things'.

One week later, they had uncovered a wall decorated with a frieze showing a raft made of balsa wood. Here was evidence not only that the people who built the pyramids were seafarers, but that they used the same type of raft that had once carried Thor Heyerdahl across the Pacific to Polynesia.

And so, with the balsa frieze of the Moche and the step pyramids of Tenerife, Heyerdahl felt that he had established evidence that ancient voyagers were plying the Pacific and the Atlantic long before Columbus – a view, of course, that accords perfectly with that of Ivar Zapp and George Erikson.

As soon as I read Heyerdahl's *Pyramids of Túcume*,[8] I emailed Rand to ask whether the site had any significance for our Atlantis blueprint. Regrettably, the answer finally turned out to be no. But while searching his atlas for Túcume Rand noticed Trujillo, where Heyerdahl had been staying when he learned of Túcume, and which fits the pattern perfectly. Rand wrote:

> Trujillo is a Giza Prime Meridian site, being 110 degrees west of the Great Pyramid. It shares this longitude with Quito (the northern end of the Inca trail) and North Bimini. It is midway between Tiahuanaco (100 degrees west of Giza), being 10 degrees to its east, and four sites a further 10 degrees to the west (at 120 degrees): Copan, Lubaantum, Quiriga and Chichen Itza.

By the time of his next email Rand had located Túcume and seen that it is several hours to the north of Trujillo. Trujillo, Peru's third largest city, is close to the huge Chimu ruins of Chan Chan, covering 11 square miles, as well as the two other major sites of the Huaca Esmeralda and Huaco del Dragon, and 6 miles to the south are the magnificent pyramids of the Sun and Moon, the former the largest in Peru, which were built 700 years earlier by the Moche. Trujillo could indeed be regarded as a major sacred site. What is significant is that Rand had identified Trujillo as a sacred site before he knew of these temples and pyramids, and this sprang out of the discovery he had made while studying the Giza prime meridian.

Heyerdahl had come upon an other equally striking piece of evidence. In September 1976, the mummy of Rameses II, the last of the great Egyptian pharaohs, who died in 1,213 BC, arrived in Paris, to form the centrepiece of an exhibition at the Museum of Mankind. Rameses had spent much of his life battling the Hittites, and the great hall of columns in the temple at Karnak is perhaps his finest memorial.

When the mummy was examined, it was found to be

deteriorating. Scientists were asked to repair the damage. One of these was Dr Michelle Lescot, of the Natural History Museum, who found herself examining a piece of mummy bandage under an electron microscope.[9] To her astonishment, she recognised grains of tobacco, which seemed odd, for tobacco first came to Europe from South America in the time of Christopher Columbus.

The announcement of her find caused a storm. Egyptologists declared that the tobacco grains must have come from the pipe of some modern scientist who was smoking as he studied the mummy, so Dr Lescot took samples from deep inside the mummy. Again she found tobacco grains. Still the 'experts' refused to admit it. They said the grains probably came from some other plant, such as henbane, which was a member of the tobacco family. Dr Lescot knew they weren't, but decided not to press her point.

Fifteen years passed, then, in 1992, German researchers in Munich began studying the materials used by the ancient Egyptians in mummification. Since they wanted to find out whether any drug was present, they turned to a forensic scientist whose expertise had often been called upon by the police in cases of suspicious deaths. Her name was Dr Svetlana Balabanova, of the Institute of Forensic Medicine in Ulm.

Dr Balabanova was not asked to study the mummy of anybody as distinguished as a great pharaoh; this was a mere priestess called Henut Taui, who died around 1,000 BC in Thebes. Her tomb was plundered by robbers in the nineteenth century, and the mummy was sold to Ludwig I, Bavaria's art-loving monarch, who gave it to the museum in Munich. Dr Balabanova tested the mummy with a method that depends on antibody reactions, and also through a machine that analyses the molecular weights of substances and shows them in the form of a graph. Both methods showed that the mummy not only contained nicotine, but also the drug cocaine.[10] Cocaine is native to the Andes. When the tired traveller arrives at a hotel in La Paz or Cuzco, he is given a cup of tea made from coca leaves, which instantly relieves the dizziness resulting from the high altitude. It looked as if the Egyptians had known about its preservative properties more than 3,000 years ago.

Lescot's findings suggested that the Egyptians must have been in contact with the natives of the east coast of America, but if Balabanova was correct, it looked as if the ancient Egyptians had made it as far as the opposite coast too. As Heyerdahl knew, the ancient Peruvians also mummified their dead.

The reception of Svetlana Balabanova's analyses was even stormier than in the case of Michelle Lescot. She received abusive and insulting letters, accusing her of being a fantasist. She replied by publishing her figures and graphs, at which the archaeological establishment fell back upon its second line of defence – contamination. When Balabanova replied that, as a forensic scientist, that was the first thing she had ruled out, they came up with another explanation: the mummy was a 'forgery', a fake concocted by enterprising Arabs. Other tests, including carbon-dating, proved that to be untrue.

Embarrassed by this publicity, the museums concerned were inclined to try and forget the whole thing. But Dr Balabanova refused. She went on testing mummies, and she regularly found traces of tobacco and cocaine. The sceptics continued to insist that it must be some other type of tobacco, native to Europe and long extinct, but that failed to explain the cocaine.

Someone else recalled that in 1975 Roman jars had been found off the coast of Brazil in a bay known as the Bay of Jars.[11] In fact, jars had been turning up there for centuries, almost certainly from a sunken Roman galley. Since Roman historians would probably have mentioned trans-Atlantic voyages if they had known about them, we can probably assume that the galley was swept out to sea by storms and carried across the Atlantic by the same westward currents that had carried Heyerdahl's *Ra*. In the case of the Egyptians, the sheer quantity of 'cocaine mummies' ruled out this explanation.

Since Egyptologists have found no other signs of tobacco or cocaine in ancient Egypt, we may probably assume that there was no regular trade in these commodities. They must have been brought to Egypt at great expense for preserving the mummies of kings and queens and guaranteeing their immortality. We must face the conclusion that the Egyptian priests were aware of the great continent across 3,000 miles of ocean, and knew that it could be reached by taking advantage of the currents. Unless they landed on the east coast, and trekked across forests and prairies and mountains to reach Peru, we must also assume they sailed around the Cape of Storms (unless they took the even longer route across the Pacific). There could hardly be stronger evidence of Hapgood's ancient ocean-going civilisation.

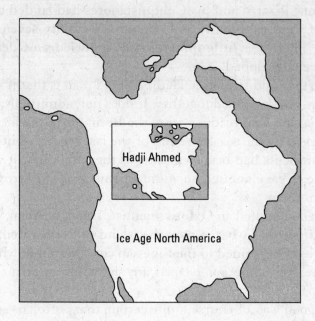

While examining the subject of America, it is interesting to consider Hapgood's *Maps of the Ancient Sea Kings* for its account of 'the remarkable map of Hadji Ahmad', which appeared in Turkey in 1559.

We note that the shape of Europe is not particularly accurate – the Mediterranean, for example, is entirely the wrong shape, and it is not clear whether the body of water running south from it is supposed to be the Red Sea or the Persian Gulf. Hapgood points out that the coast of Africa does not compare in accuracy with the Piri Reis map of nearly half a century earlier.

On the other hand, the American continent is so accurate that we could easily mistake it for a modern map. It is hard to believe that Columbus had arrived a mere sixty-seven years earlier. How had the mapmaker gained such accurate knowledge, when the continent was still mostly a vast wilderness? Above all, how had the Pacific coast been drawn with such precision? Pizarro and his Conquistadores had landed on the coast of Peru as recently as 1532, a mere twenty-seven years earlier. There was little time for such knowledge of detail to have been developed.

A further oddity of this Hadji Ahmad map is that it shows Asia and Alaska joined together. It does not, admittedly, show Beringia, the land bridge across the Bering Strait, which was submerged by the sea at the end of the last Ice Age, but if the two continents had been separate, as they are today, it would have been easy enough to indicate this with a narrow gap between them.

Hapgood quoted an Oxford scientist, Derek S. Allan,[12] who pointed out that what is now the island of Novya Zemlya is shown as being joined to the Siberian coast, and that what are now the New Siberian Islands are shown as an area of dry land.

Hapgood was, of course, quite certain that portolans such as the Hadji Ahmad map were based on far earlier maps that date back to a long-forgotten civilisation of 'ancient sea kings' – in fact, to Atlantis. Robert Temple disagrees, and in the 1998 edition of *The Sirius Mystery* puts forward his own interesting theory.[13] He accepts that ancient maps of Antarctica – such as the Piri Reis map, the Oronteus Finnaeus map, the Philip Buache map – show an Antarctica without ice, but he argues that they were not made by 'Antarcticans' (i.e., Atlanteans). His own view is that the maps are 'survivals of knowledge left by visiting extraterrestrials who were able to detect the true continental outline of Antarctica through the ice' from their orbiting spacecraft.

Rand has pointed out the objection to this theory. If Temple's spacemen surveyed Antarctica when it was under its present sheet of ice (say 600 BC), why did their survey (in the Hadji Ahmad map) show no gap between Asia and Alaska? Surely the most logical answer is that the maps were made when Lesser Antarctica and Beringia were free of ice?

Rand has here drawn attention to an important fact that Hapgood preferred to leave unstated. A map that seems to show Asia and Alaska joined together must have been made long before Hapgood's 'worldwide maritime civilisation' of 7,000 BC; it would need to have been drawn around 12,000 BC or earlier. In other words, Hapgood is implying that at least some of the portolans originated before the 'catastrophe' that Plato speaks of.

The quest of this book begins, in effect, in 1966, when Hapgood concluded *Maps of the Ancient Sea Kings* by stating that the portolans established that there must have been a worldwide maritime civilisation in 7,000 BC. If there was a *worldwide* civilisation 9,000 years ago, then it must have had origins that go back at least some time before that.

We know that Hapgood was keeping something back: his belief that Plato's Atlantis was a true story, and that therefore a maritime civilisation had existed since well before 10,000 BC. This notion accords with the views of Neil Steede and Oswaldo Rivera, the Director of Bolivian Archaeology, that

Tiahuanaco may be as much as 12,000 years old. (Steede has since revised his estimate downward to 9,000 BC – which would be, of course, after the flood.)

We may also recall Robert Bauval's view that the ancient Egyptians regarded the Nile as a reflection of the Milky Way, and placed the pyramids accordingly. And in *The Sacred Valley of the Incas: Myths and Symbols*, Fernando Salazar explains in detail how the valley of the Vilcanota River, which includes Machu Picchu and Ollentaytambo, was carefully landscaped to reflect the Milky Way, and that the astronomical knowledge encoded in it extends back to the building of Tiahuanaco. Whenever we look into the distant past, we seem to discover that ancient peoples possessed a sophisticated astronomy.

Rand's Atlantis blueprint – particularly the fact that a series of American sites are linked to a Giza prime meridian – carries Hapgood's argument one step further. If Tiahuanaco was built – as Steede now believes – around 9,000 BC, then we must suppose the Giza meridian was also in use at that time. It is, in fact, Rand's view that the Giza meridian must be 'post-flood' because all the meridians link to the North Pole.

Rand's blueprint obviously goes further than Hapgood for, if he is correct, Tiahuanaco was only one of a worldwide web of religious sites. It also seems to emerge that whoever did the 'siting' was aware of the earlier crust movements that preceded the Hudson Bay Pole. Rand's blueprint shows that many sites can be aligned on the two earlier poles, suggesting some tradition that extends back at least 100,000 years.

Let me try to give an overall picture of the theory that is beginning to emerge. The notion that our ancestors were ignorant cavemen is a misconception – they were far more intelligent than we give them credit for. Our mistake lies in identifying intelligence with the left brain. There is a deeper, more intuitive kind of intelligence, which is almost beyond our comprehension.

Compared to the intelligence of early man, the intelligence

of modern man is like a microscope compared to a telescope. Modern man *narrows* his senses to study minutiae. Our remote ancestors widened their perceptions to try to understand the cosmos. This explains, for example, why the precession of the equinoxes has been known for hundreds of generations.

Enormous and catastrophic crust movements also gave ancient man an urgent reason for studying the earth under his feet. A fairly simple 'predicter' built of posts, a 'Uriel's machine', would have served his purpose.

The 'blueprint' recognises that, while there are more than sixty sacred sites related to the Hudson Bay Pole, there are eight that are related to the Hudson Bay Pole and, at the same time, to the Yukon Pole: Byblos, Jericho, Nazca, Cuzco, Xi'an, Aguni, Pyongyang and Rosslyn Chapel.

We believe that the 'great catastrophe' took place about 9,600 BC, and that the North Pole then moved to its present position. Which implies, of course, that Atlantis (or whatever we choose to call this earlier civilisation) existed for some time before 9,600 BC. How long before? It must surely have been a long time, since the Atlanteans established more than sixty sacred sites all over the world.

Looking through the sacred sites, Rand noted that Avebury, Abydos and Nippur represented a special case. Most people are familiar with Avebury because it is 'next door' to Stonehenge, but not all of us are aware of the significance of Nippur and Abydos.

Nippur was the religious capital of the Sumerians and is where the epic of *Gilgamesh* was discovered at the end of the nineteenth century by the Babylonian Expedition from the University of Pennsylvania. Christian and Barbara Joy O'Brien, whom we met in Chapter 7, base much of their research on their translation of the Kharsag Epic, another remarkable piece of Sumerian mythology discovered at the holy city of Nippur.

The 'Osireion', a key building at Abydos (the birthplace of Osiris), was discovered in 1903 and excavated in 1913–14.

Like the Temple in front of the Great Sphinx, it was built using massive stones, many weighing 100 tons. Professor Naville, of the 1914 Egypt Exploration Fund that undertook the excavation, wrote: 'I should even say that we may call it the most ancient stone building in Egypt.'

Like the eight sites listed above, Avebury, Abydos and Nippur were linked to the Yukon Pole, but they were also, Rand observed, all slightly misaligned to the Hudson Bay Pole.

Was it possible, he wondered idly, that these three had been the 'original' sacred sites? He had already told me he suspected that the time of the Yukon Pole was regarded by later generations as a kind of Golden Age, so it would be natural that the original 'markers' should have been related to it.

He had another reason for believing these three sites to be unique. When he studied their latitudes, he realised they were all one degree 'out' when compared with the other seven earlier sites mentioned above. According to Rand's calculation, for example, in order to match the pattern of the other seven sites, Avebury should have been at 45 degrees north, but was actually at 46. Abydos and Nippur should both have been at 10, but were actually at 11.

Supposing that, during the time when Avebury, Abydos and Nippur were the only sacred sites, something extraordinary happened; some cosmic event, like a close encounter with a comet, that caused a one-degree shift in the earth's crust. We must bear in mind that one degree on the surface of the earth is about seventy miles. And if it happened fairly quickly, the result must have been fairly traumatic – although, of course, nothing like the 30-degree slide of 9,600 BC.

Such an 'earlier shift', which Rand refers to as the 'X-event', could explain why Avebury, Abydos and Nippur were misaligned by one degree. The X-event would have acted, as he put it, as a 'kick in the ass', and sixty-six more 'catastrophe-predictors' were hastily established to supplement the initial three at Avebury, Abydos and Nippur. I asked Rand: 'When do you think this X-event occurred?' His answer was: 'I don't know. All I know is that it was before 9,600 BC.'

Without a date and physical evidence to substantiate the X-event, Rand admits that this idea of 'early-warning' bases must remain pure speculation. But he points out that Enoch seemed to have foreknowledge of the coming flood when he spoke to Noah. That knowledge could plausibly have come from changes in the position of Avebury, Abydos and/or Nippur following a one-degree 'mini-displacement'.

Rand also believes that his blueprint theory can find the lost city of Atlantis.

In the second half of the 1980s the study of 'mitochondrial DNA' (DNA inherited only from females) led to the discovery that modern humans all sprang from one 'mitochondrial Eve' about 200,000 years ago. The footprints of an anatomically modern woman were discovered in South Africa in 1997; she had walked across the Langebaan Lagoon 117,000 years ago. In short, there is now a consensus that modern humans emerged before 100,000 years ago.

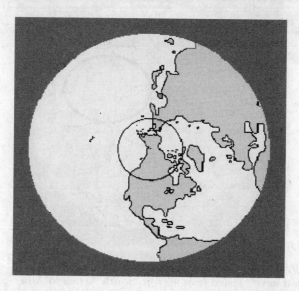

100,000 years ago the Arctic Circle was centred upon the Yukon Pole.

The usual date given for the emergence of Cro-magnons is about 40,000 years ago, when they appeared in Europe. Where were they between 100,000 years and 40,000 years ago?

Rand's suggested answer is Lesser Antarctica. According to Hapgood's *The Path to the Pole*, the North Pole was in the Yukon 100,000 years ago. Note that the Antarctic Circle extended towards southern Africa where, we know, the remains of anatomically modern humans were found. The presence there of seashells, along with the human fossils dating to 92,000 years ago, means our ancestors knew how to exploit the ocean from an early date. But how could they have travelled from southern Africa to South America and Antarctica?

Thor Heyerdahl demonstrated that the ocean currents act as silent conveyor belts, like the moving sidewalks in airports. If modern humans were exploiting sea resources on the shores of South Africa during the Yukon Pole, then it is entirely pre-dictable what would happen to them when – as was bound to

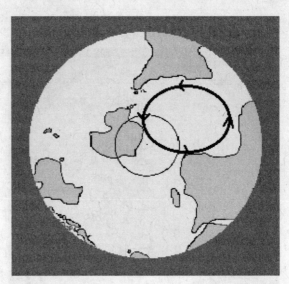

100,000 years ago, the ocean currents in the South Atlantic would have carried people from South Africa to America and Lesser Antarctica.

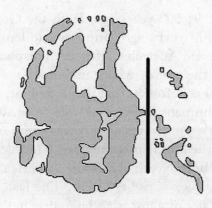

Atlantis Channel

The 'Atlantis Channel' separated mainland Antarctica from
the islands lying towards South America.

happen – some were swept out to sea. We know that Japanese
sailors made their way across the wider Pacific Ocean, landing
in California and eventually finding their way to Arizona.[14] In
1999 fossils discovered in Brazil proved to belong to an
Australian Aborigine.[15]

Ocean currents in the southern hemisphere move in a
counter-clockwise direction. The following map shows the
ocean and wind patterns prior to 91,600 BC:
People on boats or rafts could have been carried from South
Africa, up the west coast of the continent, and across the
South Atlantic, to Brazil or Argentina – and to the ice-free
regions of Lesser Antarctica. At this time there would have
been a channel between the mainland and Antarctica's chain of
islands, which Rand calls the 'Atlantis Channel'. This would
have had an impact upon the ocean and wind currents because
it would have allowed passage into the Pacific side of Lesser
Antarctica.

Now we have a scenario whereby modern humans were
transported by ocean currents to Lesser Antarctica before the

crust displacement of 91,600 years ago. With the Greenland displacement of 50,600 years ago, humans suddenly reappeared in Africa, Asia and Australia. After each displacement, people spread across the world, which may not be a coincidence. Around 91,600 BC, after a crust displacement, we find the fossil remains of humans in South Africa. The 50,600 BC displacement brought a sudden influx of people into Asia and even Australia. With the last displacement of 9,600 BC a flood of humans arrived in both North and South America, as well as (if Schwaller de Lubicz is right) Egypt. The last wave of refugees carried rich tales of a lost island paradise in the south that was destroyed by a flood.

Is it not possible, Rand asks, that modern humans evolved on Lesser Antarctica during the 40,000 years of silence in the fossil record? If so, then we should find there the remains of modern humans dating back 50,000 or possibly 125,000 years or more.

Lomas and Knight have constructed 'Uriel's machine' for studying the heavens, and they also deduced, from the words of the prophet Enoch, at what latitude the machine must have been located in 'paradise'. Their analysis of this data shows, they believe, that Enoch was taken to a place between the range of latitudes 51 and 59 degrees north.[16] They rule out the southern hemisphere because 'the first thing we could be reasonably certain of was that his latitude must be north of the equator, because the only land at these latitudes to the south would place him in Chile, Argentina, Tasmania or New Zealand, which all seemed equally improbable'.[17]

Rand points out that there would have been plenty of inhabitable land on Lesser Antarctica that would fall within these latitudes.

The authors settle on latitude 55 degrees north, which takes them to Scotland and, of course, Rosslyn Chapel. There is an unusual astronomical fact about 55 degrees that captures their imagination: 'We found it very interesting that the rising points of the sun at the summer solstice and winter solstice

316

form a perfect right-angle at the latitude of 55 degrees North, forming a "square year".'[18]

In this book we have noted that 55 degrees, 37 minutes north is a phi distance from the equator to the North Pole. Rand suggests that Lomas and Knight have found the correct latitude at which Enoch saw Uriel's machine, but Rand argues that it was on Lesser Antarctica, and that the original device may date back almost 100,000 years. (And if this assertion seems breath-taking, bear in mind that Uriel's machine is actually a simple arrangement of posts or standing stones for studying the heavens, and that this book has tried to demonstrate that ancient man has been studying the stars for tens of thousands of years.)

Rand says:

In November 1999 Rose showed me a journal article called 'Active volcanism beneath the West Antarctic ice sheet and the implications for ice-sheet stability'.[19] She thought I might be interested because of my concern for the safety of the Lesser Antarctic ice sheet. The article spoke of possible volcanoes under the ice which were undermining the stability of the ice sheet.

Then I came to the following words: 'Strikingly circular features in the Landsat images from ice stream E in West Antarctica might also be interpreted as volcanic constructs.' I was immediately alerted because this 'strikingly circular feature' was near the coast along the Ross Sea. We know that Plato's city of Atlantis was immense and circular in design and that it was carved from a small hill that stood on a plain near the ocean's shore. All these details we outlined in *When the Sky Fell*.[20] Now it seemed we might have stumbled upon the city of Atlantis by accident.

The authors of the article wrote: 'This depression is underlain by a peak in the subglacial topography that is associated with a unique magnetic signature' and brought to my mind that one of the features of Plato's Atlantis was encircling metal walls.

The authors offered the location of the 'volcano': 'Located northwest of the Whitmore Mountains (81:52:05 S, 111:18:10 W), this feature is near the proposed southern flank of the rift system, and is 100–200 km east and inslope of the initiation of ice streaming. The subglacial peak, which is 6 km wide at the base, rises 650 m above the surrounding topography to within 1,400 m of the ice surface.'[21]

Here, Rand points out, we have mountains, a rising hill on a plain and even possibly Plato's hot springs that could be the source of the 'initiation of ice streaming'.

The location of the satellite image turns out to be at 55 degrees 15 minutes south during the Yukon Pole, between Lomas and Knight's ideal of 55 degrees and the blueprint Golden Section latitude of 55 degrees, 37 minutes. Is the 'strikingly circular' structure beneath 1,400 metres of ice in Lesser Antarctica the lost city of Atlantis? The search for the lost city is a quest that has been abandoned. But the Atlantis blueprint offers a key to unlock this possible site. Like Rennes-le-Château, Nanking, Rosslyn Chapel and the 'pyramid' off the waters of Yonaguni, the ringed structures glimpsed beneath the ice of Antarctica are linked by a phi latitude to the Yukon Pole. Was the city constructed, tens of thousands of years later, to commemorate the first settlement of those early men on Antarctica?

Is there a lost city beneath the ice of Antarctica?

Appendix 1

BLUEPRINTS FROM ATLANTIS

RAND FLEM-ATH

In November of 1993 I received a fax from John Anthony West that started me on a four-year quest. The article that slipped through the fax machine that day had been written by an Egyptian-born construction engineer by the name of Robert Bauval. Little did I suspect that Bauval would soon become known for his revolutionary theory that the pyramids of Egypt were a mirror image of the constellation of Orion (see *The Orion Mystery*). However, in the article I read that day Robert had taken his idea even further. He revealed that not only the pyramids but also that most famous of all sculptures, the Sphinx, was orientated to the constellation of Orion as it appeared in 10,500 BC (see *The Message of the Sphinx*).

John followed up his fax with a telephone call – one of our earliest conversations. He had read the original manuscript of our book *When the Sky Fell* (see website at www.flem-ath.com) and had volunteered to write an Afterword. Our theory that Antarctica could hold the remains of Atlantis was framed by the concept of a geological phenomenon known as earth crust displacement about which I had spent years corresponding with Charles Hapgood. I had concluded, based on extensive research into the origins of agriculture

319

and the late Pleistocene extinctions, that 9,600 BC was the most probable date of the last displacement.

After discussing details about the Afterword for *When the Sky Fell*, John, in his usual direct manner, asked me: 'If Bauval is right that the Sphinx points to a date of 10,500 BC how do you reconcile that date with your time period of 9,600 BC for the last displacement of the earth's crust?'

John had put his finger on a very important point. If the Sphinx had been built before the crustal displacement, as Bauval's data indicated, then the monument's orientation would have been changed as the earth's crust shifted, resulting in a misalignment. But the fact remains that the Sphinx – indeed the whole Giza complex – is precisely aligned with the earth's cardinal points. 'Either Bauval's calculations of the astroarchaeology are incorrect or your date of 9,600 BC is wrong,' John said. 'How sure are you of that date? Could you be wrong by 900 years?'

'John,' I replied, 'a host of archaeological and geological radiocarbon dates indicate unequivocally that the last catastrophe occurred in 9,600 BC. I'm sticking with that. Perhaps the ancient Egyptians were memorialising an earlier date that was tremendously significant to them, not necessarily the date that the Sphinx was carved.'

In October of 1996 Robert Bauval and I continued the friendly debate at a conference in Boulder, Colorado. I was convinced that the Sphinx was constructed immediately *after* 9,600 BC and explained why. 'Imagine,' I began, 'that an asteroid or giant comet hit the United States today, utterly destroying the entire continent and throwing the whole culture back to the most primitive of living conditions. Then imagine that a team of scientists, perhaps safely under the ocean in a submarine, survived the cataclysm and decided to commemorate their nation and leave a message for the future by constructing a monument aligned to the heavens. What date would they choose to mark the memory of the United States of America? Would it be 1996, the year that their world ended? I don't think so. I believe that they would orientate their monument to 1776 – the date that the nation was born. And, in the same way, I think that although the Sphinx was created around 9,600 BC it is orientated to 10,500 BC because that date was significant to their culture.'

Appendix 1

Now it happens that inconsistencies and puzzles in science are like oxygen to my blood! My entire philosophy of science is predicated on the motto that anomalies are gateways to discovery. I usually conduct my research in a methodical and painstaking (some might say obsessive!) manner. However, over the past twenty years of investigating the problem of Atlantis and the earth's shifting crust I have discovered again and again that chance plays a critical role in discovery.

Between writing novels, Rose works part-time at the local university library and her serendipitous approach to research ideally balances my own meticulous methods. I can't begin to count the number of times that she has brought home a book that turned out to be *exactly* what I needed. So when she presented me with *Archaeoastronomy in Pre-Columbian America* I eagerly flipped it open.

Written in 1975 by Dr Anthony F. Aveni, one of the leading astroarchaeologists in the world, the book dropped a critical piece of the puzzle that I was trying to solve right into my lap. It appears that almost all of the major megalithic monuments of Meso-America are oriented *east* of true north. Aveni wrote that the people of Meso-America did 'tend to lay out many of their cities . . . oriented slightly east of true north . . . Fifty of the fifty-six sites examined align east of north.'

However, I found Aveni's explanation for this alignment wanting. He believes that the 'Street of the Dead', the famous avenue at Teotihuacan (near Mexico City) is the key to the whole mystery of why the monuments are strangely misaligned. This street, which runs directly toward the Pyramid of the Moon, is misaligned 15.5 degrees *east* of north. Because it points within one degree to the Pleiades constellation (a set of stars important to Meso-American mythology) Aveni views this skewed alignment as a kind of template, a master plan, for the rest of the megaliths throughout Meso-America. While this is true for Teotihuacan's Street of the Dead it is *not true* for the other sites that Aveni lists in his book. His argument that the other forty-nine sites are merely inadequate copies of the holy alignment of Teotihuacan rang hollow.

I had a different idea. A theory based on the science of geodesy, the study of the measurement of the shape and size of the earth.

In addition to astronomical observatories, what if these Mesoamerican sites were *also* part of a vast geographical survey? My study of ancient maps had convinced me that the Atlanteans had mapped the world. What if the orientations of the most ancient cities of Mexico were remnants of a lost science – the science of geography? What if the alignment of the ancient cities were a stone stencil – a precise blueprint of a pre-deluge earth?

Teotihuacan lies upon the longitude of 98 degrees, 53 minutes west. If we subtract the 15 degrees by which it is 'misaligned' we get a location of 83 degrees, 25 minutes west – *less than half a degree off* Charles Hapgood's location of the North Pole prior to 9,600 BC.

In other words, the Street of the Dead was 15.5 degrees west of the longitude that Hapgood had calibrated for the old pole.

When I made this discovery I was naturally very excited. Could it be that the ancient monuments of Mexico were orientated to the pole *before* the last earth crust displacement? The implications were profound. Such an orientation would point to the existence of a civilisation which must have held scientific knowledge of the earth's geography. They also must have possessed sophisticated surveying methods that they put to use in America *before* the earth's crust shifted.

I soon discovered that several important Meso-American sites (Tula, Tenayucan, Copan and Xochicalco, for instance) matched my geodetic theory. Each of their misalignments when subtracted from their current longitude yielded the longitude of the North Pole *before the last earth crust displacement* (83 degrees west). What if, I wondered, there were other sites in the Old World that were orientated to the old pole?

I began to research sites in Iraq, cradle of the most ancient civilisations.

Unlike Meso-America, these sites had not been studied in relation to their *misalignment* to the earth's cardinal points. I had to piece together the evidence from site to site, from author to author. But the tedious task was worth it to obtain the startling result. I soon discovered that many of the oldest sites in the Middle East are *west* of today's North Pole. Like the ancient sites of Meso-America they were orientated to the old pole.

The ancient city of Ur, its ziggurat (a stepped pyramid symbolising a sacred mountain) and its shrine to the moon god Nanna are orientated *west* of north (towards the 'old pole' in the Hudson Bay).

Without control of the holy city of Nippur no ruler could rightfully claim to be the King of Sumeria. The remains of the city lie south of Baghdad where some of the most famous tablets in archaeology were unearthed at the turn of century. The tablets disclosed the Sumerian belief in the existence of a long-lost island paradise called Dilmun. The myth of Dilmun, which we show in *When the Sky Fell* is remarkably similar to the mythology of the Haida people of British Columbia, relates how the island paradise is destroyed by the god, Enlil, in a great flood. Enlil's incredible power is honoured at Nippur with a temple and a ziggurat which is skewed *west of north*.

The ziggurat and 'White Temple' of the Sumerian city of Uruk also point to Hudson Bay rather than true north. The more I looked, the more ancient sites I found in the Middle East that pointed to the North Pole *before* the last earth crust displacement. Perhaps the most poignant is Jerusalem's 'Wailing Wall', the only remains of Herod's Temple, built upon the site of Solomon's Temple.

I now knew that I was looking at a unique geodetic phenomenon that demanded exploration. My next step was to calculate the former latitudes of the key megalithic and sacred sites of the world. If the latitudes were located at significant numbers then I could be sure that I really was on to something.

The first site I measured was, of course, the eternally compelling Great Pyramid at Giza. I calculated its co-ordinates against 60 degrees north, 83 degrees west (the Hudson Bay Pole). Giza had been 4,524 nautical miles from the Hudson Bay Pole, which meant its latitude was at 15 degrees north prior to 9,600 BC. I found it odd that Giza, which today lies at 30 degrees north (one-third of the distance from the equator to the Pole), should have been so neatly at 15 degrees north (one-sixth the distance) before the last earth crust displacement. So I decided to study Lhasa, the religious centre of Tibet, because I knew that this city, like Giza, lies at 30 degrees north today.

Lhasa's co-ordinates are 29 degrees 41 minutes north, 91 degrees 10 minutes east, which calculated at 5,427 nautical miles from the Hudson Bay Pole. The distance from the equator to the pole is 5,400 nautical miles (90 degrees times 60 seconds = 5,400), so Lhasa had rested just 27 nautical miles (less than half a degree) off the equator during the reign of Atlantis. This was getting spooky. The earth crust displacement had shoved Giza from 15 degrees to 30 degrees while moving Lhasa from 0 degrees to 30 degrees. Was this coincidence?

The coincidence started to become extreme when I compared the location of Giza and Lhasa (and a host of other ancient sites) with the position of the crust over *three earth crust displacements*. I was amazed to discover that latitudes like 0 degrees, 12 degrees, 15 degrees, 30 degrees, 45 degrees came up again and again. Each of these numbers divides the earth's geography by whole numbers. This seemed way beyond chance so I christened them 'sacred latitudes'. Most of these sites will be familiar to anyone who takes an interest in archaeology or the sacred sites of the world's major religions. All of these places are within 30 nautical miles (a day's walk) of sacred latitudes and are thus more accurately aligned geodetically than Aveni's astronomical calculations.

Sacred latitudes when the Pole was at Hudson Bay
(60 degrees north, 83 degrees west)

0°	Lhasa, Aguni, Mohenjo-Daro, Easter Island
5°	Byblos, Xi'an
10°	Ur/Uruk/Eridu, Thebes/Luxor, Ise, Susa
12°	Babylon, Pyongyang
15°	Giza Pyramids, Jericho/Jerusalem, Ashur, Nazca
30°	Carthage, Quito
45°	Copan, Marden

Note: Cities connected by '/' are located so close together that they yield the same results.

Sacred latitudes when the Pole was at the Greenland Sea
(73 degrees north, 10 degrees east)

0°	Quito
10°	Cuzco/Machu Picchu/Ollantaytambo
12°	Angkor
30°	Xi'an, Pyongyang
45°	Giza Pyramids, Nippur, Dahshur, Saqqara

Appendix 1

Sacred latitudes when the Pole was in the Yukon
(63 degrees north, 135 degrees west)

0°	Byblos, Machu Picchu/Cuzco/Ollantaytambo, Nazca, Abydos
5°	Tiahuanaco, Jericho/Jerusalem, Nippur, Babylon, Susa
10°	Rhodes (Knossos, on the island of Crete, is off by 41 nautical miles)
12°	Gozo (Malta)
15°	Lalibala
20°	Xi'an, Aguni
30°	Avebury/Stonehenge, Glastonbury, Pyongyang

The careful reader will note that several of these sites show up in more than one table. They are actually situated at the crossing points of two (even three) sacred latitudes. For example, Giza lies at the intersection of 15 degrees (Hudson Bay Pole) and 45 degrees north (Greenland Sea Pole) and today is at 30 degrees north. Lhasa, which today is near 30 degrees north, was at the equator during the Hudson Bay Pole and only 32 nautical miles from 30 degrees north during the Greenland Sea Pole.

Other sacred interconnections include:

Byblos (0° and 5°)	The most sacred city of the Phoenicians.
Machu Picchu/ Cuzco (0° and 10°)	A mountain-based ark in the high Andes and the holiest city of the Incas.
Nazca (0° and 15°)	Gigantic drawings visible only from the air.
Aguni (0° and 20°)	Underwater 'wall' off Japan's island of Okinawa.
Quito (30° and 0°)	Equatorial city at the north end of the Inca Trail.
Pyongyang (30° and 30° and 12°)	Capital of North Korea. Once had pyramids.
Susa (5° and 45° and 10°)	Sacred centre of Jewish learning in Iran. Capital of Elam. Prophet Daniel buried here.

Jerusalem (5° and 15°)	A site sacred to Judaism, Christianity and Islam.
Xi'an (20° and 30° and 5°)	The Chinese pyramids are located here.
Nippur (5° and 45°)	Documents relating to the lost island paradise of Dilmun were recovered from this Sumerian city.
Babylon (5° and 12°)	Site of the famous 'hanging gardens', one of the Seven Wonders of the World. Known for astronomy and astrology.

So what was going on here?

I believe that sometime before the devastating earth crust displacement, scientists in Atlantis recognised that the increasing earthquakes and rising ocean level that they were experiencing were a warning of a coming geological catastrophe. Trying to preserve their civilisation from this unavoidable disaster, they became obsessed with discovering exactly what had overtaken the globe in the remote past.

Teams of geologists fanned across the planet with a mission to gauge the *former* positions of the earth's crust. If they could determine exactly how far the crust had shifted in the past they might have some idea of what they could expect to face in the future. In the process of their investigations they left geodetic *markers* at the points they considered critical to their calculations.

After the earth crust displacement that destroyed Atlantis, the old calibrations were rediscovered by survivors who knew nothing of that forgotten and desperate geographic survey. They naturally believed that these marvellous geodetic markers from those who had gone before were messages from the gods. The sites became sacred – cities were built around them (it's no accident that 'Teotihuacan' is an Aztec term for 'Place of the Gods') and their very practical purpose was lost.

Further generations continued to worship at these huge shrines but eventually the winds of time began to erode the original structures. New altars were built on top of the remnants of the artifacts left by the surveyors from Atlantis. But during each reconstruction whispers from the past compelled the new architects to preserve the original orientations – orientations that pointed to the Hudson Bay Pole – to the time when Atlantis thrived.

The secrets buried beneath the slowly crumbling cities remained hidden for thousands of years. Eventually some intrepid souls in Egypt, Mesopotamia, India, China and America had the courage to begin excavations. The story of the remarkable discoveries uncovered by those who dared to dig under holy sites is only now emerging. The secret mission of the Knights Templar in Jerusalem is but one of these fascinating accounts.

I believe we can explain the enigmatic location of the ancient megaliths in a way that finally makes sense of their puzzling misalignments. These sacred sites, which we sense contain clues to our true history, continue to draw visitors who marvel over their awesome construction feats and wonder at the intelligence and vision of our anonymous ancestors. But my explanation covers only the tip of a very deep iceberg. There are many more sites that can be discovered using simple calculations derived from latitude changes after crustal displacements: not the least of which are sites on Atlantis itself, the island continent of Antarctica.

I never thought to find another adventure to compare with my eighteen-year search for Atlantis. But the unique placement of the earth's most sacred sites has emerged as a mystery that compels me with the same kind of fascination as that journey did. I hope to share this quest within the pages of a new book, *Finding the Future: Blueprints from Atlantis* (original working title), which will lift the veil from these ancient sites to reveal concealed time capsules – messages, records, and even blueprints – from Atlantis.

Appendix 2

LETTER TO RAND FLEM-ATH FROM CHARLES H. HAPGOOD, 16 OCTOBER 1982

Hapgood was living at 103 Davis Street (rear) in Greenfield, Massachusetts, 01301, while Rand and Rose were living at Flat 9, 9 Eldon Grove, London NW3.

I seem to have misunderstood you. *The Path of the Pole* is the second edition of *Earth's Shifting Crust*. I am working on the third edition now, and hope it will be published next year. The first edition is unobtainable, and I was flattered to learn its is [*sic*] a collector's item selling for about $100.00. However, I get no financial benefit, from that.

From the edition you have, no doubt you have realized that the way crust displacement affects evolution is that it is an accelerating factor. It opens new habitats, it clears ecological niches, it increases selection pressure. Biologists have recognized that climatic change is the leading factor in evolution and a few have realized that crust displacement at relatively short intervals provides that factor. It is unnecessary to have recourse to recondite factors to explain evolution. In some cases particular forms of life have endured for hundreds of millions of years without change. Look at the coelcanth, at the Komodo dragon lizard. There is no reason for it: it is

328

just accident. And species don't change unless they have to, and they don't die out without specific cause.

I believe that a displacement, once started, will continue until the mass of equilibrium is balanced. It then stops and a new movement awaits the development of another imbalance creating another centrifugal effect. The new movement will be in a direction unrelated to the last one; moreover there is no predetermined distance for the crust to travel. That is determined by the quantity of the centrifugal momentum acting on the crust in each case.

From examining hundreds of myths of earth upheaval I am convinced of one simple truth, that in the main they are not myths, not psychological developments, but accounts of real events, elaborated just as any event not accounted for will be accounted for by ad hoc rationalizing. Most of the catastrophe myths (for example, about Atlantis) don't bring in supernaturalism. I have recently concluded that a 'drag effect' would operate whereby the movement of the rigid crust would set in motion movements of the deeper layers, which would continue long after the movement of the crust stops, producing long-continued turbulence at the surface. Though the movement of the crust is slow there would be plenty of violent episodes, enough for any catastrophist. I think another movement has started; unfortunately for another ice age, starting several thousand years from now. A movement of the whole crust is what creates the plates and powers all their movements originally, though their movements continue long afterwards.

Your article in the *Anthropological Journal*[1] offers some good topics for discussion. I hope you don't mind my making some suggestions. On page 4 you use the phrasing, 'shifting of various parts of the earth's crust at different times, over the earth's axis'. I think it would be clearer for most people if you said 'shifting of the entire earth's crust as a unit over its semi-molten interior'.

In light of the theory of crustal displacement the western hemisphere is at a disadvantage because of geography. In the eastern hemisphere migration can occur in many different directions in accordance with the climatic changes. In the Americas the opportunities for migration are much more limited. It is not safe to depend on considerations of elevation,[2] because elevations can change greatly in a displacement. For example, it is certain that the elevations of the Andes were increased since agriculture was introduced.

Thus we find agricultural terraces at present above the line of eternal snow, and marine fauna in Lake Titicaca.

Furthermore, there is evidence that the last displacement of the crust moved both American continents southward about 30 degrees, and absolutely devastated life and civilization on them, while climatic change was much less drastic in the Old World, and more avenues of escape existed. I have found evidence of the ancient existence of agricultural cultures in the United States, in Mexico and in South America.

Furthermore, in recent exciting discoveries I believe I have convincing evidence of a whole cycle of civilization in America and in Antarctica,[3] suggesting advanced levels of science that may go back 100,000 years. I think setting any date for the beginning of agriculture is premature, anywhere on earth.[4]

A good deal of the evidence I have on this will be included in the new edition of *ESC*.[5]

Finally, I am sure you realize that I am not suggesting a sudden displacement of the crust.[6] I think it would take at least four thousand years. There could be very violent episodes during this time, such as the upheaval of the Andes must have been: but not mountain-high tidal waves.[7]

Of course, another angle that must be carefully calculated is that in any displacement maximum movement of the crust would occur along a central meridian of travel, and movement on either side would be proportional to distance from this meridian,[8] that is, to longitude, diminishing to zero at 90 from the meridian.

One of your references has great interest to me: Langway and Hansen, 1973.[9]

With best regards,

Sincerely,

Charles Hapgood

Appendix 3

SACRED SITES LINKED TO THE HUDSON BAY POLE (60 DEGREES NORTH, 83 DEGREES WEST)

RAND FLEM-ATH

These sacred sites are all within half a degree (30 nautical miles) of the former sacred latitude listed in the last column in the second table. Because so much of the world is ocean, some sites make it to this list that are the closest islands (marked with an asterisk*). Sometimes the exact co-ordinates could not be found and in these cases we put in brackets the closest known city, town or village.

We have also included two Egyptian sacred sites that were at latitude 14 degrees north since this number is so closely associated with Osiris.

Sacred sites linked to the Hudson Bay Pole, by latitude

Phi Equator (55:37)	Bimini (North), Ojai
50	Chichen Itza, Dunecht, Kilwinning/Loanhead/Rosslyn, Newgrange/Knowth/Tara, Uxmal
45	Canterbury, Copan/Quirigu, Marden
Phi Pole (34:23)	Canary Islands, Meknes
30	Carthage, Quito
25	Constantinople, Troy

Phi Pole/Pole (21:15)	Catal Huyak, Chavin, Knossos, Praisos, Rhodes
10 Phi (16:11)	Alexandria, Baalbek, Cuzco, Ehdin, Machu Picchu, Ollantaytambo, Paracas, Sidon
15	Ashur, Gilgal, Giza Pyramids, Heliopolis, Jarmo, Jericho/Jerusalem, Nazca
12	Babylon, Kish, Pyongyang
10	Eridu/Ur/Uruk/, Ise, Karnak, Kumasi, Kyoto Heian, Lagash, Luxor/Thebes, Naqada, Nara, Susa
5	Byblos, Elephantine, Lalibala, Raiatea*, Tahiti*, Xi'an
0	Aguni, Easter Island, Lhasa, Mohenjo-Daro

Sacred sites (with co-ordinates) measured by their distance to the Hudson Bay Pole

Sacred Site	Longitude/Latitude	Distance from HB Pole (nautical miles)	Former Latitude
Aguni	26:35N/127:13E	5,411	5,400 = Equator
Alexandria	31:13N/29:53E	4,428	4,429 = 10 phi
Ashur	35:29N/43:14E	4,503	4,500 = 15N
Baalbek	34:00N/36:12E	4,431	4,429 = 10 phi
Babylon	32:33N/44:25E	4,687	4,680 = 12N
Bimini (North)	25:46N/79:14W	2,059	2,063 = Phi Equator
Byblos	26:59N/49:40E	5,101	5,100 = 5N
Canary Islands	28:30N/14:10W	3,315	3,337 = Phi Pole
Canterbury	51:17N/1:05E	2,707	2,700 = 45N
Carthage	36:54N/10:16E	3,623	3,600 = 30N
Catal Huyak (Konya)	37:51N/32:30E	4,143	4,126 = Phi Pole/Pole
Chavin	9:18S/77:19W	4,157	4,126 = Phi Pole/Pole
Chichen Itza	20:40N/88:32W	2,370	2,400 = 50N
Copan	14:52N/89:10W	2,719	2,700 = 45N
Cuzco	13:32S/71:57W	4,433	4,429 = 10 phi
Dahshur	29:45N/31:14E	4,539	4,560 = 14N
Dunecht	57:10N/2:25W	2,378	2,400 = 50N
Easter Island	27:05S/109:20W	5,371	5,400 = Equator
Ehdin	34:19N/35:57E	4,408	4,429 = 10 phi
Elephantine	20:05N/32:53E	5,093	5,100 = 5N
Eridu	30:50N/46:02E	4,815	4,800 = 10N

Sacred Site	Longitude/Latitude	Distance from HB Pole (nautical miles)	Former Latitude
Gilgal	31:59N/35:27E	4,521	4,500 = 15N
Giza	29:59N/31:08E	4,524	4,500 = 15N
Heliopolis	30:03N/31:15E	4,523	4,500 = 15N
Ise	34:29N/136:41E	4,817	4,800 = 10N
Jarmo (Chamchl)	35:32N/44:50E	4,533	4,500 = 15N
Jericho	31:52N/35:27E	4,527	4,500 = 15N
Jerusalem	31:47N/35:13E	4,526	4,500 = 15N
Karnak	25:44N/32:39E	4,787	4,800 = 10N
Kilwinning	55:40N/4:42W	2,376	2,400 = 50N
Kish	32:33N/44:39E	4,692	4,680 = 12N
Knossos	35:18N/25:10E	4,098	4,126 = Phi Pole/Pole
Knowth	53:43N/6:30W	2,404	2,400 = 50N
Kyoto Heian	35:00N/135:45E	4,803	4,800 = 10N
Lagash (Tello)	31:37N/46:09E	4,774	4,800 = 10N
Lalibala	12:01N/39:05E	5,683	5,700 = 5S
Lhasa	29:41N/91:10E	5,427	5,400 = Equator
Loanhead	55:53N/3:09W	2,408	2,400 = 50N
Luxor	25:41N/32:24E	4,783	4,800 = 10N
Machu Picchu	13:08S/72:30W	4,407	4,429 = 10 phi
Marden	51:11N/0:30E	2,696	2,700 = 45N
Meknes	33:54N/5:37W	3,309	3,337 = Phi Pole
Mersea Island	51:48N/0:55E	2,671	2,700 = 45N
Mohenjo-Daro	27:17N/68:14E	5,389	5,400 = Equator

Naqada	25:52N/32:41E	4,780	4,800 = 10N
Nara	34:55N/135:49E	4,806	4,800 = 10N
Nazca	14:53S/74:54W	4,499	4,500 = 15N
Newgrange (Drogheda)	53:43N/6:21W	2,408	2,400 = 50N
Ojai	34:27N/19:15W	2,084	2,063 = Phi Equator
Ollantaytambo	13:14S/72:17W	4,414	4,429 = 10 phi
Paracas	13:50S/76:11W	4,431	4,429 = 10 phi
Praisos (Crete)	35:08N/26:07E	4,131	4,126 = Phi Pole/Pole
Pyongyang	39:00N/125:47E	4,708	4,680 = 12N
Quito	0:14S/78:30W	3,613	3,600 = 30N
*Raiatea (South Pacific)	16:50S/151:30W	5,654	5,700 = 5S
Rhodes (approx.)	36:15N/28E	4,119	4,126 = Phi Pole/Pole
Rosslyn	55:52N/3:13W	2,408	2,400 = 50N
Saqqara	29:51N/31:14E	4,533	4,560 = 14N
Sidon	33:32N/35:22E	4,437	4,429 = 10 phi
Susa	32:12N/48:20E	4,785	4,800 = 10N
*Tahiti	17:37S/149:27W	5,641	5,700 = 5S
Tara	53:34N/6:35W	2,407	2,400 = 50N
Thebes	25:41N/32:40E	4,790	4,800 = 10N
Troy	39:55N/26:17E	3,889	3,900 = 25N
Ur of the Chaldees	30:56N/46:08E	4,811	4,800 = 10N
Uruk	31:18N/45:40E	4,782	4,800 = 10N
Uxmal	20:21N/89:46W	2,395	2,400 = 50N
Xi'an (China) Pyramid	34:26:05N/108:52:12E	5,120	5,100 = 5N

Appendix 4

SACRED SITES LINKED TO THE YUKON POLE (63 DEGREES NORTH, 135 DEGREES WEST)

RAND FLEM-ATH

The Yukon Pole is more than 100,000 years old, although this does not necessarily mean that a civilisation existed at this time, as the locations of these sites might well only be geological markers left by Enoch's 'angels' a mere 12,000 years ago. On the other hand, it is possible that a civilisation at this time might have initiated the Uriel machines to 'reveal all the secrets of the depths of the earth'.

Sacred sites linked to the Yukon Pole, by latitude

Phi Equator (55:37)	City of Atlantis (South)
Phi Pole (34:23)	Kilwinning, Rosslyn
30°	Avebury, Baldock, Barbrook, Bath, Glastonbury, London, Old Sarum, Mersea Island, Pyongyang, Rollright Stones, Royston, Stonehenge, Tintagel, Vestermarie
Phi Pole/Pole (21:15)	Nanking, Rennes-le-Château
20	Aguni (Japan), No. 6 Pyramid (China)
10 Phi (16:11)	Lixus, Yonaguni
15	Abdera, Meknes

12	Gozo, Samos
10	Knossos, Raiatea
5	Alexandria, Babylon, Bassae, Jericho, Jersualem, Susa, Tiahuanaco
0	Abydos, Byblos, Cuzco, Machu Picchu, Nazca, Ollantaytambo, Tongatapu

The sacred sites in the following table are all within half a degree (30 nautical miles) of the former sacred latitude listed in the last column. Because so much of the world is ocean, some sites make it to this list that are the closest islands (marked with an asterisk*). Sometimes the exact co-ordinates could not be found and in these cases we put in brackets the closest known city, town or village. Baalbek was exactly on the sacred number 7.

Sacred sites (with co-ordinates) measured by their distance to the Yukon Pole

Sacred Site	Longitude/Latitude	Distance from Yukon (nautical miles)	Former Latitude
Abdera	40:56N/24:59E	4,506	4,500 = 15N
Abydos	26:11N/31:55E	5,427	5,400 = Equator
Aguni	26:35N/27:13E	4,204	4,200 = 20N
Alexandria	31:13N/29:53E	5,116	5,100 = 5N
Avebury	51:27N/01:51W	3,601	3,600 = 30N
Baalbek	34:00N/36:12E	4,980	4,980 = 7N
Babylon	32:33N/44:25E	5,083	5,100 = 5N
Baldock	51:59N/0:12W	3,595	3,600 = 30N
Barbrook	51:13N/3:52W	3,585	3,600 = 30N
Bassae	31:57N/35:46E	5,101	5,100 = 5N
Bath	51:23N/2:22W	3,598	3,600 = 30N
Byblos	26:59N/49:40E	5,411	5,400 = Equator
Cuzco	13:32S/71:57W	5,424	5,400 = Equator
Glastonbury	51:09N/2:43W	3,606	3,600 = 30N
*Gozo (Victoria)	36:03N/14:14E	4,692	4,680 = 12N
Jericho	31:52N/35:27E	5,105	5,100 = 5N
Jerusalem	31:47N/35:13E	5,109	5,100 = 5N
Kilwinning	55:40N/4:42W	3,329	3,337 = Phi Pole
*Knossos	35:18N/25:10E	4,841	4,800 = 10N
Lixus	35:12N/6:10W	4,435	4,429 = 10 phi
London	51:30N/0:10W	3,623	3,600 = 30N

Machu Picchu	13:08S/72:30W	5,389	5,400 = Equator
Meknes	33:54N/5:37W	4,518	4,500 = 15N
Mersea Island	51:48N/0.55E	3,616	3,600 = 30N
Nanking	32:03N/118:47E	4,126	4,126 = Phi Pole/Pole
Nazca (town)	14:53S/74:54W	5,429	5,400 = Equator
Nippur	32:10N/45:11E	5,106	5,100 = 5N
Old Sarum	51:06N/1:49W	3,621	3,600 = 30N
Ollantaytambo	13:14S/72:17W	5,400	5,400 = Equator
Pyongyang	39:00N/125:47E	3,595	3,600 = 30N
No. 6 Pyramid (China)	34:23:25N/108:44:12E	4,230	4,230 = 20N
*Raiatea	16:50S/151:30W	4,842	4,800 = 10N
Rennes-le-Château	42:55:44N/2:15:45E	4,139	4,126 = Phi Pole/Pole
Rollright Stones	52:00N/1:35W	3,575	3,600 = 30N
Rosslyn	55:52N/3:13W	3,339	3,337 = Phi Pole
Royston	52:03N/0:01W	3,594	3,600 = 30N
Stonehenge	51:11N/01:51W	3,616	3,600 = 30N
Samos	13:42N/26:59E	6,133	6,120 = 12S
Susa	32:12N/48:20E	5,101	5,100 = 5N
Tiahuanaco	16:38S/68:40W	5,671	5,700 = 5S
Tintagel	50:41N/4:46W	3,601	3,600 = 30N
Tongatapu (Nuku'alofa)	21:09S/175:14W	5,384	5,400 = Equator
Vestermarie	55:07N/14:50E	3,590	3,600 = 30N
Yonaguni	24:29N/123E	4,423	4,429 = 10 phi

Appendix 5

TRACING LOST SITES

RAND FLEM-ATH

Authors of UFO books are fond of the expression 'back-engineered'. They believe that the US government possesses at least one flying saucer and has hired experts to try to understand the underlying science of the alien crafts. This process is called 'back-engineering'. I'm not saying that a flying saucer actually exists, tucked in a secret hangar somewhere. Indeed, all my research is based upon the assumption that the past can be understood without reference to aliens or UFOs. But I do think that the idea of 'back-engineering' is appropriate to our search for lost sacred sites.

By back-engineering the Atlantis blueprint we can retrace the steps of the survivors of the flood. Hapgood's *Maps of the Ancient Sea Kings* shows maps that illustrate the shape of the continents and their positions before the displacement. Refugees from the deluge realised that to make use of this critical information they would have to update the latitudes that had been dramatically changed by the displacement. Giza, for instance, had moved from 15 degrees north to 30 degrees north. By surveying the planet from key points such as Giza, the survivors could overlay their accurate maps of the pre-flood world on to the new latitudes. This took them to specific places – places that eventually became sacred sites to following generations.

The Atlantis blueprint reveals several important sites (Copan, Quito, for example) that are linked in three ways. First, they are linked by a significant measurement to the Giza prime meridian. Copan, for example is 120 degrees west of the Great Pyramid (WGP). Second, they are located at a sacred latitude (Copan is at 15 degrees north). And third, they were also located at a sacred latitude during the Hudson Bay Pole (HBP) (Copan was at 45 degrees north). Perhaps we can extrapolate from this knowledge to find other sacred places that have remained hidden through time?

One of the most intriguing lost sites suggested by the blueprint is at 16:11S/58:52W on the border between Bolivia and Brazil, where Colonel Fawcett believed he had found the ruins of an Atlantean city. This site is promising because it lies one-quarter the distance around the globe from the Giza prime meridian and shares its latitude with Tiahuanaco. It also follows the pattern of Rosslyn Chapel (50/50 site) and Canterbury (45/45 site) in being also located at an angle that lies at a 12/12 intersection of the current and former pole.

Another site, in California, mirrors Fawcett's lost Brazilian city. The blueprint has led us to megalithic structures at 100, 110, 120, 130 and 140 degrees west of the Great Pyramid (WGP), and that's what led us to look for Brazilian sites at 90, 80 and 72 degrees WGP. If we look to the west and north we find that the 150 degrees WGP measurement cuts through southern California. The most promising latitude is the Polar Golden Section (PGS) division at 34:23N. The PGS denotes the latitude of Baalbek; Pyramid No. 6 in the Chinese province of Xi'an; Ehdin of the Kharsag epic; and one of the most sacred sites in Japan, the Shinto Temple at Ise.

During the Hudson Bay Pole, this same Californian site was located at 55:16N, which is less than half a degree from the perfect Equatorial Golden Section (EGS) latitude of 55:37N. So the mystery site in California was a double Golden Section site, being at a PGS position today and an EGS position before the flood. And it is linked to the Great Pyramid at Giza. Moreover, Kilwinning (55:40N) and Rosslyn (55:52N) are near this latitude today. Before the flood the California site shared its latitude with a tiny island off the south coast of Florida called 'North Bimini' (55:41N during the HBP). North Bimini is a site favoured by Edgar Cayce for Atlantis. It is at 110 WGP, sharing that longitude with the northern Inca capital of Quito.

When I realised this I searched a map of California for a location that was at 150 WGP at the Golden Section latitude of 34:23N. The closest city was called 'Ojai'.

I had never heard of it.

I've since discovered that Ojai (pronounced Oh-Hi) was immortalised in Frank Capra's classic 1937 film *Lost Horizon*. Capra needed the most beautiful setting that he could find to represent 'Shangri-La', the lost Tibetan city. In choosing Ojai for the site of his lost paradise, Capra was following in the footsteps of others who believed that the Ojai Valley was sacred. The Chumash people, who occupied large parts of southern California before the arrival of the white man, considered the Ojai Valley to be sacred. They called it the 'Valley of the Moon', and believed that it was 'an entry point into the land of the spirits'. As time went by Ojai became increasingly associated with spiritualism.

One of the most fascinating philosophers of the twentieth century was closely linked to the city. Born in India in May 1895, when he was eleven years old he was 'discovered' by a member of the Theosophical Society, who brought the boy to the attention of Annie Besant, a well-known leader of the Theosophical Society. She brought the boy to England and educated him there. His name was Jisshu Krishnamurti and he became a spokesperson for a radical free school of thought that advocated eliminating eventually all organised religion. His motto became 'Truth is a pathless land'.

In 1922, Krishnamurti made a visit to Ojai and fell in love with the valley, making it his life-long home. In an interview published in the *Ojai Valley News*, Krishnamurti said, 'The feeling you have is of a sacred place . . .' And 'in India, in Greece and other civilizations, when they find a beautiful spot like this, they put up a temple'.

Although there are no megalithic structures here, Ojai joins a select number of sites around the world that are linked by Golden Section divisions of the earth's dimensions (see table opposite).

APPENDIX 5

Golden Section latitudes today, during the Hudson Bay Pole and during the Yukon Pole

* = Giza Prime Meridian Site
** = City of Atlantis (see Chapter 10)

Phi Latitudes	Today	Hudson Bay Pole	Yukon Pole
10 Phi (16:11N)	Lubaantum* (16:17N)	Baalbek* (16:09N)	Yonaguni (16:17N)
	Tiahuanaco* (16:38N)	Paracas (16:09N)	Lixus (16:05N)
	Raiatea* (16:50S)	Cuzco (others – see Chapter 2) (16:07N)	
Pole to Pole (21:15N)	Wabar Tektite (21:30N)	Catal Huyak (21:26N)	Nanking (21:14N)
	Chichen Itza* (20:40)	Chavin de Huantar* (21:26N)	Rennes-le-Château (21:01N)
Pole to Equator (34:23N)	Xi'an pyramids (34:22N)	Canary Islands* (34:45N)	Rosslyn (34:23N)
	Ehdin* (34:19N)		Loanhead (34:21N)
	Baalbek* (34:00N)		Kilwinning* (34:31N)
	Ise (34:29N)		Tikal (34:31N)
	Ojai* (34:27N)		Nikko (34:03N)
Equator to Pole (55:37N)	Kilwinning* (55:40N)	North Bimini* (55:41)	
	Rosslyn (55:52N)		
		Ojai* (55:16N)	Atlantis** (55:15S)

**Lost sacred sites linked simultaneously to the Giza
prime meridian (GPM), the current and the former
position of the earth's crust/mantle**

*EGS = Equatorial Golden Section or 55:37N
**10 phi = 10 phi or 16:11N

Greenwich	GPM	Other Sites Today	Hudson Bay Pole	Other Hudson Bay Pole Sites
16:11S/58:52W (Brazil/Bolivia, one of Fawcett's Atlantean Cities)	90W	Tiahuanaco (100W)	12N	Babylon/Kish Pyongyang
34:27N/ 119:15N (Ojai, California)	150W	Ise, Xi'an, Baalbek, Ehdin (5E)	EGS*	North Bimini
45N/91:08E (Mongolia/ China)	60E	Lhasa (60E)	15N	Giza Nazca Jericho/ Jerusalem
20N/46:08E (Saudi Arabia)	15E	Ur (15E)	Equator	Easter Island Mohenjo-Daro Lhasa Aguni
15N/1:08E (Sahara Desert)	30W	Canterbury (30W)	10 phi**	Baalbek Cuzco Ollantaytambo Paracas Sidon Nineveh Machu Picchu Ehdin

Appendix 6

SPENDING TIME AND WASTING SPACE: HOW ICE CORE DATING WENT WRONG

RAND FLEM-ATH

Imagine that you have just returned from a visit to Disney World in Florida where you purchased a ticket in the state lottery. You get a phone call and are told that you have won $3,000,000! Your life has just changed. But wait, there is a problem. When you go to collect they tell you that the real figure is $400,000. Okay – it's a disappointment, but you really can't be too sad. Finally the cheque arrives in the mail and it reads $122,000. What would your reaction be? Wouldn't you want to investigate?

I tell this brief story for a serious purpose. Over the past couple of years 'experts' in ice core dating have claimed that the ice sheet on Lesser Antarctica is at least 3,000,000,[1] or 400,000,[2] or 122,000[3] years old, and therefore the theory of earth crust displacement has been falsified. People could never have lived in Lesser Antarctica a mere 12,000 years ago. But which date is the correct one? Something is very wrong here.

To find out what it is we must begin with a basic logical tool discovered by the Greek philosopher Pythagoras (circa 600 BC). He is generally regarded as the first European to claim that the earth is round and that it can be divided into climatic zones (polar, temperate and equatorial). He also introduced the notion of 'antipodes' – that people could live on the opposite side of the earth. The Greek word for 'feet' is '*pode*' and so Pythagoras called land in the southern hemisphere antipodes because the feet of the people living there were pointing in a direction that was counter to the northern hemisphere. 'Antipodes' means 'counter-footed'. This notion of antipodes is a fundamental logical tool for evaluating the reliability of the ice dating method.

Geologists almost never tire of repeating the phrase first coined by James Hutton that 'the present is the key to the past'. It remains a central concept in geology. If we wish to understand the past we must first understand the present. This is good advice and provided we remember that rates of change can vary without violating physical laws, it is advice that we need to take seriously. Today we do not find ice sheets accumulating in temperate zones (except in mountain ranges), nor do we find temperate-adapted animals living in polar zones. What we find instead is ice accumulating at the poles and only a small range of polar-adapted animals living within the polar zones.

When we look at Lesser Antarctica through the lens of ice core dating we get one set of 'facts', but when we compare these results with the evidence of the antipodes to Lesser Antarctica then other, contradictory facts emerge. What we find from the ice core dating is that Lesser Antarctica has been covered in ice for at least 122,000 years, if not more. But when we shift our attention to the opposite side of the globe and look at Siberia, Beringia and Alaska, we do not find equivalent ice sheets. Instead we find evidence of many large mammals such as horses, bison and rhinoceros swarming over grasslands. How can one part of the globe be under ice for at least 122,000 years while the exact opposite of the globe has no ice and large mammals (dating from 11,000 to 70,000 carbon-14 years ago)? This does not compute. Either the evidence from the north is wrong, or the evidence from the south is wrong.

What the 'ice core experts' are proposing is something for which we have no experience in the present: they claim that at one time, one side of the globe was under ice, while simultaneously, on the exact opposite side of the globe, large mammals were roaming on ice-free grasslands. Where on earth today can we find such a combination? We can't. If Siberia/Beringia/Alaska demonstrates evidence from a wide variety of dating methods and they all point to this area being much warmer before 9,600 BC, then we have every right to assume that the same must have been the case on Lesser Antarctica. It is simple logic as old as Pythagoras.

But the real problem that I have with those who cite ice core dating as the final word on the age of the Lesser Antarctic ice sheet is that these same people have nothing whatsoever to say about how the ice got there in the first place. They think that ice ages are simply about time and temperature changes and so they ignore the simple facts about where the ice formed and where it is today. What explanation do they offer for the fact that central Greenland and Greater Antarctica, which together hold more than 90 per cent of the world's ice, are situated in polar deserts?

The quest to solve the mystery of the ice ages has been one of the longest unsolved problems in science. Geology had been the darling of scientists in the nineteenth century, when giants such as James Hutton and Charles Lyell threw back the curtain of the earth's past to reveal time scales that staggered the public's imagination and shocked representatives of the Church. By challenging the Church's blind faith in the story of the flood and by stretching the time scale beyond the rigid confines of a world supposedly created in 4,004 BC, the uniformitarian geologists made a dramatic and lasting impact upon human consciousness.

During this time there was no challenge like geology. It was science's vanguard. Upon its foundations the likes of Charles Darwin built his radical theory of evolution. These were geology's heady days, but now the very science that once challenged the past with relentless observation and merciless logic has lost its way.

When Louis Agassiz first proposed the idea that the world had once experienced an ice age, the geological establishment laughed. Today there is no doubt that ice sheets have covered huge tracts of Europe and more than half of North America. But despite the fact that this theory is now entrenched in academic halls and is referred to daily by professors of geology, the actual cause of the ice ages remains an unsolved mystery.

Each year we are assured that this rather embarrassing state of affairs will be rectified and geology will be rid of its most persistent problem. But no one has yet been able to account for all the significant facts. When a problem such as this persists it often requires an entirely new perspective to initiate change. We believe that the problem of the ice ages has remained such a thorn in the side of geologists because it has been misconceived ever since Lyell took it over from Agassiz and transformed it into a uniformitarian theory.

Uniformitarianism is a research tradition in geology that continues to hold sway despite the fact that its logical inconsistencies were exposed in 1965. In that year, Stephen Jay Gould wrote one of his earliest published papers, entitled 'Is Uniformitarianism Necessary?'. Gould applied logic to the problem and was able to show that this idea was actually two ideas parading as one.

The early uniformitarians, like Hutton and Lyell, argued that science must not rely upon the assumption that changes of the earth could be explained through the actions of supernatural forces. They put forward a very important principle that became one of the key foundations of modern science: the idea that physical laws are invariant. What this means is that the laws of gravity, the dynamics of physics, are constant in the universe and do not change through time or space. The principle of invariance became one of the pillars not only for geology but also for science itself. It is an act of faith to believe that physical laws do not vary through time and space, but it is an act of faith that seems entirely reasonable to most scientists. We also support this notion but the problem arises when the second of uniformitarianism's dual ideas is brought into the equation.

That is the notion of gradual change. This is a theory of the earth, not a general principle of science, but uniformitarians often didn't appreciate the distinction. For them, anyone who challenges the idea of gradual change must also be challenging the notion of the invariance of physical laws. By separating the geological theory of gradualism from the scientific principle of invariance, Gould showed that uniformitarianism was ill conceived from the outset. His argument can be summarised by saying that 'invariance is true but gradualism is false'.

We need to go back to 1837 when the ice ages were first proposed by Agassiz to see how his idea was transformed into the uniformitarian theory that it is today. This historical review can help us see how ice core dating is ultimately flawed.

From the outset, Agassiz envisioned the ice ages as events that were suddenly thrust upon the earth:

A sudden intense winter, that was to last for ages, fell upon our globe; it spread over the very countries where these tropical

348

animals had their homes, and so suddenly did it come upon them that they were embalmed beneath masses of snow and ice, without time even for the decay which follows death.

Agassiz believed that the ice ages fanned out from the North and South Poles and engulfed the globe. This raised a troublesome problem. If the overall temperature of the earth had suddenly dropped, then how could the tropical animals have survived to the present day? Agassiz could not answer this question with logic, so he made a fatal error. He adopted the idea of 'special creation', which is the notion that after each catastrophic ice age God intervened in the process of evolution by repopulating the world with fresh tropical animals. By accepting the idea of 'special creation' Agassiz violated the prized principle of invariance.

Science simply would not have it.

And science was right.

As time went on, Agassiz's theory of sudden ice ages followed by special creations was replaced by Lyell's slow, gradual ice ages, which simply ignored the problem of tropical animals. This proved to be the better tactic and as a result Agassiz's catastrophic theory was absorbed into uniformitarian geology.

The problem of tropical animals is one that is still with us. And there is the equally troublesome problem of evaporation. In order to have snowfall you must first have moisture in the air and this in turn is dependent upon evaporation in the tropics. If the overall temperature of the earth falls with each ice age then the tropics also should be cooler. But if the tropics are cooler then this means there is less evaporation, and less evaporation ultimately means less snowfall. The creation of ice sheets requires substantial evaporation in the tropics. So what we really need is a theory that can provide evaporation in the tropics at the same time as snow is accumulating as ice sheets. A mantle displacement can explain these problems by replacing the simple presupposition of stable latitudes with the notion of variable latitudes. By treating the climatic zones (polar, temperate, tropical) as constants and the earth's mantle as the variable, the issue of the survival of tropical animals and the problem of evaporation in the tropics, during so-called ice ages, is resolved.

So why didn't the tropical animals disappear? And how did the snow form in the first place if the tropics were cooler? These are two simple questions that have never been properly answered by proponents of the theory that the ice ages are the result of an overall drop in the earth's temperature.

The unsolved problem is the basic unit of science, yet geology continues to ignore these two problems. For the past couple of decades scientists have repeatedly relied upon ice core dating as a tool to gauge the temperature changes that they insist must have happened to cause the ice ages. But their logic is fundamentally flawed.

The ice ages are not only about time and temperature.

They are also about space. It is really rather shocking to note that in all the discussion about the age of the ice sheets and the temperatures of the past, there is nothing said about where the ice sheets formed. It's as if this question has no bearing upon the problem. This is a ludicrous state of affairs. PhDs parading around the globe, attending conference after conference and presenting ice core evidence, all ignore the simple fact that central Greenland and eastern Antarctica, where over 90 per cent of the world's ice resides, are both polar deserts! It simply doesn't snow where the ice is! This emperor definitely has no clothes.

Some have likened ice core dating to the rings of a tree that can be counted one by one to arrive at a history of the past. There are similarities, but there are also significant differences. As each new layer of ice is laid down it adds its weight to those beneath. This does not happen with tree rings, which respond to light. Ice cores are the result of falling snow. Light is a very regular feature, unlike snowfall, which is unpredictable. The weight of each new layer of ice adds pressure to the layers beneath. This results in distortions and melting of evidence. Ice at the bottom of the ice sheet is squeezed outwards and disappears.

The thickest ice sheet on Greenland is at 72N/38W, where the ice is almost 2 miles deep. The cross-polar point from Greenland's thickest ice sheet is 72N/142E. The closest land is the New Siberian Islands (75N/140E). If we were to accept that ice core dating from Greenland was a true indicator of temperature worldwide, then the New Siberian Islands should also be under ice and could never have supported large mammals such as mammoths, lions, rhinos, bison and horse.

There is no logical reason whatsoever to prefer the ice core dating from Greenland over the physical remains of extinct mammals from the New Siberian Islands as the criteria with which to estimate the

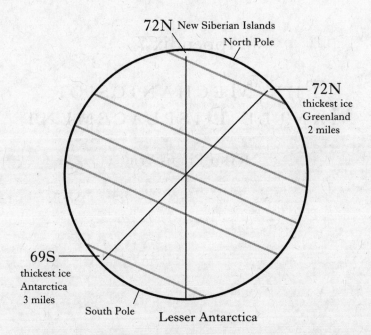

72N New Siberian Islands
North Pole

72N
thickest ice
Greenland
2 miles

69S
thickest ice
Antarctica
3 miles

South Pole

Lesser Antarctica

The thickest ice on Antarctica is antipodal to the thickest ice on Greenland. The cross-polar point to the thickest ice on Greenland is on the new Siberian Islands, which were formerly the home of a host of temperate-adapted animals. The antipodal point to the New Siberian Islands is Lesser Antarctica, which would have enjoyed a temperate climate 12,000 years ago.

world's temperature during the late Pleistocene. But this is exactly what the ice core experts do. They assume that latitudes can change only very gradually. Sudden changes such as those envisioned with a mantel displacement are beyond their consideration. They say everything must be linked to what they find on Greenland. Russian scientists, however, have seen the remains of horses, bison, etc. in Siberia and they cannot accept that the American scientists' methodology is sound.

And it isn't.

What the advocates of ice core dating have been doing is extrapolating data collected on Greenland and Greater Antarctica to the rest of the world. They have replaced investigation with extrapolation. They simply assume what they are logically obliged to prove.

Appendix 7

THE MECHANICS OF
MANTLE DISPLACEMENT

RAND FLEM-ATH

The science journal *Nature* ran a cover story on 18 July 1996 called 'Rotation of the inner core'.[1] Hardly a bestseller, this report nevertheless can explain the most perplexing problem for the earth crust displacement theory.

I first became aware of this problem just after Rose and I had done a publicity tour for the publication of *When the Sky Fell*. We had accepted an invitation to give a talk at the local bookstore in the small town of Ladysmith, British Columbia, where we live. After the talk and slide show we answered a few questions and then chatted with those still remaining. A man asked, 'How would your theory explain the hot spot under Hawaii?'

After having answered literally thousands of questions about the theory this was the first time that I came across a question that baffled me. I said, 'What do you mean?'

'Well,' he replied, 'my impression was that the Hawaiian islands were formed by a hot spot beneath the crust. As the crust moves gradually over the hot spot the rising magma pushes the crust upwards, forming islands. Since this has taken millions of years to achieve it seems to contradict your idea that the crust as a whole displaces.' I had to admit that this sounded reasonable and I said that

352

I would have to investigate the matter in more detail because his question went straight to the heart of the theory. It seemed to be an unfailing arrow.

I did investigate the problem but it wasn't until 1996 when the *Nature* article came out that I thought I might have an answer to this vexing question. In 1997, Arthur Logtenberg from Eindhoven, Holland, asked on our website[2] for my ideas on the *Nature* article, which had said that the heavy solid iron core of the earth was rotating '100,000 times faster than the fastest relative motion of the tectonic plates of the lithosphere'. What this meant was that the inner core had its own spin and axis that was only related to but not exactly the same as the spin and axis of the rest of the planet. It seemed to me that everything 'above' the inner core was vulnerable to a displacement relative to the inner core. I called this idea a mantle displacement because the mantle is the thickest part of the earth above the inner core.

This notion of a deeper level displacement offered a solution to the hot spot problem. If the displacements were that much deeper, then it didn't matter if there was a 'hot spot' beneath Hawaii, because it would move along with the rest of the mass of the earth that was displacing over the inner core.

In the summer of 1997 the question of the Hawaiian hot spot came up again. Rick Monteverde of Honolulu asked, 'Could it be that the entire globe simply shifted, interior as well as crust?' I replied: 'The Hawaiian island chain was produced by a "hot spot" beneath the surface of the crust. This poses a more serious problem for the earth crust displacement theory since a movement of the crust should result in the hot spot showing up somewhere else beneath the earth's crust. It is because of this problem that I have considered the movement of the entire mantle as a solution. A displacement of the earth's mantle (something Hapgood was considering when he wrote his last letter to me in October 1982 just weeks before he died in an automobile accident) is a much more satisfying explanation for the rapid changes and at the same time can account for the movement of the Hawaiian "hot spot" (it simply shifts along with the mantle).'

But there was still the problem of what forces might have caused the mantle displacement. In August 1997, Robert K. Morgan of San Diego asked, 'What forces would combine to break the earth's crust free of the underlying mantle?' I replied, 'In *When the Sky Fell* (Chapter 4, "Why the Sky Fell"), we review Hapgood's adoption of the idea that the weight of the ice caps positioned lop-sided to the earth's axis was *one* possible force. We also put forward two astronomical factors as additional contributing forces to the displacement of 9,600 BC. The earth's orbit was much more elliptical than it is today and thus the gravitational influence of the sun would "pull" with greater force at the immense (antipodal) ice sheets. But perhaps most importantly, the angle of the earth's tilt was at its extreme of 24.4 degrees (it goes through a 41,000-year cycle ranging from 22.8 degrees to 24.4 degrees – today we are at around 23.5 and *declining* – in other words it's getting *safer*). This meant that the *entire* earth's mass was tilted to a greater degree. This would add momentum to the centrifugal thrust of the antipodal ice sheets.'

An Extraterrestrial Solution

During the rest of 1997, while I was busy trying to unravel the Atlantis blueprint, I had temporarily to leave the question of the causes of the mantle displacement. Then in the spring of 1998 I received a letter from Donald Tim Seitz Sr, who had written a scientific paper for the Royal Astronomical Society of Canada entitled 'A Probable Cause of Crustal Shifts of the Earth: A Comet approaching the centre of mass of the Earth–Moon Gravitational System'. This appeared in *Regulus*, the journal of the society, in April 1998.

Donald had put his finger on a solution and though I was now convinced that it was a mantle rather than a crustal displacement, his theory worked perfectly. What he argued was that we tend to forget that our moon is quite large and has its own gravitational pull. If a comet or asteroid or any other extraterrestrial object is on a collision course with the earth then the force of the object is not necessarily directed to the centre of the earth, as we would normally think. The position of the moon at the point of impact upon the earth is a very important factor because its gravitational field will redirect the main thrust of the impact towards the mantle rather than the inner core of the planet.

Let's consider three cases.

If the moon is directly behind the earth when the comet collides then the force of the comet will be directed straight through the earth to the centre of the inner core. In effect, the moon doesn't matter in this case.

If the moon is between the earth and the comet then the moon will take the impact, saving the earth.

Let us imagine, however, that, as the comet is approaching, the moon is off to one side of the earth. Under these conditions the force of the comet is directed towards the upper mantle, which is the centre of gravity of the earth–moon gravitational system. This could very well dislodge the entire mantle. Donald Seitz's theory seems to be the missing piece in the puzzle of why the displacements occur.

There are a multitude of forces at work to cause a mantle displacement. The antipodal weight of the asymmetrical ice caps is one factor. The shape of the earth's orbit is another, because it brings the planet closer to the biggest gravitational force in our area of space, namely the sun. The tilt of the earth is another factor, which like the ice sheets and the shape of the orbit is an entirely predictable phenomenon.

These factors all appeared in *When the Sky Fell* but they really only set the stage for a potential displacement that must, after all, have been a mantle displacement. These astronomical preconditions are insufficient on their own to account for all the facts. When we learn, however, that the inner core has its own rotation and its own axis then the possibility for solving the hot spot problem is at hand. The discontinuity between the inner core and the rest of the mass of the planet allows us to postulate a mantle displacement, and Donald Seitz's breakthrough that the earth and the moon form a kind of 'gravity well' seems to be the final piece in the puzzle. What remains a mystery is where the comet or comets came from, where they hit the earth, how big they were, and whether others will follow in the future.

A Terrestrial Alternative

Another possibility for the cause of the mantle displacement could be the discrepancy that grows between the axis of the inner core and the axis of the rest of the planet. Today there is a 10-degree difference between the two and it is possible that at 9,600 BC, when the earth's whole axis was angled at its maximum of 24.4 degrees, the difference between it and the inner core's axis was dangerously pronounced. The earth's axis is governed by the pull of the sun, moon and other planets and follows a regular 41,000-year cycle. The peak of that cycle was reached at 9,600 BC, at which time the planet's whole axis began to decline after increasing for thousands of years.

The classic work on this subject was published in *Science* in 1976: 'Variations in the Earth's Orbit: Pacemaker of the Ice Ages' by J. D. Hays, J. Imbrie and N. J. Schackleton.[3] They showed that geological/climatic patterns coincide with the periods when the earth's tilt reaches its maximum of 24.4 degrees. The last time this occurred was around 9,600 BC, exactly the time period when Plato's 'legend' of Atlantis places the flood. When we combine this theory with the recent revelations about the inner core having its own axis, we have a much simpler idea than an extraterrestrial impact theory.

After reaching its peak angle of tilt at 24.4 degrees, in a sense the axis heads back to where it had been. The inner core is very dense and thus has more mass than the rest of the planet. Perhaps when the rest of the planet's mass starts moving towards the axis of the inner core it creates an overwhelming attraction and the mantle displaces abruptly. The axis of the inner core and the axis of the rest of the mass of the earth are reunited abruptly and catastrophically. This, no doubt, would begin slowly, but would build momentum, resulting, in the final stages, in a rapid displacement. There would be plenty of warnings, observable by any scientifically advanced civilisation experiencing it.

The arguments in favour of the 'terrestrial' force compared to 'extraterrestrial' are considerable.

The 'extraterrestrial' impact theory of a mantle displacement is unnecessarily complex. So many factors have to coincide that one can't help doubt that this idea is ad hoc and prone to constant revision and exceptions. How big must a comet or asteroid be to displace the mantle? Why would these extraterrestrial objects collide with earth on a regular basis? Where is the moon relative to the incoming object? More importantly, an impact theory of displacement really doesn't dovetail with the discoveries that the earth's geological and climatic upheavals coincide with the earth's axis tilt.

I feel certain Charles Hapgood would agree that the terrestrial model is the better theory. It explains the placement of the ice sheets and coincides with the timing developed by Hays, Imbrie and Schackleton. Hapgood seemed to be heading in this direction when he wrote to me: 'I have recently concluded that a "drag effect" would operate whereby the movement of the rigid crust would set in motion movements of the deeper layers, which would continue long after the movement of the crust stops, producing long-continued turbulence at the surface.' This indicates that Hapgood was constantly reappraising his theory and making modifications in light of new evidence. The fact that the inner core has its own axis and rotates faster than the rest of the earth's mass would surely have been factors that he would have wanted to incorporate into his theory.

For these reasons I conclude that the force that caused the mantle displacement is tied to the dynamics of the inner core of the planet coupled with the gradual oscillations of the planet's tilt cycle. Both factors can potentially reunite when the tilt of the outer earth reverses its gradual drift away from the inner core and results in a catastrophic reunion whereby both axes are brought together. The axis of the inner core and the rest of the planet are temporarily reunited and may even contribute to a regeneration of the earth's magnetic field. At this point, the pull of the sun, the moon and the rest of the planets in our solar web once again begins to gradually separate the mantle's axis from the inner core's axis and the whole cycle begins again. If this theory is correct, we can be assured that we have thousands of years (about 29,400) before another mantle displacement occurs.

NOTES

Preface

1. Pennick, *Sacred Geometry*, 1980, p. 43.
2. Cathie, *The Harmonic Conquest of Space*.
3. Michell, *City of Revelation*, p. xiii.
4. Knight and Lomas, *Uriel's Machine*, pp. 363–4.
5. Flem-Ath, Rose, *Field of Thunder*, Stoddart, Toronto, 1997.

Chapter 1: Hapgood's Secret Quest for Atlantis

1. This account of Hapgood's death is based upon a letter to Rand from Charles's cousin Beth Hapgood (2 April 1998).
2. Hapgood, *Earth's Shifting Crust*, Pantheon, New York, 1958.
3. 'Plate tectonics and earth crust displacement both share the assumption of a mobile crust. The ideas are not mutually exclusive but rather complementary. Plate tectonics explains long-term, slow changes like mountain building, volcanic activity, and local earthquakes. Earth crust displacement accepts that these processes are gradual but posits a much more dramatic and abrupt movement of the crust that can explain different problems such as mass extinctions, glaciation patterns, and the sudden rise of agriculture. In stark contrast to plate tectonics'

slow motion of individual plates, an "earth crust displacement", as postulated by Hapgood, abruptly shifts all the plates as a single unit. During this motion the core (the heavy bull's eye of the planet) doesn't change, leaving the earth's axis unaltered.' Flem-Ath, Rand and Rose, *When the Sky Fell*, p. 3.

4. Hapgood, Charles H., *Maps of the Ancient Sea Kings: Evidence of Advanced Civilization in the Ice Ages*, Chilton Books, Philadelphia/New York, 1966.
5. Hapgood, Charles H., *The Path of the Pole*, Chilton Book Company, Philadelphia/New York/London, 1970 (a revised edition of *Earth's Shifting Crust*, 1958).
6. Charles H. Hapgood Archives, Yale Collection of American Literature, Beinecke Rare Book and Manuscript Library.
7. Churchward, James, *The Lost Continent of Mu: The Motherland of Man*, William Edwin Rudge, New York, 1926.
8. Settegast, Mary, *Plato Prehistorian*, Lindisfarne Press, New York, 1990.
9. Donnelly, Ignatius, *Atlantis: The Antediluvian World*, Harper & Brothers, New York, 1882.
10. Donnelly, Ignatius, *Ragnarok: The Age of Fire and Gravel*, Harper & Brothers, New York, 1883.
11. Furneaux, p. 316.
12. Wegener, Alfred, *The Origin of the Continents and Oceans*, 1915, reissued in 1966 by Dover, New York.
13. Albert Einstein Archives, Department of Manuscripts and Archives, The Jewish National and University Library (Hapgood Correspondence, 24 November 1952).
14. Albert Einstein Archives, Department of Manuscripts and Archives, The Jewish National and University Library (Hapgood Correspondence, 8 May 1953).
15. Einstein, 'Confidential Report on Candidate for Fellowship'.
16. Ma, Ting Ying H., *Research on the Past Climate*, published by the author, Taipei, Taiwan, May 1952.
17. Reprinted in full in White, *Pole Shift*.
18. Mallery, pp .40–6.
19. Tompkins, *Secrets of the Great Pyramid*, p. 201.
20. Needham, Joseph, *Science and Civilisation in China* (three volumes), Cambridge University Press, Cambridge, 1959.
21. Hapgood, *Maps of the Ancient Sea Kings*, p. 193.

22. Pauwels, Louis, and Jacques Bergier, *The Morning of the Magicians*, Stein and Day, New York, 1964.
23. Shklovskii, Joseph, and Carl Sagan, *Intelligent Life in the Universe*, Holden Day, San Francisco, 1966.
24. In the map on pp. 32–3 of *Maps of the Ancient Sea Kings*, Hapgood numbers this 93.
25. Berlitz, Charles, *Atlantis: The Eighth Continent*, Putnam, New York, 1984.
26. See Appendix 2.

Chapter 2: The Blueprint

1. US Naval Support Force, *Introduction to Antarctica*, US Government Printing Office, Washington, DC, 1969, centrepiece.
2. Plato, *Laws*, Vol. I, Book III.
3. Flem-Ath, Rand, 'A Global Model for the Origins of Agriculture'.
4. Flem-Ath, Rand and Rose, 'The Earth Science Revolution and Pre-History'.
5. Hapgood, Charles, letter to the Flem-Aths, 3 August 1977.
6. Watkins, N. D., and J. D. Kennett, 'Antarctic Bottom Water: Major Change in Velocity during the Late Cenozoic between Australia and Antarctica', *Science*, Vol. 173, 27 August 1971, pp. 813–18; Ledbetter, M. T., and D. A. Johnson, 'Increased Transport of Antarctic Bottom Water in the Vema Channel during the last Ice Age', *Science*, Vol. 194, 19 November 1976, pp. 837–9.
7. Warren, William Fairfield, *Paradise Found: The Cradle of the Human Race at the North Pole*, Boston, 1885.
8. Tilak, Bal Gangadhar, *The Arctic Home in the Vedas*, Poona, India, 1903.
9. Hapgood, *Maps of the Ancient Sea Kings*, see n. 23 on p. 229.
10. Kuhn, Thomas S., *The Structure of Scientific Revolutions*, second edition, University of Chicago Press, Chicago, 1970.
11. Flem-Ath, Rand and Rose, *When the Sky Fell*, p. 46.
12. Schwaller de Lubicz, Rene, *The Temple of Man: Sacred Architecture and the Perfect Man*, translated by Robert and Deborah Lawlor, Inner Traditions International, Rochester, VT, 1998.

13. Fulcanelli, *The Mystery of Cathedrals*, Pauvert, Paris, 1925.

14. Schwaller de Lubicz, Rene, *Sacred Science: The King of Pharaonic Theocracy*, translated by André and Goldian VandenBroeck, Inner Traditions International, Rochester, VT, 1988, originally published in French in 1961 by Flammarion.

15. West, John Anthony, *Serpent in the Sky: The High Wisdom of Ancient Egypt*, second edition, Quest Books, Wheaton, IL, 1993.

16. Hancock, Graham, *The Sign and the Seal: The Quest for the Lost Ark of the Covenant*, Simon & Schuster, New York, 1992.

17. Roberts, Paul William, 'The Riddle of the Sphinx', *Saturday Night*, March 1993.

18. Hancock, Graham, *Fingerprints of the Gods: A Quest for the Beginning and the End*, Heinemann, London, 1995.

19. Bauval, Robert, and Adrian Gilbert, *The Orion Mystery: Unlocking the Secrets of the Pyramids*, Doubleday Canada, Toronto, 1994.

20. Wilson, Colin, *From Atlantis to the Sphinx: Recovering the Lost Wisdom of the Ancient World*, Virgin, London, 1996.

21. Hancock, Graham, and Robert Bauval, *Keeper of Genesis*, Heinemann, London, 1996 (in the US *Message of the Sphinx*, Crown, New York, 1996).

22. Barnes, John, 'Ancient purity and polygot programs', *Sunday Times*, 4 November 1984, Computing Section, p. 13; Mylrea, Paul, 'Computer helps preserve ancient Aymara language', as printed in *The Nanaimo Free Press*, 21 November 1991, p. 8.

23. Posnansky, Vol. 1, p. 2.

24. Aveni, Anthony F., *Archaeoastronomy in Pre-Columbian America*, University of Texas Press, Austin and London, 1975.

25. Tompkins, Peter, with Livio Catullo Stecchini, *Secrets of the Great Pyramid: Two Thousand Years of Adventure and Discoveries Surrounding the Mystery of the Great Pyramid of Cheops*, Galahad Books, New York, 1971.

26. Tompkins, Peter, *Mysteries of the Mexican Pyramids*, Harper & Row, New York, 1976.

27. See, for example, Michell, John, *The New View Over Atlantis*, Thames and Hudson, London, 1995 (originally published as *The View Over Atlantis* by Sago Press, UK, 1969).

28. Knight, Christopher, and Robert Lomas, *The Hiram Key*, Arrow, London, 1996.
29. Reproduced in full in Appendix 1.
30. Wilson, Colin, *Alien Dawn*, Virgin, London, 1998.

Chapter 3: The Giza Prime Meridian

1. Smyth, Charles Piazzi, 'What Shall be the Prime Meridian for the World?', *Report of the Committee on Standard Time and Prime Meridian, International Institute for Preserving and Perfecting Weights and Measures*, Cleveland, OH, June 1884, pp. 1–56.
2. Wilson, Colin, *The Atlas of Holy Places and Sacred Sites*, Penguin Studio, London, 1996.
3. Wilson, Colin, and Damon Wilson, *Unsolved Mysteries Past and Present*, NTC/Contemporary Publishing, Chicago, 1992.
4. Mitchell-Hedges, F. A., *Danger My Ally*, originally published in 1955, reissued in 1995 by Adventures Unlimited, USA.
5. Fawcett, *Exploration Fawcett*, p. 3.
6. Fawcett, *Exploration Fawcett*, p. 2.
7. Wilkins, Harold, *Mysteries of Ancient South America*, Rider & Co., London, 1946, pp. 41–6.
8. Wilkins, *Mysteries of Ancient South America*, p. 40.
9. Fleming, Peter, *Brazilian Adventure*, Jonathan Cape, London, 1933, reissued in 1999 by The Marlboro Press/Northwestern, Evanston, Illinois.
10. Fawcett, P. H., *Exploration Fawcett*, arranged from his manuscripts by Brian Fawcett, Hutchinson, London, 1953.
11. Fawcett, *Exploration Fawcett*, p. 122.
12. Fawcett, *Exploration Fawcett*, p. 263.
13. Fawcett, *Exploration Fawcett*, p. 243.
14. Fawcett, *Exploration Fawcett*, p. 260.
15. Fawcett, *Exploration Fawcett*, p. 269.
16. Fawcett, *Exploration Fawcett*, p. 269, footnote.
17. Fawcett, *Exploration Fawcett*, p. 289.
18. Fawcett, *Exploration Fawcett*, p. 293.
19. Fawcett, *Exploration Fawcett*, p. 304.
20. Wilkins, *Mysteries of Ancient South America*, p. 66.
21. The use of satellites for archaeology is increasing each year. See,

for example, Dowling, Kenven, 'Secret pyramids under the sand', *http://express.lineone.net/express/00/01/10/news/n3120sands-d.html* (10 January 2000).

Chapter 4: Thoth's Holy Chamber

1. Mendelssohn, Kurt, *The Riddle of the Pyramids*, Praeger, New York, 1974.
2. Seiss, J. A., *Miracle in Stone, of the Great Pyramid of Egypt*, Porter & Coates, Philadelphia, 1877–1878.
3. Davidson, David, *The Great Pyramid, Its Divine Message*, Williams & Norgate, 1932.
4. West, *Serpent in the Sky*, p. 1.
5. Petrie, William Matthew, *The Pyramids and Temples of Gizeh*, Field & Tuer, London, 1883.
6. Dunn, *The Giza Power Plant*, see all of Chapter 3.
7. *The Mystery of the Sphinx*.
8. West, *The Traveler's Key to Ancient Egypt*, pp. 412–18.
9. Baigent, Michael, Richard Leigh and Henry Lincoln, *The Holy Blood and the Holy Grail*, revised edition, Corgi Books, London, 1996 (originally Jonathan Cape, London, 1982).
10. Dunn, Christopher, *The Giza Power Plant: Technologies of Ancient Egypt*, Bear & Co., Santa Fe, New Mexico, 1998.
11. Bauval and Gilbert, *The Orion Mystery*, pp. 45–6.
12. In a book called *Hall of the Gods* (1998), which was withdrawn from publication.
13. Hancock and Bauval, *Keeper of Genesis*, Arrow edition, 1997, p. 314.
14. Bauval, *Secret Chamber*, pp. 14 and 28.
15. Hancock and Bauval, *Keeper of Genesis*, Arrow edition, 1997, p. 285.
16. Tomas, p. 109.
17. Kronzek, p. 5.
18. Ellis, Normandi, *Awakening Osiris*, Phanes Press, Grand Rapids, MI, 1988, as cited in Hancock and Bauval, *Keeper of Genesis*, Arrow edition, 1997, p. 339.
19. Furlong, p. 111.
20. As reproduced from McCollum in Toth, pp. 35–6.
21. Temple, *The Crystal Sun*, plate 30 and caption on pp. 216–17.

22. Dolphin, L. T., and A. H. Moussa, et al., *Applications of Modern Sensing Techniques to Egyptology*, SRI International, Menlo Park, California, 1977, as reproduced in Cayce, p. 137.

Chapter 5: 6,000 Degrees Celsius

1. Barnes and Barnes, pp. 10–11.
2. Clayton, P. A., and L. J. Spencer, 'Silica-glass from the Libyan Desert', *The Mineralogical Magazine,* 23, 501–8, 1934.
3. Wilson, *From Atlantis to the Sphinx*, p. 37.
4. Charles H. Hapgood Archives, Yale Collection of American Literature, Beinecke Rare Book and Manuscript Library (Dolphin to Lee Hammond, 24 January 1957).
5. Charles H. Hapgood Archives, Yale Collection of American Literature, Beinecke Rare Book and Manuscript Library (Dolphin to Charles Hapgood, 23 May 1957).
6. Charles H. Hapgood Archives, Yale Collection of American Literature, Beinecke Rare Book and Manuscript Library (Hapgood to Charles B. Hitchcock of the American Geographical Society, 1 January 1959).
7. White, *Pole Shift*, gives the entire text of the broadcast.
8. Wilkins, p. 183.
9. Charles H. Hapgood Archives, Yale Collection of American Literature, Beinecke Rare Book and Manuscript Library (Hapgood to Charles B. Hitchcock of the American Geographical Society, 1 January 1959).
10. Shawn Montgomery is currently researching the story of Royal Raymond Rife, an obscure American scientist who invented a revolutionary microscope. Details regarding his research can be sought at *www.writersblot.com*.
11. 1979 brochure released by Yull Brown in Christopher Bird, 'The Saga of Yull Brown – Part III', *Explore!,* Vol. 3. No. 6, 1992, p. 51.
12. Verne, Jules, *The Mysterious Island*, 1874, as reprinted in Bird, 'The Saga of Yull Brown – Part I', pp. 49–50.
13. Hapgood, Dolphin and Rennell were focused on gold (100 per cent pure) and glass (tektites). It is interesting to note that the ancient Egyptians believed that gold and glass were part of the alchemist's trade. 'In the ancient world alchemy was referred to

simply as "the sacred art". It flourished in the first three centuries AD in Alexandria, where it was the combined product of glass and metal technology, a Hellenistic philosophy of the unity of all things through the four elements (earth, air, water, fire), and "occult" religion and astrology. How the technology of coloring glass and goldsmithing – kept secret in certain families – became involved with esoteric philosophy is a long story.' Maybury-Lewis, p. 183.

14. Bird, 'The Saga of Yull Brown – Part I'.
15. Shawn Montgomery, 'Notes on Brown's Gas for Rand Flem-Ath'.
16. Sitchin, Zecharia, *The Lost Realms*, Bear & Company, Santa Fe, New Mexico, 1990.
17. Kolata, Alan L., *Valley of the Spirits: A Journey into the Lost Realm of the Aymara*, John Wiley & Sons, Inc., New York, 1996.
18. *Mysterious Origins of Man, The*. Hosted by Charlton Heston. B. C. Video Inc., 1-800-846-9682 or P. O. Box 97, Shelburne, VT, 05482, 1996.

Chapter 6: Ancient Voyagers

1. Zapp and Erikson.
2. Watkins, Alfred.
3. Heyerdahl, Thor, *The Kon-Tiki Expedition*, London, 1950, reissued in 1996 by Flamingo.
4. Lewis, David, *We, The Navigators*, 1972, reissued in 1991 by University of Hawaii Press.
5. Zapp, Ivar, and George Erikson, *Atlantis in America*, Adventures Unlimited, USA, 1998.
6. Knight and Lomas, *Uriel's Machine,* p. 106.
7. Cremo and Thompson, *Forbidden Archaeology*, p. 198.
8. Needham, Vol. 4, p. 542.
9. Barber.
10. Marshack.
11. 'When the Sahara Was Green', p.206.
12. Moran and Kelley.
13. Graves, Robert, *The White Goddess*, Farrar, Straus and Giroux, New York, 1948, reissued in 1999 by Faber & Faber, London.

14. Bailey, Jim, *The God-Kings and the Titans*, Hodder & Stoughton, London, 1973.
15. Fox, Hugh, *Gods of the Cataclysm: A Revolutionary Investigation of Man and His Gods Before and After the Great Cataclysm*, Harper's Magazine Press, New York, 1976.
16. Bailey, *Sailing to Paradise*, p. 25.
17. Patten, Donald, *The Biblical Flood and the Ice Epoch: A Study in Scientific History*, Pacific Meridian Publishing Co., Seattle, WA, 1966.
18. Chatelain, Maurice, *Our Cosmic Ancestors*, Light Technology Publications in USA, paperback edition, 1988, reissued in 1996.
19. Frawley, David, *Gods, Sages and Kings: Vedic Secrets of Ancient Civilization*, Passage Press, Salt Lake City, Utah, 1991.
20. Frawley, p. 185.
21. Sellers, Jane B., *The Death of Gods in Ancient Egypt*, Penguin Books, London, 1992.
22. Email from Sellers to Flem-Ath, 29 March 2000.
23. Wilson, Colin, *Starseekers*, Hodder & Stoughton, London, 1980.
24. Schwaller de Lubicz, Rene, *Sacred Science: The King of Pharaonic Theocracy*, translated by André and Goldian VandenBroeck, Inner Traditions International, Rochester, VT, 1988, originally published in French as *Le Roi de la theocractie Pharaonique* in 1961 by Flammarion.
25. Lash, John, *The Skies in Memory* (a work in progress).
26. Tompkins, *Mysteries of the Mexican Pyramids*, p. 301.
27. Chatelain, p. 50.
28. Morley, Sylvanus Griswold, *Introduction to the Study of Maya Hieroglyphics*, Dover Books, New York, 1975.
29. Chatelain, p. 54.
30. McCrone, John, 'Fired Up', *New Scientist*, 20 May 2000.
31. Calder, Nigel, *Timescale*, p. 241.
32. Wilson, *From Atlantis to the Sphinx*, pp. 50–52.

Chapter 7: Fallen Angels

1. *Book of the Secrets of Enoch*, p. 2.
2. *Book of the Secrets of Enoch*, p. 4.
3. Moorehead, Alan, *The Blue Nile*, Harper & Row Publishers, New York, 1962.

4. Collins, Andrew, with additional research by Richard Ward, *From the Ashes of Angels: The Forbidden Legacy of a Fallen Race*, Michael Joseph, London, 1996.
5. *Book of the Secrets of Enoch, The,* translated by W. R. Morfill and edited with an introduction by R. H. Charles, Clarendon Press, Oxford, 1896.
6. *Book of the Secrets of Enoch*, pp. 9–11.
7. O'Brien, Christian and Barbara Joy, *The Genius of the Few*, p. 90.
8. Charles, R. H., *The Book of Enoch*, Oxford University Press, Oxford, 1912, Chapter 61, Stanza 5.
9. Barton, George Aaron, *Miscellaneous Babylonian Inscriptions*, 1918.
10. O'Brien, Christian and Barbara Joy, *The Shining Ones*.
11. O'Brien, Christian and Barbara Joy, *The Genius of the Few: The Story of Those Who Founded the Garden in Eden*, Turnstone Press Limited, Wellingborough, Northamptonshire, UK, 1985.
12. O'Brien, Christian and Barbara Joy, *The Shining Ones*.
13. Knight and Lomas, *Uriel's Machine*, pp. 236–7.
14. Hawkins, Gerald, *Stonehenge Decoded*, Doubleday, New York, 1965.
15. *Daily Telegraph*, 7 August 1999.
16. Daniken, Erich von, *According to the Evidence*: *My Proof of Man's Extraterrestrial Origins,* Book Club Associates, London, 1978.
17. Hancock and Bauval, *Keeper of Genesis*, pp. 200–201.
18. Rand to Colin quoting Collins, Andrew, 'Baalbek: Lebanon's Sacred Fortress', *New Dawn*, No. 43, July–August 1997: *http:www.newdawnmagazine.com.au/Resources/arts/43c.html.*

Chapter 8: Golden Section Sites

1. Picknett, Lynn, and Clive Prince, *The Templar Revelation: Secret Guardians of the True Identity of Christ*, Simon & Schuster, New York, 1997.
2. Andrews, Richard, and Paul Schellenberger, *The Tomb of God: The Body of Jesus and the Solution to a 2,000-Year-Old Mystery*, Little, Brown & Company, London, 1996.
3. Lincoln, Henry, *Key to the Sacred Pattern: The Untold Story of Rennes-le-Château*, St Martin's Press, New York, 1998.

4. Sède, Gérard de, *Le Trésor maudit*, Editions J'ai Lu, Paris, 1968.
5. Hancock, Graham, *The Sign and the Seal: The Quest for the Lost Ark of the Covenant*, Simon & Schuster, New York, 1992.
6. Grierson and Munro-Hay.
7. Weston, Jessie L., *From Ritual To Romance*, Chapter 14; Loomis, Roger, introduction to *Chrétien's 'Perceval, or the Story of the Grail'*, Mediaeval Romances (Modern Library).
8. Lincoln, Henry, *The Lost Treasure of Jerusalem*, broadcast on BBC2 on 12 February 1972.
9. Lincoln, *Key to the Sacred Pattern*, p. 69.
10. Baigent, Michael, Richard Leigh and Henry Lincoln, *The Holy Blood and the Holy Grail*, London, originally Jonathan Cape, London, 1982, revised edition published by Corgi, 1996.
11. 'Only one planet describes a precise and regular geometric pattern in the sky – and that planet is Venus . . . and the pattern that she draws as regular as clockwork every eight years is a pentacle.' Lincoln, *The Holy Place*, p. 69.
12. Baigent, Leigh and Lincoln, *The Holy Blood and the Holy Grail*, 1996 revised edition, p. 92, which cites a letter to Lincoln from Abbé Mazières in notes, p. 517.
13. Lincoln, *Key to the Sacred Pattern*, p. 218.
14. Knight and Lomas, *Uriel's Machine*, p. 307, quoting from E. W. Barber, *The Mummies of Urumchi*, Macmillan, London, 1999.
15. Lomas and Knight, *Uriel's Machine*, p. 307.
16. Michell, *The New View Over Atlantis*, pp. 62–3.
17. *New York Times*, 28 March 1947, cited in Hausdorf, p. 112.
18. Cathie, Bruce, *The Bridge to Infinity*, America West, Bozeman, Montana, 1995.
19. Lincoln, *Key to the Sacred Pattern*, p. 148.
20. Lincoln, *Key to the Sacred Pattern*, p. 15.
21. Wood, David, *Genisis: The First Book of Revelations*, Baton Press, Tunbridge Wells, UK, 1985.
22. Fanthorpe, Lionel and Patricia, *The Holy Grail Revealed*, Newcastle Publishing, North Hollywood, 1982.
23. Baigent, Michael, Richard Leigh and Henry Lincoln, *The Messianic Legacy*, Jonathan Cape, London, 1986.
24. Wood, David, and Ian Campbell, *Geneset Target Earth*, Bellevue Books, Sunbury-on-Thames, UK, 1994.
25. Hancock and Faiia, pp. 212–21.

26. Schoch, p. 111.
27. Berriman, A. E., *Historical Metrology*, Dent, New York, 1953.
28. Lincoln, *Key to the Sacred Pattern*, pp. 215–16.
29. Henry Lincoln informs us that there are only two known copies
    of this book, both of which are now missing from the libraries
    that list them in their catalogues. See Lincoln, *Key to the Sacred
    Pattern*, pp. 69–70.

Chapter 9: What the Templars Found

1. Brydon, Robert, *The Guilds, the Masons and the Rosy Cross*,
   Friends of Rosslyn, Edinburgh, 1984.
2. Wilson, Colin, *Mysteries: An Investigation Into The Occult,
   The Paranormal & The Supernatural*, Putnam, New York,
   1978.
3. Critchlow, Keith, *Time Stands Still*, Gordon Fraser, London,
   1979.
4. Critchlow, pp. 8–9.
5. Myers, F. W. H., *Human Personality and its survival of Bodily
   Death*, University Books, New York, 1961, pp. 75–6.
6. Picknett and Prince, *The Templar Revelation*, p. 97.
7. British sacred sites (listed from west to east) on latitude 30
   degrees north during the Yukon Pole. (30N = 3,600 nautical
   miles from the pole.)

Sacred Sites	3,600 = 30N	Error
Tintagel	3,601	1
Glastonbury	3,606	6
Bath	3,598	2
Avebury	3,601	1
Stonehenge	3,616	16
Old Sarum	3,621	21
Rollright Stones	3,575	25
Baldock	3,595	5
London	3,623	23
Royston	3,594	6
Mersea Island	3,616	16

8. Michell, *The Dimensions of Paradise*, p. 28.
9. Pennick, *The Ancient Science of Geomancy*, p. 99.
10. Pennick, *The Subterranean Kingdom*, pp. 133–4.
11. Baldock and Pyongyang were both exactly 3,995 nautical miles from the Yukon Pole at latitude 29:55N.
12. Jang-jin, Hwang, 'Law proposed to preserve megalithic culture', *Korea Herald*, 25 February 1999: *http://www.koreaherald.co.kr/kh0225/m0225c01.html* (1 March 1999).
13. Parker, E. H., 'On Race Struggles in Korea', *Transactions of the Asiatic Society of Japan*, 23 (1890), pp. 137–228.
14. Nelson, p. 210.
15. University of California, *Learning about Korea*, series 1: *http://www.lib.berkeley.edu/EAL/ealknote.html* (8 May 2000).
16. Guignebert, *The Jewish World in the Time of Jesus*, 1935, p. 200.
17. Daraul: *Secret Societies*, Tandem 1965, p. 79.
18. Furneaux: *The Other Side of the Story*, London 1953, p. 132.
19. Wilson, *A Criminal History of Mankind*, 1983, p. 222.
20. Knight, Christopher, and Robert Lomas, *The Second Messiah: Templars, the Turin Shroud and the Great Secret of Freemasonry*, Century, London, 1997.
21. Picknett and Prince, *Turin Shroud: In Whose Image?*
22. Tailby.
23. Sitchin, *The Lost Realms*, p. 202.
24. Flem-Ath, Rand and Rose, *When the Sky Fell*, p. 28.
25. Prescott, *History of the Conquest of Peru*, Book 1.
26. Sitchin, *The Lost Realms*, pp. 203–4.
27. See, for example, Hancock, *Fingerprints of the Gods*, p. 230.
28. Hancock, *Fingerprints of the Gods*, p. 49.
29. Cuzco creation myth translated by Christobal de Molina (1575), quoted in Christian and Barbara Joy O'Brien, *The Shining Ones*, p. 533.
30. Prescott.
31. Prescott.
32. Prescott.
33. Prescott.
34. Sitchin, Zecharia, *The Lost Realms*, p. 202.
35. Baigent and Leigh, *Temple and the Lodge*, p. 126.

Chapter 10: The Legacy

1. Swaney, Deanna, *The Lonely Planet Guide to Bolivia*.
2. Wright, p. 4; Thorton, pp. 22–25.
3. Heyerdahl, Thor, *The Kon-Tiki Expedition*, London, 1950, reissued in 1996 by Flamingo.
4. Heyerdahl, Thor, *The Ra Expedition*, George Allen & Unwin, London, 1971.
5. Santos, Arysio Nunes dos, on his website: *http://www.atlan.org/articles/guanches/* (28 May 1999).
6. Santos, Arysio Nunes dos.
7. Heyerdahl, Thor, Daniel H. Sandweiss and Alfredo Narvaez, *The Pyramids of Tucume: The Quest for Peru's Forgotten City*, Thames and Hudson, London, 1995.
8. Heyerdahl, Thor, *The Ra Expedition*.
9. Flem-Ath, Rand and Rose, 'Contact'.
10. Balabanova, S., F. Parsche and W. Pirsig, 'First Identification of Drugs in Egyptian Mummies', *Naturwissenschaften* 79, 358, 1992.
11. Collins, *Gateway to Atlantis*, pp. 147–8.
12. Hapgood, *Maps of the Ancient Sea Kings*, p. 83, footnote.
13. Temple, *The Sirius Mystery*, pp. 20–21
14. Davis, Nancy Yaw, 'The Zuni Enigma', *New England Antiquities Research Association*, Vol. XXVII, Nos. 1 & 2, Summer/Fall 1992. Thanks to Ray Beaumont at the Frontier School Division No. 48 in Winnipeg, Manitoba, for bringing this article to Rand's attention.
15. Newton.
16. Knight and Lomas, *Uriel's Machine*, p. 151.
17. Knight and Lomas, *Uriel's Machine*, p. 146.
18. Knight and Lomas, *Uriel's Machine*, p. 172.
19. Blankenship, Donald D., Robin E. Bell, Steven M. Hodge, John M. Brozena, John C. Behrendt and Carol A. Finn, 'Active volcanism beneath the West Antarctic ice sheet and the implications for ice-sheet stability', *Nature*, Vol. 361, 11 February 1993, pp. 526–9.
20. Flem-Ath, Rand and Rose, *When the Sky Fell*, pp. 107–9.
21. Blankenship, et al.

Appendix 2: Letter to Rand Flem-Ath from Charles H.
Hapgood, 16 October 1982

1. Flem-Ath, Rand, 'A Global Model for the Origins of Agriculture', *The Anthropological Journal of Canada*, Vol. 19, No. 4, 1981, reprinted in 1995 as an appendix in *When the Sky Fell*.

2. Rand noted (following the work of Vavilov) in the above paper that the earliest experiments with agriculture seem to correspond with land that is 1,500 metres above ocean level.

3. Charles knows from Rand and Rose's first letter to him in April 1977 that they believe that Atlantis was Antarctica before the last displacement.

4. Charles is referring to Rand's article. Rand knows and believes that agriculture began in Atlantis (Antarctica) many thousand of years earlier but he cannot say this in his article and expect to be published in a scientific journal.

5. The whereabouts of this manuscript is a mystery. Rand and Colin have communicated with Hapgood's relatives and friends and have been unable to locate this important unpublished manuscript.

6. Rand and Colin both disagree with Hapgood on this point (see *When the Sky Fell* and *From Atlantis to the Sphinx*).

7. Rand had written about the correlation between altitude (1,500 metres above ocean level) and agricultural origins: 'This might be explained by crustal displacement, which would surely result in fantastic tidal waves. Any survivors would have a strong motive for staying in high mountains.' Charles took this to mean that Rand was advocating the notion of 1,500-metre-high tidal waves but what Rand meant was that any tidal waves would have the consequence of making the survivors afraid to live near the ocean.

8. Rand and Rose developed this idea in *When the Sky Fell* (pp. 49–51), calling this longitude (83 degrees west and 97 degrees east) the 'line of greatest displacement'.

9. Langway, C. C., Jr. and Lyle Hansen, 'Drilling through the Ice Cap: Probing Climate for a Thousand Centuries', in Richard Lewis and P. M. Smith, *The Frozen Future: A Prophetic Report from Antarctica*, Quadrangle Books, New York, 1973. Rand,

who now has little faith in the ice core dating method, included this book in his list of references because it contained the words 'from Antarctica'. It was his own joke on the scientific journal that was publishing his article. Rand wanted to include the idea of Atlantis but knew that any mention of the 'A' word would doom any chances of getting published. The next best thing would be to get in the words 'from Antarctica'. Charles's remarks here are a sort of wink: 'I know why you included that reference.'

Appendix 6: Spending Time and Wasting Space: How Ice Core Dating Went Wrong

1. For the date of 3,000,000 years for the Lesser Antarctic ice sheet, see Robert M. Schoch, *Voices of the Rocks: A Scientist Looks at Catastrophes and Ancient Civilizations*, Harmony Books, New York, 1999.
2. For the date of 400,000 years for the Lesser Antarctic ice sheet, see *Atlantis Reborn*, BBC2, 4 November 1999, transcript at *http://www.bbc.co.uk/horizon/atlantis2_script.shtml*.
3. For the date of 122,000 years for the Lesser Antarctic ice sheet, see Paul LaViolette, *Earth Under Fire: Humanity's Survival of the Apolcalypse*, Starburst Publications, Schenectady, New York, 1997.

Appendix 7: The Mechanics of Mantle Displacement

1. Song, Xiaodong, and Paul G. Richards, 'Seismological evidence for differential rotation of the Earth's inner core', *Nature*, Vol. 382, 1 January 1996, pp. 221–4.
2. *http:www.flem-ath.com*.
3. Hays, J. D., J. Imbrie and N. J. Schackleton, 'Variations in the Earth's Orbit: Pacemaker of the Ice Ages', Science 194 (1976), pp. 1,121–32.

BIBLIOGRAPHY

Alford, Alan, *Gods of the New Millennium: Scientific Proof of Flesh and Blood Gods*, Hodder & Stoughton, London, 1996.

Alford, Alan, *The Phoenix Solution: Secrets of a Lost Civilisation*, Hodder & Stoughton, London, 1998.

Allan, D. S., and J. B. Delair, *Cataclysm!: Compelling Evidence of a Cosmic Catastrophe in 9500 BC*, with a foreword by Rand Flem-Ath, Bear & Company, Santa Fe, New Mexico, 1997, first published under the title *When the Earth Nearly Died*, Gateway Books, Bath, UK, 1995.

Andrews, Richard, and Paul Schellenberger, *The Tomb of God: The Body of Jesus and the Solution to a 2,000-year-old Mystery*, Little, Brown & Company, London, 1996.

Ardrey, Robert, *African Genesis*, Atheneum, New York, 1961.

Ashe, Geoffrey, *Dawn Behind the Dawn: A Search for the Earthly Paradise*, A John Macrae Book/Henry Holt and Company, New York, 1992.

Atlantis Reborn, BBC2, Thursday 4 November 1999, transcript at *http://www.bbc.co.uk/horizon/atlantis2_script.shtml*.

Aveni, Anthony F., *Archaeoastronomy in Pre-Columbian America*, University of Texas Press, Austin, 1975.

Baigent, Michael, Richard Leigh and Henry Lincoln, *The Holy Blood and the Holy Grail*, revised edition, Corgi Books, London, 1996 (originally Jonathan Cape, London, 1982).

Baigent, Michael, and Richard Leigh, *The Temple and the Lodge*, Corgi, London, 1992.

Baigent, Michael, *Ancient Traces, Mysteries in Ancient and Early History*, New York, Viking, 1998.

Bailey, Jim, *The God-Kings and the Titans*, Hodder & Stoughton, London, 1973.

Bailey, Jim, *Sailing to Paradise: The Discovery of the Americas by 7000 BC*, Simon & Shuster, New York, 1994.

Balabanova, S., F. Parsche and W. Pirsig, 'First Identification of Drugs in Egyptian Mummies', *Naturwissenschaften*, 79, 358, 1992.

Barber, John, 'Oriental Enigma', *Equinox*, No. 1, January–February 1990.

Barnes, John, 'Ancient purity and polygot programs', *Sunday Times*, 4 November 1984, Computing Section, p. 13.

Barnes, Virgil E. and Mildred A., *Tektites*, Stroudsburg, Hutchinson & Ross, Inc., Dowden, PA, 1973.

Barton, George Aaron, *Miscellaneous Babylonian Inscriptions*, New Haven, Yale University Press, 1918.

Bauval, Robert, and Adrian Gilbert, *The Orion Mystery: Unlocking the Secrets of the Pyramids*, Doubleday Canada, Toronto, 1994.

Bauval, Robert, *Secret Chamber: The Quest for the Hall of Records*, Century, London, 1999.

Bellamy, H. S., *Built Before the Flood: The Problem of the Tiahuanaco Ruins*, London: Faber & Faber Limited, 1943.

Berlitz, Charles, *Atlantis: The Eighth Continent*, Putnam, New York, 1984.

Berriman, A. E., *Historical Metrology*, Dent, New York, 1953.

Besant, Annie, and C. W. Leadbeater, *Occult Chemistry: On the Chemical Elements*, Theosophical Publishing House, London, 1919.

Bird, Christopher, 'The Saga of Yull Brown – Part I', *Raum und Zeit*, Vol. 3., No. 2, 1992, pp. 49–50. (Thanks to Shawn Montgomery for sending Rand this article.)

Blankenship, Donald D., Robin E. Bell, Steven M. Hodge, John M. Brozena, John C. Behrendt and Carol A. Finn, 'Active volcanism beneath the West Antarctic ice sheet and the implications for ice-sheet stability', *Nature*, Vol. 361, 11 February 1993, pp. 526–9.

Book of the Secrets of Enoch, The, translated by W. R. Morfill and edited with an introduction by R. H. Charles, Clarendon Press, Oxford, 1896.

Bortoft, Henri, *The Wholeness of Nature: Goethe's Way of Science*, Lindisfarne Press, Hudson, NY, 1996.

Bradley, Michael, *Grail Knights of North America: On the Trail of the Grail Legacy in Canada and the United States*, Hounslow Press, Toronto/Oxford, 1998.

Bringhurst, Robert, *A Story as Sharp as a Knife: The Classical Haida Mythtellers and Their World*, Douglas & McIntyre, Vancouver/Toronto, 1999.

Brydon, Robert, *The Guilds, the Masons and the Rosy Cross,* Friends of Rosslyn, Edinburgh, 1984.

Butler, Alan, and Stephen Dafoe, *The Warriors and the Bankers: A History of the Knights Templar from 1307 to the Present*, Templar Books, Belleville, Ontario, 1998.

Calder, Nigel, *Timescale*, Viking, New York, 1983.

Cann, R., M. Stoneking and A. Wilson, 'Mitochondrial DNA and Human evolution', *Nature,* pp. 325:31–36, 1987.

Cathie, Bruce, *The Bridge to Infinity*, America West, Bozeman, Montana, 1995.

Cathie, Bruce, *The Harmonic Conquest of Space*, Nexus Magazine, 1995.

Cayce, Edgar Evans, with Gail Cayce Schwartzer and Douglas G. Richards, *Mysteries of Atlantis Revisited*, New York, St Martin's Paperbacks, 1988, with a 1997 update.

Charles, R. H., *The Book of Enoch*, Oxford University Press, Oxford, 1912.

Chatelain, Maurice, *Our Cosmic Ancestors*, Light Technology Publications in USA, paperback edition 1988, reissued in 1996.

Churchward, James, *The Lost Continent of Mu: The Motherland of Man*, William Edwin Rudge, New York, 1926.

Cieza de Leon, Pedro de, *The Incas of Pedro de Cieza de Leon*, 1553, translated by H. de Onis and edited by V. von Hagen, University of Oklahoma Press, Norman, 1959.

Clayton, P. A., and L. J. Spencer, 'Silica-glass from the Libyan Desert', *The Mineralogical Magazine,* 23, 501–8, 1934.

Clube, Victor, and Bill Napier, *The Cosmic Winter*, Universe Books, New York, 1990.

Collins, Andrew, with additional research by Richard Ward, *From the Ashes of Angels: The Forbidden Legacy of a Fallen Race*, Michael Joseph, London, 1996.

Collins, Andrew, 'Baalbek: Lebanon's Sacred Fortress', *New Dawn*, No. 43, July–August 1997: *http:www.newdawnmagazine.com.au/Resources/arts/43c.html.*

Collins, Andrew, *Gods of Eden: Egypt's Lost Legacy and the Genesis of Civilisation,* Headline, London, 1998.

Collins, Andrew, *Gateway to Atlantis: The Search for the Source of a Lost Civilisation*, Headline, London, 2000.

Cremo, Michael, and Richard L. Thompson, *Forbidden Archaeology: The Hidden History of the Human Race*, Bhaktivedanta Institute, San Diego, 1993.

Cremo, Michael (ed.), *Forbidden Archaeology's Impact,* Bhaktivedanta Book Publishing Inc., San Diego, 1998.

Critchlow, Keith, *Time Stands Still*, Gordon Fraser, London, 1979.

Däniken, Erich von, *Chariots of the Gods?: Unsolved Mysteries of the Past*, G. P. Putnam's, New York, 1968.

Däniken, Erich von, *According to the Evidence*: *My Proof of Man's Extraterrestrial Origins,* Book Club Associates, London, 1978.

Davidson, David, *The Great Pyramid, Its Divine Message*, Williams & Norgate, 1932.

Davis, Nancy Yaw, 'The Zuni Enigma', *New England Antiquities Research Association*, Vol. XXVII, Nos. 1 & 2, Summer/Fall 1992.

Dolphin, L. T., and A. H. Moussa, et al., *Applications of Modern Sensing Techniques to Egyptology,* SRI International, Menlo Park, California, 1977.

Donnelly, Ignatius, *Atlantis: The Antediluvian World*, Harper & Brothers, New York, 1882.

Donnelly, Ignatius, *Ragnarok: The Age of Fire and Gravel*, Harper & Brothers, New York, 1883.

Dowling, Kenven, 'Secret pyramids under the sand': *http://express.lineone.net/express/00/01/10/news/n3120sands-d.html* (10 January 2000).

Dunn, Christopher, *The Giza Power Plant: Technologies of Ancient Egypt*, Bear & Company, Santa Fe, New Mexico, 1998.

Einstein, Albert, correspondence with Charles H. Hapgood, Albert Einstein Archives, Department of Manuscripts and Archives, The Jewish National and University Library.

Einstein, Albert, in John Simon Guggenheim Memorial Foundation, 'Confidential Report on Candidate for Fellowship', dated 18 November 1954 and received at the Foundation on 20 November 1954.

Eliade, Mircea, *Shamanism: Archaic Techniques of Ecstasy*, translated from the French by Willard R. Trask, Pantheon Books, New York, 1964.

Ellis, Normandi, *Awakening Osiris*, Phanes Press, Grand Rapids, 1988.

Ellis, R., *Thoth: Architect of the Universe*, Edfu Books, Dorset, UK, 1997.

Falkner, R. O., *The Ancient Egyptian Coffin Texts*, Oxford University Press, Oxford, 1969.

Fanthorpe, Lionel and Patricia, *The Holy Grail Revealed*, Newcastle Publishing, North Hollywood, 1982.

Fawcett, P. H., *Exploration Fawcett*, arranged from his manuscripts by Brian Fawcett, Hutchinson, London, 1953.

Fix, William R., *Pyramid Odyssey*, John Wiley & Sons Canada Limited, Toronto, 1978.

Flem-Ath, Rand and Rose, 'The Earth Science Revolution and Pre-History', July 1977 (unpublished paper for Charles Hapgood).

Flem-Ath, Rand, 'A Global Model for the Origins of Agriculture', *The Anthropological Journal of Canada*, Vol. 19, No. 4, 1981, reprinted in 1995 as an appendix in *When the Sky Fell*.

Flem-Ath, Rand and Rose, *When the Sky Fell: In Search of Atlantis*, Stoddart, Toronto, 1995.

Flem-Ath, Rand, *Atlantis and the Earth's Shifting Crust* (video), LL Productions, Bellevue, Washington, USA (1-800-243-1483 in the US and 425-455-1053 outside the US), 1995.

Flem-Ath, Rand and Rose, 'Contact', *New Dawn Magazine*, 1997.

Flem-Ath, Rand, 'Blueprints from Atlantis', *Atlantis Rising*, February 1998.

378

Flem-Ath website: *www.flem-ath.com*.

Flem-Ath, Rose, *Field of Thunder*, Stoddart, Toronto, 1997.

Fleming, Peter, *Brazilian Adventure*, Jonathan Cape, London, 1933, reissued in 1999 by The Marlboro Press/Northwestern, Evanston, Illinois.

Fowden, Garth, *The Egyptian Hermes*, Princeton University Press, New Jersey 1993.

Fox, Hugh, *Gods of the Cataclysm: A Revolutionary Investigation of Man and His Gods Before and After the Great Cataclysm*, Harper's Magazine Press, New York, 1976.

Frawley, David, *Gods, Sages and Kings: Vedic Secrets of Ancient Civilization*, Passage Press, Salt Lake City, Utah, 1991.

Fulcanelli, *The Mystery of Cathedrals*, Pauvert, Paris, 1925.

Furlong, David, *The Keys to the Temple: Pyramids, Ley Patterns and the Atlantean Heritage*, Piatkus, London, 1997.

Furneaux, Rupert, *The World's Strangest Mysteries*, Ace Books, New York, 1961.

George, Andrew, *The Epic of Gilgamesh: A New Translation*, Allen Lane/The Penguin Press, London, 1999.

Graves, Robert, *The White Goddess*, Farrar, Straus and Giroux, New York, 1948, reissued in 1999 by Faber & Faber.

Great Builders of Egypt, The, a documentary made for A&E by Greystone Communications Inc., 1998. Produced by Louis C. Tarantino, Lauren E. Herz and Cathy Ward. Broadcast on A&E, 7 February 1999.

Grierson, Roderick, and Stuart Munro-Hay, *The Ark of the Covenant*, Weidenfeld & Nicolson, London, 1999.

Hall, Edward, *The Dance of Life*, Anchor Press/Doubleday, Garden City, New York, 1983.

Hall, Manly Palmer, *The Secret Teachings of All Ages*, The Philosophical Research Society Inc., Los Angeles, 1977.

Hancock, Graham, *The Sign and the Seal: The Quest for the Lost Ark of the Covenant,* Simon & Schuster, New York, 1992 (1993 edition).

Hancock, Graham, *Fingerprints of the Gods: A Quest for the Beginning and the End*, Heinemann, London, 1995.

Hancock, Graham, and Robert Bauval, *Keeper of Genesis*,

Heinemann, London, 1996 (paperback edition published by Arrow, 1997; in the US published as *Message of the Sphinx*, Crown, New York, 1996).

Hancock, Graham, *The Mars Mystery: The Secret Connection Between Earth and the Red Planet*, Crown, New York, 1998.

Hancock, Graham, and Santha Faiia, *Heaven's Mirror: Quest for the Lost Civilization*, Michael Joseph, London, 1998.

Hapgood, Charles H., *The Earth's Shifting Crust*, Pantheon, New York, 1958.

Hapgood, Charles H., *Maps of the Ancient Sea Kings: Evidence of Advanced Civilization in the Ice Ages*, Chilton Books, Philadephia/New York, 1966.

Hapgood, Charles H., *The Path of the Pole*, Chilton Book Company, Philadelphia/New York/London, 1970 (a revised edition of *Earth's Shifting Crust*, 1958).

Hapgood, Charles H., Charles H. Hapgood Archives, Yale Collection of American Literature, Beinecke Rare Book and Manuscript Library.

Hapgood, Charles H., letter to the Flem-Aths, 3 August 1977.

Hapgood, Charles H., letter to Rand Flem-Ath, 16 October 1982.

Hapgood, Elizabeth (Beth), Letter to Rand Flem-Ath, 2 April 1998.

Hausdorf, Hartwig, *The Chinese Roswell*, New Paradigm Books, Boca Raton, Florida, 1998.

Hawkins, Gerald, *Stonehenge Decoded*, Doubleday, New York, 1965.

Hayes, Mike, *The Infinite Harmony*, Weidenfeld & Nicolson, London, 1994.

Hays, J. D., and N. J. Schackleton, 'Variations in the Earth's Orbit: Pacemaker of the Ice Ages', *Science*, 194, 1976, pp. 1,121–32.

Heyerdahl, Thor, *The Kon-Tiki Expedition*, London, 1950, reissued in 1996 by Flamingo.

Heyerdahl, Thor, *The Ra Expedition*, George Allen & Unwin, London, 1971.

Heyerdahl, Thor, *Early Man and the Ocean*, Doubleday, Garden City, NY, 1979.

Heyerdahl, Thor, Daniel H. Sandweiss and Alfredo Narvaez, *Pyramids of Tucume: The Quest for Peru's Forgotten City*, Thames & Hudson, London, 1995.

How Far Is It?: *http://www.indo.com/distance/*.

Ivimy, John, *The Sphinx and the Megaliths,* Turnstone, London, 1974.

Jang-jin, Hwang, 'Law proposed to preserve megalithic culture', *Korea Herald*, 25 February 1999: *http://www.koreaherald.co.kr/ kh0225/m0225c01.html* (1 March 1999).

Jaynes, Julian, *The Origin of Consciousness in the Breakdown of the Bicameral Mind*, Houghton Mifflin, New York, 1976.

Jung, Carl, *Memories, Dreams, Reflections*, Vintage Books, New York, 1961.

Keller, Werner, *The Bible as History*, originally published in German in 1978 as *Und die Bibel hat doch recht* by Econ Verlag GmbH, translated by William Neil, second edition, Morrow, New York, 1981.

Kenyon, Kathleen, *Beginning in Archaeology*, Phoenix, 1953.

Kerisel, Jean, 'The Pyramid of Cheops: Further Research', October/December 1992, extract from his paper in *Revue Française d'Egyptologie*, 1993.

Kirkpatrick, Sidney D., *Lords of Sipan: A True Story of Pre-Inca Tombs*, Morrow, New York, 1992.

Knight, Christopher, and Robert Lomas, *The Hiram Key*, Arrow, London, 1996.

Knight, Christopher, and Robert Lomas, *The Second Messiah: Templars, the Turin Shroud and the Great Secret of Freemasonry*, Century, London, 1997.

Knight, Christopher, and Robert Lomas, *Uriel's Machine: The Prehistoric Technology that Survived the Flood*, Century, London, 1999.

Kolata, Alan L., *Valley of the Spirits: A Journey into the Lost Realm of the Aymara*, John Wiley & Sons, Inc., New York, 1996.

Kramer, Samuel Noah, *History Begins at Sumer*, Thames & Hudson, London, 1958, reissued in 1981 by the University of Pennsylvania Press, Philadelphia.

Krings, M., et al., 'Neanderthal DNA sequence and the origins of modern humans', *Cell*, 90, pp. 19–30, 1997.

Kronzek, Allan Zola, *The Secrets of Alkazar: A Book of Magic*, Four Winds Press, New York, 1980.

Kuhn, Thomas S., *The Structure of Scientific Revolutions*, second edition, University of Chicago Press, Chicago, 1970.

Langway, C.C. Jr., and Lyle Hansen, 'Drilling through the Ice Cap: Probing Climate for a Thousand Centuries', in Richard Lewis and P. M. Smith, *The Frozen Future: A Prophetic Report from Antarctica*, Quadrangle Books, New York, 1973.

Lash, John, *The Skies in Memory*, a work in progress.

LaViolette, Paul, *Earth Under Fire: Humanity's Survival of the Apocalypse*, Starburst Publications, Schenectady, New York, 1997.

Lawton, Ian, and Chris Ogilvie-Herald, *Giza: the Truth*, Virgin, London, 1999.

Lawlor, Robert, *Sacred Geometry: Philosophy and Practice*, Thames and Hudson, London, 1982.

Lawrence, T. E., *Seven Pillars of Wisdom*, Jonathan Cape, London, 1952.

University of California, *Learning about Korea*, series 1: *http://www.lib.berkeley.edu/EAL/ealknote.html* (8 May 2000).

Ledbetter, M.T., and D. A. Johnson, 'Increased Transport of Antarctic Bottom Water in the Vema Channel during the last Ice Age', *Science*, Vol. 194, 19 November 1976, pp. 837–9

Lehner, Mark, *The Complete Pyramids,* Thames and Hudson, London, 1997.

Lewis, David, *We, The Navigators*, 1972, reissued in 1991 by University of Hawaii Press.

Lincoln, Henry, *The Holy Place: Discovering the Eighth Wonder of the Ancient World*, Arcade Publishing/Little, Brown & Company, New York, 1991.

Lincoln, Henry, *Key to the Sacred Pattern: The Untold Story of Rennes-le-Château*, St Martin's Press, New York, 1998.

Loomis, Roger, introduction to *Chrétien's 'Perceval, or the Story of the Grail'*, Mediaeval Romances (Modern Library) Columbia University Press, New York, 1952.

Ma, Ting Ying H., *Research on the Past Climate*, published by the author, Taipei, Taiwan, May 1952.

Magnus, Rudolf, *Goethe as Scientist*, translated by Heinz Norden, Henry Schuman, New York, 1949.

Mallery, Arlington, *Lost America: The Story of the Pre-Columbian Iron Age in America*, Overlook Co., Washington, DC, 1951.

Marshack, Alexander, *The Roots of Civilisation*, McGraw-Hill Book Company, New York, 1972.

Marx, Robert F., and Jenifer G. Marx, *In Quest of the Great White Gods: Contact Between the Old and New World from the Dawn of History*, Crown, New York, 1992.

Marris, Sarah, *Curse of the Cocaine Mummies*. Written and directed by Sarah Marris. Produced by Hilary Lawson and Maureen Lemire. Narrated by Hilary Kilberg. A TVF Production for Channel Four in association with the Discovery Channel, 1997.

Maybury-Lewis, David, *Millennium: Tribal Wisdom and the Modern World*, New York, Viking, 1992.

McCollum, Rocky, *The Giza Necropolis Decoded*, Michigan, 1975.

McCrone, John, 'Fired Up', *New Scientist*, 20 May 2000.

Mead, G. R. S., *Thrice Great Hermes: Studies in Hellenistic Theosophy and Gnosis*, Samuel Weiser Inc., North Beach, Maine, 1992.

Mendelssohn, Kurt, *The Riddle of the Pyramids*, Praeger, New York, 1974.

Michell, John, *City of Revelation*, Ballantine Books, New York, 1972.

Michell, John, *The Earth Spirit: Its Ways, Shrines and Mysteries*, Crossroads, New York, 1975.

Michell, John, *Megalithomania*, Cornell University Press, Ithaca, New York, 1982.

Michell, John, *The Dimensions of Paradise: The Proportions and Symbolic Numbers of Ancient Cosmology*, Harper & Row, San Francisco, 1988.

Michell, John, *At the Center of the World: Polar Symbolism Discovered in Celtic, Norse and Other Ritualized Landscapes*, Thames and Hudson, London, 1994

Michell, John, *The New View Over Atlantis*, Thames and Hudson, London, 1995, (originally published as *The View Over Atlantis* by Sago Press, UK, 1969).

Mitchell-Hedges, F. A., *Danger My Ally*, originally published in 1955, reissued in 1995 by Adventures Unlimited, USA.

Moran, Hugh A. and Kelley, David, *The Alphabet and the Ancient Calendar Signs*, Palo Alto Daily Press, 1969.

Morfill, W. R., *The Book of the Secrets of Enoch*, translated by W. R. Morfill and edited with an introduction by R. H. Charles, Clarendon Press, Oxford, 1896.

Montgomery, Shawn, 'Interview with Yull Brown', June 1996.

Montgomery, Shawn, 'Notes on Brown's Gas for Rand Flem-Ath', 30 January 1997.

Moorehead, Alan, *The Blue Nile*, Harper & Row Publishers, New York, 1962.

Mylrea, Paul, 'Computer helps preserve ancient Aymara language', as printed in *The Nanaimo Free Press*, 21 November 1991, p. 8.

Mysterious Origins of Man, The. Hosted by Charlton Heston. B.C. Video Inc., 1-800-846-9682 or P. O. Box 97, Shelburne, VT, 05482, 1996.

Mystery of the Sphinx, The. Copyright The Sphinx Project, Inc., Magic Eye/North Tower Films Production, 1993.

Narby, Jeremy, *The Cosmic Serpent: DNA and the Origins of Knowledge*, Jeremy Tarcher/Putnam, New York, 1998.

Needham, Joseph, *Science and Civilisation in China* (five volumes), Cambridge University Press, Cambridge, 1959.

Nelson, Sarah Milledge, *The Archaeology of Korea*, Cambridge University Press, Cambridge, 1993.

Newton, Gregg, 'Ancient Skull: An Americas Mystery', Reuters, 21 September 1999: *http://abcnews.go.com/sections/science/Daily News/luiza990921.html* (26 September 1999).

North, John, *Stonehenge: Neolithic Man and the Cosmos*, HarperCollins Publishers, London, 1996.

O'Brien, Christian and Barbara Joy, *The Genius of the Few: The Story of Those Who Founded the Garden in Eden*, Turnstone Press Limited, Wellingborough, Northamptonshire, UK, 1985.

O'Brien, Christian and Barbara Joy, *The Shining Ones*, Dianthus Publishing Limited, Kemble, Cirencester, Gloucestershire, UK, 1997.

Oppenheimer, Stephen, *Eden in the East: The Drowned Continent of Southeast Asia*, Weidenfeld & Nicolson, London, 1998.

Ovchinnikov, Igor V., Anders Gotherstroms, Galina P. Romanova,

Vitaliy M. Kharitonov, Kerstin Lidens and William Goodwin, 'Molecular analysis of Neanderthal DNA from the northern Caucasus', *Nature*, Vol. 404, 30 March 2000, pp. 490–93.

Patten, Donald, *The Biblical Flood and the Ice Epoch: A Study in Scientific History*, Pacific Meridian Publishing Co., Seattle, WA, 1966.

Pauwels, Louis, and Jacques Bergier, *The Morning of the Magicians*, Stein and Day, New York, 1964.

Pennick, Nigel, *The Ancient Science of Geomancy: Living in Harmony with the Earth*, CRCS Publications, Sebastopol, California, and Thames and Hudson Ltd., London, 1979.

Pennick, Nigel, *Sacred Geometry: Symbolism and Purpose in Religious Structures*, Harper & Row, San Francisco, 1980.

Pennick, Nigel, *The Subterranean Kingdom: A Survey of Man-made Structures Beneath the Earth*, Turnstone Press Limited, Wellingborough, Northamptonshire, 1981.

Petrie, William Matthew, *The Pyramids and Temples of Gizeh*, Field & Tuer, London, 1883.

Picknett, Lynn, and Clive Prince, *Turin Shroud: In Whose Image?*, Acacia Press, Melbourne and Los Altos, California, 1994.

Picknett, Lynn, and Clive Prince, *The Templar Revelation: Secret Guardians of the True Identity of Christ*, Simon & Schuster, New York, 1997.

Picknett, Lynn, and Clive Prince, *The Stargate Conspiracy*, Little, Brown & Company, 1999.

Plato, *Timaeus and Critias*, translated by Desmond Lee, Harmondsworth, Middlesex, Penguin, 1977.

Posnansky, Arthur, *Tihuanacu, the Cradle of American Man*, translated by James F. Shearer, Austin, 1945.

Prescott, William Hickling, *History of the Conquest of Peru*: *http://sunsite.doc.ic.ac.uk/public/media/literary/collections/project_gutenberg/gutenberg/etext98/hcpru10.txt*.

Rehlen, Merritt, 'Voices from the Past', *Natural History*, March 1987.

Reymond, E. A. E., *Mythical Origin of the Egyptian Temple*, Manchester University Press, Barnes and Noble Inc., New York, 1969.

Roberts, Paul William, 'The Riddle of the Sphinx', *Saturday Night*, March 1993.

Ruby, Robert, *Jericho: Dreams, Ruins, Phantoms*, Henry Holt & Company, New York, 1995.

Rux, Bruce, *Architects of the Underworld: Unriddling Atlantis, Anomalies of Mars, and the Mystery of the Sphinx*, Frog Limited, Berkeley, California, 1996.

Salazar, Fernando, *The Sacred Valley of the Incas: Myths and Symbols*, Chelsea Green Publishing Company, Post Mills, VT, 1990.

Santillana, Georgio de, and Hertha von Dechend, *Hamlet's Mill: An Essay Investigating the Origins of Human Knowledge and its Transmission through Myth*, Nonpareil Books, Boston, 1977 (originally 1969).

Santos, Arysio Nunes dos, website: *http://www.atlan.org/articles/guanches/* (28 May 1999).

Schoch, Robert M., *Voices of the Rocks: A Scientist Looks at Catastrophes and Ancient Civilizations*, Harmony Books, New York, 1999.

Schwaller de Lubicz, Rene, *Sacred Science: The King of Pharaonic Theocracy*, translated by André and Goldian VandenBroeck, Inner Traditions International, Rochester, VT, 1988, originally published in French in 1961 as *Le Roi de la theocractie Pharaonique* by Flammarion.

Schwaller de Lubicz, Rene, *The Temple of Man: Sacred Architecture and the Perfect Man*, translated by Robert and Deborah Lawlor, Inner Traditions International, Rochester, VT, 1998.

Sède, Gérard de, *Le Trésor maudit*, Editions J'ai Lu, Paris, 1968.

Seiss, J. A., *Miracle in Stone, of the Great Pyramid of Egypt*, Porter & Coates, Philadelphia, 1877–8.

Seitz, Donald Tim (Senior), 'A Probable Cause of Crustal Shifts of the Earth: A Comet Approaching the Centre of Mass of the Earth–Moon Gravitational System', Regulus, Ontario, April 1998.

Sellers, Jane B., *The Death of Gods in Ancient Egypt*, Penguin Books, London, 1992.

Sellers, Jane B., email to Rand Flem-Ath, 28 July 2000.

Shklovskii, Joseph, and Carl Sagan, *Intelligent Life in the Universe*, Holden Day, San Francisco, 1966.

Sitchin, Zecharia, *The 12th Planet*, Santa Fe, New Mexico, Bear & Company, 1976.

Sitchin, Zecharia, *The Wars of Gods and Men*, Avon, New York, 1985.

Sitchin, Zecharia, *The Lost Realms*, Bear & Company, Santa Fe, New Mexico, 1990.

Sitchin, Zecharia, *Genesis Revisited*, Bear & Company, Santa Fe, New Mexico, 1991.

Smyth, Charles Piazzi, *The Great Pyramid: Its Secrets and Mysteries Revealed*, Crown, New York, 1978 (originally published 1880).

Smyth, Charles Piazzi, 'What Shall be the Prime Meridian for the World?', *Report of the Committee on Standard Time and Prime Meridian, International Institute for Preserving and Perfecting Weights and Measures*, Cleveland, OH, June 1884, pp. 1–56.

Song, Xiaodong, and Paul G. Richards, 'Seismological evidence for differential rotation of the Earth's inner core', *Nature*, Vol. 382, 1 January 1996, pp. 221–4.

Sullivan, William, *Secret of the Incas: Myth, Astronomy, and the War Against Time*, Crown, New York, 1997.

Swaney, Deanna, *The Lonely Planet Guide to Bolivia*, Lonely Planet, London, 1996.

Taylor, John, *The Great Pyramid: Why Was It Built? & Who Built It?*, Longmans, Green, London, 1864.

Tailby, S. R., *A Brief History of Lodge Mother Kilwinning No. 0*, Kilwinning, 1944.

Temple, Robert, *The Sirius Mystery: New Scientific Evidence for Alien Contact 5,000 Years Ago*, Arrow, London, 1998 (originally published in 1976).

Temple, Robert, *The Crystal Sun: Rediscovering a Lost Technology of the Ancient World*, Century, London, 2000.

Thom, A., *Megalithic Sites in Britain*, Oxford University Press, Oxford, 1968.

Thorton, Russell, *American Indian Holocaust and Survival*, University of Oklahoma Press, Norman, 1987.

Tilak, Bal Gangadhar, *The Arctic Home in the Vedas*, Poona, India, 1903.

Tomas, Andrew, *Atlantis From Legend to Discovery*, Robert Hale, London, 1972.

Tompkins, Peter, *Mysteries of the Mexican Pyramids*, Harper & Row, New York, 1976.

Tompkins, Peter, with Livio Catullo Stecchini, *Secrets of the Great Pyramid: Two Thousand Years of Adventure and Discoveries Surrounding the Mystery of the Great Pyramid of Cheops*, Galahad Books, New York, 1971.

Torkain, M., email to Rand Flem-Ath, 13 March 1998.

Toth, Max, *Pyramid Prophecies*, Warner Destiny Books, New York, 1979.

Tyler, Major F. C., OBE, *The Geometrical Arrangement of Ancient Sites*, Simpkin Marshall Ltd, London, 1939.

University of California, *Learning about Korea*, series 1: *http://www.lib.berkeley.edu/EAL/ealknote.html* (8 May 2000).

US Naval Support Force, *Introduction to Antarctica*, US Government Printing Office, Washington, DC, 1969.

Velikovsky, Immanuel, *Worlds in Collision*, Doubleday, New York, 1950.

Wallace-Murphy, Tim, and Marilyn Hopkins, *Rosslyn: Guardians of the Secrets of the Holy Grail*, Element, Shaftesbury, Dorset, 1999.

Warren, William Fairfield, *Paradise Found: The Cradle of the Human Race at the North Pole*, Boston, 1885.

Watkins, Alfred, *The Old Straight Track: Its Mounds, Beacons, Moats, Sites and Mark Stones*, Methuen & Co. Ltd, Great Britain, 1925, reissued in 1974 by Abacus, London.

Watkins, N. D., and Kennett, J. D., 'Antarctic Bottom Water: Major Change in Velocity during the Late Cenozoic between Australia and Antarctica', *Science,* Vol. 173, 27 August 1971, pp. 813–18.

Watson, Lyall, *Supernature,* Anchor Press, Garden City, NY, 1973.

Wegener, Alfred, *The Origin of the Continents and Oceans*, 1915, reissued in 1966 by Dover, New York.

West, John Anthony, *Serpent in the Sky: The High Wisdom of Ancient Egypt*, second edition, Quest Books, Wheaton, IL, 1993.

BIBLIOGRAPHY

West, John Anthony, in *Mystery of the Sphinx*, video, NBC, directed by Bill Cote, 1993.

West, John Anthony, *The Traveler's Key to Ancient Egypt*, Quest Books Edition, Wheaton, Illinois, 1995 (originally published 1985).

Weston, Jessie L., *From Ritual To Romance*, Cambridge University Press, 1920.

'When the Sahara Was Green', *The World's Last Mysteries*, Reader's Digest, Pleasantville, New York, 1977.

White, John, *Pole Shift*, Doubleday, New York, 1980.

Wilkins, Harold T., *Mysteries of Ancient South America*, Rider & Company, London, 1946.

Wilkins, Harold T., *Secret Cities of Old South America: Atlantis Unveiled*, Library Publishers, New York, 1952.

Wilson, Colin, *Mysteries: An Investigation into the Occult, the Paranormal and the Supernatural*, Putnam, New York, 1978.

Wilson, Colin, *Starseekers*, Hodder & Stoughton, London, 1980.

Wilson, Colin, and Damon Wilson, *Unsolved Mysteries Past and Present*, NTC/Contemporary Publishing, Chicago, 1992.

Wilson, Colin, *From Atlantis to the Sphinx: Recovering the Lost Wisdom of the Ancient World*, Virgin, London, 1996.

Wilson, Colin, *The Atlas of Holy Places and Sacred Sites*, Penguin Studio, London, 1996.

Wilson, Colin, *Alien Dawn*, Virgin, London, 1998.

Woolley, Sir C. Leonard, *Ur of the Chaldees*, Ernest Benn, London, 1929.

Wood, David, *Genisis: The First Book of Revelations*, Baton Press, Tunbridge Wells, Kent, 1985.

Wood, David, and Ian Campbell, *Geneset Target Earth*, Bellevue Books, Sunbury-on-Thames, 1994.

Wright, Ronald, *Stolen Continents: The 'New World' Through Indian Eyes*, Penguin Books, London, 1992.

Zapp, Ivar, and George Erikson, *Atlantis in America, Navigators of the Ancient World,* Adventures Unlimited Press, 1998.

Zink, David, *The Stones of Atlantis*, Prentice-Hall Canada, Toronto, 1978.

INDEX

Page numbers in **bold** denote illustration.

ABOUT THE AUTHORS

COLIN WILSON, author of such international bestsellers as *The Outsider* and *The Occult*, also writes on archaeology, astronomy, and cosmology. His recent book, *From Atlantis to the Sphinx,* reaches number five on the London *Times* bestseller list. He lives in Cornwall, England, with his wife.

RAND FLEM-ATH, a Canadian librarian, is one of the world's leading researchers in catastrophe myths; he is the author of *When the Sky Fell: In Search of Atlantis.* He lives on Vancouver Island with his wife, Rose, and their two dogs and two cats.